Warriner's English Grammar and Composition

LIBERTY EDITION

Second Course

Warriner's English Grammar and Composition

LIBERTY EDITION

John E. Warriner

Second Course

 Harcourt Brace Jovanovich, Publishers

Orlando   San Diego   Chicago   Dallas

THE SERIES:

English Grammar and Composition: First Course
English Grammar and Composition: Second Course
English Grammar and Composition: Third Course
English Grammar and Composition: Fourth Course
English Grammar and Composition: Fifth Course
English Grammar and Composition: Complete Course

Annotated Teacher's Edition, Part I; Teacher's Edition, Part II for each above title.

CORRELATED SERIES:

English Workshop: First Course
English Workshop: Second Course
English Workshop: Third Course
English Workshop: Fourth Course
English Workshop: Fifth Course
English Workshop: Review Course

Composition: Models and Exercises, First Course
Composition: Models and Exercises, Second Course
Composition: Models and Exercises, Third Course
Composition: Models and Exercises, Fourth Course
Composition: Models and Exercises, Fifth Course
Advanced Composition: A Book of Models for Writing, Complete Course

Vocabulary Workshop: First Course
Vocabulary Workshop: Second Course
Vocabulary Workshop: Third Course
Vocabulary Workshop: Fourth Course
Vocabulary Workshop: Fifth Course
Vocabulary Workshop: Complete Course

John E. Warriner taught English for thirty-two years in junior and senior high schools and in college. He is chief author of the *English Grammar and Composition* series, coauthor of the *English Workshop* series, general editor of the *Composition: Models and Exercises* series, and editor of *Short Stories: Characters in Conflict*. His coauthors have all been active in English education.

To the Student

A long time ago when education did not have to be so complicated as it must be today, the main subjects in school were referred to as the three R's: reading, 'riting, and 'rithmetic. As a familiar song says, they were "taught to the tune of a hickory stick." The hickory stick, fortunately, is not much used any more, but the three R's remain. Two of them, reading and writing, make up a large part of the school subject called English.

If someone were to ask you the unlikely question, "What do you do in English?" your reply might be something like this: "In English we read stories and poems and stuff like that. We learn about nouns and verbs and, well, subjects and predicates, I guess. We write our own stories and poems and themes. And we give talks in front of the class." This answer is a fairly good account of what you do in English.

A teacher, however, would use different terms in answering the same question. Instead of mentioning just stories and poems, a teacher might say you study *literature*. Noun, verb, subject, and predicate are terms used in the study of *grammar*. Writing stories, poems, and themes is practicing written *composition*. Talks in front of the class are a means of improving your *speech*. The four main areas of English, then, are literature, grammar, composition, and speech.

This book deals mainly with the last three of the four areas, grammar, composition, and speech. To use a language well, you need to know how it works. By studying grammar, you learn how the language works. This knowledge will help you to improve both your writing and your speech.

Although you write much less often than you speak, written composition demands a large amount of English time because writing is hard to learn. Each year in school you will be expected to do more written work in most of your classes, but it is only in English class that you learn how to write.

By writing well, you communicate with others. By speaking (and listening) well, you also communicate with others. Speech skills are a vital part of your education because you spend so much of every day talking with others.

Mastering the three areas in this textbook—grammar, composition, and speech—is not an easy task. However, you can do it if you have sound guidance. Your teacher is your most helpful guide, but your textbook is also an important guide. Study it, follow the rules, do the practice exercises, and whenever you write or speak put to use what you have learned. You will find your work will improve steadily.

J. W.

CONTENTS

Part One: GRAMMAR

6. The Clause 145
INDEPENDENT AND SUBORDINATE CLAUSES

7. The Kinds of Sentence Structure 172
THE FOUR BASIC SENTENCE STRUCTURES

Part Two: USAGE

Usage Mastery Review: Cumulative Test   307

Part Three: MECHANICS

13. Capital Letters   313
RULES FOR CAPITALIZATION

14. Punctuation   335
END MARKS, COMMAS, SEMICOLONS, COLONS

15. Punctuation

Part Five: COMPOSITION:
The Writing Process

20. Writing Paragraphs 491

STRUCTURE AND DEVELOPMENT OF
PARAGRAPHS

21. **Writing Paragraphs** 540

FOUR TYPES OF PARAGRAPHS

22. Writing Stories 571

USING NARRATION AND DESCRIPTION

23. Writing Exposition   607

THE WHOLE COMPOSITION

24. Writing Exposition   652

SUMMARIES AND REPORTS

25. Writing Letters   686
SOCIAL LETTERS, BUSINESS LETTERS

Part Six: AIDS TO GOOD ENGLISH

26. Using the Dictionary   713

ARRANGEMENT OF A DICTIONARY, INFORMATION
IN A DICTIONARY

29. Spelling 778

IMPROVING YOUR SPELLING

30. Studying and Test Testing 802

SKILLS AND STRATEGIES

Part Seven: SPEAKING AND LISTENING

PART ONE

GRAMMAR

CHAPTER 1

The Sentence

SUBJECT AND PREDICATE, KINDS OF SENTENCES

Suppose that you began to read a story that opened as follows:

> Awakened in study hall John leaped from his seat into the balcony above him came the marching band led by the drum major playing the "Star Spangled Banner" on his tall hat a great plume nodded to John it was a rude awakening.

Your difficulty in understanding the story comes not from a failure to understand the words but from a failure to understand the writer's units of thought. If the writer told the story to you, the meaning could be conveyed by vocal expression and by pauses at the right places. Writing differs from speaking in that writers have only their words and punctuation as a means of communication. Thus, writers need to use patterns that are familiar to their readers—to write complete sentences that are set off clearly by punctuation.

There is a second important difference between speaking and writing. In conversation you often leave a sentence unfinished and begin it over again. You think as you speak. In writing, you have to think before you begin. In general, you will find that writing requires more care than speaking usually does.

DIAGNOSTIC TEST

A. Identifying Subjects and Predicates. Number your paper 1–10. After the proper number, write each italicized group of words, and indicate whether it is the subject or the predicate of the sentence. If it is the subject, underline the simple subject. If it is the predicate, underline the simple predicate, or verb.

EXAMPLES 1. *The mean dog next door* barks fiercely.
1. *The mean <u>dog</u> next door—subject*
2. The mean dog next door *barks fiercely.*
2. *<u>barks</u> fiercely—predicate*

1. Mr. Adams *gave me his old croquet set.*
2. Why did *that large new boat* sink on such a clear day?
3. *Trees and bushes all over the neighborhood* had been torn out by the storm.
4. On his way to school, Bill *was splashed by a passing car.*
5. *My old bicycle with the ape-hanger handlebars* is rusting away in the garage now.
6. *The creek behind my house* rises during the summer rains.
7. Sandy's little sister *bravely dived off the high board at the community pool.*
8. *Does* Max *want another serving of pie?*
9. My cousins and I *played basketball and walked over to the mall yesterday.*
10. *Fridays and other test days* always seem longer than regular school days.

B. Identifying Sentences by Purpose. Number your paper 11–20. After the proper number, identify each sentence as *declarative, interrogative, imperative,* or *exclamatory.*

EXAMPLE 1. What did you say?
1. *interrogative*

11. That may have been the longest string of train cars I have ever seen.
12. Follow these directions exactly.
13. No, I haven't seen Jenny all day.

14. Run for it—Tommy just knocked down a wasps' nest!
15. What's wrong with the television set?
16. I don't care.
17. Take this book down to Mrs. Esteva's office.
18. Mai Lin and her family suffered many hardships at sea.
19. Ouch, that hurts!
20. May my dog have the rest of your sandwich?

THE SENTENCE

1a. A *sentence* **is a group of words expressing a complete thought.**

A sentence begins with a capital letter and concludes with an end mark: a period or a question mark or an exclamation point. Sometimes a group of words looks like a sentence when it is not. You must examine the group of words closely to be sure that it expresses a complete thought. Reading it aloud will help you.

NOT A SENTENCE   The music of Scott Joplin. [This is not a complete thought. What about the music of Scott Joplin?]

SENTENCE   The music of Scott Joplin is popular again.

NOT A SENTENCE   Upon hearing Jose Feliciano. [The thought is not complete. Who heard Feliciano? What was the response?]

SENTENCE   Upon hearing Jose Feliciano, the audience applauded.

NOT A SENTENCE   After she worked a long time. [The thought is not complete. What happened after she worked a long time?]

SENTENCE   After she worked a long time, Louise Nevelson completed the sculpture.

EXERCISE 1. Identifying and Writing Sentences. Read the following groups of words and decide which are sentences and which are not. (Capital letters and end punctuation marks have been purposely omitted.) If a group of words is a sentence, write it after the proper number, using a capital letter and end punctuation. If the group of words is not a sentence, write *NS* after the proper number. Then write the group of words, adding whatever is necessary to complete the thought and make it a sentence.

EXAMPLES
1. living alone in the mountains
1. *NS—Living alone in the mountains, the couple make their own furniture and clothes.*
2. classes in mountain climbing will begin soon
2. *Classes in mountain climbing will begin soon.*

1. catching the baseball with both hands
2. in the back of the room stands a tall pile of boxes
3. a long narrow passage with a trapdoor at each end
4. after waiting for six hours
5. the gymnasium is open
6. last night there were six television commercials every half-hour
7. instead of calling the doctor about her sore throat
8. beneath the tall ceiling of the church
9. are you careless about shutting off unnecessary lights
10. doing the multiplication tables
11. practice your writing
12. her sister studies engineering at the college
13. discussing the dance in February
14. probably forty guests
15. the governor was elected
16. when the chorus began singing
17. she is tired
18. after the frightening movie when the lights were still dim
19. beneath the truck on the highway
20. everyone shared the remaining cookies

EXERCISE 2. Identifying Sentences. Number your paper 1–20. After each number on your paper, write *S* if the group of words is a sentence and *NS* if it is not a sentence.

1. One of the best-known women in our history is Sacajawea. **2.** A member of the Lemhi band of the Shoshoni Indians.   **3.** She is famous for her role as interpreter for the Lewis and Clark expedition.   **4.** Which was seeking the Northwest Passage.

5. In 1800 the Lemhis had encountered a war party of the Hidatsa.   **6.** Who captured some of the Lemhis, including Sacajawea.   **7.** Later, with Charbonneau, her French-Canadian husband, and their two-month old son.   **8.** Sacajawea joined the Lewis and Clark expedition in what is now North Dakota.   **9.** Her knowledge of Indian languages enabled the explorers to communicate with various tribes.   **10.** Sacajawea also searched for eatable plants.   **11.** And once saved valuable instruments during a storm.   **12.** As they traveled further.   **13.** The explorers came across the Lemhis.   **14.** From whom Sacajawea had been separated years before.   **15.** The Lemhis helped the explorers.   **16.** By giving them guidance.

17. After they returned from the expedition.   **18.** Clark tried to establish Sacajawea and Charbonneau in St. Louis.   **19.** However, the couple moved back to Sacajawea's native land. **20.** Where this famous woman died in 1812.

EXERCISE 3. Writing Interesting Sentences.   The following groups of words are not sentences. On your paper, add whatever is necessary to make interesting sentences.

EXAMPLE   1. at the the last minute
           1. *At the last minute they remembered the secret message.*

1. on the last day of summer
2. found only in the country
3. a graceful ballerina
4. burning out of control
5. in the dark theater
6. the old building by the lake
7. which calmed our nerves
8. up and down the street

9. when the principal entered the room
10. with their hats pulled down over their eyes

THE SUBJECT

You have learned that a sentence is a group of words expressing a complete thought. In order to express a complete thought, a sentence must have a subject and a predicate.

1b. The *subject* of a sentence is the part about which something is being said.

EXAMPLES
subject
A line of people | waited to see the movie.

subject
Standing in line were | several sailors.

Since the subject is that part of the sentence about which something is being said, you can usually locate it by asking yourself *Who?* or *What?* Who waited to see that movie? Who was standing in the line? Notice that the subject comes at the beginning of the first example and at the end of the second.

In the subject part of each of these sentences, one word stands out as essential; in the first sentence, *line;* in the second sentence, *sailors.* These two words, which cannot be removed from the subject parts of the sentences, are called *simple subjects.* The simple subject and the other words that belong with it, taken together, are called the *complete subject.*

1c. The *simple subject* is the main word in the complete subject.

The simple subjects in the following sentences are printed in boldface (heavy type).

complete subject
My **date** for the dance | arrived late.

complete subject
The long, hard **trip** across the desert | was finally over.

complete subject

Pacing back and forth in the cage was │ a hungry **tiger**.

When the subject is only one word or one name, the complete subject and the simple subject are the same.

complete subject

EXAMPLE   **Patsy Mink** │ was elected to office in Hawaii.
She │ was chosen congresswoman.

EXERCISE 4. Identifying Complete Subjects and Simple Subjects.

Write the complete subject in each sentence. Then underline the simple subject.

EXAMPLE   1. The day of the performance arrived.
1. *The day of the performance*

1. A tense excitement filled the air.
2. Several students had been nervous all day.
3. The crew in charge of sets got ready for the first act.
4. The director of the play told everyone to "break a leg."
5. The curtain inched slowly upward.
6. Everyone in the audience stopped talking.
7. The lights flooded the stage.
8. On the stage stood the actors.
9. They said their lines with confidence.
10. The first performance of the play was a great success.

As has been pointed out, the most important word in the complete subject is the simple subject. Without the simple subject there could be no sentence, because the simple subject is needed to state a complete thought. From now on in this book, the word *subject* will refer to the simple subject.

EXERCISE 5. Identifying the Subject.

Number your paper 1–20. After the proper number, write the subject (simple subject) of each sentence. Ask yourself what or whom the sentence says something about.

1. Mark Twain wrote many entertaining stories.   2. Among them is "The Celebrated Jumping Frog of Calaveras County."

3. One of the characters in this story will apparently believe anything. **4.** In a broken-down mining camp, this character meets Mr. Simon Wheeler. **5.** To the kindly old man, he asks a simple question. **6.** Instead of a simple answer, Mr. Wheeler gives a long, fantastic, and funny reply. **7.** This reply is in the form of a humorous tall tale. **8.** The tale features Jim Smiley, the owner of a very athletic frog. **9.** Mr. Smiley trained this frog for jumping contests. **10.** Confidently, Mr. Smiley bragged about his frog's leaping ability. **11.** Soon someone challenged Smiley's frog. **12.** The challenger, however, did not have a jumping frog for the contest. **13.** To Smiley, this was no problem. **14.** In a nearby swamp he found a frog for the challenger. **15.** Each creature was held on the starting line. **16.** Then, with a shout, each man released his frog. **17.** But Smiley's famous frog never jumped. **18.** The ordinary frog from the swamp easily won the contest. **19.** Smiley had been fooled by a trick. **20.** You will enjoy reading this story.

THE PREDICATE

The subject is one of the two essential parts of a sentence; the other essential part is the predicate.

1d. The *predicate* of a sentence is the part that says something about the subject.

EXAMPLES
$\qquad$ *predicate*
N. Scott Momaday | wrote several books.

$\qquad$ *predicate*
My whole family | heard Marian Anderson sing.

$\qquad$ *predicate*
On either side of me were | my two friends.

To find the predicate in a sentence, ask *What is being said about the subject?* or *What happened?* In the normal order of an English sentence, the predicate follows the subject, but in some sentences the predicate comes before the subject. (See the sentence above.)

The Simple Predicate, or Verb

Just as the simple subject is the most important part of the complete subject, so the simple predicate is the most important part of the complete predicate. The simple predicate is usually called the *verb* of the sentence.

1e. The *simple predicate,* or *verb,* is the main word or group of words in the predicate.

In each of the following sentences the simple predicate, or verb, is in boldface.

    complete subject   *complete predicate*
The movie star | **signed** autographs for hours.

    complete subject   *complete predicate*
A whirlwind | **swept** through the town.

    complete subject   *complete predicate*
The trees | **sagged** beneath the weight of the ice.

The simple predicate may be a one-word verb, or it may be a verb of more than one word, such as *has signed, did sweep, will be sagging.* A simple predicate that has more than one word is called a *verb phrase.* Note the verb phrases in boldface in the following sentences:

The famous novel *Frankenstein* **was written** by Mary Wollstonecraft Shelley.

After the concert the guitarist **will sign** autographs.

Your vocabulary **can be increased** by the study of the origins of words.

The complete predicate, which consists of the verb or verb phrase and the other words that belong with it, usually comes after the subject, but it sometimes can appear at the beginning of a sentence, as in the following sentences.

complete predicate   *complete subject*
There on its back **was** | a large **tortoise.**

complete predicate   *complete subject*
At the top of the tree **is** | a bird's **nest.**

The subject may come in the middle of the predicate so that part of the predicate is on one side of the subject and the rest is on the other side. In the following examples, the complete predicate is in boldface.

During the winter many birds **fly south.**
Do sparrows **fly south**?

The words *not* and *never,* which are frequently used with verbs, are not verbs. They may be part of the predicate, but they are never part of a verb or a verb phrase.

EXAMPLES   She **did** not **believe** me.
We **had** never **met.**

From now on in this book, the simple predicate will be called the verb.

EXERCISE 6. Identifying Complete Predicates.   Write the complete predicate from each of the following sentences. Then underline the verb or verb phrase twice.

EXAMPLE   1. A ton and a half of groceries may seem like a big
order for a family of five.
1. *may seem like a big order for a family of five*

1. Such a big order is possible in the village of Pang.
2. This small village is located near the Arctic Circle.
3. The people of Pang receive their groceries once a year.
4. A supply ship can visit Pang only during a short time each year.
5. In spring, families order their year's supply of groceries by mail.
6. The huge order is delivered to Pang a few months later.
7. The people store the groceries in their homes.
8. Frozen food is kept outdoors.

9. Too costly for most residents is the air-freight charge of two dollars a kilogram.

10. Villagers also hunt for wild game or fish in the icy water.

WRITING APPLICATION A:
Expressing Your Ideas in Complete Sentences

Did anyone ever hold out two closed fists for you to choose the one that contained a surprise? When you communicate your thoughts to others, you offer them a surprise. You are sharing a thought that is unique and special because you are unique and special. In conversations, you can tell by your listener's expression whether or not your message is clear. In writing, however, you cannot see your reader's expression. Therefore, when you communicate your thoughts in writing, you should use complete sentences to express your thoughts completely.

EXAMPLES   *Groups of Words:* Terrible day. She'd been gone. Black and white. Missing for several days. Boy across the street. There on the side of the road.

                        Sentences: Boots, our beautiful black and white cat, had been missing several days. We hoped that someone had found her and that they were taking care of her. Then, on that terrible Saturday morning, the boy who lived across the street knocked on our door. He told us that he had seen Boots. She had been hit by a car and was on the side of the road.

Writing Assignment

Sometimes you really do not know how you feel about something until you put your thoughts into words. Writing down your ideas in complete sentences helps you organize your thinking. You may even discover thoughts that you did not know you had. Discover what you think about the following subjects by making a complete sentence out of each group of words. Some groups are subjects, and some groups are predicates.

1. the way to beat feeling lonely
2. always makes a class more interesting
3. dark, rainy days
4. earning extra spending money
5. is my favorite hobby
6. really gets on my nerves
7. watching television
8. my idea of a good friend
9. a subject that my parents and I don't agree on
10. is a game that appeals to me

EXERCISE 7. Identifying Verbs and Verb Phrases. Number your paper 1–20. After the proper number, write the verb or verb phrase in each of the following sentences:

1. At one time the *exemplum* was a popular kind of tale. **2.** The *exemplum* is a tale with a moral. **3.** One popular *exemplum* is told by the Pardoner in Chaucer's *Canterbury Tales*. **4.** According to the Pardoner's story, three young men were looking for Death. **5.** During their search they met an old man. **6.** He directed them to an oak tree. **7.** There they would find Death. **8.** The young men hurried to the tree. **9.** But the only thing under the tree was a heap of gold. **10.** Now the young men no longer looked for Death. **11.** Instead, they thought of the money. **12.** Each wanted all the money for himself. **13.** The youngest of the men was sent into town on an errand. **14.** On his return he was killed by the other two. **15.** Then these two drank a toast to their good fortune. **16.** Soon they too died. **17.** The youngest man had poisoned their wine. **18.** Thus, all three men found Death. **19.** Greed is the source of much evil. **20.** This, of course, is the moral of the *exemplum*.

EXERCISE 8. Identifying Subjects and Verbs. Write the subject and the verb of each of the following sentences. Underline the subject once and the verb twice.

EXAMPLE   1. In 1825 a famous diary was published in six volumes.
           1. *diary* <u>*was published*</u>

1. For many years the diary had been written in a secret shorthand.
2. This secret shorthand was decoded after several years of hard work.
3. Samuel Pepys wrote this diary between 1660 and 1669.
4. A personal look at life in England during the seventeenth century is given in his diary.
5. Some of the entries tell about funny incidents of daily life.
6. Other entries are very serious.
7. In fact, in entries during 1666, Pepys described the great London fire.
8. What have accounts of the fire told us about this tragedy?
9. Pepys contributed his diaries and other works to Cambridge University.
10. These works are still read by people today.

EXERCISE 9. Identifying Subjects and Verbs. Find the subject and the verb in each sentence and write them on your paper after the proper number.

1. Carla's mother drove us to the theater.
2. The bumblebee carries pollen from one plant to another.
3. A strong, gusty wind is blowing out to sea this morning.
4. My sister accidentally locked her keys inside the car.
5. From Maine to California the bicyclists made a cross-country journey.
6. The Medusa of Greek mythology was one of the three Gorgons, terrible in appearance.
7. For many centuries she has been pictured with a head of snakes.
8. The picture of the Medusa with her snaky hair appears in many books on mythology.

9. According to myth, a glance at the Medusa would turn a mortal to stone.
10. She was slain by Perseus with the aid of the goddess Athena.

EXERCISE 10. Writing Complete Sentences. Some of the following word groups are complete subjects and some are complete predicates. Write each group of words on your paper, adding whatever part is needed to make it a sentence. Then underline the subject once and the verb twice.

EXAMPLE   1. marched for five hours
        1. *The* <u>members</u> *of the band* <u>marched</u> *for five hours.*

1. the videotape of the rock concert
2. should not be left alone
3. are fascinating stories
4. the vacant lot down the street
5. some students in Los Angeles
6. danced across the floor
7. looked mysteriously at us
8. their best player
9. the woman in the blue uniform at the ticket window
10. rescued the cat from the oak tree in front of the old brick building

THE SENTENCE BASE

You have been studying the two most important parts of the sentence: the subject and the verb. Because these two parts are essential to the sentence, they are called the *sentence base.* All other parts of the sentence are attached to the sentence base.

Sentence base: **Dogs play.**

Sentence base with other parts attached: Every day two frisky **dogs** named Bison and Stark **play** for hours on our front lawn.

The parts that were added give additional information, but they would be meaningless without the sentence base.

EXERCISE 11. Using the Sentence Base. The following subjects and verbs are sentence bases that state complete thoughts. Add other parts to each of these sentence bases. Notice how the sentence base holds the other parts together.

EXAMPLE   1. Balloons floated.
> 1. *At dawn, fifty hot-air balloons floated over Nashville.*

1. Sparks flashed.
2. Car swerved.
3. Lion roars.
4. Band played.
5. Runner was sprinting.
6. Flower bloomed.
7. Girl laughed.
8. Child jumped.
9. Riders were sitting.
10. Years have passed.

COMPOUND SUBJECTS AND COMPOUND VERBS

Some sentences have more than one subject.

ONE SUBJECT   **Alicia** carried her book.
TWO SUBJECTS   **Alicia** and **Joy** carried their books.
THREE SUBJECTS   **Alicia, Joy,** and **Carmen** carried their books.

ONE SUBJECT   **New York City** is our destination.
TWO SUBJECTS   Either **New York City** or **Niagara Falls** is our destination.

Notice that when two or more subjects have the same verb, a connecting word—usually *and* or *or*—is used between them. The connected subjects are referred to as a *compound subject*.

1f. A *compound subject* consists of two or more connected subjects that have the same verb. The usual connecting words are *and* and *or*.

COMPOUND SUBJECT The **Senate** and the **House** are in session.
[There are two subjects—*Senate* and *House*. They are joined by a connecting—*and*—and have the same verb—*are*.]

EXERCISE 12. Identifying Compound Subjects. On your paper, write the compound subject, together with the connecting words, from each of the following sentences. Then write the verb or verb phrase that goes with both subjects.

EXAMPLE 1. Cicely Tyson and Paul Winfield starred in a film together.
1. *Cicely Tyson and Paul Winfield—starred*

1. Florida and California have world-famous amusement parks.
2. Records and tapes were sold at a discount.
3. The Aztecs, the Mayas, and the Incas developed impressive Indian cultures in Central and South America.
4. Garlic or oregano may be used in the recipe.
5. Scarlett O'Hara and Melanie Wilkes were created by Margaret Mitchell.
6. On Tuesday the mayor and the governor were at the conference.
7. Suddenly, the sleet and the hail poured from the dark clouds.
8. Neither Jim nor Carol must take the test for science class.
9. In the center ring were ten clowns, five acrobats, and three elephants.
10. Hawaii, Maui, and Oahu are three of the Hawaiian Islands.

Just as a sentence may have a compound subject, so it may have a compound verb.

1g. A *compound verb* consists of two or more connected verbs that have the same subject.

ONE VERB Surfing **has become** a very popular sport.

COMPOUND VERB The dog **barked** and **growled** at the thief.
[There are two verbs—*barked* and *growled*—

joined by *and*. Both verbs have the same subject—*dog*.]

COMPOUND VERB   The man **was convicted** but later **was found** innocent of the crime. [There are two verb phrases—*was convicted* and *was found*—joined by *but*. Both verb phrases have the same subject—*man*.]

EXERCISE 13. Identifying Compound Verbs. Write the compound verb, together with the connecting word(s), from each of the following sentences. Then write the subject of the verb.

EXAMPLE   1. The hikers loaded their backpacks and studied the map of the mountain trails.
1. *loaded and studied—hikers*

1. Linda wrote her essay and practiced the piano last night.
2. Miami is the largest city in southern Florida and has been a popular resort area since the 1920's.
3. According to Greek mythology, Arachne angered Athena and was changed into a spider.
4. Martina Arroyo has sung in major American opera halls and has made appearances abroad.
5. The players either were bothered by the cold or were having a bad day.
6. During special sales, shoppers arrive early at the mall and search for bargains.
7. Maria Montessori studied medicine in Italy and developed new methods for teaching children.
8. Jim Rice autographed baseballs and made a short speech.
9. General Lee won many battles but lost the war.
10. In the summer many students go to music camps and improve their skills.

Sometimes you will see a sentence that has a compound subject and a compound verb. In such a sentence both of the subjects go with both of the verbs.

EXAMPLE
$$\overset{S}{}\quad\overset{S}{}\quad\overset{V}{}$$
The **captain** and the **crew battled** the storm and

$$\overset{V}{}$$
prayed for better weather. [Notice that both *captain* and *crew* performed both actions—*battled* and *prayed*.]

EXERCISE 14. Identifying Compound Subjects and Compound Verbs. Write the following sentences on your paper, underlining the subjects once and the verbs or verb phrases twice.

EXAMPLE   1. Several fine poems and novels were written by the Brontë sisters.

1. *Several fine <u>poems</u> and <u>novels</u> <u>were written</u> by the Brontë sisters.*

1. Charlotte and Emily are the most famous Brontë sisters.
2. Originally, they wrote and published under pen names.
3. *Jane Eyre* and *Wuthering Heights* are their well-known books.
4. In Charlotte Brontë's novel, Jane Eyre endured and overcame many hardships.
5. Emily Brontë's *Wuthering Heights* saddens me and makes me tearful.
6. Catherine Earnshaw and Heathcliff stand as unforgettable characters.
7. As children they wandered and explored the moor.
8. Catherine loved Heathcliff but married Edgar.
9. *Jane Eyre* and *Wuthering Heights* became movies.
10. I watched the movies and then read the books again.

EXERCISE 15. Writing Sentences with Compound Subjects and Compound Predicates. Using titles, words, and characters of songs, books, and poems, write ten sentences—five with compound subjects and five with compound predicates. Underline subjects once and verbs twice.

EXAMPLE   1. *<u>Tom Sawyer</u> and <u>Becky Thatcher</u> <u>were</u> childhood sweethearts.*

EXERCISE 16. Writing Complete Sentences. Write complete sentences by adding predicates to the following subjects. Vary your sentences by using some compound predicates. You may also add to the subjects, making them compound if you wish. Underline subjects once and verbs twice. Capitalize the first word of each sentence.

EXAMPLE   1. the bats
      1. *At midnight the <u>bats</u> <u><u>flew</u></u> out of the damp cave.*

1. the African elephant
2. the park near the lake
3. a group of hungry campers
4. my favorite movie star
5. an angry cat
6. the singer for the band
7. the grades for the semester
8. Jennifer
9. ten contestants
10. the teacher

CLASSIFYING SENTENCES BY PURPOSE

1h. Sentences may be classified according to purpose. There are four kinds of sentences.[1]

(1) A *declarative sentence* makes a statement. It is followed by a period.

EXAMPLES   Miriam Colon founded the Puerto Rican Traveling Theater.
Amelia Earhart was born in 1897.
Curiosity is the beginning of knowledge.

(2) An *interrogative sentence* asks a question. It is followed by a question mark.

EXAMPLES   What do you know about glaciers?
Why do we see only one side of the moon?
Who was the mother of Perseus?

[1] The classification of sentences according to structure (simple, compound, complex, compound-complex) is taught in Chapter 7.

(3) An *imperative sentence* gives a command or makes a request. It is followed by a period. Strong commands are followed by exclamation points.

EXAMPLES Do your homework each night.
             Watch out!
             Finish your work, John.

At first glance, none of these sentences seems to have any subject. Actually, the person addressed in each case is the subject. The subject *you* is said to be "understood" in such sentences.

(You) Do your homework each night.
(You) Watch out!
John, (you) finish your work, please.

(4) An *exclamatory sentence* shows excitement or expresses strong feeling. It is followed by an exclamation point.

EXAMPLES What a sight the sunset is!
             They're off!
             Sarah won the videotape player!

Many students have a tendency to overuse the exclamatory sentence. Be sure to save your exclamation points for sentences that really do show strong emotion. If overused, the exclamatory sentence loses its significance.

EXERCISE 17. Classifying Sentences. Each of the following items is a famous quotation. Number your paper 1–10. After each number, write the kind of sentence it is and give the punctuation mark that should follow the sentence.

EXAMPLE 1. The only thing we have to fear is fear itself
                           —FRANKLIN D. ROOSEVELT
        1. *declarative.*

1. Shall I compare thee to a summer's day
                       —WILLIAM SHAKESPEARE
2. Tact is after all a kind of mindreading—SARAH ORNE JEWETT
3. Sail on, O Ship of State—HENRY WADSWORTH LONGFELLOW

4. The history of every country begins in the heart of a man or woman—WILLA CATHER
5. What happiness is there which is not purchased with more or less of pain—MARGARET OLIPHANT
6. Bring me my bow of burning gold—WILLIAM BLAKE
7. No one can make you feel inferior without your consent
—ELEANOR ROOSEVELT
8. Since when was genius found respectable
—ELIZABETH BARRETT BROWNING
9. Never leave that till tomorrow which you can do today
—BENJAMIN FRANKLIN
10. An expert is one who knows more and more about less and less—NICHOLAS MURRAY BUTLER

WRITING APPLICATION B:
Adding Variety to Your Sentences by Placing the Subject in New Positions

Have you really looked at your room lately? You probably haven't unless something has been changed. When you see the same items in the same places over and over, you usually stop paying attention to them. This reaction to repetition is also true in writing. If you start every sentence with the subject, your reader may begin to lose interest. In other words, you need to liven up your writing to hold your reader's interest. One way to do this is to place the subject of your sentence in a new place, perhaps in the middle or at the end of the sentence.

EXAMPLES   "In spite of everything, **I** still believe that people are really good at heart."—ANNE FRANK

Across the bottom of the television picture came the **words** Tornado watch.

In the first example, the subject I is in the middle of the sentence. In the second example, the subject words is near the end of the sentence.

Writing Assignment

You have probably read several good biographies. The lives of other people—even ordinary people—are often a source of entertainment and sometimes of inspiration, too. Write a mini-biography of a friend or relative. Add variety by occasionally placing the subject in the middle or at the end of your sentences.

DIAGRAMING THE SUBJECT AND VERB

A diagram shows the structure of a sentence as a kind of picture. Making a diagram of the subject and the verb is a way of showing that you understand these two parts of the sentence.

PATTERN

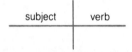

EXAMPLE   Lions roar.

EXAMPLE   People speak.

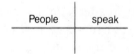

Notice that the parts of the sentence base—the subject and the verb—are placed on a horizontal line with a vertical line separating the subject from the verb. The capital marking the beginning of the sentence is used, but not the punctuation.

To diagram a sentence, first pick out the subject and the verb and then write them on the horizontal line, separated by a crossing vertical line.

EXAMPLES   1. The energetic reporter dashed to the fire.

2. Have you been studying for the final test?

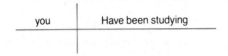

3. Listen to the beautiful music.

EXERCISE 18. Diagraming Simple Subjects and Verbs.

Diagram the simple subjects and verbs in the following sentences. Omit all other words from your diagram. Draw your diagrams with a ruler, and leave plenty of space between the diagrams.

1. Midas is a character in Greek mythology.
2. He was the king of Phrygia.
3. One of the gods gave Midas a magic power.
4. With this power, Midas could turn anything into gold.
5. This could be done with a simple touch of Midas' hand.
6. For a while, this gift pleased Midas.
7. Soon it became a curse.
8. Do you know why?
9. Read the story of King Midas in a mythology book.
10. Today, people with "the Midas touch" can make money in any project at all.

The following example shows how to diagram a sentence with a compound subject. Notice the position of the connecting word *and*.

EXAMPLE   Vines and weeds grew over the old well.

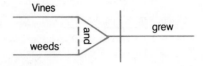

To diagram a sentence with a compound verb, follow a similar pattern.

EXAMPLE   The model walked across the platform and turned around.

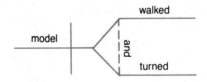

If the sentence has both a compound subject and a compound verb, it is diagramed this way:

EXAMPLE   Ken and Marti dived into the water and swam across the pool.

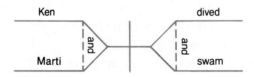

EXERCISE 19. Diagraming Subject and Verbs. Diagram the simple subjects and the verbs or verb phrases in the following sentences:

1. We ran to the railroad station and barely caught the train.
2. The students and the faculty combined their efforts and defeated the proposal.
3. The plane circled above the landing field but did not descend.
4. Pencil and paper are needed for tomorrow's assignment.
5. The actress and her costar prepared for the scene.

6. The students either wrote in ink or typed their compositions.
7. The President and the Congress approved the bill and provided the necessary money.
8. In the evening the crickets and frogs make loud noises.
9. She will write or call this week.
10. The workers and the management argued for hours but never reached an agreement.

REVIEW EXERCISE A. *Oral Drill.* **Identifying Subjects and Predicates.** Identify the complete subject and the complete predicate. Then identify the simple subject and the verb or verb phrase. Some sentences have compound subjects and verbs.

1. Collies and German shepherd dogs guard and herd sheep.
2. One German shepherd responded to one hundred commands.
3. Another dog could do about one hundred and fifty things.
4. People at the Gaines Research Center called Tubby the most useful animal in the United States.
5. It herded cattle, gathered firewood, and carried messages.
6. The trainer would scatter fifteen objects on the floor.
7. The dog would bring each object on command and drop it at the trainer's feet.
8. It hardly ever missed a command.
9. Other dogs have become famous for their intelligence.
10. Lassie and Rin Tin Tin are known to many movie fans.

REVIEW EXERCISE B. Identifying Complete Subjects and Predicates. Write the following sentences on your paper. Separate the complete subject from the complete predicate with a vertical line. Then underline the simple subject once and the verb twice.

EXAMPLE 1. Legends and folk tales have been repeated and enjoyed throughout the Americas.
   1. *Legends and folk tales* | *have been repeated* and *enjoyed throughout the Americas.*

1. The Chorotega people lived in Nicoya, Costa Rica, hundreds of years ago.
2. One Chorotega folk tale tells the story of Nicoya's treasure and praises Princess Nosara for her protection of it from the enemy.
3. The warriors of the Chireños landed on the Nicoyan peninsula and attacked the Chorotegas.
4. The Indians of Nicoya were surprised and could not react quickly.
5. Nosara grabbed the treasure in her father's house.
6. Nosara and her suitor took a bow and arrow and fled into the woods.
7. The two ran from the enemy all night and at last reached a river.
8. The brave girl dashed into the mountains, hid the treasure, and returned to the river.
9. The enemy killed the princess and her friend.
10. The murderous tribe never found the gold.

REVIEW EXERCISE C. Classifying Sentences and Identifying Subjects and Verbs. Write the following sentences, putting in the correct end punctuation. Then underline the simple subject once and the verb twice. After the sentence, write what kind of sentence it is.

EXAMPLE 1. Turn left at the corner
         1. (*you*) *Turn* left at the corner.—*imperative*

1. Several recent movies have shown the problems of life on a farm
2. How many times have they tried to win the championship
3. Imagine a ride in the space shuttle
4. Because of its funny appearance, the frilled lizard looks like a comical monster
5. Can you give me directions to the post office
6. How fresh the air feels after a storm
7. Think about both sides of the problem

8. Many large museums in America have pottery from New Mexico by Maria Martinez
9. What teams are playing in the World Series
10. What a fantastic world lies beneath the waves

CHAPTER 1 REVIEW: POSTTEST 1

A. Identifying Subjects and Predicates. Number your paper 1–15. After the proper number, write each italicized group of words and indicate whether it is the subject or the predicate of the sentence. If it is the subject, underline the simple subject. If it is the predicate, underline the simple predicate, or verb.

EXAMPLES   1. The little boy in the baseball uniform *ran up the stairs.*
1. *ran up the stairs*—predicate
2. *The little boy in the baseball uniform* ran up the stairs.
2. The little *boy* in the baseball uniform—subject

1. *Thursday's baseball game* was the longest one our team has played.
2. *The newborn sparrows in the nest* chirped hungrily.
3. *Does* Jill *know my brother*?
4. *My scout troop* will hike down to the lake and camp overnight.
5. My father's old lawnmower *never starts easily.*
6. *Look at that*!
7. *The striped gray cat or the bobtail black one* ate Benny's fish.
8. *Every Saturday night* my older sister *baby-sits for the family on the corner.*
9. *Perhaps* that way *would be easiest.*
10. My friend's hamster *spends hours in its little exercise wheel.*
11. Did *the clerk with the black hair or the clerk with the red hair* pack these groceries?
12. *This lake* is my favorite fishing spot.

13. *After dinner* my brother *gave me a ride to the bowling alley and treated me to a free game.*
14. No, *that one* is the wrong answer.
15. Past the bridge and a mile down the dirt road lay *some of the most beautiful woods in our state.*

B. Identifying Sentences by Purpose. Number your paper 16–25. After the proper number, identify each sentence as *declarative, interrogative, imperative,* or *exclamatory.*

EXAMPLE 1. Wow, what a beautiful day!
          1. *exclamatory*

16. Look up that word in the dictionary.
17. How can I find it if I don't know the spelling?
18. You can try several spellings until you discover the right one.
19. I'll never find it that way!
20. Yes, you will.
21. It'll take me all day though, won't it?
22. If you use your knowledge of spelling rules, it shouldn't take you too long.
23. That's easy for you to say!
24. Just calm down and use your head.
25. Oh, okay, I'll give it a try.

CHAPTER 1 REVIEW: POSTTEST 2

A. Identifying Subjects and Predicates. Number your paper 1–15. After the proper number, write each italicized group of words and indicate whether it is the subject or the predicate of the sentence. If it is the subject, underline the simple subject. If it is the predicate, underline the simple predicate, or verb.

EXAMPLES 1. *My aunt in Florida* took us to Sea World.
           1. *My aunt in Florida—subject*
           2. My aunt in Florida *took us to Sea World.*
           2. *took us to Sea World—predicate*

Our whole family (1) *drove down to my aunt's house in Florida last summer.* (2) *The long drive and the steamy heat, especially in the southern states,* wore out all of us.

The first two days at my aunt's house, (3) *my mother and father and my brother and I* spent almost all of our time in my aunt's air-conditioned back room. Lounging on the couch, we (4) *could look out the wall of windows at the lake and palm trees in the back yard.* My brother, (5) *naturally, was bored and pestered everyone.* (6) *Does* your little brother *always act that way, too*?

On the third day there, (7) *all of us* rode up to Sea World. (8) *The various exhibits and shows* featured all kinds of strange and wonderful animals. Many animals, particularly dolphins and killer whales, (9) *performed tricks and seemed very intelligent.*

In one huge tank swam (10) *scary-looking sharks.* A clear glass or plastic tunnel (11) *went right through the middle of the shark tank.* My mother and brother (12) *did not like the tunnel.*

(13) *My brother's favorite part of Sea World* was the pirate ship. He (14) *ran and played all over the ship with a bunch of other children his age.* Even after a whole day there, (15) *none of us* wanted to leave.

B. Identifying Sentences by Purpose.   Number your paper 16–25. After the proper number, identify each sentence as *declarative, interrogative, imperative,* or *exclamatory.*

EXAMPLE   1. Write your name at the top of your paper.
          1. *imperative*

16. Where have all the flowers gone?
17. The bears had ransacked our camp and eaten all our food supplies.
18. I give up!
19. Maria plans to study architecture at the state university after she graduates.
20. Don't ever let me hear you say that again.
21. This isn't the right answer, is it?
22. No, it definitely is not!

23. Clean up your room this instant, and don't make up any excuses or try to get out of it.
24. I can't right now, Mom; everybody's waiting for me down at Andy's house.
25. Is she the girl he asked to the dance?

CHAPTER 1 REVIEW: POSTTEST 3

Writing a Variety of Sentences. Write ten of your own sentences according to the guidelines given for each number. Make the subjects and predicates different for each sentence.

1. A declarative sentence with a compound subject
2. An imperative sentence with a compound predicate
3. A declarative sentence with a single subject and a single predicate
4. An interrogative sentence with a compound subject
5. An interrogative sentence with a compound predicate
6. An exclamatory sentence with a single subject and a single predicate
7. An imperative sentence with a single subject and a single predicate
8. A declarative sentence with a compound predicate
9. An exclamatory sentence with a compound predicate
10. A declarative sentence with a compound subject and a compound predicate

CHAPTER 2

The Parts of Speech

NOUN, PRONOUN, ADJECTIVE

There are many thousands of different words in the English language, but there are only eight different *kinds* of words. These eight kinds, which are called "parts of speech," are the *noun,* the *pronoun,* the *adjective,* the *verb,* the *adverb,* the *preposition,* the *conjunction,* and the *interjection.* In this chapter you will study three of these eight parts of speech: the *noun,* the *pronoun,* and the *adjective.*

DIAGNOSTIC TEST

Identifying Nouns, Pronouns, and Adjectives. Number your paper 1–20. After the proper number, write each italicized word in the following sentences and indicate whether it is a noun, a pronoun, or an adjective. Use the abbreviations *n.* (noun), *pron.* (pronoun), and *adj.* (adjective).

EXAMPLE 1. The airplane had two *wings* and a *wooden* propeller.
  1. *wings—n., wooden—adj.*

1. Sometimes I don't feel well when *it* gets cloudy and the *dark* sky threatens rain.

2. My little sister, *afraid* of thunder and *lightning,* hid under the bed.
3. Inger's mother gave *each* of us a tall glass of *cold* milk.
4. One by one, *each* husky ventured out into the *cold.*
5. *Who* went to church *Sunday* morning?
6. While the *Wilsons* were on vacation, Julio fed *their* dog and parakeet.
7. The house across the street has been up for *sale* again since *Tuesday.*
8. Under the *rotten* pine flooring my *brother-in-law* found a small tin canister.
9. *That* rifle doesn't belong to *anyone.*
10. *That* is a *Persian* cat.
11. Give me *some iced* tea, please.
12. *Somebody* said that there would be no more *discount* movie tickets.
13. I got a *discount* on *our* tickets, though.
14. *Mr. Taylor* donated the *sports* equipment.
15. Barney is going to try out for track and several *other sports.*
16. *Everyone* liked one painting or the *other.*
17. June went to the *mall* by *herself.*
18. Hobbies take up so *much* time that they often become *work.*
19. My father's *work* schedule often takes *him* out of town.
20. *This* parakeet screeches if you don't give him *enough* seed.

THE NOUN

One of the first things that happened to you after you were born was that you were given a name. More than likely, the first words that you learned to speak were also names of people and things. If you were to travel to a foreign country where a language other than English is spoken, you would soon find yourself asking,

"What's that called?" Knowing the names of things is basic to communication. A word that names something is called a *noun*.

2a. A *noun* is a word used to name a person, place, thing, or idea.

Persons	Helen Hayes, Dr. Lacy, child, architect
Places	Wyoming, Mexico, Europe, home, city
Things	money, shell, wind, worm, desk
Ideas	courage, love, freedom, sorrow, luck

Notice that some kinds of nouns name things that you can see, while others do not. The nouns that name unseen things, like ideas, can be more difficult to identify.

EXERCISE 1. Identifying Nouns.   Number your paper 1–10. Pick out fifty nouns from the following sentences. (*Which, they,* and *all* are not nouns.)

EXAMPLE   1. Both children and adults enjoyed the comedy.
　　　　　　1. *children, adults, comedy*

1. Rods, reels, and lines are called tackle.
2. Mines are important to the economy and industry of Utah.
3. Hobbies teach many people new skills and provide hours of entertainment.
4. During the war, women in our country worked in hospitals, factories, and offices.
5. The pollution of the air and the water has been a serious problem for many years.
6. Computers have become a part of the daily lives of both children and adults.
7. Huge crowds of people attended the Olympics last year.
8. All responsible citizens in a democracy should exercise the right to vote in elections.
9. Armadillos have an excellent sense of smell, which they use in their daily searches for food such as insects, lizards, and other small creatures.

10. A person never knows when courage will be needed in the face of danger or of a personal problem.

EXERCISE 2. Identifying Nouns. Number your paper 1–10. Pick out at least forty nouns from the following famous quotations. List each noun in order after the proper number. (The words *I, me, our, you, him,* and *it* are not nouns.)

EXAMPLE   1. The health of nations is more important than the wealth of nations.   —WILL DURANT
           1. *health, nations, wealth, nations*

1. The whole of science is nothing more than a refinement of everyday thinking.   —ALBERT EINSTEIN
2. The birthday of my life.
   Is come, my love is come to me.   —CHRISTINA ROSSETTI
3. Beauty is in the eye of the beholder.
         —MARGARET WOLFE HUNGERFORD
4. 'Tis education forms the common mind:
   Just as the twig is bent, the tree's inclined.
         —ALEXANDER POPE
5. You yet may spy the fawn at play,
   The hare upon the green;
   But the sweet face of Lucy Gray
   Will never more be seen.   —WILLIAM WORDSWORTH
6. I lift my lamp beside the golden door.   —EMMA LAZARUS
7. The snow had fallen thick over everything; in the pale starlight the line of bluffs across the wide, white meadows south of the town made soft, smoke-colored curves against the clear sky.   —WILLA CATHER
8. The paths of glory lead but to the grave.   —THOMAS GRAY
9. He was seated at one of those little bamboo tables decorated with a Japanese vase of paper daffodils.
         —KATHERINE MANSFIELD
10. Oh, talk not to me of a name great in story—
    The days of our youth are the days of our glory. . . .
          —GEORGE GORDON, LORD BYRON

Compound Nouns

Sometimes a single noun is made up of two or more words. These words may be written as a single word (redwood), as two words (red pepper), or with a hyphen (self-esteem). Nouns that are names of particular people or things also often consist of more than one word: Rose Fitzgerald Kennedy (a three-word noun), Buckingham Palace (a two-word noun), *The Adventures of Huckleberry Finn* (the name of a book; a five-word noun). Nouns, such as these, that have more than one word are called *compound nouns*. The only way to be sure that two or more words are a compound noun is to look them up in your dictionary.

Proper Nouns and Common Nouns

There are two main classes of nouns: common nouns and proper nouns. While the *common noun* names a class or a group of persons, places, or things, the proper noun names a particular person, place, or thing. The *proper noun* begins with a capital letter. If it consists of more than one word, each important word is capitalized *(Declaration of Independence)*.

COMMON NOUNS	PROPER NOUNS
poem	"To a Skylark"
country	Kenya
man	Roberto Clemente
ship	*Mayflower*
newspaper	*New York Times*
ocean	Pacific Ocean
street	Market Street
date	November 6, 1985
city	Los Angeles

EXERCISE 3. Identifying Nouns. Number your paper 1–10. After each number, list the nouns you find in the corresponding sentence. (*Note: One* and *their* are not nouns.)

EXAMPLE 1. Forests come in many different shapes, kinds, and sizes.
1. *forests, shapes, kinds, sizes*

1. Trees in a tropical jungle have an ample supply of water.
2. Rain forests are usually located in tropical regions.
3. However, one rain forest is on a peninsula in the northwestern state of Washington.
4. Along the coast of California grow the famous redwoods, the tallest trees in the world.
5. The forests in Canada contain mostly evergreens, which adapt well to a cold climate.
6. Forests in the temperate zones have evergreens and also trees that shed leaves, such as oaks, beeches, and maples.
7. The giant Douglas fir, an evergreen tree, is a valuable source of lumber.
8. Many other types of plants are dependent on trees for their life.
9. Forests swarm with insects, mammals, birds, and reptiles.
10. A national park such as Sequoia National Park protects large areas of forest.

REVIEW EXERCISE A. Classifying Nouns. Make two columns on your paper. Label one column *Proper Nouns* and the other column *Common Nouns*. Under the appropriate heading, list the nouns from the following paragraph.

Each day several thousand people visit the Lincoln Memorial in Washington. The monument was designed by Henry Bacon and was dedicated on Memorial Day. Located in West Potomac Park, the Lincoln Memorial consists of a large marble hall that encloses a lifelike statue of Abraham Lincoln. The figure, which was made from blocks of white marble by Daniel Chester French, a distinguished sculptor, is sitting in a large armchair as if in deep meditation. On the north wall is found a famous passage from an inaugural address by Lincoln, and on the south wall is inscribed the Gettysburg Address.

THE PRONOUN

Once you can recognize nouns, you can learn to identify pronouns. A *pronoun* is a word that stands for a noun. Without pronouns we would be forced to repeat the same nouns again and again.

EXAMPLE   When Kelly saw the signal, Kelly pointed the signal out to Teresa.
When Kelly saw the signal, **she** pointed **it** out to Teresa.

2b. A *pronoun* **is a word used in place of one or of more than one noun.**

Name the nouns that the pronouns in the following sentences stand for.

1. Gail read the book and returned **it** to the library.
2. The models bought **themselves** new dresses.
3. "Students," the teacher said, "**you** should keep vocabulary notebooks."
4. Sharon and Pat went fishing. **Both** caught six bass.

The noun that a pronoun stands for is called the *antecedent*. Sometimes the antecedent is not stated.

EXAMPLES
antecedent   pron.   pron.
Catherine told **her** father **she** would be late.

antecedent   pron.
Juanita, did **you** do the lesson?

pron.
You can't sleep now. [no antecedent stated]

There are several kinds of pronouns. The following pronouns are the *personal pronouns:*

I, me, mine, my, myself
you, your, yours, yourself, yourselves
he, him, his, himself
she, her, hers, herself

it, its, itself
we, us, our, ours, ourselves
they, them, their, theirs, themselves

In this book, pronouns that come directly before nouns and show possession (*my, his, her, its, your, their*) are called *possessive pronouns*. Your teacher may prefer that you call them *possessive adjectives*.

Make sure that you learn the differences between *its* and *it's* and between *their, they're*, and *there*. Avoid using *hisself* and *theirselves*, which are not standard English.[1]

Other common pronouns are

who, whom, whoever, whomever
everybody, everyone, someone, somebody,
no one, nobody, none, others

The following words are pronouns when they are used in the place of nouns:

what, which, whatever, whichever, whose
this, that, these, those
one, each, some, any, other, another
many, more, much, most
both, several, few, all, either, neither

EXERCISE 4. Identifying Pronouns.   Number your paper 1–10. List the pronouns in each of the following sentences after the appropriate number. After each pronoun, write the noun or nouns that the pronoun refers to.

EXAMPLE   1. Beth saw the kittens in the snow, and she decided
                to bring them inside.
            1. *she—Beth*
               them—kittens

---

[1] *Standard* and *nonstandard* are the terms used in this book to describe kinds of usage. This book teaches standard English. The word *standard* suggests a model with which things can be compared. In this case, the model—standard English—is the set of usage conventions most widely accepted by English-speaking people. All other kinds of usage are called *nonstandard* English. These are variations in usage that are not suitable in formal writing and formal speaking.

1. When the luggage cart fell on its side, the bags and their contents scattered everywhere.
2. The passengers scrambled to find their luggage; they even got down on their hands and knees to pick up the belongings.
3. One salesperson shouted, "This bag belongs to me! It has my name on it."
4. "Are you sure these socks are yours?" asked another traveler. "I have a pair just like them."
5. One couple asked, "Who owns a pink-and-yellow shirt? This isn't ours."
6. As a crowd of people gathered, many just laughed, but several offered to help.
7. The travelers found themselves quibbling over toothbrushes, combs, and magazines.
8. "Where's my hairbrush!" exclaimed one irate person.
9. One worried traveler asked, "Where are the birthday presents for my cousin? He will be disappointed if I lose them."
10. Finally, the problem was resolved, and no one was unhappy or angry.

WRITING APPLICATION A:
Using Pronouns to Avoid Unnecessary Repetition

Sometimes people don't realize that they are telling you the same things over and over. At times they even repeat the exact words. How do you feel when this happens? You probably get irritated and impatient. You might want to say, "You've told me that three times already!" In your writing, you can use pronouns to avoid irritating your reader with unnecessary repetition of nouns. Skillful use of pronouns makes your writing smoother and more interesting—and certainly less monotonous. You can see in the following example that the use of pronouns would make the information on Poe much smoother.

Edgar Allan Poe had a sad life. Edgar Allan Poe was the son of professional actors. Edgar Allan Poe was an orphan at age three. Edgar Allan Poe was raised and educated by a wealthy couple in Virginia. Edgar Allan Poe could not get along with Poe's foster father. Edgar Allan Poe's young wife died of tuberculosis. Edgar Allan Poe did not take good care of Edgar Allan Poe, and Edgar Allan Poe survived Poe's wife by only two years.

Writing Assignment

Select a well-known person from public life, the entertainment field, or sports. Describe this person without revealing his or her name until the end of your paragraph. Have the class guess who the person is.

EXERCISE 5. Writing Pronouns in Sentences. Rewrite the following paragraphs by filling in the blanks with appropriate pronouns. If necessary, refer to the lists of pronouns on page 40.

Let —— tell —— about the experience that —— of my friends, Mary Tam, had on vacation. —— was taking a group tour through the dense Australian forests. After traveling for hours at night through wilderness, —— in the group wanted to make camp, but the guide insisted that —— continue. Finally, —— agreed to travel for just one more hour.

Soon —— were rewarded for the trip. At the edge of the forest, the guide pointed to the top of a large tree where several koalas were feeding. —— of the animals swung from one tree to ——.

The tour watched —— from the ground. —— dared to speak a word. The koalas munched happily on the leaves of the trees. —— held onto branches with their sharp claws. —— of the animals carried a cub on her back. —— was feeding the cub while she also fed ——.

Although —— of the koalas have been hunted ruthlessly, a —— of the animals thrive within remote Australian forests. —— of the tour members marveled at the unique appearance of the koalas. —— look different from any other animal in the world.

EXERCISE 6. Identifying Pronouns. Number your paper 1–10. List the pronouns in each of the following sentences after the proper number. Underline the possessive pronouns.

EXAMPLE 1. What do you know about her life?
         1. *What, you, <u>her</u>*

1. On our way home from school, we heard the sirens of twelve fire engines.
2. Rats are the ugliest creatures one can imagine; they are also very dangerous.
3. Both of them were delighted to see their names in the newspaper.
4. They give us a swimming lesson during each of the gym periods.
5. Do you think she noticed the ink stain on my new plaid shirt?
6. Most of your efforts in school will help you later in college and in a career.
7. He immediately complimented them on their beautiful dancing.
8. Please tell me if someone is going to make breakfast for all of us.
9. Because everyone else is rooting for the underdog team, I am cheering for the team expected to win.
10. She and Dan like summer best, but I can't wait for it to be over.

REVIEW EXERCISE B. Identifying Pronouns. Number your paper 1–10. Write the pronouns from each sentence after the corresponding number. Circle all possessive pronouns.

1. All of us saw Rosemary Casals play in the tennis tournament.
2. Many of the spectators watching in the stands play tennis themselves.
3. Who would not like to be on the court playing during one of the sets?
4. Casals began to play, and the crowd was awed by the strength of her serve.
5. People were amazed that anyone could play with that much stamina.
6. Casals played such a strong game that she seemed to be rewarding us for our support.
7. Did you know that Rosemary Casals has played in many tennis tournaments?
8. I remembered that Casals had won my admiration by fighting for equal rights for women in professional tennis.
9. Several people in the audience showed by their enthusiasm that they had enjoyed watching the matches.
10. We met them for dinner after the tournament.

THE ADJECTIVE

Jennie goes fishing, and after an exciting struggle she reels in a trout that is over twenty inches long and weighs almost five pounds. She will not be content with describing her catch merely as a trout. Rather, she will call it a *large* trout or even a *huge* trout.

Allen and Sonia have just finished the final exam for the history course they are taking. Neither of them will be satisfied with saying merely that it was a test. Rather, they will describe the test as being *long* or *difficult* or even *unfair*.

Often we are not satisfied with just naming things—*trout, test.* We like to make a noun more definite by describing it in some way. The words that we use to make a noun more definite are called *adjectives*. When a noun is described by an adjective, it is said to be *modified*. Since a pronoun may be used in place of a noun, it too may be described, or modified, by an adjective.

2c. An *adjective* is a word used to modify a noun or a pronoun.

An adjective often answers one of these questions: *What kind? Which one? How much?* or *How many?*

WHAT KIND?	WHICH ONE?	HOW MUCH? OR HOW MANY?
a *tall* woman	the *other* one	*five* times
a *steep* mountain	*this* year	*many* mistakes
a *long* hike	the *last* answer	*several* others
an *eager* clerk	*those* people	*no* supplies
a *tired* dog	*that* dress	*few* marbles

The most frequently used adjectives are *a, an,* and *the.* These three adjectives are called *articles*.

EXERCISE 7. Writing Appropriate Adjectives. Rewrite the following sentences, replacing the italicized questions with adjectives that answer the questions.

EXAMPLE 1. They sold *how many?* tickets for the *which one?* show and *how many?* tickets for the *which one?* one.
   1. *They sold fifty tickets for the first show and seventy-five tickets for the last one.*

1. Even though we had run *how many?* laps around the track, we still had to run *how many?* others.
2. *Which one?* weekend, *how many?* hikers went on a *what kind?* trip to the *what kind?* park.
3. We rode in a *what kind?* van that carried *how many?* people and went *how many?* miles to the basketball game.
4. There was *how much?* time left when I started to answer the *which one?* question on the test.
5. During the *what kind?* afternoon we washed more than *how many?* cars and earned *how many?* dollars.

In Exercise 7, all adjectives preceded the nouns they modified. However, an adjective sometimes follows the word it modifies. Note the position of the adjectives in the following sentences. An arrow is drawn from the adjective to the word it modifies.

Each one of the students brought **used books** for the auction.

The **books,** although **old** and **worn,** were quickly bought.

EXERCISE 8. Identifying Adjectives and the Words They Modify.

Write the following sentences, underlining the adjectives. Then draw an arrow from each adjective to the noun it modifies. Do not underline *a, an,* and *the,* but remember that they are adjectives.

EXAMPLE 1. It was a stormy night by the time the weary hikers reached the campground.

1. *It was a stormy night by the time the weary hikers reached the campground.*

1. Melville described whaling in his famous novel *Moby Dick*.
2. Whaling used to be considered an exciting and romantic adventure.
3. Whalers took long voyages on sailing ships with tall masts.
4. Modern whaling is a different kind of adventure.
5. Today, ships that hunt for whales are huge floating factories.
6. Sharp harpoons are shot from guns and carry explosive tips.
7. In the nineteenth century, the products of whaling had great value, but today the products are not in much demand.
8. Some types of whales are becoming a rare sight in the oceans of the world.
9. Of the nine species of whales, six are now on the list of endangered species.
10. Citizens, both young and old, have been working for a long time to protect whales.

EXERCISE 9. Identifying Adjectives. There are twenty-five adjectives in the following paragraph. Make a list of them as they appear. Do not list articles.

1. The ancient Greeks and Romans worshiped twelve major gods. 2. The one with the most power was Zeus, or Jupiter, who lived on a high mountain, Mount Olympus. 3. From the cloudy peak he surveyed the various affairs of the world. 4. He rode in a great chariot that was drawn by four white horses. 5. Whenever he liked, he called for a great assembly of the gods. 6. At the huge assembly would be Poseidon, or Neptune, the god of the sea; Hades, or Pluto, the god of the shadowy land of the dead; Hera, or Juno, the beautiful but quarrelsome wife of Zeus; Apollo, the handsome god of the sun; Artemis, or Diana, the swift goddess of the hunt, who in time became known as the goddess of the moon; Hermes, or Mercury, the swift messenger of the gods; Hestia, or Vesta, the goddess of the hearth, who became a special protector of the home; Ares, or Mars, the dreadful god of war; Athena, or Minerva, the favorite daughter of Zeus, who was noted for her great wisdom; Hephaestus, or Vulcan, the ugly god, who was the useful god of fire and of the forge; and Aphrodite, or Venus, the lovely goddess of beauty.

EXERCISE 10. Writing Sentences with Adjectives. Except for *a, an,* and *the,* the following sentences contain no adjectives. Rewrite each sentence and, wherever possible, add interesting adjectives to modify the nouns and pronouns.

EXAMPLE 1. The children took a nap.
1. *The five grumpy children took a long nap.*

1. Carolyn gave a cat to her aunt.
2. The car stopped, and a woman stepped out.
3. We walked for hours until we reached a farm.
4. Luis donated books and jeans for the sale.
5. We watched the parade pass under our window.
6. The heat made everyone leave the auditorium.

7. The fielder caught the ball and made a throw to the catcher.
8. The dancer leaped across the stage.
9. After sewing for hours, Michele finished the costumes for the party.
10. The award was given to the brothers.

Proper Adjectives

When you speak of the poetry of Homer, you use a proper noun, but when you say *Homeric* poetry, you use a proper adjective. A *proper adjective* is formed from a proper noun, and like a proper noun, it begins with a capital letter.

PROPER NOUN	PROPER ADJECTIVE
Mexico	**Mexican** capital
Africa	**African** nations
China	**Chinese** calendar
President	**Presidential** powers
Islam	**Islamic** law

EXERCISE 11. Identifying Proper Nouns and Proper Adjectives. Number your paper 1–10. If a sentence contains a proper noun, write the noun after the corresponding number. If the sentence contains a proper adjective, write both the adjective and the noun it modifies. Some sentences contain both proper nouns and proper adjectives.

EXAMPLE 1. In recent years many American tourists have visited the Great Wall in China.
   1. *American tourists, Great Wall, China*

1. The Colorado beetle has destroyed many potato crops in the United States.
2. The professor of African literature gave a lecture on the novels of Camara Laye, a writer who was born in Guinea.
3. Marian McPartland, a jazz pianist from New York City, played several songs that Scott Joplin wrote.
4. The program about the Egyptian ruins was narrated by an English scientist and a French anthropologist.

5. The exchange students from Europe were fascinated by the video games in America.
6. The society of Victorian England was the subject of many British novels in the late 1800's.
7. During the press conference the President commented on the Congressional vote.
8. My friend from Tokyo gave me a Japanese kimono.
9. We saw a display of Appalachian crafts in the public library.
10. I fell asleep during the Shakespearean drama at the theater.

WRITING APPLICATION B:
Making Writing More Exact Through the Careful Use of Adjectives

Some words, especially adjectives, have been used so many times that they no longer carry much meaning. If you describe a friend with words like *nice, great,* and other common adjectives, you are not being very specific. One way to increase your word power is to keep a notebook of new adjectives. Using these adjectives in your writing and speaking will help you in two ways: You will learn new words that will enable you to communicate more information, and you will be more exact.

EXAMPLE   The people of Florida would not allow the old capitol to be destroyed. They raised money to restore the interior to the way it had been in 1845. Red, white, and blue were the original colors, but they had been natural colors and soft pastels. The ceiling over the entry hall has been painted in a *terra-cotta* red.

Do you know what *terra cotta* is? Other specific color adjectives include *azure, mauve, cerise, taupe,* and *scarlet.*

Writing Assignment

Having seen advertisements and commercials nearly all your life, you can probably write one of your own. Make up a new product that would be a magnificent discovery. Write a sales pitch or some other kind of advertisement for this product. Use at least three lively, exact adjectives describing your new product. Underline these adjectives.

Changing Parts of Speech

Sometimes nouns are used as adjectives: *Marian's* book, *airplane* ride, *school* mascot. *Marian, airplane,* and *school* are nouns, but they act as adjectives when they are put in front of nouns. The way that a word is used in a sentence determines what part of speech it is. Whenever a noun is used as an adjective in exercises dealing with parts of speech, label such a noun as an adjective.

Words such as *each, some,* and *whose* are sometimes pronouns and sometimes adjectives, depending on their use in a sentence. When they are used in place of nouns, they are pronouns; when they modify nouns, they are adjectives. If they are adjectives, they always precede a noun.

PRONOUN **Each** did the assignment.
ADJECTIVE **Each** person did the assignment.

PRONOUN **Some** have gone to their dressing rooms.
ADJECTIVE **Some** actors have gone to their dressing rooms.

PRONOUN **Whose** are these?
ADJECTIVE **Whose** gloves are these?

EXERCISE 12. Identifying Adjectives and Pronouns. In each of the following sentences, decide whether the word in italics is used as an adjective or as a pronoun. Number your paper 1–10. Beside the appropriate number, write *adj.* when the word is an adjective and *pron.* when the word is a pronoun.

EXAMPLE 1. Say *whatever* you think.
　　　　　 1. *pron.*

1. *Both* passed the test.
2. At the tryouts *each* one of the students recited the lines from the first act.
3. *Many* high schools offer driver training.
4. It's hard to know what *one* should do in this situation.
5. *Some* twins do not look exactly alike.
6. After several days in Paris, *each* of the tourists flew to London.
7. They took *both* bicycles to be repaired.
8. Sally asked *another* friend to the party.
9. *Many* of us volunteered to help the teacher.
10. A unicycle has only *one* wheel, making it difficult to ride.

REVIEW EXERCISE C. Identifying Adjectives. There are twenty adjectives in the following sentences. Number your paper 1–10. Write the adjectives in each sentence after the corresponding number on your paper. Do not list articles. Be careful not to confuse adjectives with pronouns.

1. There are many ideas and interesting predictions about the future. **2.** Some people say that television will play a larger part in our lives. **3.** Those people predict that in the future we will never have to leave our comfortable homes. **4.** In fact, even today few homes are without a television. **5.** One day, however, we may buy new clothes or read our favorite books through television. **6.** We may even vote in national elections from our homes. **7.** We may also study English literature or learn another language on TV. **8.** Would it be much fun to study school subjects this way? **9.** Imagine never meeting good friends whose jokes make you laugh or going to an exciting game between rival schools. **10.** Then again, these predictions may never happen.

DIAGRAMING NOUNS AND ADJECTIVES

Diagraming, as you recall from Chapter 1, is a way of showing that you understand the relationships between words and groups of words. When you first studied the adjective, you drew an arrow from the adjective to the noun that it modified. This relationship can also be expressed in a diagram.

PATTERN

EXAMPLES   bright star   a special person

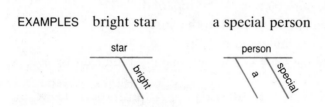

Two or more adjectives joined by a connecting word are diagramed this way.

PATTERN

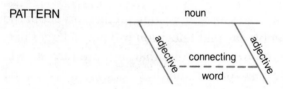

EXAMPLES   her red and white boots

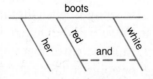

Notice that possessive pronouns are diagramed in the same way adjectives are.

EXERCISE 13. Diagraming Nouns and Adjectives.
Diagram the following items. Draw your diagrams with a ruler and allow plenty of space between diagrams.

1. mighty warrior
2. big blue ox
3. a narrow path
4. long, exciting movie
5. his one purpose

6. the last one
7. blue and silver streamers
8. many others
9. my final offer
10. the slow but persistent turtle

EXERCISE 14. Diagraming Sentences. Diagram the following sentences.

EXAMPLE   1. A funny clown performed.

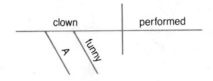

1. Our Swedish visitor arrived.
2. Several answers were given.
3. The angry dog growled.
4. Each one agreed.
5. Our problem has been solved.
6. The small, shy boy won.
7. The poor but generous woman helped.
8. A house and a large barn have burned.
9. The noisy crowd jeered and shouted.
10. My favorite candidate will speak.

REVIEW EXERCISE D. Identifying Nouns, Pronouns, and Adjectives. Write the following paragraph on your paper, leaving an extra line of space between lines of writing. Over each noun, write *n.;* over each pronoun, write *pron.;* and over each adjective, write *adj.* Disregard the articles *a, an,* and *the.*

Charles Drew developed techniques that are used in the separation and preservation of blood. His research saved numerous lives during World War II. After he received his medical degrees, he taught at Howard University in Washington, D.C. He set up centers in which blood could be stored.

The British government asked him to develop a storage system in England. During the war, Dr. Drew was director of an important effort for the American Red Cross that involved the donation of blood. Dr. Drew was also chief surgeon at Freedman's Hospital. We are indebted to this scientist for his great contributions. Many people who have needed blood owe their lives to his methods.

REVIEW EXERCISE E. Diagraming Sentences.   Diagram the following sentences:

1. Every minute counts.
2. Many famous politicians attended.
3. Five days and five nights passed.
4. The powerful motor shook and roared.
5. The golden clock struck.
6. A few people have left.
7. Several dark clouds can be seen.
8. The ventriloquist and the dummy talked and sang.
9. My favorite comedian is performing.
10. Black and white horses have been sold.

CHAPTER 2 REVIEW: POSTTEST 1

Identifying Nouns, Pronouns, and Adjectives.   Number your paper 1–25. After the proper number, write each italicized word in the following sentences, and indicate whether it is a noun, a pronoun, or an adjective. Use the abbreviations *n.* (noun), *pron.* (pronoun), and *adj.* (adjective).

1. Jenna prepared supper *herself this* morning.
2. *Everybody* says that *high school* will be more work, but more fun, too.
3. *This* is the biggest mistake *they* ever made.
4. Jackie became a *high-school* senior *last* year.
5. Does *anybody* know *whose* bicycle this is?
6. *Mr. Lander* owns a grove of citrus trees.

7. That *German shepherd dog* is a *vicious* animal.
8. The lady across the street owns a *German* clock that has *ivory* numbers.
9. Vincent lived in *Los Angeles* before *his* family moved here.
10. This is *their* fault because they ignored all the *danger* signals.
11. I'm telling you, *you* are in *danger*.
12. *It* seemed that *whatever* happened always turned out all right.
13. The answer, *plain* and simple, is that *somebody* needs to do more work.
14. Give me *some* candy out of that *old* jar, will you?
15. The *football* player had to retire after his third knee *injury*.
16. Are you going to the *dance Saturday* night?
17. I told him to give you *something* for *your* stomachache.
18. The dogcatcher picked up *my* dog last *Saturday*.
19. *Each* student was required to take *English*.
20. *Each* of them believed that the *best* response would be no response at all.
21. *No one* gave Ms. Lucas *any* trouble.
22. *That* drummer is the *best*.
23. The *waiter* brought dessert even though Richard had said that he didn't want *any*.
24. *Mama* said to turn off the *television,* Billy.
25. I learned a new *dance* step from that *television* show.

CHAPTER 2 REVIEW: POSTTEST 2

Identifying Nouns, Pronouns, and Adjectives. Number your paper 1–25. The italicized words in the following paragraphs have been numbered. After the proper number, write each italicized word, and indicate whether it is a noun, a pronoun, or an adjective. Use the abbreviations *n.* (noun), *pron.* (pronoun), and *adj.* (adjective).

The (1) *first* week of (2) *school* is always confusing. (3) *Many* of the students are trying to find their classes, while the teachers and school (4) *staff* are busy adjusting to new schedules. Often, the bells ring at (5) *odd* times, (6) *which* creates additional confusion.

(7) *This* year my first class is (8) *English.* For (9) *some* reason I had difficulty finding the (10) *right* classroom the first few days. By the end of the first week my (11) *English* teacher had dubbed (12) *me* the "late arrival." At (13) *first* I thought that she was angry with me; however, I soon realized that (14) *she* was only joking.

By the end of the (15) *second* week (16) *most* students are settled into their new routines. (17) *Some,* though, take longer to get (18) *themselves* adjusted. One of my friends always finds it (19) *difficult* to leave (20) *summer* behind. We usually ride (21) *our* bikes to school together, and she often is not ready on time during the first (22) *few* weeks of the year.

Nevertheless, she always gets (23) *good* grades. Although she may seem confused sometimes, I wonder whether she is really confused at all, or whether she simply wants (24) *summer* vacation to last a little (25) *bit* longer.

CHAPTER 2 REVIEW: POSTTEST 3

Writing Sentences with Nouns, Pronouns, and Adjectives. Use each of the following words as a noun, a pronoun, or an adjective in two sentences. Write the part of speech of the word after each sentence.

EXAMPLE   1. this
      1. *This bicycle is mine.   adjective*
      2. *This cannot be the right answer.   pronoun*

1. game	6. that	11. first	16. one
2. their	7. green	12. paper	17. many
3. American	8. school	13. lake	18. money
4. right	9. mine	14. square	19. date
5. anybody	10. they	15. bicycle	20. government

CHAPTER 3

The Parts of Speech

VERB, ADVERB, PREPOSITION, CONJUNCTION, INTERJECTION

In Chapter 2 you studied two of the workhorses of the sentence—the *noun* and the *pronoun*—and the part of speech that makes the noun or pronoun more definite—the *adjective*. In this chapter you will learn about the other workhorse of the sentence—the *verb*—and the remaining four parts of speech—*adverb, preposition, conjunction*, and *interjection*.

DIAGNOSTIC TEST

Identifying Verbs, Adverbs, Prepositions, Conjunctions, and Interjections. Number your paper 1–20. After the proper number, write each italicized word or word group in the following sentences and indicate whether it is a verb, an adverb, a preposition, a conjunction, or an interjection. Use the abbreviations *v.* (verb), *adv.* (adverb), *prep.* (preposition), *conj.* (conjunction), and *interj.* (interjection). For each verb, indicate whether it is an action verb, a linking verb, or a helping verb.

EXAMPLE 1. That girl has *traveled widely* with her family.
　　　　　 1. *traveled—v. (action), widely—adv.*

57

Turn to page 281

1. Rosie *hit* a home run *and* tied up the score.
2. *Wow,* that's the best meal I've eaten *in* a long time!
3. School *can* be fun *sometimes.*
4. *Neither* Carlos *nor* Jan wanted to go *very* far out in the water.
5. That dog *looks* mean *in spite of* his wagging tail.
6. Have you *ever* seen any wild animals *around* here?
7. If Ken will *not* help us, then he cannot *share* in the rewards.
8. My older sister *was* a cheerleader *during* her senior year.
9. The road that runs *close* to the railroad tracks is *usually* crowded.
10. Several *of* my friends *enjoy* working at the mall.
11. No one could *do* much to help, *for* the damage had already been done.
12. *Where* have you been *putting* the corrected papers?
13. *Oh,* I didn't know he had *already* volunteered.
14. Jodie *was* taking in the wash *for* her mother.
15. *Surely,* Ms. Johnson doesn't *expect* us to finish by tomorrow.
16. *May* I have a glass of milk and a combination sandwich *without* onions?
17. James *became* impatient, *but* he waited quietly.
18. My uncle *almost* always brings us something when he *visits* during the holidays.
19. The car swerved *suddenly, yet* the driver remained in control.
20. Everybody was amazed *at* what a fighter she *became* when angered.

THE VERB

You know that the verb is one of the parts of a sentence base. It helps to make a statement about its subject. Some verbs do this by expressing the action of the subject: girl *ran;* monkeys *chatter;* sun *sets.* Other verbs help to make a statement without expressing action: I *am* an eighth-grader; this *is* good; they *seem* happy.

3a. A *verb* is a word that expresses action or otherwise helps to make a statement.

Action Verbs

The action expressed by a verb may be physical action or mental action.

PHYSICAL ACTION   jump, shout, search, carry, run

MENTAL ACTION   worry, think, believe, imagine

The action verbs in the following sentences are in boldfaced type.

Langston Hughes **wrote** volumes of poetry.
Julia Child **makes** gourmet cooking fun.
A distinguished cinematographer, James Wong Howe, **filmed** the movie.
We **listened** to the *Jupiter* Symphony by Mozart.
They **watched** all of Julie Andrews' movies.
She **remembered** the song.

EXERCISE 1. Identifying Action Verbs. Number your paper 1–11. After the proper number, write the verb or verbs in each sentence. There is a total of twenty verbs in the passage. They are all action verbs.

1. In the winter our house makes strange noises.   **2.** Doors on old brass hinges creak as they open and close.   **3.** Pipes in the basement shudder when the water heater starts up.   **4.** Loose floorboards crack from the weight of footsteps.   **5.** The window curtains rustle softly when the winds blow outside.   **6.** The old china cabinet clatters each time a truck passes by.   **7.** Beams and rafters in the attic strain and groan during the cold, windy nights.
8. Often members of my family sit silently and listen for these noises of the house.   **9.** We disconnect the television and the appliances.   **10.** Each of us makes a list of the various sounds.

11. Sometimes we pretend that ghosts lurk upstairs and cause the eerie noises.

Linking Verbs

Many important verbs do not express action. Instead, they help to make a statement by acting as links between a subject, which normally comes before the verb, and a word in the predicate, which usually follows the verb. Such verbs are called *linking verbs* because they link their subjects with nouns or adjectives in the predicate.

EXAMPLES   The star's name **is** Ruby Dee. [name = Ruby Dee]

Marie Curie **became** a famous scientist. [Marie Curie = scientist]

Wild animals **remain** free on the great animal reserves in Africa. [free animals]

The student from Germany **seemed** lonely and unhappy. [lonely and unhappy student]

The watermelon **looks** ripe. [ripe watermelon]

The verb most commonly used as a linking verb is the verb *be.* You should memorize its various forms.

Forms of the Verb Be

am, is, are, was, were, be, being, been

Any verb ending in *be* or *been* is a form of *be: shall be, will be, can be, might be, has been, have been, had been, would have been, might have been,* etc.

In addition to *be,* there are several other verbs that are often used as linking verbs:

seem, appear, look	taste, feel, smell, sound
become, grow	remain, stay

EXERCISE 2. Writing Linking Verbs.   Write the following sentences, inserting a linking verb in each blank. Use a different

verb for each sentence. Be prepared to tell what word each verb links to its subject.

EXAMPLE   1. Judith Jamison —— calm during the premiere of the dance.

           1. *Judith Jamison <u>remained</u> calm during the premiere of the dance.* [*Remained* links *Jamison* and *calm.*]

1. The first day —— long.
2. Your suggestion —— good to me.
3. Our room —— festive after we decorated it for the party.
4. The orange —— a little too sweet.
5. In the novel the main character —— a doctor, and he returns home to set up a clinic.
6. Before a storm the air —— wet and heavy.
7. Did she —— happy living in Florida?
8. The diver —— more confident with each dive she made.
9. They —— interested in the guest speaker.
10. The lilacs —— lovely.

Most linking verbs may also be used as action verbs. Whether a verb is used to express action or to link words depends on its meaning in a given sentence.

LINKING   The tiger **looked** tame.
ACTION   The tiger **looked** for something to eat.

LINKING   The soup **tasted** good.
ACTION   I **tasted** the soup.

LINKING   She **grew** tired of playing.
ACTION   She **grew** into a fine woman.

EXERCISE 3. Identifying Action Verbs and Linking Verbs.

Number your paper 1–10. In the following sentences, the verbs are used either as action verbs or as linking verbs. When the verb is used as an action verb, write the verb and its subject beside the appropriate number. When the verb is used as a linking verb, write the verb, its subject, and the word or words that the verb links to its subject.

EXAMPLES   1. Ms. Brody appeared suddenly in the classroom.
              1. *appeared, Ms. Brody*
              2. Ms. Brody appeared quite cheerful.
              2. *appeared, Ms. Brody—cheerful*

1. At Marla's request, we tasted the chili.
2. The chili tasted very spicy.
3. The cook looked unhappy about our comments.
4. She looked at her sister Joan suspiciously.
5. Yesterday the chili looked good, but it was too spicy.
6. Marla looked at Joan then, too.
7. Joan felt mischievous.
8. She felt a laugh in the back of her throat.
9. The doorbell sounded down the hall.
10. Marla's voice sounded angry because Joan had added too much chili powder to her recipe again.

EXERCISE 4. Writing Sentences with Linking Verbs and Action Verbs. Write two sentences for each of the following verbs. In the first sentence, use the verb as a linking verb; in the second, use it as an action verb.

EXAMPLE   1. remained
            1. *The animals remained calm after the clap of thunder.*
            We remained in our seats after the bell rang.

1. tastes   3. appear   5. feels
2. smelled   4. looked

EXERCISE 5. Identifying Verbs. Number your paper 1–14. After the proper number, list the verb or verbs that appear on that line. If the verb is a linking verb, list also the subject and the word or words which the verb links to its subject.

1   Matt is a young musician who loves all kinds of music.
2   According to his parents, he practices the piano every day.
3   No one knows how many hours he plays each week, al-
4   though many people guess at least fifteen. His parents

5   worry about him. They think he remains indoors too much.
6   Still, Matt seems happy.
7   One day Matt becomes restless. The notes sound wrong,
8   and everything appears impossible. However, Matt seems
9   confident. He grabs some sheets of music paper and then
10 writes down some notes. After some careful revisions Matt
11 forms the notes into an original harmony.
12   Later that night he performs his song for his parents.
13 They exclaim, "Matt, we are so proud of our son, the pianist
14 and composer!"

WRITING APPLICATION A:
Using Verbs That Make Your Writing Fresh and Lively

Verbs are vital to communication. They express the action taken or experienced by the subject in a sentence. To make your writing lively and original, select your verbs with care. Try to use verbs that catch your reader's attention. Sportswriters often vary their verbs to give their reports more action and excitement.

EXAMPLES   Celtics **rip** past Lakers
                Mississippi State **bashes** Michigan

Writing Assignment

When you use chronological order, you tell what happened by placing events in the order in which they occurred. Write a summary of an incident from a book, a movie, or a television show that you consider to be exciting. Present the incident in chronological order, using verbs that are fresh and lively. Underline three of these verbs.

Helping Verbs

So far in this chapter you have been studying one-word verbs, sometimes called *main verbs*. Without these verbs there could be no sentences. Frequently, though, the main verb is accompanied by other verbs called *helping verbs*. The main verb and the helping verbs together make up a *verb phrase*. Each of the following main verbs is made into a verb phrase through the use of helping verbs. Notice that the main verb may change its form when a helping verb is added.

MAIN VERB **crawl**
VERB PHRASE **will crawl**

MAIN VERB **listen**
VERB PHRASE **have been listening**

MAIN VERB **find**
VERB PHRASE **would have been found**

You see that a verb phrase consists of a main verb preceded by one or more helping verbs. Here is a list of the most commonly used helping verbs.

be (am, is, are, etc.)	shall	should	must
has	will	would	do
have	can	could	did
had	may	might	does

The verb *be* in its various forms is the most frequently used helping verb. *Be* used as a helping verb is very easy to distinguish from *be* used as a linking verb. When *be* is used as a helping verb, there is always a main verb used with it; but when *be* is used as a linking verb, it is itself the main verb.

HELPING VERB **are found**
LINKING VERB **are**

HELPING VERB **have been tasted**
LINKING VERB **have been**

The following sentences contain verb phrases. The helping verbs and the main verbs are in boldface; the main verbs are also underlined.

Seiji Ozawa **has been praised** for his fine conducting.
His recordings **should be heard** by anyone interested in classical music.

He **will** <u>**conduct**</u> many outstanding orchestras.
He **is** <u>**making**</u> music important to young people.

EXERCISE 6. Identifying Verb Phrases. Number your
paper 1–10. Write the verb phrases in the order in which they
appear in the following paragraph:

Many people are earning their livings at unusual jobs.
Even today people can find positions as shepherds, inventors,
and candlestick makers. It may seem strange, but these
people have decided that ordinary jobs can become too
tedious for them. Some people have been working as messen-
gers. You may have seen them when they were wearing
costumes such as gorilla suits. Other people have been finding
work as mimes. With a little imagination, anyone can find an
unusual job.

Sometimes the verb phrase is interrupted by other parts of
speech, as in the following examples:

Because of the fog, we **could** not **see** the road.
Parachuting **has** quickly **become** an important sport.
People **may** someday **communicate** with dolphins.
How much **do** you **know** about Lucy Stone, the suffragist?
Have you ever **read** a biography of Elizabeth I?

EXERCISE 7. Identifying Verb Phrases. Number your
paper 1–20. List the twenty verb phrases that appear in the
following paragraph. Some of the verb phrases are interrupted by
other parts of speech. Be sure that you include the entire verb
phrase.

EXAMPLE   1. People have been using ham radios for many years.
          1. *have been using*

Ham radio operators must know Morse code and radio
theory, and they must pass a test before they can receive a
license. Recently, more people have been taking the Novice
test. The test may often seem hard to people who have been

afraid of mathematics all their lives. However, a little extra effort can be richly rewarded and can even result in a Novice license. After radio operators have received their licenses, they can talk to people all over the world. Many friendships are formed this way. Does a knowledge of other languages help operators when they are talking to people in other countries? In a way, Morse code can be considered another language. It may seem difficult at first, but people of all ages have mastered Morse code and have become operators. People who have enjoyed ham radio may continue their studies and eventually they can earn advanced licenses.

REVIEW EXERCISE A. Labeling Linking Verbs and Action Verbs. Number your paper 1–20. List the verbs and the verb phrases that appear in the following paragraph. After each action verb or verb phrase, write *a.v.*; after each linking verb or verb phrase, write *l.v.*

The term *Viking* was used for all sailors of the North, whether they were Norwegians, Swedes, or Danes. The Vikings were a fierce people who roamed the seas for about three hundred years. For several centuries people considered the Vikings the scourge of Europe because they invaded and pillaged the countries to the south. They worshiped such fierce gods as Thor and Odin, and they hoped that they would die in battle. The Vikings believed that when they died in battle, they went to Valhalla, where they could eternally enjoy battles and banquets. The Vikings thought that each day the warriors in Valhalla would go out to the battlefield and would receive wounds time and time again. Then, in spite of their injuries, at the end of each day they would all meet back at the banquet hall, where their wounds would promptly heal and they could boast about their great bravery in battle.

REVIEW EXERCISE B. Labeling Parts of Speech. Write the following sentences on every other line of your paper. Underline the italicized words in each sentence. Over each word that you underline, write an abbreviation to show which part of speech it is: *n.* for noun, *pron.* for pronoun, *adj.* for adjective, *a.v.* for action verb, and *l.v.* for linking verb. Treat proper names and verb phrases as one word.

EXAMPLE   1. *Mary McLeod Bethune is* a *major figure* in American history.

n.   l.v.   adj.   n.

1. <u>*Mary McLeod Bethune*</u> <u>*is*</u> a <u>*major*</u> <u>*figure*</u> in American history.

1. Mary Bethune *dedicated* her *life* to helping *young* people.
2. In her *early years* she *began* a teaching *career.*
3. In 1904 *she moved* to Florida and *opened* a *school* of *her* own.
4. The school eventually *became* the Bethune-Cookman College, and *Bethune* served as its *president.*
5. In 1930 Bethune *was invited* to a *Presidential conference* on child health and protection.
6. Then, during Roosevelt's *administration, she helped* in the establishment of the *National Youth Administration.*
7. Her *outstanding efforts* impressed Roosevelt, and *he established* an *important* office on minority affairs.
8. This office *granted funds* to *serious students* so that they could continue *their* education.
9. In 1945 she *was* an observer at the *conference* that *organized* the *United Nations.*
10. Bethune *remained* interested in education, and her *notable* efforts earned her *national recognition.*

THE ADVERB

3b. An *adverb* is a word used to modify a verb, an adjective, or another adverb.

An *adverb* usually answers one of these questions: *Where? When? How? To what extent (how much or how long)?*

WHERE?	WHEN?
The fire started **here**.	The police arrived **promptly**.
The couple was married **nearby**.	**Then** the suspects were questioned.
The thief fell **down**.	He writes **daily**.

HOW?	TO WHAT EXTENT (HOW MUCH OR HOW LONG)?
The accident occurred **suddenly**.	We should **never** deceive our friends.
The Prime Minister spoke **carefully**.	The escaped panther ran **far**.
The train stopped **abruptly**.	She has **scarcely** begun the lesson.

(1) An adverb modifies a verb more often than it modifies an adjective or an adverb.

Notice how an adverb makes the meaning of the verb more definite.

EXAMPLES The man crawled **down**. [The adverb tells *where* the man crawled.]

He crawled **slowly**. [The adverb tells *how* he crawled.]

Now we are busy. [The adverb tells *when* we are busy.]

The speaker droned on **endlessly**. [The adverb tells *to what extent* the speaker droned.]

Adverbs are sometimes used to ask questions.

EXAMPLES **Where** are you going?
How did you do on the test?

EXERCISE 8. Writing Adverbs in a Sentence. Number your paper 1–10. Write an adverb for each blank in the following sentences. After each adverb, write what the adverb tells: *Where? When? How?* or *To what extent (how much* or *how long)?* the action was done. Use a different adverb for each blank and include all four kinds.

EXAMPLE   1. We sang —— .
              1. *loudly—how?*

1. They tiptoed —— and spoke —— .
2. The motor ran —— .
3. My report was due —— .
4. —— the door slammed.
5. Their players could —— catch the ball.
6. —— will the dentist call?
7. —— the scouts —— hiked the Bear State Trail.
8. Lisa's rabbit jumped —— and then ate the carrots —— .
9. After the girl —— washed the car, she —— polished it.
10. The speaker laughed —— as she told the story of her first school dance.

EXERCISE 9. Identifying Adverbs That Modify Verbs.
The following sentences contain twenty adverbs, all modifying verbs. Number your paper 1–9. After the proper number, write the adverbs in that sentence.

1. The snowstorm has completely blocked traffic and has temporarily grounded airplanes today.
2. How can you develop into a strong runner now?
3. Yesterday three police officers secretly followed the suspect.
4. The doctor came immediately, but the patient had already recovered.
5. Gymnastics has recently attracted many students, and the equipment is always in use.
6. The coach argued violently, but the umpire calmly ignored him.
7. February is never a warm month in Maine.
8. Her luncheon was well attended, and her speech was applauded loudly afterward.
9. Today astronomers can accurately chart the courses of planets, yet the motions of some celestial bodies are still a mystery.

(2) An adverb sometimes modifies an adjective.

An adverb is sometimes needed to make the meaning of an adjective more definite. An *extremely* good dancer is quite different from a *fairly* good dancer.

EXAMPLES   The skaters put on a **very** exciting show. [The adjective *exciting* modifies the noun *show;* the adverb tells *how exciting* the show was.]

An **unusually** fast starter, Karen easily won the hurdles event. [The adjective *fast* modifies the noun *starter;* the adverb tells *how fast* the starter was.]

Our committee is **especially** busy at this time of year. [The adjective *busy* modifies the noun *committee;* the adverb tells *how busy* the committee is.]

EXERCISE 10. Identifying Adverbs That Modify Adjectives.
Number your paper 1–10. After the proper number, write the adverbs that modify adjectives in each sentence. After each adverb, write the adjective that it modifies.

EXAMPLE   1. Because so many bicycles have been stolen, the principal hired a guard.
    1. *so, many*

1. The team is extremely proud of its record.
2. All frogs may look quite harmless, but some are poisonous.
3. The class was unusually quiet today.
4. Newborn animals are very clumsy at first.
5. The coach said we were too careless when we made the routine plays.
6. The situation seemed utterly futile.
7. When kittens are with their mother, they look thoroughly contented.
8. Weekends are especially hectic for me when all of my teachers assign homework.
9. The lecture seemed much longer than one hour.

10. The new exchange student who comes from Norway is surprisingly fluent in English.

EXERCISE 11. Writing Adverbs to Modify Adjectives.
The adverb *very* is used far too often to modify adjectives. Write an adverb to modify each adjective below. Do not use *very*.

EXAMPLE 1. strong
          1. *incredibly strong*

1. cheerful   4. messy   7. heavy   9. calm
2. sour   5. honest   8. long   10. graceful
3. wide   6. timid

(3) An adverb occasionally modifies another adverb.

EXAMPLES   Elena finished the problem **more** quickly than I did.
           [The adverb *quickly* modifies the verb *finished* and
           is, in turn, modified by the adverb *more,* which tells
           how quickly Elena finished the problem.]

           Our guest left **quite** abruptly. [The adverb *abruptly*
           modifies the verb *left* and is modified by *quite,* which
           tells *how abruptly* our guest left.]

**EXERCISE 12. Identifying Adverbs That Modify Other
Adverbs.**   Number your paper 1–10. Beside the appropriate
number, list the adverbs that modify other adverbs in the
following sentences. Then, after each adverb, write the adverb
that it modifies.

EXAMPLE 1. The new swimming pool is most certainly an im-
            provement over the old one.
          1. *most, certainly*

1. Condors, an endangered species, are very rarely seen in
   California.
2. In fact, these birds are almost entirely extinct in the United
   States.
3. They are more frequently seen soaring over the Andes
   Mountains in South America.

4. Their wings enable them to glide quite noiselessly on the thermal air currents.
5. Condors are the largest living birds, and some people think that they are most assuredly the ugliest.
6. Although they can eat live animals, they feed quite often on carrion.
7. Condors, like most other vultures, circle their prey very slowly before they descend to eat.
8. People should protect endangered species more forcefully, or hundreds of species will disappear.
9. Even though condors have not been welcomed too enthusiastically into the hearts of people, they still need protection.
10. The balance of nature quite definitely depends on all kinds of animals, even on the ones that are not cute and cuddly.

REVIEW EXERCISE C. Identifying Adverbs. Number your paper 1–10. Beside the appropriate number, list the adverbs in the order that they appear in each of the following sentences. After each adverb, write the word or expression that the adverb modifies. Some sentences have more than one adverb.

EXAMPLE   1. The movie ended too quickly.
   1. *too, quickly; quickly, ended*

1. I have been a fan of mystery stories since I was very young.
2. My favorite stories are about detectives who cleverly match wits with equally clever villains.
3. Some stories are incredibly exciting from start to finish, but others slowly build suspense.
4. If I like a story, I can hardly put the book down until I finish it.
5. I should never become involved in a story if I have tons of homework to do because then I am too tempted to read.
6. If I am not able to guess the ending, I can scarcely prevent myself from peeking at the last chapter.
7. I restrain myself unusually well when this temptation comes near.

8. I wonder if I would have the nerve to creep around and look for clues in a terribly dark, spooky basement.
9. Clues are often found in carefully guarded places.
10. How do the mystery detectives find the answers to some of the most complicated cases?

DIAGRAMING VERBS AND ADVERBS

The verb, like the noun and pronoun, always appears on a horizontal line. The adverb is diagramed on a slanting line under the word it modifies.

1. An adverb modifying a verb:

EXAMPLES   studies hard   does not exercise daily

2. An adverb modifying an adjective:

EXAMPLES   extremely strong wind   much better swimmer

3. An adverb modifying another adverb:

EXAMPLES   tried rather hard   flew almost too high

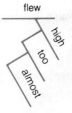

EXERCISE 13. Diagraming Verbs and Adverbs. Diagram the following groups of words. Use a ruler and leave plenty of space between diagrams.

1. answered quickly
2. badly worn sail
3. listened quite intently
4. worked very late
5. dangerously sharp curve

6. never plans very carefully
7. walked proudly away
8. somewhat rickety bridge
9. may possibly happen
10. drove rather slowly

EXERCISE 14. Diagraming Sentences. Diagram the following sentences. Use a ruler and leave plenty of space between diagrams.

1. The plane landed smoothly.
2. The guide limped noticeably.
3. The extremely nervous passenger collapsed.
4. Our turn finally came.
5. They tried very hard.
6. The shutters rattled quite noisily.
7. The new automobile had been slightly damaged.
8. We are definitely leaving tomorrow.
9. The tired motorist drove much too far.
10. The unbelievably slow turtle got there first.

THE PREPOSITION

3c. A *preposition* is a word used to show the relationship of a noun or a pronoun to some other word in the sentence.

Notice how a change in the preposition changes the relationship between *package* and *tree* in each of the following sentences.

The package **under** the tree is mine.
The package **in** the tree is mine.
The package **near** the tree is mine.

Learn to recognize the following words, which are commonly used as prepositions.

Commonly Used Prepositions

aboard	behind	from	throughout
about	below	in	to
above	beneath	into	toward
across	beside	like	under
after	between	near	underneath
against	beyond	of	until
along	but (except)	off	unto
amid	by	on	up
among	down	over	upon
around	during	past	with
at	except	since	within
before	for	through	without

Occasionally you will find compound prepositions—prepositions of more than one word. A compound preposition may be considered as one word.

Compound Prepositions

because of	according to
on account of	instead of
in spite of	out of

EXERCISE 15. Identifying Prepositions. Number your paper 1–10. List the prepositions beside the appropriate number in the order in which they appear in each of the following sentences. Be sure that you include all parts of any compound prepositions you find.

EXAMPLE 1. Many Roman myths were adaptations of Greek myths.
1. *of*

1. Mars, the god of war, is perhaps the most Roman god in Roman mythology.
2. Many Roman gods were borrowed from Greek mythology.
3. According to legends, Mars was the father of Romulus and Remus, twin brothers.

4. When the twins were babies, an evil ruler threw them into the Tiber River.
5. Romulus and Remus were rescued from the river, then were fed by a wolf, and were raised under the care of a shepherd.
6. The twins fought against each other in a deadly rivalry.
7. Instead of working with his brother, Romulus killed Remus.
8. It is said that Romulus founded the city of Rome around 753 B.C.
9. Throughout the centuries people have read about the legend of Romulus and Remus.
10. Out of hundreds of legends, this one has remained among the best known.

A preposition is always followed by a noun or a pronoun that the preposition relates to another word in the sentence. The noun or the pronoun following the preposition is called the *object* of the preposition. Words that modify the object may come between the preposition and the object. Taken together, the preposition, its object, and the modifiers of the object are called a *prepositional phrase*.

EXAMPLE across the dusty prairie [The entire prepositional phrase includes the preposition *across,* its object *prairie,* and two adjectives modifying the object *the dusty.*]

EXERCISE 16. Identifying Prepositional Phrases. Each of the following sentences contains a prepositional phrase. Number your paper 1–10, and after the proper number, write the phrase. Underline each preposition.

EXAMPLE 1. Walt Whitman wrote a very moving poem, "O Captain! My Captain!" about Abraham Lincoln.
1. *about Abraham Lincoln*

1. In this poem the ship's captain represents Abraham Lincoln.
2. The ship has just completed a voyage through rough weather.
3. On the shore, people celebrate the ship's safe arrival.
4. One member of the ship's crew addresses his captain.

5. "For you they call, the swaying mass, their eager faces turning. . . ."
6. Everyone except the captain can hear the rejoicing.
7. He has died during the voyage.
8. The ship represents the ship of state.
9. The ship's voyage across rough seas symbolizes the Civil War.
10. Lincoln, the captain, directed his ship toward a safe harbor.

WRITING APPLICATION B:
Using Prepositional Phrases To Create Vivid Similes

When you were in elementary school, you probably learned to color with crayons and paints. Then, as you learned to read, perhaps you were given a picture with instructions to color certain items blue, red, yellow, or some other particular color. Color can add considerable appeal and interest to a picture. To create the same kind of vivid impression in your writing, try experimenting with *similes*. To form a simile, use *like* or *as* to show how one thing is similar to another thing, even though the two items are basically different. Notice how the following similes are expressed in prepositional phrases beginning with *like*.

EXAMPLES   Her coat was red and silky, and there was a blaze of white down her chest and a circle of white around her throat. Her face was wrinkled and sad, **like a wise old man's.**

JAMES STREET

For nearly a year, I sopped around the house, the Store, the school and the church, **like an old biscuit.**

MAYA ANGELOU

Writing Assignment

Have you ever heard of a *tall tale*? It is a highly improbable humorous story that stretches the facts beyond any hope of belief. Tall tales include people as tall as mountains, woodsmen who use trees as toothpicks, and other impossible situations. Write a tall tale in which you use at least three similes that are given in prepositional phrases beginning with *like* or *as*. Underline these similes.

Sometimes the same word may be used as either a preposition or an adverb. It is easy to tell the adverb from the preposition if you remember that a preposition must always be followed by a noun or pronoun object.

ADVERB   The plane circled above.
PREPOSITION   The plane circled above the field. [Note the object of the preposition—*field*.]

ADVERB   We remained within.
PREPOSITION   We remained within the shelter. [Note the object of the preposition—*shelter*.]

EXERCISE 17. Writing Sentences with Adverbs and Prepositions. Use each of the following words in two sentences, first as an adverb and then as a preposition. Underline the designated word.

EXAMPLE   1. along
              1. *"Why can't I go along?" asked the child.*
                 Wildflowers were blooming along the riverbank.

1. off   2. across   3. below   4. above   5. into

You must also be careful not to confuse a prepositional phrase beginning with *to* (*to town, to her club,* etc.) with a verb form beginning with *to* (*to run, to be seen, to have completed,* etc.). Again, remember that a prepositional phrase always ends with a noun or pronoun.

THE CONJUNCTION

3d. A *conjunction* **is a word that joins words or groups of words.**

Conjunctions joining single words:

> brush **and** paint
> hot **or** cold
> small **but** comfortable

Conjunctions joining groups of words:

> through a forest **and** across a river
> wanted to notify **but** not to alarm
> camping out **or** staying in motels

Conjunctions joining groups of words that are sentences:

> The stars seem motionless, **but** actually they are moving rapidly through space.
> One leader was very powerful, **and** the other was very weak.
> Sharon typed her paper herself, **or** she had her sister type it for her.

Conjunctions are of three kinds: *coordinating, correlative,* and *subordinating.*

The *coordinating conjunctions* are *and, but, or, nor, for, so,* and *yet.*

EXAMPLES   The cave explorers carried ropes **and** torches.
You may take the test now, **or** you may wait until later.
Our auction was very successful, **for** every student brought something to be sold.

Notice that when *for* is used as a conjunction, it connects groups of words that are sentences. On all other occasions, *for* is used as a preposition.

CONJUNCTION   We wrote to the tourist bureau, **for** we wanted information on places to visit.
PREPOSITION   We waited patiently **for** a reply.

Correlative conjunctions are always found in pairs that have other words dividing them: *either . . . or, neither . . . nor, both . . . and, not only . . . but also.*

EXAMPLES   Our class will furnish **either** the punch **or** the cookies for the party.
Both cats **and** dogs make good pets.
Clare Boothe Luce was **not only** a playwright **but also** an ambassador.

Subordinating conjunctions occur in complex sentences and are explained on page 158.

EXERCISE 18. Writing Conjunctions in Sentences.   Number your paper 1–10. After each number, write a coordinating or correlative conjunction to fill the blanks in the corresponding sentence.

EXAMPLE   1. —— you —— I will have to clean up the mess.
1. *Both, and*

1. We will serve —— fruit juice —— milk with lunch.
2. Gabby Hayes —— Andy Devine were popular sidekicks to cowboy heroes in many western movies.
3. We sang —— before the game —— during the half-time festivities.
4. I'm not sure whether it was Charlotte Brontë —— George Eliot who wrote *Silas Marner*.
5. Phyllis McGinley wrote poetry —— published essays.
6. —— Memphis —— Knoxville is the capital of Tennessee.
7. My parents are watching the football game, —— I am studying for a test.
8. —— the clowns —— the dancing bears made us laugh.
9. The last gymnast did the floor exercise perfectly —— ended her routine with a smile.
10. The young man did not ask for help, —— did he want any advice.

EXERCISE 19. Identifying Coordinating and Correlative Conjunctions.   Number your paper 1–20. After the proper

number, write the coordinating or correlative conjunctions in each sentence. Be prepared to tell what words or groups of words each conjunction joins. Treat a pair of correlative conjunctions as one conjunction.

EXAMPLE   1. Our teacher bought either a jeep or a pickup truck.
              1. *either—or*

1. The disc jockey played records and tapes for us.
2. Neither the Ferris wheel nor the roller coaster was safe to ride.
3. Some people prefer water-skiing, but others like snow-skiing.
4. We are working hard on the project, for the science fair starts tomorrow.
5. Both our team and the visitors played well at last week's game.
6. Our club members will either make the decorations or bring refreshments.
7. Many players and coaches would like to change the rules.
8. Ms. Whiting is both a teacher and a mother.
9. The girls' basketball team not only won the game but also scored the most points in our school's history.
10. If the girls rehearse, they will perform at the game and at the dance on Saturday.
11. Sarah speaks French or German.
12. I hope I improve my grades, for I have been studying hard.
13. They must practice fielding and batting.
14. We will be working on the balance beam or the trampoline this week in gym class.
15. I didn't receive a letter from my cousin today, nor did I really expect one.
16. The drivers braked and swerved to avoid the dog.
17. Either you or I should send the invitations.
18. The people waited patiently for the bus, but it never came.
19. The artist used neither oils nor acrylics to paint this picture.
20. The principal was excited, for the school board had approved his plan for a new cafeteria.

THE INTERJECTION

3e. An *interjection* is a word that expresses emotion and that is not related grammatically to other words in the sentence.

EXAMPLES   **Oh!** You surprised me.
                 Wow! Am I tired!
                 Well, I did my best.

DETERMINING PARTS OF SPEECH

You have now finished a study of the eight parts of speech. On page 83 is a chart that briefly summarizes what you have learned.

3f. A word's use determines its part of speech.

Although words are given as examples of particular parts of speech in the chart that follows, you cannot really tell what part of speech a word is until you know how the word is used in a sentence. You have seen in your study of Chapters 2 and 3 that the same word can be used as a pronoun and an adjective or as an adverb and a preposition. Only when you see how a word is used in a sentence can you label it as a particular part of speech.

EXAMPLES   **Each** did his part. [pronoun]
                 Each student baked a cake. [adjective]

                 The tired shoppers sat **down** for a while. [adverb]
                 The ball rolled **down** the hill. [preposition]

                 A member of the crew has spotted **land.** [noun]
                 The pilot can **land** here safely. [verb]

                 We didn't find her, **for** she had left. [conjunction]
                 Everybody searched **for** the lost child. [preposition]

                 Well, he seems to have recovered. [interjection]
                 He doesn't look **well** to me. [adjective]

SUMMARY OF PARTS OF SPEECH

Rule	Part of Speech	Use	Examples
2a	noun	names a person, a place, a thing, or an idea	Wilma, cave, Asia, freedom, honesty
2b	pronoun	takes the place of a noun	she, ourselves, who, anyone
2c	adjective	modifies a noun or pronoun	sick, tiny, purple, smooth
3a	verb	shows action or helps to make a statement	play, study, were, become
3b	adverb	modifies a verb, an adjective, or another adverb	very, too, usually, quickly
3c	preposition	relates a noun or a pronoun to another word; begins a prepositional phrase	beside [her], to [town], for [John], with [them]
3d	conjunction	joins words or groups of words	and, but, either . . . or
3e	interjection	shows strong feeling	Well! Wow! Oh!

REVIEW EXERCISE D. Identifying Parts of Speech.
Number your paper 1–20. After each number, write the italicized word from the corresponding sentence. Then write the part of speech of the word. Be prepared to explain your answer to the class.

EXAMPLES 1. The *ship* entered the harbor slowly.
1. *ship—noun*
2. Did they *ship* the package to Dee and Tom?
2. *ship—verb*

1. The English test was easy *for* him.
2. He didn't go to the movies, *for* he wanted to practice on the drums.
3. It was a steep *climb,* but we made it to the top of the hill.
4. June and I *climb* the stairs for exercise.
5. *Some* volunteered to sell tickets.
6. We donated *some* clothes to the rummage sale.
7. Looking for shells, the girl strolled *along* the shore.
8. When we went sailing, Raul and Manuel came *along.*
9. I lost *my* book report!
10. *My!* This is not a good day!
11. The little girl sat *still* during the concert.
12. She photographed the *still* waters of the lake.
13. Most club members voted in favor of the hayride, but *many* voted against it.
14. Christie has *many* lovely quilts in her room.
15. The *plan* for the trip has been confirmed.
16. My parents *plan* to attend the school play.
17. The hospital is located *nearby.*
18. After the movie we went to a *nearby* restaurant.
19. When the batter hit the ball, it popped *up.*
20. The neighbor's dog chased Fluffy *up* the crabapple tree.

REVIEW EXERCISE E. Using Different Parts of Speech in Sentences. Write a short sentence for each of the following words, using the word as the part of speech that is indicated. Underline the word in your sentence.

EXAMPLE   1. *praise* as a noun
          1. *Our club received a lot of <u>praise</u> for our winning float.*

1. *tire* as a verb
2. *tomorrow* as an adverb
3. *all* as an adjective
4. *stars* as a noun
5. *aboard* as an adverb

6. *drop* as a verb
7. *few* as a pronoun
8. *within* as a preposition
9. *well* as an interjection
10. *for* as a conjunction

REVIEW EXERCISE F. Identifying Different Parts of Speech.

Number your paper 1–50. After the proper number, write each of the italicized words in the following paragraphs. After each word, write what part of speech it is. Be able to explain your answer by giving the use of the word in the sentence. Use the following abbreviations:

n.	noun	*adv.*	adverb
pron.	pronoun	*prep.*	preposition
v.	verb	*conj.*	conjunction
adj.	adjective	*interj.*	interjection

Dancing may be (1) *easy* for (2) *some,* but I have (3) *always* had (4) *two* left (5) *feet.* (6) *Yesterday* after (7) *school,* one of my friends (8) *tried* to teach (9) *me* the latest dance. (10) *Well!* I was (11) *so* embarrassed I could have hidden (12) *in* the (13) *closet.* My feet (14) *have* (15) *minds* of (16) *their* own, and (17) *they* do (18) *not* behave well.

Today I (19) *thought* (20) *about* this (21) *problem* (22) *throughout* lunch. (23) *Later* I thought about it (24) *during* math class. I have considered every (25) *possible* solution. I have (26) *even* wanted to put (27) *down* cutouts of (28) *paper* feet (29) *with* numbers on them.

My (30) *mother* has (31) *shown* me (32) *some* dances that (33) *were* popular when (34) *she* was my age. I've tried (35) *hard* (36) *many* times to follow the (37) *steps,* (38) *but* all my efforts have (39) *seemed* (40) *useless.*

"Either you are (41) *too* tense when you dance, (42) *or* you are trying too hard. (43) *You* should (44) *relax* more," people say to me.

(45) "*What!* (46) *How* can I relax?" I groan. (47) "*No one* can relax when the body goes (48) *left* and the feet go right!" At

that point, I usually (49) *decide* to give up, but I always try (50) *again* the next day.

CHAPTER 3 REVIEW: POSTTEST 1

Identifying Verbs, Adverbs, Prepositions, Conjunctions, and Interjections. Number your paper 1–25. After the proper number, write each italicized word or word group in the following sentences, and indicate whether it is a verb, an adverb, a preposition, a conjunction, or an interjection. Use the abbreviations *v.* (verb), *adv.* (adverb), *prep.* (preposition), *conj.* (conjunction), and *interj.* (interjection). For each verb, indicate whether it is an action verb, a helping verb, or a linking verb.

EXAMPLE   1. I am *reading* a book *about* dinosaurs.
          1. *reading—v. (action), about—prep.*

1. We watched the skywriter *spell* out the letters *carefully*.
2. *Both* the dog *and* the cat *are* dirty and need baths.
3. His cousins don't *know* much *about* sports.
4. When the horse reared *back*, the girl held *onto* its mane.
5. The teacher *would* have been late if the bell had rung on time *yesterday*.
6. *Well*, I plan to help Andrea, *for* I believe in her cause.
7. Clever replies *never* occur to me until the situation is *long* past.
8. If I had *known* how to identify verbs, I would have gotten a better grade *on* that test.
9. *When* do you usually *feel* your best—mornings or afternoons?
10. He won't go, *nor* will he *willingly* cooperate.
11. Juan exercised *daily* for twenty minutes *before* breakfast.
12. Our history books contain some *very* informative graphs and charts *about* American business.
13. One of the runners *almost tripped* over the hurdle, *yet* he still placed third.

14. There are times when Jill thinks that she *cares* almost *too* much about making the team.
15. *Whoops!* I dropped my ring, and it rolled *under* the counter.
16. My scout leader said that she *had* never tasted stew like mine *before*.
17. Although *not* many people *like* the heat, the desert can be beautiful.
18. Be sure that you *sharpen* your pencil *now* because you won't be allowed to leave your seat after the test begins.
19. *Did* you bring a note *from* your parents?
20. Jeff loaned Anne a dollar and *then* found out that he didn't have *quite* enough money for his own lunch.
21. The girl *tried* again *in spite of* her previous difficulty.
22. My mom took me *aboard* the ship where she *used* to work.
23. Nguyen *does* not wish to intrude, nor does he *feel* fully at ease in such situations.
24. The fish *quickly* darted *under* a rock.
25. *Hey!* hold it *right* there.

CHAPTER 3 REVIEW: POSTTEST 2

Identifying Verbs, Adverbs, Prepositions, Conjunctions, and Interjections.   Number your paper 1–25. After the proper number, write each italicized word or word group in the following sentences, and indicate whether it is a verb, an adverb, a preposition, a conjunction, or an interjection. Use the abbreviations *v.* (verb), *adv.* (adverb), *prep.* (preposition), *conj.* (conjunction), and *interj.* (interjection). For each verb, indicate whether it is an action verb, a linking verb, or a helping verb.

EXAMPLE   1. We *played* baseball *nearly* all day.
          1. *played—v. (action), nearly—adv.*

1. That *was* a *very* helpful reply.
2. The clouds *gathered* into a huge thunderhead that *soon* turned as black as asphalt.

3. Mr. Beaumont grew angry, *but* still the boys would *not* stop talking and laughing.
4. *Gee,* I didn't know there was a snake *under* that rock.
5. The car started at once, *yet* it wouldn't run *for* very long.
6. We were not *quite there* when my brother *finally* fell asleep on the back seat.
7. My dad *says* that he *will* never ask me to cut his hair again.
8. *After* the storm ended, we went *outside*.
9. Where *are* you going *today*?
10. No one can repair an engine *more* quickly than she can, *nor* can anyone do a better job.
11. I *guess* that I had better get my gear *together* for our camping trip this weekend.
12. *How* far should we *drive* in this direction?
13. My father can *coach* the team *tomorrow* if we can't find somebody else.
14. You should *never* talk *with* your mouth full.
15. Why *fertilize* the lawn when fertilizer just makes it grow faster so that we have to cut it more *often*?
16. *Yes,* that *appears* to be the right answer.
17. *During* the storm last week, the huge silver oak tree in our front yard fell *down*. $\mathcal{L}$
18. Our dog *chased* the neighbor's cat down the street *again* last night.
19. *How* should I know what she *is* planning?
20. Melinda gave a *somewhat* better answer than Erin had *given* for that question.
21. Nobody knew where she had gone, *for* she *left* without telling anyone.
22. My dog *became* sick after he ate *that* toad.
23. The monkey *carefully* peeled back the wrapper and *tasted* the granola bar.
24. His parents give him *so* many things that he *has* become spoiled.
25. I *think* I'll have a sandwich *instead of* a hamburger for lunch.

CHAPTER 3 REVIEW: POSTTEST 3

Writing Sentences Using Different Parts of Speech.
Write two sentences using each of the following words as the parts of speech given in parentheses. Underline the word in the sentence, and write the part of speech of the word after the sentence.

EXAMPLE   1. over (adv. and prep.)
   1. *The skies began to clear when the storm was <u>over</u>.*
      adverb
      The horse jumped <u>over</u> the fence. preposition

1. but (conj. and prep.)
2. like (v. and prep.)
3. run (n. and v.)
4. well (adv. and interj.)
5. that (pron. and adj.)
6. more (adj. and adv.)
7. last (v. and adj.)
8. one (adj. and pron.)
9. near (v. and prep.)
10. around (prep. and adv.)
11. all (pron. and adj.)
12. past (n. and prep.)
13. so (interj. and adv.)
14. for (conj. and prep.)
15. fight (n. and v.)
16. even (v. and adv.)
17. since (prep. and adv.)
18. taste (n. and v.)
19. boy (n. and interj.)
20. any (pron. and adj.)

CHAPTER 4

Complements

DIRECT AND INDIRECT OBJECTS, SUBJECT COMPLEMENTS

As you learned in Chapter 1, every sentence has a sentence base. The sentence base always consists of at least a verb and its subject. In many sentences this subject-verb base is enough.

    S   V
John shouted.

       S   V
The squirrels scampered across the campus.

The sentence base often has another part, in addition to the subject and verb, called a *complement*. The word *complement* means "completer." A complement completes the meaning begun by the subject and verb. Notice that the following word groups are not complete, even though they have subjects and verbs.

    S   V
Marlene brought [what?]

S V
I met [whom?]

    S   V
Her friend is [what?]

Here a complement completes the meaning of each.

     S   V   C
Marlene brought a cake.

S V   C
I met Carlos.

       S   V   C
Her friend is a painter.

DIAGNOSTIC TEST

Identifying Direct Objects, Indirect Objects, and Subject Complements. Number your paper 1–20. After the proper number, write the italicized word or word group in the following sentences. Correctly identify each, using these abbreviations: *d.o.* (direct object), *i.o.* (indirect object), *p.n.* (predicate nominative, or *p.a.* (predicate adjective).

EXAMPLES 1. The rancher raised prize-winning *cattle*.
            1. *cattle—d.o.*
            2. The rancher became a rich *man*.
            2. *man—p.n.*

1. Brenda caught the *ball* and threw it to first base.
2. Your cousin seems *nice*.
3. I'm not the *one* who did that.
4. The sun grew *hotter* as the day went on.
5. Mrs. Ford gave *me* a failing grade.
6. That hamburger meat smells *bad* to me.
7. Jane's father and mother are both *truck drivers*.
8. Have you bought your *tickets* yet?
9. My mother won't let me ride your *trail bike*.
10. The irate customer sent the *store manager* a letter of complaint.
11. The nurse gave *Virgil* a flu shot.
12. Earl often doesn't feel *well* on Monday mornings.
13. With his calloused hands he often cannot feel the *texture* of fine cloth.

14. Her grades are always *higher* than mine.
15. Heather, who is new at our school, is the nicest *girl* I know.
16. Overhead, the vultures circled the injured *gazelle*.
17. Throw *Eric* a screen pass.
18. When left in the sun, plums become *prunes*.
19. Why did Mr. Santos loan *Arnie* five dollars?
20. Ms. Rossetti will be our Spanish *teacher* this fall.

4a. A *complement* is a word or a group of words that completes the meaning begun by the subject and verb.

Jody redecorated her **room.** [*Room* completes the meaning by telling *what* Jody redecorated.]

My aunt sent **me** a **postcard** from Amsterdam. [*Me* and *postcard* complete the meaning by telling *what* was sent and *to whom* it was sent.]

The Ephron sisters are humorous **writers.** [*Writers* completes the meaning by telling something about the subject *sisters*.]

The *Mona Lisa* is very **famous.** [*Famous* completes the meaning by describing the subject *Mona Lisa*.]

In these four sentences, you see two kinds of complements. In sentences (1) and (2) you see complements that are affected by the action of the verb. In sentences (3) and (4) you see complements that refer to the subject. A noun, a pronoun, or an adjective can serve as a complement, but an adverb can never be a complement.

The bus is **here.** [*Here* is an adverb, not a complement.]

A complement, like a subject, is never in a prepositional phrase.

Sarah is reading the **dictionary.** [*Dictionary* is a complement; it completes the meaning begun by the subject and verb.]

Sarah is thumbing through the dictionary. [*Dictionary* is in the phrase *through the dictionary*; it is not a complement.]

Helen is an expert **skier** and **skater**. [*Skier* and *skater* are complements; they complete the meaning begun by the subject and verb.]

Helen is in Colorado. [*Colorado* is in the phrase *in Colorado;* it is not a complement.]

EXERCISE 1. **Identifying Subjects, Verbs, and Complements.** Make three columns on your paper. Label the first *Subject,* the second *Verb,* and the third *Complement.* Write in the appropriate columns these three parts of the base of each of the following sentences. Remember that a complement is never in a prepositional phrase.

1. We usually take the bus to school.
2. The driver of a school bus must be patient.
3. The distance between school and home is not long.
4. The walk from school is unpleasant in bad weather.
5. Usually I meet one of my friends at the corner.
6. On Mondays everyone in school seems sleepy.
7. A seat in the last row is sometimes desirable.
8. Jan and Flo have always been good friends.
9. Can you remember the name of the principal?
10. Alice bought a loaf of bread on her way home.
11. Sometimes we read a story in the afternoon.
12. This new book is full of animal adventures.
13. Did anyone guess the ending of the story?
14. My brother borrows a lot of library books.
15. His overdue book is a very long novel.

EXERCISE 2. **Identifying Subjects, Verbs, and Complements.** Make three columns on your paper. Label the first *Subject,* the second *Verb,* and the third *Complement.* Find the base of each of the following sentences, and enter the parts of the base in the appropriate columns. Remember that a complement is never in a prepositional phrase.

1. In Shakespeare's time, plays were very popular in England.
2. Many people watched plays at the Globe Theater in London.

3. William Shakespeare was one of the owners of the Globe.
4. The playhouse looked quite different from most of our modern theaters.
5. It was a building with eight sides.
6. The building contained an inner courtyard.
7. The stage was a platform at one end of the courtyard.
8. Many people in the audience did not have seats during a performance.
9. The people without seats filled the courtyard in front of the stage.
10. Many of them watched the action of the play from a position next to the stage.

EXERCISE 3. Writing Sentences with Subjects, Verbs, and Complements. Write five sentences using the following sentence bases. Add enough words to make *interesting* sentences.

SUBJECT	VERB	COMPLEMENT
girl	delivered	telegram
days	are	long
Pam	won	contest
runner	appeared	tired
Venus	is	planet

DIRECT AND INDIRECT OBJECTS

There are two kinds of complements that are affected by the action of the verb: the *direct object* and the *indirect object*.

4b. The *direct object* receives the action expressed by the verb or names the result of the action.

Dorothea Lange photographed **farmers** in the Midwest during the Depression. [*Farmers* is the direct object; it receives the action of the verb *photographed*.]

Lange built an impressive **collection.** [*Collection* is the direct object; it names the result of the action *built*.]

Direct objects follow action verbs only. They answer the question *What?* or *Whom?* after an action verb. Lange, in the first sentence, photographed whom? She photographed *farmers*; therefore, *farmers* is the direct object. In the second sentence, Lange built what? She built a *collection*; therefore, *collection* is the direct object.

EXERCISE 4. Identifying Direct Objects. Number your paper 1–10. Write the action verb and its object in each sentence. Say the verb to yourself and ask *What?* or *Whom?* Remember that objects are complements and will never be in a prepositional phrase.

EXAMPLE   1. The volunteers distributed food to the flood victims.
　　　　　　1. *distributed—food*

1. On the plains the Cheyenne hunted buffalo for food and clothing.
2. We watched a performance of Lorraine Hansberry's *A Raisin in the Sun.*
3. During most of its history the United States has welcomed refugees from other countries.
4. Cyrano wore a hat with a large plume.
5. Are you helping or hurting the environment?
6. After the game the coach answered questions from the sports reporters.
7. Did you see her performance on television?
8. The researchers followed the birds' migration from Mexico to Canada.
9. Mayor Fiorello La Guardia governed New York City during the Depression.
10. Have the movie theaters announced the special discount for teen-agers yet?

4c. The *indirect object* of the verb precedes the direct object and tells *to whom* or *what* or *for whom* or *what* the action of the verb is done.

Sarita bought **us** a chess set. [*Us* is the indirect object because it tells *for whom* Sarita bought a chess set.]

Dad gave the **car** a coat of paint. [*Car* is the indirect object because it tells *to what* Dad gave a coat of paint.]

Notice that these two sentences contain direct objects as well as indirect objects. This is usually the case. The indirect object normally precedes the direct object.

The guide gave **me** clear **directions**. [*Me* is the indirect object; *directions* is the direct object.]

The indirect object, like the direct object, is never in a prepositional phrase.

She sent her **mother** some of her earnings. [*Mother* is an indirect object, telling *to whom* she sent some of her earnings.]

She sent some of her earnings to her mother. [*Mother* is not an indirect object; it is in the prepositional phrase *to her mother* and is the object of the preposition *to*.]

EXERCISE 5. Identifying Direct Objects and Indirect Objects. Number your paper 1–10. Write the direct objects and the indirect objects from the following sentences. Write *d.o.* after each direct object and *i.o.* after each indirect object. Not every sentence has an indirect object.

EXAMPLE   1. They gave us their solemn promise.
           1. *us, i.o.; promise, d.o.*

1. Sue's parents shipped her the books she had forgotten.
2. They sent me on a wild-goose chase.
3. Gloria mailed the company a check yesterday.
4. The speaker showed the audience the slides of Niagara Falls.
5. Juan would not deliberately tell you a lie.
6. Luckily, we had asked three of our friends to help.
7. I sent my cousins some embroidered pillows for their new apartment.
8. They praised the new student's artwork.

9. Carly and Doreen taught themselves the importance of hard work.
10. In European countries, Americans must carry their passports for identification.

REVIEW EXERCISE A. Identifying Direct and Indirect Objects. The following sentences contain ten direct objects and five indirect objects. Number your paper 1–10. After the proper number, write the object or objects in the sentence. Label direct objects *d.o.* and indirect objects *i.o.*

1. Mr. Luis told us many interesting stories about his childhood in Puerto Rico.
2. Yesterday's mathematics assignment on decimals was very difficult, and no one in the class finished it.
3. Allow yourselves more time for your homework assignments.
4. Television viewers in our country can watch events as they happen in any part of the world.
5. Who told you that ridiculous story about the gorilla in the gymnasium?
6. A permanent member of the United Nations Security Council can veto any resolution.
7. The Panama Canal greatly shortened the trip by boat between Europe and Japan.
8. Rudolf Diesel's first motor exploded during his experiments and nearly killed him.
9. The jeweler, Mrs. Adams, offered me a hundred dollars for my pearl necklace.
10. I brought her my antique silver bracelet, but she was not interested in it.

Diagraming Direct and Indirect Objects

All complements except the indirect object are diagramed on the main horizontal line with the subject and the verb as part of the sentence base. The direct object is diagramed on the horizontal line with a vertical line preceding it. The vertical line stops at the horizontal line to distinguish it from the line separating the subject and the verb.

PATTERNS

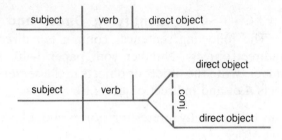

EXAMPLES   1. The rain cleaned the street.

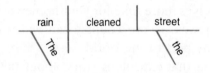

2. We sold lemonade and oranges.

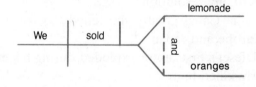

EXERCISE 6. Diagraming Sentences with Direct Objects.
Diagram the following sentences, which contain direct objects. Use a ruler and leave plenty of space between diagrams.

1. We completed our assignment.
2. The quarterback made the touchdown.
3. The distinguished conductor directed his own composition.
4. Our class collects leaves and rocks.
5. The audience saw a serious one-act play and two amusing skits.

6. The school of fish paid no attention to the diver.
7. I have heard programs from Germany on my shortwave set.
8. Bill read several articles on surfboarding and waterskiing.
9. A few people still plant corn by the light of the moon.
10. We grow orchids and ferns in our greenhouse.

To diagram an indirect object, write it on a short horizontal line below the verb. Connect it to the verb by a slanted line.

PATTERNS

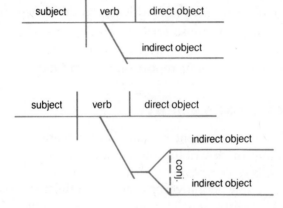

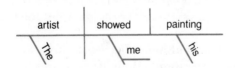

EXAMPLES 1. The artist showed me his painting.

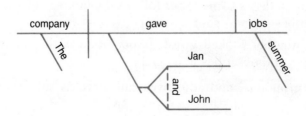

2. The company gave Jan and John summer jobs.

EXERCISE 7. Diagraming Sentences with Direct and Indirect Objects. Diagram the following sentences. Not every sentence has an indirect object.

1. The lifeguard gave us lessons.
2. Cara's sister taught her the rules.
3. The cashier handed the children balloons.
4. The judges awarded Jean and Rae the prizes.
5. Snow gives motorists and pedestrians trouble.
6. At the dime store we bought Japanese lanterns.
7. The police sold my parents tickets to the dance.
8. Josie built a doghouse for her two puppies.
9. Ms. Thompson lent Charles her binoculars.
10. Have you given your report on the pyramids of Egypt?

SUBJECT COMPLEMENTS

Sometimes a complement completes the meaning of a sentence by explaining or describing the subject. Such a complement is called a *subject complement*. While the direct and the indirect object can follow action verbs only, the subject complement can follow linking verbs only. (If you need to review the list of linking verbs, turn to page 60.)

4d. A *subject complement* is a word which follows a linking verb and refers to (explains or describes) the subject.

Alice Tseng is a **teacher**. [*Teacher* follows the linking verb *is*, and explains something about *Alice Tseng*.]

We are the **ones**. [*Ones* follows the linking verb *are* and refers to the subject *we*.]

A lemon tastes **sour**. [*Sour* follows the linking verb *tastes* and describes *lemon*—sour lemon.]

The weather looked **good**. [*Good* follows the linking verb *looked* and describes *weather*.]

Nouns, pronouns, and adjectives can serve as subject complements.

Predicate Nominatives and Predicate Adjectives

There are two kinds of subject complements—*predicate nominatives* and *predicate adjectives*.

(1) If the subject complement is a noun or a pronoun, it is called a *predicate nominative.*

EXAMPLES   Tuesday is my **birthday.** [*Birthday* is a predicate nominative. It is a noun referring to the subject *Tuesday.*]

He is **one** of the best players. [*One* is a predicate nominative. It is a pronoun referring to the subject *he.*]

Like subjects and objects, predicate nominatives never appear in prepositional phrases.

The result was a **declaration** of war. [The predicate nominative is *declaration,* not *war.* Not only is *war* part of a prepositional phrase, but the *result* was just a *declaration,* not the war itself.]

(2) If the subject complement is an adjective, it is called a *predicate adjective.* A predicate adjective modifies the subject.

EXAMPLES   An atomic reactor is very **powerful.** [*Powerful* is a predicate adjective modifying the subject *reactor.*]

This ground looks **swampy.** [*Swampy* is a predicate adjective modifying the subject *ground.*]

EXERCISE 8. Identifying Predicate Nominatives and Predicate Adjectives. Write the linking verb and the subject complement from each of the following sentences. If the complement is a predicate nominative (noun or pronoun), write *p.n.* after it. If it is a predicate adjective, write *p.a.* after it.

EXAMPLE   1. The raincoat looked too short for me.
          1. *looked, short—p.a.*

1. My dog is playful.
2. I am the one who called you yesterday.
3. Many public buildings in the East are proof of I. M. Pei's architectural skill.
4. The downtown mall appeared especially busy today.
5. Sally Ride sounded confident during the television interview.
6. The package felt too light to be a book.
7. These questions seem easier to me than the ones on the last two tests.
8. The singer's clothing became a symbol that her fans imitated.
9. Some poems, such as "The Bells" and "The Raven," are delightfully rhythmical.
10. While the mountain lion looked around for food, the fawn remained perfectly still.

Some verbs, such as *look, grow,* and *feel,* may be used as either linking verbs or action verbs. They are followed by predicate nominatives or predicate adjectives only when the nouns or adjectives that follow them refer back to the subject. They are followed by objects only when the nouns that follow them receive the action of the verb or name the result of the action.

LINKING VERB   The sailor **felt happy.** [*Happy* is a predicate adjective after the linking verb *felt. Happy* refers back to sailor.]

ACTION VERB   The sailor **felt** the **breeze.** [*Breeze* is a direct object after the action verb *felt,* and names what the sailor felt.]

WRITING APPLICATION:
Using Predicate Adjectives to Help Organize
a Description

If you are like most people, you probably cannot, without planning, sit down and write a perfectly organized paragraph. You have most likely found that it is worth taking the time to jot down your ideas, think about them, revise them, and plan the best order for them before you begin writing. This kind of planning is called *prewriting*. Prewriting refers to the thinking, the organizing, and all of the other activities that precede writing. If you were going to write a paragraph of description, you might think about your subject in terms of a compound predicate adjective. The pattern you would use would be SUBJECT—LINKING VERB—PREDICATE ADJECTIVES.

EXAMPLE   A computer can be fun, challenging, and occasionally frustrating.

Using this pattern for the beginning sentence of your paragraph, you then could supply facts, reasons, or details that develop the adjectives into an organized description.

Writing Assignment

When you have spare time, what do you enjoy doing? Describe this activity in a paragraph that begins with a sentence containing a compound predicate adjective with three adjectives as in the example above.

EXAMPLE   The game *Trivial Pursuit* is fast-moving, educational, and sometimes funny.

Underline the predicate adjectives in your beginning sentence, and in your paragraph tell why or how each adjective describes the activity you are describing.

EXERCISE 9. Identifying Subject Complements.   Seven of the sentences in this exercise contain a subject complement—a predicate nominative or a predicate adjective. If a sentence has a subject complement, write the complement after the proper number; if not, leave the space blank after the number.

EXAMPLE   1. The soup tasted salty.
            1. *salty*

1. After the audience had left, the empty theater seemed eerily quiet.

2. We grew fond of the mongrel puppies.
3. The tired runner rubbed her swollen ankle.
4. The inventor's contraptions, exhibited in the library, were those of an imaginative person.
5. Lately, the television commercials sound louder than the shows.
6. The judges looked critically at all the science projects in the fair.
7. The audience grew restless as the delay continued.
8. After they discovered the mistakes, the officials appeared worried about the public reaction to the news stories.
9. Virginia Dare was the first child born to English parents in the New World.
10. A picture of a skier was on the cover of our literature book.

REVIEW EXERCISE B. Identifying Subject Complements.

Number your paper 1–15. After the appropriate number, write the subject complement or complements in each of the following sentences. Be sure that your complements follow a linking verb and refer to the verb's subject.

EXAMPLE   1. The child was very restless.
           1. *restless*

1. Some varieties of apples that grow in the United States taste tart.
2. Several dishes at the potluck supper were spicy, but others seemed bland.
3. Exotic orchids can be surprisingly easy to grow.
4. Cheese is a valuable source of protein.
5. After connecting the batteries to the engine, we will see whether our machine is a success.
6. If the sky is clear and the water is warm enough, we will be ready for a day at the beach.
7. It could be worse.
8. The saxophone is the most popular instrument in the jazz band.

9. Silver dollars, which are no longer pure silver, have long been favorites among coin collectors.
10. According to some, the new style looks ugly.
11. Most of my friends like avocados, but they will not eat artichokes, which I think are very delicious.
12. Perhaps next year our team will be the undisputed champions in our league.
13. The disposal of hazardous wastes has become a controversial issue in many states.
14. After climbing the mountain, we looked down at the valley, which seemed peaceful at that distance.
15. The children grew weary and the adults were cranky, but I remained cheerful during the snow storm.

Diagraming Subject Complements

A subject complement is diagramed somewhat like a direct object. But the short vertical line separating it from the verb is slanted toward the subject to show that the complement refers to the subject.

PATTERNS

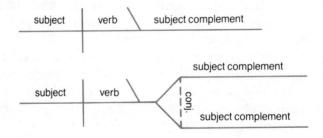

EXAMPLES   1. The dancers are graceful.

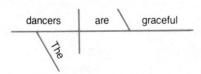

2. The contestants are Joan and Dean.

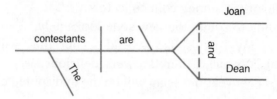

EXERCISE 10. Diagraming Subject Complements. Diagram the following sentences:

1. The lights were dim.
2. Who are they?
3. The girls became lifeguards.
4. The cave was cold and damp.
5. Our speaker was a teacher and a writer.
6. We felt qualified for the job.
7. One of the most daring explorers of the sixteenth century was Sir Francis Drake.
8. The chimpanzees seem happy in their new environment.
9. My shoes looked worn and dusty after the long walk.
10. John Donne was a famous poet and a great preacher.

REVIEW EXERCISE C. Identifying Verbs and Their Objects or Subject Complements. Number your paper 1–15. After the proper number, write the verb or verbs in the sentence. If a verb has one or more objects, write each object after it. If a verb is a linking verb, write the subject complement after it. Then identify each object or complement as direct object (*d.o.*), indirect object (*i.o.*), predicate adjective (*p.a.*), or predicate nominative (*p.n.*).

EXAMPLE 1. I have never seen a live manatee, but in pictures they look gentle.
    1. *have seen, manatee—d.o.; look, gentle—p.a.*

1. The embarrassed guest accidentally broke the antique Chinese vase.
2. The symphony conductor is the speaker for today.

3. After thieves had stolen his money, the store owner installed a burglar alarm.
4. Five of my relatives are politicians, but I would never cast my vote for any of them.
5. This American sports car has many new features.
6. The ladder by the doorway looks sturdier than the one in the corner.
7. India seems mysterious, but its people share many problems that are common to us.
8. With the permission of the museum director, we can take pictures of the new exhibit.
9. Do you remember the end of that joke?
10. These are only some of the popular songs from ten years ago.
11. The performing seals gave us a good laugh.
12. White gloves were once common in stylish circles.
13. Whenever something is beautiful, some people will feel a need to destroy it.
14. My little cousin always finds some treasure at my house, such as a rock or a bottle cap.
15. The book club sent me the wrong selection this month.

REVIEW EXERCISE D. Diagraming Complete Sentences. Diagram these sentences:

1. The lifeguard gave the rescued boy artificial respiration.
2. We deposited our money at the bank.
3. You seem very cheerful today.
4. Her mother was a ballerina with a famous ballet troupe.
5. Don and Maria acted the parts of Romeo and Juliet.
6. The origin of the Gypsies remains a great mystery.
7. The girls made themselves bracelets and necklaces for the dress rehearsal.
8. Two of the most famous canals in the world are the Suez Canal and the Panama Canal.
9. We proudly displayed our best paintings along the sidewalk.
10. The clown's shoes were long and wide.

REVIEW EXERCISE E. Writing Sentences with Subject Complements or Objects. Fill in the blanks in the following paragraph with words that will make a funny or ridiculous story. Write on your paper the words that you want in the blanks. After each word, write what kind of complement it is: *p.n., p.a., d.o.,* or *i.o.* Before you begin writing, read quickly through the entire paragraph so that you can plan what you will write.

With the rain drenching me thoroughly, I peered through the trees and spotted a ——. It looked ——. As I walked closer, the wind howled and gave —— a ——. But I felt ——. When I opened ——, a spider's cobweb hit ——. Then I became ——. The door creaked and a mouse scurried away. Finally, I decided it was not ——. I went back outside and found ——.

CHAPTER 4 REVIEW: POSTTEST 1

Identifying Direct Objects, Indirect Objects, Predicate Nominatives, and Predicate Adjectives. Number your paper 1–25. After the proper number, write the italicized words in the following sentences. Correctly identify each, using these abbreviations: *d.o.* (direct object), *i.o.* (indirect object), *p.n.* (predicate nominative), or *p.a.* (predicate adjective).

EXAMPLE 1. The pitcher threw a curve *ball.*
2. *ball—d.o.*

1. A pronoun is a *word* that takes the place of a noun.
2. Much foliage stays *green* during the winter in Florida.
3. Don't you know the *answer?*
4. I gave *Marsha* my doll collection.
5. This fly rod can cast a *lure* all the way across the river.
6. My books got soaking *wet* in the storm yesterday.
7. Turn in your *papers* now.
8. Our house is bright *blue.*
9. Throughout the day the principal interrupted *classes* with announcements over the intercom.

10. Brothers and sisters can be a *pain* in the neck.
11. Several sports magazines have sent *me* subscription order blanks lately.
12. Just *what* does that mean?
13. The message sounded *urgent* to me.
14. Michael Jackson is my favorite *singer*.
15. Frank asked *Angela* to the dance.
16. The baby sitter read the *children* a story.
17. My uncle took *all* of us to the carnival last week.
18. When I returned to the house where we used to live, it seemed *smaller*.
19. She is the most active *member* of our club.
20. The eerie noise gave *me* quite a scare.
21. The sign hanging on the post looks *crooked* from here.
22. The committee asked each *applicant* several questions.
23. Let me hear your *excuse*.
24. Halloween was my favorite *holiday* when I was younger.
25. You always think you know the *answer*.

CHAPTER 4 REVIEW: POSTTEST 2

Identifying Direct Objects, Indirect Objects, Predicate Nominatives, and Predicate Adjectives. Number your paper 1–25. The italicized words in the following paragraphs have been numbered. After the proper number, write each italicized word and indicate whether it is a direct object, an indirect object, a predicate nominative, or a predicate adjective. Use the abbreviations *d.o.* (direct object), *i.o.* (indirect object), *p.n.* (predicate nominative), *p.a.* (predicate adjective).

Girls aren't the only (1) *ones* who know how to cook. My mom got a (2) *job* last summer, so she gave (3) *me* cooking lessons before school began this year. At first, I felt (4) *reluctant* about learning what I considered a "girl's job." I've always thought that boys who cook are (5) *sissies*. I couldn't remember when my dad had ever cooked a (6) *meal*. However, he reminded me that he makes a (7) *number* of his specialties, and he said that cooking lessons would be a good (8) *idea* for me. Boy, was he ever (9) *right*!

When I began, I could hardly boil (10) *water* without fouling up, but my mom remained (11) *patient* and carefully showed her bumbling (12) *son* the correct and easy ways to do things. For example, did you know that water will boil faster if it has a little (13) *salt* in it or that cornstarch makes an excellent thickening (14) *agent* in everything from batter to gravy? These are just a (15) *couple* of the tips I have learned. Cooking involves a lot (16) *more* than I ever imagined.

My first attempts tasted (17) *awful,* but gradually I've become a fairly good (18) *cook.* Probably my best complete meal is beef (19) *stew.* Although stew doesn't require the highest (20) *grade* of beef, a good cut of chuck roast will give (21) *it* a much better taste. I am always very (22) *careful* about picking out the vegetables too. Our grocer probably thinks I am too (23) *picky* when I hunt for the best (24) *ingredients* I can find. I don't care, though, because when I serve my (25) *family* my stew, they say it is their favorite dish.

CHAPTER 4 REVIEW: POSTTEST 3

Writing Sentences with Direct Objects, Indirect Objects, and Subject Complements. Write sentences according to the following guidelines. Underline the direct object, the indirect object, or the sentence complement in each sentence.

1. a declarative sentence with a direct object
2. a declarative sentence with a predicate nominative
3. an interrogative sentence with a predicate adjective
4. an imperative sentence with a direct object
5. an exclamatory sentence with a predicate adjective

CHAPTER 5

The Phrase

PREPOSITIONAL, VERBAL, AND APPOSITIVE PHRASES

In Chapters 2 and 3, you studied single-word modifiers: the adjective and the adverb. Whole groups of words also may act as modifiers. Just as a verb phrase acts as a single verb, so an adjective phrase acts as a single adjective, and an adverb phrase acts as a single adverb. An entire phrase may also serve as a noun, either as a subject or as an object within a sentence. This chapter will focus on how to identify and use phrases in writing.

DIAGNOSTIC TEST

Classifying Phrases. Number your paper 1–20. After the proper number, write each italicized phrase in the following sentences and indicate what kind of phrase it is. Use the abbreviations *prep.* (prepositional phrase), *part.* (participial phrase), *inf.* (infinitive phrase), *ger.* (gerund phrase), and *app.* (appositive phrase). Do not identify a prepositional phrase that is part of a larger phrase.

EXAMPLE   1. He tried *to do his best*.
           1. *to do his best—inf.*

1. *Fishing for bass* is my father's favorite pastime.
2. The seagulls *gliding through the air* looked like pieces of paper caught in the wind.
3. The school bus was on time *in spite of the traffic jam.*
4. Ms. Hoban, *my science teacher,* got married last week.
5. There is no time left *to answer your questions.*
6. *Under a white flag* of truce, the defeated soldiers glumly emerged from the fort.
7. My brother plans *to marry Maureen in June.*
8. Nobody seems to be interested in *going to the fireworks display.*
9. Have you seen my cat, *a striped Persian with pale yellow eyes?*
10. Joel said that he can go *to the dance or the movies* on Friday.
11. *Hoping for a new bicycle and a toy robot,* my brother couldn't sleep at all on Christmas Eve.
12. Tom Sawyer tricked his friends into *painting the fence for him.*
13. In America, citizens have the right *to speak their minds.*
14. My aunt's car, *an old crate with a beat-up interior and a rattly engine,* used to belong to my grandfather.
15. Debbie's sister denied *taking the cookies.*
16. Last Sunday, we all piled in the car and went *to the beach, the bowling alley, and the mall.*
17. The shark *chasing the school of fish* looked like a hammerhead.
18. Nobody wanted to read the book, *a thick hardback with a faded cover.*
19. All of the invitations *sent to the club members* had the wrong date on them.
20. Buddy's cousin ran off *to join the circus.*

5a. A *phrase* is a group of related words that is used as a single part of speech and does not contain a verb and its subject.

You have already studied the *verb phrase*, which is introduced by a helping verb (*have* bought). You have also been introduced to the *prepositional phrase*. In this chapter you will learn more about the prepositional phrase, and you will meet several new kinds of phrases—the *participial phrase*, the *infinitive phrase*, the *gerund phrase*, and the *appositive phrase*.

THE PREPOSITIONAL PHRASE

5b. A *prepositional phrase* **is a group of words that begins with a preposition and usually ends with a noun or pronoun.**

In the following examples, the prepositional phrases are in boldface.

> We prepared treats **for them.**
> **During the night** the horse ran off.
> Marian wore white pajamas **with red stripes.**

Of course, a single prepositional phrase may contain two or more objects.

> The dish is filled **with crackers and rice cookies.**
> The group traveled **through Spain and Italy.**

EXERCISE 1. Identifying Prepositional Phrases. Number your paper 1–13, using every other line. After the appropriate number, write the prepositional phrases in the following sentences. There are twenty-five phrases.

1. The daily schedule prepared by the camp directors was followed from dawn until late evening.
2. We were awakened at six by a bugle, played with cold fingers by a sleepy camper.
3. Linda Sanchez sometimes woke the camp in the morning with her saxophone.
4. Standing attentively outside our cabins, we shivered in the early morning breeze coming across the lake.
5. After exercises, everyone swam in the icy water.

6. Fearing death from freezing, we raced back and dressed for breakfast.
7. Inspection followed the cleaning of cabins.
8. Activity period included classes in painting, crafts, music, drama, and folklore.
9. The rest of the morning was devoted to sports.
10. After lunch, we spent an hour in our cabins.
11. Then we had two hours of water sports.
12. The time between water sports and dinner was free.
13. At night, talented campers and counselors entertained us.

The Adjective Phrase

Some prepositional phrases are called *adjective phrases* because they act like adjectives; that is, they modify nouns and pronouns.

5c. An *adjective phrase* **is a prepositional phrase that modifies a noun or a pronoun.**

Notice that the adjectives and the adjective phrases in boldface in the following sentences do the same work: they modify a noun.

ADJECTIVE The **lighthouse** beacon stayed on all night.

ADJECTIVE PHRASE The beacon **from the lighthouse** stayed on all night.

ADJECTIVE Their **varsity** players are bigger than our players.

ADJECTIVE PHRASE The players **on their varsity** are bigger than our players.

ADJECTIVE I met some **Asian** students.

ADJECTIVE PHRASE I met some students **from Asia.**

Like the adjective, an adjective phrase is usually located next to the word it modifies. But while the adjective generally precedes the word it modifies, the adjective phrase usually follows the word it modifies.

EXERCISE 2. Identifying Adjective Phrases. Each of the following sentences contains an adjective phrase. Number your paper 1–10. After the proper number, write the adjective phrase and the noun or pronoun it modifies.

EXAMPLE   1. The dancers on the stage were thrilling.
              1. *on the stage, dancers*

1. The strait between the Pacific Ocean and San Francisco Bay is called the Golden Gate.
2. The Golden Gate Bridge spans this narrow body of water.
3. San Francisco was once a small village on the bay but is now a busy metropolitan center.
4. The California gold rush of 1849 swelled San Francisco's population.
5. The 1906 earthquake destroyed the homes of many people.
6. Today sightseers from many different nations crowd San Francisco's streets.
7. Some of the streets are very steep.
8. San Francisco's Chinatown is an attraction for visitors.
9. This city beside the bay has many charms.
10. Do you know any songs about San Francisco?

EXERCISE 3. Writing Sentences with Adjective Phrases. Construct sentences using each of the following word groups as an adjective phrase. Underline the noun or pronoun that the adjective phrase modifies.

EXAMPLE   1. by the river
              1. *The <u>tree</u> by the river is a willow.*

1. down the street
2. under the bridge
3. like us
4. with bright lights
5. in the pup tent
6. near the fireplace
7. through the hallway
8. around the cottage
9. for our kitten
10. at the store

Sometimes one adjective phrase follows another. The second phrase usually modifies the object in the first phrase.

EXAMPLE   Sicily is an island **off the coast of Italy.**

EXERCISE 4. Identifying Adjective Phrases.   Each of the following sentences contains two adjective phrases. Number your paper 1–10, and write the adjective phrases after the appropriate numbers. After each phrase, write the word it modifies.

EXAMPLE   1. Sharon read a book on the origins of words.
              1. *on the origins, book; of words, origins*

1. You will find the book on the right side of the shelf.
2. My sister Connie, a real terror with a whale of a temper, shouts "Beans!" when something goes wrong.
3. Ms. Ford, our teacher during the second semester of English, uses many different expressions.
4. Some terms for the expression of anger were originally Latin or Greek words.
5. Many of us in the class wanted to discuss how people express their annoyance.
6. Imagine what would happen if everybody in every house in the city had a bad day.
7. The fireworks in the sky over the entire area would surely flare and pop then.
8. That would be an excellent time to become an exchange student on the other side of the planet.
9. The funniest expression we heard was "as mad as a wet hen on top of a picket fence."
10. Even though the topic was interesting, we agreed that the best thing to do is to avoid people with chips on their shoulders.

The Adverb Phrase

When a prepositional phrase is used as an adverb to modify a verb, adjective, or adverb, it is called an *adverb phrase*. Like a single-word adverb, the adverb phrase answers the question *How? When? Where?* or *To what extent?*

5d. An *adverb phrase* is a prepositional phrase that modifies a verb, an adjective, or an adverb.

EXAMPLES The snow fell **like feathers.** [The adverb phrase modifies the verb *fell,* telling *how* the snow fell.]

Her dress is too long **in the back.** [The adverb phrase modifies the adjective *long,* telling *where* the dress is too long.]

We arrived early **in the morning.** [The adverb phrase modifies the adverb *early,* telling *when* we were early.]

Adverb phrases modify verbs more often than they modify adjectives and adverbs.

EXERCISE 5. Identifying Adverb Phrases. Each of the following sentences contains an adverb phrase. Number your paper 1–10. After the appropriate number, write the adverb phrase from each sentence. Then write the verb, adjective, or adverb that the phrase modifies.

EXAMPLE 1. Our town was built over a river.
1. *over a river, was built*

1. The Cheery Oh, a new restaurant, has opened across the road.
2. The food is fantastic beyond belief.
3. Almost everyone has gone to the new place.
4. At the Cheery Oh you can eat exotic food.
5. People sit late into the night drinking tropical fruit juices and chatting.
6. They enjoy themselves in the friendly atmosphere.
7. People appear happy with the service.
8. Some say in all seriousness that it resembles an English coffeehouse.
9. For three weeks the Cheery Oh has been crowded.

10. If the famous writers John Dryden and Joseph Addison were alive today, they could probably be found at this charming restaurant.

EXERCISE 6. Writing Sentences with Adverb Phrases. Construct sentences in which you use the following phrases as adverbs modifying verbs. Underline the verb or verb phrase that is modified.

EXAMPLE   1. above the clouds
1. *The huge jet soared above the clouds.*

1. during the storm	6. about an hour ago
2. outside the cabin	7. beside the path
3. after several weeks	8. down the river
4. without any help	9. through our efforts
5. by their teammates	10. in the laundry

EXAMPLE   Animals move **to a warm place during the winter months.**

The adjective phrase almost always follows immediately after the word it modifies, but the adverb phrase may be separated from the word it modifies by other words. Adverb phrases may be moved about in the sentence.

EXAMPLES   **For many centuries** people searched **for a way** to make gold.
People searched **for many centuries for a way** to make gold.
For a way to make gold, people searched **for many centuries.**

EXERCISE 7. Identifying Adverb Phrases. Number your paper 1–7. After the proper number, write the adverb phrase or phrases in each sentence. After each adverb phrase, write the word or phrase it modifies.

EXAMPLE   1. I am going to camp during vacation.
1. *to camp—am going; during vacation—am going*

1. Mount Vernon is interesting for its history.
2. It is near Washington, D.C.
3. The house was named Mount Vernon by Lawrence Washington, who lived there for many years.
4. Somewhat later, George and Martha Washington moved to Mount Vernon.
5. After Washington's death the house was owned by a series of people.
6. In 1858, it was bought by the Mount Vernon Ladies' Association, which restored it.
7. The buildings and grounds are open to the general public.

Diagraming Adjective and Adverb Phrases

An adjective or adverb phrase is diagramed below the word it modifies. Write the preposition on a line slanting down from the modified word. Then write the object of the preposition (the noun or pronoun following the preposition) on a horizontal line extending from the slanting line. Modifiers within a phrase are diagramed in the usual way.

PATTERNS

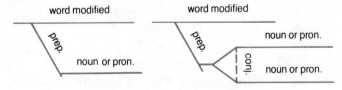

EXAMPLES   1. walked along the road

2. paintings by famous artists

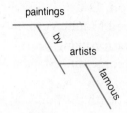

3. went with Hollis and Dave

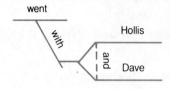

When a prepositional phrase modifies the object of another prepositional phrase, the diagram looks like this:

EXAMPLE   camped on top of a mountain

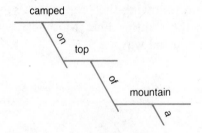

EXERCISE 8. Diagraming Prepositional Phrases. Diagram the following word groups, which contain prepositional phrases. Use a ruler, and leave plenty of space between diagrams.

1. invited to the celebrations
2. everyone but her
3. date of the wedding
4. a glimpse of the famous ruler
5. was by my favorite singer
6. hiked for twenty miles

7. one of the people in the room
8. the day before the trial
9. read about King Midas and his golden touch
10. drove to a village near Paris

EXERCISE 9. Diagraming Sentences with Adjective Phrases and Adverb Phrases. Diagram the following sentences, each of which contains an adjective phrase or an adverb phrase or both.

EXAMPLE The company of actors performed in front of a large audience.

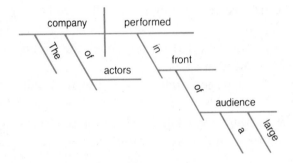

1. The film was made in Spain.
2. The number of whales is decreasing.
3. One of the candidates withdrew from the race.
4. Ocean tides are controlled by the moon.
5. Pompeii was destroyed by a volcano.
6. Citrus fruits are grown in California and Florida.
7. Many historic events have been decided by sudden changes in the weather.
8. The defeat of the Spanish Armada resulted from a violent ocean storm.
9. Some familiar animals can be found only in zoos.
10. Hundreds of species have vanished from the earth.

REVIEW EXERCISE A. Identifying Adjective Phrases and Adverb Phrases. After the proper number, list in order the adjective phrases and adverb phrases in the following sentences.

After each phrase, write the word or expression it modifies. Be ready to tell whether it is an adjective phrase or an adverb phrase.

EXAMPLE 1. Through old journals, our understanding of the pioneers has increased.

        1. *Through old journals, has increased; of the pioneers, understanding*

1. Few of us appreciate the determination and courage shown by the pioneers who traveled west to make new homes.
2. The word *travel* comes from the French word *travailler,* which means "to work hard."
3. On the trip westward only the smallest children rode in the wagons.
4. Everyone else traveled on foot over the mountains, which were covered with snow.
5. Sometimes a wagon train would stop in a valley and then spend the winter in houses that were built quickly.
6. In one account of a harsh winter, a pioneer recorded an incident of a roof that collapsed under the weight of the snow.
7. Food was often scarce for many families, and hundreds never recovered from the hardships.
8. A typical day's chores began long before dawn.
9. The pioneers who did survive by sheer determination often continued their journey.
10. At their western destination, many families often shared the same cabin and would make plans to build their homes.

VERBALS AND VERBAL PHRASES

When you studied the eight parts of speech, you learned how a verb functions in a sentence. In addition to their usual function, some forms of a verb may also act as a noun, an adjective, or an adverb. A verb form that acts as one of these other parts of speech is called a *verbal.* There are three kinds of verbals: the *participle,* the *gerund,* and the *infinitive.*

The Participle

5e. A *participle* is a verb form that can be used as an adjective.

There are two kinds of participles—present participles and past participles. Present participles end in *–ing.* Past participles often end in *–ed, –d,* or *–t.*

EXAMPLES The horses **trotting** past were not frightened by the crowd. [*Trotting* (a form of the verb *trot*) modifies, like an adjective, the noun *horses—trotting horses.*]

Buried by pirates, the treasure was undiscovered for centuries. [*Buried* (a form of the verb *bury*) modifies, like an adjective, the noun *treasure—buried treasure.*]

Do not confuse participles used as in the examples above with participles used in a verb phrase.

PARTICIPLE **Broken,** the toy still ran.
VERB PHRASE The toy **was broken** but still ran.

PARTICIPLE **Planning** their trip, the class learned some geography.
VERB PHRASE While they **were planning** their trip, the class learned some geography.

The participle in a verb phrase is part of a verb and does not act as an adjective.

EXERCISE 10. Identifying Participles. Number your paper 1–10. After the proper number, write the participle from each of the following sentences. After each participle, write the noun or pronoun it modifies. Be prepared to tell whether the participle is a present participle or a past participle.

EXAMPLE 1. We heard the train whistling and chugging in the distance.
1. *whistling, train; chugging, train*

1. Records, cracked and warped, were in the old trunk in the attic.
2. Shouting loudly, Becky warned the pedestrian to look out for the car.
3. The sparkling water splashed in our faces.
4. The papers, aged and yellowed, are kept in the file.
5. For centuries the ruins remained there, still undiscovered.
6. Smiling politely, she gave directions to the post office.
7. The charging bull thundered across the field.
8. Cheering and clapping, the spectators greeted their team.
9. The children, fidgeting noisily, waited eagerly for recess.
10. Recently released, the movie has not yet come to our local theaters.

The Participial Phrase

When a participle introduces a group of related words that act together as an adjective, this word group is called a *participial phrase.*

5f. A *participial phrase* is a group of related words that contains a participle and that acts as an adjective.

A prepositional phrase often follows the participle. When it does, it is considered a part of the participial phrase. In the following examples, an arrow is drawn from each participial phrase (shown in boldface) to the word that it modifies.

Seeing itself in the mirror, the duck seemed bewildered.

It stood in front of the mirror, **watching its image closely.**

Then, **disgusted with the other duck,** it began to peck the mirror.

Finally, **giving up in dismay,** it backed cautiously away from its strange opponent.

WRITING APPLICATION A:
Using Participial Phrases to Combine Closely Related Sentences

Do you have a sample of your handwriting from your elementary school days? If you do, you are probably amused at how different it is from the way you write now. As you mature, your handwriting is not the only part of your writing to change; your sentence structure also changes. When you were younger, you probably wrote mostly short, choppy sentences that contained simple ideas. As you have grown older, you have learned to combine ideas to pack more information into your sentences. One way you do this is by using participles.

EXAMPLE   I sat down at the table. Mother was at the table. I took out my class schedule for next year. Mother and I discussed my classes. These classes were offered for ninth-graders. [The style of this example is short and choppy.]

Sitting down at the table, I took out my class schedule to show Mother. She and I discussed the classes **offered for ninth-graders next year.** [This is one way to improve the short, choppy sentences. Notice the participial phrases in boldface.]

Writing Assignment

Before people begin activities of various kinds, they often have warm-ups. This is true whether they are getting ready to swim in a race, play in a band concert, or perform in a dance recital. Describe either a person or a group of persons warming up. Use at least three participial phrases, and underline these phrases.

EXERCISE 11. Identifying Participial Phrases.   Number your paper 1–10. After the proper number, write the participial phrase in each sentence and the noun or pronoun that the phrase modifies.

1. Defeated badly, the team walked slowly from the field.
2. Looking over the audience, Carolyn saw several familiar faces.
3. A bear, standing in the road, stopped traffic.
4. The heavy rains predicted by the weather bureau did not come.
5. Washed overboard by an enormous wave, the skipper was rescued by the crew.
6. The family left early, forgetting to lock the back door of the house.
7. Grabbing her coat, Melissa rushed out the door.
8. Mailed on March 4, your letter did not arrive until April 1.
9. We offered a ride into town to two students waiting for the bus.
10. Named for her mother, Catherine has always been called Katie.

EXERCISE 12. Identifying Participial Phrases. Number your paper 1–10. After the appropriate number, write the participial phrase in each sentence. After the phrase, write the word or words that it modifies.

1. Noted for her beauty, Venus was sought by all the gods as a wife.
2. Jupiter, knowing her charms, nevertheless married her to Vulcan, the ugliest of the gods.
3. Bathed in radiant light, Venus brought love and joy wherever she went.
4. Mars, known to the Greeks as Ares, was the god of war.
5. Terrified by Ares' power, many Greeks did not like to worship him.
6. They saw both land and people destroyed by him.
7. Observing his path, they said that Ares left blood, devastation, and grief behind him.
8. The Romans, having great respect for Mars, made him one of their three chief deities.

9. They imagined him dressed in shining armor.
10. Mars, supposed to be the father of the founders of Rome, has a month named after him.

EXERCISE 13. Writing Sentences with Participial Phrases. Use the following participial phrases in sentences of your own. Place each phrase as close as possible to the noun or pronoun that it modifies. If you use a participial phrase to begin a sentence, put a comma after the phrase, and follow it closely with the word that is modified.

EXAMPLE 1. standing in line
1. *Standing in line, we waited twenty minutes for the store to open.*

1. printed on Thursdays
2. waiting for the bus in the rain
3. passing the store window
4. invited to her party on Saturday
5. planning the escape
6. stored in the hall closet
7. jumping from stone to stone
8. angered by the remarks
9. inscribed on the inside
10. hearing the whistle blow and feeling the train lurch forward

The Gerund

Besides acting as participial modifiers, verbs ending in *–ing* can also be another kind of verbal called a *gerund*. Gerunds function as nouns in sentences.

5g. A *gerund* is a verb form ending in *–ing* that is used as a noun.

EXAMPLES   **Fishing** can be a hobby or an occupation. [subject]
My favorite exercise is **jogging**. [predicate nominative]

> Lock the door before **leaving.** [object of preposition]
>
> Did they go **hiking?** [direct object]

Because the gerund acts as a noun, it can be modified by adjectives and adjective phrases.

EXAMPLES My father and I enjoyed the **excellent** fishing. [The adjective *excellent* modifies the gerund *fishing.*]

The **quiet** gurgling **of the aquarium** was restful. [The adjective *quiet* and the adjective phrase *of the aquarium* both modify the gerund *gurgling.*]

Because gerunds are also verb forms, they can be modified by adverbs and adverb phrases, too.

EXAMPLES Practicing **regularly** will help you perfect your skill. [The adverb *regularly* modifies the gerund *practicing.*]

We crossed the stream by stepping **carefully from stone to stone.** [The adverb *carefully* and the adverb phrase *from stone to stone* both modify the gerund *stepping.*]

Remember that gerunds are nouns. Do not confuse gerunds with participles used as verbs or as adjectives.

EXAMPLE **Pausing,** the deer was **sniffing** the wind before **stepping** into the open meadow.

Pausing is a participle modifying *deer,* and *sniffing* is part of the verb phrase *was sniffing. Stepping* is a gerund, serving as the object of the preposition *before.*

EXERCISE 14. Identifying Gerunds.

Number your paper 1–10. After the appropriate number, write the gerund in each of the following sentences. If there is no gerund in the sentence, write *none.*

EXAMPLE 1. Typing is a useful skill.
           1. *Typing*

1. Their singing caused the dogs to howl.
2. Jerry has been practicing pole vaulting every day after school.
3. My sister has always enjoyed horseback riding.
4. In the past, working took up most people's time six days a week.
5. I look forward to resting after this tiring job is done.
6. Uncle Eli's specialty is barbecuing on the outdoor grill.
7. Nobody could stand the child's unceasing whine.
8. The colonel will be commending the scout for volunteering for the dangerous mission.
9. Studying usually pays off in higher scores.
10. Considering the choices, Melinda decided on walking.

The Gerund Phrase

A gerund may be accompanied by modifiers and complements, which together with the gerund form a *gerund phrase.*

5h. A *gerund phrase* **includes the gerund and all the words related to the gerund.**

A gerund is formed from a verb. It may be modified by an adverb and may also have a complement, usually a direct object. Since a gerund functions as a noun, it may be modified by an adjective. A gerund phrase includes the gerund and all of its modifiers and complements.

EXAMPLES   **Shouting at people** does not make them understand you better. [*Shouting* is a gerund, and *at people* is a prepositional phrase acting as an adverb that modifies *shouting.* Together, *shouting at people* is a gerund phrase that acts as the complete subject of the sentence.]

Most of the players obeyed **the stern warning from the coach.** [The gerund *warning* is modified by the article *the,* the adjective *stern,* and the prepositional phrase *from the coach.* The word group, *the stern* *warning from the coach* is a gerund phrase that serves as the object of the verb *obeyed.*]

The child spelled her name by **carefully printing each letter.** [The gerund *printing* is modified by the adverb *carefully* and has the direct object *each letter.* Together, the gerund phrase *carefully printing each letter* is the object of the preposition *by.*]

☞ **NOTE** Since a gerund acts as a noun, any noun or pronoun that comes immediately before it should be in the possessive case.

EXAMPLES   **Michael's** cooking is the best I've ever tasted.
The vultures didn't let anything disturb **their** feeding.

EXERCISE 15. Identifying Gerund Phrases.   Number your paper 1–10. After the appropriate number, write the gerund phrase in each of the following sentences.

EXAMPLE   1. The rain interrupted their building of the bonfire.
1. *their building of the bonfire*

1. Vincent's pleading never influenced his mother's decision.
2. The man was given a ticket for driving the wrong way on a one-way street.
3. We sat back and enjoyed the slow rocking of the boat.
4. The blue jay's screeching at the cat woke us up at dawn.
5. My cousin and I look forward to going downtown to the movie tonight.
6. When did that piercing clanging begin?
7. The frantic darting of the fish indicated that a shark was nearby.
8. She is considering running Patty's campaign for class president.

9. Ants try to protect their colonies from storms by piling up sand against the wind.

10. The wading egret was intently searching for frogs and other small animals during its early morning feeding.

EXERCISE 16. Writing Sentences with Gerund Phrases.
Write each of the following gerund phrases in a sentence of your own. Underline the gerund phrase in each sentence, and identify it as a subject, a predicate nominative, a direct object, or an object of a preposition.

EXAMPLE   1. Hiking up the hill
          1. *Hiking up the hill* took us all morning.   *subject*

1. getting up in the morning
2. arguing among themselves
3. selling tickets to the concert
4. driving recklessly
5. refusing any help with the job
6. looking for a good deal
7. asking directions to the bus stop
8. walking slowly across the lawn
9. sharpening my pencil
10. playing a trick on my best friend

WRITING APPLICATION B:
Using Gerunds to Explain Activities Involving Action

Paper clips are quite versatile. They can be used to fasten together pieces of paper, to hang up lightweight pictures, to retrieve lost items, and to perform a number of other tasks. Similarly, gerunds can be used in a variety of ways—as subjects, objects, predicate nominatives, and in any other way that a noun is used. When you need a noun that expresses action, a gerund can be very helpful.

EXAMPLES   **Learning to play a violin** is harder than I thought it would be. [gerund phrase used as subject]

> My brother dislikes **taking out the trash.** [gerund phrase used as object of the verb]

Writing Assignment

If you could have any job when you finish school, what would it be? Write a paragraph telling about this job, why you would choose it, and why you think you are suited for it. Use three gerund phrases, and underline these phrases.

The Infinitive

Besides the participle, which is a verbal that acts as an adjective, and the gerund, which is a verbal that acts as a noun, there is a third kind of verbal called the *infinitive*. An infinitive can act as an adjective, a noun, or an adverb.

5i. **An *infinitive* is a verb form that can be used as a noun, an adjective, or an adverb.**

Instead of ending in *–ing* (as participles and gerunds do), an infinitive has the word *to* directly before the plain form of the verb, as in *to win, to go,* and *to consider.*

To determine what part of speech an infinitive is, closely examine how the infinitive is used in the sentence.

Infinitives used as nouns: She expected to finish the race, but not to win. [*To finish* and *to win* are objects of the verb expected.]

To forgive does not always mean to forget. [*To forgive* is the subject of the sentence; *to forget* is the predicate nominative.]

Infinitives used as adjectives: The best time **to visit** Florida is December through April. [*To visit* modifies *time.*]

If you want information about computers, that is the magazine **to read.** [*To read* modifies *magazine.*]

Infinitives used as adverbs: They were eager **to try.** [*To try* modifies the adjective *eager.*]

The caravan stopped at the oasis **to rest.** [*To rest* modifies the verb *stopped.*]

☞ **USAGE NOTE**   *To* plus a noun or a pronoun (*to class, to them, to the dance*) is a prepositional phrase, not an infinitive. Be careful not to confuse infinitives with prepositional phrases beginning with *to.*

INFINITIVE   I want **to go.**
PREPOSITIONAL PHRASE   I want to go **to town.**

EXERCISE 17. Identifying Infinitives.   Number your paper 1–10. After the appropriate number, write the infinitive in each sentence. If a sentence does not contain an infinitive, write *none.*

EXAMPLE   1. June doesn't know how to dance.
        1. *to dance*

1. After school June and I like to walk home together.
2. Usually, we go to my house or her house to listen to tapes.
3. Sometimes I get up to move with the music, but June never does.
4. One day I asked her to join me.
5. She said that she had never been to dancing school or learned any steps.
6. "Do you want me to show you some?" I asked.
7. "I'm ready to try," she answered.
8. I didn't know which steps to start with.
9. After trying to teach her for three weeks, I gave up.
10. It's a good thing that June doesn't plan to become a dancer.

The Infinitive Phrase

An infinitive may be followed by a group of related words, which together with the infinitive form an *infinitive phrase.*

5j. An *infinitive phrase* consists of an infinitive together with its complements and modifiers.

Because an infinitive may be a noun, an adjective, or an adverb, it may be modified by an adjective or an adverb. As a verb form, an infinitive may also have a complement. Together, an infinitive and its modifiers and complements make up an infinitive phrase. The entire infinitive phrase may act as an adjective, an adverb, or a noun.

EXAMPLES **To lift those weights** takes a lot of strength. [The infinitive phrase *to lift those weights* is used as a noun that is the subject of the sentence. The infinitive *to lift* has an object, *weights,* which is modified by *those.*]

Peanuts and raisins are good snacks **to take on a camping trip.** [The infinitive phrase *to take on a camping trip* is used as an adjective modifying *snacks.* The infinitive *to take* is modified by the prepositional phrase *on a camping trip.*]

The crowd grew quiet **to hear the speaker.** [The infinitive phrase *to hear the speaker* is used as an adverb modifying the adjective *quiet.* The infinitive *to hear* has the complement *the speaker.*]

EXERCISE 18. Identifying Infinitive Phrases. Number your paper 1–10. After the appropriate number, write the infinitive phrase in each of the following sentences, and identify whether it is a noun, an adjective, or an adverb. If there is no infinitive phrase in the sentence, write *none.*

EXAMPLE 1. My uncle taught me to take care of my bicycle.
      1. *to take care of my bicycle—noun*

1. Taking care of your bicycle will help to make it last longer.
2. We used machine oil to lubricate the chain.
3. He said to place a drop of oil on each link.
4. Then he showed me the valve to fill the inner tube.
5. Using a hand pump, we added air to the back tire.

6. We were careful not to put in too much air.
7. Next, we got out wrenches to tighten several bolts.
8. My uncle warned me not to pull on the wrench too hard.
9. Overtightening can cause as much damage to a bolt as not tightening it enough can.
10. I thanked my uncle for taking the time to give me tips about taking care of my bicycle.

EXERCISE 19. Writing Sentences with Infinitives. Write each of the following infinitive phrases in a sentence of your own. Underline the infinitive phrase and identify it as a noun, an adjective, or an adverb.

EXAMPLE 1. to leave school early on Tuesday
1. *The principal gave me permission to leave school early on Tuesday.—adj.*

1. to give the right answers
2. to go home after school
3. to run after the bus
4. to read the entire book over the weekend
5. to buy a new pair of shoes
6. to eat all my vegetables
7. to spend the night at my cousin's house
8. to write with a pen
9. to memorize my address and telephone number
10. to get better grades

REVIEW EXERCISE B. Identifying and Classifying Verbals and Verbal Phrases. Number your paper 1–10. After the appropriate number, write the verbal or verbal phrase in each of the following sentences. Identify each verbal or verbal phrase as a *gerund, gerund phrase, infinitive, infinitive phrase, participle,* or *participial phrase.*

EXAMPLE 1. Raising his head, the steer looked across the field.
1. *Raising his head—participial phrase*

1. Even the people in charge didn't know what to do.
2. My brother took us all to the skating rink last week.
3. Brad received a letter of commendation for organizing the clean-up campaign.
4. What did you say to her to make her so mad?
5. According to a number of experts, swimming is the best form of exercise for many people.
6. One of the women taking tickets at the door gave us directions to our seats.
7. The old hermit preferred living alone in the forest.
8. The tourists looked exhausted, but they didn't stop for a rest.
9. One solution may be to offer them more money.
10. His constant complaining grated on everyone's nerves.

Diagraming Verbals and Verbal Phrases

Participial phrases are diagramed as follows:

EXAMPLE **Shaking her head,** my older sister winked at me.

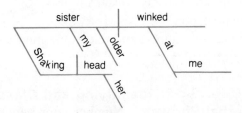

Gerunds and gerund phrases are diagramed as follows:

EXAMPLE **Being slightly ill** is no excuse for **missing two days of practice.** [Gerund phrases used as subject and as object of preposition. The first gerund has a subject complement (*ill*); the second gerund has a direct object (*days*).]

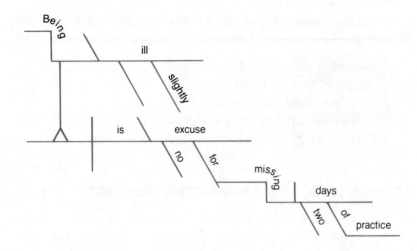

Infinitives and infinitive phrases used as modifiers are diagramed like prepositional phrases.

EXAMPLE   He was the first one **to solve that tricky problem.**

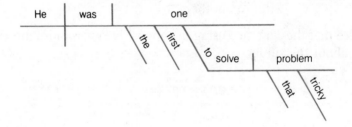

Infinitives used as nouns are diagramed as follows:

EXAMPLE   Marge was hoping **to go with us.**

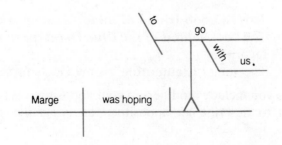

EXERCISE 20. Diagraming Sentences with Verbal Phrases. Diagram the following sentences:

1. Taking that shortcut will cut several minutes off the trip.
2. I am going to watch that program tonight.
3. That is my cat licking its paws.
4. Did they say what to do about this?
5. Checking the time, Wynetta rushed to the gym.

APPOSITIVES AND APPOSITIVE PHRASES

When you want to explain more exactly who or what you are talking about, you usually give additional information. You have already learned to add information by using complements. Another way is to use an *appositive* or an *appositive phrase*. Study these two ways to add information:

COMPLEMENT Mrs. Collins is **my English teacher.**

APPOSITIVE Mrs. Collins, **my English teacher,** went to school with my mother.

Notice that the sentence using the appositive gives more information about the subject.

5k. An *appositive* **is a noun or a pronoun that explains the noun or pronoun it follows.**

Appositives are often set off from the rest of the sentence by commas. However, when an appositive is necessary to the meaning of the sentence or is closely related to the word it follows, no commas are necessary.

EXAMPLES Troy, **a good friend of mine,** is camping with us.

The book ***Island of the Blue Dolphins*** is one of my favorites.

The song **"Clementine"** is my Dad's favorite.

Sometimes you include modifiers in your appositive. When words are added to describe an appositive, an *appositive phrase* is created.

5l. An *appositive phrase* is made up of an appositive and its modifiers.

EXAMPLE   The Newbery Medal, **an award for outstanding children's books,** was named for a man who sold children's books in the 1700's.

Diagraming Appositives and Appositive Phrases

Diagraming an appositive or an appositive phrase is not hard. Identify the appositive in the sentence. Then write it in parentheses after the word it explains.

EXAMPLE   "The Bill Cosby Show," **my favorite program,** is about a family like mine.

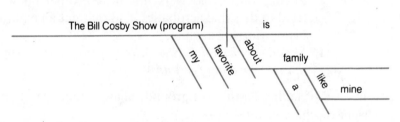

EXERCISE 21. Identifying Appositives and Appositive Phrases.

Number your paper 1–10. After the appropriate number, write the appositive or appositive phrase in each of the following sentences. If a sentence has no appositive or appositive phrase, write *none*.

EXAMPLE   1. My dog, the mutt with floppy ears, can do tricks.
            1. *the mutt with floppy ears*

1. Don't lock that door, the exit out the back of the gym.
2. This is just the color blue I've been looking for.
3. Two men, a truck driver and a fisherman, helped my father push the car off the road.
4. I'll have a sandwich, tuna salad on rye bread, please.
5. Ollie has the same class, American history, this afternoon.
6. My sister's friend forgot her sweater and her books.
7. Dee wondered where her friend Bonnie had gone.

8. Somebody reported the hazard, a pile of trash containing broken bottles, to the police.
9. Be sure to bring exact change, fifty cents.
10. We sang the song "I've Been Working on the Railroad" over and over all the way down the path.

REVIEW EXERCISE C. Identifying Verbals and Appositives. Number your paper 1–10. After the appropriate number, write verbals and appositives that appear in each of the following sentences. Write only the appositive or the verbal, not any of its modifiers or complements. In parentheses after each word, identify it as *appositive, infinitive, gerund,* or *participle.*

EXAMPLE 1. Skating on the sidewalk, my little brother Shawn tried to do some acrobatics, and that put an end to his playing for a while.

1. *Skating (participle), Shawn (appositive), to do (infinitive), playing (gerund)*

1. Instead of falling on the soft ground, Shawn managed to hit right on the concrete.
2. The concrete, broken and crumbling, cut him in several places, mostly his knees and elbows.
3. We heard his piercing wail all the way up at our house, and my mother and I rushed to see what had happened.
4. By the time we got to him, all the cuts had started bleeding, and he was struggling to get his skates off.
5. Bending down, my mother pulled the skates off and dabbed at the seeping red cuts and scrapes.
6. Shawn, a brave little boy usually, could not control his crying.
7. Mom carried Shawn back to the house, and I followed with the new skates, bent and ruined on the first day he used them.
8. After cleaning Shawn's cuts, Mom decided to take him to the emergency clinic.
9. The doctor, an Indian lady, said that she would have to close two of the cuts with stitches.

10. When we got home, Mom told Shawn that she wasn't going to get him another pair of skates until he was old enough to pay his own doctor bills.

CHAPTER 5 REVIEW: POSTTEST 1

Identifying Prepositional, Verbal, Appositive Phrases. Number your paper 1–25. After the proper number, write the italicized phrase in each of the following sentences, and indicate what kind of phrase it is. Use the abbreviations *prep.* (prepositional phrase), *part.* (participial phrase), *ger.* (gerund phrase), *inf.* (infinitive phrase), and *app.* (appositive phrase). Do not identify a prepositional phrase that is part of a larger phrase.

EXAMPLE   1. *Walking along Oak Street yesterday,* I found a dime on the sidewalk.
    1. *Walking along Oak Street yesterday—part.*

1. *Setting up camp* took us all morning.
2. Any business *run for profit* must be carefully managed.
3. Do you know Liz, *the new girl with red hair and green eyes?*
4. We went *to the drive-in movie* over by the highway.
5. One of my chores is *to take out the garbage.*
6. At the zoo we saw a hyena *pacing back and forth in its cage.*
7. The playground will not reopen *until the first day of school.*
8. Everyone wanted *to congratulate the winner of the race.*
9. Dad and I chopped down the elm tree *growing along the property line between our house and Mr. Monat's.*
10. All of the members were dedicated to *making a success of the club project.*
11. Nobody said that this was going *to be easy.*
12. Please hand me those jogging shoes, *the blue ones with the red laces.*
13. The skiers decided not to return to the lodge *in spite of the cold.*

14. It was sunny, but the air remained cool *throughout the day.*
15. *To try your best* is all that you can do.
16. The officer *leading the charge* signaled to his men.
17. My father told Mrs. O'Hara, *the owner of the grocery store on the corner,* that some boys had knocked down her sign.
18. Don't try *giving her any excuses.*
19. Nobody said anything about *offering him another chance.*
20. The sun, *shining bright and warm,* stood directly overhead.
21. We all paid *for our tickets and our meals.*
22. Lilly asked to ride that horse, *the strawberry roan with the cropped mane.*
23. In China, *brewing tea properly* is an art.
24. Out of the entire class June and she were chosen *to represent our school at the science fair.*
25. Henry's grandmother sent him one of the family's treasured heirlooms, *a Civil War cavalry saber.*

CHAPTER 5 REVIEW: POSTTEST 2

Identifying Prepositional, Verbal, and Appositive Phrases. Number your paper 1–25. After the proper number, write each italicized phrase in the following paragraphs, and indicate what kind of phrase it is. Use the abbreviations *prep.* (prepositional phrase), *part.* (participial phrase), *ger.* (gerund phrase), *inf.* (infinitive phrase), and *app.* (appositive phrase). Do not identify a prepositional phrase that is part of a larger phrase.

EXAMPLES   After (1) *driving past the intersection,* my father had
            (2) *to drive over a mile farther before the next turn.*
            1. *driving past the intersection—ger.*
            2. *to drive over a mile before the next turn—inf.*

Jill, (1) *my best friend since elementary school,* and I decided (2) *to go to the mall after school yesterday.* Jill suggested (3) *taking the back way* so that we could jog, but I was wearing sandals (4) *instead of my running shoes,* so we just walked. Along the way we saw Cathy (5) *sitting on her front porch* and asked her if she wanted (6) *to join us.* She was earning a little spending money by (7) *baby-sitting her neighbor's children,* though, and couldn't leave.

(8) *Walking up to the wide glass doors at the mall,* Jill and I looked in our purses (9) *for our wallets and student passes.* We both had a few dollars and our passes, so we stopped (10) *to get a glass of orange juice* while we checked what movies were playing. None of the four features— (11) *a western, two spy stories, and a space movie*—looked (12) *interesting to us.* However, John Bowers, (13) *a friend from school and an usher at the theater,* said that there would be a sneak preview (14) *of a   new adventure film* later, and we told him we'd be back then.

Since most stores do not allow customers (15) *to bring in food or drinks,* Jill and I gulped down our orange juice before (16) *going into our favorite dress shop.* We looked (17) *through the sale racks,* but none of the dresses, (18) *all of them formal or evening gowns,* appealed to us. The salesclerk (19) *working behind the counter* asked if we were shopping (20) *for something special.* After (21) *checking with Jill,* I told the clerk we were just looking, and we left.

We walked past a couple of shops— (22) *the health food store and a toy store*—and went into Record World. (23) *Seeing several cassettes of my favorite group,* I picked out four tapes. Unfortunately, (24) *buying them all* was impossible because I didn't have enough money. By the time we walked out of Record World, I'd spent all my money, so we never did get (25) *to go to the movie that day.*

CHAPTER 5 REVIEW: POSTTEST 3

Writing Sentences with Prepositional, Verbal, and Appositive Phrases. Write ten sentences using the following phrases. Follow the directions in the parentheses.

1. after the game *(use as an adverb phrase)*
2. instead of your good shoes *(use as an adjective phrase)*
3. in one of Shakespeare's plays *(use as an adjective phrase)*
4. going to school every day *(use as a gerund phrase as the subject of the sentence)*
5. living in a small town *(use as a gerund phrase as the object of a preposition)*
6. walking through the empty lot *(use as a participial phrase)*
7. dressed in authentic costumes *(use as a participial phrase)*
8. to drive a car for the first time *(use as an infinitive phrase as the direct object of the sentence)*
9. the best athlete in our school *(use as an appositive phrase)*
10. my favorite pastime *(use as an appositive phrase)*

CHAPTER 6

The Clause

INDEPENDENT AND SUBORDINATE CLAUSES

In Chapter 5 you studied the phrase, a group of related words without a verb and its subject. In a sentence there may also be other groups of related words, called *clauses,* which do contain a verb and its subject.

PHRASES   **on the tugboat** [no subject or verb]
            have been laughing [no subject]

CLAUSES   **as the tugboat crossed the river** [a verb—*crossed*—and its subject—*tugboat*]
            who have been laughing [a verb—*have been laughing*—and its subject—*who*]

In this chapter you will learn about independent and subordinate clauses.

DIAGNOSTIC TEST

Identifying Independent and Subordinate Clauses; Classifying Subordinate Clauses.   Number your paper 1–20. After the proper number, identify each of the italicized clauses in the following sentences as an independent clause or a subordinate clause. Classify each italicized subordinate clause according to how it functions in the sentence. Use the abbreviations *adj. cl.* (adjective clause), *adv. cl.* (adverb clause), and *n. cl.* (noun clause).

EXAMPLES
1. The customer thumbed through the book, but *it didn't seem to interest her.*
   1. *independent clause*
2. Anyone *who gets a high score on this test* will not have to take the final exam.
   2. *subordinate clause, adj. cl.*

1. *After it had been snowing for several hours,* we took our sleds out to Sentry Hill.
2. The ring *that I lost at the beach last summer* had belonged to my great-grandmother.
3. If he doesn't get here soon, *I'm leaving.*
4. *Who do you think* she is?
5. Nobody has seen Shawn *since the football game ended last Saturday night.*
6. *In the morning they gathered their belongings and left* before the sun rose.
7. Nobody knew *that John had worked out the solution.*
8. *The dogs chased the deer onto the ice,* which was more than two feet thick.
9. My dad says never to trust strangers *who seem overly friendly.*
10. *That he had been right* became obvious as the problem grew worse.
11. Julio knew the right answer *because he looked it up in the dictionary.*
12. Our assignment was to write a three-paragraph composition on *how a bill becomes a law.*
13. On our vacation we visited my dad's old neighborhood, *which is now an industrial park.*
14. *It just doesn't seem right* that I have to do all this work without getting paid.
15. Did you get the message *that your mother called*?

16. Andy raked up the leaves *while his father stuffed them into plastic bags.*
17. Before the program began, *the band tuned their instruments,* and the audience got refreshments.
18. We will be over to your house *as soon as Sandy finishes his lunch.*
19. That is the man *whose dog bit my sister.*
20. Free samples were given to *whoever asked for them.*

6a. A *clause* **is a group of words that contains a verb and its subject and is used as a part of a sentence.**

Every clause, like every sentence, has a subject and a verb; however, every clause does not express a complete thought, as all sentences do. Clauses that do express a complete thought are called *independent clauses.* Some clauses do not make complete sense by themselves and must be linked to an independent clause to express a complete thought. Clauses that do not express a complete thought by themselves are called *subordinate clauses.* Subordinate clauses, like phrases, can serve as nouns, adjectives, and adverbs. In this chapter you will become better acquainted with both independent and subordinate clauses.

THE INDEPENDENT CLAUSE

6b. An *independent* **(or** *main***)** *clause* **expresses a complete thought and can stand by itself as a sentence.**

If you can recognize a sentence, you will have no trouble recognizing independent clauses. Independent clauses are sentences when they stand alone. They are usually called independent clauses only when they are part of a sentence.

SENTENCE **I baked her a cake.**

INDEPENDENT CLAUSE Since it was my mother's birthday, **I baked her a cake.**

Study the following sentences, in which the independent clauses are in boldface. Notice that the third sentence has more than one independent clause.

If you have worked with the soil, **you are familiar with humus.**
Humus comes from a Latin word that means "earth."
Humilis means "on the ground," and **from this Latin word we derive the word "humility."**
When you are humble, **you are "on the ground."**

THE SUBORDINATE CLAUSE

Although an independent clause can stand alone as a complete thought, a subordinate clause cannot stand alone.

SENTENCE   Writers gathered at the home of Gertrude Stein when she lived in Paris.

INDEPENDENT CLAUSE   Writers gathered at the home of Gertrude Stein. [can stand alone]

SUBORDINATE CLAUSE   when she lived in Paris [cannot stand alone]

6c. A *subordinate* **(or** *dependent***)** *clause* **does not express a complete thought and cannot stand alone.**

The word *subordinate* means "lesser in rank or importance." Since a subordinate clause cannot stand by itself, it is considered "below the rank" of an independent clause.

Study the following sentences, which contain subordinate clauses set in boldface. Notice that the subordinate clauses all contain verbs and their subjects. Some subordinate clauses begin with words such as *since, when, if,* or *as.* (You will learn more about these words later on in this chapter.)

         S   V
As the monster appeared from beneath a huge rock, all of us in the movie theater held our breath.

S   V
Since most plants die without light, we moved our house plants closer to the window.

Some subordinate clauses begin with words such as *who, which,* or *that.* (You will learn more about these words later on in this chapter.)

S V
The animals **that I saw in the game preserve** were protected from hunters.

S   V
Michele, **who was on the debating team last year,** won her argument with the teacher.

S   V
People **who live in glass houses** should not throw stones.

In the last two examples, notice that the word *who* is both the introductory word in the clause and the subject of the clause.

EXERCISE 1. Identifying Independent Clauses, Subordinate Clauses, and Phrases. Some of the following expressions are sentences, although they are written without capital letters and periods; some are subordinate clauses; and some are phrases. Number your paper 1–20. If the expression is a sentence, write *S* after the proper number; if it is a subordinate clause, write *C;* if it is a phrase, write *P.*

EXAMPLE   1. as I answered the telephone
           1. *C*

1. we memorized the lyrics
2. by the back porch
3. if no one is coming
4. who was born on Valentine's Day
5. through the years
6. after last year's flood
7. the singer wore a silk scarf
8. when the lights were flickering
9. who ran into a tree
10. beside the lion's cage

11. as the jet landed on the runway
12. should have been told
13. since the first time we talked
14. inside the core
15. we can relax
16. if the bus arrives on time
17. as I stared out the window
18. away from the crowds
19. everyone laughed
20. when the snow has fallen

EXERCISE 2. Identifying Subordinate Clauses and Their Subjects and Verbs. Number your paper 1–10. After the proper number, write the subordinate clause from each of the following sentences. Underline the subject of the clause once and the verb twice.

EXAMPLE   1. In history class we learned about the plague that spread across Europe in the fourteenth century.
1. that spread across Europe in the fourteenth century

1. In October 1347, trading ships arrived on the Mediterranean island of Sicily from Caffa, which was a port city on the Black Sea.
2. As they emerged from the boats, many of the sailors carried a strange illness.
3. No medicine could save the sailors, who died quickly and painfully.
4. In the same year, many other people became sick and died as the plague spread across Sicily and Europe.
5. Even doctors caught the illness when they hurried to the bedsides of sick patients.
6. If a person traveled to another city in Europe, the disease probably traveled too.
7. The fast-spreading, deadly plague terrified the survivors, who thought the world was coming to an end.

8. Since it originated in the Black Sea area, the plague was called the Black Death.
9. No one is sure of the total number of people who died from the dreaded plague.
10. Since medicine offers new ways for controlling plague, the spread of this disease is unlikely today.

EXERCISE 3. Writing Sentences with Independent and Subordinate Clauses. Add an independent clause to each of the following subordinate clauses, and write the whole sentence on your paper. Draw one line under the subject of each clause and two lines under the verb.

EXAMPLES
1. who came late
1. *Susie is the volunteer who came late.*
2. as the horn blared
2. *As the horn blared, I was running out the door.*

1. when the ice melts
2. if my teacher approves
3. since the record was made
4. when they act silly
5. who borrowed my notes
6. as she began to shout
7. when we performed on stage
8. who gave the report
9. since I sleep soundly
10. that I bought yesterday

THE ADJECTIVE CLAUSE

Like an adjective or an adjective phrase, a clause may modify a noun or a pronoun. In the following word groups, you see first an adjective phrase, then an adjective clause.

ADJECTIVE PHRASE   the woman **in the car**
ADJECTIVE CLAUSE   the woman **who is in the car**

ADJECTIVE PHRASE   a tree **with red blossoms**
ADJECTIVE CLAUSE   a tree **which has red blossoms**

ADJECTIVE PHRASE   a day **for fishing**
ADJECTIVE CLAUSE   a day **that was made for fishing**

6d. An *adjective clause* is a subordinate clause used as an adjective to modify a noun or a pronoun.

Observe how the adjective clauses in the following sentences modify nouns or pronouns. Notice that adjective clauses usually follow immediately after the words that they modify.

Helen Keller was a remarkable woman **who overcame blindness and deafness**.

Ms. Jackson showed slides **that she had taken in Egypt**.

The ones **whose flight was delayed** spent the night in Detroit.

The Relative Pronoun

Adjective clauses are easy to identify because they are almost always introduced by a special kind of pronoun: the *relative pronoun.* *Who, whom, whose, which,* and *that* are called *relative* pronouns because they *relate* to another word or idea in the sentence.

EXAMPLES   Leonardo da Vinci was the artist **who painted the Mona Lisa**. [The relative pronoun *who* begins the clause and relates to the noun *artist*.]

Everything **that could be done** was done. [The relative pronoun *that* begins the clause and relates to the pronoun *everything*.]

EXERCISE 4. Identifying Adjective Clauses.   Write the adjective clauses from the following sentences. Circle the relative pronouns. After each clause, write the word that the pronoun refers to.

EXAMPLE   1. Our friends have a canary that is named Neptune.
             1. (that) is named Neptune, canary

1. Proverbs are sayings that usually give advice.
2. Trivia questions have been organized into games that have become quite popular.
3. A black hole, which results after a star has collapsed, can trap energy and matter.
4. A special award was given to the student whose work had improved most.
5. Frances Perkins, who served as Secretary of Labor, was the first woman to hold a Cabinet position.
6. The problem that worries us now is the pollution of underground sources of water.
7. We enjoyed the poems of Gwendolyn Brooks, who for years has been poet laureate of Illinois.
8. Through his book *Walden*, Thoreau shared a philosophy that has influenced many people.
9. Athena, who ranked as an important Greek goddess, protected the city of Athens.
10. A friend is a person whom you can trust.

WRITING APPLICATION A:
Using Adjective Clauses to Make Your Writing Specific

When your teachers showed films a few years ago, they likely used projectors and reels. Now they probably use VCR's and cassettes. Videocassettes are an improvement because they are smaller and easier to use but contain just as much as reels of film do. As you become more experienced in writing, you learn how to pack more information into smaller spaces. Specific facts, for example, can sometimes be compressed into adjective clauses.

EXAMPLE   The first library, *which contained a dining room, private studies, laboratories, and a walkway for strolling,* was located in Alexandria, Egypt.

Writing Assignment

In some cases people misunderstand each other because they do not have in mind the same meanings for words. For example, what *you* think is a *good* report card may not be the same as what your *parents* think is a *good* report card. Write a brief paragraph defining one of the following terms. Use at least two adjective clauses, and underline these clauses.

a clean room   an ideal pet
a good teacher   a fun weekend
a loyal friend   a good-looking outfit

Sometimes the relative pronoun is preceded by a preposition. The preposition has actually been moved from the end of the clause to the beginning. Many writers think that the clause sounds better and is more correct with the preposition at the beginning.

the day **which we looked forward to**
the day **to which we looked forward**

my friend, **whom I would do anything for**
my friend, **for whom I would do anything**

the politician **whose speech the public is interested in**
the politician **in whose speech the public is interested**

EXERCISE 5. Identifying Adjective Clauses.

Write the adjective clause from each of the following sentences. Circle the relative pronoun, following the example in Exercise 4. Remember that a relative pronoun may sometimes be preceded by a preposition.

1. Coco Chanel is the woman for whom the perfume is named.
2. Darth Vader, the enemy that Luke Skywalker fought, was an evil villain in *Star Wars*.
3. The cello, to which I could listen for hours, was an instrument of joy in the hands of Pablo Casals.
4. Ella Fitzgerald, who started singing in New York City, is famous throughout the world.

5. Christopher Marlowe wrote of Helen of Troy, "Was this the face that launched a thousand ships?"
6. Anita was one of the sopranos who performed in the school musical.
7. In the play *My Fair Lady,* Eliza Doolittle, a poor flower merchant, becomes a woman whom everyone admires.
8. The Kinderhook was the creek in which we found the small striped bass.
9. Janet Flanner, whose pen name was Genêt, wrote dispatches from Paris.
10. The astronauts, to whom travel in the space shuttle is routine, must always keep in shape.

EXERCISE 6. Writing Adjective Clauses in Sentences.
Complete each of the following sentences by supplying an adjective clause for the blank. Write the complete sentence on your paper. Remember that a clause must have a subject and a verb. Underline each relative pronoun.

EXAMPLE 1. Pineapples —— thrive in Hawaii.
1. *Pineapples, which do not grow in many parts of the United States, thrive in Hawaii.*

1. Our club sponsored a dance ——.
2. The car —— is the sportiest one on the block.
3. Cruelty to animals —— is a serious problem.
4. The paramedic quickly gave first aid to the motorist ——.
5. The woman —— was once a famous author.
6. Suits of armor —— weigh hundreds of pounds.
7. We watched the videotape ——.
8. Rita and Jon met the professional football player ——.
9. Our school band —— was invited to lead the Memorial Day parade.
10. They gave the books to the librarian ——.

EXERCISE 7. Identifying Adjective Clauses. Write the adjective clauses in the following sentences. After each clause, write the word that it modifies.

EXAMPLE   1. Many apartment buildings that do not permit pets do allow Seeing Eye dogs.
        1. *that do not permit pets—buildings*

1. All rookies must learn to accept the advice that they receive from their experienced teammates.
2. For many months we had been practicing for the talent show that was interrupted by a power failure during our act.
3. We are going to see that movie which you saw yesterday.
4. Each time that we talk, I learn something new about you.
5. In gym class we were graded not only on our skills but also on our attitude, which the teacher considers important.
6. We were proud of the students who made the daring rescue.
7. The wheelchair races, which took place last week, were broadcast live on television.
8. Interest in space has increased among people who have always dreamed of riding in a spaceship.
9. By the time that I finish this novel about international spies, I will have learned a lot about espionage.
10. Everyone in the group was encouraged by the enthusiastic support that we received from the community.

THE ADVERB CLAUSE

Like an adverb or an adverb phrase, a subordinate clause may modify a verb, an adjective, or an adverb. Such a clause is called an *adverb clause*.

ADVERB PHRASE   **During the winter** many animals hibernate.
ADVERB CLAUSE   **When winter sets in,** many animals hibernate.

6e. An *adverb clause* is a subordinate clause used as an adverb.

An adverb clause may modify a verb, an adjective, or an adverb in one of the following ways: *how, when, where, why, to what extent* (*how much* or *how long*), or *under what conditions*.

The truck moves **as if it is hauling a heavy load.** [The adverb clause tells *how* the truck *moves.*]

There was a great sea wave **when the volcano erupted.** [The adverb clause tells *when* there *was* a great sea wave.]

We stood **where we could see all of the track.** [The adverb clause tells *where* we *stood.*]

Because the day was very hot, the cool water felt good. [The adverb clause tells *why* the water *felt* good.]

We worked **until we were completely worn out.** [The adverb clause tells *how long* we *worked.*]

If it does not rain tomorrow, we will go to see Crater Lake. [The adverb clause tells *under what condition* we *will go* to see Crater Lake.]

As these examples show, the adverb clause may be placed at various places in the sentence. When it begins the sentence, an adverb clause is usually followed by a comma.

WRITING APPLICATION B:
Using Adverb Clauses to Explain a Process

It's fun to browse in bookstores. To help you find the books you want, most bookstores are divided into sections, such as science fiction, romance, westerns, and young adult fiction. A large and growing section in most bookstores is called "self-help." In the self-help section, you can find how-to books. You can read about how to build things, how to cook, how to study, and even how to get over a broken heart! Adverb clauses are useful in explaining how to do something. They help a reader understand exactly how one thing is related to another in an explanation. Notice in the following example how the subordinating conjunction *if* helps relate the information in the adverb clause to information in the rest of the sentence.

EXAMPLE   *If you want a tasty, nourishing dessert,* you should try combining an orange, an apple, and some pecans in gelatin.

Writing Assignment

Write a paragraph explaining a process that you have used. Be sure to list any equipment your reader would need to complete the process, and include all of the steps. Use at least three adverb clauses, and underline these clauses. Circle the subordinating conjunctions that introduce the clauses. Here are some ideas:

> How to Clean a Trumpet
> How to Pack for a Beach Trip
> How to Study for a Test

The Subordinating Conjunction

In Chapter 3, you learned to recognize two kinds of conjunctions: coordinating conjunctions, such as *and* and *but,* and correlative conjunctions, such as *either . . . or* and *neither . . . nor.* There is a third kind of conjunction, called a *subordinating conjunction,* which introduces an adverb clause. Just as a relative pronoun, such as *who* or *which,* introduces an adjective clause, so a subordinating conjunction, such as *since* or *if,* introduces an adverb clause.

The following words are commonly used to begin adverb clauses. Remember that *after, before, since, until, as,* and many other subordinating conjunctions may also be used as prepositions.

Subordinating Conjunctions

after	as though	so that	whenever
although	because	than	where
as	before	though	wherever
as if	if	unless	while
as long as	in order that	until	
as soon as	since	when	

EXERCISE 8. Identifying Adverb Clauses.
Write the adverb clause from each of the following sentences. Circle the subordinating conjunction, and draw one line under the subject

and two lines under the verb of each clause. Be prepared to tell what word the clause modifies.

EXAMPLE   1. I exercise every morning before I go to school.
      1. (before) I go to school

1. When the workers began digging the foundation for the building, they found pieces of ancient pottery.
2. Near the finish of the marathon, the leading runner felt as if every muscle in his body were screaming in pain.
3. After Lillian had worked for weeks, she finally completed her science project.
4. The girls stopped at the gas station so that they could fill their bicycle tires with air.
5. The children had never tasted Chinese food until their aunt took them to the restaurant.
6. Because Sherry loved the ballet, she read everything she could find in the library about George Balanchine's dance troupe.
7. We told jokes as we waited for the bus.
8. Some paintings would have been ruined if museums had not had the facilities and people to restore them.
9. Many people bought souvenirs while they were on vacation in Europe.
10. Whenever a stranger approaches the puppies, their mother guards them closely.

EXERCISE 9. Identifying Adverb Clauses.   There are ten adverb clauses in the following paragraph. Write the number of the line on which the clause begins. Then write the clause. In each clause, underline the subject once and the verb twice.

EXAMPLE   1   While we were listening to the radio,
      2   we heard the news bulletin.
      1. *While we were listening to the radio*

1   What countries would you visit if you could travel any-
2 where in the world? After you had thought about all the

3 possibilities for a few minutes, you would probably list some
4 of the countries in Europe. Of course, England, France,
5 Spain, Germany, or Italy would likely be on your list, since
6 you have heard much about them. As you studied a map of
7 Europe, you might also notice Liechtenstein and Andorra.
8 Although you might need a magnifying glass to see them,
9 these two European countries could go on your list. When
10 you search for places to visit, you can often overlook some of
11 the less famous areas. However, there are many charming
12 spots in the world. Give some consideration to these when-
13 ever you make your travel plans. Because the world is so vast
14 and full of interesting people and lands, it is worthwhile to
15 search for different possibilities so that you can have a
16 choice. When you are planning which places to visit, look
17 beyond the obvious ones and consider some of the many
18 small treats hidden away all over the world.

EXERCISE 10. Writing Adverb Clauses in Sentences.
Add an adverb clause to each of the following sentences, which
are all independent clauses. Write the entire sentence on your
paper. Then circle the subordinating conjunctions, and underline
the subject of each adverb clause once and the verb twice.
Remember that your adverb clauses will tell *how, when, where,
why, how much,* or *under what conditions.*

EXAMPLE 1. The movie finally ended.
　　　　　1. (After) we spent three hours in the theater, the movie
　　　　　　 finally ended.

1. The alarm clock rang.
2. Our choir sang.
3. Members of the Drama Club auditioned.
4. Erica speaks three languages.
5. We prepared moussaka, a dish with lamb and eggplant, for
   our Cooking Club's international supper.
6. The Goldmans had flown to Acapulco many times.
7. Donna reread her library book.

8. We had lost the game.
9. Jill daydreams in class.
10. No one went hungry.

THE NOUN CLAUSE

In addition to acting as modifiers, subordinate clauses may also serve as nouns. A subordinate clause that acts as a subject, a predicate nominative, a direct object, an indirect object, or the object of a preposition in a sentence is called a *noun clause*.

6f. A *noun clause* is a subordinate clause used as a noun.

Notice how noun clauses can replace nouns in the following sentences:

NOUNS	NOUN CLAUSES
Subject Ann's **anger** was obvious.	**That Ann was angry** was obvious.
Predicate nominative Three dollars is their **offer**.	Three dollars is **what they offer**.
Direct object The judges determined the **winner**.	The judges determined **who won**.
Indirect object The sheriff gave each **volunteer** a flashlight.	The sheriff gave **whoever volunteered** a flashlight.
Object of preposition They agreed with his **statements**.	They agreed with **whatever he said.**

Most noun clauses are introduced by *that, what, whatever, who, whom, whoever,* and *whomever.*

EXAMPLES   They told him what he should do. [The introductory word *what* is the direct object of the noun clause—*he should do what.* The entire noun clause *what he should do* is the direct object of the verb *told.*]

Give a free pass to whoever asks for one. [The introductory word *whoever* is the subject of the noun clause—*whoever asks for one*. The entire noun clause *whoever asks for one* is the object of the preposition *to*.]

Their complaint was that the milk smelled sour. [The introductory word *that* simply introduces the noun clause and has no other function in the clause. The noun clause *that the milk smelled sour* is the predicate nominative, referring to the subject of the sentence—*complaint*.]

EXERCISE 11. Identifying and Classifying Noun Clauses. Number your paper 1–10. After the proper number, write the noun clause in each of the following sentences. Then tell how the entire noun clause is used in the sentence: as *subject, predicate nominative, direct object, indirect object,* or *object of the preposition*. If there is no noun clause in the sentence, write *none*.

EXAMPLE 1. We couldn't find what was making the noise in the car.

      1. *what was making the noise in the car—direct object*

1. Whatever you decide will be fine with us.
2. My uncle was who took us to the beach.
3. Do you know what happened to the rest of my tuna fish sandwich?
4. Stu is looking for whoever owns that red bicycle.
5. Checking our supplies, we discovered that we had forgotten the flour.
6. The worst flaw in the story is that it doesn't have a carefully developed plot.
7. Unfortunately, these results are not what we had planned.
8. The painter gave whatever spots had dried another coat of enamel.
9. At the end of practice on Thursday, the coach announced the name of who will be the new team captain.
10. That anyone could doubt his story seemed to amaze Michael.

Diagraming Subordinate Clauses

Diagram an adjective clause by connecting it with a broken line to the word it modifies. Draw the broken line between the relative pronoun and the noun that it relates to.

EXAMPLE   The grades that I got last term pleased my father.

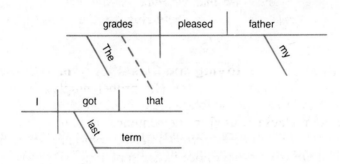

Diagram an adverb clause by using a broken line to connect the adverb clause to the word it modifies. Place the subordinating conjunction that introduces the adverb clause on the broken line.

EXAMPLE   When I come home from school, I usually eat a sandwich.

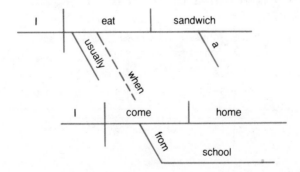

Diagram a noun clause according to how it is used in the sentence. Connect the noun clause to the independent clause with a solid line, as shown in the following two examples.

EXAMPLE   Olive knew what she wanted. [The noun clause *what she wanted* is the direct object of the independent clause. The word *what* is the direct object in the noun clause.]

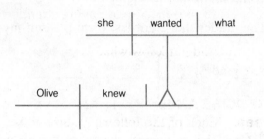

When the introductory word of the noun clause does not have a specific function in the noun clause, the sentence is diagramed in this way:

EXAMPLE   The problem is that they lost the map. [The noun clause *that they lost the map* is the predicate nominative of the independent clause. The word *that* has no function in the noun clause except as a introductory word.]

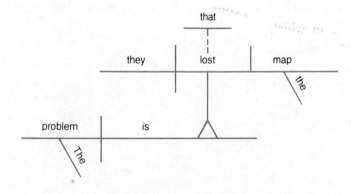

EXERCISE 12. Diagraming Sentences with Subordinate Clauses. Diagram the following sentences.

1. The test that we took on Friday was hard.
2. If I had not studied Thursday night, I could not have answered half the questions.
3. Our teacher announced what would be on the test.
4. Several friends of mine were not paying attention when the teacher gave the assignment.
5. My friends who did not know what to study are worried now about their grades.

REVIEW EXERCISE A. Identifying Adjective, Adverb, and Noun Clauses. Each of the following quotations contains at least one adjective clause, adverb clause, or noun clause. Write the clause or clauses after the proper number. Write *adj. cl., adv. cl.,* or *n. cl.* where appropriate.

1. It's no use shutting the barn door after the horse is gone.—
   OLD PROVERB
2. For fools rush in where angels fear to tread.—ALEXANDER POPE
3. Never say anything that will not improve on silence.—
   EDMUND MUSKIE
4. They also serve who only stand and wait.—JOHN MILTON
5. You gain strength, courage and confidence by every experience in which you really stop to look fear in the face.—
   ELEANOR ROOSEVELT
6. And so, my fellow Americans, ask not what your country can do for you; ask what you can do for your country.—JOHN F. KENNEDY
7. Let me not criticize any man until I have walked a mile in his moccasins.—OLD INDIAN PROVERB
8. I believe that man will not merely endure: he will prevail.—
   WILLIAM FAULKNER
9. Every fact that is learned becomes a key to other facts.—
   E. L. YOUMANS
10. Rhythm might be described as, to the world of sound, what light is to the world of sight.—DAME EDITH SITWELL

REVIEW EXERCISE B. Identifying Subordinate Clauses.

There are twenty subordinate clauses in the following paragraphs. Write the number of the line in which the first word of the
clause appears. Then write the clause. Write *adj. cl.* after each
adjective clause, *adv. cl.* after each adverb clause, and *n. cl.* after
each noun clause.

```
 1      Robert Browning, who was a poet of the Victorian
 2   period, wrote a poem about Childe Roland, a daring knight
 3   who set out on a dangerous quest for the Dark Tower. Many
 4   brave knights had been killed searching for the tower, but
 5   Roland was determined that he would find it.
 6     After Roland had searched for years, he came upon an old
 7   man who pointed the way to the tower. Following the old
 8   man's directions, Roland came upon what proved to be a
 9   land horrible beyond belief. As he passed across the eerie
10   wasteland, he saw all around him that savage struggles had
11   taken place there in the past. Although Roland now felt
12   doomed, he rode on. He saw sights that would have con-
13   vinced whoever ventured there, even the bravest of knights,
14   to turn back. However, Roland would not give up while he
15   had strength to continue.
16      Finally, when he had become discouraged, a large black
17   bird swooped down over his head. Watching it fly away, he
18   saw in the distance what he had been seeking. Lying in a
19   valley, the Dark Tower loomed up before him as a rocky
20   shelf might appear to a sailor who knows that his ship is
21   about to crash into it. While Roland paused to look, he
22   heard ringing in his ears the names of all those who had died
23   in the quest for the tower. Then, on the hillsides, he saw in a
24   sheet of flame the figures of the knights who had perished. In
25   spite of the horror, Roland raised his horn to his lips and
26   blew: "Childe Roland to the Dark Tower came."
```

REVIEW EXERCISE C. Writing Sentences with Indepen-
dent and Subordinate Clauses.   Write your own sentences
according to the instructions that are given.

EXAMPLE   1. A sentence with an adjective clause beginning with *that*
         1. *Here is the money that I owe you.*

1. A sentence with an independent clause and no subordinate clauses
2. A sentence with one independent clause and one subordinate clause
3. A sentence with an adjective clause beginning with *which*
4. A sentence with an adjective clause beginning with *who*
5. A sentence with an adverb clause beginning with a subordinating conjunction
6. A sentence with an introductory adverb clause
7. A sentence with an adverb clause and an adjective clause
8. A sentence with a noun clause used as an object
9. A sentence with a noun clause used as a predicate nominative
10. A sentence with a noun clause and either an adjective clause or an adverb clause

CHAPTER 6 REVIEW: POSTTEST 1

Identifying Independent and Subordinate Clauses; Classifying Subordinate Clauses. Number your paper 1–25. After the proper number, identify each of the italicized clauses in the following sentences as an independent clause or a subordinate clause. Tell whether each italicized subordinate clause functions as a noun, an adjective, or an adverb. Use the abbreviations *n. cl.* (noun clause), *adj. cl.* (adjective clause), and *adv. cl.* (adverb clause).

EXAMPLES   1. *The pilot ejected safely from the jet* before it crashed.
         1. *independent clause*
         2. The pilot ejected safely from the jet *before it crashed.*
         2. *subordinate clause—adv. cl.*

1. We never thought *that we'd see him again*.
2. Before I was halfway through the test, *my pen ran out of ink*.
3. That road looks *as if it may be too rough for our station wagon*.
4. This is right or *it is not right*, but it can't be both.
5. Whoops! The jar *that had pickled eggs in it* fell on the floor and broke.
6. *What I liked best about elementary school* was recess.
7. *After Matt got his new camera for Christmas,* he joined the Photography Club.
8. Ms. Adams said that she has never seen anyone *who complains as much as you do*.
9. *My brother's girlfriend knitted me a sweater* that fits me perfectly.
10. Overhead, a huge flock of geese was flying south *before the heavy snows came*.
11. Don't try to tell me *that you did your best*.
12. Kevin's grandmother is very particular about the way *that her tea is brewed*.
13. *Wherever Steve wants to go bowling* will be fine with me.
14. Most of the students had bought tickets *as soon as they could*.
15. Are these all the people *who plan to participate*?
16. Be sure to get several extras *so that we don't run short*.
17. *I'm not going*, no matter what anyone says.
18. All those *whose lockers failed inspection* are to report to the principal's office.
19. *This has to be the hardest test* I've ever taken.
20. Would you please tell me *why we have to do this*?
21. Mr. DiAngelo said not to disturb him *unless it was an emergency*.
22. On our trip out West we visited a ghost town, *which had been abandoned sometime during the 1870's*.
23. The instructions were very vague about *what step came next*.

24. *After it was all over,* nobody knew what had happened.
25. *Give her a hand with that job* whenever you get a chance, or we'll never get finished.

CHAPTER 6 REVIEW: POSTTEST 2

Identifying Independent and Subordinate Clauses; Classifying Subordinate Clauses. Number your paper 1–25. After the proper number, identify each of the italicized clauses in the following paragraphs as an independent clause or a subordinate clause. Tell whether each italicized subordinate clause functions as a noun, an adjective, or an adverb. Use the abbreviations *n. cl.* (noun clause), *adj. cl.* (adjective clause), and *adv. cl.* (adverb clause).

EXAMPLES   When my father got a new job, (1) *we had to move to another town.*
1. *independent clause*
(2) *When my father got a new job,* we had to move to another town.
2. *subordinate clause—adv. cl.*

Earlier this year I had to transfer to another school (1) *because my father got a new job.* This is the fourth time (2) *that I have had to change schools*, and every time I've wished (3) *that I could just stay at my old school.* (4) *As soon as I make friends in a new place*, I have to move again and leave them behind. Then at the new school (5) *I am a stranger all over again.*

We lived in our last house for three years, (6) *which is the longest time we've spent in any one place* (7) *since I was little.* Living there so long, (8) *I had a chance to meet several people* (9) *who became good friends of mine.* My two best friends, Chris and Marty, said (10) *that they would write to me*, and I promised to write to them, too. However, the friends (11) *that I had before* always promised to write, but after a letter or two (12) *we lost touch.* (13) *Why this happens* is a mystery to me, but it has happened every time.

I dreaded registering at my new school two months (14) *after the school year had begun*. By then, everyone else would already have made friends, and (15) *I would be an outsider*, (16) *as I knew from past experience*. There are always some students who bully and tease (17) *whoever is new at school* or anyone else (18) *who is different*. Back in elementary school I would get angry and upset (19) *when people would pick on me*. Since then, I've learned how to fit in and make friends (20) *in spite of whatever anyone does to hassle me or make me feel uncomfortable*.

Everywhere (21) *that I've gone to school,* some students always are friendly and offer to show me around. (22) *I used to be shy*, and I wouldn't take them up on their invitations. Since they didn't know (23) *whether I was being shy or unfriendly,* they soon left me alone. Now (24) *whenever someone is friendly to me at a new school or in a new neighborhood,* I fight down my shyness and act friendly myself. It's still hard to get used to new places and new people, but (25) *it's a lot easier with a little help from new friends*.

CHAPTER 6 REVIEW: POSTTEST 3

Writing Sentences with Independent and Subordinate Clauses. Write your own sentences according to each of the following instructions. Underline the subordinate clauses.

EXAMPLE 1. A sentence with an independent clause and an adjective clause
1. I am going to the game with Jim, *who is my best friend*.

1. A sentence with an independent clause and no subordinate clauses
2. A sentence with an independent clause and one subordinate clause
3. A sentence with an adjective clause that begins with a relative pronoun

4. A sentence with an adjective clause in which a preposition precedes the relative pronoun
5. A sentence with an introductory adverb clause
6. A sentence with an adverb clause and an adjective clause
7. A sentence with a noun clause used as a direct object
8. A sentence with a noun clause used as a subject
9. A sentence with a noun clause used as the object of a preposition
10. A sentence with a noun clause and either an adjective clause or an adverb clause

The Kinds of Sentence Structure

THE FOUR BASIC SENTENCE STRUCTURES

In Chapter 1 you learned that sentences may be classified according to their purpose: *declarative, interrogative, imperative,* and *exclamatory.* Another way to classify sentences is according to their construction—the kind and number of clauses they contain. In this chapter you will study the four kinds of sentence structure: *simple, compound, complex,* and *compound-complex.*

DIAGNOSTIC TEST

Identifying the Four Kinds of Sentence Structure. Number your paper 1–20. Identify each of the following sentences as simple, compound, complex, or compound-complex.

EXAMPLE 1. We bought a new computer program that helps with spelling and grammar.
    1. *complex*

1. Nancy wanted to go to the dance, but she had to baby-sit.
2. When the rabbit saw us, it ran into the bushes.
3. Beyond that building and around the corner, the line stretched all the way down the block to the movie theater.

4. Either buy a new bicycle, or fix your old one.
5. Judy said that this was the shortest route, but I think that she's wrong.
6. There was no way to tell what had really happened.
7. Yes, that seems like the right answer to me.
8. The steer broke out of its pen and trampled my mother's vegetable garden.
9. Do you know who wrote this?
10. I'm not sure what you said, but I think I agree.
11. Nobody is worried about that, for it will never happen.
12. Whatever you decide will be fine with me.
13. Is the movie that we wanted to see playing at the drive-in, or do we have to go to the theater in the mall?
14. Leroy knew the plan, and he assigned us each a part.
15. Amphibians and some insects can live both on the land and in the water.
16. The detective searched for the man who had been wearing a beret, but there weren't many clues.
17. The tornado cut across the edge of the housing development, and seven homes were destroyed.
18. Until then, everyone had agreed with his main argument.
19. Before the game started, all the football players ran out on the field, and everyone cheered.
20. My father stopped to help the family whose car had broken down on the highway.

THE SIMPLE SENTENCE

From your study of clauses in Chapter 6, you will remember that a clause is a sentence part that contains a verb and its subject. An independent clause expresses a complete thought and may stand alone. A subordinate clause does not express a complete thought and cannot stand alone. When an independent clause stands alone with no other clauses attached to it, it is called a *simple sentence*.

7a. A *simple sentence* has one independent clause and no subordinate clauses.

In the following examples, the subjects and verbs are printed in boldface. Notice that a simple sentence may have a compound subject (sentence 2), a compound verb (sentence 3), or both (sentence 4).

EXAMPLES   The **hair stylist gave** John a new look.

Beth Heiden and **Sheila Young won** Olympic medals. [compound subject: *Beth Heiden* and *Sheila Young*]

Lawrence caught the ball but then **dropped** it. [compound verb: *caught* but *dropped*]

The **astronomer** and her **assistant studied** the heavens and **wrote** reports on their findings. [compound subject: *astronomer* and *assistant;* compound verb: *studied* and *wrote*]

EXERCISE 1. Identifying Subjects and Verbs in Simple Sentences.   Number your paper 1–10. After the proper number, write the subjects and the verbs of the following sentences. Some sentences have compound subjects and verbs.

EXAMPLE   1. The first combustion engines were quite different from those of today.
1. *engines, were*

1. No kitten or puppy compares to my pet boa constrictor.
2. Officers in uniform boarded the ship in the harbor.
3. We gave apples to the trick-or-treaters.
4. Often juniors or seniors serve as tutors.
5. The amount of food will depend on the number of guests.
6. The first mayor of our town was elected in 1854 and won by a unanimous vote.
7. The accident occurred during the late-afternoon rush hour.
8. The Olympic Games inspired pride in our athletes and renewed interest in the support and training of amateur athletes in the United States.

9. Soldiers waiting for orders and volunteers waiting for supplies organized a system to help the flood victims.
10. After the dance the students, remembering their manners, thanked the chaperons.

THE COMPOUND SENTENCE

Sometimes two or more independent clauses appear in the same sentence without any subordinate clauses. Such a sentence is called a *compound sentence*.

7b. A *compound sentence* has two or more independent clauses but no subordinate clauses.

The independent clauses are usually joined by the coordinating conjunctions *yet, and, but, or, nor, for,* or *so.*

EXAMPLES **Thad prepared the slides,** and **Ines examined them.** [two independent clauses joined by the conjunction *and*]

According to legend, Betsy Ross made our first flag, but **there is little evidence.** [two independent clauses joined by the conjunction *but*]

The whistle blew, the drums rolled, and **the crowd cheered.** [three independent clauses, the last two joined by the conjunction *and*]

EXERCISE 2. Identifying Subjects, Verbs, and Conjunctions in Compound Sentences. Number your paper 1–10. After each number, write the subject and verb of the first independent clause, the coordinating conjunction that joins the independent clauses, and the subject and verb of the next clause. Insert a comma before the conjunction. Underline subjects once and verbs twice.

EXAMPLE 1. A director of a theater-in-the-round visited our class, and we listened to his humorous stories for almost an hour.
1. *director visited, and we listened*

1. Many strange things happen backstage during a performance, but the audience usually does not know about them.
2. Audiences at theaters-in-the-round add to the director's problems, for they are seated very close to the stage.
3. Members of the audience sometimes use stage ashtrays, or they hang their coats on the actors' coat racks.
4. Sometimes these actions are overlooked by the stagehands, and the results can be very challenging for the actors.
5. The main clue in a certain mystery play depended on a scarf left lying on the stage floor, but the audience had gathered on the stage during intermission.
6. During the scene after the intermission, the detective in the play counted three scarves instead of one, but the actor showed no surprise.
7. Directors are not always able to predict the reactions of the audience, nor can they always control the audience.
8. During the performance of another mystery drama, a spectator in the front row became too excited about the action of the play, for at one point, leaping up on the stage, the spectator tackled the killer.
9. The workers in charge of properties are usually alert and efficient, but they do sometimes make mistakes.
10. In one production of *Romeo and Juliet,* the character Juliet prepared to kill herself with a dagger, but unfortunately there was no dagger on the stage.

Sentences with Compound Parts

Although it consists of two or more subjects joined by a conjunction, a compound subject is still one subject. Similarly, a compound verb is still one verb. A simple sentence, which has only one subject and one verb, is still a simple sentence even when its subject or verb is compound. Do not confuse a simple sentence containing a compound subject or a compound verb with a compound sentence, which has a subject and a verb in each of its independent clauses.

SIMPLE SENTENCE   Bill and Joe increased their speed and passed the other runners. [compound subject and verb]

COMPOUND SENTENCE   Bill led half the way, and then Joe took the lead.

EXERCISE 3. Distinguishing Between Compound Sentences and Compound Subjects and Verbs. Number your paper 1–10. After the proper number, write each subject and verb in the following sentences. Underline the subjects once and the verbs twice. Then write *S.* if the sentence is a simple sentence or *Cd.* if it is a compound sentence.

EXAMPLES 1. David Attenborough has studied many unusual creatures around the world and has photographed their unique habitats and behavior.

    1. *David Attenborough has studied, has photographed—S.*

    2. Some preferred the program "Life on Earth," but others liked "The Living Planet" better.

    2. *Some preferred, others liked—Cd.*

1. He always manages to find unusual animals, and he rarely misses a chance to observe them in their natural environments.

2. He has traveled to tundra regions and tropical rain forests, for his study of living creatures includes all forms of nature.

3. According to photographs, the Walbiri people living in the central desert of Australia often paint pictures on cliffs, and the colors of their paintings are mineral ochers.

4. One photograph shows Punan forest hunters in central Borneo and depicts their hunting methods.

5. Other kinds of life, such as horseshoe crabs, have been photographed, but none is more interesting than the three-toed sloth in Panama.

6. Some people avidly read books about nature and look forward to learning more.

7. David Attenborough has written books, too, and he has contributed many of the outstanding photographs in them.
8. He has boundless curiosity about living creatures, yet he treats them with respect.
9. Many of his television programs focus on animal life, but several include information about plants and geology.
10. Perhaps someday everyone will have the same enthusiasm for life on this planet, and then people will take care of the environment.

Diagraming Compound Sentences

If you can diagram a simple sentence, you can easily learn to diagram a compound sentence, for the independent clauses in a compound sentence are diagramed like simple sentences. The second clause is diagramed below the first and is joined to it by a coordinating conjunction diagramed as shown. The coordinating conjunction is placed on the horizontal line.

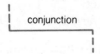

EXAMPLE   The quarterback threw a good pass, but the end did not catch it.

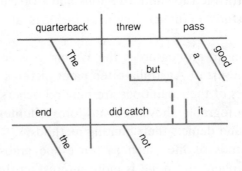

EXERCISE 4. Diagraming Compound Sentences. Diagram the following compound sentences.

1. I want a motorboat, but Jan prefers a sailboat.
2. The bus stopped at the restaurant, and everyone got off.
3. Our club is very small, but it is growing.
4. Shall we meet you at the station, or will you take a taxi?
5. In Arizona the temperature is often high, but the humidity always remains low.

THE COMPLEX SENTENCE

Like a compound sentence, a complex sentence contains more than one clause. However, unlike the compound sentence, the complex sentence has at least one subordinate clause.

7c. A *complex sentence* **has one independent clause and at least one subordinate clause.**

A subordinate clause may be an adjective clause (pages 151–52), an adverb clause (pages 156–57), or a noun clause (pages 161–62).

Adjective clauses usually begin with a relative pronoun: *who, whom, whose, which, that.* Adverb clauses usually begin with a subordinating conjunction such as *after, although, because, if, until, when, where.* Noun clauses usually begin with *that, what, whatever, who, whoever, whom,* or *whoever.*

In the following examples, the subordinate clauses are printed in boldface.

EXAMPLE **When I watch Martha Graham's dances,** I feel like studying dance.

One independent clause I feel like studying dance

Subordinate clause When I watch Martha Graham's dances

EXAMPLE Some of the sailors **who took part in the mutiny on the British ship *Bounty*** settled Pitcairn Island.

One independent clause Some of the sailors settled Pitcairn Island

Subordinate clause who took part in the mutiny on the British ship *Bounty*

EXAMPLE **Since the ballads that have come down to us are usually sad,** ballad singers often dress in black or other somber colors.

One independent clause   ballad singers often dress in black or other somber colors

Two subordinate clauses   Since the ballads are usually sad; that have come down to us

EXERCISE 5. Identifying Independent and Subordinate Clauses in Complex Sentences. Write the following complex sentences. Draw one line under each independent clause and two lines under each subordinate clause. Circle subordinating conjunctions and relative pronouns. Be prepared to identify the subject and the verb in each clause. A sentence may have more than one subordinate clause.

EXAMPLES   1. China is a largely agricultural country which has a population of more than one billion people.

        1. *China is a largely agricultural country* (*which*) *has a population of more than one billion people.*

        2. Although my brother bought one of those coins for his collection, it was nearly worthless.

        2. (*Although*) *my brother bought one of those coins for his collection, it was nearly worthless.*

1. The detective show appeared for several weeks on television before it became popular with viewers.
2. Most of the albums that we have from the 1960's are sitting in the corner of the basement behind the broken refrigerator.
3. Richard E. Byrd is but one of the explorers who made expeditions to Antarctica.
4. As studies continued, many important facts about nutrition were discovered.
5. Singers, who donated their time, recorded a song that made people aware of the problems in Ethiopia.
6. The players who were sent back to the minor leagues received a chance to improve their skills.

7. After we have written our report on the history of computers, we may be able to go to the picnic.
8. Although few students or teachers knew about it, a group of sociologists visited our school to study the relationship between the classroom environment and students' grades.
9. While the stage crew was constructing the sets, the performers continued their rehearsal, which continued into the night.
10. Because the park is maintained by the city, the citizens have complained to the mayor about vandalism.

Diagraming Complex Sentences

To diagram complex sentences, you need to know how to diagram subordinate clauses. The methods for diagraming subordinate clauses—adjective clauses, adverb clauses, and noun clauses—have been covered on pages 163–64.

Here is how to diagram each of the three kinds of subordinate clauses in a complex sentence:

EXAMPLES We had lunch in the student cafeteria when we visited the college. [complex sentence containing an adverb clause]

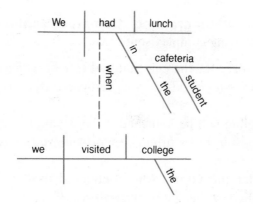

Blair has a ring that belonged to her great-grandmother. [complex sentence containing an adjective
clause]

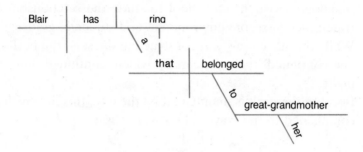

All of the children believed that they had actually
seen Santa Claus. [complex sentence containing a
noun clause]

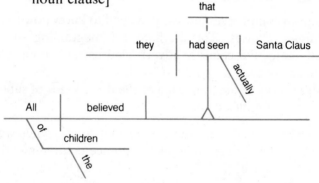

EXERCISE 6. **Diagraming Complex Sentences.** Diagram the following complex sentences.

1. We felt sorry for the cub that had caught its leg in a trap.
2. When we stood beside the redwood tree, we felt very small.
3. The satellite will be launched if the weather remains good.
4. The knight in black armor fought whoever would challenge him.
5. Alexander the Great, who conquered most of the known world, died at the age of thirty-three.

THE COMPOUND–COMPLEX SENTENCE

A compound-complex sentence, as the name suggests, is a combination of the compound sentence and the complex sentence. Like a compound sentence, it has a least two independent clauses; like a complex sentence, it has at least one subordinate clause.

7d. *A compound-complex sentence* **has two or more independent clauses and at least one subordinate clause.**

EXAMPLE   Isabel began painting only two years ago, but she has already been asked to hang one of her paintings at the art exhibit that is scheduled for next month.

Two independent clauses   Isabel began painting only two years ago, but she has already been asked to hang one of her paintings at the art exhibit
Subordinate clause   that is scheduled for next month

EXERCISE 7.   Identifying Clauses in Compound-Complex Sentences.   The following sentences are compound-complex. Write each clause separately, and identify it as *independent* or *subordinate*.

EXAMPLE   1.   When they returned from their vacation, they collected their mail at the post office, and they went to the laundromat.
   1.   *When they returned from their vacation—subordinate*
      they collected their mail at the post office—independent
      they went to the laundromat—independent

1.   Before we conducted the experiment, we asked for permission to use the science lab, but the principal insisted on teacher supervision of our work.

2. Inside the old trunk up in the attic, which is filled with boxes and toys, we found some dusty photo albums, and one of them contained pictures from the early 1900's.
3. The instant that the train stopped at the platform, the passengers quickly climbed aboard, for they were anxious to find good seats.
4. Some picnic tables under the trees were empty because sap had fallen on them and their tops were all sticky.
5. The little-theater group was happy with the performances, and everyone immediately set to work to find new plays so that next season would be successful, too.
6. Later in the fall, we went up to the mountains to photograph the colorful trees, and from the pictures that we took of the maples, we chose three, which we had enlarged so that we could hang them in the dining room.
7. We told them that their plan wouldn't work, but they wouldn't listen to us.
8. Every expedition that had attempted to explore that region had vanished without a trace, yet the young adventurer was determined to map the uncharted jungle.
9. Did you see what happened, or did you only hear about it?
10. The smoke, which grew steadily thicker and darker, billowed through the dry forest, and the animals ran ahead of it as the fire spread quickly.

WRITING APPLICATION:
Using Different Kinds of Sentences to Achieve Variety

Would you like to wear the same kind of clothes every day? Sometimes the same thing over and over can become boring. Your writing can get repetitious and boring if you use the same kind of sentence over and over. One way to give freshness and variety to your writing is to vary your sentences. Try to include complex and compound-complex sentences along with ones that are simple and compound. In the following example, notice how revising the sentence structure helps to add variety.

EXAMPLE   O. Henry had an unusual life. He grew up in North Carolina. He became a pharmacist's apprentice. He moved to Texas and became a rancher, a bank teller, and a newspaper writer. He was accused of embezzlement. He fled to Honduras. He returned to Texas. His wife was dying. He went to prison. He wrote short stories there. He wrote more than two hundred short stories. They became very popular. (The paragraph uses all simple sentences.)

O. Henry had an unusual life. [simple] He grew up in North Carolina, and he became a pharmacist's apprentice. [compound] After moving to Texas, he became a rancher, a bank teller, and a newspaper writer before he was accused of embezzlement. [complex] He fled to Honduras, but he returned to Texas because his wife was dying. [compound–complex] While he was in prison, he wrote short stories. [complex] His stories—more than two hundred—became very popular. [simple]

Writing Assignment

Write a summary of the life of an American author. In your summary, include the four kinds of sentences—simple, compound, complex, and compound–complex. At the end of each sentence, write in parentheses the kind of sentence it is. Here are some ideas for a subject:

James Thurber   Emily Dickinson
Edgar Allan Poe   Robert Frost
Mark Twain   Gwendolyn Brooks

REVIEW EXERCISE. Identifying Simple, Compound, Complex, and Compound-Complex Sentences. Number your paper 1–20. Identify the kinds of sentences—simple, compound, complex, or compound-complex—in the following paragraphs. Use the abbreviations *S., Cd., Cx.,* and *Cd.–Cx.*

1. People who are learning a new sport often begin by mastering basic skills, and they usually are very enthusiastic. **2.** During the beginning stage there are many approaches to learning, and there are many kinds of advice. **3.** After people have been practicing the basic skills for several weeks or months, they may progress to more difficult moves. **4.** At this point a beginner is likely to become discouraged, and the temptation to quit grows strong.

5. One of the most common problems that beginners face is coordination. **6.** All of the different movements become confusing as the novice tries to remember the instructor's directions. **7.** If the beginner is determined and does not give up, the movements eventually feel comfortable and start to come naturally and easily.

8. Sometimes the muscles hurt a little. **9.** If the student is not careful, the muscles can be injured, but the strenuous activity usually strengthens the muscle tissues. **10.** Fortunately, sports medicine has contributed to our knowledge of the body. **11.** When enough oxygen reaches the warmed-up muscles, the danger of injury is lessened, and the muscles grow in size. **12.** Now, computerized equipment is used by athletes who want to reduce the risk of injury.

13. Another benefit of learning a new skill is confidence. **14.** The hours of practice that a beginner puts in often result in noticeable improvements and consequently help build the person's confidence.

15. When people have been playing a sport for a time, they sometimes reach a plateau. **16.** Then they may become discouraged. **17.** In general, athletes who have reached a plateau should be patient with themselves. **18.** They will soon start to improve again. **19.** Obviously, learning something new takes time and work, or it would not be worthwhile. **20.** In sports, as in most activities, persistence and patience can earn rewards.

CHAPTER 7 REVIEW: POSTTEST 1

Identifying the Four Kinds of Sentence Structure. Number your paper 1–25. After the proper number, identify each of the following sentences as simple, compound, complex, or compound-complex.

EXAMPLE 1. The delivery van brought the new water bed that Willa got for her birthday.
1. *complex*

1. Pat hit a foul ball over the fence, and it broke Mrs. Broward's window.
2. My brother was in such a hurry that he forgot his lunch, and Mom had to take it to him later.
3. No one said that we couldn't play here.
4. Just slow down, and pay attention to what you're doing.
5. Over the door hung a worn, rusty horseshoe and a majestic set of deer antlers.
6. We wanted to help, yet we didn't want to interfere.
7. The two dogs barked at each other from midnight until the sun came up, so my mother went to talk to their owner this morning.
8. Reluctantly, two of the boys stepped forward and admitted that they were responsible.
9. Our cat turns his nose up at anything but cooked food.
10. None of the dresses had any style, nor were they reasonably priced.
11. As far as I know, it belongs to anyone who wants to haul it away.
12. Why do we always have to do it her way?
13. Stainless steel thermos bottles cost more, but they're worth the extra money.
14. In spite of our differences, Margaret and I have been good friends since the third grade.
15. Whoever wins this set will go on to the finals.

16. The truck roared past our car and cut back into our lane, nearly running us off the road.
17. Don't put latex paint over enamel unless you sand all the gloss off the enamel and use a top-quality primer first.
18. When you get there, unlock the gate and open it.
19. We had already done a lot of work, yet there was still much more to do.
20. Let me have that mug with the flowers all around the rim.
21. They weren't sure where they were headed, but they kept going anyway.
22. The stoplight turned green before we were halfway across the street.
23. Underneath her calm exterior burned an anger that she could barely control, so she spent much of her time alone.
24. Will the bus pick us up, or should we ask one of our parents for a ride?
25. George and I went to the store and bought new engines for our model airplanes.

CHAPTER 7 REVIEW: POSTTEST 2

Identifying the Four Kinds of Sentence Structure. Number your paper 1–25. After the proper number, identify each of the following sentences as simple, compound, complex, or compound-complex.

EXAMPLE 1. When my grandmother came to visit at Christmas time, we decided to make our own ornaments for the Christmas tree.
    1. *complex*

(1) Last year my grandmother came to stay with us from the middle of December until my brother's birthday in January. (2) While we were getting out the Christmas decorations, Grandma told us all about how she and her family used to make their own decorations when my mother was a girl. (3) Mom said that she

remembered making Christmas decorations and that it used to be fun, so we decided to try making some.

(4) My dad, my brother, and I drove out to the woods to gather pine cones. (5) We had forgotten to ask Grandma what size pine cones to get, and since Dad had never made decorations in his family, he didn't know. (6) We decided to play it safe and get all different sizes, which was easy to do because there were pine cones everywhere. (7) My brother picked up all the hard little ones, and my dad and I threw about a hundred medium and big ones into the trunk of the car. (8) When Mom and Grandma saw how many we had, they laughed and said there were enough for ten Christmases!

(9) First we sorted the cones into two piles: the little hard ones and the other bigger ones. (10) Dad and I painted the little ones silver, and Mom and Grandma painted stripes, dots, and all sorts of designs on them. (11) Then we tied strings to the tops of them, and later, when we put up our tree, they made great ornaments. (12) Every year, some of our glass ornaments get broken, but our pine-cone ornaments are just about indestructible.

(13) We painted the bigger pine cones all different colors and glued on cranberries and beads, which made each cone look like a miniature Christmas tree. (14) We saved some of the smaller ones to hang on our big Christmas tree, and we put most of the others around on the windowsills and all over the house. (15) My brother took some to school, too.

(16) Besides the pine-cone decorations, we made some strings to hang on the tree. (17) My mom got some needles and a spool of heavy thread out of her sewing basket, and we all strung the rest of the cranberries on six-foot lengths of the thread.

(18) Dad said that all this work was making him hungry, and Grandma suggested that we make some popcorn. (19) We popped a big bowlful, which Dad, my brother, and I immediately began eating. (20) When Grandma and Mom kept on making more popcorn, Dad and I told them to stop because we had had enough. (21) Grandma said that they had other plans for the popcorn.

(22) Mom and Grandma cut off more pieces of thread, and we made strings of popcorn, just like our strings of cranberries. (23) We left some of the strings white and painted the others different colors.

(24) Decorating our tree was even more fun than usual, and I think that the tree looked prettier, too, with all our homemade ornaments. (25) From now on, we're going to make decorations every year.

CHAPTER 7 REVIEW: POSTTEST 3

Writing a Variety of Sentence Structures.   Write your own sentences according to the following instructions:

1. A simple sentence with a compound subject
2. A simple sentence with a compound predicate
3. A compound sentence with two independent clauses joined by *but*
4. A compound sentence with two independent clauses joined by *or*
5. A complex sentence with an adjective clause beginning with the relative pronoun *that*
6. A complex sentence with an adjective clause beginning with the relative pronoun *who*
7. A complex sentence with an adverb clause at the beginning of the sentence
8. A complex sentence with an adverb clause at the end of the sentence
9. A complex sentence with a noun clause
10. A compound-complex sentence

GRAMMAR
MASTERY REVIEW: Cumulative Test

A. PARTS OF SPEECH. Number your paper 1–10. After the proper number, write each italicized word in the following passage, and indicate what part of speech it is. Use the abbreviations *n.* (noun), *pron.* (pronoun), *v.* (verb), *adj.* (adjective), *adv.* (adverb), *prep.* (preposition), *conj.* (conjunction), and *interj.* (interjection).

One day I was bouncing a tennis ball (1) *against* the house. My father was (2) *inside* working on some papers, (3) *and* he yelled to me to stop. I (4) *went* around to the (5) *garage* and began bouncing the ball there. When I heard the (6) *back* door slam, I missed my catch, and the ball rolled out in the street where a car ran over (7) *it*. Behind me, I (8) *heard* my father laugh and say, "(9) *Well*, that's the way the ball bounces, (10) *Son*."

B. SUBJECTS AND VERBS. Number your paper 11–15. After the proper number, write the subject and the verb in each of the following sentences. Underline each subject once and each verb twice. Be sure to include all helping verbs and all parts of a compound subject or verb.

11. My uncle drives a huge truck.
12. Sometimes my aunt and my uncle go places in the truck together.
13. In the last few years they have driven all over the United States and Canada.
14. My aunt can drive the big rig by herself and can work on the engine, too.
15. Have you ever ridden in a big tractor-trailer truck?

C. COMPLEMENTS. Number your paper 16–20. After the proper number, write the complement or complements in each of the following sentences and label them. Use the following abbreviations to identify each complement: *p.a.* (predicate adjective), *p.n* (predicate nominative), *d.o.* (direct object), *i.o* (indirect object).

16. My friend's parents took us out on a sailboat last weekend.
17. Since I can't swim very well, I was a little frightened.
18. Pat's mother gave me a life jacket.
19. The light breeze and sea air felt cool and clean.
20. By the end of the day, all of us had become tired sailors.

D. PHRASES. Number your paper 21–30. After the proper number, write each italicized phrase in the following sentences, and indicate what kind of phrase it is. Use the abbreviations *prep.* (prepositional phrase), *part.* (participial phrase), *ger.* (gerund pharse), *inf.* (infinitive phrase), and *app.* (appositive phrase).

21. Colors can influence the way people feel *about a place or a thing*.
22. A room *painted white or almost any light color* can often seem bigger than a darker-colored room the same size.
23. Green, *the color of leaves, plants, and many things in nature*, can make people feel relaxed.
24. According to studies, more men than women prefer blue, while women seem *to prefer red*.
25. *Painting something bright yellow or orange* makes people notice it more.
26. Because of traffic lights, nearly everyone has learned *to associate green with approval or permission and red with disapproval or prevention*.
27. Beige and tan hues can often give a person the feeling of *being warm and cozy*.
28. Long ago, pink became the traditional color *of blankets and other baby things for girls*.
29. Of course, red, white, and blue, *the colors of the American flag*, have a special meaning for us Americans.
30. *Studying the effects of color on people*, scientists have made interesting discoveries about human nature.

E. CLAUSES. Number your paper 31–40. After the proper number, identify each of the italicized clauses in the following sentences as an independent clause or a subordinate clause. Then tell how each italicized subordinate clause functions in the sentence. Use the abbreviations *adj. cl.* (adjective clause), *adv. cl.* (adverb clause), and *n. cl.* (noun clause).

31. *Just after we had gone to bed during a big storm one night*, a lightning bolt hit our electric line and blew out our television set.
32. The next day the repairman looked at our television and said *that he would have to order parts for our set.*
33. *We asked Dad to rent another set* while ours was being repaired, but he said no.
34. Instead, he and Mom thought up some things *that we could all do* rather than watch TV.
35. We played a trivia game the first night, but my sister and I didn't have much fun *because we didn't know many of the answers.*
36. The next night we all went to a movie, *which was a lot more fun than playing the trivia game.*
37. *Over the weekend we camped out in the national forest*, where we couldn't have watched television anyway.
38. By the time we got back on Sunday and got unpacked, *we had begun to get used to not having a television.*
39. *When the repairman returned with the set a few days later*, we were glad to have it back, but we had learned to live without it.
40. Now, the program schedule doesn't decide *what we watch on television;* we do.

F. SENTENCES. Number your paper 41–50. After the proper number, identify each of the following sentences as simple, compound, complex, or compound-complex.

41. Every year since we were ten, either my cousin has visited me during the summer, or I have visited him.

42. Before then, we used to live near each other until his father got a new job down in Texas.
43. This year I am going to visit him, and I look forward to going horseback riding.
44. When I visited two years ago, he had his own pony, and my mother sent money for me to rent one for a whole month.
45. We went riding almost every day, all around the stable and out on a big pasture.
46. Since then, he's gotten another pony and still has his first pony, too, so I'll be riding the first one this summer.
47. Besides going riding, we are also going to listen to his cassettes and the ones that I bring with me.
48. Luckily, we share the same taste in music and can trade tapes with each other.
49. I know that we will have a lot of fun together because we always have.
50. We've been best friends all of our lives, and we're going to keep on being best friends forever.

PART TWO

USAGE

CHAPTER 8

Agreement

SUBJECT AND VERB, PRONOUN AND ANTECEDENT

Certain words in a sentence are closely related. The verb is closely related to its subject. A pronoun is closely related to the noun it stands for. Such closely related words have matching forms. When the related words are correctly matched, we say that they *agree*. One way in which such words agree is in *number*. In this chapter, rule 8a explains the meaning of *number*.

DIAGNOSTIC TEST

A. Identifying Verbs That Agree with Their Subjects. Number your paper 1–10. In each of the following sentences, a verb has been italicized. If an italicized verb agrees with its subject, write *C* after the proper number. If an italicized verb does not agree with its subject, write the correct form of the verb after the proper number.

EXAMPLES 1. Ms. Suarez, our gym teacher, *don't* know what happened.
     1. *doesn't*
     2. The answers to that question don't make sense.
     2. *C*

1. Neither of the plants *need* water yet.
2. Everyone who wears eyeglasses *is* having vision tests today.
3. Two minutes *are* long enough to boil an egg.
4. Mr. Adams said that it *don't* look like rain today.
5. My baseball and my catcher's mitt *is* back in my room.
6. Neither Esteban nor Tina *have* tried out yet for the play.
7. All of the programs *have* been on television before.
8. *Don't* the team captain plan to put her into the game?
9. One of the men *have* decided to get his car washed.
10. The Bill of Rights *give* American citizens the right to worship where they please.

B. Identifying Pronouns That Agree with Their Antecedents.

Number your paper 11–20. In each of the following sentences, a pronoun has been italicized. If an italicized pronoun agrees with its antecedent, write *C* after the proper number. If an italicized pronoun does not agree with its antecedent, write the correct pronoun after the proper number.

EXAMPLES 1. Each of the boys brought *their* permission slips.
          1. *his*
          2. One of the does was accompanied by *her* fawn.
          2. *C*

11. Have all the girls taken *their* projects home?
12. Paul, Mike, and Chip each sent in *their* application.
13. Many of the trees had lost *its* leaves.
14. Neither Sally nor Marilyn had worn *their* gym suit.
15. Every dog had a tag hanging from *their* collar.
16. Someone in the Boy Scout troop camped near poison ivy and has gotten it all over *themselves*.
17. A few of the carpenters had brought tools with *them*.
18. My dog was one of the winners who had *its* picture taken.
19. According to the teacher, both of those titles should have lines drawn underneath *it*.
20. No one was sure which of the streets had *its* names changed.

AGREEMENT OF SUBJECT AND VERB

Singular and Plural Number

8a. When a word refers to one person, place, thing, or idea, it is *singular* in number. When a word refers to more than one, it is *plural* in number.

SINGULAR   book, woman, fox, one, I, he
  PLURAL   books, women, foxes, many, we, they

EXERCISE 1. Classifying Nouns and Pronouns According to Number. Number your paper 1–20. After each number, write *S* if the word is singular and *P* if it is plural.

EXAMPLE   1. cat
          1. *S*

1. tomatoes	8. basis	15. he
2. coach	9. girl	16. mosquito
3. they	10. mice	17. assignments
4. universities	11. we	18. light bulbs
5. I	12. parents	19. it
6. sailboat	13. saucers	20. tapes
7. many	14. surfboard	

EXERCISE 2. *Oral Drill.* Classifying Nouns and Pronouns by Number. Read the following expressions aloud. Tell whether each is singular or plural.

1. The lion yawns.	9. They have.
2. The cubs play.	10. The actors rehearse.
3. We listen.	11. The play opens.
4. No one stays.	12. Everyone goes.
5. The refugees arrive.	13. The curtain rises.
6. She wins.	14. All applaud.
7. The flower blooms.	15. People laugh.
8. I am.	

8b. A verb agrees with its subject in number.

(1) Singular subjects take singular verbs.

EXAMPLES   The **candle burns** slowly.
The **car comes** to a sudden stop.
On that route **the plane flies** at a low altitude.
[The singular subjects *candle, car,* and *plane* take
the singular verbs *burns, comes,* and *flies.*]

(2) Plural subjects take plural verbs.

EXAMPLES   The **candles burn** slowly.
The **prisoners walk** in the exercise yard.
Again and again the **dolphins leap** playfully.

[The plural subjects *candles, prisoners,* and *dolphins*
take the plural verbs *burn, walk,* and *leap.*]

Generally, subjects ending in *s* are plural (*candles, prisoners, dolphins*), and verbs ending in *s* are singular (*burns, comes, flies*). The verb *be* is a special case.

SINGULAR	PLURAL	SINGULAR	PLURAL
I am	we are	I was	we were
you are	you are	you were	you were
he is	they are	she was	they were
Luis is	the boys are	Linda was	the girls were

EXERCISE 3. Identifying the Correct Number of Verbs.
Number your paper 1–10. After the proper number, write the
word in parentheses that agrees with the given subject.

EXAMPLE   1. it (is, are)
1. *is*

1. this (costs, cost)
2. plants (grows, grow)
3. the batter (swings, swing)
4. we (considers, consider)
5. the men (was, were)
6. she (asks, ask)
7. these (needs, need)
8. those colors (seems, seem)
9. that ink (lasts, last)
10. days (passes, pass)

Prepositional Phrases Between Subject and Verb

Errors in agreement often occur because words in prepositional phrases are mistaken for the subjects of verbs.

NONSTANDARD[1] The many lights on the Christmas tree makes it look very festive. [*Lights,* not *tree,* is the subject.]

STANDARD The many **lights** on the Christmas tree **make** it look very festive.

8c. The number of a subject is not changed by a prepositional phrase following the subject.

Remember that a word in a prepositional phrase can never be the subject of a verb. If a sentence confuses you, imagine that the prepositional phrase is enclosed by parentheses, and go directly from the subject to the verb.

EXAMPLE The **silence** (in the halls) is unusual.

EXERCISE 4. *Oral Drill.* Using the Correct Number for Verbs in Sentences with Phrases Following the Subjects.   Read each of the following sentences aloud, stressing the italicized words. Be able to tell whether the subject and the verb are singular or plural.

1. Many dogwood *trees* on my street *are* in bloom.
2. Her *paper* on rare American stamps *needs* editing.
3. Your *opinion* of the candidates *gives* the pollster important information.
4. The *scientists* at Cape Canaveral *work* many extra hours during a launch.
5. Some *students* in the class *volunteer* for extra projects.
6. *One* of the tests *shows* a flaw in the computer.
7. The *owner* of the factories *asks* for weekly reports from the managers.

[1] For explanation of nonstandard and standard, see footnote, page 40.

8. The *chimes* in the tower *play* every hour.
9. The *temperature* inside the caverns *stays* at fifty degrees all year long.
10. A good *book* on plants *costs* very little.

EXERCISE 5. Identifying Subjects and Verbs That Agree in Number in Sentences with Phrases Following the Subjects. Number your paper 1–10. After the proper number, write the subject and then the correct form of the verb. Remember that the subject is never part of a prepositional phrase.

EXAMPLE 1. The houses on my block (has, have) two stories.
1. *houses, have*

1. The launch of a space shuttle (attracts, attract) the interest of people throughout the world.
2. The thermos bottle in the picnic basket (is, are) filled with apple juice.
3. My favorite collection of poems (is, are) *Where the Sidewalk Ends.*
4. The cars on the assembly line (needs, need) to have seat belts installed.
5. The starving children of the world (needs, need) food and medicine.
6. The cucumbers in my garden (grows, grow) very quickly.
7. The koalas of Australia (eats, eat) eucalyptus leaves.
8. The principal of each school (awards, award) certificates to honor students.
9. Ceramic tiles from Mexico (makes, make) a beautiful trivet for a Mother's Day gift.
10. The house beside the city park (is, are) where my grandfather was born.

Indefinite Pronouns

Certain pronouns do not refer to a definite person, place, thing, or idea and are therefore called *indefinite* pronouns.

You should learn the number of all the indefinite pronouns so that you will not make an error in agreement when an indefinite pronoun is the subject of the sentence.

8d. The following common pronouns are singular and take singular verbs: *each, either, neither, one, everyone, everybody, no one, nobody, anyone, anybody, someone, somebody.*

Pronouns like *each* and *one* are frequently followed by prepositional phrases. Remember that the verb agrees with the subject of the sentence, not with a word in a prepositional phrase.

EXAMPLES **One** of the chairs **looks** comfortable.
Either of the answers **is** correct.
Everyone with passports **was** accepted.
Someone in the stands **has been waving** at us.

8e. The following common pronouns are plural and take plural verbs: *both, few, several, many.*

EXAMPLES **Many** of the students **walk** to school.
Both of the apples **are** good.
Few of the guests **know** of the robbery.

8f. The words *some, any, none, all,* **and** *most* **may be either singular or plural.**

This rule is an exception to rule 8c because the number of the subjects *some, any, none, all,* and *most* is determined by a word in the prepositional phrase that follows the subject . If the word the subject refers to is singular, the subject is singular; if the word is plural, the subject is plural.

EXAMPLES **All** of the fans **rush** home.
All of my work is finished.

Some of the birds **have** gone south.
Some of the glare **has** disappeared.

WRITING APPLICATION A:
Using Indefinite Pronouns Correctly in Narration

Sometimes when you write, you may not want to use specific names because names are not important in what you are writing or because so many people are involved that using all their names would be confusing. In these cases, you probably will use indefinite pronouns, which do not refer to a particular person, place, thing, or idea. When you use these pronouns, be sure to proofread carefully to make certain that you have not made errors in agreement.

EXAMPLE   Many of the students enjoys the water slide.
[The indefinite pronoun *many* does not agree with the singular verb *enjoys*.]

Many of the students **enjoy** the water slide.
[The plural pronoun *many* agrees with the plural verb *enjoy*.]

Writing Assignment

Write a narrative in the present tense telling about a real or imaginary class or club trip. In your paragraph, use at least four indefinite pronouns, such as *many, few, several, either, all,* and *some*. Here is an idea about how you can begin:

Every year, at the end of May, my chorus class takes a trip to the beach. *Some* students bring fishing gear. *Many* bring inflatable rafts to float on. A *few* pack lotion to help prevent bad sunburns.

EXERCISE 6. Identifying Verbs That Agree with Indefinite Pronouns Used as Subjects. Number your paper 1–10. After the proper number, write the subject and then the correct one of the verbs in parentheses.

1. All of my friends (has, have) had the chicken pox.
2. Everyone at the party (likes, like) the cottage cheese and vegetable dip.

3. Both of Fred's brothers (celebrates, celebrate) their birthdays in July.
4. Some of my classmates (takes, take) tennis lessons after school.
5. None of those rosebushes (blooms, bloom) in February.
6. Several of those colors (appeals, appeal) to me.
7. Many of Mrs. Taniguchi's students (speaks, speak) fluent Japanese.
8. Nobody in the beginning painting class (displays, display) work in the annual art show.
9. Most of the appetizers on the menu (tastes, taste) delicious.
10. One of Georgia O'Keeffe's paintings (shows, show) an animal's skull.

REVIEW EXERCISE A. Proofreading Sentences for Subject-Verb Agreement Number your paper 1–20. Read each sentence aloud. If the verb agrees with the subject, write *C* after the proper number on your paper. If the verb does not agree with the subject, write the correct form of the verb after the proper number. Some sentences have more than one verb for you to consider.

EXAMPLES   1. One of the women practice medicine.
                1. *practices*
                2. Both of them work hard.
                2. *C*

1. The beaches of Florida and the mountains of Colorado is favorite vacation spots of college students.
2. All of the chorus members harmonize very well.
3. Neither Hector nor Julio want the lead part in the class play.
4. The curtains inside all school buildings is made of flame-retardant material.
5. Several of the eighth-grade track stars also compete in the swimming meets.
6. Britain's prehistoric monument Stonehenge challenges tourists to uncover its mysteries.

7. Everybody want to know who erected the massive stones.
8. Most of the visitors assumes that the ancient Druids built Stonehenge.
9. Many of the archaeologists studying Stonehenge believe that it was built before the time of the Druids.
10. None of the tour guides explain the secrets of the monument.
11. All of the tourists wonders why the structure was built.
12. Few of the visitors leave without forming their own theory.
13. One of Justin's grandmothers visit Stonehenge once a year.
14. The stones in Stonehenge weighs as much as fifty tons.
15. Some of Jill's cousins plans a trip to England when they graduate from high school.
16. No one like to be left at home while the rest of the family travels abroad.
17. Either Scotland or Ireland is the country Mr. McCoy would like to visit.
18. The trains in London run very efficiently.
19. Does any of the trains provide a dining car or snack bar?
20. Everyone who travels by train comment on how punctual they are.

Compound Subjects

Most compound subjects that are joined by *and* name more than one person or thing; therefore, they are plural and require a plural verb.

8g. Subjects joined by *and* are plural and take a plural verb.

EXAMPLES **Antonia Brico** and **Sarah Caldwell are** famous conductors. [Two people are conductors.]
Last year a **library** and a **museum were** built in our town. [Two things were built.]

If the items in a compound subject actually refer to only one person or are thought of as one thing, the verb is singular.

EXAMPLES The **captain** and **quarterback** of the team is the speaker. [One person is both the captain and the quarterback.]

Chicken and dumplings is a favorite southern dish. [Chicken and dumplings is one dish.]

EXERCISE 7. Choosing Verbs That Agree in Number with Compound Subjects. Number your paper 1–10. Decide whether the compound subjects of the following sentences are singular or plural. Choose the correct verb form in parentheses, and write it after the proper number.

EXAMPLE 1. Cleon and Pam (is, are) here.
1. *are*

1. March and April (is, are) windy months.
2. My mother and the mechanic (is, are) discussing the bill.
3. Virginia Wade and Tracy Austin (plays, play) today.
4. Steak and eggs (is, are) my favorite breakfast.
5. (Does, Do) Carla and Jean take dancing lessons?
6. (Is, Are) the knives and forks in the drawer?
7. English and science (requires, require) hours of study.
8. (Here's, Here are) our star and winner of the meet.
9. Where (is, are) the bread and the honey?
10. (Does, Do) an Austrian and a German speak the same language?

8h. Singular subjects joined by *or* or *nor* take a singular verb.

EXAMPLES A **pen or** a **pencil** is needed for this test. [Either one is needed.]

Neither Miami nor Jacksonville is the capital of Florida. [Neither one is the capital.]

EXERCISE 8. Choosing Verbs That Agree in Number with Compound Subjects. Number your paper 1–10. From each pair of verbs in parentheses, choose the one that agrees with the subject.

EXAMPLE 1. Either tea or coffee (is, are) fine with me.
   1. *is*

1. Either Mrs. Gomez or Mr. Ming (delivers, deliver) the welcome speech on the first day of school.
2. Our guava tree and our fig tree (bears, bear) more fruit than our entire neighborhood can eat.
3. Tuskegee Institute or Harvard University (offers, offer) the best courses in Chester's field.
4. Armadillos and anteaters (has, have) tubular mouths and long sticky tongues for catching insects.
5. Either the president or the vice-president of the class (calls, call) roll every morning.
6. Georgia's frog and Sam's frog (jumps, jump) out of the aquarium.
7. Red and royal blue (looks, look) nice in this bedroom.
8. Bridge or canasta (is, are) my favorite card game.
9. Neither my sister nor I (mows, mow) the lawn without protesting.
10. The tulips and the daffodils (blooms, bloom) every April.

8i. **When a singular subject and a plural subject are joined by** *or* **or** *nor* **the verb agrees with the nearer subject.**

EXAMPLES Either Joan or her **friends are** mistaken. [The verb agrees with the nearer subject, *friends*.]

Neither the players nor the **director was** on time for rehearsal. [The verb agrees with the nearer subject, *director*.]

Whenever possible, avoid this kind of construction. The second sentence can be rewritten to read: *Both the players and the director were late for rehearsal.*

EXERCISE 9. Choosing Verbs That Agree with Singular and Plural Compound Subjects.   Number your paper 1–10. From each pair of verbs in parentheses, choose the one that agrees with the subject, and write it after the proper number.

1. Either Sylvia or her brothers (washes, wash) the kitchen floor each Saturday morning.
2. Grapefruit and papaya (tastes, taste) sour after the sweet, fresh strawberries.
3. Chicken or shrimp (is, are) always Mr. Cortez's choice for his birthday dinner.
4. This bread and this cereal (contains, contain) no preservatives or dyes.
5. Elizabeth and Nancy (fixes, fix) bicycles after school to earn money.
6. Kim or Danny (shouts, shout) the loudest at the pep rallies.
7. (Was, Were) Abraham Lincoln or Andrew Jackson our sixteenth president?
8. Either the students or the teacher (reads, read) aloud during the last ten minutes of each class period.
9. The heavy rainclouds and the powerful winds (indicates, indicate) that a hurricane is approaching.
10. Neither the seal nor the clowns (catches, catch) the ball that the monkey throws into the circus ring.

REVIEW EXERCISE B. Choosing Verbs That Agree with Singular and Plural Subjects. Number your paper 1–20. Then choose from the words in parentheses the verb that agrees with the subject, and write it after the proper number.

1. Either the squirrels or the dog (digs, dig) a new hole in the yard at least once a day.
2. Jeffrey and his dad (builds, build) fireplaces for clients throughout the summer months.
3. Someone (puts, put) the bricks around the fireplaces.
4. None of the bricks (cracks, crack) if they are installed very carefully.
5. Yellowstone National Park in Wyoming (fascinates, fascinate) many people.
6. The grizzly bears and coyotes (terrifies, terrify) would-be hikers.

7. A car or camper (provides, provide) protection from animals.
8. Some of the tourists foolishly (approaches, approach) the wild bears to give them food.
9. Unfortunately, several of these generous people (has, have) been killed or maimed by the bears.
10. Most of the park's visitors now (realizes, realize) that wild bears are truly wild.
11. However, everybody (acknowledges, acknowledge) that the wild bears often look like large teddy bears.
12. The mountains in the park (offers, offer) excellent hiking trails.
13. Anyone who hikes these trails (carries, carry) water, snacks, and a camera.
14. Many of the hikers (shoots, shoot) award-winning photographs in the park.
15. Some of these photographs (circulates, circulate) in art shows throughout the United States.
16. The mountains and the wildflowers (present, presents) excellent subjects for interesting photographs.
17. A geyser or a wandering elk (makes, make) a nice composition for another photograph.
18. The Grand Teton Mountains or the Yellowstone River (appeals, appeal) to children and adults who enjoy various activities.
19. Each of us (leaves, leave) the park with a renewed respect for the land and its wildlife.
20. Both of my aunts (plans, plan) a week-long hiking trip in Yellowstone National Park next summer.

Other Problems in Agreement

8j. Collective nouns may be either singular or plural.

A collective noun names a group of persons or things and is singular in form.

Common Collective Nouns

army	club	family	squadron
assembly	crowd	group	swarm
audience	fleet	herd	team
class	flock	public	troop

A collective noun takes a plural verb when the noun refers to the individual parts or members of the group. A collective noun takes a singular verb when the noun refers to the group as a unit.

EXAMPLES   The **family were arguing** about where to spend the next vacation. [*Family* here refers to individuals acting separately.]

The **family was** calmed down by the grandparents. [*Family* here refers to a group considered as a unit.]

EXERCISE 10. Writing Sentences with Collective Nouns. Select five collective nouns. Use each noun as the subject of two sentences. In the first, make the subject singular in meaning so that it calls for a singular verb. In the second, make the subject plural in meaning so that it takes a plural verb.

8k. A verb agrees with its subject, not with its predicate nominative.

Sometimes the subject and the predicate nominative of a sentence are different in number. In this case the verb agrees with the subject, not with the predicate nominative. The subject usually comes *before* the linking verb and the predicate nominative *after*.

EXAMPLES   The happiest **time** of my life **was** my childhood days. My childhood **days were** the happiest time of my life.

8l. When the subject follows the verb as in sentences beginning with *there* and *here* and in questions, find the subject and make sure that the verb agrees with it.

EXAMPLES   Here **is** my **seat**.
             Here **are** our **seats**.
             There **is** an exciting **ride** at the fair.
             There **are** exciting **rides** at the fair.
             Where **are** the programs?

Be especially careful when you use the contractions *here's* and *there's*. These contain the verb *is* and should be used only with singular subjects.

NONSTANDARD   There's the books.
   STANDARD   There **are** the **books**.

EXERCISE 11. Choosing Verbs That Agree in Number with Singular and Plural Subjects.
Number your paper 1–10. After the proper number, write the correct verb for each sentence.

1. The audience (loves, love) the mime performance.
2. (Here's, Here are) the answers to Chapter 8.
3. The club (sponsors, sponsor) a carwash each September.
4. Andy's gift to Jynelle (was, were) two roses.
5. (Here's, Here are) the letters I have been expecting.
6. The public (differs, differ) in their opinions on the referendum.
7. (There's, There are) only three people in the contest.
8. The tennis team (plays, play) every Saturday morning.
9. His legacy to us (was, were) words of wisdom.
10. (Where's, Where are) the bell peppers for the salad?

WRITING APPLICATION B:
Checking for Correct Agreement When the Subject Follows the Verb

One of the reasons that people from foreign countries sometimes have difficulty learning English is that the word order, or syntax, of English sentences can vary. The subject, the verb, and any modifiers may appear at the beginning, in the middle, or at the end of a sentence. For example, in sentences that begin with *here* or *there,* the subject usually follows the verb. In your writing, you need to proofread to make certain that each verb agrees with its subject in number, particularly when the verb comes *before* the subject.

INCORRECT　There has been many exciting TV shows lately about historical figures. [The subject *shows* is plural; it does not agree in number with the singular verb *has been.*]

　CORRECT　There **have been** many exciting TV **shows** lately about historical figures. [The plural verb *have been* agrees with the plural subject *shows.*]

Writing Assignment

Pretend that you are welcoming a group of people to a new time or a new place. Explain to them the strange new things they will encounter. Start at least four sentences with *here* or *there.* Be sure to proofread for agreement errors. Here are several ideas for new times and places for your explanation:

1. The twenty-second century
2. A new, previously unknown planet
3. A spaceship from another planet
4. Your home when you are twenty-five years old
5. The school your children attend in the year 2010

8m. *Don't* **and** *doesn't* **must agree with their subjects.**

Use *don't* with plural subjects and with the pronouns *I* and *you.*

EXAMPLES　These gloves **don't** fit.
　　　　　　You **don't** speak clearly.
　　　　　　I **don't** like that record.

Use *doesn't* with other subjects.

EXAMPLES　The **music box doesn't** play.
　　　　　　She doesn't like cold weather.
　　　　　　It doesn't matter.

The most frequent errors in using *don't* and *doesn't* are made when *don't* is incorrectly used with *he, she,* or *it.* Remember always to use *doesn't* with these singular subjects: *he doesn't, she doesn't, it doesn't.*

EXERCISE 12. *Oral Drill.* **Using** *Doesn't* **with Singular Subjects.** Read the following sentences aloud. By getting accustomed to hearing the correct use of *doesn't* and *don't,* you will get into the habit of using these two words correctly.

1. It doesn't look like a serious wound.
2. She doesn't call meetings often.
3. One doesn't interrupt a speaker.
4. She doesn't play records loudly.
5. Doesn't the television set work?

EXERCISE 13. Writing *Doesn't* **and** *Don't* **with Subjects.** Number your paper 1–10. After the proper number, write the subject of each sentence and write the correct verb, *doesn't* or *don't.*

EXAMPLE   1. —— they go to our school?
　　　　　　1. *they, Don't*

1. —— anyone in the class know about Susan B. Anthony?
2. My three-year-old sister —— use good table manners.
3. They —— have enough people to form a softball team.
4. Pearl and Marshall —— need to change their schedules.
5. It —— hurt to practice the piano an hour a day.
6. —— you think that the music is too loud?
7. Those snow peas —— look crisp.
8. Hector —— win every track meet, but he often places second.
9. —— anyone know the time?
10. They —— know the shortest route from Dallas to Peoria.

REVIEW EXERCISE C. Proofreading Sentences for Subject-Verb Agreement. Number your paper 1–20. Some of the following sentences are correct, while others have mistakes in agreement. If a sentence is correct, write *C* on your paper after the proper number. If the sentence is incorrect, write the correct form of the incorrect verb.

EXAMPLE 1. There is a man and a woman here to see you.
         1. *are*

1. Walter or one of his assistants replaces the bald tires.
2. Leilani and Yoshi doesn't know how to swim.
3. Either Maribeth or Wade are expected to win the speech contest.
4. The flock of geese flies over the lake at dawn.
5. The Seminole Indians of Florida sews beautifully designed quilts.
6. Here's the sweaters I knitted for you.
7. Neither Frank nor his classmates thinks the test is fair.
8. The windmill generates power.
9. Each of the ten-speed bicycles cost more than one hundred dollars.
10. Few of the boxers leave the ring without some bruises.
11. Most of the puddle disappear after the sun comes out from behind the clouds.
12. Somebody in this room know where the car keys are hidden.
13. The team of soccer players celebrate each victory with a pizza party.
14. The wheelchair division of the six-mile race was won by Randy Nowell.
15. The caribou and the reindeer is closely related.
16. Don't you think three hours of homework is enough?
17. Both of the doctors agrees that she must have her tonsils removed.
18. Any of those dresses look nice on you.
19. All of those books smells musty from being stored in the basement.
20. Where's the bus schedule for downtown routes?

AGREEMENT OF PRONOUN AND ANTECEDENT

Every pronoun refers to another word, called its *antecedent*. For example, in the phrase *the car with its windows open,* the pronoun *its* refers to the antecedent *car.* Whenever you use a pronoun, make sure that it agrees with its antecedent.

8n. A pronoun agrees with its antecedent in number and gender.

Some singular personal pronouns have forms that indicate gender. *He, him,* and *his* refer to masculine antecedents, while *she, her,* and *hers* refer to feminine antecedents. *It* and *its* refer to antecedents that are neither masculine nor feminine.

Here are several sentences containing pronouns that agree with their antecedents in both number and gender:

EXAMPLES **Bryan** lost **his** book.

Dawn loaned **her** book to Bryan.

The **book** had Dawn's name written inside **its** cover.

The antecedent of a personal pronoun can be another kind of pronoun, such as *each, either,* or *one.* To determine the gender of a personal pronoun that refers to one of these other pronouns, you may need to look in a phrase that follows the antecedent pronoun.

EXAMPLES **Each** of the men put on **his** hard hat.

Neither of those women got what **she** wanted.

Some antecedents may be either masculine or feminine, while others may be both. When referring to such antecedents, the masculine form of the personal pronoun may be used, or both the masculine and the feminine may be used.

EXAMPLES **No one** on the committee gave **his** approval.

or **No one** on the committee gave **his or her** approval.

Everyone in the class wanted to know **his grade**.

or **Everyone** in the class wanted to know **his or her** grade.

In conversation, you may be more accustomed to using a plural pronoun to stand for a singular antecedent that may be either masculine or feminine. Such usage is becoming more acceptable in writing, too, and may someday be considered acceptable in standard written English.

EXAMPLES   **Everybody** rode **their** bicycle.
Each student paid for **their** ticket.

(1) Use a singular pronoun to refer to *each, either, neither, one, everyone, everybody, no one, nobody, anyone, anybody, someone,* **or** *somebody.*

EXAMPLES   **Nobody** in the three classes would admit **his** (*or* **his or her***)* guilt.

Each of the birds built **its** own nest.

As these examples show, a prepositional phrase does not affect the number of the antecedent. In both examples, the antecedent is singular and, therefore, takes a singular pronoun to agree with it.

(2) Two or more singular antecedents joined by *or* **or** *nor* **should be referred to by a singular pronoun.**

EXAMPLES   **Julio or Van** will bring **his** football.
Neither **the mother nor the daughter** had forgotten **her** umbrella.

☞ **USAGE NOTE**   Rules (1) and (2) are often disregarded in conversation; however, they should be followed in writing.

---

(3) Two or more antecedents joined by *and* **should be referred to by a plural pronoun.**

EXAMPLES   My **mother and father** send **their** regards.
My **dog and cat** never share **their** food.

EXERCISE 14. Identifying Antecedents and Writing Pronouns That Agree with Them. Number your paper 1–10. After the proper number, write a pronoun that will complete the meaning of the sentence. Then, write the antecedent for that pronoun. Follow the rules for standard written English.

EXAMPLE　1. Ann and Margaret wore——cheerleader uniforms.
　　　　　　1. *their, Ann and Margaret*

1. The trees lost several of —— branches in the storm.
2. Each of these magazines has had the President's picture on —— cover.
3. Has anyone turned in —— paper yet?
4. The mob raised —— voices in protest.
5. The creek and the pond lost much of —— water during the drought.
6. One of my uncles always wears —— belt buckle off to one side. ——
7. No person should be made to feel that —— is worth less than someone else.
8. None of the dogs had eaten all of —— food.
9. A few of my neighbors have fenced —— backyards.
10. The fire engine and the police car went rushing by with —— lights flashing.

EXERCISE 15. Proofreading Sentences for Pronoun-Antecedent Agreement Number your paper 1–10. Most of the following sentences contain errors in pronoun-antecedent agreement. After the proper number, write *C* if the sentence is correct. If the sentence is incorrect, write the antecedent after the number; then, write the correct form of the pronoun. Follow the rules for standard written English.

EXAMPLE　1. Everyone in my English class has to give their oral report on Friday.
　　　　　　1. *Everyone—his* (or *his or her*)

1. Either Don or Buddy will be the first to give their report.
2. Several others, including me, volunteered to give mine first.

3. Everybody else in class wanted to put off giving their report as long as possible.
4. Last year my best friend Sandy and I figured out that waiting to give our reports was worse than actually giving them.
5. I am surprised that more people didn't volunteer to give his or her reports first.
6. Someone else will be third to give their report; then I will give mine.
7. A few others in my class are going to try to get out of giving his or her reports at all.
8. However, my teacher, Mrs. Murray, said that anyone who does not give an oral report will get an "incomplete" as their course grade.
9. Most of us wish that he or she did not have to give an oral report at all.
10. Since no one can get out of giving their report, though, I'd rather get it over with as soon as possible.

REVIEW EXERCISE D. Proofreading Sentences for Pronoun-Antecedent Agreement. Number your paper 1–20. Most of the following sentences contain errors in pronoun-antecedent agreement. After the proper number, write *C* if the sentence is correct. If the sentence is incorrect, write the antecedent after the number; then, write the correct form of the pronoun. Follow the rules for standard written English.

1. Each member of the President's Cabinet gave their advice about what to do.
2. Nearly every one of the girls had their hair cut short.
3. At the zoo we saw the kangaroo and the koala bear in its natural environment.
4. A few women working at the factory enrolled her children in the day-care center.
5. Was Mr. Avery or Mr. Jones going to show their classes that film today?
6. The guard said that anybody who didn't have their pass could not get in.

7. Some of the Boy Scouts had built an authentic Indian wigwam for their shelter.
8. Neither of those trees needs their limbs trimmed.
9. Every one of the soldiers carried extra rations in their pack.
10. Have you ever talked to Rosa or Flo about what they really thought?
11. The llama and the sheep are both valued for its wool.
12. Nobody I know wants other people ordering them around.
13. Andrea, Tammy, and Laura trade outfits so that she can always have something different to wear.
14. All of the volunteers quickly went to work at his or her jobs.
15. Either of those singers can break a glass with their voice.
16. A person should weigh their words carefully before criticizing someone else.
17. Did Ms. Chambers tell you what songs Alicia and Pamela plan to sing for their part of the program?
18. Somebody left their dirty sneakers on the hall rug.
19. Everybody ate his lunch in the shade of the pine trees.
20. Why didn't anyone pay their dues on time?

CHAPTER 8 REVIEW: POSTTEST 1

A. Identifying Verbs That Agree with Their Subjects.
Number your paper 1–15. In each of the following sentences, a verb has been italicized. If an italicized verb agrees with its subject, write *C* after the proper number. If an italicized verb does not agree with its subject, write the correct form of the verb after the proper number.

EXAMPLES 1. The people on the bus have all been seated.
                  1. *C*
                  2. The fish, bass and perch mostly, *has* started feeding.
                  2. *have*

1. Pencil and paper *is* needed for this test.
2. Either Sol or Anthony *have* been assigned to give a report.
3. *Doesn't* any of the children ride the bus?
4. Mrs. Holmes and Mr. Davis *assigns* homework almost every night.
5. Nearly every cat, no matter what breed, *go* crazy for catnip.
6. James Fenimore Cooper's *Leatherstocking Tales is* a famous collection of stories about the early American wilderness.
7. None of the answers you gave *was* correct.
8. Up until recently hardly anyone *have* been able to own a personal computer.
9. The club often *argues* among themselves about finances.
10. Every player on the varsity teams *go* to daily exercise.
11. Somebody said that he, of course, *don't* approve.
12. There *is* probably a few children who don't like strawberries.
13. My spelling lessons and science homework sometimes *takes* me hours to finish.
14. The mice or the cat *has* eaten the cheese that was left out.
15. The swarm of bees *have* deserted its hive.

B. Identifying Pronouns That Agree with Their Antecedents.

Number your paper 16–25. In each of the following sentences, a pronoun has been italicized. If an italicized pronoun agrees with its antecedent, write *C* after the proper number. If an italicized pronoun does not agree with its antecedent, write the correct pronoun after the proper number.

EXAMPLES 1. Either of the men could have offered *their* help.
      1. *his*
      2. Both of the flowers had spread their petals.
      2. *C*

16. Why doesn't somebody raise *their* hand and ask for directions?
17. In most cases, a dog or a cat that gets lost in the woods can take care of *themselves*.
18. One of the birds had lost most of *their* tail feathers.

19. By the end of the day, all of the streets in our neighborhood had new yellow lines painted along *its* edges.
20. Everyone who will be going will need to bring a note from *their* mother.
21. I don't understand how chameleons sitting on a green leaf or a bush change *their* color.
22. Each of these tests has *their* own answer key.
23. Please ask some of these girls to pick up *her* own materials from the supply room.
24. The air conditioner and the refrigerator have switches that turn *it* off and on automatically.
25. The audience clapped *its* hands in approval.

CHAPTER 8 REVIEW: POSTTEST 2

Writing Sentences with Subject-Verb and Pronoun-Antecedent Agreement. Number your paper 1–25. After the proper number, rewrite each of the following sentences according to the directions in parentheses. Whenever necessary, change each verb to make it agree with its subject, and change each pronoun to make it agree with its antecedent.

EXAMPLES
1. Every player on both teams has to wear protective gear. (Change *Every player* to *All players*.)
1. *All players on both teams have to wear protective gear.*
2. Only one of the boys wore his uniform. (Change *Only one* to *Only two*.)
2. *Only two of the boys wore their uniforms.*

1. Both of the rockets had used up their fuel before leaving the earth's gravity. (Change *Both* to *One*.)
2. There are not supposed to be any cars parked in the driveway. (Change *any cars* to *a car*.)
3. One of the roosters ruffled his feathers and crowed. (Change *One* to *Several*.)

4. Has Annie or Miguel signed up yet? (Change *or* to *and*.)
5. Someone has numbered her answer sheets in the wrong corner. (Change *Someone* to *Some students*.)
6. When the storm was over, none of the boats was still afloat. (Change *none* to *few*.)
7. Neither the birds nor the monkey wants to live in the same tree. (Change *the birds nor the monkey* to *the monkey nor the birds*.)
8. Would you please tell each of the members to bring her dues to the next meeting? (Change *each* to *all*.)
9. Not one of the children could feed himself. (Change *Not one* to *A few*.)
10. The crowd voiced its unanimous disapproval. (Change *The crowd* to *Members of the crowd*.)
11. The yogurt has been eaten. (Change *yogurt* to *cups of yogurt*.)
12. Ms. Tranh asked both Stan and Ryan what they had seen. (Change *both Stan and Ryan* to *either Stan or Ryan*.)
13. The school of sharks circled their prey. (Change *school of sharks* to *a shark*.)
14. The older boys don't seem to have as much fun as we do. (Change *boys* to *boy*.)
15. Several of the sales offer good buys. (Change *Several* to *Not one*.)
16. The family could not decide which selections it wanted. (Change *family* to *family members*.)
17. Only some of the tickets have been sold. (Change *some* to *one*.)
18. Don't any of you want to help? (Change *any of you* to *anyone*.)
19. The men in the lifeboat had been conserving their water. (Change *men* to *man*.)
20. The seals barked as the keeper threw raw fish to them. (Change *seals* to *seal*.)
21. From what I hear, everybody in our school wants to get a copy of that album. (Change *everybody* to *all the students*.)

22. The ceiling panels over my head are made of stainless steel. (Change *panels* to *panel*.)
23. Either you or your friends have to clean up this room. (Change *you or your friends* to *your friends or you*.)
24. Neither of those paths had trees and flowers growing alongside it. (Change *Neither* to *Both*.)
25. The change in my pocket doesn't add up to much. (Change *change* to *coins*.)

CHAPTER 9

Using Verbs Correctly

PRINCIPAL PARTS, REGULAR AND IRREGULAR VERBS

Few errors in speaking or writing are more obvious than verb errors. Students who write *she done it, he begun, they drownded,* or *it bursted* immediately tag themselves as people who do not know the standard usages of their language.

DIAGNOSTIC TEST

A. Writing the Past and Past Participle Forms of Verbs.
Number your paper 1–15. After the proper number, write the past or past participle of the verb given before the sentence.

EXAMPLES   1. *take*   We don't know why it —— them so long.
1. *took*
2. *take*   We don't know why it has —— them so long.
2. *taken*

1. *lie*   The cat —— down in front of the warm fire.
2. *raise*   Since the storm began, the river has —— four feet.
3. *go*   Did you see which way they —— ?
4. *write*   Liang should have —— you a note to let you know we were coming.

5. *break*   Two runners on our track team have —— the school record for the mile run.

6. *burst*   When the manager unlocked the door, a mob of shoppers —— into the store to take advantage of the sale.

7. *shrink*   Larry washed his wool sweater in hot water, and it —— .

8. *see*   The witness said that she —— the blue car run through the red light.

9. *rise*   Look in the oven to see if the cake has —— yet.

10. *ring*   Everyone should be in class after the bell has —— .

11. *know*   You have all —— for a week that we were going to have a test today.

12. *lay*   Jeanette carefully —— her coat across the back of the chair.

13. *freeze*   Usually, by January the lake has —— hard enough to skate on it.

14. *choose*   No one could understand why Terry —— the striped one instead of the others.

15. *swim*   So far, Dena has —— fifteen laps around the pool.

B. Correcting Verbs in the Wrong Tense. Number your paper 16–20. In each of the following sentences, the italicized verb is in the wrong tense. After the proper number, write the italicized verb in the correct tense.

EXAMPLE   1. He looked out the window and *sees* the storm approaching.
    1. *saw*

16. Jan was late, so she *decides* to run the rest of the way.

17. The man at the gate *takes* our tickets and said that we were just in time.

18. My uncle often travels in the Far East and *brought* me some fascinating souvenirs.

19. When his mother told the little boy it was his bedtime, he *throws* a temper tantrum.

20. The waitress brought my order and *asks* me if I wanted anything else.

THE PRINCIPAL PARTS OF A VERB

Besides naming an action, a verb also shows its time. This expression of time by the verb is called *tense*. To express different times, a verb has different tenses. These tenses are formed from four *principal parts* of the verb.

9a. The principal parts of a verb are the *infinitive*, the *present participle*, the *past*, and the *past participle*.

From these four principal parts all the tenses of our language are formed. The four principal parts of *sing* are *sing* (infinitive), *singing* (present participle), *sang* (past), and *sung* (past participle). Notice in the following sentences how the four principal parts are used to express time.

I **sing** in the school glee club.
We **are singing** at the music festival tonight.
Mahalia Jackson **sang** gospels at Carnegie Hall.
We **have sung** all over the state.

Here are the principal parts of two familiar verbs:

INFINITIVE	PRESENT PARTICIPLE	PAST	PAST PARTICIPLE
work	working	worked	(have) worked
eat	eating	ate	(have) eaten

Notice that the present participle always ends in *–ing*. The past participle is the form used with *has, have,* or *had*.

THE SIX TENSES

By using the four principal parts of the verb, along with various helping verbs, you can form six tenses for every verb. When you give the forms for the six tenses of a verb, you are *conjugating* that verb.

Conjugation of **Write**

Principal parts: write, writing, wrote, (have) written.

Present Tense

Singular	*Plural*
I write	we write
you write	you write
he, she, *or* it writes	they write

Past Tense

Singular	*Plural*
I wrote	we wrote
you wrote	you wrote
he, she, *or* it wrote	they wrote

Future Tense

Singular	*Plural*
I will (shall) write	we will (shall) write
you will write	you will write
he, she, *or* it will write	they will write

Present Perfect Tense

Singular	*Plural*
I have written	we have written
you have written	you have written
he, she, *or* it has written	they have written

Past Perfect Tense

Singular	*Plural*
I had written	we had written
you had written	you had written
he, she, *or* it had written	they had written

Future Perfect Tense

Singular	*Plural*
I will (shall) have written	we will (shall) have written
you will have written	you will have written
he, she, *or* it will have written	they will have written

REGULAR VERBS

9b. A regular verb forms its past and past participle by adding
–ed or *–d* to the present form.

INFINITIVE	PRESENT PARTICIPLE	PAST	PAST PARTICIPLE
follow	following	followed	(have) followed
date	dating	dated	(have) dated
miss	missing	missed	(have) missed

Pay careful attention to pronunciation of the past and past
participle. Avoid nonstandard pronunciation, which usually follows two patterns: (1) adding an extra syllable—*drownded* for
drowned, attackted for *attacked;* (2) not pronouncing the *–ed*
ending—*ask* for *asked, suppose* for *supposed.*

**EXERCISE 1. *Oral Drill.* Pronouncing the Past and Past
Participle Forms of Regular Verbs Correctly.** The following sentences contain regular verbs that are often mispronounced. Read *aloud* every sentence, stressing the pronunciation
of the italicized words, especially their endings.

1. The troops *attacked* the fort.
2. Our speaker was *supposed* to arrive at six o'clock.
3. How many people have *drowned* in this lake?
4. Rosa has often *used* her knowledge of geography.
5. The accident *happened* at night.
6. The brave woman *risked* her life to save her son.
7. You *asked* me that question yesterday.
8. This shampoo has *lasted* a long time.
9. Private detectives have sometimes *tracked* criminals for the
   police.
10. Have you *washed* the car?

**EXERCISE 2. *Oral Drill.* Forming the Past and Past
Participle Forms of Regular Verbs.** Use the following
verbs in sentences. Put each verb in the past tense, or use the past
participle and the helping verb *have* or *has.*

1. hope	3. call	5. walk	7. decide	9. support
2. talk	4. gallop	6. own	8. finish	10. love

IRREGULAR VERBS

9c. An *irregular verb* forms its past and past participle in a different way than a regular verb does.

Irregular verbs form their past and past participle in several ways:

1. by a vowel change: *ring, rang,* (have) *rung*
2. by a consonant change: *make, made,* (have) *made*
3. by a vowel and consonant change: *bring, brought,* (have) *brought*
4. by no change: *burst, burst,* (have) *burst*

If you do not know the principal parts of irregular verbs, you may make errors like this:

NONSTANDARD   She has drank all her milk. [*Drunk,* not *drank,* is the past participle.]

To avoid errors, memorize the principal parts of irregular verbs. Include *have* with the past participle because this helping verb is often used with the past participle.

Irregular Verbs Frequently Misused

INFINITIVE	PRESENT PARTICIPLE	PAST	PAST PARTICIPLE
begin	beginning	began	(have) begun
blow	blowing	blew	(have) blown
break	breaking	broke	(have) broken
bring	bringing	brought	(have) brought
burst	bursting	burst	(have) burst
choose	choosing	chose	(have) chosen
come	coming	came	(have) come
do	doing	did	(have) done
drink	drinking	drank	(have) drunk
drive	driving	drove	(have) driven

eat	eating	ate	(have) eaten
fall	falling	fell	(have) fallen
freeze	freezing	froze	(have) frozen
give	giving	gave	(have) given
go	going	went	(have) gone
know	knowing	knew	(have) known
lie	lying	lay	(have) lain
ride	riding	rode	(have) ridden
ring	ringing	rang	(have) rung
rise	rising	rose	(have) risen
run	running	ran	(have) run
see	seeing	saw	(have) seen
set	setting	set	(have) set
shrink	shrinking	shrank	(have) shrunk
sing	singing	sang	(have) sung
sit	sitting	sat	(have) sat
speak	speaking	spoke	(have) spoken
steal	stealing	stole	(have) stolen
swim	swimming	swam	(have) swum
take	taking	took	(have) taken
throw	throwing	threw	(have) thrown
write	writing	wrote	(have) written

Caution: Be careful not to confuse irregular verbs with regular ones. Never say *knowed, throwed, shrinked,* or *bursted.*

EXERCISE 3. Writing the Past and Past Participle Forms of Irregular Verbs. As your teacher or a classmate reads aloud to you the infinitive forms of the thirty-two irregular verbs just listed, write the past and the past participle forms on your paper.

Merely knowing the principal parts of irregular verbs is not enough. You need to practice using them in sentence patterns. Use the following example to help you practice usage of irregular verbs.

Today I **bring** lunch.
Yesterday I **brought** lunch.
Often I **have brought** lunch.

EXERCISE 4. Identifying the Correct Forms of Irregular Verbs.

Number your paper 1–20. Choose the correct one of the two verbs in parentheses, and write it after the proper number on your paper. After your paper has been corrected, read each sentence *aloud* several times, stressing the correct verb.

EXAMPLE   1. The bread (rised, rose) as it cooked.
             1. *rose*

1. Ray Charles, a blind musician, has (wrote, written) many beautiful songs.
2. Olympic champion Mary Lou Retton (began, begun) her gymnastics training when she was eight years old.
3. A gust of wind (blowed, blew) his glasses off his head.
4. The mail carrier (brung, brought) me a present from Bob.
5. Leigh (came, come) to visit us last Friday.
6. She (knew, knowed) we had planned a busy day.
7. We (drove, drived) to my uncle's ranch in the country.
8. Mr. Cuevas (spoke, spoken) at our Wednesday meeting.
9. Maria Tallchief (chose, choosed) a career as a dancer.
10. The newborn fawn (run, ran) into the secluded thicket.
11. The bell (ringed, rang) before I could finish the test.
12. She (taked, took) her textbook to class but forgot her workbook.
13. My woolen socks (shrinked, shrank) when I washed them in hot water.
14. He (eat, ate) chicken salad on whole-wheat bread for lunch.
15. The jacket (falled, fell) from the coat rack.
16. She (drank, drunk) all the orange juice I was planning to serve for breakfast.
17. The monkey had (stole, stolen) the food from its brother.
18. Henry and Tonya (sang, sung) a duet in the eighth-grade talent show.

19. The shy turtle (came, come) closer to me to reach the lettuce I was holding.
20. When I heard the suspicious noise, I (froze, freezed) where I was standing.

EXERCISE 5. **Writing the Past and Past Participle Forms of Verbs.** Number your paper 1–20. After the proper number, write the past or the past participle of the verb given before each sentence to complete the sentence correctly.

EXAMPLE   1. *do*   Nobody knew why he —— that.
            1. *did*

1. *ring*   The telephone —— just as I stepped into the shower.
2. *throw*   The outfielder —— the ball to home plate.
3. *swim*   Diana Nyad —— sixty miles from the Bahama Islands to Florida.
4. *choose*   Did he say why he had —— that one?
5. *drive*   We have —— all night to attend my sister's college graduation exercises.
6. *write*   I have —— a letter of complaint to the manufacturer.
7. *drown*   He would have —— if the lifeguard hadn't noticed the splashing in the waves.
8. *begin*   Kay —— her training by running beside her dog.
9. *know*   She —— that she could run the three-mile race.
10. *run*   On the day of the race, she —— the course in less than twenty minutes.
11. *drink*   After she finished the race, she —— three glasses of water.
12. *break*   He —— his arm when he fell on the pavement.
13. *burst*   The balloon —— when it strayed too near the flame.
14. *freeze*   The catfish —— in the pond last winter.
15. *go*   I have —— from one room to another looking for my lost shoe.

16. *blow* The siren —— long and loud to warn the residents of danger.
17. *ride* Derek —— his snowmobile up to the remote mountain cabin.
18. *sit* Peter —— quietly throughout the entire discussion.
19. *see* Marianne —— that he disagreed with her.
20. *steal* Our dog had —— a steak from the grill while we were inside.

REVIEW EXERCISE A. Writing Sentences Using the Past and Past Participle Forms of Irregular Verbs. Write two original sentences, using correctly the past and past participle forms of each verb that you missed in Exercises 4 and 5. After your sentences have been checked for accuracy, read them aloud until you feel that you have mastered the troublesome verbs.

REVIEW EXERCISE B. Proofreading Sentences for Correct Verb Forms. Number your paper 1–20. Write *C* after the number of each correct sentence. Write the correct form of the verb after the number of each incorrect sentence.

EXAMPLES 1. I broke a water glass.
1. *C*
2. We rung the door bell.
2. *rang*

1. Sally give me a menu from the new downtown restaurant.
2. I had spoke to my parents last week about trying this restaurant.
3. We had never went there before.
4. My big brother Mark drove us there in Mom's car.
5. We had almost reached the restaurant when Mark hit a curb.
6. We falled off the curb with a big bounce.
7. We all seen that he was very embarrassed.
8. I shrinked down in the back seat so that he wouldn't notice that I was laughing.
9. When we arrived at the restaurant, I runned ahead of everyone to tell the hostess we needed five seats.

10. The waiter had brought our menus before we all sit down.
11. We drunk water with lemon slices in the glasses.
12. Have you ever ate spaghetti with clam sauce?
13. Dad chose the ravioli.
14. My little sister Emily taked two helpings of salad.
15. The waiter bringed out our dinners on a huge platter.
16. Mark give me a taste of his eggplant parmigiana.
17. Emily stealed a bite of my lasagna.
18. Mom breaked the last breadstick in half so that Emily and I could share it.
19. Dad writed on the bill that the food was delicious.
20. We had made a good decision to try that new restaurant.

SPECIAL PROBLEMS WITH VERBS

Sit and Set

Study the principal parts of the verbs *sit* and *set*. Notice that *sit* changes to form the past tense, but *set* remains the same in the past and the past participle.

INFINITIVE	PRESENT PARTICIPLE	PAST	PAST PARTICIPLE
sit (to rest)	sitting	sat	(have) sat
set (to place)	setting	set	(have) set

Sit and *set* are verbs that are often confused. You will not make mistakes with these two verbs if you remember two facts about them:

(1) *Sit* means "to rest in an upright, seated position," while *set* means "to put or place (something)."

Let's **sit** under the tree.
Let's **set** the bookcase here.

The tourists **sat** on benches.
The children **set** the dishes on the table.

We **had sat** down to eat when the telephone rang.
We **have set** the reading lamp beside the couch.

(2) *Sit* is almost never followed by an object, but *set* often does take an object.

My aunt **sits** in the large chair. [no object]
She **sets** the chair in the corner. [Sets what? *Chair* is the object.]

The audience **sat** near the stage. [no object]
The stagehand **set** a microphone near the Judds. [Set what? *Microphone* is the object.]

EXERCISE 6. *Oral Drill*. Using the Forms of *Sit* and *Set* Correctly. Read the following sentences aloud, paying particular attention to the meaning of *sit* and *set*. Pronounce each verb distinctly.

1. Let's sit down here.
2. Look at the dog sitting on the porch.
3. Our teacher set a deadline for our term projects.
4. Have you set the clock?
5. I have always sat in the front row.
6. Please set the carton down inside the doorway.
7. She has set a high standard for her work.
8. The woman sits by the window every day.
9. The referee is setting the ball on the fifty-yard line.
10. After I set the mop in the closet, I sat down to rest.

EXERCISE 7. Using the Correct Forms of *Sit* and *Set*. Number your paper 1–10. After the proper number, write the correct one of the two words in parentheses. If the verb you choose is a form of *set*, write its object after it.

EXAMPLE 1. Please (sit, set) the serving platter on the table.
  1. *set, platter*

1. Will you (sit, set) down here?
2. It's Aaron's turn to (sit, set) the table for dinner.
3. Carolyn (sat, set) her notebook on the kitchen counter.
4. I have been (sitting, setting) here all day.
5. (Sit, Set) the fine crystal in the china cabinet.

6. Jennifer promised her little sister she would (sit, set) her hair for the party.
7. The cat cautiously (sat, set) beside the Great Dane.
8. Zachary (sits, sets) up in bed at night while he reads another chapter from his library book.
9. Let's (sit, set) that aside until later.
10. They have been (sitting, setting) there for fifteen minutes without saying a word to each other.

EXERCISE 8. Writing Sentences Using *Sit* and *Set* Correctly. Use correctly each of the following verbs in sentences of your own.

1. sits	4. was setting	7. have sat	9. will set
2. sets	5. sat	8. have set	10. will sit
3. was sitting	6. set		

Lie and Lay

Study the principal parts of *lie* and *lay*.

INFINITIVE	PRESENT PARTICIPLE	PAST	PAST PARTICIPLE
lie (to recline)	lying	lay	(have) lain
lay (to put)	laying	laid	(have) laid

Like *sit*, *lie*[1] has to do with resting, and it has no object. *Lay* is like *set* because it means "to put (something) down" and because it may have an object.

The cows **are lying** in the shade. [no object]
The workers **are laying** the foundation for the building. [*Are laying* what? *Foundation* is the object.]

The soliders **lay** very still while the enemy passed by. [No object—*lay* here is the past tense of *lie*.]
The soldiers **laid** a trap for the enemy. [*Laid* what? *Trap* is the object.]

---

[1] The verb *lie* meaning "to tell a falsehood" is a different word. Its past forms are regular: *lie, lying, lied, lied.*

The injured man **had lain** in the cave for weeks. [no object]
The lawyer **had laid** the newspaper next to her briefcase.
[*Had laid* what? *Newspaper* is the object.]

EXERCISE 9. *Oral Drill.* **Using the Forms of** *Lie* **and** *Lay*
Correctly. Read each of the following sentences aloud several
times. Be able to explain why the verb is correct.

1. The delegates laid the groundwork for future conferences.
2. She lay in bed until eleven o'clock.
3. Don't lie in the sun too long!
4. You shouldn't lay your papers on the couch.
5. The lion had been lying in wait for an hour.
6. The senator laid her notes aside after her speech on careers in politics.
7. He had lain still for a few minutes.
8. He has laid his books on his desk.
9. Our cat lies on the radiator.
10. She lays the sharp knives on the top shelf.
11. The cook laid the meat on the grill.
12. The exhausted swimmer lay helpless on the sand.
13. Lie down for a few minutes before supper.
14. She laid her pen on the edge of the desk.

EXERCISE 10. Writing the Correct Forms of *Lie* **and**
Lay. Number your paper 1–10. After the proper number, write
the correct form of *lie* or *lay* for each of these sentences.

1. The television journalist —— aside her career while her children were young.
2. My dad was —— down when I asked for my allowance.
3. We need to —— down some club rules.
4. Have you ever —— on a water bed?
5. Andrew —— his keys beside his wallet.
6. My cat loves to —— in the tall grass behind our house.
7. My brother left his clothes —— on the floor until they began to smell.

8. The alligator —— in the sun on the bank of the stream.
9. The groundskeeper has —— new sod on the golf course.
10. The newspaper had —— in the yard until the sun faded it.

EXERCISE 11. Writing Sentences Using Forms of *Lie* and *Lay*. Use each of the following verbs or verb phrases correctly in a sentence of your own.

1. lies
2. laid
3. was laying
4. has lain

5. lays
6. has been lying
7. lay (past tense of *lie*)

8. have laid
9. will lie
10. are lying

Rise and Raise

Study the principal parts of *rise* and *raise*.

INFINITIVE	PRESENT PARTICIPLE	PAST	PAST PARTICIPLE
rise (to go up)	rising	rose	(have) risen
raise (to lift up)	raising	raised	(have) raised

The verb *rise* means "to go up" or "to get up." Rise, like *lie*, never has an object. *Raise*, which means "to lift up" or "to cause to rise," may, like *lay*, have an object.

My neighbors **rise** very early in the morning. [no object]
Every morning they **raise** their shades to let the sunlight in. [*Raise* what? *Shades* is the object.]

The moon **rose** slowly last night. [no object]
Last year Ana and Bill **raised** corn and tomatoes in their garden. [*Raised* what? *Corn* and *tomatoes* are the objects.]

The senators **have risen** from their seats to show respect for the Chief Justice. [no object]
The wind **has raised** a cloud of dust. [*Has raised* what? *Cloud* is the object.]

EXERCISE 12. *Oral Drill*. Using the Correct Forms of *Rise* and *Raise*. Repeat each of the following correct sentences aloud several times, stressing the italicized verbs and thinking of the meanings of the verbs.

1. The reporters *rise* when the President enters the room.
2. The reporters *raise* their hands to be recognized.
3. The reporter who was recognized *rose* to her feet.
4. She *has raised* an interesting question.
5. Another reporter *was rising*.
6. Several reporters *rose* at the same time.
7. Who *had risen* first?
8. The President recognized the one who *rose* first.
9. Will Congress *raise* taxes this year?
10. Everyone *rises* as the President leaves.

EXERCISE 13. Writing the Correct Forms of *Rise* and *Raise*. Number your paper 1–10. After the proper number, write the correct one of the two verbs in parentheses. If the verb you choose is a form of *raise*, write its object after it.

1. The steam was (rising, raising) from the pot of soup.
2. That comment (rises, raises) a very good question.
3. The child's fever (rose, raised) during the night.
4. The sun (rises, raises) later each morning.
5. The teacher will call only on students who (rise, raise) their hands.
6. We must (rise, raise) the flag before school begins.
7. The student body's interest in this subject has (risen, raised) to new heights.
8. The kite has (risen, raised) above the power lines.
9. My father promised to (rise, raise) my allowance if I pull the weeds.
10. The store (rose, raised) the price on that radio the last week.

EXERCISE 14. Writing the Correct Forms of *Rise* and *Raise*. Number your paper 1–10. After the proper number, write the correct form of *rise* or *raise* in each blank in the following paragraphs.

We girls —— early to start our hike to Lookout Mountain. From our position at the foot of the mountain, it looked as though it —— straight up to the heavens.

But we had not —— at daybreak just to look at the high peak. We —— our supply packs to our backs and started the long climb up the mountain. With every step we took, the mountain seemed to —— that much higher. Finally, after several hours, we reached the summit and —— a special flag that we had brought for the occasion. When our friends at the foot of the mountain saw the flag —— , they knew that we had reached the top safely. They —— their arms and shouted.

Although we could not see them, we heard voices that seemed to —— from the valley below. Then we felt glad that we had —— early enough to climb to the top of Lookout Mountain.

WRITING APPLICATION A:
Using Irregular Verbs Correctly When Writing About Experiences in the Past

When you talk with other people and when you write, you often deal with personal experiences. These experiences involved you (or people you know) in the past. One of the most common errors in English usage is misuse of the past and past participle forms of irregular verbs. Since these verbs do not add a simple –ed for the past tense, you have to memorize their correct forms.

EXAMPLE   Drivers in England *have* always *drove* on the left side of the street. [The past participle *driven* should be used with the helping verb *have*.]

Drivers in England *have* always *driven* on the left side of the street. [The error in agreement is corrected.]

Writing Assignment

Select one of the irregular verbs discussed in this chapter. Using the correct forms of this verb, write a paragraph about a personal experience. Following are some ideas.

Learning to Swim   A Horseback Ride
Making Ice Cream   The Time I Ate Too Much

REVIEW EXERCISE C. Using the Correct Forms of *Sit*
and *Set,* *Lie* **and** *Lay,* **and** *Rise* **and** *Raise.*   Number your
paper 1–20. Choose the correct verb from the two in parentheses,
and write it after the proper number. If a sentence has two verbs,
write both of them on the same line in the order in which they
occur. Be prepared to explain your choices in class.

1. The sun has (risen, raised), and you are still (lying, laying) in
   bed.
2. While their grandmother (sat, set) in the shade, Marilyn and
   Ed (sat, set) the table for the picnic.
3. The water level of the stream has not (risen, raised) since last
   summer.
4. Cooks often (lie, lay) their stirring spoons in special spoon
   rests.
5. Key West (lies, lays) off the southwestern coast of Florida.
6. To study how solar energy works, our class (sit, set) a solar
   panel outside the window of our classroom.
7. The golfer carefully (sits, sets) the ball on the tee.
8. Since I have gotten taller, I have (rose, raised) the seat on my
   bicycle.
9. We all (sit, set) in alphabetical order in algebra class.
10. (Lie, Lay) the grass mats on the sand so that we can (lie, lay)
    on them.
11. (Sit, Set) the groceries on the table while I start dinner.
12. The squirrels (rose, raised) their heads when they heard me
    tapping on the window.
13. (Rise, Raise) the car a little higher so that we can change the
    tire.
14. When the sun (rises, raises), I sometimes have difficulty
    (sitting, setting) aside my covers and getting up.
15. When the sun had (sit, set), I wearily (lay, laid) on the hard
    earth in my tent.

16. I (lay, laid) my flashlight beside my sleeping bag.
17. My dog Beau (lay, laid) just outside the tent.
18. We (sat, set) under a beach umbrella so that we wouldn't get sunburned.
19. Mr. DeLemos (lay, laid) the foundation for our new patio.
20. Your grades must (rise, raise), or you will not make the honor roll this term.

CONSISTENCY OF TENSE

You should never shift tenses needlessly. When you are writing about events in the past tense, you should use the past tense consistently unless there is some reason for you to change tenses. You should not shift without reason to the present tense.

9d. Do not change needlessly from one tense to another.

NONSTANDARD	After we were comfortable, we begin to do our homework. [*Were* is past tense and *begin* is present.]
STANDARD	After we **were** comfortable, we **began** to do our homework. [Both *were* and *began* are in the past tense.]
NONSTANDARD	Suddenly the great door opened, and an uninvited guest comes into the dining hall. [*Opened* is past tense and *comes* is present.]
STANDARD	Suddenly the great door **opens,** and an uninvited guest **comes** into the dining hall. [Both *opens* and *comes* are in the present tense.]
STANDARD	Suddenly the great door **opened,** and an uninvited guest **came** into the dining hall. [Both *opened* and *came* are in the past tense.]

EXERCISE 15. Proofreading a Paragraph to Make the Tenses of the Verbs Consistent. Read the following paragraph, and decide what tense you should use to tell about the

events. Prepare to read the paragraph aloud, making the verb tense consistent throughout.

> At my grandparents' house that morning, I wake up before anyone else and quietly grabbed the fishing pole and head for the pond. Across the water, I saw ripples. "I have to catch that fish," I say to myself. I threw my lure near where I see the ripples and reeled in the line. The fish don't seem interested. I saw more ripples and throw the line in the water again. "I've got a strike!" I shout to the trees around me. As I reeled in the line, a beautiful trout jumps out of the water and spit out the hook. Discouraged, I go back to the house. Grandpa was sitting at the table with a bowl of hot oatmeal for me. I say, "Maybe tomorrow we'll have trout for breakfast."

WRITING APPLICATION B:
Being Consistent in Using Verb Tenses

How do you know when it's time for lunch? Your stomach usually gives you a signal in the form of a hunger pang. Every day you encounter many things that indicate the time, such as sunrise, bells, and alarm clocks. The way you signal the time to your readers is through the use of *tense*. Avoid shifting tenses unless you have a good reason. An important rule to remember is *be consistent*.

EXAMPLE   In *The Secret Life of Walter Mitty,* by James Thurber, the main character *was henpecked* by his wife. [past tense] When she *fusses* at him, [present tense] he *will dream* about being some famous person. [future tense]

In this example, the tenses are not consistent. They switch from past to present to future. The example could be corrected by writing all three verbs in either the present or the past tense to make them consistent.

Writing Assignment

Select a story or book that you have read recently. Write a paragraph summarizing the plot. Proofread your paragraph to make sure that you have been consistent in the use of verb tense.

REVIEW EXERCISE D. Using the Correct Verb and the Correct Verb Form. Number your paper 1–20. Select from each sentence the correct one of the verb forms in parentheses, and write it after the proper number on your paper. Some sentences have more than one verb.

1. He (knew, knowed) he would not get his wish even though he (blew, blowed) out all his birthday candles.
2. Buffy Sainte-Marie has (sang, sung) professionally for more than twenty years.
3. Have you (began, begun) your homework yet?
4. Cindy Nicholas was the first woman who (swam, swum) the English Channel both ways.
5. I'm glad you (come, came) with us to the lake.
6. When the baby sitter (rose, raised) her voice, the children (knew, knowed) it was time to behave.
7. After we had (saw, seen) all the exhibits at the county fair, we (ate, eat) a snack and then (went, go) home.
8. The egg (burst, bursted) in the microwave oven.
9. I was very nervous when I (go, went) on the ski lift for the first time.
10. He (lay, laid) his lunch money on his desk.
11. When he tried to claim the money later, he found that it had been (stole, stolen).
12. The loud noise (breaked, broke) my concentration.
13. Grandma (give, gave) me a belt for my birthday.
14. For the creative writing assignment, I had (wrote, written) a story about my deep-sea fishing trip.

15. Robbie had (chose, chosen) to take band this year.
16. The thirsty plants (drank, drunk) all the rainwater.
17. The truck has (rode, ridden) over the rough country road with ease.
18. We had (rode, ridden) halfway across the desert when I began to wish I had (brought, brung) more water.
19. The beautiful oranges had (froze, frozen) on the trees last winter.
20. We liked that movie so much that we (sat, set) through it three times on Saturday.

REVIEW EXERCISE E. Using the Correct Verb and the Correct Verb Form. Number your paper 1–20. After the proper number, write the form of the verb at the left that correctly fills the blank in each sentence. In some instances you must choose the correct verb as well as the correct form.

1. *blow*   The pollen had —— in my face, causing me to sneeze.
2. *sing*   Stevie Wonder —— at the concert hall here last week.
3. *swim*   The otters have —— in their pool all day.
4. *run*   Have you ever —— in a race with Alberto Salazar?
5. *break*   Pearl Moore —— a record in basketball by scoring 4,061 points during her college career.
6. *fall*   The newly hatched sparrow —— from its nest.
7. *come*   Chris —— over to my house just as I was leaving for my violin lesson.
8. *steal*   The bandits —— over seven million dollars in cash.
9. *lie, lay*   At the end of the busy day, she finally —— down to rest.
10. *sit, set*   Whenever Uncle Olaf —— in the oversize arm chair, we gather around his feet to listen to tales of his native land.
11. *burst*   Some of his stories were so funny that we —— out laughing.

12. *ride* We had —— for hours before we realized that we had forgotten our toothbrushes.

13. *shrink* The meat patties —— while they were being cooked.

14. *write* I have —— a poem about my cat Mittens.

15. *ring* The child cried each time a Halloween goblin —— the doorbell.

16. *see* I —— a prism in these pieces of broken glass.

17. *speak* Have you —— to the counselor about your schedule for next year?

18. *take* Who —— a bite from my blueberry muffin?

19. *bring* Ms. Kaneshige —— her Japanese kimono to show the class.

20. *do* He —— the best he could on the paper but received only a B for his efforts.

CHAPTER 9 REVIEW: POSTTEST 1

A. Writing the Past and Past Participle Forms of Verbs.

Number your paper 1–15. After the proper number, write the past or past participle of the verb given before the sentence.

EXAMPLES 1. *ride* Roy Rogers —— a horse named Trigger.

1. *rode*

2. *ride* Most of the ranch hands had —— back to the bunkhouse by dark.

2. *ridden*

1. *bring* Everyone —— a gift for the hostess.

2. *take* Very few people knew what had actually —— place.

3. *know* If I had —— you were sleeping, I would have been quieter.

4. *do* We all believe that you —— the right thing.

5. *raise* Many of the farmers had —— so many cattle that the price of beef went down.

6. *begin*   Just after the cheering ——, the team ran out onto the field.

7. *freeze*   The scientists found a saber-toothed tiger —— in the glacier.

8. *see*   Tell your brother that we —— him drive by our house last night.

9. *throw*   My mother has —— out most of my old comic books.

10. *drink*   We were so thirsty that we must have —— three gallons of water that day.

11. *sing*   Both my brother and my sister —— in the choir last year.

12. *fall*   If a tree has —— when no one is there, how can you know that it made any noise?

13. *choose*   It appears that the fish have —— to ignore our lures.

14. *sit*   Some of the store's merchandise —— on the shelves for years.

15. *give*   Eating all those berries —— me a stomachache.

B. Determining the Correct Forms of *Lie—Lay, Sit—Set,* and *Rise—Raise* in Sentences.

Number your paper 16–20. Read each of the following sentences, and determine whether it is correct. If it is correct, write *C* after the proper number. If it is incorrect, write the correct form.

EXAMPLES   1. The cat lay on its back and licked its paws.
          1. *C*
          2. The carpenter lay his hammer on the windowsill.
          2. *laid*

16. Would you please set the sofa down here?
17. The people in front of me raised up in their seats to get a better look.
18. You'd better set down while I tell you this.
19. He ran out of the house and left his books laying on the table.
20. The crane raised the steel beam into place.

C. Correcting Verbs in the Wrong Tense.
Number your paper 21–25. In each of the following sentences, the italicized verb is in the wrong tense. After the proper number, write the correct tense of the italicized verb.

EXAMPLE   1. The crow squawked at us and then *flies* away.
           1. *flew*

21. The police officer asked if we were lost and then *takes* us home.
22. Not many people *knew* what happened, but they all ask a lot of questions.
23. The fence runs alongside the parking lot down to the street and then *curved* left along the curb.
24. The mountain looked beautiful in the sunset and *makes* me feel at home.
25. They *send* me a free sample and then asked me to pay for it.

CHAPTER 9 REVIEW: POSTTEST 2

A. Writing the Past and Past Participle Forms of Verbs.
Number your paper 1–15. After the proper number, write the past or past participle of the verb given before the sentence.

EXAMPLES   1. *run*   The deer —— across the road in front of our car.
           1. *ran*
           2. *run*   Her dog has —— away from home.
           2. *run*

1. *shrink*   The older girl —— from the responsibility of caring for her younger brothers and sister.
2. *write*   Have you —— your history report yet?
3. *eat*   I don't think I should have —— that last handful of sunflower seeds.
4. *sit*   The blue jay that —— on the telephone wire called to its mate.

5. *know*   She is the nicest person I have ever —— .

6. *break*   When the medicine finally began to work, his fever —— .

7. *ring*   That phone has —— every five minutes since I got home.

8. *come*   Earl thought and thought, but the answer never —— to him.

9. *freeze*   If that had happened to me, I would have —— with fear.

10. *sing*   Through the murky depths the whales —— to one another.

11. *give*   The coach —— us all a pep talk before the game.

12. *begin*   We knew that it would rain soon because the crickets had —— chirping.

13. *take*   That job shouldn't have —— you all day.

14. *bring*   Everyone else had —— along a warm sweater.

15. *fall*   Though he had —— from the top of the tree, the baby squirrel was all right.

B. Writing the Correct Forms of *Lie—Lay, Sit—Set,* and *Rise—Raise* in Sentences. Number your paper 16–20. Choose the correct verb from the two verbs given in parentheses, and write it after the proper number on your paper.

EXAMPLE   1. My cat (lies, lays) around the house all day.
           1. *lies*

16. We had to wait for the drawbridge to (rise, raise) before we could sail out to the bay.

17. (Sit, Set) that down in the chair, will you?

18. The treasure had (lay, lain) at the bottom of the ocean for more than four hundred years.

19. My grandfather and grandmother like to (sit, set) on the porch and talk.

20. Look on the other side of any logs (lying, laying) in the path to avoid stepping on a snake.

C. Correcting Verbs in the Wrong Tense. Number your paper 21–25. In each of the following sentences, the italicized verb is in the wrong tense. After the proper number, write the italicized verb in the correct tense.

EXAMPLE   1. My father looked at his watch and *decides* that it
                  was time to leave.
            1. *decided*

21. Marjorie's sister refused to give us a ride in her car, and then she *asks* us to loan her some money for gas.
22. He says he's sorry, but he *didn't* mean it.
23. The trees grow close together and *had* straight trunks.
24. When the show ended, we *get* up to leave, but a crowd had already gathered.
25. Several mechanics worked on my aunt's car before one of them finally *finds* the problem.

CHAPTER 10

Using Pronouns Correctly

NOMINATIVE AND OBJECTIVE CASE FORMS

The case of a noun or a pronoun depends on how the noun or pronoun is used in the sentence. A word used as a subject is in the *nominative* case; a word used as an object is in the *objective* case; and a word used to show ownership or relationship is in the *possessive* case.

The case of nouns presents no problem because a noun has the same form in the nominative and objective cases.

The **woman** [nominative] said she saw another **woman** [objective] in the park.

The possessive case of a noun usually requires only the addition of an apostrophe and an *s*.

The **woman's** friend has arrived.

The case of personal pronouns, however, does present a problem, because they change form in the different cases. To use these pronouns correctly, you must know their various case forms and know when to use them.

DIAGNOSTIC TEST

Using Pronouns Correctly in Sentences. Number your paper 1–20. After the proper number, write the correct one of the two pronouns in parentheses.

EXAMPLE 1. Just between you and (I, me), I think he's wrong.
1. *me*

1. When I got home, a package was waiting for (I, me).
2. Everyone thought that (she, her) was very intelligent.
3. We saw (they, them) riding their bikes to school.
4. The winners in the contest turned out to be Jill and (I, me).
5. The wasp flew in the window and bit (he, him) on the arm.
6. Elton and (she, her) will give reports this morning.
7. The two scouts who have earned the most merit badges are Angelo and (he, him).
8. Several people in my neighborhood helped (we, us) boys clear the empty lot and measure out a baseball diamond.
9. Nina has promised to give Ralph and (I, me) some help with our music lessons.
10. My father and (he, him) are planning to go into business together.
11. We thought that we'd be facing (they, them) in the finals.
12. May I sit next to Marvin and (he, him)?
13. After class the teacher asked Kim and (she, her) to help erase the chalkboard.
14. My little sister always gives (me, I) a lot of trouble.
15. Did you know that it was (I, me) who called?
16. Corey's mother and my father said that (we, us) could go on the field trip.
17. The bears wanted (we, us) to feed them the rest of our sandwiches.
18. Invite (she, her) and the new girl in class to the party.
19. We hoped that the job would fall to Leon and Greg instead of (we, us).
20. The best soloists in the band are (they, them), apparently.

THE CASE FORMS OF PERSONAL PRONOUNS

Study the following list of pronouns to see how their forms differ in the three cases.

Personal Pronouns

NOMINATIVE CASE	OBJECTIVE CASE	POSSESSIVE CASE
Singular		
I	me	my, mine
you	you	your, yours
he, she, it	him, her, it	his, her, hers, its
Plural		
we	us	our, ours
you	you	your, yours
they	them	their, theirs

The pronouns *you* and *it* cause few usage problems because their forms remain unchanged in the nominative and objective cases. The possessive case forms, which show ownership or relationship, need care in spelling. (See pages 383–84.) Omitting *you* and *it* and the possessive pronouns from the above list leaves the following pronouns, which have different forms in the nominative and objective cases. Memorize the list for each case.

NOMINATIVE CASE	OBJECTIVE CASE
I	me
he	him
she	her
we	us
they	them

THE NOMINATIVE CASE

10a. The subject of a verb is in the nominative case.

EXAMPLES **I** like music. [*I* is the subject of the verb *like*.]

He and **she** sold tickets. [*He* and *she* are the subjects of the verb *sold*.]

> **They** called while **we** were away. [*They* is the subject of *called; we* is the subject of *were.*]

Pronoun usage errors occur most frequently when the subject is compound. It is easy to say, "Lois and me study together" when you should say, "Lois and I study together." "Lois and I" is a compound subject. If you test the pronoun by itself with the verb, you can tell which form is correct.

EXAMPLE   Lois and me study together. [me study—nonstandard]
          [I study—standard] Lois and **I** study together.

Use the same test in sentences such as "We girls work together" and "Us girls work together." Use the pronouns alone before the verb. "Us work together" is incorrect. "We work together" is correct; consequently, "We girls work together" is correct.

EXERCISE 1. *Oral Drill.* Practicing Correct Pronoun Usage.
Read the following sentences aloud, stressing the italicized pronouns.

1. *He* and *she* collect seashells.
2. My grandmother and *I* are painting the boat.
3. Both *they* and *we* were frightened.
4. Did Sally or *she* answer the phone?
5. *We* girls are giving a fashion show.
6. *You* and *I* will stay behind.
7. Where are *he* and *she?*
8. My parents and *they* are good friends.
9. *She* and *I* deliver newspapers.
10. Do you and *she* like to fish?

EXERCISE 2. Writing Pronouns in Sentences.   Number your paper 1–10. Beside the proper number, write a pronoun that will correctly fill the blank. Use a variety of pronouns. Do not use *you* or *it*.

EXAMPLE   1. —— and —— will have a debate.
          1. *We, they*

1. Yesterday she and —— went shopping.
2. Our cousins and —— are ready for the race.
3. Neither —— nor Kathy was nominated.
4. —— and Margie have copies of the book.
5. When are —— and —— coming?
6. Everyone remembers when —— won the big game.
7. Someone said that —— and —— are finalists.
8. Did you or —— ride in the hot-air balloon?
9. Both —— and —— gave excellent speeches.
10. Has —— or Eduardo seen that movie?

10b. A predicate nominative is in the nominative case.

A *predicate nominative* is a noun or a pronoun that completes the meaning of a linking verb. A pronoun used as a predicate nominative usually follows a form of the verb *be (am, is, are, was, were)* or a verb phrase ending in *be* or *been,* such as *will be* or *has been*.

Read these examples aloud; stress the boldfaced words.

It may be **she** at the door. [*She* is a predicate nominative following the linking verb *may be.*]

The speakers are **she** and **I.** [*She* and *I* are predicate nominatives following the linking verb *are.*]

Do you think it was **they**? [*They* is a predicate nominative following the linking verb *was.*]

EXERCISE 3. Identifying Correct Pronoun Usage for Predicate Nominatives. Number your paper 1–10. Write the linking verb in each sentence and then write the correct pronoun.

EXAMPLE   1. It was (I, me) at the door.
       1. *was, I*

1. We hoped it was (her, she).
2. That stranger thinks I am (she, her).
3. Luckily, it was not (them, they) in the accident.

4. It could have been (she, her) that he called.
5. Everyone believed it was (we, us) students.
6. It might have been (him, he), but I'm not sure.
7. Our opponents could have been (them, they).
8. I thought it was (they, them) to whom he spoke.
9. If the singer had been (her, she), I would have listened.
10. Was that Claudia or (she, her)?

☞ USAGE NOTE   You should understand two facts about English usage. First, some usages are acceptable in conversational English, but not in written English. Second, from time to time usage changes, so that expressions that were once considered nonstandard may become standard. The application of rule 10b provides examples of both these facts. The expressions *It's me, That's her, It was them,* etc., although they violate the rule and were once considered nonstandard, have now become acceptable spoken English. In writing, however, standard usage still follows the rule except for *It's me,* which is often acceptable and which almost never appears in writing anyway.

SPOKEN   No one would believe it was her. (him, etc.)
WRITTEN   No one would believe it was she. (he, etc.)

Of course, it would be correct to use *she* in speaking, even though *her* is acceptable.

In doing the exercises in this book, base your answers on the usage of written English.

THE OBJECTIVE CASE

10c. Direct and indirect objects of a verb are in the objective case.

EXAMPLES   You surprised **us.** [*Us* is the object of the verb *surprised.*]

Our neighbor gave **her** and **me** a job. [*Her* and *me* are indirect objects; they tell *to whom* our neighbor gave a job.]

The ranger guided **us** boys to the camp. [*Us* is the object of the verb *guided*. Using the pronoun alone after the verb shows that the ranger guided *us* (not *we*) to the camp.]

Most errors in the use of the objective case occur when the object is compound. You can often avoid making an error with a compound object by trying each pronoun separately with the verb, as in the following example.

The representative met (she, her) and (he, him).

NONSTANDARD   The representative met she.
                            The representative met he.

STANDARD   The representative met **her.**
                    The representative met **him.**
                    The representative met **her** and **him.**

EXERCISE 4. *Oral Drill.* Practicing Correct Pronoun Usage for Objects.

Read the following sentences aloud at least twice, stressing the italicized pronouns. When your ear becomes accustomed to hearing the right pronouns, you will be able to choose the correct forms more easily.

1. The hot soup burned Gail and *me*.
2. Karen showed *her* and Allen her houseplants.
3. The dog followed *her* and *him* to school.
4. Did you expect *us* or *them*?
5. The doctor gave *her* and *me* flu shots.
6. The president of the club called *us* girls to a special meeting.
7. Let's help Sarah and *him* with their chores.
8. Have you seen the Romanos or *them*?
9. The mayor thanked you and *him*.
10. The cook made *us* boys a special dessert.

EXERCISE 5. Writing Pronouns as Direct and Indirect Objects. Number your paper 1–10. After the appropriate numbers, write correct pronouns for the blanks in the following sentences. Be sure to use a variety of pronouns, but do not use *you* and *it*. When your answers have been checked, read aloud at least three times the corrected form of each sentence you missed.

EXAMPLE   1. The teacher asked —— some hard questions.
          1. *us*

1. The judges picked —— and —— as the winners.
2. They asked —— and Ms. Shore for permission.
3. Rita can usually find Alberto and —— at our house.
4. Did you know Jarvis and ——?
5. My grandmother helped —— girls make homemade bread.
6. Aunt Aggie took —— and —— to the zoo.
7. The driver left my sister and —— at the corner.
8. Should we call Mark and ——?
9. Do you remember —— and ——?
10. The dog chased Adam and ——.

WRITING APPLICATION:
Using Pronouns Correctly in Compound Subjects and Objects

Have you ever seen someone whose socks didn't match? When you are in a hurry, sometimes it's easy to make a mistake. Pronoun usage errors often occur when writers are in too much of a hurry. These mistakes are particularly easy to make when a subject or an object is compound.

EXAMPLE   Me and Jana waited for a tennis court so that we could play. [The pronoun *me* should not be used as the subject of a verb.]

          Jana and I waited for a tennis court so we could play. [The nominative case pronoun *I* is correct as the subject of the verb *waited*.]

Writing Assignment

Do you have a best friend? Write a paragraph about an incident that involved you and that friend. Supply as many details as you can that make you remember this incident. As you write, include two compound subjects and two compound objects. Underline these constructions. Be sure to use nominative case pronouns for subjects and objective case pronouns for objects.

10d. The object of a preposition is in the objective case.

A prepositional phrase begins with a preposition and ends with an object, which is always a noun or a pronoun. When the object is a pronoun, you must be careful to use the objective case. The following prepositional phrases have their objects printed in boldface.

with **me**	near **her**	except **them**
to **him**	by **us**	for **us**

Most errors in usage occur when the object of the preposition is compound. Notice that in the prepositional phrases in the following exercise all pronouns are in the objective case.

EXERCISE 6. *Oral Drill.* **Practicing Correct Pronoun Usage.**
Read each of the following sentences several times, stressing the correct, italicized pronouns.

1. The safari continued without *her* and *me*.
2. Everyone except *us* counselors had left the camp.
3. We stood beside their families and *them* during the ceremony.
4. Do you have any suggestions for Jane or *me*?
5. The clowns talked to Claire and *him*.
6. Behind *us* girls was a playful bear cub.
7. Give this to either your father or *her*.
8. With the help of Juan and *her,* we built a fire.
9. The group sat in a circle around the scouts and *them* while they danced and sang.
10. There was a spelling bee between *us* and *them*.

EXERCISE 7. Writing Pronouns as Objects of Prepositions in Sentences. Number your paper 1–10. After each number, write the prepositional phrase in the corresponding sentence. Then add a pronoun that will complete the phrase correctly. Use a variety of pronouns, but do not use *you* or *it*.

EXAMPLE 1. We could not find all of ——.

         1. *of them*

1. You always give advice to Bob and ——.
2. I made an appointment for —— and you.
3. There are some seats behind Jenny and ——.
4. No one except —— and Beth was studying.
5. I couldn't have done it without you and ——.
6. Why didn't you speak to —— and Christie?
7. Our team has played soccer against the Jets and ——.
8. I was near you and —— during the parade.
9. Just between you and ——, I think our chances are good.
10. About your cousin and ——, there is no doubt.

REVIEW EXERCISE A. Identifying Correct Pronoun Usage in Sentences. Number your paper 1–20. After the proper number, write the pronoun of the two in parentheses that will make the sentence correct. After each answer, write an abbreviation showing how the pronoun is used: *subj., p.n., d.o., i.o., obj. prep.*

EXAMPLE 1. Say hello to (she, her) and Ann.

         1. *her, obj. prep.*

1. The mayor congratulated (we, us) volunteers for our effort.
2. The election resulted in a tie between Diane and (he, him).
3. Last year's winner was (she, her).
4. Where should you and (I, me) meet after school?
5. The audience clapped for (he, him) and Ned.
6. (We, Us) sisters should help Dad with the lawn.
7. The best singer in the choir is (she, her).
8. We beat Betty and (they, them) at tennis.
9. The poet dedicated the book to Greg and (she, her).

10. The film editor showed the visitors and (we, us) students around the television station.
11. Deborah and (he, him) will recite next.
12. Have you given Arlene and (they, them) directions?
13. Please invite your cousin and (they, them) to the horse show this Saturday.
14. She sewed Aunt Elsie and (I, me) matching vests.
15. The one by the yellow car is (he, him).
16. The officer gave (we, us) girls a ride to the gas station.
17. The oldest members are Jerry and (she, her).
18. Tomorrow you and (they, them) can distribute posters.
19. I was standing by Consuelo and (she, her).
20. For English class I wrote a story about my great-grandmother and (he, him).

REVIEW EXERCISE B. Writing Sentences with Pronouns. Write ten original sentences, using the following pronouns correctly. After each sentence, identify the use of the pronoun or pronouns: *subj., p.n., d.o, i.o., obj. prep.*

1. you and I
2. you and me
3. her friend and she
4. his friend and him
5. him and her
6. Gail and they
7. us students
8. our parents and we
9. Susan and her
10. our teacher and us

REVIEW EXERCISE C. Identifying Correct Pronoun Usage. Number your paper 1–20. After the proper number, write the correct one of the two pronouns in parentheses.

EXAMPLE 1. It was news to (I, me).
1. *me*

1. Craig and (he, him) are washing the car.
2. Honorable mention was given to Mary and (I, me).
3. The first speakers will be you and (she, her).
4. Members of the decorating committee for the dance include four juniors and (we, us).

5. Everyone except Steve and (I, me) will be at the game.
6. Did you get these books from Cindy or (she, her)?
7. She will tell (we, us) runners when to line up.
8. It was (they, them) who rescued you.
9. That could have been (they, them) at the store.
10. The Jensens and (we, us) watched the fireworks display.
11. The studio sent (she, her) and her husband to Argentina.
12. The cartoonist made a sketch of Ida and (she, her).
13. The counselors lent (we, us) girls their canoe.
14. Both Erica and (she, her) speak French.
15. That set of piggy banks came from Amanda and (he, him).
16. The girls in the ticket booth are (they, them).
17. Did you call Sharon and (I, me)?
18. Hank and (I, me) have invited our parents.
19. It's always (we, us) girls who are early.
20. Never argue with (she, her) and Julie.

CHAPTER 10 REVIEW POSTTEST 1

Using Pronouns Correctly in Sentences. Number your paper 1–25. After the proper number, write the correct one of the two pronouns in parentheses.

EXAMPLE 1. For some time after the game had ended, we could still hear (they, them) cheering.
1. *them*

1. My sister June and (I, me) are getting our own rooms.
2. The basketball bounced off the rim and hit (she, her) on the forehead.
3. Don't send (they, them) an invitation to the party.
4. The only one who hasn't had a turn is (he, him).
5. The ranger showed (we, us) scouts around the wildlife preserve.
6. Ramon brought his camera and took pictures of Dennis and (I, me).

7. My father's company transferred (he, him) to another city.
8. Neither Clay nor (we, us) could tell the difference between the twins.
9. Could it have been (they, them) who did that?
10. The cook gave an extra portion to (he, him).
11. Why didn't Isa and (I, me) get second servings?
12. Mr. Willis sent (I, me) here to pick up his order.
13. The player that has the highest average is (she, her).
14. The rain nearly blinded (we, us) when we were caught outdoors.
15. The entire class was punished on account of (she, her).
16. (We, Us) cheerleaders have a lot of fun.
17. As Jackson was walking in back of (we, us), he spilled his milk down my back.
18. They heard the special twang of the guitar and knew that it must be (he, him).
19. Have you told (they, them) about the dance on Friday?
20. One of the winners, I hope, will be (I, me).
21. Tell (we, us) the secret of your success.
22. The man in the car asked if Dinah and (she, her) knew how to get to the mall.
23. We were all waiting for Mr. Burch to give (we, us) the assignment.
24. Didn't you forget to call Charlene and (she, her)?
25. Since I don't feel well, you'd better go on without (I, me).

CHAPTER 10 REVIEW: POSTTEST 2

Determining the Proper Case of Pronouns in Sentences.
Number your paper 1–25. Most of the following sentences contain an incorrect pronoun. After the proper number, write the incorrect pronoun and then its correct form. If the sentence is correct, write *C*.

EXAMPLE   1. The teacher told Jim and I to stop talking.
            1. *I—me*

1. Several people have asked if you and me are related.
2. The winning science project had been entered by Shannon and he.
3. That announcer always irritates my father and I.
4. Did you give she the answer?
5. The last person I would have suspected was him.
6. Let's ask Neil and him for help.
7. The coach taught we linemen not to budge an inch.
8. We split the pie between him and I.
9. Shirley and him generously donated their time to the fund drive.
10. The ones who deserve a reward are the Thompsons and them.
11. After they had read the inscription, they awarded she the plaque.
12. Us teammates have to stick together, right?
13. When my mother finally found me sitting on the curb, she was mad at me.
14. Would they suggest what Irene and me should make for dinner?
15. The shop teacher said he was particularly pleased with Ling and I.
16. Why don't they give we girls a chance?
17. At the movies we met Julia and she while buying popcorn.
18. The strongest discus thrower we have is him.
19. I am afraid that you will have to go to the lake without Ben and I.
20. Why does the teacher always assign she the easiest reports?
21. Was that Hank or him?
22. Both of my brothers and him promised to take me along.
23. My mother never tires of telling Mary Anne and I what it was like when she was our age.
24. We happened to be standing next to Elijah and her when the lightning struck.
25. The people who stand to gain the most are them.

Using Modifiers Correctly

COMPARISON AND PLACEMENT

You know from your study of Chapters 2 and 3 that adjectives and adverbs are called modifiers. A modifier describes or makes more definite the meaning of another word. Adjectives modify nouns or pronouns, and adverbs modify verbs, adjectives, or other adverbs. You also know from your study of Chapters 5 and 6 that phrases and clauses, as well as individual words, may be used as modifiers. This chapter will help you learn to use modifiers more correctly and effectively.

DIAGNOSTIC TEST

A. Using the Correct Comparative and Superlative Forms. Number your paper 1–10. The following sentences contain errors in the use of comparison modifiers. After the proper number, write the incorrect words from each sentence. Then write the correct form, adding or omitting words if necessary. In some cases you may need to write the entire sentence.

EXAMPLES 1. Sara is more neater than her sister is.
      1. *more neater—neater*
      2. I never get to have no fun.
      2. *never, no—I never get to have fun.*

1. Of all the carnival rides, the roller coaster was the most funnest.
2. Alan thinks that this pie tastes gooder than the others.
3. I couldn't hardly believe she said that.
4. Yoshi is the tallest of the twins.
5. The detective kept getting curiouser about the suspect's alibi.
6. The movie doesn't cost much, but I don't have no money.
7. They offer so many combinations that I don't know which one I like more.
8. The house on Drury Avenue is the one we like the bestest.
9. There's nothing I like more better than barbecued ribs.
10. Why doesn't the teacher give us questions that are more easier?

B. Revising Sentences by Correcting Misplaced and Dangling Modifiers.

Each of the following sentences contains a dangling or misplaced modifier in italics. After the proper number, revise each sentence by placing the italicized modifier where it will make the meaning of the sentence logical and clear. In some cases you will need to add or omit words.

EXAMPLE 1. *Waiting at the curb for the bus,* a car splashed water on me.
   1. *Waiting at the curb for the bus, I had water splashed on me by a car.*
   or
   1. *A car splashed water on me while I was waiting at the curb for a bus.*

11. *Under the doormat,* I looked for the key.
12. The library has several books about dinosaurs *in our school.*
13. *Sleeping soundly,* Howard woke his father when supper was ready.
14. We did not know one person at the party *who was there.*
15. Aunt Joan sent away a coupon for a free recipe book *in a magazine.*

16. *From where I was standing,* the truck crossed the yellow line and smashed into the fence.
17. *Left alone for the first time in his life,* strange sounds in the night scared my little brother.
18. Many people go to the beach or the mountains *when they are on vacation.*
19. *Often slaughtered only for their tusks,* many African nations prohibit the hunting of elephants.
20. *Sitting in the bleachers,* the outfielder caught the ball right in front of us.

GOOD AND WELL

11a. Distinguish between *good* and *well* as modifiers.

Use *good* to modify a noun or a pronoun; never use *good* to modify a verb. Use *well* to modify a verb.

NONSTANDARD   Doris bowls good.
   STANDARD   Doris bowls **well.**

NONSTANDARD   The orchestra played very good.
   STANDARD   The orchestra played very **well.**

In the following examples, *good* is correct because it is a predicate adjective modifying the subject. Like all predicate adjectives, it follows a linking verb.

STANDARD   The pie tastes especially **good.** [good pie]
STANDARD   Over the microphone her voice sounds **good.** [good voice]

Well can also be used as an adjective when it refers to a person's health or appearance.

EXAMPLES   Doug feels **well** today. [*Well* is a predicate adjective modifying the subject *Doug.*]
           You look **well** in red. [*Well* is a predicate adjective modifying the subject *you.*]

EXERCISE 1. *Oral Drill.* **Practicing the Correct Use of the Modifier** *Well.* Read aloud each of the following sentences, stressing the italicized words. This exercise will train your ear and check your tendency to use *good* as the modifier of a verb.

1. Everyone did *well* on the test.
2. We work *well* together.
3. Do you sing as *well* as your sister does?
4. I can't water-ski very *well*.
5. How *well* can you write?
6. The pilot landed the plane *well*.
7. All went *well* until the actor forgot his lines.
8. Our class pictures turned out *well*.
9. The freshman quarterback can pass as *well* as the senior.
10. The plans for the square dance are working out quite *well*.

EXERCISE 2. Identifying the Correct Use of *Good* **and** *Well.* Number your paper 1–10. If *good* or *well* is correctly used in a sentence, write *C* after the corresponding number. If *good* or *well* is not correctly used, write the correct word.

EXAMPLE 1. We danced good at the recital.
           1. *well*

1. Peg did not run as good during the second race.
2. The casserole tasted good to us.
3. How good does she play the part?
4. I didn't answer the questions very well.
5. He certainly looks well in spite of his illness.
6. I gave them directions as well as I could.
7. The children behaved very good.
8. Spinach salad always tastes good to them.
9. The debate did not go as good as we had hoped.
10. How good the pool looks on such a hot day!

COMPARISON OF MODIFIERS

Adjectives and adverbs may be used in comparing two or more things.

Richard is **heavier** than Bob.
This is the **heaviest** box of the three.

Maria spoke **more clearly** than Alicia.
Of all the speakers, Hazel spoke **most clearly**.

When adjectives and adverbs are used to make comparisons, they express degrees of comparison. *Degrees of comparison* show the degree to which one word states a quality, as compared with another word that states the same quality.

This building is **tall**.
This building is **taller** than that one.
This building is the **tallest** one in the world.

I ski **frequently**.
I ski **more frequently** than she does.
Of the three of us, I ski **most frequently**.

11b. There are three degrees of comparison of modifiers: *positive, comparative,* and *superlative.*

POSITIVE	COMPARATIVE	SUPERLATIVE
weak	weaker	weakest
ancient	more ancient	most ancient
loud	louder	loudest
loudly	more loudly	most loudly
good	better	best
bad	worse	worst

There are two regular ways to compare modifiers. To form the comparative degree, the letters *–er* may be added to the end of a word, or the word *more* may precede it. To form the superlative, the letters *–est* may be added to the end of a word, or the word *most* may precede it.

(1) Most one-syllable modifiers form their comparative and superlative degrees by adding *–er* and *–est*.

POSITIVE	COMPARATIVE	SUPERLATIVE
near	nearer	nearest
meek	meeker	meekest

(2) Some two-syllable modifiers form their comparative and superlative degrees by adding _-er_ and _-est,_ but most two-syllable modifiers form their comparative and superlative degrees by means of _more_ and _most._

POSITIVE	COMPARATIVE	SUPERLATIVE
simple	simpler	simplest
drowsy	drowsier	drowsiest
modern	more modern	most modern
pleasant	more pleasant	most pleasant

When you are in doubt about which way a modifier forms its degrees of comparison, consult a dictionary.

(3) Modifiers having three or more syllables form their comparative and superlative degrees by means of _more_ and _most._

POSITIVE	COMPARATIVE	SUPERLATIVE
ignorant	more ignorant	most ignorant
happily	more happily	most happily

EXERCISE 3. Forming the Degrees of Comparison of Modifiers. Write the forms for the comparative and superlative degrees of the following modifiers:

EXAMPLE   1. long
            1. _longer, longest_

1. slow
2. cautious
3. agilely
4. thankful
5. possible
6. short
7. easy
8. confident
9. forcefully
10. plain

(4) Comparisons to indicate _less_ and _least_ of a quality are accomplished by using the words _less_ and _least_ before the modifier.

POSITIVE	COMPARATIVE	SUPERLATIVE
skillful	less skillful	least skillful
delicate	less delicate	least delicate

Irregular Comparison

When adjectives and adverbs do not follow the regular methods of forming their comparative and superlative degrees, they are said to be compared irregularly. You should learn the comparative and superlative degrees of these five modifiers:

POSITIVE	COMPARATIVE	SUPERLATIVE
bad	worse	worst
good	better	best
well	better	best
many	more	most
much	more	most

REVIEW EXERCISE A. Writing the Comparative and Superlative Degrees of Modifiers. Write the comparative and superlative degrees of the following modifiers. When in doubt about words of two syllables, consult a dictionary.

EXAMPLE 1. wasteful
     1. *more wasteful, most wasteful*

1. sheepish
2. simply
3. much
4. surely
5. gracious
6. quick
7. weary
8. suddenly
9. many
10. frequently
11. furious
12. enthusiastic
13. easily
14. tasty
15. generous
16. hot
17. good
18. well
19. near
20. old

Use of Comparative and Superlative Forms

11c. Use the *comparative* degree when comparing two things; use the *superlative* when comparing three or more.

Comparing two things:
> The second problem is **harder** than the first.
> She is **more studious** than her sister.
> This book is **more carefully** written than that one.

Comparing three or more things:
> This road is the **narrowest** of the three we've traveled.

Of all the performers, she was the **best.**
This is the **simplest** recipe for bread that I've seen.

Most mistakes in the use of modifiers are made when two things are being compared. Remember that the comparative degree should be used when two things are compared.

NONSTANDARD   Of the two soups, this is the best one.
STANDARD   Of the two soups, this is the **better** one.

NONSTANDARD   Marie is the youngest of the two girls.
STANDARD   Marie is the **younger** of the two girls.

When comparing one thing with a group to which it belongs, do not omit the word *other*.

NONSTANDARD   She is taller than any girl on her team. [She is a member of her team, and she obviously cannot be taller than herself.]
STANDARD   She is taller than any **other** girl on her team.

WRITING APPLICATION A:
Using Modifiers Correctly When Comparing Two Things

It's fun to have a friend come over to spend the night. Perhaps your parents let you put up a tent in the backyard or let you roll out sleeping bags in front of the TV. Sometimes, though, it's difficult to decide which friend to invite. When you narrow your decision down to *two* people and then select one, you make comparisons. To form the comparative degree of a modifier, you add –*er* to the end of the word or use the word *more* before it.

EXAMPLES   My new room is *bigger* than my old room.
I think soccer is *more* exciting than basketball.

Writing Assignment

Select two books, two movies, or two TV shows that interest you. Write a comparison of the two. Use comparative forms to give specific reasons why you prefer the one to the other. Proofread for inaccuracies in the use of modifiers.

11d. Avoid the double comparison.

A *double comparison* occurs when *–er* or *–est* is added to a modifier and, at the same time, the modifier is preceded by *more* or *most*. Words should be compared in only one of these two ways; you should never use both ways at the same time.

NONSTANDARD   Our dog is more smaller than yours.
  STANDARD   Our dog is **smaller** than yours.

NONSTANDARD   It was the most beautifulest waterfall I had ever seen.
  STANDARD   It was the **most beautiful** waterfall I had ever seen.

EXERCISE 4. Identifying Correct Usage of Degrees of Comparison. Number your paper 1–10. Write *C* after the number of each correct sentence. After the number of each incorrect sentence, revise the sentence, using the correct form of comparison.

EXAMPLE   1. It's the most homeliest dog in the world.
        1. *It's the homeliest dog in the world.*

1. The rehearsals are getting more longer every day.
2. Judith, the pitcher, is worse at bat than any member of the team.
3. That modern sculpture is the most strangest that I've ever seen.
4. After watching the two kittens for a few minutes, Rudy chose the most playful one.
5. This morning was more sunnier than this afternoon.
6. Your cough sounds worser today.
7. The music on this album is better for dancing than the music on that one.

8. New York City has a larger population than any city in the United States.
9. I can see more better with my new glasses.
10. She was the most talented singer in the show.

EXERCISE 5. Writing Sentences with Comparatives and Superlatives. Use the first five words as modifiers in sentences comparing two things. Use the second five in sentences comparing three or more things.

1. well   4. cold   7. carefully   9. clever
2. nosy   5. unexpected   8. often   10. polite
3. useful   6. dreary

THE DOUBLE NEGATIVE

Words like the following ones are called negatives: *no, not, none, never, no one, nothing, hardly, scarcely.* (Notice that many negatives begin with the letter *n.*). When such a word is used in a sentence, it makes an important change in the meaning.

I have found the wallet that I lost.
I have **never** found the wallet that I lost.

11e. Avoid the use of double negatives.

We often make negative statements such as "I never ran in a race." Negative statements in standard English require only one negative word. Use of more than one negative word is called a *double negative.* For example, the sentence "I never ran in no race" contains a double negative. Double negatives are considered nonstandard English.

NONSTANDARD   We don't have no extra chairs.
STANDARD   We have **no** extra chairs.
STANDARD   We **don't** have any extra chairs.

NONSTANDARD   He couldn't hardly talk.
STANDARD   He **could hardly** talk.

EXERCISE 6. Correcting Sentences with Double Negatives. Revise the following sentences, eliminating the double negatives.

EXAMPLE 1. We don't hardly have time to relax.
1. *We hardly have time to relax.*
or *We don't have time to relax.*

1. Josie hasn't never been to Tennessee.
2. Because of the heavy rain, we couldn't scarcely find our way home.
3. He never had no problem with public speaking.
4. The athletes don't hardly have a break between events.
5. Don't use no forks to get toast out of the toaster.
6. By the time I had made sandwiches for everyone else, I didn't have nothing left for me.
7. I never hardly listen to gossip.
8. Your answer doesn't make no difference to me.
9. Don't never say *not* and *scarcely* together.
10. The goalie doesn't have no excuse.

WRITING APPLICATION B:
Using Modifiers Correctly When Comparing More Than Two Things

All through your life you are faced with decisions. Some are just small decisions, such as whether to order chicken, beef, or fish. Other decisions, however, such as whether to go to college, get a job, or volunteer for military service, can be much more serious. When you are describing a decision involving more than two options, use the superlative degree of modifiers instead of the comparative degree.

EXAMPLE I plan to work with children. Of the three activities, teacher helper, candy striper, and camp assistant, I think being a teacher helper will best prepare me for my career. [The use of the modifier *best* is correct because more than two things are being compared.]

Writing Assignment

Even though graduation is a long way off, you may have given some thought to what you would like to do after you graduate. Sometimes your goal can affect what subjects you take in high school. Select three possible career choices. Write a paragraph comparing these three. Based on this comparison, indicate which job you think would suit you best. Remember to use the superlative degree for your modifiers.

REVIEW EXERCISE B. Correcting Improperly Used Modifiers. Revise the incorrect sentences in the following exercise, eliminating errors in the use of modifiers. If a sentence is correct, write *C* after the corresponding number. You should have thirteen revised sentences.

EXAMPLE 1. We don't never stay after school.
           1. *We never stay after school.*

1. Rick is the most smartest boy in science class.
2. Which did you like best—the book or the movie?
3. Gina has more ideas for the festival than anyone else has.
4. Since the defeat, we have worked more harder.
5. I can't hardly reason with her.
6. Jean and Frank work good as a team.
7. Jim was the stronger swimmer of the two.
8. Lana's bruise looks worse today than it did yesterday.
9. Inga is the best dancer of the pair.
10. They haven't said nothing to us about it.
11. Carlos did so well in his speech that other groups have invited him to speak.
12. Of the two singers, Rose has the best voice.
13. Which has better sound, your stereo or mine?
14. Sean doesn't want nothing to do with the plan.
15. The cast performed extremely well.
16. Which of the four desks is the sturdiest?
17. Asia is much more larger than Australia.

18. Which of the two videotapes plays longest?
19. Whenever we see her, she seems more funny.
20. Lewis is more politer than Dan.

PLACEMENT OF MODIFIERS

Notice how the meaning of the following sentence changes when the phrase *from Canada* is moved about in the sentence.

> The professor **from Canada** gave a televised lecture on famous writers.
> The professor gave a televised lecture on famous writers **from Canada.**
> The professor gave a televised lecture **from Canada** on famous writers.

The first of the three sentences above says that the *professor* was from Canada; the second sentence, that the *famous writers* were from Canada; the third, that the *televised lecture* came from Canada. As you can see, shifting the position of the modifying phrase has resulted in important changes in meaning.

11f. Place modifying phrases and clauses so that they clearly and sensibly modify a word in the sentence.

Prepositional Phrases

You know that prepositional phrases are used as adjectives and adverbs. To make a sentence clear and sensible, you should place a prepositional phrase near the word it modifies.

☞ NOTE As was said on page 118, adverb phrases are more flexible than adjective phrases and do not have to come immediately after the modified word. However, to avoid confusion, an adverb phrase should be placed near the modified word. Often, as in the second standard sentence in the following examples, it precedes the modified word.

NONSTANDARD The vase was set in the middle of the table with flowers. [*With flowers* should go with *vase*, not *table*.]

STANDARD The vase **with flowers** was set in the middle of the table.

NONSTANDARD I read about the lost puppy that was found in today's newspaper. [The puppy was not found in the newspaper.]

STANDARD **In today's newspaper** I read about the lost puppy that was found.

Be careful to avoid having a prepositional phrase come between two words that it might modify. Instead, place it next to the *one* word that you intend it to modify.

UNCLEAR She said in the morning she was going to Chicago.

CLEAR She said she was going to Chicago **in the morning.**

CLEAR **In the morning** she said she was going to Chicago.

EXERCISE 7. Identifying the Appropriate Placement of Modifiers.
The meaning of each of the following sentences is not clear and sensible, because the modifying phrase is in the wrong place. Decide where the phrase belongs; then revise the sentence.

EXAMPLE 1. I read about the satellite that was launched in the news today.

1. *I read in the news today about the satellite that was launched.*

1. The nature photographer told us about filming a herd of water buffalo in class today.
2. Inside the ring we watched the antics of a comical dancing bear.
3. The robotic mannequins drew a huge crowd in the futuristic window display.
4. Hundreds of people were watching the show in their cars.
5. The assignment required three articles from magazines on the Statue of Liberty.

6. My aunt promised me on Saturday she would take me to the symphony.
7. There is one gymnast who can tumble as well as vault on the gymnastics team.
8. The marathon runner twisted his ankle with the blue T-shirt.
9. The model posed gracefully in front of the statue in the designer gown.
10. We saw the trapeze artist swinging dangerously through our field binoculars.

Participial Phrases

A participial phrase, like an adjective, modifies a noun or pronoun. When a participial phrase begins the sentence, it modifies the noun or pronoun immediately following it. Notice that the participial phrases below are separated from the other parts of the sentences by commas. (For a review of participles, see page 123.)

EXAMPLES **Screaming wildly,** the bandits chased the stage-coach.

Arriving after the others, we waited until intermission to be seated.

When you begin a sentence with a participial phrase, you should be sure that it modifies the noun or pronoun that immediately follows it; otherwise, your sentence will have a *dangling participle.* A dangling participle is a participle that is not closely connected to the noun or pronoun it modifies.

DANGLING Coming in for a landing, the tower contacted the plane. [The participial phrase dangles because the *tower* was not coming in for a landing.]

CORRECTED **Coming in for a landing,** the plane was radioed by the tower.

CORRECTED The tower radioed the plane **coming in for a landing.**

DANGLING	Broken in many pieces, I saw my watch lying on the floor. [The participial phrase dangles because *I* was not broken in many pieces.]
CORRECTED	**Broken in many pieces,** my watch was lying on the floor.

EXERCISE 8. Identifying the Correct Placement of Participial Phrases in Sentences.

All of the following sentences contain participial phrases. Some of the sentences are nonsensical or awkward because they contain dangling participial phrases. If a sentence is correct, write *C* after the proper number. Revise all incorrect sentences so that the participial phrases modify the right words. (You may have to supply some words.) A participial phrase beginning a sentence should be followed by a comma.

EXAMPLE   1. Dressed in our costumes, the police officer waved to us clowns.

         1. *The police officer waved to us clowns dressed in our costumes.*

1. Standing on the dock, a boat almost sank right in front of us.
2. Exploring the old house, Janet and Patty found a secret passageway.
3. Having bolted the cabin door, the hungry bear never really frightened us.
4. Punctured by a nail, I had to repair my bicycle tire.
5. Surrounded by reporters, many questions were asked of the governor.
6. Suffering from blisters, the race was lost by last year's winner.
7. After practicing for several hours, my recital for tonight was ready.
8. The old suit hanging in the closet would make the perfect costume for the play.
9. Balancing precariously on the wire, the tightrope walker performed amazing tricks.

282 < Using Modifiers Correctly

10. Exhausted after our exercises, a tall, cool glass of water was what we craved.

EXERCISE 9. Writing Sentences with Introductory Participial Phrases. Use correctly the following introductory participial phrases in sentences of your own.

EXAMPLE   1. Sitting near the stage,
             1. *Sitting near the stage, I was able to see the dancers clearly.*

1. Locked in the old trunk,
2. Hanging from the ceiling,
3. Expecting a phone call from her boyfriend,
4. Almost lost in the confusion,
5. Looking toward the sunset,
6. Driving by the park,
7. Not wanting a gift,
8. Destined for a future in the spotlight,
9. Responding to the emergency call,
10. Inspired by the speech,

Clauses

Like modifying phrases, adjective and adverb clauses should be placed as close as possible to the words they modify. Notice in the following examples how the confusion resulting from misplaced clauses is cleared up when the clauses are placed near the words they modify.

MISPLACED   My parents traded an old television for a new tape recorder that they no longer wanted. [The parents no longer wanted the new tape recorder?]

CORRECTED   My parents traded an old television **that they no longer wanted** for a new tape recorder.

MISPLACED   The book was about insects that we read. [Did you read the insects?]

CORRECTED   The book **that we read** was about insects.

EXERCISE 10. Correcting the Placement of Clauses in Sentences. Read each of the following sentences. Decide which word the misplaced clause should modify; then write the sentence, placing the clause near the right word.

EXAMPLE
1. I retyped the first draft on clean paper which I had corrected.
1. *I retyped the first draft, which I had corrected, on clean paper.*

1. The soldiers were far from their base camp who had volunteered for the mission.
2. We tiptoed over the ice in our heavy boots, which had begun to crack.
3. The spaniel belongs to my friend Bernie that won the dog show.
4. Several gospel songs were presented at yesterday's assembly that were often sung by Mary Lou Williams.
5. The telethon had achieved its goal that ran for thirty-six hours.
6. The game was canceled by the two schools that was scheduled for tomorrow.
7. The strange messenger gave Mr. Johnson a dozen balloons who was dressed as a chicken.
8. When I worked in the school office, I typed a report for the principal that was sixty pages long.
9. My married sister Becky came for the weekend to see me who lives in Michigan.
10. The documentary was filmed at several locations which will be broadcast in the fall.

REVIEW EXERCISE C. Identifying the Correct Use of Modifiers in Sentences. In each of the following sentences, a modifier is used incorrectly. The mistake may result from (1) a confusion of *good* and *well*, (2) incorrect comparison, (3) the use of a double negative, or (4) a dangling or misplaced modifier. Revise the sentences, correcting the mistakes.

EXAMPLE 1. This one is the most interesting of the two articles.
    1. *This one is the more interesting of the two articles.*

1. During last night's concert, the singing group was protected from being swarmed by guards.
2. You can't hardly imagine how upset some of the fans were by these measures.
3. Attempting to raise money for the homeless, many sad songs were sung by the group.
4. Their recorded interviews with homeless people also worked very good for raising contributions.
5. However, the group itself attracted the most biggest crowd of people on the road tour.
6. Sometimes the group sang their old hits, and other times they introduced new songs that had made them famous.
7. Years ago the singers wore strange costumes and makeup so that fans couldn't hardly tell what their faces looked like.
8. Using brilliant strobe lights, the identities of the singers had been hidden.
9. When the fans began to tire of these gimmicks, the singers tried out a new look who were also tired of the gimmickry.
10. They finally chose the most simply tailored look of the two they had considered.
11. Warned about the fickleness of fans, a different style of singing was also practiced by the group.
12. Few fans could tell the first time they appeared in public after changing their style how nervous the singers were.
13. "That was the most scariest performance of my career," one singer remarked.
14. Without makeup, the audience had seen the singers' faces for the first time.
15. The audience relieved the singers' fears when they cheered heartily.

16. Taking a chance on the group's new image, a great deal of money was raised by the concert's organizers.
17. Of all the benefit concerts, the one last night earned the most highest amount for the city's homeless people.
18. Encouraged by last night's success, many other concerts for good causes are being planned by the group.
19. Both the concert and the fund raising ended exceptionally good.
20. Fans will likely be seeing benefit concerts that are more larger than that one in the future.

CHAPTER 11 REVIEW: POSTTEST 1

A. Using the Correct Comparative and Superlative Forms. Number your paper 1–15. The following sentences contain errors in the use of comparison modifiers. After the proper number, write the incorrect word or words from the sentence. Then write the correct form, adding or omitting words if necessary. In some cases you may need to write the entire sentence.

EXAMPLES 1. This has been one of the worstest days in my life.
    1. *worstest—worst*
    2. They don't know nothing about that.
    2. *don't, nothing—They know nothing about that.*
        or *They don't know anything about that.*

1. Move that chair over more nearer to the wall.
2. Peaches, pears, and apples all taste good, but I like apples better.
3. Most of the class couldn't hardly finish on time.
4. There are few things more worse to drink than sour milk.
5. My father said I can't go over there no more.
6. She is a better fielder than any player on the team.

7. The king cobra is one of the most deadliest snakes in the world.
8. Which do you like best, boots or loafers?
9. Mattie didn't want none of the peaches.
10. I don't think Ms. Bains is more nicer than Mr. Jones.
11. That meal tastes worse than any meal I've ever eaten.
12. She tested both perfumes on her wrist and decided that the first one, Moonlit Jungle, was best.
13. The boulder was so big that the bulldozer couldn't hardly budge it.
14. What crop grows better here—corn, wheat, or rice?
15. My sister likes iced lemonade better than any cold drink.

B. Revising Sentences by Correcting Misplaced and Dangling Modifiers.

Each of the following sentences contains an italicized dangling or misplaced modifier. After the proper number, revise each sentence by placing the italicized modifier where it will make the meaning of the sentence logical and clear. In some cases you will need to add or omit words.

EXAMPLE 1. *On the way home from school,* Mom asked me to stop at the store and pick up a loaf of bread.
　　　　 1. *Mom asked me to stop at the store on the way home from school and pick up a loaf of bread.*

16. Mario explored the woods that stretch all the way down to the lake *last Saturday.*
17. The witness told her side of the story, facing the jury *giving all the details.*
18. The huge herds of bison ranged across the open prairies *which railroad passengers gunned down for sport.*
19. *Carried away in a stream of water,* I lost my gold bracelet down the drain.
20. *Taking a rest break,* the cool breeze refreshed us.
21. The porcupine sat stubbornly in the road *with its tail poised to attack.*
22. The warriors killed the rogue lion *from the village.*

23. Phan found something she liked in every state *traveling around the country.*
24. *In spite of our differences,* a compromise was worked out.
25. The concert had to be postponed until next week, *which will feature my favorite band.*

CHAPTER 11 REVIEW: POSTTEST 2

A. Using the Correct Comparative and Superlative Forms. Number your paper 1–15. The sentences in the following paragraphs contain double negatives and errors in the use of comparative and superlative modifiers. After the proper number, write the incorrect word or words. Then write the correct form, adding or omitting words if necessary.

EXAMPLES 1. We don't want none of that food.
           1. *don't, none—We don't want any of that food.*
           2. Gail was even more later than I was.
           2. *more later—later*

(1) The wonderfullest place in the whole world is my grandmother's house. (2) We used to live there when we didn't have no apartment of our own. (3) Since her house is bigger than any house in the neighborhood, we all had plenty of room. (4) My grandmother was glad to have us stay because my dad can fix things so that they're gooder than new. (5) He plastered and painted the walls in one bedroom so that I wouldn't have to share a room no more with my sister. (6) I don't know which was best—having so much space of my own or having privacy from my sister.

(7) My grandmother can sew better than anybody can. (8) She taught my sister and me how to make the beautifullest clothes. (9) She has three sewing machines and my mother has one, but I like Grandma's older one better. (10) We started with the more simpler kinds of stitches. (11) After my sister and I could do those, Grandma showed us elaborater stitches and sewing tricks. (12) For instance, she taught us to wrap thread behind buttons we

sew on so that they will be more easier to button. (13) We learned how to make dresses, skirts, blouses, and all sorts of things, until now there isn't hardly nothing we can't make.

(14) I was sad when we left Grandma's house, but I like our new apartment more better than I thought I would. (15) Luckily, we moved to a place near my grandmother's, and after school I can go over there or go home—whichever I want to do most.

B. Revising Sentences by Correcting Misplaced and Dangling Modifiers.

Each of the following sentences contains a misplaced modifier or a dangling modifier. After the proper number, revise each sentence by placing the misplaced or dangling modifier where it will make the meaning of the sentence logical and clear. In some cases you will need to add or omit words.

EXAMPLE 1. Tearing away his umbrella, Mr. Perez became drenched in the storm.
1. *Tearing away his umbrella, the storm drenched Mr. Perez.*

16. Our teacher told us that she had been a nurse in class today.
17. The woman helped us who runs the store.
18. Destroyed by the fire, the man looked sadly at the charred house.
19. To get to school on time after missing the bus my mother gave me a ride in the car.
20. The fox escaped from the hounds pursuing him with a crafty maneuver.
21. Walking through the park, the squirrels chattered at me.
22. My uncle lives in Germany who is in the Army.
23. The squid fascinated the students preserved in formaldehyde.
24. Keeping track of the race with binoculars, the blue car with a yellow roof pulled into the lead.
25. We watched the snow pile up in drifts inside our warm house.

Glossary of Usage

COMMON USAGE PROBLEMS

This chapter contains a short glossary of English usage, supplementing the material in Chapters 8–11. The words and expressions in this glossary are listed in alphabetical order so that you can find them easily. You may, if you wish, study the glossary and use the exercises at the end of the chapter to test your knowledge of the various items. However, the glossary is included in the book mainly for you to use as a reference when you are uncertain about a question of usage.

Several kinds of usage problems are treated in this glossary. Some require the writer or speaker to choose between two words, according to the meaning intended. Others involve a choice between two words in which one word is less acceptable than the other. A few of the words and expressions discussed here should be avoided altogether. (Spelling problems arising from the confusion of similar words are treated in Chapter 29.)

DIAGNOSTIC TEST

Revising Sentences by Correcting Errors in Usage. In each of the following sets of sentences, one sentence contains an error in usage. After the proper number, write the letter of the sentence that contains an error, and revise the sentence. Make sure that your revisions follow standard formal usage.

EXAMPLE 1. (a) I rode a unicycle. (b) Everyone came except Michael. (c) The side affects of the medicine are well know.

   1. *(c) The side effects of the medicine are well known.*

1. (a) They bought themselves new pens. (b) The balloon busted. (c) Use less flour.
2. (a) She did not feel well. (b) Jack ought to help us. (c) John hisself bought that.
3. (a) Tom could of come. (b) This book has fewer pages. (c) He sang well.
4. (a) We had already been there. (b) She feels alright now. (c) We looked everywhere for him.
5. (a) He behaved badly. (b) She felt badly about being late. (c) There is no talking between classes.
6. (a) We saved ten dollars between the four of us. (b) Bring a salad when you come. (c) The chair broke.
7. (a) She set down. (b) This news may affect his decision. (c) They left less milk for me.
8. (a) I cannot go unless I finish my work first. (b) Your my friend. (c) She laid the packages on the table.
9. (a) My father use to play the piano. (b) We have a long way to go. (c) Yesterday I read in the newspaper that the governor is in town.
10. (a) I know how come she left. (b) It's windy. (c) He likes this kind of movie.
11. (a) I am somewhat hungry. (b) Will you learn me how to ski? (c) Do as the leader does.
12. (a) She looks as though she is exhausted. (b) Meet me outside of the building. (c) He wrote the letter and mailed it.
13. (a) The reason he works is that he wants to save money for a trip. (b) Your backhand has improved somewhat. (c) Their are not enough chairs.

14. (a) I just bought those shoes. (b) This here ride is broken. (c) Try to relax.
15. (a) I am real happy. (b) Study now. Then go outside. (c) They're new in school.
16. (a) Take the report when you go. (b) She might have gone. (c) Mr. Bennigan he is my English teacher.
17. (a) We worked for a hour. (b) She accepted your invitation. (c) They can hardly see the sign.
18. (a) Where do you study? (b) Divide the tasks among the two of us. (c) If he had been there, I would have seen him.
19. (a) You should have come. (b) Less sugar is needed. (c) It's pedal is stuck.
20. (a) He likes these kinds of ties. (b) It looks like a rabbit. (c) She raised up on her tiptoes.

LEVELS OF USAGE

To use the glossary properly, you will need to be familiar with the terms *standard English, formal English, informal English, non-standard English, slang, colloquialisms,* and *jargon.*

Standard English

Standard English is the form of English most widely accepted by educated people. It conforms to the rules and conventions given throughout this textbook, such as those concerning subject-verb agreement, pronoun-antecedent agreement, and pronoun usage.

EXAMPLE   Marc and **I** [not *me*] ate lunch in the park.

Formal English is the standard English used most often in formal writing or speaking situations, such as in formal reports that have footnotes and bibliographies, formal essays, and speeches given on serious occasions. Formal English avoids contractions and slang. Presidential State of the Union speeches are examples of formal English.

Informal English is the standard English that most of us use every day in our conversation and in much of our personal writing. It is used in many newspapers, magazines, and books; on radio and television; by professional and business people; and by students. Informal English is inappropriate for formal occasions.

INFORMAL   He looks kind of tired.
 FORMAL   He looks **somewhat** tired.

Nonstandard English

Nonstandard English is the form of language that does not conform to the rules and conventions discussed in this text-book.

EXAMPLE   Our house is more smaller than yours. [nonstan-
          dard]
          Our house is **smaller** than yours. [standard]

Special Uses of English

Slang, colloquialisms, and jargon are most often found in informal English.

Slang consists of new words, or old words in new uses, that are adopted because they seem colorful and clever and they show that the user is up to date. Slang is often found in the speech of young people and those who belong to groups set apart from the community.

EXAMPLE   My older brother always **hassles** me.

Colloquialisms are words or phrases usually found in the speech, but not in the writing, of educated speakers. Colloquialisms are more widespread than slang.

EXAMPLE   Let's **put our heads together** to solve this prob-
          lem.

Jargon consists of words and phrases used in a particular ac-tivity, such as a sport, hobby, or field of study, or by people engaged in a particular profession or occupation. Often jargon assigns a specified meaning to a word already in widespread use.

EXAMPLE   The base runner tried to **steal** second base.

In doing the exercises in this chapter, use standard formal English.

USAGE GLOSSARY

a, an   Use *a* before words beginning with consonant sounds; use *an* before words beginning with vowel sounds.

EXAMPLES   Mike will stay at **a** hotel.
I live on **a** one-way street.
Susan is **an** honest person.
My older sister gave me **an** orange sweater.

accept, except   *Accept* is a verb; it means "to receive." *Except* may be either a verb or a preposition. As a verb, it means "to leave out" or "to omit"; as a preposition, it means "excluding."

EXAMPLES   I **accept** your apology.
Some students will be **excepted** from this assignment.
Mark has written all his friends **except** John.

affect, effect   *Affect* is a verb meaning "to influence." *Effect* used as a verb means "to accomplish." Used as a noun, *effect* means "the result of some action."

EXAMPLES   His score on this test will **affect** his final grade.
Bo and Alice's hard work **effected** a solution to the problem.
The **effects** of the hurricane would not be known for days.

ain't   Avoid this word in speaking or writing; it is nonstandard English.

all ready, already   *All ready* means "completely prepared" or "in readiness." *Already* means "previously."

> EXAMPLES   We had **already** seen that film.
> The soup is **all ready** to be served.

all right   Used as an adjective, *all right* means "satisfactory" or "unhurt." Used as an adverb *all right* means "satisfactory." *All right* is always two words. *Alright* is not an acceptable spelling.

> EXAMPLES   Your work is **all right.** [adjective]
> Maria fell, but she is **all right.** [adjective]
> You did **all right** at the track meet. [adverb]

anywheres, everywheres, nowheres, somewheres   Use these words without the final *s.*

> EXAMPLE   I didn't go **anywhere** [not *anywheres*] yesterday.

as   See **like, as.**

as if   See **like, as if.**

at   Do not use *at* after *where.*

> NONSTANDARD   Where will you be at?
> STANDARD   Where will you be?

bad, badly   *Bad* is an adjective; in most uses, *badly* is an adverb. The distinction between the two forms should be observed in standard formal usage.

> EXAMPLES   The fish tastes **bad.** [The adjective *bad* modifies *fish.*]
> The boy's wrist was sprained **badly.** [The adverb *badly* modifies *was sprained.*]

In informal usage, however, the expression "feel badly" has become acceptable, though ungrammatical, English.

> INFORMAL   Marcia felt badly about her low grade.
> FORMAL   Marcia felt **bad** about her low grade.

because   See **reason . . . because.**

between, among   Use *between* when you are thinking of two things at a time, even though they may be part of a group consisting of more than two.

EXAMPLES   In English, Marc sits **between** Bob and me.

Some players practice **between** innings. [Although there are more than two innings, the practice occurs only *between* any two of them.]

Next year we will study the War **Between** the States. [Although thirty-five states were involved, the war was *between* two sides.]

I could not decide which of the four pairs of jeans to buy, as there was not much difference **between** them. [Although there are more than two pairs of jeans, each one is being thought of and compared with the others separately.]

Use *among* when you are thinking of a group rather than of separate individuals.

EXAMPLES   There was disagreement **among** the players about the coach's decision. [The players are thought of as a group.]

We saved up twenty dollars **among** the three of us. [The three people together saved twenty dollars.]

bring, take   *Bring* means "to come carrying something." *Take* means "to go carrying something." Think of *bring* as related to *come* and of *take* as related to *go*.

EXAMPLES   Please **bring** my book when you come.
Take this dish when you go.

bust, busted   Avoid using these words as verbs. Use a form of either *burst* or *break*.

EXAMPLES   The balloon **burst** [not *busted*] when June sat on it.
The dish **broke** [not *busted*] when I dropped it.

can't hardly, can't scarcely   The words *hardly* and *scarcely* are negative words. They should never be used with another negative word.

EXAMPLES   I **can** [not *can't*] **hardly** read Jack's handwriting.
We **had** [not *hadn't*] **scarcely** enough food for everyone.

could of   *Could have* sounds like *could of* when spoken. Do not write *of* with the helping verb *could.* Write *could have.* Also avoid *ought to of, should of, would of, might of,* and *must of.*

EXAMPLE   Sally **could have** [not *of*] played the piano.

effect   See **affect, effect.**

everywheres   See **anywheres,** etc.

fewer, less   *Fewer* is used with plural words, *less* with singular words; *fewer* tells "how many," *less* "how much."

EXAMPLES   We have **fewer** balloons than we need.
This recipe calls for **less** flour.

good, well   *Good* is always an adjective. Never use *good* to modify a verb; use *well,* which is an adverb.

NONSTANDARD   Nancy sang *good* at the audition.
STANDARD   Nancy sang **well** at the audition.

Although it is usually an adverb, *well* is used as an adjective to mean "healthy."

EXAMPLE   He did not feel **well** yesterday. [predicate adjective meaning "healthy"]

☞ USAGE NOTE   *Feel good* and *feel well* mean different things. *Feel good* means "to feel happy or pleased." *Feel well* means "to feel healthy."

EXAMPLES On a sunny day, I feel **good.**
I felt **good** when I received an A in English.
He went to the doctor because he didn't feel
well.

The use of *good* as an adverb is increasing in conversational
English, but it should not be so used in writing.

had of See **of.**

had ought, hadn't ought Unlike other verbs, *ought* is not used
with *had.*

NONSTANDARD Gary had ought to help us; he hadn't ought to
have missed our meeting yesterday.
STANDARD Gary **ought to** help us; he **oughtn't to have**
missed our meeting yesterday.
or
Gary **should** help us; he **shouldn't have**
missed our meeting yesterday.

he, she, they In writing, do not use an unnecessary pronoun
after a noun. This error is called the *double subject.*

NONSTANDARD Mrs. Pine she is my mother's friend.
STANDARD Mrs. Pine is my mother's friend.

hisself *Hisself* is nonstandard English. Use *himself.*

EXAMPLE Ira bought **himself** [not *hisself*] a yellow tie.

how come In informal English, *how come* is often used instead
of *why;* but in formal English, *why* is always preferable.

INFORMAL I don't know how come she's not here.
FORMAL I don't know **why** she is not here.

its, it's *Its* is a personal pronoun in the possessive form. *It's* is a
contraction of *it is* or *it has.*

EXAMPLES **Its** window is broken. [*Its* is a possessive pro-
noun.]
It's a hot day. [*It's* means "it is."]
It's been a good trip. [*It's* means "it has."]

kind, sort, type In writing, the demonstrative words *this, that, these,* and *those* must agree in number with the words *kind, sort,* and *type*.

EXAMPLE Maria likes **this kind** of book better than any of **those** other **kinds.**

kind of, sort of In informal English, *kind of* and *sort of* are used to mean "somewhat" or "rather"; but in formal English, *somewhat* or *rather* is always preferable.

INFORMAL It was kind of embarrassing.
FORMAL It was **somewhat** embarrassing.

WRITING APPLICATION:
Using *Kind Of* Correctly in Writing Definitions

If you are not a basketball fan, you might not know what a *slam-dunk* is. If you are not a climber, you have probably never heard of *chimneying*. Sometimes words are familiar only to people who have a special interest in a particular subject. Your reader might be eager to learn about a new subject that you know much about. To explain a particular subject, you would give a definition of it. Definitions often include the phrase *kind of,* which should not be followed by *a*.

EXAMPLE A piranha is a **kind of** tropical fish that attacks and destroys its prey with very sharp teeth. [Notice that *kind of* is not followed by *a*.]

Writing Assignment

Write a paragraph in which you define a term that is familiar to you but may not be well known to other people. Here are some ideas:

woofer *or* tweeter   Siamese cat   word processor   ceramics

Use the phrase *kind of* at least twice, and underline it each time you use it.

---

learn, teach *Learn* means "to acquire knowledge." *Teach* means "to instruct" or "to show how."

> EXAMPLES I am **learning** how to use this computer.
> My father is **teaching** me how.

less See **fewer, less.**

lie, lay See pages 237–38.

like, as *Like* is a preposition, introducing a prepositional phrase. In informal English, *like* is often used as a conjunction meaning "as"; but in formal English, *as* is always preferable.

> EXAMPLES This tastes **like** pineapple juice. [Like is a preposition introducing the phrase *like pineapple juice.*]
>
> Please do **as** he suggests. [*He suggests* is a clause and needs the conjunction *as* (not the preposition *like*) to introduce it.]

like, as if In formal written English, *like* should not be used for the compound conjunctions *as if* or *as though*.

> EXAMPLE You looked **as though** [not *like*] you knew the answer.

might of, must of See **could of.**

nowheres See **anywheres,** etc.

of Do not use *of* with prepositions such as *inside, off,* and *outside*.

> EXAMPLE He quickly walked **off** [not *off of*] the stage.
> She waited **outside** [not *outside of*] the school.
> What is **inside** [not *inside of*] this large box?

Of is also unnecessary with *had*.

> EXAMPLE If I **had** [not *had of*] seen her, I would have said hello.

ought to of   See **could of.**

real   In informal English, *real* is often used as an adverb meaning "very" or "extremely"; but in formal English, *very* or *extremely* is preferable.

> INFORMAL   I am real tired.
> FORMAL   I am **very** tired.

reason . . . because   In informal English, *reason . . . because* is often used instead of *reason . . . that.* In formal English, use *reason . . . that,* or revise your sentence.

> INFORMAL   The reason why I did well on the test was because I had studied hard.
> FORMAL   The **reason** I did well on the test was **that** I had studied hard.
>
> *or*
>
> I did well on the test **because** I had studied hard.

rise, raise   See page 239.

shall, will   Some people prefer to use *shall* with first person pronouns and *will* with second and third person in the future and future perfect tenses. Nowadays, most Americans do not make this distinction. *Will* is acceptable in the first person as well as in the other two.

sit, set   See pages 235–36.

so   Because this word is usually overworked, avoid it in your writing whenever you can.

> INFORMAL   I want to get a good grade, so I will study tonight.
> FORMAL   Because I want to get a good grade, I will study tonight.
>
> *or*
>
> I want to get a good grade; therefore, I will study tonight.

some, somewhat   In writing, do not use *some* for *somewhat* as an adverb.

NONSTANDARD   My math has improved some.
STANDARD   My math has improved **somewhat.**

than, then   Do not confuse these words. *Than* is a conjunction; *then* is an adverb.

EXAMPLES   Margo is a faster runner **than** I am.
First, we went to the department store; **then** we went to the library.

their, there, they're   *Their* is the possessive form of *they*. *There* is used to mean "at that place" or to begin a sentence. *They're* is a contraction of *they are*.

EXAMPLES   **Their** team won the game.
We will go **there** in the spring.
There were twenty people at the party.
They're the best players on the team.

theirself, theirselves   *Theirself* and *theirselves* are nonstandard English. Use *themselves*.

EXAMPLE   They bought **themselves** [not *theirself* or *theirselves*] new basketballs.

them   *Them* should not be used as an adjective. Use *these* or *those*.

EXAMPLE   I gave you **those** [not *them*] records yesterday.

this here, that there   The *here* and the *there* are unnecessary.

EXAMPLE   Do you like **this** [not *this here*] shirt or **that** [not *that there*] one?

this kind, sort, type   See **kind,** etc.

try and   In informal English *try and* is often used for *try to;* but in formal English *try to* is always preferable.

INFORMAL   Try and be early.
FORMAL   **Try to** be early.

use to, used to   Be sure to add the *d* to *use*. *Used to* is the past form.

EXAMPLE   We **used to** [not *use to*] own a dog.

very   Avoid overusing this word. Try to use more precise words in its place.

EXAMPLES   I was **trembling** [instead of *very* afraid].
He was **delighted** [instead of *very* happy] with his gift.

way, ways   Use *way*, not *ways*, in referring to a distance.

EXAMPLE   They still had a long **way** [not *ways*] to go.

when, where   Do not use *when* or *where* incorrectly in writing a definition.

NONSTANDARD   Listening is when a person pays close attention to what the other person is saying.
STANDARD   Listening is paying close attention to what the other person is saying.

where   Do not use *where* for *that*.

EXAMPLE   I read in our newspaper **that** [not *where*] John will be the new sportswriter.

which, that, who   Remember that the relative pronoun *who* refers to people only; *which* refers to things only; *that* refers to either people or things.

EXAMPLES   She is the student **who** had the lead in the school play. [person]
I rode my bike, **which** has ten speeds. [thing]
This is the pen **that** I want to buy. [thing]
He is the person **that** can help you. [person]

without, unless   Do not use the preposition *without* in place of the conjunction *unless*.

EXAMPLE   I will not be able to go to the party **unless** [not *without*] I finish my homework first.

would of   See **could of.**

your, you're   *Your* is the possessive pronoun of *you. You're* is the contraction of *you are.*

EXAMPLES   **Your** dinner is on the table.
You're one of my closest friends.

CHAPTER 12 REVIEW: POSTTEST 1

Revising Sentences by Correcting Errors in Usage.   In each of the following sets of sentences, one sentence contains an error in usage. After the proper number, write the letter of the sentence that contains an error, and revise the sentence. Make sure that your revisions follow standard formal usage.

EXAMPLE   1. (a) The chicken tastes bad. (b) Where is the book at? (c) There was agreement among the five dancers.
1. *(b) Where is the book?*

1. (a) Bring your notes when you come. (b) The dish busted. (c) He could have danced.
2. (a) I drew an apple. (b) The cold affects the plant. (c) We are already to go.
3. (a) Mike feels alright today. (b) She went everywhere. (c) We have fewer chairs than we need.
4. (a) They danced good at the party. (b) If I had sung, you would have laughed. (c) You ought to help.
5. (a) It's cold. (b) He made it hisself. (c) Its knob is broken.
6. (a) Teach me the song. (b) That story is kind of funny. (c) The dog lay down.

7. (a) Mr. Barnes is here. (b) I know why he left. (c) This kinds of bikes are expensive.

8. (a) These taste like oranges. (b) Sing as she does. (c) She might of moved.

9. (a) Please come inside the house. (b) I am real happy. (c) The reason she laughed was that your dog looked funny.

10. (a) I wanted the book, but someone had lost such. (b) Your forehand has improved somewhat. (c) He sings better than I do.

11. (a) Your coat is beautiful. (b) You're a fast runner. (c) I cannot leave without I wash the dishes first.

12. (a) She is the student which plays the violin. (b) We only have a short way to go. (c) We read in our newspaper that a new store is opening in town.

13. (a) I use to read mysteries. (b) Set that crate down here. (c) This hat is old.

14. (a) I gave you them books. (b) They bought themselves new shirts. (c) There is the cat.

15. (a) Sit down. (b) They're smiling. (c) There team is good.

16. (a) Gail did not feel well. (b) Have a orange. (c) You invited everyone except Sue.

17. (a) I raised at 8:00 this morning. (b) Have you read about the effects of the sun's rays? (c) We already read the book in class.

18. (a) You did all right. (b) They went nowheres. (c) He looks as if he is sad.

19. (a) Nancy's ankle was hurt bad. (b) We listened to the discussion among the three governors. (c) The pipe burst.

20. (a) I cannot hardly dance. (b) Warm days make me feel good. (c) It's pretty.

21. (a) He must be somewhere. (b) I can scarcely ride this bike. (c) The reason why I like him is because he is kind.

22. (a) We have fewer shelves than we need. (b) Those kinds of shirts are warm. (c) This morning I laid in bed too long.

23. (a) Pat always lays her books on the couch. (b) Learn how to play this game. (c) Do like he does.

24. (a) They are inside of the house. (b) I will have a sandwich. (c) He set the chair down.
25. (a) Their my cats. (b) Do you need those books? (c) This house has fourteen rooms.

CHAPTER 12 REVIEW: POSTTEST 2

Revising Sentences by Correcting Errors in Usage. The following sentences contain many of the common errors you have been studying. Revise each sentence, using formal standard English.

1. Marc plays the cello good.
2. Anita had ought to help us finish the scenery.
3. You have less books to carry than I do.
4. If I had of missed the game, I would have been disappointed.
5. We have looked everywheres for Plato.
6. Do you know how come Sharon will not be there?
7. Jack hisself built that doghouse.
8. Its too hot to ride our bikes today.
9. Mr. Parker he is the mail carrier.
10. He had lain his papers on his desk.
11. I was kind of embarrassed when I bumped into Jack.
12. This kinds of coats are the warmest.
13. Please learn me how to do that dance.
14. They have risen the price of the shoes.
15. After the show John looked like he were tired.
16. Please wait for me outside of the doctor's office.
17. Your a good soccer player.
18. She is the student which won the poster contest.
19. When my brother completed the marathon, I was real happy.
20. Did you read in the newspaper where the mayor will be in town tomorrow?

21. Pete wants to go to Mike's house after dinner, so he will finish his homework now.
22. A *simile* is when a person uses a figure of speech in which one thing is compared to another.
23. Their never on time.
24. The reason why I do not have my homework is because the dog ate it.
25. I have read more of his books then you have.

USAGE
MASTERY REVIEW: Cumulative Test

A. AGREEMENT. Number your paper 1–10. In most of the following sentences, either a verb does not agree with its subject, or a pronoun does not agree with its antecedent. Copy the incorrect verb or pronoun after the proper number; then write the correct form. If a sentence is correct, write *C* after the proper number.

EXAMPLES   1. Has many of the runners finished the race?
            1. *Has—Have*
            2. *Fay or Pinar forgot her purse.*
            2. *C*

1. Neither the cat nor the dog have had a rabies shot.
2. Everyone brought their books to class today.
3. Tanya, of all people, don't need to eat any more sweets.
4. There's sure to be some children at the playground.
5. A few of the mice always prefer eating by itself.
6. The committee for the school carnival unanimously agrees on the date that it will be held.
7. Why have Mr. Chiano and Mr. Katz decided to open his business there?
8. After dinner tonight all of the dishes and silverware has to be washed immediately.
9. Can you tell me why each of us have to help?
10. One of the girls who took swimming lessons yesterday forgot their bathing cap.

B. CORRECT PRONOUN USAGE. Number your paper 11–20. After the proper number, write the correct one of the two pronouns given in parentheses.

EXAMPLE   1. The solution was known only by Maggie and (she, her).
            1. *her*

11. Everybody knew that the true leader of that group was (she, her).
12. Why don't you just go ahead and give (he, him) your old tennis racket?
13. Hardly anyone guessed it would be (they, them) who would have the best chance of winning.
14. Please don't leave any more of those tedious chores for (we, us) assistants to do.
15. The baseball coach introduced Felipe and (I, me) to the Major League recruiter.
16. His friends and (he, him) have decided to form a sandlot team.
17. Well, just between you and (I, me), the chances of getting in free don't look good.
18. Everybody always said that (we, us) guitar players would be the stars of the show.
19. Has your dog or my dog been chasing (they, them) out of the yard?
20. The athletic director said that every girl except (she, her) would run the cross-country course.

C. **USING THE CORRECT FORM OF THE VERB.** Number your paper 21–30. After the appropriate number, write the past or past participle of the verb given before each sentence. When two verbs are given, you will need to choose the correct verb as well as the correct form.

EXAMPLES 1. *break* By the middle of January my brother had —— most of his Christmas toys.
          1. *broken*
          2. *sit/set* That's where Ms. Matthews always —— in the park.
          2. *sat*

21. *know*   All of the members —— the pledge by heart.
22. *shrink* Shyly, Rosa —— from taking any of the credit.
23. *lie/lay* After he had —— down for a while, he felt refreshed.

24. *rise/raise*   Those pigs have been born and —— on this farm.

25. *ride*   Now I wish we had —— the bus instead of walking.

26. *drink*   I think that Elliot —— all the lemonade.

27. *bring*   Did you see all the clothes he —— with him for just an overnight stay?

28. *lie/lay*   The painters carefully —— dropcloths over the furniture.

29. *throw*   The flames of the bonfire licked the night sky after the rest of the wood had been —— onto the pile.

30. *Sit/Set*   —— that vase on the table near the door.

D. CORRECT USAGE OF MODIFIERS. In most of the following sentences, modifiers are either incorrect or misplaced. After the proper number, write the incorrect word, then the correct one; or revise the sentence to make the meaning clear and logical. If the sentence is correct, write *C*.

EXAMPLES   1. That was the bestest sundae I ever ate.
           1. *bestest—best*
           2. The spectators cheered the runners in the stands.
           2. *The spectators in the stands cheered the runners.*

31. The courthouse is the most oldest building in our town.

32. Yesterday morning the fog got so thick that I couldn't hardly see on the way to school.

33. Our soccer team plays better than any team in town.

34. The large spider frightened my aunt crawling up the curtain.

35. If you have a choice between the king-size box and the jumbo size, take the jumbo because it contains the most soap.

36. The pigeons belong to my brother and sister that live on the roof.

37. The majorette leading the band never dropped her baton once.

38. Vast stretches of space have been explored by scientists using sophisticated equipment beyond our Milky Way.
39. My mother said that I can't go nowhere this afternoon.
40. Swarming out of the hive I had knocked down, I got chased all the way home by the bees.

E. STANDARD FORMAL USAGE OF EXPRESSIONS.

Number your paper 41–50. Most of the following sentences contain errors in usage. After the proper number, write the incorrect form of the words or expressions; then write the correct form beside it. If a sentence is correct, write *C*.

EXAMPLE   1. I could of guessed that you'd say that.
        1. *could of—could have*

41. No one knew how the chemical pollution would effect the fish and other wildlife.
42. Why don't they mind they're own business?
43. Casey always does good on true-false tests.
44. It usually takes a while to get use to a new school.
45. The make-up quiz was even harder then the test was.
46. Hey, get off of that fence!
47. One of the reasons she didn't go was because she didn't have fun there the last time she went.
48. We couldn't find any canned peaches anywheres in the store.
49. Ronnie didn't do too well on her science project.
50. The players looked like they'd just been through a war.

PART THREE

MECHANICS

Capital Letters

RULES FOR CAPITALIZATION

Capital letters indicate important words—the beginnings of sentences and quotations, titles, and other words that deserve special attention. You have probably already mastered most of the rules for capitalization. Perhaps there are some that you find still troublesome. In this chapter you will review the rules for using capital letters correctly.

DIAGNOSTIC TEST

Correcting Sentences by Using Capitalization Correctly.
Number your paper 1–20. Each of the following sentences contains incorrect capitalization. After the proper number, write the word or words correctly, supplying capitals where they are necessary or omitting capitals where they are unnecessary.

EXAMPLE 1. The Maxwells enjoyed visiting the southwest, particularly the Alamo in San Antonio.
1. *Southwest*

1. Dr. Powell's office is at the corner of Twenty-first street and Oak Drive.

2. On labor day we always go to Three Trees State Park.
3. We invited aunt Mae and her two children to go with us.
4. Our junior high school had a much more successful carnival than Lakeside junior high school did.
5. When our class read *a Tale of two Cities,* we also studied the French Revolution.
6. My cousin joined the Peace corps and lived in a small village on the west coast of Africa for a year.
7. No fish live in the Great salt lake in Utah.
8. One famous hero of World War I is sergeant Alvin York.
9. We have studied Japanese culture and the shinto religion.
10. This year I have English, American History, Spanish, and shop in the afternoon.
11. On sunday my mother and I went to an antique car show.
12. The Robinsons live near route 41 just off the Memorial Parkway on the south side of town.
13. At our Wednesday night meeting, the reverend Terry Witt gave a short talk on the beliefs of Lutherans.
14. Did you see the president speak on television last night?
15. Thursday was named after the Norse God Thor.
16. An icy gust of Winter air chilled the scouts to the bone.
17. Dale Evans and Roy Rogers always sang "Happy trails to you" at the end of their television programs.
18. Ms. Morelli's class has studied the Supreme court.
19. Both of my uncles served in the U.S. Army during the War in Vietnam.
20. The American revolution took place toward the end of the Age of Enlightenment in the eighteenth century.

13a. Capitalize the first word in every sentence.

In order to capitalize the first word in a sentence, you must be able to identify the beginning of a sentence. If you are not sure of your ability to do this, the section on run-on sentences (pages 409–10) will help you.

INCORRECT	More and more people are discovering the benefits of exercise daily workouts at the gymnasium, on the running track, or on the tennis court strengthen the heart these workouts also help control weight.
CORRECT	More and more people are discovering the benefits of exercise. **D**aily workouts at the gymnasium, on the running track, or on the tennis court strengthen the heart. **T**hese workouts also help control weight.

The first word of a sentence that is a direct quotation is capitalized even if the quotation begins within a sentence.

EXAMPLE   Elinor shouted, "**W**e did it!"

For a fuller explanation of this rule, see the section on writing quotations, pages 372–373.

☞ **NOTE**   Traditionally, the first word in a line of poetry is capitalized, whether or not the word begins a sentence:

*W*hen I am dead, my dearest,/*S*ing no sad songs for me . . .

Some modern poets do not follow this style. When copying a poem, be sure to follow the capitalization the poet used.

13b. Capitalize the pronoun *I*.

EXAMPLES   Recently **I** have begun to enjoy classical music.
May **I** help you?

13c. Capitalize the interjection *O*.

The interjection *O* is most often used on solemn or formal occasions. Notice that it is most often used with a word in direct address and that no mark of punctuation follows it.

EXAMPLES   Hear our prayer, **O** Lord.
Protect us in the battle, **O** great Athena!

The interjection *oh* requires a capital letter only at the beginning of a sentence. It is usually followed by a comma.

EXAMPLES **Oh,** wait till you see tomorrow's assignment.
We haven't seen her for some time—**oh,** perhaps two or three months.

13d. Capitalize proper nouns.

The proper noun, which you studied on page 37, names a particular person, place, or thing. It is always capitalized. The common noun is capitalized only when it begins a sentence or is part of a title.

PROPER NOUNS	COMMON NOUNS
Cicely Tyson	actress
February	month
Tennessee	state

(1) Capitalize the names of persons.

EXAMPLES **J**ames **B**aldwin is my favorite writer.
Is **A**lice coming, too?
According to **P**at **S**andoz, **A**nnie **S**ullivan is a good subject for a biography.

(2) Capitalize geographical names.

Cities, Towns: **J**amestown, **S**an **D**iego, **A**kron
States: **G**eorgia, **I**daho, **H**awaii
Countries: **G**hana, **N**icaragua, **T**hailand
Sections of the Country: the **M**idwest, the **N**orth

> ☞ NOTE Do *not* capitalize *east, west, north, south,* or any combination like *southwest* when these words indicate direction; do capitalize them when they indicate a region: *If you travel west across the Pacific Ocean, you will arrive in the Far East.*

Islands: Isle of Wight, Molokai, Wake Island, Attu
Bodies of Water: Danville Reservoir, Tennessee River, Lake Erie, Niagara Falls, Tampa Bay, Indian Ocean, Puget Sound, Bering Sea
Streets, Highways: Cherry Lane, Taconic Avenue, Crescent Circle, West Ninety-fourth Street, Route 44, Skyline Drive

---

☞ **NOTE**   In a hyphenated street number, the second word begins with a small letter: *East Seventy-eighth Street, South Forty-third Place*

Parks: Estes Park, White Mountain National Forest
Mountains: Big Horn Mountains, Mount Washington, Sawtooth Range, Pikes Peak, Great Smokies
Continents: North America, Europe, Africa, Asia

(3) Capitalize names of organizations, business firms, institutions, and government bodies.

EXAMPLES   Debating Club
Air National Guard
Garcia's Hardware Store
United Tool and Die Corporation
Cary Memorial Hospital
Hillcrest School
Antioch College
Department of Agriculture
Governor's Council

☞ **NOTE**   Do *not* capitalize words like *school, circus, restaurant, club* unless they are part of a proper name: *an elementary school—Irving Elementary School; a circus—Ringling Brothers' Circus.*

---

(4) Capitalize special events and calendar items.

EXAMPLES   World Series   Fourth of July
                National Chess Tournament   Friday
                Rockland Lobster Festival   October

☞ **NOTE** Do *not* capitalize the names of seasons: *We go on fishing trips in the spring and the fall.*

---

(5) Capitalize historical events and periods.

EXAMPLES   Ice Age, Revolutionary War, Battle of Bunker Hill, Middle Ages, Renaissance, Crusades

(6) Capitalize the names of nationalities, races, and religions.

EXAMPLES   Spanish, Egyptian, Caucasian, Eskimo, Lutheran

(7) Capitalize the brand names of business products.

EXAMPLES   Cannon towels, Buick sedan, Ivory soap [Notice that only the brand name is capitalized; the common noun following it begins with a small letter.]

(8) Capitalize the names of ships, planets, monuments, awards, and any other particular places, things, or events.

Monuments, Memorials: Washington Monument, Vietnam Veterans Memorial
Awards: Pulitzer Prize, Newbery Medal
Ships, Trains: U.S.S. *Maine, Queen Elizabeth, Silver Rocket*
Planets, Stars: Venus, Saturn, the Milky Way, the Big Dipper

☞ **NOTE** Planets, constellations, stars, and groups of stars are capitalized; *sun, moon,* and *earth* are not capitalized unless they are listed with other heavenly bodies.

EXERCISE 1. Writing Common Nouns and Proper Nouns.

Number your paper 1–20. For each proper noun, write a corresponding common noun. For each common noun, write a proper noun.

EXAMPLES   1. Chien Shiung Wu
            1. *physicist*
            2. city
            2. *San Francisco*

1. basketball team
2. Fourth of July
3. museum
4. *Great Expectations*
5. Super Bowl
6. lake
7. Geraldine Ferraro
8. historical event
9. river
10. month
11. North Dakota
12. Ethiopia
13. Washington Monument
14. planet
15. poem
16. IBM computer
17. cereal
18. television set
19. Environmental Protection Agency
20. Christianity

EXERCISE 2. Using Capital Letters Correctly.

Number your paper 1–25. After the proper number, write each of the following expressions, using capital letters where they are needed. Do not capitalize the first word unless it requires a capital.

EXAMPLE   1. a member of the peace corps
           1. *a member of the Peace Corps*

1. veterans day ceremony
2. decisions of the united states supreme court
3. eastern half of iowa
4. eleanor roosevelt park
5. ambassador to an african nation
6. cree indians of north america
7. boulder dam
8. graduate of bryn mawr college

9. a member of the house of representatives
10. the statue of liberty
11. fullback for the denver broncos
12. yellowstone national park
13. enid bagnold
14. saint patrick's day parade
15. general foods corporation
16. one street east of north fairview drive
17. 512 west twenty-fourth street
18. state farm insurance companies
19. pictures of saturn sent by *voyager II*
20. the hawaiian island called maui
21. the great lakes
22. a catholic
23. sealtest cottage cheese
24. monday, april 29
25. the stone age

EXERCISE 3. Correcting Sentences by Capitalizing Words. Number your paper 1–10. After the proper number, write and capitalize all words that need capital letters in the sentence.

EXAMPLE 1. our class visited abraham lincoln's home in spring-field, illinois.

1. *Our, Abraham Lincoln's, Springfield, Illinois*

1. according to the federal aviation administration, united states airlines are the safest in the world.
2. ethel waters spent most of her childhood in chester, pennsylvania.
3. the sacred muslim city of mecca is one of the two capitals of saudi arabia.
4. in chicago, the sears tower and the museum of science and industry attract many tourists.
5. the detroit tigers won the world series in 1984.
6. the valentine's day dance is always the highlight of the winter.

7. several of my friends bought new converse tennis shoes at the big sporting goods sale in the mall.
8. the city-wide food pantry is sponsored and operated by protestants, catholics, and jews.
9. the second-place winners will receive polaroid cameras.
10. jane bryant quinn writes a magazine column on money management.

13e. Capitalize proper adjectives.

A proper adjective, which is formed from a proper noun, is always capitalized.

PROPER NOUN	PROPER ADJECTIVE
China	Chinese doctor
Egypt	Egyptian cotton
Ireland	Irish wolfhound
Middle East	Middle Eastern tour
Brazil	Brazilian artist

EXERCISE 4. Correcting Sentences by Capitalizing Proper Nouns and Proper Adjectives.

Number your paper 1–10. After the appropriate number, write and capitalize all proper nouns and proper adjectives in the sentence.

EXAMPLE 1. A finnish architect, eliel saarinen, designed a number of buildings in the detroit area.
1. *Finnish, Eliel Saarinen, Detroit*

1. Have you seen the exhibit of african art at the library?
2. The egyptian and israeli leaders met in jerusalem.
3. The european cities I plan to visit are paris and vienna.
4. Our english literature book includes hopi poems and cheyenne legends.
5. The south american rain forests contain many different kinds of plants and animals.
6. Maria has watched several of the shakespearean plays on television.

7. The alaskan wilderness is noted for its majestic beauty.
8. Our program will feature irish and scottish folk songs.
9. The language most widely spoken in brazil is not spanish but portuguese.
10. The baptist leader discussed the ruling of the supreme court.

13f. Do *not* capitalize the names of school subjects, except languages and course names followed by a number.

EXAMPLES   I have tests in English, science, and math.
You must pass History II before taking History III.
Next year we will have algebra and Latin.

EXERCISE 5. Correcting Phrases by Capitalizing Words.
Number your paper 1–10. After the proper number, write each phrase, inserting capitals where they are needed.

1. a lesson in spanish
2. take a creative-writing course
3. report for english II
4. teacher of social studies and french
5. a program on chinese customs
6. homework for mathematics
7. problems in geometry
8. courses in civics II, algebra, and modern history
9. lab experiments in science II
10. studying latin, history, chemistry, and government II

13g. Capitalize titles.

(1) Capitalize the title of a person when it comes before a name.

EXAMPLES   There will be a short address by Governor Halsey.
Report to Lieutenant Engstrom, please.
Did you know that Dr. Politi has a new associate, a Ms. Tam?

This is the church in which the **R**everend Henry Ward Beecher preached.

How many terms did **P**resident Cleveland serve?

Does **Q**ueen Sofia live in the Netherlands or in Spain?

(2) Capitalize a title used alone or following a person's name only if it refers to a high official or to someone to whom you wish to show special respect.

EXAMPLES   The **S**ecretary of **L**abor will hold a news conference this afternoon. [*Secretary of Labor* is a high government office.]

Since 1800 the White House has been the official residence of the **P**resident. [The word *President* is usually capitalized when it refers to the President of the United States.]

Martha Layne Collins, **G**overnor of **K**entucky, was elected to her office on November 6, 1984. [Although it follows the person's name, the title is that of a high office.]

The **t**reasurer of our scout troop has the measles. [The title is not that of a high office.]

Ellen Rafferty, **c**hairperson of the program committee, reported on plans for the Winter Carnival. [The office is not a high one.]

☞ **NOTE**   When a title is used instead of a name in direct address, it is usually capitalized: *Could you tell me how my sister is feeling, Nurse?*

(3) Capitalize words showing family relationships when used with a person's name but *not* when preceded by a possessive.

EXAMPLES   **A**unt Christine, **G**randfather Smith
Maria's **m**other, our **b**rother, her **a**unt

Exception: When family-relationship words are *usually* used before a name, so that they are considered a part of the name, they are capitalized even when preceded by a possessive.

EXAMPLE Kim's **Aunt Betty**

When family-relationship words are used in place of a person's name, they may or may not be capitalized.

EXAMPLE Ask **Mother**, *or* Ask **mother**. [Either is correct.]

(4) Capitalize the first word and all important words in titles of books, magazines, newspapers, poems, stories, movies, paintings, and other works of art.

Unimportant words in a title are *a, an, the,* and prepositions and conjunctions of fewer than five letters. Such words should be capitalized only if they come first or last in the title.

EXAMPLES My sister asked me to read Denise Levertov's poem, "**With Eyes at the Back of Our Heads.**"

Katharine Hepburn and Humphrey Bogart star in *The African Queen.*

Curtain Going Up! is a biography of Katharine Cornell.

Exception: When you write the names of newspapers and magazines within a sentence, do not capitalize the word *the* before the name.

EXAMPLES May I borrow your copy of the *Reader's Digest*?

Is that the late edition of the *New York Times*?

(5) Capitalize words referring to the Deity.

EXAMPLES Lord, Jehovah, the Creator, Son of God, Allah

> ☞ **NOTE** The word *god* is not capitalized when referring to gods in mythology: *The Roman god of war was Mars.*

EXERCISE 6. Correcting Sentences by Capitalizing Words. Number your paper 1–10. After the proper number, write and capitalize the words requiring capitals.

1. Our drama club produced the play *cheaper by the dozen* this spring.
2. Do you read the *chicago sun-times* or the *chicago tribune*?
3. During Woodrow Wilson's term as president of the united states, sheep grazed on the front lawn of the White House.
4. Uncle Otis and aunt Lennie are still living on their farm.
5. Not all people worship god in the same way.
6. Was Carrie Fisher in *return of the jedi*?
7. Many of my teachers are members of the denver classroom teachers' association.
8. Both the governor and the secretary of state spoke at the convention.
9. The reporter interviewed dr. Lee, a physician highly respected for her work in cardiology.
10. What room is my mother in, doctor?

EXERCISE 7. Correcting Sentences by Capitalizing Words. Number your paper 1–10. After the proper number, write and capitalize the words requiring capitals. If a sentence is correct, write *C*.

1. The president of the united states explained the tax proposal.
2. When aunt Jo visits, she often shows slides of her most recent trip.
3. All of these pronunciations are taken from the *american heritage dictionary*.
4. Some of the gods in greek mythology were also worshiped in ancient asian and egyptian cultures.
5. Did you hear commissioner of education smathers' speech recommending a longer school day?
6. The vice-president is to speak at the governors' conference.
7. After the secretary read the minutes, the treasurer reported on the club's budget.

8. Lillian Hellman wrote *watch on the rhine*.
9. My older brother subscribes to *field and stream*.
10. The first politician to make a shuttle flight was senator Jake Garn of Utah.

REVIEW EXERCISE A. Correcting Sentences by Capitalizing Words. Number your paper 1–10. After the proper number, write and capitalize the words requiring capitals.

1. mr. arroyo is a vice-president of atom electronics.
2. lieutenant betty leifheit visited our class and told us about her experiences at the united states naval academy at annapolis, maryland.
3. my friend John is attending a summer camp at tulsa junior college, where he is taking classes in biology, journalism, music, and american literature.
4. is your mother still teaching an art appreciation class at the swen parson gallery?
5. have you read margaret walker's poem "childhood"?
6. one volume of anne morrow lindbergh's diaries and letters is titled *hour of gold, hour of lead*.
7. we took these pictures at uncle dave's cabin at green lake last summer with our kodak camera.
8. next week the class officers will meet with principal adams.
9. alice yen has been elected treasurer of our club.
10. the city park is bounded on the north by highway 23 and on the south by tilton park drive.

REVIEW EXERCISE B. Correcting Sentences by Capitalizing Words. Number your paper 1–10. After the proper number, write and capitalize the words requiring capitals.

1. Our friends the browns hosted an exchange student from argentina.
2. The king ranch in texas is as large as rhode island.
3. Ms. epstein is taking courses in computer programming I, french, and english at rand community college.

4. The sixth day of the week, friday, gets its name from a norse goddess.

5. Both the christian holiday of christmas and the jewish holiday of hanuka are celebrated in december.

6. My uncle ron was stationed in the south pacific when he was an ensign in the united states navy.

7. The liberty bell, which is on display in independence hall in philadelphia, was rung to proclaim the boston tea party and to announce the first public reading of the declaration of independence.

8. Many people consider the bible great literature as well as the word of god.

9. Emily dickinson and robert frost, both new england poets, are among the best-loved american poets.

10. I walk to the eagle supermarket each sunday for the *miami herald* and a quart of tropicana orange juice.

WRITING APPLICATION:
Using Capital Letters Correctly to Make Your Writing Clear

Using capital letters correctly helps you make your writing clear. A capital letter signals your readers that you are referring to a specific person, place, or thing. Compare the following pairs of sentences:

EXAMPLES   Exit at the third street ramp.
Exit at the Third Street ramp.

This new Mexican bracelet was a gift.
This New Mexican bracelet was a gift.

She perched on the back of the mustang to have her picture taken.
She perched on the back of the Mustang to have her picture taken.

To make your meaning clear, always proofread your writing carefully to make sure that you have used capital letters correctly.

Writing Assignment

Write ten sentences, using one of the items in the following list in each sentence. Proofread the sentences carefully to make sure that you have used capital letters correctly to make your meaning clear.

1. The name of a magazine
2. A business
3. A mountain range
4. The title of a person
5. The title of a book
6. A geographical section of the country
7. The name of a street
8. A language and two other school subjects
9. A historical event
10. A continent

REVIEW EXERCISE C. Correcting Sentences by Correcting Capitalization Errors. Number your paper 1–20. For each sentence, write in order the words that should be capitalized and capitalize them. Also write the words that are incorrectly capitalized and omit the capitals.

1. The president's saturday talks from the white house were broadcast on the radio.
2. In History class, we learned about women suffragettes such as elizabeth cady stanton, susan b. anthony, and lucretia c. mott.
3. A great many words came into the english language from greek and latin.
4. At elgin larkin high school, students must complete three years of Math, three of Science, and four of English.
5. Each summer a group from the methodist youth fellowship travels to appalachia to help poor people in the area.
6. The empire state building is 265.5 feet taller than the eiffel tower.

7. In April, the cherry blossom festival will be celebrated by a Parade in the heart of the City.

8. The 1984 summer olympics were held in los angeles, California.

9. The rio grande flows along the Southern border of Texas; it is one of the most famous rivers in north america.

10. jane addams, an American Social Reformer who founded hull house in chicago, was awarded the 1931 nobel peace prize.

11. Many of the countries of europe are smaller than some states in our country.

12. The President of the local volunteer society received the volunteer-of-the-year award two years in a row.

13. My parents subscribe to *national geographic* and *time*.

14. William Least Heat Moon began his journey around America in the southeast.

15. Seeing the Redwood forests was a highlight of our trip to California.

16. Bonds were sold to raise money for the construction of a new Junior High School in Sycamore.

17. A new general electric plant, to be built South of lincoln highway, will employ six hundred people.

18. The University was the site of a convention of african and south american scientists.

19. The panama canal connects the atlantic ocean and the pacific ocean; the new york state barge canal connects the hudson river and lake erie.

20. Edna Ferber's *so big, cimarron,* and *giant* give a colorful picture of american life during times of rapid growth.

CHAPTER 13 REVIEW: POSTTEST 1

Correcting Sentences by Using Capitalization Correctly.
Number your paper 1–25. Each of the following sentences contains an error in capitalization. After the proper number,

write the word or words correctly, supplying capitals where they are necessary and omitting capitals where they are unnecessary.

EXAMPLE   1. The shubert Theater is located at 225 West Forty-fourth Street in New York.
      1. *Shubert*

1. On June 6, 1944, the Allies invaded Normandy and began marching toward victory in world war II.
2. Elena always got high scores in mathematics, while Dee did well in english.
3. Several of the planets in our solar system were named after Roman Gods.
4. When we drove to Alaska, we visited several old mines that had been abandoned after the yukon Gold Rush.
5. In history class we had to memorize the Capitals of all the states.
6. Uncle Ron owns one of the first honda motorcycles that was sold in America.
7. Knowing that I am a sports fan, my cousin gave me a terrific book, *Rules of the game,* which illustrates the rules of all sorts of games.
8. My grandmother makes delicious boston brown bread.
9. The coach yelled, "run out for a long bomb, Slater."
10. Rajiv Gandhi, the prime minister of India, visited Washington, D.C., in June of 1985.
11. The Indus river flows from the Himalaya Mountains to the Arabian Sea.
12. Appearing on television and writing popular books, dr. Carl Sagan has done much to increase public interest in science.
13. In the afternoons we used to help Mrs. Parkhurst deliver the *Evening Independent,* a local Newspaper.
14. Some people think that the first woman president of the United States will be elected before the turn of the century.
15. Stavros and several of his friends belong to the Civil air Patrol.

16. As economic conditions changed, people began leaving Northern states and moving to the South and West.
17. Everybody is looking forward to the big fourth of July picnic.
18. I can hardly wait for Summer vacation, when I will get to stay at my grandparents' farm.
19. Are we going to eat at tides restaurant tonight, mom?
20. Two of my friends attended the olympics in Los Angeles.
21. Who do you think will win the World series this year?
22. *Romeo and Juliet* is the first shakespearean play that I have read.
23. Ernest Hemingway and Robert Service are two of the famous writers who served in the red cross during the Spanish Civil War.
24. My brother owns an IBM computer with a zenith monitor and an Olympia printer.
25. Many charitable organizations are helping the people affected by the famine in africa.

CHAPTER 13 REVIEW: POSTTEST 2

Correcting Sentences by Using Capitalization Correctly. Number your paper 1–25. Each of the following sentences contains one or more errors in capitalization. After the proper number, write the word or words correctly, supplying capitals where they are necessary and omitting capitals where they are unnecessary.

EXAMPLE   1. We had french toast, orange juice, and apples for breakfast at aunt Gwen's house.
   1. *French, Aunt*

1. Next year my sister will graduate from mayfair high school and go to the university in the state capital.
2. When we found the injured german shepherd, we took it to our veterinarian, dr. Rita Molina.

3. Could you please tell me how to get to the chrysler Factory on highway 21 and riverside road?
4. I used to read my brother's copies of *boys' life* when he was in the boy Scouts.
5. Throughout europe during the dark ages, it was considered sinful to charge interest on loans.
6. The woman in the bait shop said to steer the boat North across the lake to the mouth of Fisheating creek.
7. For father's day, we bought Dad a new power saw.
8. Elizabeth asked, "Why can't I stay up and see the new year's show at Midnight, too?"
9. Joyce does volunteer work at good samaritan hospital on Weekends and Tuesday Evenings.
10. Have you ever seen any of the original Donald duck cartoons that they show in the theater on main street in Disney World?
11. My grandfather was an army Lieutenant in the Battle of the bulge.
12. Last year we studied the hapsburg empire and learned how Bavaria and other states joined together to become Germany.
13. My Aunt has seen every super Bowl, even the first one between the Green Bay packers and the Kansas City chiefs.
14. From the time I was six until I was fourteen, my Parents sent me to camp nikamongo every Summer.
15. The Ohio department of education provided buses to help evacuate the victims of the tornado in June.
16. Anwar Sadat was one of the most famous egyptian leaders in Modern Times.
17. On our trip to new York, we visited the Museum of natural history, the statue of Liberty, and many other famous Sights.
18. In the south, the civil war is sometimes called the war between the States.

19. The saint Lawrence Seaway connects the Atlantic ocean and the great lakes.
20. When We read "fire and ice" by Robert Frost, I understood what the Poem meant.
21. At the beginning of their long journey, the Pioneer families knelt beside their wagons and prayed to god for guidance.
22. The secretary of state advised the president against taking any Military action.
23. Before you can take Advanced computer programming I, you have to take Calculus and basic computer Programming I.
24. When I ate Supper at Cam's house, I tried *nuoc mam,* a vietnamese fish sauce.
25. To get to woodside mall, turn left at the deep pit barbecue palace; then turn right at park street, and you'll see the Mall on the Left.

SUMMARY STYLE SHEET

This list gives examples of the rules of capitalization in this chapter. Use it as a review by studying each item and explaining the use of each capital or small letter. The list will also be convenient for quick reference.

Johnson City	a city in Tennessee
Aztec Motel	a motel in Miami
Second Street	a street in Pasadena
Milton Pond	a pond in Milton
the Northeast	a northeast gale
North Dakota	north of South Dakota
the Music Club	a club for musicians
Slater Woolen Company	a woolen company
Topeka High School	a high school in Topeka
the Korean War	a war in Korea
the John Hancock Building	an insurance building
Washington's Birthday	Christine's birthday
the Industrial Revolution	a revolution in manufacturing
God, our Father	the gods of Greek mythology
the Winter Prom	a prom in the winter
the Sophomore Class	a class of sophomores
French, English, Russian	mathematics, music, geography

Science II	a lesson in **science**
Principal Harris	Ms. **Harris**, the **principal**
the **President** of the **United States**	the **president** of the company
Will you call **Mother** (*or* **mother**)?	My **mother** is here.
Aunt Marie	her **aunt**
the *American Girl*	a monthly **magazine**
the *Dallas Times Herald*	a **newspaper**
The War of the Worlds	an exciting **book**
customs of the **Japanese**	national **customs**
an **Episcopalian**	a sermon in **church**
Ford truck	a **pickup** truck

Punctuation

END MARKS, COMMAS, SEMICOLONS, COLONS

In spoken language the voice indicates pauses and full stops, but in written language punctuation does the work. Although it might seem as if writing would be easier without using periods or commas or other marks of punctuation, the result would be very difficult to read. In this chapter and the next one, you will learn to master punctuation so that your writing will be clear.

DIAGNOSTIC TEST

Correcting Sentences by Adding End Marks, Commas, Semicolons, and Colons. Write the following sentences, inserting end marks, commas, semicolons, and colons where they are needed.

EXAMPLE   1. Have you seen our teacher Ms. O'Donnell today
           1. *Have you seen our teacher, Ms. O'Donnell, today?*

1. My neighbor, the lady with red hair used to be my baby-sitter when I was younger and I still visit her sometimes
2. We made a salad with the following vegetables from our garden lettuce cucumbers carrots and celery
3. Running after the bus Melody tripped and fell in a puddle

4. My first pet which I got when I was six was a beagle I named it Bagel

5. You in the back row Randy hush up right now

6. The award was given for the best-written most interesting report about air pollution

7. My mother said that we could go to the lake however it looks like it's going to rain

8. Does anyone know where the crank that we use to open the top windows is

9. The chickens clucked the dogs barked and the ducks squawked

10. Over the weekend I saw Charly's twin brother who used to work at the grocery store at the motocross bike course

11. Wow That's the longest homer I've ever hit

12. After the rain stopped falling the blue jays hopped around the lawn in search of worms

13. Wasn't President John F. Kennedy assassinated on November 22 1963

14. Why wasn't Sid's last letter which was mailed May 5 delivered until June 5

15. Everybody had told her of course that it was useless to try

16. The jetliner filled with fuel and preparing for takeoff rolled slowly toward the runway

17. Hand in your test your answer sheet and your scratch paper.

18. What shall we do after 3:00 when school lets out Yolanda

19. Her address is 142 Oak Hollow Court Mendota CA 93640

20. My cousins will stay here tonight or they will drive on to Aunt Cindy's house

---

END MARKS

14a. A statement is followed by a period.

EXAMPLES The lens is the most important part of a camera.
One of the figure skaters was Sonja Henie.

14b. A question is followed by a question mark.

EXAMPLES   Have you watched Barbara Walters**?**
               Is photography a science or an art**?**

14c. An exclamation is followed by an exclamation point.

EXAMPLES   What a good time we had**!**
               Wow**!** What a view**!**

14d. An imperative sentence is followed by either a period or an exclamation point.

EXAMPLES   Please give me the scissors**.** [making a request]
               Give me the scissors**!** [showing strong feeling]

EXERCISE 1. Correcting Paragraphs by Adding End Marks. Number your paper 1–20. In the following paragraphs, sentences have been run together without end marks. Write the last word of every sentence and the first word of the next sentence, inserting the proper end mark. There are twenty end marks to supply. Use one line of your paper for each end mark.

Have you ever visited New Salem Park in Illinois There you will find a reproduction of the little village of New Salem, just as it was when Abraham Lincoln lived there If you do visit this village, you will find that life in Lincoln's time was much harder than it is today

What tiny, crude cabins the people lived in The twenty-three cabins include ten shops, a school, and a sawmill There is also a carding mill, where wool fibers were cleaned and straightened before they were spun into cloth

The cabin of the Onstats is not a reproduction but the original cabin where Lincoln spent many hours In that living room, on that very floor, young Abe Lincoln studied with Isaac Onstat The rest of the Onstat family were also there It was the cabin's only room

Across the way a big kettle hangs under a porch This is the original kettle used by Mr. Waddell for boiling wool Mr. Waddell, the hatter of the village, made hats of wool and fur

If you look into the various cabins, you will see rough floors and walls and uncomfortable-looking furniture You might wonder how you would enjoy living in such a home In almost every cabin there is a ladder running up to the loft, where some of the family slept How cold it was up there in winter and how hot in summer

Do any of you feel you would like to go back to those days What endurance those people must have had Could we manage to live as they did

14e. **An abbreviation is followed by a period.**

EXAMPLES	min.	minute	Neb.	Nebraska
	St.	Street	in.	inch
	Dr.	Doctor	Mr.	Mister
	Aug.	August	Co.	Company

Note that *Miss* preceding a woman's name is not an abbreviation and is not followed by a period. Similar titles—*Mr., Mrs., Ms.*—are abbreviations. Initials used with a name are abbreviations of names and should be followed by periods.

EXAMPLES Miss Ellsworth
A. B. Guthrie
Ms. Angstrom

COMMAS

A comma does not indicate a full stop, as a period does. Instead, it divides a sentence into readable parts by indicating pauses. If you master the use of the comma, your written work will improve in clarity. One word of warning: Do not use commas carelessly. Have a reason for every comma you put into a sentence.

Items in a Series

14f. Use commas to separate items in a series.

Words, phrases, and clauses in a series should be separated by commas so that the reader can tell where one item in the series ends and the next item begins.

(1) Use commas to separate words in a series.

EXAMPLES We have read poems by Longfellow, Teasdale, and Dickinson this week.

Tobacco, hammock, canoe, and *barbecue* are four of the many words that English-speaking people owe to American Indians.

In the early morning, the lake looked cold, gray, and uninviting.

Get in the habit of using a comma before the *and* joining the last two items in a series. Although many writers omit this comma, it is sometimes necessary to make your meaning clear.

UNCLEAR Next year we will study algebra, civics, French and American history. [No comma used; will we study the French language or French history?]

CLEAR Next year we will study algebra, civics, French, and American history.

CLEAR Next year we will study algebra, civics, French history, and American history.

(2) Use commas to separate phrases in a series.

EXAMPLES We found seaweed in the water, on the sand, under the rocks, and even in our shoes.

It makes no difference whether that hamster is in a cage, on a string, or under a net—it always escapes.

(3) Use commas to separate subordinate clauses and short independent clauses in a series.

EXAMPLES   Everyone wondered when he had been in the house,
            what he had wanted, and where he had gone.

            We worked, we played, and we rested.

(4) If all items in a series are joined by *and* or *or*, do not use commas to separate them.

EXAMPLE   Have you read *Huckleberry Finn* or *Tom Sawyer* or *A
           Connecticut Yankee in King Arthur's Court*?

EXERCISE 2. Correcting Sentences by Adding Commas.
Number your paper 1–10. After the proper number, show where
commas are needed in each sentence by writing the word before a
necessary comma and adding the comma. Two of the sentences
do not require commas. Write *C* after the number of each of
those sentences.

EXAMPLE   1. Each American eats an average of 117 pounds of
              potatoes 116 pounds of beef and 100 pounds of
              fresh vegetables each year.
           1. *potatoes, beef,*

1. Have you heard of vitamin K vitamin T or vitamin H?
2. Carlos and Anna and Francie ran across the park climbed
   over the fence and hurried to the bus stop.
3. You can learn more about photography ham radios art or
   chess by joining one of the school clubs.
4. The three states that have produced the most U.S. Presidents
   are Virginia and Ohio and New York.
5. The school band includes clarinets saxophones trumpets
   trombones tubas flutes piccolos and drums.
6. Check to see if that coin is stamped with the letter *D* the
   letter *S* or no letter at all.
7. That information indicates whether the coin was minted in
   Denver in San Francisco or in Philadelphia.
8. Are you taking home economics or woodworking or drama
   this year?

9. Most flutes used by professional musicians are made of sterling silver 14-carat gold or platinum.
10. We discussed what we would write about where we would find sources and how we would organize our reports.

EXERCISE 3. Correcting Sentences by Adding Commas.

Number your paper 1–10. After the proper number, show where commas are needed in each sentence by writing the word before a necessary comma and adding the comma.

EXAMPLE 1. Find out when the picnic is what we should take and who wants to ride with us.
       1. *is, take,*

1. No one knew what had started the argument when the two had begun to fight or why they were now both laughing loudly.
2. Financial writer Sylvia Porter has written a book explaining how to earn money and how to spend it borrow it and save it.
3. Yesterday Maxine raked the leaves Tasha mowed the lawn and then we all went swimming.
4. According to the weather forecast the front will move through our area this evening the skies will clear and the temperature will turn cool.
5. Last summer I read *The Red Badge of Courage The Wizard of Earthsea The Virginian* and *A Wrinkle in Time.*
6. We are learning how to select a subject how to limit it and how to gather information.
7. Tammy and Necia plan to check the card catalog to prepare lists of possible sources and to take detailed notes.
8. The San Joaquin kit fox the ocelot the Florida panther and the red wolf are some of the endangered mammals in North America.
9. I would like to visit Thailand Nepal China and Japan, the Land of the Rising Sun.
10. Swimming biking and brisk walking are all excellent forms of exercise.

14g. Use a comma to separate two or more adjectives preceding a noun.

EXAMPLES   An Arabian stallion is a fast, beautiful horse.
The early rancher often depended on the small, tough, sure-footed mustang.

When the final adjective is so closely connected to the noun that the words seem to form one expression, do not use a comma before the final adjective.

EXAMPLE   Training a frisky colt to become a gentle, dependable riding horse takes great patience. [No comma is used between *dependable* and *riding* because the words *riding horse* are closely connected in meaning and may be taken as one term.]

A comma should never be used between an adjective and the noun immediately following it.

INCORRECT   Mary O'Hara wrote a tender, suspenseful, story about a young boy and his colt.

CORRECT   Mary O'Hara wrote a tender, suspenseful story about a young boy and his colt.

EXERCISE 4. Correcting Sentences by Adding Commas.
Write the following sentences, inserting commas where needed.

EXAMPLE   1. A squat dark cooking stove stood in one corner of the kitchen.
1. *A squat, dark cooking stove stood in one corner of the kitchen.*

1. The cool misty drizzle was a welcome change after the heat wave.
2. Jose has a quick lively sense of humor.
3. The children made a clubhouse in the empty unused storage shed.
4. This book describes the harsh isolated lives of pioneer women in Kansas.
5. What a lovely haunting melody that tune has!

6. A group of proud smiling parents watched the nervous young musicians take their places on the stage.
7. The breakthrough resulted from the scientists' long hard years of work.
8. The delicate colorful wings of the ruby-throated humming-bird vibrate up to two hundred times each second.
9. Have you read May Swenson's clever tantalizing poems?
10. In the attic they discovered an old trunk filled with shabby faded out-of-style clothes.

Compound Sentences

14h. Use a comma before *and, but, or, nor, for,* and *yet* when they join independent clauses.

EXAMPLES   The musical comedy originated in America, and it has retained a distinctly American flavor.

Grand opera is a popular form of entertainment in Europe, but few Americans take the opportunity to see live productions of operas.

Singers must devote many years to training and practice, for a musical career is a demanding one.

If the clauses in a compound sentence are very short, the comma before the conjunction may be omitted.

EXAMPLE   Hammerstein wrote the words and Rodgers wrote the music.

To follow comma rule 14h, you must be able to distinguish a compound sentence from a simple sentence with a compound verb.

COMPOUND SENTENCE Margo likes tennis and golf, but she doesn't enjoy archery. [comma between independent clauses joined by a conjunction]

SIMPLE SENTENCE WITH COMPOUND VERB Margo likes tennis and golf but doesn't enjoy archery. [no comma between parts of compound verb joined by a conjunction]

EXERCISE 5. Correcting Compound Sentences by Adding Commas. Number your paper 1–10. After the proper number, write the words in the sentence that should be followed by commas. Add the commas. Several sentences do not require commas. Write *C* after the number of each of those sentences.

EXAMPLE   1. Have you read this article in *Nature* or do you want me to tell you about it?
1. *Nature,*

1. Human beings must study to become architects yet some animals build amazing structures by instinct.
2. The male orange-crested gardener bird builds a complex structure and decorates it carefully to attract a mate.
3. This bird constructs a dome-shaped garden in a small tree and underneath the tree it lays a carpet of moss covered with brilliant tropical flowers.
4. As a finishing touch, the bird gathers twigs and arranges them in a three-foot-wide circle around the display.
5. Prairie dogs might be called the city planners of the plains for they create huge networks of underground burrows.
6. These burrows may stretch hundreds of miles and house millions of prairie dogs.
7. The prairie dogs do not often leave their own small territories within the complex but they can somehow tell their neighbors from strangers.
8. The female European water spider builds a waterproof nest underwater and it stocks the nest with air bubbles.
9. This air supply is very important for it allows the spider to hunt underwater.
10. The water spider also lays its eggs in the waterproof nest and they hatch there.

Phrases and Clauses

Participial phrases, as you learned on page 123, act as adjectives to modify nouns or pronouns. Subordinate clauses may also act as adjectives (see page 152).

In some sentences, the participial phrase or adjective clause is essential to the thought. It cannot be removed without destroying the meaning of the sentence.

EXAMPLES   All farmers **growing hybrid corn** owe a debt to an Austrian monk named Gregor Mendel. [The participial phrase in boldfaced type tells which farmers. It is essential to the meaning of the sentence.]

Mendel made the discoveries **that have become the basis of modern genetics.** [The adjective clause modifies *discoveries*. It cannot be removed without destroying the meaning of the sentence.]

In other sentences, the participial phrase or adjective clause is *not* essential to the thought. Such a phrase or clause can be removed without changing the basic meaning.

EXAMPLES   Sometimes seeds and nuts**, forgotten by the squirrels that hid them,** germinate far away from their parent plants. [The participial phrase can be removed without changing the basic meaning of the sentence: *Sometimes seeds and nuts germinate far away from their parent plants.*]

Migrating birds**, which often fly hundreds or thousands of miles,** are one of the main carriers of seeds. [The adjective clause can be removed without changing the basic meaning of the sentence: *Migrating birds are one of the main carriers of seeds.*]

14i. Use commas to set off participial phrases and adjective clauses that are not essential to the basic meaning of the sentence. Do not use commas with phrases or clauses that are essential to the meaning.

To set off with commas means to separate from the rest of the sentence. If the phrase or clause comes in the middle of the sentence, a comma is needed before and after it. If the phrase or clause comes at the end, a comma is needed before it; if the phrase or clause comes at the beginning of the sentence, a comma is needed after it.

EXAMPLES   A new spider web**,** **shining in the morning light,** is an impressive example of engineering. [nonessential participial phrase; commas needed]

Anyone **who finishes early** may start on tomorrow's assignment. [essential adjective clause; no commas needed]

If a participial phrase or adjective clause is preceded by a proper noun, a comma is ordinarily needed to separate it from the noun.

EXAMPLE   Cybill reported on *Insects and Plants***,** which was written by Elizabeth Cooper.

EXERCISE 6. Correcting Sentences by Adding Commas to Set Off Participial Phrases and Adjective Clauses.

Number your paper 1–20. Write *C* after the numbers of sentences that are correctly punctuated. After the numbers of other sentences, write the words that should be followed by commas and add the commas.

1. Ynes Mexia hoping to find new kinds of plants explored the dense jungles of Brazil.
2. The plants that she collected were carefully dried and preserved.
3. Traveling and working alone for many months she found a tremendous variety of new and unusual plants.
4. Mrs. Nina Floy who was an assistant to Ynes Mexia kept detailed records of Mexia's jungle discoveries.
5. Ynes Mexia who spent a year in search of unknown plants on the South American continent collected nearly one thousand new varieties of plants on her expedition.
6. Louis Pasteur studying spoilage in liquids developed a method for killing disease-producing bacteria.
7. Pierre and Marie Curie are the scientists who discovered both radium and polonium.
8. Marie Sklodowska Curie who was awarded the Nobel Prize twice devoted her life to her work.

9. Irene Curie who was the daughter of Pierre and Marie also was awarded the Nobel Prize.
10. Mount McKinley rising 20,320 feet in Alaska is the highest mountain in the United States.
11. The citizens who named the towns of Waterproof, Louisiana, and Why, Arizona, must have had a good sense of humor.
12. Which state is the only one named after a U.S. President?
13. The word *bonnet* which in the United States means a type of hat in Great Britain means the hood of a car.
14. Do you know any other words that mean one thing in the United States and another in Great Britain?
15. President Carter whose full name is James Earl Carter prefers to be known as Jimmy.
16. He was born in Plains which is a small town in Georgia.
17. Carter who graduated from the U.S. Naval Academy studied nuclear physics.
18. After his Navy service he returned to Georgia serving first as a state senator and later as Governor.
19. Winning the Democratic Party's nomination for the Presidency Carter defeated President Ford in the 1976 election.
20. Carter whose family owned several businesses in Plains returned to live there in 1981.

14j. Use a comma after a participial phrase or an adverb clause that begins a sentence.

EXAMPLES **Forced onto the sidelines by a torn ligament,** Harris was restless and unhappy. [introductory participial phrase]

When March came, the huge ice pack began to melt and break up. [introductory adverb clause]

An adverb clause that comes at the end of a sentence does not usually need a comma.

EXAMPLE The huge ice pack began to melt and break up **when March came.**

EXERCISE 7. Correcting Sentences by Adding Commas to Set Off Participial Phrases and Introductory Clauses.

Number your paper 1–10. After the proper number, if a comma is needed in a sentence, supply it by writing the word before it and adding the comma. If no comma is needed, write *C* after the number.

EXAMPLE 1. Stopping at the post office I mailed the letters.
1. *office,*

1. Although mail delivery is as old as recorded history the first postage stamps were not used until the nineteenth century.
2. The idea of using prepaid postage stamps was adopted after it was suggested by a British educator.
3. Originally picturing government officials or national symbols stamps soon began to feature a wide variety of other items.
4. Stamp collecting became a popular hobby when stamps became more varied.
5. Because stamps provide a colorful record of many parts of life they are fascinating.
6. Although most stamps are issued to pay for the delivery of mail special issues are produced for sale to collectors.
7. Enjoyed by more than twenty million people in the United States alone stamp collecting is a favorite pastime of both young and old.
8. Collectors can always look forward to adding new stamps because new designs are issued often.
9. Since a collection of every type of stamp ever issued would be too bulky many collectors concentrate on a single topic such as religion or flowers or fish.
10. Filling albums with their treasures collectors enjoy examining their first stamps as well as their latest ones.

Interrupters

When an expression such as *of course* or *well* or a person's name interrupts a sentence, commas are needed to set off the interrupter. If the interrupting expression comes in the middle of the sentence, two commas are needed. If it comes first or last, only one comma is needed.

14k. Use a comma after a word such as *well, yes, no, why* when it begins a sentence.

EXAMPLES   Why, you really should know about Sarah Winnemucca!
Yes, she helped her Piute people.
No, I have not heard about her.
Well, she opened a school in Nevada.

> ☞ NOTE Words such as *well, yes, no,* and *why* are not followed by a comma if they do not interrupt the sentence; that is, if no pause follows them: *Why is Rebecca early?*

14l. Use commas to set off an expression that interrupts a sentence.

(1) Appositives and appositive phrases are usually set off by commas.

An *appositive* is a word that means the same thing as the noun it follows; usually it explains or identifies the noun. An appositive phrase is an appositive plus the words that go with it.

EXAMPLES   Have you ever been in Texas, **the Lone Star State**? [*The Lone Star State* is an appositive meaning the same thing as *Texas.*]

The Rio Grande, **one of the major rivers of North America,** forms part of the border between Texas and Mexico. [*One of the major rivers of North America* is an appositive phrase meaning the same thing as *Rio Grande.*]

> ☞ **NOTE** When an appositive is closely related to the word it follows, no comma is needed. Such appositives are usually one word: *my sister Odelite.*

EXERCISE 8. Correcting Sentences by Adding Commas to Set Off Appositives. After the proper number, write the sentences that require commas. Insert the commas. If a sentence is correct, write *C.*

EXAMPLE   1. The dog a boxer is named Brindle.
          1. *The dog, a boxer, is named Brindle.*

1. The composer Mozart wrote five short piano pieces when he was only six years old.
2. Katy Jurado the actress has appeared in many fine motion pictures.
3. Harper Lee the author of *To Kill a Mockingbird* was born in Alabama.
4. Did you know that the card game canasta is descended from mah-jongg an ancient Chinese game?
5. Jupiter the fifth planet from the sun is so large that all the other planets in our solar system would fit inside it.
6. Parrots the best-known talking birds rarely learn more than twenty words.
7. The writing of Elizabeth Bowen an Irish novelist shows her keen, witty observations of life.
8. Charlemagne the king of the Franks in the eighth and ninth centuries became Emperor of the Holy Roman Empire.
9. The family next door has two unusual pets a skunk and a tarantula.
10. What grade did you get on the history quiz the one on world capitals?

(2) Words used in direct address are set off by commas.

When someone speaks directly to another person, using that person's name, commas precede and follow the name.[1]

EXAMPLES Would you rather go to Africa or South America, **Hazel**?

Mrs. Clarkson, I just want to get to the beach.

Can you tell me, **Sir,** when the next bus is due?

EXERCISE 9. Correcting Sentences by Adding Commas to Set Off Words in Direct Address.
Number your paper 1–10. After the proper number, write the words in the sentence that should be followed by a comma, and add the comma.

EXAMPLE 1. Are you hungry Jan or have you already had lunch?

1. *hungry, Jan,*

1. Ms. Wu will you schedule me for the computer lab tomorrow?
2. Have you signed up for a baseball team yet Aaron?
3. Did you remember Rose to list all the sources you used for your report?
4. Your time was good in the hurdles Juanita but I know you can do better.
5. Yvette and Lori please draw the shades so that we can watch the film.
6. You rascal that was no shortcut you took us on.
7. Do you have to work late tonight Mother or will you be home for supper?
8. Be sure to wear sturdy shoes girls; those hills are hard on the feet!
9. Run Susan; the bus is pulling out!
10. Boys have you cleaned your room yet?

(3) Parenthetical expressions are set off by commas.

Occasionally a sentence is interrupted by an expression such as *to tell the truth, in my opinion, in fact*. Such expressions are

---

[1] For rules governing the use of commas in dialogue, see page 374.

called *parenthetical* because, like words enclosed in parentheses, they are not grammatically related to the rest of the sentence. These expressions are set off by commas.

EXAMPLES   The President said**, off the record,** that he was deeply disappointed.

To be honest, I thought the movie was fairly good. It wasn't very good**, in my opinion.**

The following expressions are often used parenthetically.

in fact	however
mind you	for example
as I was saying	to tell the truth
of course	nevertheless
on the contrary	I suppose (*or* know *or* believe
for instance	*or* hope)
in my opinion	if you ask me

Such expressions are not always parenthetical. Be careful to use commas only if they are needed.

EXAMPLES   What**, in her opinion,** is the best closing hour? [a parenthetical expression set off by commas]

I have no faith **in her opinion.** [not a parenthetical expression; no comma needed]

Traveling by boat may take longer**, however.** [a parenthetical expression, preceded by a comma]

However you go, it will be a delightful trip. [*However* not used parenthetically; no comma needed]

EXERCISE 10. Correcting Sentences by Adding Commas to Set Off Parenthetical Expressions.

Number your paper 1–10. After the proper number, write the words in the sentence that should be followed by commas, and add the commas.

EXAMPLE   1. Mathematics I'm afraid is my hardest subject.
 1. *Mathematics, afraid,*

1. The situation is if you ask me very unfortunate.
2. Your subject I think should be limited further.

3. I'm not saying mind you that I agree with their methods.
4. Yes Mary Wells Lawrence has been extremely successful in advertising.
5. You will come back soon I hope and visit us again.
6. Why those soldiers are only children!
7. Flying however will be more expensive.
8. No I do not enjoy murder mysteries.
9. His confession in fact cost him his TV privileges for a week.
10. Nevertheless his honesty pleased his parents.

14m. Use a comma in certain conventional situations.

The conventions of English usage require that commas be used in dates, in addresses, and after the salutations and closings of letters.

(1) Use a comma to separate items in dates and addresses.

EXAMPLES   The delegates to the Constitutional Convention signed the Constitution on September 17, 1787, in Philadelphia, Pennsylvania.

The Passover holiday begins on Wednesday, April 14, this year.

My friend has just moved to 6448 Higgins Road, Chicago, Illinois.

In an address, you should leave some space between the ZIP code and the state (unless you are writing it in a sentence). No comma should come before it.

EXAMPLE Jackson Heights, New York   11372

> ☞ **NOTE** If a preposition is used between items of an address, a comma is not necessary: *He lives at 144 Smith Street in Moline, Illinois.*

(2) Use a comma after the salutation of a friendly letter and after the closing of any letter.

EXAMPLES   Dear Aunt Margaret,
               Sincerely yours,
               Yours truly,

EXERCISE 11. Correcting Dates, Addresses, and Letter Parts by Adding Commas. After the proper number, write the following items on your paper, inserting commas wherever needed.

1. 11687 Montana Avenue Los Angeles CA 90049
2. 1615 West Touhy Avenue Chicago IL 60626
3. Monday December 2 1985
4. after January 1 1986
5. Dresser Road at North First Street in Lynchburg Virginia
6. Memorial Day 1985
7. from December 1 1985 to March 15 1986
8. either Thursday April 18 or Monday April 22
9. Dear Joanne
10. Sincerely yours

WRITING APPLICATION A:
Using Commas to Separate Items

Using commas between words, phrases, and short independent clauses signals your reader that each item is a separate one. Compare the following examples:

EXAMPLES   We invited Mary Beth Hardy and Bill.
               We invited Mary Beth, Hardy, and Bill.
               We invited Mary, Beth, Hardy, and Bill.

The first sentence indicates that two persons were invited. The second sentence shows that three were invited, while the third sentence increases the guest list to four. As you can see, using commas to separate items can make a big difference in the meaning of a sentence. When you proofread your writing, be sure that you have used commas correctly to make your meaning clear.

Writing Assignment

Write a paragraph describing a busy scene, using words that appeal to the senses—sight, sound, touch, taste, and smell. After you revise your paragraph, proofread it carefully to be sure that you have used commas correctly to make your meaning clear. Then prepare a clean copy of your paragraph.

REVIEW EXERCISE A. Correcting Sentences by Adding Commas. Number your paper 1–20. If a comma is needed in a sentence, supply it by writing the word before it and adding the comma. If a sentence is correctly punctuated, write *C*.

1. Determined to succeed in life John set strict goals for himself.
2. He practiced the piano two hours every day read books on many subjects and kept a detailed journal.
3. Some of the qualities that make a person a good friend are loyalty tact and humor.
4. Someday Ann hopes to write a novel that will sell millions of copies.
5. She will have to work hard to improve her writing of course.
6. Although Ms. Delano's tests are not easy they are fair.
7. Members of the drama club the newspaper staff and the science club will have their pictures taken at 10:00 A.M. on Friday November 8.
8. The club sponsors who will be excused from their teaching duties will be included in the pictures.
9. The student-faculty basketball games are exciting hilarious events.
10. When the game was over, the players tired and disappointed walked slowly to the showers.

11. Hoping to be chosen for the swimming team Ramon practiced his diving daily.
12. Ms. Strubhart the school principal was the most enthusiastic fan in the stands.
13. Watching the acrobats soar through space, Earline decided that circus life was for her.
14. We have driven through the Blue Ridge Mountains several times and we always enjoy the scenery.
15. Requiring large investments farming has become very expensive.
16. The heavily wooded hills are lovely in the spring, but they are even more beautiful in the fall.
17. The students whose projects have been chosen for the county science fair will meet after school today.
18. Rainbows can be seen only when the sun is 40 degrees or less above the horizon.
19. Since oats, corn, and wheat are all grasses most cereal is grass!
20. Most sugar also comes from a grass sugar cane.

REVIEW EXERCISE B. Correcting Sentences by Adding Commas and End Marks. Number your paper 1–20. After the proper number, supply commas and end marks in the following sentences by writing the word before a mark of punctuation and adding the comma or end mark.

1. If we include New York City in our vacation plans we will certainly go to the Statue of Liberty
2. Yes Marilyn the statue should be restored by then
3. The famous statue was dedicated on October 18 1886
4. Few people know its full name the Statue of Liberty Enlightening the World
5. The statue which was given to the United States by France has become a symbol of freedom
6. Have you ever made the long tiring trip up the stairs to the head of the statue Alan

7. What a view of the nation's largest city you get from there Mary

8. Fred stopping for lunch now will make us late for the tour of Montreal

9. When you travel in Canada Joe you will know you are no longer in the United States

10. Notice for example the signs that allow speeds up to 100 kilometers per hour

11. How fast is that in miles per hour

12. Well it converts to about 62 miles per hour I think

13. Some states have passed laws requiring the use of seat belts and others are considering such laws

14. Bicycles stairs and doors cause more home accidents than any other objects

15. If people kept stairways clear put games and equipment away and watched where they were going there would be fewer home accidents

16. Brenda and Beverly the twins next door have given their old bikes to Goodwill

17. Horseback riding swimming and reading are my three favorite activities

18. A trip on the space shuttle in my opinion would be the ultimate vacation for it would really be getting away from it all

19. Imagine being able to gaze at the earth instead of the moon

20. Excited by the idea of such an experience I decided to write a story about it

REVIEW EXERCISE C. Correcting Sentences by Adding Commas and End Marks. Number your paper 1–20. After the proper number, supply commas and end marks in the following sentences by writing the word before a mark of punctuation and adding the comma or end mark.

1. Burning nine million tons of gas each second the sun is expected to burn itself out eventually

2. If a piece of a supernova the size of a baseball were brought to earth it would weigh more than the Empire State Building does

3. The blue whale weighs as much as thirty elephants grows as long as three buses and has a bone in its upper jaw three feet long

4. Turtles crocodiles alligators frogs and dolphins must breathe air in order to survive

5. Lanolin a smelly fatty substance taken from the wool of sheep is used in many cosmetics

6. Although they were much bigger than other animals dinosaurs had very small brains

7. The duckbill platypus is a strange puzzling animal for it is similar to both birds and mammals

8. For example the platypus lays eggs has a bill and has webbed feet

9. However the animal also nurses its young has fur and possesses claws

10. Its call is a throaty cluck but it can also growl

11. A giraffe which can run faster than a horse can go without water longer than a camel can

12. On May 29 1953 Sir Edmund Hillary a New Zealand explorer became the first person to climb Mount Everest the highest point on the earth's surface

13. Jim Whittaker became the first American to reach this point on May 22 1963

14. Junko Tabei one of a team of Japanese women reached the summit in 1975

15. Many people who love climbing have been inspired by these feats

16. Will the first day of the twenty-first century begin officially on January 1 2000 or on January 1 2001 Sarah

17. That depends I suppose on when the twentieth century officially began

18. You can send orders to the company at 111 Berkshire Drive Sierra Madre CA 91024

19. What a great fireworks display that was
20. Students pay attention when I am speaking

REVIEW EXERCISE D. Correcting Sentences by Adding Commas and End Marks. Number your paper 1–20. If a sentence has been punctuated correctly, write *C* after the proper number. Supply commas and end marks in the other sentences by writing the word before a mark of punctuation and adding the comma or end mark.

1. When we move our new address will be 2120 Mirror Lake Drive Iowa City IA 52240.
2. Meredith, have you met the new student?
3. Peggy Guggenheim the art collector owned a beautiful palace in Venice.
4. The volunteers will, of course, wear name tags.
5. What a lot of work we have done
6. Well Melba you remember how it felt to be the youngest
7. The tournament will be held from Thursday December 26 to Monday December 30
8. The monitor will pass out the tests, explain the directions, and collect the papers.
9. The poem that we recited from memory was Rudyard Kipling's "If."
10. Angelina who is the president of the art club drew the mural.
11. Our treasury as a matter of fact has more funds than ever before
12. Increasing her pace Eva crossed the finish line first.
13. George Hannah Dennis and Fran your poems have been accepted by the editor
14. Puzzled until the final page Margo closed the book with a sigh
15. The girl who wrote that composition revised her work carefully.
16. The car our first new one was a Pontiac.
17. Why Joline have I said something funny
18. The rain ended the sun came out and we went for a walk

19. No, I hadn't heard about your poetry award Dan.
20. Did you know that Alice Walker won the Pulitzer Prize in 1983 Sue

SEMICOLONS

The semicolon, as you can tell from its appearance, is part period and part comma. It signals a pause stronger than a comma but not as strong as a period.

14n. Use a semicolon between independent clauses in a sentence if they are not joined by *and, but, or, nor, for, yet.*

EXAMPLES On our first trip to Houston I wanted to see the Astrodome; my little brother wanted to visit the Johnson Space Center.

Our parents settled the argument for us; they took us to see a rodeo in a nearby town.

A period (and capital) between the independent clauses would change each of these examples into two sentences. Creating two sentences would be correct, but it would not show how closely related the ideas are.

☞ NOTE Very short independent clauses without conjunctions may be separated by commas: *The leaves whispered, the brook gurgled, the sun beamed benignly.*

14o. Use a semicolon between independent clauses joined by such words as *for example, for instance, that is, besides, accordingly, moreover, nevertheless, furthermore, otherwise, therefore, however, consequently, instead, hence.*

EXAMPLES Shirley Hufstedler became Secretary of Education in 1979; moreover, she was the first person to hold this cabinet position.

Mary Ishikawa decided not to stay at home; instead, she went to the game.

The popular names of certain animals are misleading; for example, the koala bear is not a bear.

The early Christians refused to worship the Roman emperor as a god; therefore, they were persecuted by the Romans.

English was Louise's most difficult subject; accordingly, she gave it more time than any other subject.

14p. **A semicolon (rather than a comma) may be needed to separate the independent clauses of a compound sentence if there are commas within the clauses.**

The mark of punctuation that is ordinarily used to indicate a separation between independent clauses is a comma. However, if commas are used within the clauses, it may be difficult to distinguish between these commas and a comma indicating the end of a clause. In such a case, a different, stronger signal—the semicolon—is needed.

EXAMPLE   A tall, slender woman entered the large, drafty room; and a short, slight, blond woman followed her.

EXERCISE 12. Correcting Sentences by Using Semicolons Between Independent Clauses.   Number your paper 1–10. After the proper number, indicate that the sentence requires a semicolon by writing the words before and after the semicolon and inserting the mark of punctuation. If the sentence does not require a semicolon, write *C*.

EXAMPLE   1. The gym is on the ground floor the classrooms are above it.
          1. *floor; the*

1. Map makers have explored almost all areas of the earth, they are now exploring the floors of the oceans.
2. Some scientists predict the development of undersea cities, but this prediction seems at least questionable.

3. In the future, perhaps, people will choose to live in a city in space, or they may prefer to have an apartment in an undersea city.

4. Roger Maris hit his sixty-first home run during the last game of the 1961 baseball season, until then Babe Ruth had held the record for the most home runs in a season.

5. Some reptiles like a dry climate, but others prefer a wet climate.

6. Many of today's office buildings look like glass boxes, they appear to be made entirely of windows.

7. In April 1912, a new "unsinkable" ocean liner, the *Titanic,* struck an iceberg in the North Atlantic, as a result, 1,493 persons lost their lives.

8. The *Titanic* carried nearly 2,200 passengers and crew, however, it had only enough lifeboats to accommodate 950.

9. The tragedy brought stricter safety regulations for ships, for example, the new laws required more lifeboats and better training of crews.

10. Today's shipwrecks can produce a different kind of tragedy, for instance, if a large oil tanker is wrecked, the spilled oil damages beaches and kills wildlife.

COLONS

The colon says, in effect, "Note what follows."

14q. Use a colon before a list of items, especially after expressions like *as follows* or *the following*.

EXAMPLES   Minimum equipment for camping is as follows: bedroll, utensils for cooking and eating, warm clothing, sturdy shoes, jackknife, rope, and flashlight.

This is what I have to do on Saturday: clean my room, shop for a birthday present for my sister, baby-sit for Mrs. Magill for two hours, do my Spanish homework, and make dinner.

14r. Use a colon in certain conventional situations.

(1) Use a colon between the hour and the minute when you write the time.

EXAMPLES 11**:**30 P.M.
4**:**08 A.M.

(2) Use a colon after the salutation of a business letter.

EXAMPLES Gentlemen**:**
Dear Ms. Gonzalez**:**
Dear Sir**:**

☞ **NOTE** The friendly letter requires a comma, not a colon, after the salutation.

REVIEW EXERCISE E. Correcting Sentences by Adding Semicolons, Colons, and Commas. Number your paper 1–10. Supply necessary semicolons, colons, and commas by writing the word before a mark of punctuation and adding the punctuation. If a sentence is correct, write *C*.

1. Even before the auction the hall was busy already bidders were poking among the piles of housewares and furniture.
2. Part of the play was funny part was sad.
3. During the field trip our teacher pointed out the following trees sugarberry pawpaw silverbell and mountain laurel.
4. Our teacher enjoys the outdoors she knows all of the types of trees in our area.
5. Anyone completing the test early may work on her or his report.
6. The first lunch period begins at 11 00 A.M. the second begins at 11 30 A.M.

7. These foreign languages are offered at our local high school Latin Spanish French and German.

8. Georgia was nervous during the first game of the match but she soon settled down and played well.

9. The scavenger hunt required us to bring back the following items a purple shoe a hula hoop a dozen unmatched socks and a hard-boiled egg.

10. Dogs require care time and attention cats do too.

WRITING APPLICATION B:
Using Semicolons to Join Closely Related Ideas

Using semicolons between independent clauses signals your reader that the ideas in the clauses are closely related. However, few ideas are so closely related that they are equal in importance. Thus, you will probably not use the semicolon often. When you do, be sure that you have used it correctly. Compare the following examples:

EXAMPLES   The rain began before dawn; I went shopping.
The rain began before dawn; it lasted all day.

The connection between the two ideas in the first example may have had meaning for the writer, but the relationship is not at all clear to the reader. Therefore, the semicolon is used incorrectly. The second sentence correctly combines two closely related ideas with a semicolon. When you use a semicolon, always check to make sure that the ideas it combines are closely related.

Writing Assignment

Write a paragraph explaining how something you said or did brought about an unexpected event. After you revise your paragraph, proofread it carefully to make sure that you have used semicolons to connect only closely related ideas. Then make a clean copy of your paragraph.

CHAPTER 14 REVIEW: POSTTEST 1

Placing End Marks and Commas in Sentences. Rewrite the following sentences, inserting end marks and commas as needed.

EXAMPLE   1. The teacher called Scott's name twice but Scott didn't answer
            1. *The teacher called Scott's name twice, but Scott didn't answer.*

1. Marshall won first prize in the free-skating event which is very competitive
2. The children looked for Easter eggs behind bushes on lower tree branches on the lawn chairs and under fallen leaves
3. Send your order to Best-Made Pet Products P.O. Box 113 Indianapolis IN 46204
4. Hey Don't do that
5. Has anyone seen our school mascot a small goat on a leash run by here
6. The ostrich which is the largest bird in the world can run much faster than a person can
7. The plankton that huge whales feed on for example are microscopic
8. Lori where did you put the keys
9. Although the Declaration of Independence was adopted on July 4 1776 some delegates did not sign it until later that year
10. Our new family doctor is Dr. Aki Matsuo a friendly and understanding woman from San Francisco
11. Looking through the Sunday newspaper Patti found sales on shoes swimming suits and beach towels
12. What an amazing exciting story he told
13. Is it possible for one person to be in the band the orchestra and the chorus
14. The letter was signed "Your favorite tennis partner Jeremy" and had a picture of a tennis racket at the bottom

15. My best friend Barbara moved to Ava a small town in New York
16. To be honest I don't think they have a chance of winning
17. Rozene didn't want to go swimming nor did she want to play volleyball
18. Why do they keep that old refrigerator which hasn't worked for years and could be dangerous to small children
19. Stop Frisky Come back here
20. Left behind in the nest the eaglets squirmed and cried hungrily
21. The gnu also called a wildebeest is a large African antelope
22. Nobody enjoys doing these chores but everybody has to do them sometime
23. As the train pulled into the station the whistle gave a loud blast
24. Why don't you ask him to help you with the project Stacy
25. That is not I think the best way to handle your problem

CHAPTER 14 REVIEW: POSTTEST 2

Correcting Sentences by Adding End Marks, Commas, Semicolons, and Colons. Rewrite the following paragraphs, inserting end marks and commas as needed.

EXAMPLE
1. Did I ever tell you how our washing machine which usually behaves itself once turned into a foaming monster
1. *Did I ever tell you how our washing machine, which usually behaves itself, once turned into a foaming monster?*

(1) "Oh no The basement is full of soapsuds!" my younger sister Sheila yelled (2) When I heard her I could tell how upset she was (3) Her voice had that tense strained tone that I know so well (4) Running downstairs to the basement I immediately saw

why she was excited (5) Imagine the following scene the washing machine was completely hidden in a thick foamy flow of bubbles (6) I ran across the slippery floor fought my way through the foam and turned off the machine

(7) This of course only stopped the flow (8) Sheila and I now had to clean up the mess for we didn't want Mom and Dad to see it when they got home (9) We mopped up soapsuds we sponged water off the floor and we dried the outside of the washing machine (10) After nearly an hour of exhausting effort we were satisfied with our work and decided to try the washer

(11) Everything would have been fine if the machine had still worked however it would not even start (12) Can you imagine how upset we both were then (13) Thinking things over we decided to call a repair shop

(14) We frantically telephoned Mr Hodges who runs the appliance-repair business nearest to our town (15) We told him the problem then we asked him to come to 21 Crestview Drive Ellenville as soon as possible

(16) When he arrived Mr Hodges inspected the machine asked us a few questions and said that we had no real problem (17) The wires had become damp and we were to let the machine sit for a day before we tried to use it again

(18) Surprised and relieved we thanked Mr Hodges and started toward the stairs to show him the way out (19) He stopped us however and asked if we knew what had caused the problem with the suds (20) We didn't want to admit our ignorance but our hesitation gave us away (21) Well Mr Hodges suggested that from now on we should measure the soap instead of just pouring it into the machine

(22) Looking at the empty box of laundry powder I realized what had happened (23) It was I believe the first time Sheila had used the washing machine by herself and no one had told her to read the instructions on the box

(24) This incident occurred on November 10 1983 and we have never forgotten it (25) Whenever we do the laundry now we remember the lesson we learned the day the washer overflowed.

CHAPTER 15

Punctuation

ITALICS, QUOTATION MARKS, APOSTROPHES, HYPHENS

Just as you use different facial expressions, gestures, and intonations to convey meaning when you speak, you need a variety of different marks of punctuation to make the meaning of your writing clear. In this chapter you will study the use of four more marks of punctuation.

DIAGNOSTIC TEST

A. Proofreading Sentences for the Correct Use of Apostrophes and Hyphens.   Number your paper 1–10. Each of the following sentences contains one or two errors in the use of apostrophes or hyphens. After the proper number, write each sentence correctly.

EXAMPLE   1. Rays mother said that hed have to mow the lawn before he could play soccer.
    1. *Ray's mother said that he'd have to mow the lawn before he could play soccer.*

1. Marsha is this years captain of the girls basketball team.
2. The plants leaves had wilted and its stem had shriveled.

3. At one time or another, Ive tried to play the piano, the guitar, and the clarinet.
4. We couldnt have done the job without you're help.
5. Mrs. Frasers strict about being on time.
6. On my older brothers last birthday, he turned twenty one.
7. Wed have forgotten to turn off the computer if Gabriel hadnt reminded us.
8. The recipe said to add two eggs, a teaspoon of salt, and three fourths cup of milk.
9. My fathers office is on the twenty second floor.
10. The soldiers supplies had run out, and its doubtful whether they could have survived without reinforcements.

B. Proofreading Sentences for the Correct Use of Quotation Marks and Underlining (Italics).

Number your paper 11–20. Each of the following sentences contains one or two errors in the use of quotation marks or underlining (italics). After the proper number, rewrite each sentence correctly.

EXAMPLE 1. Mary asked, "Did you read Robert Frost's poem Nothing Gold Can Stay out loud in class?"

1. *Mary asked, "Did you read Robert Frost's poem 'Nothing Gold Can Stay' out loud in class?"*

11. Uncle Ned reads the Wall Street Journal every day.
12. Fill in all the information on both sides of the form, the secretary said.
13. How many times have you seen the movie of Margaret Mitchell's novel Gone with the Wind?
14. Many of the students enjoyed the humor and irony in O. Henry's short story The Ransom of Red Chief.
15. My little sister asked, Why can't I have a hamster?
16. Please don't sing I've Been Working on the Railroad.
17. Over the summer my older sister played in a band on a Caribbean cruise ship named Bright Coastal Star.
18. "Read E. B. White's essay The Decline of Sport, and answer the study questions," the teacher announced.

19. Dudley Randall's poem Ancestors questions why people always seem to believe that their ancestors were aristocrats.
20. "Wait here," the clerk said, while I go to check the price.

UNDERLINING (ITALICS)

Italics are printed letters that lean to the right, *like this*. In handwritten or typewritten work, italics are indicated by underlining. If your composition were to be printed in a book or some other publication, the typesetter would use italics for underlined words. For example, if you wrote

Born Free is the story of a lioness that became a pet.

the printed version would look like this:

Born Free is the story of a lioness that became a pet.

15a. Use underlining (italics) for titles of books, periodicals, works of art, plays, films, television programs, ships, and so on.

EXAMPLES   *Big Red* is a book about an Irish setter.
Van Gogh's *Sunflowers* is a well-known painting.
The *Philadelphia Inquirer* has won many of the nation's top journalism awards.
Jacques-Yves Cousteau has outfitted the *Calypso* as a seagoing research lab.
Star Wars was one of the most popular movies ever made.

☞ NOTE When writing the title of a newspaper or a magazine within a sentence, underline the title. Do not underline or capitalize the word *the* with the name of a newspaper or magazine within a sentence. The name of a city in a newspaper title is usually, but not necessarily, underlined.

EXAMPLE   My parents subscribe to two newspapers published in other cities: the *St. Louis Post-Dispatch* and the *San Francisco Chronicle.*

EXERCISE 1. Using Underlining to Indicate Titles.
Number your paper 1–10. After the proper number, write and underline the words in the sentence that should be in italics.

EXAMPLE   1. Have you read The Call of the Wild?
          1. *The Call of the Wild*

1. Popular Mechanics, Sports Illustrated, and Seventeen are all popular magazines in our library.
2. In Wednesday's edition of the Globe-Democrat there is a section on baking bread.
3. The final number will be a medley of excerpts from George Gershwin's opera Porgy and Bess.
4. Elizabeth Speare won the Newbery medal twice, for her books The Witch of Blackbird Pond and The Bronze Bow.
5. Picasso's painting Guernica is named for a Spanish town that was destroyed during the Spanish Civil War.
6. Katharine Graham, the publisher of the Washington Post, is one of this year's commencement speakers.
7. The first battle between ironclad ships took place between the Monitor and the Merrimac in 1862.
8. Have you seen both versions of the movie Close Encounters of the Third Kind?
9. Betty Comden and Adolph Green have written such Broadway shows as Bells Are Ringing and Fade Out, Fade In.
10. The magazine rack held current issues of National Wildlife, Time, Popular Photography, Ladies Home Journal, and The Runner.

WRITING QUOTATIONS

Quotations are words spoken or written by someone and reported directly. In your writing you will often find it necessary to tell what someone has said, whether you are describing a true happening or writing an imaginary story. The rules in this section explain how to write quotations in a standard form that can be easily read by others.

15b. Use quotation marks to enclose a direct quotation—a person's exact words.

Quotation marks before and after a person's words show exactly what was said.

EXAMPLES "Has anyone in the class swum in the Great Salt Lake?" asked Ms. Estrada. [Ms. Estrada's exact words]

"I swam there last summer," said June. [June's exact words]

Do not confuse a person's exact words with a rewording of the person's speech. If you tell what someone said without repeating the exact words, you are using an *indirect* quotation. No quotation marks are needed for an indirect quotation.

INDIRECT Pauline asked for **my interpretation of the poem.** [not Pauline's exact words; no quotation marks needed]

DIRECT Pauline asked, **"What is your interpretation of the poem?"** [Pauline's exact words; quotation marks needed]

INDIRECT I told her that **I thought the poet was expressing awe at the power of nature.**

DIRECT **"I think the poet is expressing awe at the power of nature,"** I said.

15c. A direct quotation begins with a capital letter.

EXAMPLES Jimmy shouted, "**A** parade will be held here tomorrow!"

"**I**s it true?" asked Sandra.

Carla groaned, "**O**h, I won't be able to be there!"

15d. When a quotation is divided into two parts by an interrupting expression such as *he said* or *Mother asked,* **the second part begins with a small letter.**

EXAMPLES   "What are some of the things," asked Mrs. Perkins, "that the astronauts who walked on the moon discovered?"

"One thing they discovered," answered Gwen, "was that the moon is covered by a layer of dust."

"Gee," George added, "my room at home is a lot like the moon, I guess."

If the second part of an interrupted quotation starts a new sentence or if it begins with a word that ordinarily requires a capital, it should start with a capital letter.

EXAMPLES   "Anything that is dangerous is exciting, too," remarked Mrs. Perkins. "Space travel is no exception." [The second part begins with a capital because it is a new sentence.]

"In my opinion," Tony said, "Mars is more fascinating than the moon." [The second part begins with a capital because *Mars*, a proper noun, is always capitalized.]

EXERCISE 2. Correcting Sentences by Adding Capital Letters and Punctuation.

Write the following sentences, supplying whatever capitals and marks of punctuation are needed. For the two sentences that require no changes, write *C.*

EXAMPLE   1. Now, said the teacher, you may go to the library.
         1. *"Now," said the teacher, "you may go to the library."*

1. I hope, said Elizabeth, that we will reach Atlanta soon.
2. if the traffic does not get worse, the driver predicted, we should be there in half an hour.
3. practice your saxophone every day said Ms. Noonan your playing will improve rapidly.

4. We took the injured young owl into the house, said Dick, and we made a nest for it in a basket.

5. Mrs. Yamasaki, our physical education teacher, told us we would begin the volleyball unit Monday.

6. That will be fun, said Patrick I enjoy playing volleyball

7. I want to learn how to improve my serve said Catherine hitting a good serve is harder than it looks.

8. Yes, Patrick agreed, for it takes practice.

9. Catherine commented that you have to know how to position your hands.

10. Proper wrist motion, Patrick added, is also important.

15e. A direct quotation is set off from the rest of the sentence by commas or by a question mark or exclamation point.

EXAMPLES   "I've just finished reading a book about Narcissa Whitman," Ellen said.

"Was she one of the early settlers in the Northwest?" asked Janet.

"What an adventure!" exclaimed Carol.

15f. A period or a comma following a quotation should be placed inside the closing quotation marks.

EXAMPLES   Ramon said, "Hank Aaron was better than Babe Ruth because he hit more home runs in his career."

"But Hank Aaron never hit sixty in one year," countered Paula.

15g. A question mark or an exclamation point should be placed inside the closing quotation marks if the entire quotation is a question or an exclamation. Otherwise, it should be placed outside.

EXAMPLES   "What is the time difference between Los Angeles and Chicago?" asked Ken. [The quotation is a question.]

Linda exclaimed, "I thought everyone knew that!"
[The quotation is an exclamation.]

Is the right answer "two hours"? [The whole sentence is a question, but the quotation is not.]

If a sentence contains two questions, you still use only one question mark: Who said, "What's in a name?"

EXERCISE 3. **Correcting Sentences by Adding Capital Letters and Punctuation.** Revise the following sentences, supplying capitals and marks of punctuation as needed.

EXAMPLE   1. Why she asked can't we leave now
           1. *"Why," she asked, "can't we leave now?"*

1. Mother, will you take us to the soccer field asked Libby
2. Of course, Libby replied Mother if you have done your homework, I'll take you there now
3. Please hold my viola case for a minute, Dave Josh said I need to tie my shoelace
4. Did you say Forget it
5. What a game that was exclaimed the coach
6. You're out shouted the umpire
7. Cary asked What is pita bread
8. Did Therese answer It's a round, flat Middle Eastern bread
9. Run Run cried the boys a tornado is headed this way
10. Cassie announced her sister Marcia is on the telephone for you

15h. When you write dialogue (conversation), begin a new paragraph each time you change speakers.

EXAMPLE   "What did you think of that movie about Japan?" Sara asked Ron as they left the school building.

"I was surprised at the scenes in Tokyo. I didn't know it was so much like Chicago or New York."

"I guess a lot of the young people don't wear traditional Japanese clothes nowadays," Sara said.

"I hope the use of kimonos doesn't disappear completely—they are so pretty."

"How would you like to wear one to school?" asked Ron. "You'd be the center of attention."

15i. When a quotation consists of several sentences, put quotation marks only at the beginning and at the end of the whole quotation, not around each sentence in the quotation.

INCORRECT   "Memorize all your lines for Monday." "Have someone at home give you your cues." "Enjoy your weekend!" said Ms. Goodwin.

CORRECT   "Memorize all your lines for Monday. Have someone at home give you your cues. Enjoy your weekend!" said Ms. Goodwin.

EXERCISE 4. Punctuating and Paragraphing Dialogue.

Revise the following dialogue, punctuating and paragraphing it correctly.

Lynette, did you enjoy reading *The Yearling* Miss Bishop asked I think it's the best book I have ever read, Miss Bishop Can you tell us why you liked it The characters seemed so real Lynette replied and their struggles made me like them even more What were some of the struggles Jody and his family faced They struggled to raise crops and to gather food to get through the winter Jody struggled with loneliness until he found Flag What conflicts did keeping the deer as a pet cause Flag ate some of the crops, and Jody struggled with his father to keep the deer Jody loved his pet and had trouble admitting it couldn't live with the family Good, Lynette

15j. Use single quotation marks to enclose a quotation within a quotation.

EXAMPLES   "I said, 'The quiz will cover Unit 2 and your special reports,'" repeated Mr. Allyn.

"What poem begins with the line, 'I'm going out to clean the pasture spring'?" Carol asked.

15k. Use quotation marks to enclose titles of chapters, articles, short stories, poems, songs, and other *parts* of books or magazines.[1]

EXAMPLES   Irwin Shaw's "Strawberry Ice-Cream Soda" is a story of an older and a younger brother.

Our assignment for tomorrow is the first part of Chapter 11, "Americans Create New States out of the Wilderness."

Helen can still recite several stanzas of "Paul Revere's Ride," which she memorized last year.

The poetry of Elizabeth Madox Roberts is the subject of an article called "A Tent of Green" in the *Horn Book Magazine*.

EXERCISE 5. Using Punctuation Marks, Quotation Marks, and Underlining (Italics).
Write the following sentences, inserting punctuation marks and quotation marks where needed. Underline words that should be in italics.

EXAMPLE   1. We sang Greensleeves for the assembly.
          1. *We sang "Greensleeves" for the assembly.*

1. The chapter The War to End All Wars is about World War I.
2. Jane said that the article Autumn Above the Timbers features some beautiful photographs of the mountains.
3. Do you know the poem To Make a Prairie?
4. Has anyone read the story To Build a Fire asked the teacher.
5. I have said Eileen. It was written by Jack London.
6. Do you know who said Ask not what your country can do for you; ask what you can do for your country asked Candace.
7. The New Yorker magazine features excellent short stories.
8. How many times has the United States launched space shuttles asked Peggy.

[1] For the use of italics for titles, see rule 15a on page 370.

9. Did you read asked Ms. Carlson the article Animal Architects in the St. Louis Post-Dispatch?
10. My dental appointment has been changed said Les Now I won't be able to go with you.

REVIEW EXERCISE A. Correcting Sentences by Adding Punctuation and Capital Letters. If a sentence is punctuated and capitalized correctly, write *C* after its number on your paper. Revise the incorrect sentences, making all necessary corrections.

1. Mother told us "When I was in 4-H, we had to complete projects in public speaking and community development.
2. "Won't you stay," pleaded Wynnie, "there will be refreshments and music later."
3. "Why, Jason," said Irv, "you play the drums like an expert!"
4. That parked car is rolling downhill yelled Will
5. The girls asked if we needed help finding our campsite.
6. "Elise, do you know who said The thoughts of youth are long, long thoughts" asked the teacher.
7. We left early I explained but we got lost.
8. "Hurray," shouted Rita. "We've won the contest!"
9. It would be better if we studied now I suggested. We will be too tired if we wait until later.
10. "What a wonderful day for a picnic!" exclaimed Susan.
11. Dear me whispered Connie doesn't this speaker know when to say In conclusion.
12. Cindi asked, what are you planning to wear, Barb.
13. Father asked if we had packed our toothbrushes.
14. When President Lincoln heard of the South's defeat, he requested that the band play Dixie.
15. The latest issue of National Geographic has an article on rain forests.
16. What can have happened to Linda this time, Tina Didn't she say I'll be home long before you are ready to leave?
17. Langston Hughes's Dream Deferred is a moving poem.

18. "Keeping a writer's journal is a good idea, Mrs. Elliott. I'm glad you had us begin one this semester," said Sandra.
19. "What a clear explanation Jay gave us!" exclaimed the teacher.
20. "Not so fast, Dave," said Miss Rivera, you have not turned in your homework yet."

WRITING APPLICATION A:
Using Dialogue in Narration

Using dialogue helps make your readers feel as though they are hearing an actual conversation. The way people express themselves often reveals their personalities. When you write narration, using dialogue that is natural and realistic can help develop the personalities of your characters. Remember to proofread your narration carefully to make sure that you have used quotation marks and paragraphing correctly. Otherwise, your readers may not be able to tell which character is which.

Writing Assignment

Write a one-page narrative using dialogue between two characters to reveal their personalities. After you revise what you have written, proofread it carefully to make sure that you have used quotation marks and paragraphing correctly. Then make a clean copy of your paper.

APOSTROPHES

The *apostrophe* has two uses: to show ownership or relationship, and to show where letters have been omitted in a contraction.

The Possessive Case

The possessive case of a noun or pronoun shows ownership or relationship. The following nouns and pronouns are in the possessive case.

OWNERSHIP   Sandra's boat
Mother's job
a book's title

RELATIONSHIP   an hour's time
Julio's father
person's responsibility

☞ **NOTE** Personal pronouns in the possessive case require no apostrophe: Is this bat *ours, yours,* or *theirs?*

15l. To form the possessive case of a singular noun, add an apostrophe and an *s*.

EXAMPLES   a dog's collar
a country's natural resources
a moment's thought
one cent's worth
Charles's typewriter

Exception: A proper name ending in *s* may take only an apostrophe to form the possessive case under the following conditions:

1. The name consists of two or more syllables.
2. Adding '*s* would make the name awkward to pronounce.

EXAMPLES   Mr. and Mrs. Rogers' house
Marjorie Kinnan Rawlings' novels
Hercules' feats

EXERCISE 6. Supplying Apostrophes in Possessive Nouns.

Number your paper 1–10. After the proper number, write the noun or nouns that are in the possessive case and supply the necessary apostrophes.

EXAMPLE   1. The dogs leash is too short.
               1. *dog's*

1. The squirrels tail is crooked.
2. That trucks taillights are broken.
3. Toms book is on the counter.
4. The judges were impressed with Veronicas project.
5. Last weeks meals were meatless ones.
6. Margos dream is to have a horse like her sisters palomino.
7. Hanks locker is next to the science lab.
8. Are we going to Aunt Mays cottage this weekend?
9. An astronauts life is adventurous.
10. Please pack your mothers books and Joans toys.

15m. To form the possessive case of a plural noun ending in *s,* add only the apostrophe.

EXAMPLES   friends' invitations
            citizens' committee
            pupils' records

The few plural nouns that do not end in *s* form the possessive just as singular nouns do, by adding an apostrophe and an *s.*

EXAMPLES   men's suits
            mice's tracks
            children's voices

☞ **NOTE**   Do not use an apostrophe to form the *plural* of a noun. The apostrophe shows ownership or relationship, not number.

INCORRECT   The new car's are sporty this year.
  CORRECT   The new cars are sporty this year. [plural]
  CORRECT   The new car's styling is sporty. [possessive]

A noun in the possessive case (shown by an apostrophe) is usually followed by a noun.

EXAMPLES   car's styling   women's group
            book's cover   Jean's friends

EXERCISE 7. Forming Plural Possessives. Number your paper 1–10. After the proper number, write the possessive for each of the following plural expressions.

EXAMPLE 1. artists paintings
          1. *artists' paintings*

1. boys boots
2. women careers
3. friends comments
4. three days homework
5. girls parents
6. Joneses cabin
7. men shoes
8. children games
9. cities mayors
10. oxen yokes

EXERCISE 8. Writing Singular Possessives, Plurals, and Plural Possessives. Number your paper 1–20. Divide your paper into three columns. Label the columns *Singular Possessive, Plural,* and *Plural Possessive.* In each column, write the form of the following nouns that the column label calls for.

1. stove
2. puppy
3. captain
4. library
5. life
6. donkey
7. mouse
8. child
9. voter
10. teacher
11. calf
12. soprano
13. buyer
14. potato
15. elephant
16. citizen
17. tooth
18. berry
19. school
20. valley

Contractions

15n. Use an apostrophe to show where letters have been omitted in a contraction.

A *contraction* is a word made by combining or shortening two words. An apostrophe takes the place of the letters that are omitted.

EXAMPLES **Where is** the exit?
          Where's the exit?

> **We will** have gone by then.
> **We'll** have gone by then.
>
> She **might have** let us know.
> She **might've** let us know.

The word *not* is contracted *n't*. This is often added to a verb to form a contraction. Usually the spelling of the verb is unchanged.

is not	isn't	has not	hasn't
are not	aren't	have not	haven't
does not	doesn't	had not	hadn't
do not	don't	should not	shouldn't
was not	wasn't	would not	wouldn't
were not	weren't	could not	couldn't

However, in some cases the spelling does change, as in the following contractions:

shall not	shan't
will not	won't
cannot	can't

Contractions may also be formed with nouns or pronouns and verbs:

I am	I'm	you will	you'll
you are	you're	they are	they're
she would	she'd	Ann is	Ann's

Its and It's

The word *its* is a pronoun in the possessive case. It does not have an apostrophe.

   The word *it's* is a contraction of *it is* or *it has* and requires an apostrophe.

EXAMPLES   **Its** right front tire is flat. [*Its* is a possessive pronoun.]
   It's wet paint. [*It's* means *it is.*]
   It's been a long time. [*It's* means *it has.*]

Whose and *Who's*

The word *whose* is a pronoun in the possessive case. It does not have an apostrophe.

The word *who's* means *who is* or *who has*. Since it is a contraction, it requires an apostrophe.

EXAMPLES **Whose** idea was it? [*Whose* is a possessive pronoun.]

Who's next in line? [*Who's* means *who is*.]

Who's been in my room? [*Who's* means *who has*.]

Your and *You're*

The word *your* is a possessive pronoun. It does not have an apostrophe.

You're is a contraction of *you are*. It requires an apostrophe to show where the letter *a* is omitted.

EXAMPLES **Your** paper shows great improvement, Leon. [*Your* is a pronoun in the possessive case.]

You're going to get a better mark this term. [*You're* means *you are*.]

Plurals

15o. Use an apostrophe and *s* to form the plurals of letters, numbers, and signs, and of words referred to as words.

EXAMPLES Doesn't he know the ABC's?
Your 2's look like 5's.
Don't use &'s in place of *and*'s.

EXERCISE 9. Correcting Sentences by Adding Apostrophes.

Number your paper 1–10. Rewrite the items that require apostrophes in the following sentences, and insert the apostrophes where they belong.

EXAMPLE 1. Do you know what youre doing?
1. *you're*

1. The girls didn't say when they'd be back.
2. Let's find out when the next game is.
3. Dorothy usually gets all A's and B's on her report card.
4. It isn't correct to use &'s in your compositions.
5. Many of the scores were in the 80's and 90's.
6. They can't come with us; they're studying.
7. They'll meet us later if its all right to tell them where were going.
8. Who's signed up for the talent show?
9. Don't those 2's look like z's to you?
10. Your capital L's and F's are hard to tell apart.

WRITING APPLICATION B:
Using Underlining, Quotation Marks, and Apostrophes to Make Your Writing Clear

Using underlining, quotation marks, and apostrophes correctly helps make your writing clear. Compare the following sets of sentences.

EXAMPLES   Have you seen the sun today?
Have you seen the *Sun* today?

He said he cannot go with us.
He said, "He cannot go with us."

Well, take care of it right away.
We'll take care of it right away.

As you can see, the punctuation makes a great deal of difference in the meaning of the sentences in each pair. Always proofread your writing carefully to make sure that you have used punctuation marks correctly to make your meaning clear.

Writing Assignment

Write six sentences, using one of the following words in each sentence: *its, it's, whose, who's, your, you're.* Proofread your sentences to make sure that you have used the words correctly.

HYPHENS

15p. Use a hyphen to divide a word at the end of a line.

Sometimes you will find that there is not enough space for a whole word at the end of a line. When this happens, you may divide the word, using a hyphen to indicate the division.

EXAMPLES How long has the building been under construction?
If you want to know, look it up in the almanac.

Be careful to divide words only between syllables. For the rules on dividing words, see page 447.

15q. Use a hyphen with compound numbers from twenty-one to ninety-nine and with fractions used as adjectives.

EXAMPLES There were twenty-one ducks in that flock.
A two-thirds majority will decide the issue, and the other one third will have to abide by the decision. [In the first use, *two-thirds* is a compound adjective modifying *majority*; in the second use, *third* is a noun modified by the single adjective *one*.]

EXERCISE 10. Hyphenating Numbers and Fractions. Number your paper 1–10. After the proper number, write the words from the following expressions that require hyphens. Supply hyphens. If an expression is correct, write *C*.

1. a three fourths majority
2. one half of the money
3. one hundred twenty five contestants
4. eighty nine
5. Twenty third Street
6. forty eight decorated eggs
7. one fourth of the audience

8. three fourths of the voters
9. eight and six tenths centimeters
10. one third of the class

REVIEW EXERCISE B. Forming Contractions. Number your paper 1–20. Form contractions from the following groups of words.

1. will not	6. are not	11. you are	16. I am
2. there is	7. it is	12. does not	17. had not
3. who will	8. should not	13. he would	18. she is
4. they are	9. let us	14. shall not	19. you will
5. who is	10. can not	15. we are	20. could not

REVIEW EXERCISE C. Inserting Apostrophes and Hyphens. Number your paper 1–20. After the proper number, write the words in the following sentences that require apostrophes or hyphens. Supply the apostrophes and hyphens.

1. Theres where they live.
2. Whose experiment is this, Doreens or Lauras?
3. Wholl volunteer to participate in next weeks anti-litter campaign?
4. The Lockwood sisters golden retriever is named Storm.
5. Isnt there enough gas to drive seventy four miles?
6. One third of Hollys allowance goes into the bank.
7. Wouldnt it be wonderful if the person whos taken my wallet returned it?
8. From Fifty third Street down to Forty fifth there are ninety seven businesses.
9. He either cant or wont answer the question.
10. Ive read Stevens story, but wheres yours?
11. Youve got to see our float to believe what weve done!
12. Twenty six student council members (more than a two thirds majority) voted to change the school song that theyd selected.
13. Shelly signed up for the writing class because shed heard how helpful it was.

14. If two thirds of the class has a score below seventy five, well all have to retake the test.
15. Our new neighbors hadnt realized how close our apartment building is to the railroad tracks.
16. Allans staying with you this evening while Im at the gym.
17. Its cushions are worn, but its comfortable.
18. I dont know whos responsible, but Ill find out.
19. Lets see whats happening at the park today.
20. Ninety seven years ago my great-grandparents left Scotland for the United States.

REVIEW EXERCISE D. Correcting Sentences by Adding Punctuation. Rewrite the following sentences, supplying punctuation marks, including quotation marks, where they are needed.

1. Ill see you at the sale tomorrow at Sport World said Vera Its on the corner of Thirty ninth and Vine.
2. Today's Geneva Gazeteer has a story about the fire at the Pattersons home; its roof was destroyed.
3. Belinda, Bill, Don, and Vickie have each read at least twenty one books since last years book fair.
4. I cant imagine remarked Judy a more terrifying short story than The Most Dangerous Game.
5. Seventy three percent of the legislators voted to extend the school day.
6. Lisa reported that one third of the students interviewed said they usually had no homework, while a two thirds majority said that they had too much.
7. Although I offered to help with the cleanup, Renee explained, Brian said that he could manage alone.
8. Augusta Savages Lift Every Voice and Sing is the sculpture Id most like to see for myself.
9. Larues eyes twinkled as he replied Why, Ive no idea what youre talking about nobodys planning a party.
10. Shell ride to todays meeting with us.

CHAPTER 15 REVIEW: POSTTEST 1

A. Proofreading Sentences for the Correct Use of Apostrophes and Hyphens.   Number your paper 1–15. Each of the following sentences contains one or two errors in the use of apostrophes or hyphens. After the proper number, write each sentence correctly.

EXAMPLE   1. Ms. Morris didnt finish her tomato juice.
    1. *Ms. Morris didn't finish her tomato juice.*

1. Everyones order for a school sweatshirt must be sent out this afternoon.
2. The explorers thirty five mile hike through the jungle took them ten days.
3. We are looking for a lost puppy; its brown with white spots.
4. Soccer practice begins at 4:00 P.M.; dont forget to bring your kneepads.
5. Wallys team included Francine, Lani, and George.
6. Whos going with us to help select a present for Grandmothers fiftieth birthday?
7. Karl lost points on the spelling test because his *i*s looked like *e*s.
8. The director of the Drama Clubs spring play asked us to find a womans portrait.
9. Although Mr. Crawford listened to Maxines plan, he didnt like it.
10. The clocks hands stopped because it's cord was unplugged.
11. The forty five minute wait will pass quickly; youll see.
12. The winner of the contest received a years supply of paper towels and twenty one free meals at the Antler Restaurant.
13. Lets evacuate before the river floods the house.
14. Well meet Pablos cousins when they come to visit him.
15. According to our study, one third of students time is spent on school activities.

B. Proofreading Sentences for the Correct Use of Quotation Marks and Underlining (Italics).
Number your paper 16–25. Each of the following sentences contains one or two errors in the use of quotation marks or underlining (italics). After the proper number, write each sentence correctly.

EXAMPLE   1. Mother asked, Are you going, Jill?
            1. *Mother asked, "Are you going, Jill?"*

16. The ending of Liam O'Flaherty's short story The Sniper shocked everyone.
17. Ms. Morton asked Vic, In what year did Columbus reach the West Indies in the Santa Maria?"
18. Deborah sang New York, New York in the talent show.
19. "This may seem easy to you, Bryan said, but I don't think I can do it."
20. The best chapter in Cook Up Something Healthful is "How to Make Wholesome Snacks.
21. Look at this! my father shouted. "Who used my best tie as a kite tail?"
22. "In what poem does a raven say, Nevermore, over and over?" Mr. Burrows asked the class.
23. Although Willie Wonka and the Chocolate Factory is a children's movie, my father and mother enjoy watching it.
24. Karen leaned over and whispered, This is boring; let's leave.
25. Bob always prints because he has trouble making capital letters such as S's and Q's in cursive writing.

CHAPTER 15 REVIEW: POSTTEST 2

A. Proofreading Sentences for the Correct Use of Apostrophes and Hyphens.
Number your paper 1–15. Each of the following sentences contains one or two errors in the use of apostrophes or hyphens. After the proper number, write each sentence correctly. Some will require respelling.

EXAMPLE 1. Our ad appeared in todays paper, but our phone number wasnt included.

          1. *Our ad appeared in today's paper, but our phone number wasn't included.*

1. The dog's havent been fed yet.
2. The games three categories are *animal, vegetable,* and *mineral.*
3. The decoration committees purchases included crepe paper, confetti, and seventy two balloons.
4. Didnt the directions say to add only one half cup of milk to the dry ingredients?
5. It's battery was dead; the car wouldn't start.
6. Wed have been here sooner, but its farther than we thought.
7. Alinas sister looked at all the greeting cards and finally took the one shed selected to the cashier.
8. You're tour of Chicago should include a drive along Lake Michigan to see the citys skyline.
9. For this class youll need a ruler and a protractor.
10. This work cant wait any longer; well have to do it now.
11. There was a big party at the Rogers house when Mr. Rogers was forty seven years old.
12. My great-grandfather often tells us to mind our *p*s and *q*s.
13. Do you have any idea whos going to the parade?
14. My aunt, who's job takes her all over the world, sends me postcards from the places she visits.
15. More than one half of the students stories were about they're pets.

B. Proofreading Sentences for the Correct Use of Quotation Marks and Underlining (Italics).

Number your paper 16–25. Each of the following sentences requires underlining (italics), quotation marks, or both. After the proper number, write each sentence correctly.

EXAMPLE 1. Ted, can you answer the first question? Ms. Simmons asked.

1. *"Ted, can you answer the first question?" Ms. Simmons asked.*

16. The best chapter in our vocabulary book is the last one, More Word Games.

17. "I answered all the questions, Todd said, but I think that some of my answers were wrong."

18. There is a legend that the band on the Titanic played the hymn Nearer My God to Thee as the ship sank into the icy sea.

19. Mr. Washington asked Connie, "What flag included the slogan Don't Tread on Me?"

20. Star Wars was more exciting on the big movie screen than it was on our small television set.

21. Play the Gene Autry tape again, Mom, Jonathan said, grinning at his mother.

22. Wendy wrote an article called Students, Where Are You? for our local newspaper, the Morning Beacon.

23. In the short story The Tell-Tale Heart, Edgar Allan Poe explores the theme of guilt.

24. "Can I read Treasure Island for my book report? Carmine asked.

25. Every Christmas Eve my uncle recites The Night Before Christmas for the children in the hospital.

MECHANICS
MASTERY REVIEW: Cumulative Test

A. CAPITALIZATION. Number your paper 1–15. Each of the following sentences contains one or two errors in capitalization. After the proper number, write the word or words correctly, supplying capitals where they are necessary and omitting them where they are unnecessary.

EXAMPLE 1. We drove East until we reached the Atlantic ocean.
      1. *east, Ocean*

1. Sometimes on a cloudy or rainy sunday, I enjoy watching old movies like *The caine Mutiny.*
2. Three days a week my little sister takes Ballet lessons at the Tinkerbell Dance academy.
3. After the russians launched the first Satellite in 1957, the United States hurried to catch up in the space race.
4. Wynetta is going to sign up for algebra I, American Government, and biology next year.
5. Is dr. Renalda Gazi's office on the corner of sixty-sixth Street?
6. At our last halloween party, Bernie dressed as napoleon.
7. My aunt has driven volkswagen cars ever since she was stationed in Europe.
8. Jacques Cousteau spent many months searching for the lost Continent of atlantis, but he found no trace of it.
9. Some aztec indians offered human sacrifices to their gods.
10. Did norse sailors discover America before Christopher Columbus reached the west Indies?
11. The faces of the presidents on mount Rushmore are familiar to most Americans.
12. People from earth will colonize not only mars but also planets far beyond our solar system some day.

13. Many people believe that they see the work of god in nature.
14. My Grandmother enjoys working the crossword puzzle in the *Los Angeles times* every morning.
15. Brad's father owns a winchester rifle that once belonged to Buffalo Bill.

B. END MARKS AND COMMAS. Number your paper 16–30. Each of the following sentences contains one or two errors in the use of end marks or commas. After the proper number write each sentence correctly.

EXAMPLE 1. Did you see that Carrie
　　　　　 1. *Did you see that, Carrie?*

16. My dog will sit up on command but it won't fetch
17. When we finally reached the store most of the sale shirts were gone
18. Wow That soup is hot
19. The first human space flight took place on April 12 1961 and was soon followed by others.
20. Who is that man the mysterious one wearing the trench-coat
21. There's no way to know I suppose what actually happened.
22. The carpet which was a mottled brown and green was worn through in several spots.
23. At the fair Glenda won a stuffed dog a baseball cap and nine keychains.
24. Grumbling in the distance the thunder seemed to be getting closer
25. Yes my brother's pen pal is a boy, who lives in New Zealand.
26. That was probably the longest most boring speech I've ever heard and I think that the next one will be even worse.
27. They gave the Best Dog of the Show prize to Ms. Kennedy's poodle a nasty animal with an annoying bark

28. Hurry, Bonnie come here before it's too late

29. Armed with nothing but a book of matches and a sheath knife she survived for three days on the hostile wind-swept mountain.

30. Why can't we leave early and get there before the crowd gets too large

C. SEMICOLONS AND COLONS. Number your paper 31–35. Each of the following sentences contains one or two errors in the use of semicolons or colons. After the proper number, write each correctly. You may need to delete a comma in order to add a semicolon or a colon.

EXAMPLE   1. They did not believe Roy, however, they could not prove that he was lying.

   1. *They did not believe Roy; however, they could not prove that he was lying.*

31. The following students are to report to the office Rita Funez, Leon Patterson, and Jay Wheeler.

32. Mario tried several different ways to enter the program into the computer, it still would not run.

33. We leave for school at 7 15 A.M. every day.

34. The secretary files papers, takes dictation, and types letters, and the receptionist answers the phone, greets people, and makes appointments.

35. We thought that it was going to be an adventure story, instead, it's a silly romance.

D. ITALICS AND QUOTATION MARKS. Number your paper 36–45. Each of the following sentences contains one or two errors in the use of italics or quotation marks. After the proper number, write each sentence correctly.

EXAMPLE   1. "Has anyone here read The Odyssey? Ms. Hall asked.

   1. *"Has anyone here read The Odyssey?" Ms. Hall asked.*

36. I can't solve this puzzle without help! Mike insisted.
37. Stella said that the article More Tips on Bike Maintenance should be read by every bicycle owner.
38. "Did you buy a copy of the record We Are the World to help hungry people?" Joy asked.
39. "This was not what I had in mind, Uncle Cliff exclaimed, when I asked you to wash my car!"
40. For the answer to that question, look under the World Biography section of the almanac.
41. Eli turned around and asked, "How many times have you seen Close Encounters of the Third Kind?
42. "Have you read the latest Science Digest article on cloning? Paula asked.
43. My uncle carries in his wallet a copy of the poem Nothing Gold Can Stay.
44. Please don't tell me that you've forgotten your assignment again, Roger, Mr. Carmichael said.
45. As the students entered the theater, the teacher said, You may recognize some of the music you'll be hearing this afternoon in Bizet's opera Carmen."

E. **APOSTROPHES AND HYPHENS.** Number your paper 46–50. Each of the following sentences contains one or two errors in the use of apostrophes or hyphens. After the proper number, write the sentence correctly.

EXAMPLE   1. Our school year lasts thirty six weeks.
           1. *Our school year lasts thirty-six weeks.*

46. Everyones hat blew off when the wind gusted up Fifty seventh Street.
47. Im never sure how many *ss* there are in *Mississippi*.
48. Dont you think its too hot to lie in the sun?
49. Well do well on the test if we study the notes we took in Ms. Joness class.
50. Consuela won the election by a two thirds majority.

PART FOUR

COMPOSITION:
Writing and Revising
Sentences

CHAPTER 16

Writing Complete Sentences

SENTENCE FRAGMENTS AND RUN-ON SENTENCES

When you speak, you signal the end of a sentence by making your voice rise or fall and by pausing between sentences. When you write, the signals you use are end marks: periods, question marks, and exclamation points. If you use these marks incorrectly, you give your reader the wrong signals. You can eliminate many of your punctuation problems by reading aloud what you have written and listening for the signals your voice gives.

Two frequent errors that occur in written composition are the *sentence fragment* and the *run-on sentence*. When you put a period, question mark, or exclamation point after a group of words that is not a complete sentence, you have made the error of writing a sentence fragment. When you omit end marks between two or more separate sentences, you are writing a run-on sentence. To avoid these errors, apply the "sentence sense" you use when you speak.

FRAGMENTS

A sentence expresses a complete thought. When only a part of a sentence is written as a complete sentence, the resulting error is a sentence fragment. A fragment almost always belongs with the sentence that precedes it.

16a. A *fragment* is a separated sentence part that does not express a complete thought.

To decide whether or not a group of words is a sentence, ask yourself these two questions: (1) Does it have a verb and its subject? (2) Does it express a complete thought? If the answer to either question is "no," the group of words is not a sentence but a fragment of a sentence.

Each of the following examples contains a sentence and a fragment, which is printed in italics. Note that all the fragments, except the one in the third example, do not contain verbs and their subjects. The third one, which is a subordinate clause, has a verb and its subject, but it does not express a complete thought.

The newspaper staff worked late. *Putting out a special edition.* [The fragment contains no main verb or subject.]

We looked forward to meeting Ms. Case. *Our new physics teacher.* [The fragment contains no verb or subject.]

As the horses neared the gate. The excitement increased. [The fragment contains a verb and a subject, but it does not express a complete thought. It leaves the reader wondering what happened *as the horses neared the gate.*]

Since these fragments all belong to the sentences they precede or follow, you can correct them by joining them to these sentences.

The newspaper staff worked late **putting out a special edition.**

We looked forward to meeting Ms. Case, **our new physics teacher.**

As the horses neared the gate, the excitement increased.

EXERCISE 1. Identifying Sentences and Fragments; Correcting Fragments. Seven of the italicized groups of words that follow are fragments, while three are complete sentences. Indicate a complete sentence by placing a *C* after the proper number. Correct each fragment by writing the entire item and making the fragment part of the sentence.

EXAMPLES   1. Dolphins are intelligent animals. *That are being closely studied today.*
         1. *Dolphins are intelligent animals that are being closely studied today.*
         2. The study of this aquatic mammal has already shown surprising results. *The dolphin has been trained as a diver's seagoing partner.*
         2. *C*

1. The man who has done the most research on the dolphin is Dr. John C. Lilly. *Who is attempting to devise a method of communication between humans and dolphins.*
2. *By putting a partially paralyzed dolphin into a tank with other dolphins.* Dr. Lilly discovered the dolphin's distress call.
3. The disabled dolphin emitted its distress call. *When it began to sink.*
4. It was immediately assisted by two other dolphins. *They lifted it to the surface for air.*
5. Dolphins usually stay together in groups. *Helping each other out in times of trouble.*
6. A baby dolphin is looked after by two adults. *Its mother and an assistant mother serve as nurses.*
7. Even a deadly shark is no match for two angry mother dolphins. *Circling and striking at their foe with their hard, beaklike noses.*
8. *In addition to having unusual ability to mimic the human voice.* The dolphin is of extreme interest because of its streamlined body structure and its amazing built-in sonar system.
9. Nuclear-powered submarines have been designed in the same general shape as the dolphin. *It is the most perfectly streamlined animal known.*
10. The dolphin possesses a built-in sonar apparatus. *Which is as accurate as sonar equipment used by scientists.*

EXERCISE 2. Identifying and Correcting Fragments.

Write the following paragraph, joining fragments to the sentences to which they belong. You might have to leave out several words as you rewrite a sentence to correct the fragment.

> Everyone is interested in the pony express. Which operated for eighteen months and during that time lost only one saddlebag. There were 308 runs made by the pony express. One of the fastest runs that was made by the riders. It was made in 1861. When Lincoln's first inaugural address was carried across the country. The trip covered 1,966 miles. And required seven days and seventeen hours for the riders to go from St. Joseph, Missouri, to Sacramento, California. Do you think postal rates are high today? Compare our rates today with those of the pony express. Which first charged five dollars per half ounce of mail but later reduced its rate to one dollar per half ounce.

Three Kinds of Fragments

The *subordinate clause,* the *verbal phrase,* and the *appositive phrase* are three kinds of fragments that often appear in student writing. Once you recognize that these three word groups cannot stand alone as complete sentences, you will have gone a long way toward eliminating fragments from your writing.

The Subordinate Clause

16b. A subordinate clause must not be written as a sentence.

As you learned on page 148, a subordinate clause contains a verb and its subject but does not express a complete thought. It cannot stand by itself but must always be attached to an independent clause. *As she turned the corner* is a subordinate clause. If you read this word group aloud, you will hear at once that it is not a complete sentence. Read the following subordinate clauses aloud. Do they sound like complete sentences? Then notice the difference when they are joined to independent clauses.

When it rains during a football game [What happens then?]

Who directed us to our seats [If a question is intended, the word group is a sentence. If not, it is a fragment.]

When it rains during a football game, the stadium looks like a patchwork quilt of umbrellas.

We gave our tickets to an usher, **who directed us to our seats.**

Remember that relative pronouns *(who, whom, whose, which, that)* or subordinating conjunctions (see the list on page 158) introduce subordinate clauses. These are very important words, for they can change a sentence into a fragment.

SENTENCE   It rains during a football game.
FRAGMENT   When it rains during a football game.

SENTENCE   An usher directed us to our seats.
FRAGMENT   An usher who directed us to our seats.

EXERCISE 3. Correcting Subordinate Clause Fragments.
The following paragraphs contain ten fragments. Each fragment is a subordinate clause incorrectly written as a sentence. Write the paragraphs, attaching the fragments to the related independent clauses.

Fifteen very young dinosaurs were waiting in a nest. While their mother went looking for food. Before the adult dinosaur could return to its young. Disaster struck. The small prehistoric creatures all perished. When a volcano buried the nest in debris.

Scientists recently uncovered the fossils of these small dinosaurs. Which lived 70 million years ago. After they studied the remaining fragments of bones. Scientists reconstructed the appearance of the dinosaurs. The name given to these extinct lizards was *hadrosaur.* Which means ''duck-billed lizard.'' Adult hadrosaurs were plant eaters. That could scoop up vegetation from watery swamps.

The discovery of these small fossils was important. Because it shed light on one of the great mysteries about dinosaurs. Before this recent discovery was made. Scientists debated whether dinosaurs were coldblooded or warmblooded animals. Fossil evidence shows these tiny hadrosaurs were living in a nest. They were likely warmblooded. Because few coldblooded animals are fed by their parents or protected in nests.

EXERCISE 4. Correcting Subordinate Clause Fragments.
Make each of the following fragments into a complete sentence by adding an independent clause to go with the subordinate clause. Write each sentence on your paper, using punctuation and capital letters correctly.

EXAMPLE 1. Because I missed the bus by seconds.
      1. *I was twenty minutes late to school because I missed the bus by seconds.*

1. Who broke her glasses.
2. Because the lights on the stage went out during the performance.
3. While Jolene was rehearsing her part.
4. After the fish got away.
5. Who is president of the student council.
6. That are working on a clean-up campaign for the school.
7. If you want to own a pet.
8. Which were racing across the lake.
9. Because the library closes at six o'clock.
10. Whom I met at your party.

The Verbal Phrase

16c. A verbal phrase must not be written as a sentence.

As you learned in Chapter 5, present participles and gerunds are verbals that end in –*ing* (*coming, working, being*). Past participles are verbals that usually end in –*d*, –*ed*, –*t*, –*n*, or –*en* (*looked*, *slept, broken).* Infinitives are verbals that usually consist of *to* plus the verb *(to go, to play).*

A verbal phrase is a phrase containing a verbal. It is often mistaken for a sentence because the verbal is often mistaken for a main verb. However, a phrase does not have both a subject and a verb and, therefore, cannot express a complete thought. By itself, a verbal phrase is a fragment.

FRAGMENTS   Lying lazily on the beach
              Built of bamboo
              Waiting patiently at the doctor's office
              To see a movie

Like subordinate clauses, verbals depend on independent clauses to make their meaning complete.

SENTENCES   **Lying lazily on the beach,** I fell asleep.
              A house **built of bamboo** cannot withstand a heavy wind.
              Waiting patiently at the doctor's office is difficult for me.
              They wanted **to see a movie.**

EXERCISE 5. Correcting Verbal Phrase Fragments. The following items are verbal phrases incorrectly written as sentences. Write ten complete sentences by adding an independent clause to each of the verbal phrases. Use punctuation and capital letters correctly. Underline the verbal in each sentence.

1. Standing alone.
2. Seeing the exit sign.
3. Expecting guests.
4. Waiting for the bus.
5. Painted bright colors.
6. Sparkling in the sunlight.
7. To go to the concert.
8. Chosen as the captain of the debating team.
9. Walking on the hot pavement.
10. To buy a bike.

EXERCISE 6. Correcting Verbal Phrase Fragments. The following paragraphs contain ten verbal phrases incorrectly used as sentences. Revise the paragraphs, joining the fragments to the proper independent clauses.

Alice's Adventures in Wonderland is a literary classic. Read by college students as well as elementary-school students. Every child enjoys this story. Missing some of the fun but laughing at many of the comic incidents. When children grow up, they read the story again. Finding more humor in it this time.

In one of the most famous episodes in the book, Alice finds herself at an unusual tea party. Given by the Hatter. Being very lazy. The Hatter and his companions, the March Hare and the Dormouse, have allowed dirty dishes to pile up all over. The Dormouse tells a long story. Falling asleep in the middle. The March Hare offers Alice wine. Alice is told that there is no wine. After accepting the offer. For a while the three creatures ask her riddles. Having no answers. Then they ignore her. Carrying on a ridiculous conversation among themselves. Finally, Alice manages to escape. Thoroughly exhausted.

The Appositive Phrase

16d. An appositive phrase must not be written as a sentence.

An appositive phrase, an appositive with its modifiers, identifies or explains the noun or pronoun it follows (see pages 138–139). Neither an appositive nor an appositive phrase can stand alone as a sentence; it should be set off from the rest of the sentence by a comma or commas.

FRAGMENT   The eighteen sailors rowed 3,618 miles to Timor. *An island near Java.*

SENTENCE   The eighteen sailors rowed 3,618 miles to Timor, **an island near Java.** [*An island near Java* is an appositive phrase explaining *Timor* and should be joined to the rest of the sentence.]

FRAGMENT   We had dinner at the Banana Tree. *An interesting restaurant near Key West.*

SENTENCE   We had dinner at the Banana Tree, **an interesting restaurant near Key West.** [*An interesting restaurant near Key West* is an appositive phrase explaining *Banana Tree.*]

EXERCISE 7. Correcting Appositive Phrase Fragments.
Revise the following expressions, attaching the appositive phrases to the independent clauses from which they have been separated. Change punctuation and capital letters wherever necessary. Some of the appositive phrases belong in the middle of sentences.

1. Rachel and I enjoy playing *Parcheesi.* A game from India.
2. The entrance to the Mediterranean is guarded by Gibraltar. A rocklike peninsula.
3. Astronomers have long been intrigued by Saturn. The first planet known to have rings.
4. Thursday was named for Thor. The Norse god of thunder.
5. We saw two movies. A science fiction thriller and a western.
6. In 1818 Mary Wollstonecraft Shelley wrote *Frankenstein.* The famous horror novel.
7. The Battle of Marathon was won by the Greeks. One of the most famous battles in the history of the world.
8. Coretta King has become as well known as her husband for the advocacy of civil rights. The widow of Dr. Martin Luther King, Jr.
9. The world's largest cactus plants often reach a height of sixty feet and live for two hundred years. The huge saguaros in Arizona.
10. Pumpkins were a staple of the Native American diet and still appear in the supermarkets every fall. Members of the squash family.

REVIEW EXERCISE A. Correcting Fragments. Revise the following items, eliminating fragments by attaching them to independent clauses. Then write whether each fragment is a *subordinate clause*, a *verbal phrase*, or an *appositive phrase*.

1. As I was driving home. I saw a turtle in the middle of the highway.
2. It had been rolled over on its back by a car. While trying to cross the road.
3. Now it was lying there in the middle of the highway. Helplessly moving its feet back and forth.
4. Because I remembered that a turtle cannot get off its back on a smooth surface. I stopped the car and picked the animal up.
5. It immediately drew its feet and head under its shell. So that I could see nothing more than two eyes. Staring at me from inside the shell.
6. The turtle that I had found was a box turtle. A very shy land dweller.
7. I took it to Tall Oaks. My parents' cottage in the mountains. Because I wanted to observe it for a while.
8. Arriving there, I put the turtle down on a rug. Which covers most of the living room floor.
9. The turtle slowly began to stick its feet and head out from its shell. After being still for almost ten minutes.
10. As soon as it felt safe, it crawled very awkwardly but quickly across the rug. Heading for a corner of the room.

REVIEW EXERCISE B. Identifying Sentences and Fragments. Some of the following groups of words are sentences; others are subordinate clauses, verbal phrases, or appositive phrases incorrectly written as sentences. Number your paper 1–25. After the proper number, write *S* for each complete sentence and *F* for each fragment. Be prepared to tell how you would correct each fragment by making it part of a related sentence.

1. Almost every book on art includes a reproduction of the *Mona Lisa.* **2.** One of the most famous paintings in the world. **3.** The *Mona Lisa* was painted by Leonardo da Vinci. **4.** Who worked on it for four years (1503–1506). **5.** The painting

was never quite finished.   **6.** After working for several hours.
7. Leonardo would sit down in front of the *Mona Lisa* to quiet his
nerves.   **8.** Some people say that Leonardo did not finish the
painting.   **9.** Because he wanted an excuse to keep it with him.

10. There is a mysterious smile on the face of the woman in
the painting.   **11.** Which has intrigued people for centuries.
12. Although no one knows the true explanation of the
smile.   **13.** Several legends have grown up about it.   **14.** One
story says that the woman was smiling sadly when she sat for the
portrait.   **15.** Because her child had died.   **16.** Another story,
however, goes on to say that Leonardo hired musicians to play
during the sittings.   **17.** Flutists and violin players.   **18.** So that
he could capture the young woman's rapt expression.

19. When Leonardo left Italy and moved to France.   **20.** He
took the painting with him.   **21.** The French king persuaded him
to sell the painting.   **22.** Which now hangs in the Louvre.   **23.**
An art museum in Paris.

24. The *Mona Lisa* has been exhibited in several countries.
25. So that many people have had a chance to see the woman
with the mysterious smile.

RUN–ON SENTENCES

Another common writing fault that you can avoid by using your
sentence sense is the *run-on sentence*. Run-on sentences occur
when the writer fails to recognize the end of a sentence and runs
on into the next sentence without proper punctuation or, sometimes, without any punctuation at all.

16e. A *run-on sentence* consists of two or more sentences
separated only by a comma or by no mark of punctuation.

RUN-ON   Romare Bearden is a prominent artist his collage is
in the museum.

CORRECTED   Romare Bearden is a prominent artist. **H**is collage
is in the museum.

RUN-ON   Lee Trevino was playing in the golf tournament, I hoped I could go.

CORRECTED   Lee Trevino was playing in the golf tournament. I hoped I could go.

A comma marks a break in a sentence, not the end of the sentence. Thus a comma should not be used between two sentences.

EXERCISE 8. Revising Run-on Sentences. Revise the following run-ons. Number your paper 1–10. After the proper number, write the last word in the first sentence and place a period after it; then write the first word of the next sentence, beginning it with a capital letter.

EXAMPLE   1. The Virgin Islands' weather is perfect, daytime temperatures are in the 80's year round.

                1. *perfect. Daytime*

1. In nineteenth-century England there were two types of English pepper moths one type was all black, and the other had gray and white speckles.
2. The black variety was extremely rare, most people had only seen speckled pepper moths.
3. The moths lived on the bark of surrounding trees, most trees in England had a gray moss covering them.
4. The speckled moths blended into this background the birds that ate pepper moths could not see them against the gray moss.
5. The black moths could be easily seen they were frequently killed by birds.
6. The Industrial Revolution in England produced many factories, when the smoke and soot created by the factories filled the air, it covered the neighboring trees.
7. The amount of soot, two tons per square mile, was enough to color the trees black, the speckled moths could now be easily seen by birds searching for food.
8. The black moths blended into the background of the black trees, the birds began to dine on the speckled variety.

9. Within fifty years, the black variety outnumbered the speck-led moths 99 to 1, the advantage of a particular color for protection had completely reversed.

10. Other animals use protective coloration certain kinds of fish have the same color as their surroundings and can blend with the background to escape enemies.

EXERCISE 9. Revising Run-on Sentences. Each of the following passages contains several run-on sentences. You will find the passages hard to read because run-on sentences always interfere with the clear expression of ideas. After you have decided where each sentence should end, write the last word of each complete sentence on your paper. Place the appropriate end mark after the word; then write the first word of the next sentence, beginning it with a capital letter.

EXAMPLE 1. *Jest* once had a different meaning than it does today, in medieval times the English used the word to refer to a brave act or the story of such a deed, by the sixteenth century it meant "to jeer or mock" now, of course, a *jest* is a joke.

    1. *today. In*
    deed. By
    mock." Now

1. Our word *humor* has an interesting history, it comes from the Latin word for liquid, in the Middle Ages people believed that four liquids in the body made up one's character, thus a person with too much of one humor might be quite odd or eccentric.

2. Our word *paper* comes from the French word *papier,* this word can be traced back to the Greek *papyros,* which is the name of an Egyptian plant, part of this plant was sliced into strips and then soaked in water, finally, it was pressed and pasted into a writing material that was used by the Egyptians, Greeks, and Romans.

3. The comma can be traced back to the Greek language, our word *comma* comes from the Greek word *komma,* which

412 < Writing Complete Sentences

means "a piece cut off" when you use a comma, you cut off an expression from the rest of the sentence.

4. The word *rigmarole* came from a group of documents called *ragman roll* written in 1291, Scottish lords signed these documents to prove their loyalty to King Edward I of England since many of the documents were so full of signatures that they were confusing and hard to read, the word *rigmarole* came to mean "a series of confused or foolish statements."

5. Have you ever wondered about the origin of the word *sandwich,* it came into use during the eighteenth century, John Montagu, the Earl of Sandwich, was addicted to gambling, so addicted that he often would not stop for his meals, during one of his twenty-four-hour gambling sessions, he instructed someone to bring him slices of bread with roast beef inserted between them because the Earl of Sandwich did not want to stop gambling long enough to go to dinner, the world gained the sandwich.

EXERCISE 10. Revising Run-on Sentences. Of the following sentences, five are correct and five are run-ons. After the proper number, write only the run-ons, making whatever corrections are necessary.

1. The Amazon is the second longest river in the world, it flows through South America for 3,900 miles.

2. When the runner broke the school's record, everyone in the stadium stood up to cheer him.

3. There is an old belief that birds begin to choose their mates on February 14 perhaps this legend is responsible for our association of romance with Valentine's Day.

4. Have you ever heard of Six Mile that's a strange name for a town.

5. Hank Aaron was born in Mobile, Alabama, which is the birthplace of several other former Major League stars.

6. My grandfather says that we will have six more weeks of winter because the groundhog saw its shadow on February 2.

7. The winner of the soccer World Cup is decided every four years, hundreds of millions of people watch the tournament on television.
8. Before the airplane was invented, many people made wings, but no one succeeded in flying.
9. Aladdin had a magic lamp, and when he rubbed it, two jinn appeared to do his bidding.
10. "The albatross is a bird that is popular in legend and literature," our teacher explained, "it is the largest of the sea birds."

REVIEW EXERCISE C. Identifying Sentences, Fragments, and Run-ons. Some of the following expressions are sentences. Others are fragments or run-ons. Number your paper 1–10. After the proper number, write *S* (sentence), *F* (fragment), or *R* (run-on). Be prepared to tell how you would correct the fragments and run-ons.

1. All cats are able to climb trees, some spend most of their time in trees.
2. Others prefer to spend more time on the ground.
3. Most cats have the ability to draw back their claws and shield them.
4. When the claws are not in use.
5. A notable feature of the cat family.
6. Most cats have long tails.
7. That they use for balance.
8. Many cats are tailless, their hind legs are longer than their forelegs.
9. Nearly all cats have good vision and excellent hearing.
10. Few cats catch their prey by outrunning it, they stalk their victims patiently and silently.

REVIEW EXERCISE D. Identifying Sentences, Fragments, and Run-ons. Some of the following expressions are sentences. Others are fragments or run-ons. Number your paper 1–20. After the proper number, write *S* (sentence), *F* (fragment), or *R* (run-on). Be prepared to tell how you would correct the fragments and run-ons.

1. Medusa and her two sisters were three horrible monsters who had at one time been beautiful women.
2. The most beautiful of the three, Medusa, was very proud, she boasted that she was even more beautiful than the goddess Athena.
3. Because of her pride, she and her two sisters were turned into monsters.
4. Who had hissing serpents for hair.
5. No one dared look upon Medusa and her sisters.
6. Because anyone who did turned to stone.
7. Lying all about them were stones that had once been men.
8. Medusa and her two sisters menaced the land for years finally they were challenged by Perseus.
9. A young, handsome warrior.
10. Having been given magic weapons by the gods.
11. Perseus set out to kill Medusa.
12. The only mortal one of the three sisters.
13. When he approached the area in which the monsters lived.
14. Perseus put on a magic cap that made him invisible, he held up a shield that had been given to him by Athena.
15. Studying the reflection of Medusa and her sisters in his shield.
16. Perseus slowly approached the monsters.
17. Luckily, they were sleeping.
18. Still using the shield as a mirror, he cut off Medusa's head with a single stroke he put the head into a special pouch.
19. Which had also been given to him by Athena.
20. The other sisters awoke but could not see him, therefore he escaped with the head of Medusa.

REVIEW EXERCISE E. Revising Fragments and Run-ons in Your Own Writing. Pretend that you are writing to a person who has never seen a comic strip. Write a paragraph in which you describe one of the main characters in your favorite comic strip. After you have finished writing the paragraph, read each sentence aloud, one by one, to be sure that you have not carelessly written a fragment or a run-on. Make the necessary corrections on your paper.

CHAPTER 17

Writing Effective Sentences

SENTENCE COMBINING AND REVISING

As you continue in school and your writing assignments become more demanding, you should develop the habit of writing at least two drafts of a composition. In the first draft, express what you have to say. In the revised draft, concentrate on writing clearly and well and on eliminating faults in style. Watch especially for groups of choppy, abrupt sentences and for rambling sentences held together by a string of conjunctions. Such sentences, while occasionally effective, become monotonous and tiresome if used too often. This chapter will show how to recognize such poorly written sentences and how to revise them.

CORRECTING A CHOPPY STYLE BY COMBINING SENTENCES

Short sentences are often effective in a composition, but a long series of short sentences tends to irritate readers. They slow the reader down and make it difficult to focus on what is being said. Such choppy sentences are often similar in construction and thus are monotonous in their effect. The following passage of choppy sentences would irritate most readers.

Victor visited Williamsburg, Virginia. Marsha also went. The visit took place during the summer. They both visited for the first time. They toured the buildings together. Marsha was studying the antiques collection. Victor was examining the architecture. They began to share each other's interest. The architecture was from the colonial period. The antiques were from the colonial period.

This passage is very choppy. By combining sentences that are closely related, the passage could be revised as follows:

During the summer, Victor and Marsha visited Williamsburg, Virginia, for the first time. As they toured the buildings together, Marsha was studying the antiques collection, but Victor was examining the architecture. They began to share each other's interest because both the architecture and the antiques were from the colonial period.

Several methods have been used in revising the passage. For example, the first four sentences in the original version have been combined into one sentence containing a compound subject and two prepositional phrases. To improve your writing style, you should be familiar with each of the ways to combine short, related sentences.

17a. Combine short, related sentences by inserting adjectives, adverbs, or prepositional phrases.

WEAK   At half time, the coach gave the players confidence in themselves.
       The players had been discouraged.
BETTER At half time, the coach gave the discouraged players confidence in themselves. [The adjective *discouraged* in the second sentence is inserted into the first sentence.]

WEAK   In the second half, the team improved.
       They improved rapidly.
BETTER In the second half, the team improved rapidly. [The adverb *rapidly* in the second sentence is inserted into the first sentence.]

WEAK The solar-energy panels were installed yesterday.
They are on the garage roof.

BETTER The solar-energy panels were installed yesterday on the garage roof. [The prepositional phrase *on the garage roof* in the second sentence is inserted into the first sentence.]

When you join short sentences by inserting adjectives, adverbs, or prepositional phrases, be sure the new sentence reads smoothly. (Review the rule concerning commas separating adjectives on page 342.)

EXERCISE 1. Combining Sentences by Inserting Adjectives, Adverbs, or Prepositional Phrases. Combine each group of short, related sentences into one sentence by inserting adjectives, adverbs, or prepositional phrases. There may be more than one correct way to combine the sentences. Add commas where they are necessary.

EXAMPLE 1. The bird sings in the cage.
The bird is yellow.
It sings sweetly.
The cage is by the window.
1. *The yellow bird sings sweetly in the cage by the window.*

1. Melissa chains her bike to a post.
The post is steel.
2. The sun descended into the horizon.
The sun was bright.
The horizon was hazy.
3. The fans filed into the rows.
They filed noisily.
4. The guitarist tuned her instrument.
She was on the stage.
5. The two parties argued their cases.
The parties were angry.
They argued in front of the judge.

6. Conservation laws protect wildlife.
   The laws are strong.
   They protect wildlife inside state parks.
7. We will make the decorations.
   We will do this shortly.
   The decorations are for Flag Day.
8. Miguel wrote his letter.
   He wrote it on Saturday.
   It was a letter to the mayor.
9. Poland has one of the tallest structures. *on Earth*
   It is one of the tallest structures on earth.
   Poland is in northeastern Europe. *on a mirror*
10. The tallest structure is an antenna.
    It is a very thin antenna.
    It is a radio-station antenna.

17b. Combine closely related sentences by using participial phrases.

A participial phrase (see page 124) is a group of related words that contains a participle and that acts as an adjective, modifying a noun or a pronoun. In the following examples, all the words in boldfaced type are part of the participial phrase.

EXAMPLES **Grinning from ear to ear,** Michelle trotted off the stage. [*Grinning* is a present participle.]

Battered by the high seas, the small ship limped into port. [*Battered* is a past participle.]

Two closely related sentences can be combined by making one of the sentences a participial phrase.

EXAMPLE The librarian answered our question.
He was whispering in low tones.

Whispering in low tones, the librarian answered our question.

A participial phrase must be placed close to the noun or pronoun it modifies. Otherwise, the phrase may confuse the reader.

MISPLACED Caught in the chicken coop, the farmer cornered the fox.

IMPROVED The farmer cornered the fox caught in the chicken coop.

☞ NOTE Use a comma after a participial phrase that begins a sentence.

EXAMPLE Embarrassed by our loss, our team sat in the locker room.

EXERCISE 2. **Combining Sentences by Using a Participial Phrase.** Combine each of the following groups of sentences into one sentence by using a participial phrase. Make sure that the participial phrase is not misplaced. There may be more than one correct way to combine the sentences. Add commas where they are necessary.

EXAMPLE 1. The class worked quickly.
They divided up the job.
1. *Dividing up the job, the class worked quickly.*
or *Working quickly, the class divided up the job.*

1. The referee signaled a score.
   She was standing beneath the basket.
2. The secretary called a meeting.
   He was troubled by the press reports.
3. The audience applauded loudly.
   They were interrupting the singer.
4. Betty captured the flag.
   She ruined the other team's late comeback.
5. Ellis wrote a thank-you note.
   It expressed his joy over the visit.

6. The students voted yesterday.
   They were electing a class president.
7. Susan ran downstairs.
   She was startled by the noise.
8. The town is safe and secure.
   It nestles beneath two mountains.
9. I was puzzled by the rules of the game.
   I decided not to play.
10. The team on the passing bus started to sing.
    They drowned out the teacher's voice.

17c. Combine short, related sentences by using appositive phrases.

Appositive phrases (see page 139) are useful for explaining or identifying nouns or pronouns. The following sentence contains an appositive phrase in boldfaced type.

EXAMPLE   At the movie theater I saw Mrs. Jacovina, **our next-door neighbor.**

Two related sentences can be combined by using an appositive phrase.

TWO SENTENCES   Marlene won the competition.
                She is an excellent tennis player.
ONE SENTENCE   Marlene, an excellent tennis player, won the competition.

EXERCISE 3. Combining Sentences by Using an Appositive Phrase.   Combine each group of sentences by using an appositive phrase. Place the phrase next to the noun or pronoun it explains or modifies. Put commas at the beginning and end of each appositive phrase to set it off from the rest of the sentence.

EXAMPLE   1. Karen bought me a sweater for my birthday.
             She is my good friend.
          1. *Karen, my good friend, bought me a sweater for my birthday.*

1. Juan won the citywide spelling bee.
   He is an excellent speller.
2. Lena Jackson lived in Japan before moving here.
   She is our new doctor.
3. I finally spoke to Mr. Powell.
   He is the store manager.
4. Jack read my composition.
   He is my brother's friend.
5. Joan made the lasagna.
   It was the most popular dish at the picnic.
6. Bob was at the last baseball game.
   He is the sportswriter for our newspaper.
7. Have you ever been to Redwood National Park?
   It is a national park in California.
8. I am reading *The Adventures of Huckleberry Finn*.
   It is a book written by Mark Twain.
9. *Carnival of Autumn* is in the Museum of Fine Arts in Boston.
   It is a painting by Marsden Hartley.
10. Ms. Mangan was at the fair, too.
    She is my music teacher.

Another method of combining short, related sentences is to join the subjects to make a compound subject or to join the verbs to make a compound verb.

17d. Combine short, related sentences by using compound subjects.

A compound subject (see page 17) consists of two or more simple subjects joined by a conjunction such as *and* or *or* and having the same verb.

EXAMPLE   This **table** and that **chair** are ready for the movers.

Often two short sentences may contain similar verbs but different subjects.

EXAMPLE   The radio report predicted rain.
          The television news also predicted it.

You can combine these short sentences by writing a single sentence with a compound subject.

EXAMPLE　**Both the radio report and the television news** predicted rain.

Words that connect a compound subject are *and, or, both—and, either—or,* and *neither—nor.* The choice of the conjunction depends on the meaning of the sentence.

Compound subjects must agree with the verb in the sentence.

EXAMPLES　Paul has missed the bus.
His sister has missed it also.

Paul **and** his sister have missed the bus. [Subjects joined by *and* or *both—and* take a plural verb.]

An almanac gives the answer.
An atlas gives the answer.

Either an almanac **or** an atlas gives the answer. [Singular subjects joined by *or, either—or,* or *neither —nor* take a singular verb.]

EXERCISE 4. **Combining Sentences by Using a Compound Subject.**　Combine each pair of sentences by writing one sentence with a compound subject. Be sure the subject and the verb agree in number.

EXAMPLE　1.　Arlene will not be at the party tomorrow.
Margery will not be there either.

1.　*Neither Arlene nor Margery will be at the party tomorrow.*

1. Rugby is played in England.
Soccer is played there also.
2. Soda is not allowed in the stands.
Popcorn is not allowed either.
3. My sister went to the zoo.
I went there with her.
4. The sun is a reliable source of energy.
Coal is another reliable source.

5. Engineering might be Teng's career choice.
Medicine might be his career choice instead.
6. Tracy Austin will play in the tournament.
Björn Borg will play also.
7. Listening to music is one of my favorite pastimes.
Reading is another of my favorites.
8. The treasurer could be responsible for the minutes.
The secretary could be responsible instead.
9. Maples grow well in this area.
Birches grow well too.
10. Chewing gum is not allowed in class.
Whispering is not allowed either.

17e. Combine short, related sentences by using compound verbs.

A compound verb (see page 18) consists of two or more verbs that have the same subject and are joined by a conjunction. In the following example, the compound verb is printed in boldface.

EXAMPLE   The senator **voted** for the conservation law but **lost** the election.

You can combine two sentences by writing one sentence with a compound verb.

EXAMPLE   He backed the car down the driveway.
He lurched to a stop in the street.

He **backed** the car down the driveway and **lurched** to a stop in the street.

The conjunctions used most frequently to join compound verbs are *and, but, or, either—or, neither—nor,* and *both—and.* The choice of the conjunction depends on the sentence meaning.

EXERCISE 5. Combining Sentences by Using a Compound Verb. Combine each pair of short sentences into a single sentence with a compound verb. Use connecting words that clearly state the relation between sentences.

EXAMPLE   1. In February Teresa visited her grandparents in
             Puerto Rico.
             She also toured Everglades Park in Florida.
          1. *In February Teresa both visited her grandparents in*
             Puerto Rico and toured Everglades Park in Florida.

1. He repaired the bicycle yesterday.
   He raced with it today.
2. Ruth had a better plan.
   She proposed it during class.
3. Elgin finished dinner before everyone else.
   He stayed at the table anyway.
4. I had heard of polecats.
   I had never seen one before.
5. The guard did not hear the car approaching.
   She was taken completely by surprise.
6. This worthless timetable may be misprinted.
   It may be out of date.
7. The train was late leaving the station.
   It still arrived on time.
8. Mr. Verris casually crossed the hall.
   He entered the room and quietly handed out the tests.
9. The giant wave swamped the boats in the harbor.
   It also toppled the lighthouse.
10. She will announce the field trip soon.
    She will wait another week.

**REVIEW EXERCISE A. Revising a Passage by Combining
Sentences.**   The following passage contains several short, related sentences. Revise the passage, combining the sentences by
the methods you have learned thus far. Your new passage should
not change the meaning of the original. Add commas where they
are necessary.

   The Majestic River runs between the mountains. It is a
deep river. It runs swiftly. The mountains are high. Lush,
green vegetation crowds the river's shores. The vegetation

also grows up the mountain slopes./Campers fish in the river's pools. Day hikers also fish there. The pools are clear. The pools are beneath the rapids./Canoes can navigate the river. Rafts can also do this. The rafts are rubber./Canoes and rafts can navigate the river from High Falls to Bolt's Landing.

17f. Combine short, related sentences by making them into a compound sentence.

A compound sentence (see page 175) is really two or more simple sentences joined together. When simple sentences are joined together in a compound sentence, they are called independent clauses. The following sentence has two independent clauses.

EXAMPLE Tractor drivers bulldozed a barrier around the forest fire, and helicopter crews drenched the fire with chemicals.

Two simple sentences closely related in meaning may be joined into one compound sentence.

EXAMPLE The quarterback threw a long pass.
A defender intercepted the ball.

The quarterback threw a long pass, but a defender intercepted the ball.

The conjunctions used to join the parts of a compound sentence are usually *and, but, or,* or *nor.* The choice of the conjunction depends on the meaning of the sentence.

Be sure that the ideas you connect in the compound sentence are closely related and equal in importance. If you attempt to correct a choppy passage by connecting unrelated ideas, the result will be even worse than the original choppy version.

UNRELATED IDEAS I read the entire television schedule.
I like to watch news documentaries.

RELATED IDEAS I read the entire television schedule.
I could not find one interesting program.

UNEQUAL IDEAS   Lynn was elected class president.
Cara didn't vote.
EQUAL IDEAS   Lynn was elected class president.
Peter became secretary.

☞ **NOTE** Do not forget to put a comma before *and, but, or,* or *nor* when they join independent clauses (see page 343).

EXAMPLE   Alice brought her new water skis, and Tina borrowed her parents' ski boat.

EXERCISE 6. Combining Sentences by Making Them into a Compound Sentence.

Most of the following items consist of two or more closely related ideas. Combine these ideas into a single compound sentence, using *and, but,* or *or* as the connecting word. Add commas where they are necessary. A few items contain unrelated or unequal ideas. In such cases, write *U* after the proper number on your paper to show that the ideas are better expressed in two separate sentences.

1. Other nations use the metric system for weights and measures.
   The United States has decided to use the same system.
2. International trade depends on a uniform system of weights and measures.
   The United States leads the world in scientific research.
3. The United States is slowly converting to the metric system.
   This process is called metrification.
4. We can resist the change until the last possible moment.
   We can learn to use the metric system now.
5. The metric system is actually very easy to use.
   A decimeter is one tenth of a meter.
6. Metric weights are based on the kilogram.
   Metric lengths use the meter as the basic unit.

7. Many citizens still use the old system of measurement.
   Many professions and corporations have switched to the metric system.
8. All metric measurements are based on the number 10.
   Some baseball parks measure their distances in meters.
9. Counting by tens is second nature to most people.
   The metric system still seems complicated to many.
10. Metrification will be a difficult process.
    Careful planning will help.

Compound sentences can combine equal items from two separate sentences. When combining unequal ideas, however, it is best to use complex sentences.

17g. Combine short, choppy sentences into a complex sentence. Put one idea into a subordinate clause.

A complex sentence (see page 179) has an independent clause and at least one subordinate clause.

(1) Use an adjective clause to combine sentences.

An adjective clause (see page 152) is a subordinate clause that, like an adjective, modifies a noun or a pronoun. In the following example, the adjective clause is in boldfaced type.

EXAMPLE   The girl **who just waved to me** is my first cousin.
[The adjective clause modifies *girl*.]

Adjective clauses begin with one of the relative pronouns—
who, whom, whose, which, or *that.* Study the following examples of the relative pronoun used in a sentence.

EXAMPLES   Mr. Allen praised Tom, **who** had written an excellent paper.
Mr. Bingley gave a slide show, **which** the entire class enjoyed.
The answer **that** she gave was an abrupt and definite "no."

When two sentences are closely related, the second sentence may help to modify a noun, pronoun, or adjective in the first sentence.

EXAMPLE   Nora played her favorite record.
            I had given it to her. [This sentence modifies *record* in the first sentence.]

You can combine these two sentences by turning the second sentence into an adjective clause and inserting it into the first sentence.

> Nora played her favorite record, **which I had given to her.**

☞ **NOTE** Use commas to set off adjective clauses that are not essential to the basic meaning of the sentence. Do not use commas with clauses that are essential to the meaning. (See page 345.)

EXAMPLES   This is my favorite coin, **which I bought four years ago.** [nonessential clause]
             This is the coin **that I told you about.** [essential clause]

EXERCISE 7. Combining Sentences by Using an Adjective Clause.

Combine each of the following groups of sentences into a single sentence by putting one of the ideas into an adjective clause. Use commas where they are necessary.

EXAMPLE   1. Wendy Quon won the championship.
               She is a great athlete.
            1. *Wendy Quon, who is a great athlete, won the championship.*

1. The girl spoke to me.
   I did not know her.
2. The motion was passed by the Student Council.
   I had stated it.

3. Mr. Belleck is our new minister.
   He finished divinity school last year.
4. Julie dived in to help Jan.
   Julie is the best swimmer in our crowd.
5. I helped with the campaign of Senator Blake.
   She was the best candidate for the office.
6. Peter was the best dancer at the party.
   He studies ballet.
7. Mrs. Morrison swims all year.
   She does not look like an athlete.
8. "The Tell-Tale Heart" is my favorite story.
   It was written by Edgar Allan Poe.
9. She gave us some advice.
   It hindered more than it helped.
10. This statue is the most expensive item in the store.
    It is made of pure gold.

(2) Use an adverb clause to combine sentences.

An adverb clause (see page 156) is a subordinate clause that, like an adverb, modifies a verb, an adjective, or an adverb.

EXAMPLE   She sings **whenever she is alone.**

Adverb clauses, like adverbs, may tell *how, when, where, why, to what extent,* or *under what condition* an action is done. They begin with a subordinating conjunction. In the example, *whenever* is a subordinating conjunction. Study the following list:

Subordinating Conjunctions

after	before	than	whenever
although	if	unless	where
as	since	until	wherever
because	so that	when	while

Examine these two sentences:

The conductor stopped the orchestra.
The violins were not in tune.

You can combine these two sentences by turning the second sentence into an adverb clause and inserting it into the first sentence.

The conductor stopped the orchestra because the violins were not in tune.

When you combine two short sentences by turning one of them into an adverb clause, be careful to choose the correct subordinating conjunction. (The common subordinating conjunctions are *because, although, since, if, unless, when, before,* and *after.*) Because a subordinating conjunction shows the relationship between clauses, a poorly chosen conjunction will show a false or meaningless relationship. For example, a number of subordinating conjunctions could be used to join the following two sentences, but not all of them would show a relationship that makes sense.

EXAMPLE   Mario is industrious.
             He receives high grades.
UNCLEAR   Unless Mario is industrious, he receives high grades.
CLEAR   **Since** Mario is industrious, he receives high grades.

☞ NOTE   A comma is used after an adverb clause placed at the beginning of a sentence.

EXAMPLE   Although her head ached, she continued dancing.

EXERCISE 8. Combining Sentences by Using an Adverb Clause.
Combine each of the following groups of sentences into a single complex sentence by putting one idea into an adverb clause. Refer to the lists of subordinating conjunctions on pages 158 and 430.

EXAMPLE   1. Rosa saw the fox near the tree.
                She photographed it.
             1. *When Rosa saw the fox near the tree, she photographed it.*

1. Her ankle pained her sharply.
   She kept on playing.
2. Doris did not go to the movie.
   She had a headache.
3. He saw the truck rolling down the hill toward him.
   He jumped onto the curb.
4. The temperature dropped sharply.
   We kept right on skating.
5. Jane's mother motioned to us.
   We walked across the street.
6. The baby threw the plate on the floor.
   Sam rushed to the kitchen.
7. Mrs. White was just about to start the test.
   We ran into the room.
8. My eyes were growing tired.
   I did not stop studying.
9. Cathy held the tent up straight.
   Jeannette hammered down the stakes.
10. Norm forgot the time of the party.
    We were late.

REVIEW EXERCISE B. **Using Sentence-Combining Methods.** Combine each of the following groups of sentences into one sentence, using the sentence-combining methods you have learned. Do not change the meaning of the sentences you combine. Add commas where they are necessary.

EXAMPLE   1. The jury returned its verdict.
              The prisoner was set free.
              The real criminal was arrested.
           1. *When the jury returned its verdict, the prisoner was set free, and the real criminal was arrested.*

1. The umpire called a strike.
   The batter left the plate.
   The fans protested.
   The fans were angry.
   They protested with loud screams.

2. Mary grabbed the rope.
   She pulled in the sail.
   Sue held the tiller.
   She held it tightly.
   She is the captain.
3. The day was over.
   It was a hard day.
   The Brimwells sat together.
   They sat by the fire.
   They told stories.
   The stories were about their ancestors.
4. Federal Bank sponsors a refresher course.
   The course is in mathematics.
   The course is open to every student.
5. The President wants to fight inflation.
   He gave a speech on television.
   He did this last night.
   The people want action, not words.

REVIEW EXERCISE C. Using Sentence-Combining Methods. Combine each of the following groups of sentences into one smooth, clear sentence by using the sentence-combining methods you have learned. Do not change the meaning of the sentences you combine. Add commas where they are necessary.

1. No one has ever solved the mystery.
   It is the mystery of the ship *Mary Celeste*.
   It set sail in 1872 bound for Europe.
   It set sail from New York.
2. The ship was found.
   It was floating in the Atlantic Ocean.
   It was found without a crew.
3. The crew may have been murdered.
   The crew may have deserted.
   No sign of a struggle was found.
   There was no reason to desert.

4. A child's toys lay undisturbed.
They lay on the bed.
It was the captain's bed.
The toys suggest that the child left suddenly.
5. People still look for clues.
These people are curious.
The clues may explain the crew's disappearance.

REVIEW EXERCISE D. Revising a Paragraph by Combining Sentences. The following paragraph contains choppy sentences. Revise the paragraph by combining sentences to create clear, varied sentences, but be careful not to change the meaning of the paragraph. Use the sentence-combining methods you have learned. Add commas where they are necessary.

Wayne felt nervous asking questions in class. He had helpful questions to ask. He had interesting questions to ask. Today Wayne took a chance. He raised his hand. He asked the question calmly. He didn't feel nervous. The class session finished. Wayne got up. He turned to his friend, Boyd. He said, "That wasn't so bad, after all."

REVIEW EXERCISE E. Revising a Paragraph by Eliminating Choppy Sentences. Revise the following paragraph to eliminate choppy sentences, but be careful not to change the meaning of the original paragraph. Use the sentence-combining methods you have learned. Add commas where they are necessary.

Robert Frost wrote many poems. Frost grew up in New England. Many of his poems are about the countryside in winter. One poem has been popular with students. It is titled "Stopping by Woods on a Snowy Evening." In this poem a traveler pauses on a journey. The traveler pauses for a moment. The journey is by horse. The traveler watches the snow. It is falling in the woods. The woods are far from the nearest village. People disagree about the poem's meaning. They enjoy it immensely. It seems to touch on a deep truth about life. It describes a common, everyday experience.

CORRECTING A MONOTONOUS STYLE

If you look at the first passage on page 417, you will notice that each sentence in the paragraph begins in the same way, with a subject followed by a verb. In the revised passage, however, each sentence begins differently. The first sentence begins with a prepositional phrase, the second sentence begins with a subordinate clause, and so on. This was done to avoid a monotonous style.

17h. Correct a monotonous style by varying the beginnings of sentences.

A series of sentences that begin in the same way produces a monotonous style. Young writers often write a paragraph of sentences all of which begin with the subject. To avoid such monotony, you can revise some sentences to begin with a modifier: an adverb, an adverb clause, a prepositional phrase, or a participial phrase. You will not need to revise them all, however. If all the sentences were changed to begin with an adverb, for example, the passage would be as monotonous as before. Moreover, you should never write an unclear or awkward sentence merely for the sake of variety. If a sentence sounds best with the subject first, you should leave it that way and try to revise some of the sentences near it, if necessary.

(1) Vary sentences by beginning them with adverbs.

EXAMPLES She paid her debts willingly.
Willingly she paid her debts.

She said sorrowfully, "We're leaving."
Sorrowfully she said, "We're leaving."

(2) Vary sentences by beginning them with adverb clauses.

EXAMPLES The pain eased after the tooth was pulled.
After the tooth was pulled, the pain eased.

He was not afraid to fight, although he was small.
Although he was small, he was not afraid to fight.

EXERCISE 9. Beginning Sentences with an Adverb or Adverb Clause. Revise the following sentences by beginning them with either an adverb or an adverb clause.

1. She agreed to his proposal reluctantly.
2. The puppy started whining instantly.
3. We went fishing whenever work permitted.
4. He carefully sharpened the carving knife.
5. She lived in Mexico before she moved here.
6. Tim was polite although they had angered him.
7. She will wash the car if you wish.
8. She wisely pretended not to hear.
9. He will go to college if he gets a scholarship.
10. She gave him a tip although she had little money.

(3) Vary sentences by beginning them with prepositional phrases.[1]

EXAMPLES   A portrait of our mother hung on the wall.
On the wall hung a portrait of our mother.

A police officer sat in the car.
In the car sat a police officer.

Sometimes when you move a prepositional phrase, you may want to change the position of the verb also.

EXAMPLE   A kettle hung above the fire.
Above the fire hung a kettle.

(4) Vary sentences by beginning with participial phrases.[2]

A participial phrase is usually separated from the rest of the sentence by a comma.

EXAMPLES   The fielder, **leaping up,** caught the ball.
Leaping up, the fielder caught the ball.

---

[1] If you need to review the prepositional phrase, turn to pages 113–17.
[2] If you need to review the participial phrase, turn to page 124.

> She sang for the crowd, **accompanying herself on the piano.**
>
> **Accompanying herself on the piano,** she sang for the crowd.
>
> They stared at each other in bewilderment, **stunned by the news.**
>
> **Stunned by the news,** they stared at each other in bewilderment.

(5) Vary sentences by beginning them with infinitive phrases.[1]

EXAMPLES **To get to Homer's Fish Market,** turn left at the next corner.

To stay on the team, you must attend every meeting.

EXERCISE 10. Beginning Sentences with an Adverb, a Phrase, or a Clause. All of the following sentences begin with the subject. For the sake of variety, revise them with an adverb, a phrase, or a clause at the beginning.

1. Alice practices the piano after she finishes her homework.
2. She sang in her shrill voice to annoy me.
3. The rainmaker, jumping from his chair, smiled with satisfaction as he pointed at the dark clouds massing overhead.
4. The mechanic will repair your car if you tell him what you want done.
5. I arrived early to surprise him.
6. The general wore a Medal of Honor around his neck.
7. The scouts were singing loudly and happily as they were hiking back to camp.
8. She kept score, watching the players on the field intently.
9. Her parents said, finally, that she could go hiking on Saturday afternoon if she finished painting the fence.
10. Aunt Martha took the twins to the new swimming pool on the very next day.

[1] If you need to review the infinitive phrase, turn to page 133.

EXERCISE 11. Writing Sentences with Introductory Adverbs or Adverb Clauses. Use the following adverbs and adverb clauses to begin sentences of your own.

1. Carefully,
2. Proudly,
3. Happily,
4. Unwillingly,
5. As soon as Carmen heard the news,
6. Because he felt tired,
7. If we had plenty of time,
8. Suddenly,
9. After she thought it over,
10. Whenever my grandparents visit us,

EXERCISE 12. Writing Sentences with Introductory Phrases. Use the following prepositional and participial phrases to begin sentences of your own.

1. On her day off,
2. Resisting temptation,
3. Strolling around the zoo,
4. In shocked surprise,
5. Wrapping around his arm,
6. Inside the old valise,
7. At the bottom of the well,
8. Delighted with the new coat,
9. Picking up the cards,
10. To make the team,

REVIEW EXERCISE F. Combining Sentences; Varying Sentence Beginnings. Revise choppy and monotonous sentences in the following paragraphs by combining short sentences into longer sentences and by varying the beginnings of sentences. It may not be necessary to revise every sentence. Your aim should be a series of sentences that are clear, show variety, and are pleasing to read.

A lens is different from an ordinary pane of glass. A pane of glass has a flat surface. A lens is curved. Rays of light go through a pane of glass without much change. Rays of light are bent, or refracted, in a lens. This refraction may change both the shape and the size of an image. The curve of the lens determines the size of the image. A concave lens curves inward. It is called a reducing glass. A convex lens curves outward. It is a magnifying glass. Lenses often combine the qualities of a concave and a convex lens. Lenses may be concave on one side and convex on the other. A lens may also have one flat surface. A planoconcave lens is flat on one side and concave on the other, for example.

An optical lens must be made from glass of high quality. It must be manufactured by highly trained experts. Optical glass is first tested for flaws. It is then molded into discs. A disc is first ground roughly, then precisely, to give it the correct shape. It is finally polished with ferric oxide. This substance is called rouge by glassmakers.

Two or more lenses are combined in a microscope so that we can see very small objects. One lens is called the objective. It produces the primary image. The second lens is the eyepiece, or ocular. It magnifies the primary image. A microscope is judged not only by its magnifying power. It is also judged by its resolving power. This is its power to show separation between things that are very close together.

CORRECTING RAMBLING SENTENCES

Sometimes you may try to avoid a choppy style by stringing many short sentences together, using the conjunctions *and, but,* and *so* to join them. Such rambling sentences are just as irritating and monotonous to read as short, choppy sentences. Learn to avoid them in your writing.

17i. Correct rambling sentences by combining ideas and avoiding the overuse of *and, but, and so.*

Since rambling sentences are usually choppy sentences joined by conjunctions, the methods of correcting choppy sentences may also be applied to rambling sentences. Think of a rambling sentence as a series of choppy sentences as you review it. Combine some of the clauses into compound or complex sentences. Study the following rambling sentence to see how it was revised.

RAMBLING   I saw a television program last night, and it was about invaders from another planet and my little brother

Ted became frightened so Mom calmed him down and told him that there is little evidence of life on other planets but that there may be life on Mars but few people believe that life exists there either.

REVISED Last night I saw a television program which was about invaders from another planet. When my younger brother Ted became frightened, Mom calmed him down. She told Ted that there is little evidence of life on other planets. Mom added that there may be life on Mars but that few people believe that life exists there either.

As with choppy sentences, the first step in revising a rambling sentence is to recognize it as bad writing. When you review your compositions, watch for long sentences in which the conjunctions *and, but,* or *so* are used a great deal. Usually you will find that the independent clauses are not very closely related. These clauses should be rewritten to show a closer relationship, or, sometimes, they should be allowed to stand as complete sentences. The final step in revising rambling (or choppy) sentences is to read aloud what you have written. If the passage does not sound right, you have more revising to do.

EXERCISE 13. Revising a Rambling Style. Revise the rambling style of the following passages. Break the sentences down into clauses, and combine some clauses into compound or complex sentences. Let other clauses stand as complete sentences. To avoid a monotonous style, vary the beginnings of some sentences. Then read the passages aloud to see if the sentences flow smoothly and have variety.

1. Paul bought some skis, and he decided he must systematically learn to ski, and so he asked himself what to do first. The answer was to consult an instructor, and the instructor pointed out that it was dangerous to ski if you didn't know how to fall down properly, and so Paul thanked her, and he went home, and he dressed in his new ski clothes, and he went down the slopes and practiced falling down all day. He sprained his wrist at 3:00, and he twisted his leg at 4:36, and

he left the slopes at 4:38, and now the skis are mine. I bought them from Paul for a song, and so tomorrow I plan to take my first fall at 9:30 sharp.

2. Joan thinks she can speak French, but she made a funny mistake the other day when Lisa came limping into class with a bandage on her ankle, and she had sprained it while playing hockey, so Joan thought she would show off her French. She meant to say, *"C'est dommage,"* and it means "That's too bad," but she said, *"C'est fromage"* instead, and it means "That's cheese," but Joan was quite proud of herself until Mrs. Stevens pointed out her mistake.

REVIEW EXERCISE G. Revising a Passage by Eliminating Choppy and Rambling Sentences. There are both choppy and rambling sentences in the following passage. Revise it so that the sentences are clear, well written, and varied. Read your revised version aloud to see if the sentences flow smoothly.

The dam is not a modern invention. It was used in ancient times. It was used very early in Egypt. It was used to dam the Nile River. The first dam recorded in history was built about 2600 B.C. It was a large stone dam. It was located about eighteen miles south of Memphis. This dam was an engineering failure. Other Egyptian kings built other dams to store water. Their dams created Lake Moeris.

The Babylonians also built dams to control the Tigris and Euphrates rivers, and the Romans built dams, and the dams lasted for centuries. Emperor Nero directed the building of a dam, and it lasted for 1,300 years, but the Arabians built a dam that lasted more than 1,000 years, and it was two miles long and 120 feet high so it was the greatest dam ever built.

Two of the largest dams in the world today are in the United States. One is the Hoover Dam, and it is near Las Vegas, Nevada. The other is the Grand Coulee Dam, and it is in the state of Washington. Each dam is an important source of electrical power. Both serve American cities. They produce over 10,000 megawatts of power each year.

PART FIVE

COMPOSITION:
The Writing Process

CHAPTER 18

Manuscript Form

STANDARDS FOR WRITTEN WORK

A manuscript is any handwritten or typewritten composition. In your schoolwork this year and during the years ahead, you will be writing more and more manuscripts. Learn standard form for your written work now and follow it in all your papers.

18a. **Follow accepted standards in preparing manuscripts.**

Your teacher will find it easier to read and evaluate your papers if they are properly prepared. There is no single correct way to prepare a paper, but the following rules are widely used and accepted. Follow them unless your teacher requests you to do otherwise.

1. Unless you type your compositions, write them on standard size (8½- x 11-inch) lined paper. For typewritten papers, use standard size white typing paper.

2. Write on only one side of a sheet of paper.

3. Write in blue or black ink, or type. If you type, double-space the lines.

4. Leave a margin of about two inches at the top of a page and margins of about one inch at the sides and bottom. The

left-hand margin must be straight. The right-hand margin should be as straight as you can make it.

5. Indent the first line of each paragraph about one-half inch from the left margin.

6. Follow your teacher's instructions for placing your name, the class, and the date on the manuscript.

7. If your paper has a title, write it in the center of the first line. Do not enclose the title in quotation marks. Skip a line between the title and the first line of your composition.

8. If the paper is more than one page, number the pages after the first one. Place the number in the upper right-hand corner, about one-half inch from the top.

9. Write legibly and neatly. If you are using unlined paper, try to keep the lines straight. Form your letters carefully, so that *n*'s do not look like *u*'s, *a*'s like *o*'s, and so on. Dot the *i*'s and cross the *t*'s. If you have to erase, do it neatly.

18b. Learn the rules for using abbreviations.

In your writing, you should spell out most words rather than abbreviate them. A few abbreviations, however, are commonly used and are considered acceptable in written work.

The following abbreviations may be used with a name: *Mr., Mrs., Ms., Dr., Jr.,* and *Sr.* If they do not accompany a name, spell out the words instead of using the abbreviations.

EXAMPLES   **Mr.** Arroyo   **Dr.** Doris Yen
               Mrs. Galzone   Charles Grant, **Jr.**

               Have you met the **doctor**?
               Rosa is a **junior** partner of the firm.

The abbreviations A.M. (*ante meridiem*—before noon), P.M. (*post meridiem*—after noon), A.D. (*anno Domini*—in the year of the Lord), and B.C. (*before Christ*) are acceptable when they are used with numbers.

EXAMPLES   The meeting is called for 3:30 **P.M.**

               Augustus Caesar lived from 63 **B.C.** to **A.D.** 14. [Note that the abbreviation A.D. precedes the number, but B.C. follows it.]

Abbreviations for organizations are acceptable if they are generally known.

EXAMPLE   That woman is an agent for the **FBI**. [Abbreviations for government agencies are usually written without periods.]

18c. Learn the rules for writing numbers.

Numbers of more than two words should be written in numerals, not words. If, however, you are writing several numbers, some of them one word and some more than one, write them all the same way. Always spell out a number that begins a sentence.

EXAMPLES   Dana and I used **twenty-three** rolls of film this week.
From San Mateo, take Route **280.**
Karen started with **120** baby chicks, but now she has only **90**.
Two hundred and fifty-seven people were staying at the hotel during the week of the convention.

Write out numbers like *seventh, fifty-third,* and so on. If they represent the day of the month, however, it is customary to use numerals only.

EXAMPLES   I was the **first** [not 1st] customer at the bank this morning.
Flag Day is June **14**.

18d. Learn the rules for dividing words at the end of a line.

Dividing a word at the end of a line in order to keep an even margin should generally be avoided, but sometimes it must be done.

1. Divide a word between syllables (pronounceable parts) only. If you are in doubt about the syllables in a word, look the word up in the dictionary. Never divide a one-syllable word.

INCORRECT   scream-   [*Screamed* is a one-syllable word.]
                     ed

INCORRECT	buil- ding	[The syllables of *building* are
CORRECT	build- ing	*build* and *ing*.]

INCORRECT	bewitch- ed	[We do not pronounce the word
CORRECT	be- witched	bewitch-ed.]

2. Do not divide a word so that only one letter is left on a line.

INCORRECT	man- y	i- magine

18e. Learn the standard correction symbols.

In marking your papers, your teacher may use some or all of the following symbols. If you are not sure how to correct your error, use the index of your book to find the section that you need to review.

ms	error in manuscript form or neatness
cap	error in use of capital letters
p	error in punctuation
sp	error in spelling
frag	sentence fragment
ss	error in sentence structure
k	awkward sentence
nc	not clear
rs	run-on sentence
gr	error in grammar
w	error in word choice
¶	new paragraph
t	error in tense
∧	something left out

Writing and Thinking

THE WRITING PROCESS

A *process* is an orderly series of actions that someone carries out to produce or create something. Most writers follow the steps of a process. They begin by thinking and planning. After gathering and organizing information, they write their ideas in sentences and paragraphs. Then, they make changes and improvements in their writing. Next, they check for mistakes such as misspelled words and incomplete sentences. Finally, they prepare a clean, correct copy of their writing.

In this chapter you will learn about the steps in this writing process, and you will practice important skills that will help you become a better writer. As you progress, you will discover that critical thinking is a big part of the writer's job. At every stage in the writing process, writers make important decisions and judgments that affect the writing they produce. Throughout this chapter you will practice many of these *critical thinking skills.*

THE WRITING PROCESS

The writing process can be divided into five major stages: these are *prewriting, writing, revising, proofreading,* and *preparing the final copy.* Several of these stages also include important smaller steps. The following list shows all the stages in the writing process and the steps in each stage.

PREWRITING

1. Deciding on a purpose, or reason, for writing
2. Thinking about the audience's needs and interests
3. Choosing a subject for writing
4. Limiting the subject to a suitable topic
5. Gathering ideas and information on the topic
6. Organizing ideas for your paper

WRITING THE FIRST DRAFT

7. Expressing your ideas in sentences and paragraphs

REVISING

8. Reexamining the ideas, organization, and word choice in your first draft
9. Making changes to improve the first draft

PROOFREADING

10. Checking the revised draft of your paper for errors in grammar, usage, and mechanics
11. Correcting errors

MAKING THE FINAL COPY

12. Following directions for the final copy of your paper
13. Copying the final draft of your paper
14. Proofreading the paper again, if necessary

This chapter presents the steps in the writing process as they are shown on the chart—even though writers do not always complete the steps in the same order. They may skip steps, complete two steps at the same time, or move back and forth from one step to another.

How you apply the process depends on what you are writing and on your own habits as a writer. Every time you write, you face a different situation and make different decisions. If you are writing a quick note to your mother, you may spend only a minute or two planning your message. If you are writing an important report, you may spend several days on prewriting or you may discover as you revise your report that you need more information, and move back to the prewriting stage.

EXERCISE 1. Understanding the Writing Process. The following entries from a writer's journal (notebook) show how she used the writing process to prepare her first article for the school newspaper. Use the chart of the writing process on page 450 to answer the questions following these entries.

Tuesday—I've spent an hour brainstorming subjects for my next article for the school newspaper. I think kids would be interested in the summer space-camp Brian attended. I can talk to Brian tomorrow and find out more about the camp.

Wednesday—Wow! Brian really had a lot to say about the model rockets they launched, their experiments with weightlessness, and the simulated space shuttle mission. I think I have plenty of information. All I have to do is write it up.

Thursday—I wrote half of my first draft, but when I read over it I wasn't thrilled. It's too disorganized. I thought I could tell what happened at camp day by day, but I got off the track. Maybe I should stop and organize my notes.

Friday—I finished writing my second draft and started revising. I decided I needed more details about the simulated space shuttle mission; I called Brian and got more information.

Saturday—Finished proofreading and correcting mistakes in the article. I can write the final copy Monday.

1. What stage was the writer at on Tuesday? What step did she complete?
2. On what day did the writer move to the *writing* stage?
3. On Thursday the writer moved from the *writing* stage back to *prewriting*. Why?
4. Why did she move from *revising* back to *prewriting* on Friday?
5. What step in the writing process should the writer devote more time to when she writes her next article?

PREWRITING

Prewriting is the stage in which you prepare to write. Prewriting includes all the thinking and planning that occurs before writers start to record their ideas in the words and sentences of a first draft. During this stage writers search for a topic, read, take notes, and plan and organize their ideas.

In this stage of the writing process, you should consider all of the following questions: your purpose (Why am I writing?), your audience (Who will read what I write?), the subject and topic (What will I write about?), content or information (What will I say about the topic?), and arrangement (How will I organize my ideas?). Understanding and making sound decisions about each of these questions will help you produce strong writing.

There is no rule that says how you should think about these five questions. Often, the order in which you complete these steps will vary. Begin with what you know about the writing task. If your English teacher asks you to write a description that will interest your classmates, you know your purpose (to describe) and audience (your classmates). With these in mind, you can search for an appropriate topic and gather details that will interest your classmates.

THINKING ABOUT THE PURPOSE OF WRITING

When you think about why you are writing, you think about your *purpose*. You will find that having a clear purpose in mind will help you select ideas and information to communicate to your readers.

Understanding the Four Purposes

19a. Understand the four purposes of writing.

In a one-paragraph composition, you could *describe* the elephant you saw at the zoo, *tell what happened* when the elephant approached you, *explain* what you learned about the elephant, or *persuade* your readers to raise money for zoo programs. These reasons—to describe, to tell a story about what happened, to explain, or to persuade—are the four common purposes for writing. Each of these has a name.

1. *Narrative* writing tells a story about what happened.

EXAMPLE   We had just finished our picnic lunch when my uncle hollered, "Look at that!" Lumbering down the path toward us was an elephant. We thought the animal was loose until we saw one of the zookeepers walking beside her. The zookeeper explained that the elephant, named Tiny, was simply out for a stroll. As we talked, Tiny stood quietly waving her huge gray ears back and forth like fans, curling and uncurling her trunk. When the zookeeper tapped Tiny's front leg, she rose up on her hind legs and turned in a circle almost as if she were dancing.

2. *Descriptive* writing is writing that describes.

EXAMPLE   Tiny was at least three or four feet taller than the zookeeper. Her bulky gray body was covered with wrinkled, tough skin that hung in loose, baggy folds around her short, thick legs. In contrast, her ears were like two paper-thin palm leaves attached to each side of her head.

3. *Expository* or *Explanatory* writing is writing that explains.

EXAMPLE   An elephant uses its trunk the way we use our hands. Because the trunk is strong and flexible, an elephant can lift and carry a six-hundred-pound log simply by curling its trunk around the log. Using the delicate knob at the end of its trunk, an elephant can locate and pick up an object as small as a dime. In the jungle heat an elephant cools off by filling its trunk with water and shooting the water across its back. An adult elephant can store a six-gallon shower in its trunk.

4. *Persuasive* writing is writing that tries to persuade readers.

EXAMPLE   Many wildlife experts predict that the elephant—along with the cheetah, the Siberian tiger, and the rhinoceros—will disappear within the next twenty-five years. Few people realize that more than a thousand varieties of wild animals are threatened with extinction. The threats to these animals include the clearing of more than 100,000 acres of jungle every day, illegal hunting, and the poisoning of the environment with pesticides and powerful fertilizers. Unless people around the world support conservation groups such as the World Wildlife Fund and the zoo's Save the Animals program, seeing a live elephant or tiger may become as difficult as seeing a live dinosaur.

Occasionally, it may seem that the writing you are planning does not fit these four purposes. Your purpose for keeping a journal may be to express your thoughts, feelings, and reactions. Yet, if you look closely at your entries, you will find that some describe something, others tell about events that happened to you, and still others explain what you have learned or read. If you write an amusing paper, you may have decided that your purpose is to entertain readers. However, as your work progresses, you will probably discover that you are writing to achieve one of these four basic purposes. Perhaps you will amuse readers by persuading them to do something silly, by telling a funny story, or by describing an amusing scene.

EXERCISE 2. Identifying Purposes for Writing. Read each of the following pieces of writing carefully. Then decide if the writer's purpose is to describe, to narrate, to explain, or to persuade.

1

It was a perfect Halloween night. From behind the gray edges of the clouds, a round orange moon lit up a starless sky. The moonlight outlined the bare twisted limbs of the apple tree in the yard. The wind whistled and moaned, scattering dead leaves and rattling in the dry weeds along the fence. Somewhere in the distance an owl hooted.

2

As we put on our Halloween costumes last night, we heard a loud scratching at the living-room window. My sister crept across the room, cautiously pulled back the curtain, and peered into the darkness. Nothing. Then we heard more scratching. When a face suddenly appeared for a moment, we all screamed and dived behind the couch. Finally, we mustered enough courage to peek over the top of the couch. Several seconds passed before we realized that the face pressed against the glass was only my dad, up to some Halloween tricks.

3

Several Halloween customs can be traced back to the Celts, who lived in England over a thousand years ago. The Celts believed dangerous spirits were allowed to roam the countryside on October 31, the night before their new year. To protect themselves from these wandering spirits, the Celts stayed at home and put good things to eat outside their doors. If they had to go out, they dressed up in unusual disguises, hoping any evil spirit they encountered would mistake them for other wandering spirits.

4

Parents whose children will be trick-or-treating can take measures to ensure their children's safety. Children are more visible to motorists if their costumes are light-colored or have reflecting tape sewn on the edges. Make sure masks do not obscure children's vision; paint or makeup is a good alternative. Trick-or-treaters should always be accompanied by an adult and should visit only homes in their neighborhood or the homes of family friends.

5

Some students and parents want to do away with trick-or-treating because candy or fruit can be tampered with—but marching around town in costumes is half the fun of Halloween! I think we should continue to trick-or-treat but accept only donations for UNICEF. We could all meet at school and divide into groups with one adult in each group. Later we could come back to the gym for a community Halloween party with games and refreshments. We could even turn the locker room into a "haunted house."

Most of the writing you do will have a single major purpose. Sometimes, part of a long piece of writing may have a separate purpose. For example, the major purpose of your science report on the Asiatic elephant may be to explain—to share information with the rest of your class. However, in one paragraph of your report you might describe an elephant. If the main purpose of a newspaper article is to persuade students to attend a workshop on bicycle safety, the reporter might begin by telling about an accident that occurred because someone did not follow the rules for safe bicycling.

Determining Your Purpose

19b. Determine your purpose for writing.

Defining your purpose for writing will help you make sound decisions about the kinds of details and information you will need to gather for your paper. Writing that describes includes details about how something looks, tastes, smells, sounds, or feels when touched. Writing that tells what happened emphasizes events and actions. Writing that explains gives readers new and specific facts and information. In writing that persuades, you will want to include reasons that support your opinion.

Understanding your purpose for writing is important for a second reason. Some topics are more appropriate for one purpose than another. If you recently watched a magician perform several magic tricks, you might describe the magician's appearance or tell what happened during the act. It would be more difficult, based only on your observations, to write a persuasive paper or to explain how each trick was performed. If you know you must write a paper for a particular purpose, you can select an appropriate topic.

EXERCISE 3. Identifying Purposes for Writing. Imagine that you have decided to write a one- or two-page paper about each of the following topics. Then describe what your major purpose for writing about each topic would be.

1. The sights and sounds of a hayride on a crisp autumn evening
2. Why your school needs a larger gymnasium
3. What your grandmother looks like
4. Major events in your great-grandmother's life
5. What happened at last Friday's pep rally
6. Information about German life that you learned from talking to your great-grandmother and reading in the library
7. The training required to become a veterinarian
8. The time your aunt, who is a veterinarian, was knocked over by a cow
9. A typical day in the life of a country veterinarian
10. Why dog owners should not allow their pets to roam at large

IDENTIFYING YOUR AUDIENCE

19c. Identify the audience who will read your writing.

Another important step in prewriting is thinking about your *audience*—the person or persons who will read your writing. Are you writing for one person or a group? Are your readers adults who already know something about your topic or children who will be confused by long, complicated sentences or technical terms? What feelings do the members of your audience have about your topic? Are they interested or will you have to arouse their interest?

Good writers plan their writing to fit their audience's age, knowledge, interests, and opinions. Last week one student completed three pieces of writing:

A letter to Exotic Pets, Inc., about food for her new parrot
A one-page science report about the habits of tropical birds
A letter to her six-year-old cousin, who has the measles

She did not write the same way for all three audiences. When she wrote to her young cousin, she used simple words and short sentences that he could understand. To amuse him, she told a funny story about her new parrot. In her letter to Exotic Pets, Inc., she stated clearly what seeds and bird food she wanted. Because this was a business letter, she included only the information needed to fill her order. Since her teacher is interested in what she has learned about parrots, she wrote a report about their habits and behavior. She included scientific names and terms in the report to show that she knew what these meant and how they are used. In each situation, what she knew about her reader's age, education, interests, and opinions influenced how she handled her topic, the kind of information and details she included, and the language she used.

EXERCISE 4. How Audience Affects Writing. Imagine that the following statements are details about your school and recent activities. Look over the list and decide what details you would include in your first letter to a new Japanese pen pal who has never been to the United States. Then go over the list again and select the details you would include in a letter to a former classmate who has just moved to a town fifty miles away.

1. We watched the breakdancing on the river walk.
2. In winter I ride the bus, because we have a lot of snow and the temperature is often below zero.
3. We took a field trip to the farm museum and watched a demonstration of plowing with horses.
4. The junior high band will perform at the Spring Festival.
5. Saturday I played Pacman with Enrique and his sister at the arcade in the mall.
6. School starts at 7:30 in the morning and ends at 3:15.
7. Every day I have five classes, each taught by a different teacher.
8. Thursday there was a tornado warning. A siren went off, but nothing happened.
9. Everyone dresses casually at school—running shoes, blue jeans, and loose sweaters.

10. There are two high schools and three junior high schools in town.

11. In spring and fall when the weather is nice, I ride my bicycle to school.

EXERCISE 5. Rewriting a Paragraph for an Adult Audience. The following paragraph was written for young readers and is not suitable for an adult audience. Read the paragraph carefully, keeping in mind what you have learned about the needs of different audiences. Decide what changes you would make if you were writing about this topic for an adult audience. Then rewrite the paragraph. (Additional information about the Statue of Liberty appears on pages 474–75 and 477 in this chapter.)

> The Statue of Liberty stands on an island in the water near New York City. The statue is of a woman holding a bright torch above her head. This famous statue was built one hundred years ago in France. Then it was taken apart and sent to the United States. It was a present from the French people to the people of America. The outside of the statue is made of thin pieces of copper. Inside the statue is an iron frame like the scaffold a builder or painter uses. The statue needs to be fixed. Parts have rusted. The torch may fall apart. The work will be finished soon.

EXERCISE 6. Rewriting a Paragraph for a Younger Audience. The paragraph about Halloween customs on page 455 was written for an eighth-grade audience. Read the paragraph carefully; then rewrite it for an audience of third-grade students.

CHOOSING A SUBJECT

Do not overlook your own experiences when you are searching for a subject for your writing. Beginning writers sometimes assume their own experiences are too dull or ordinary to be good subjects for writing. Experienced writers, on the other hand, know they often produce their best work when they write about what they know well. The writer of the following paragraph used her experience with ice skating to explain how skates should fit. Because she knows her topic well, she can provide helpful details and information.

> Beginners who wobble around the rink or can't balance on their blades often assume they have weak ankles. Actually, the problem is usually skates that are too big. When you rent skates, remember that skate sizes normally run larger than shoe sizes. Ask for skates that are a half size smaller than your shoe size. Lace the bottom two or three eyes of the skate loosely. Then lace the skate tightly up to your ankle and tie a half knot. Lace the rest of the skate loosely and stand up. You should be able to wiggle your toes, but if you can move your heel up and down inside your skates, your skates are too big.

Starting with Yourself

19d. Consider your own experiences when you choose a subject for writing.

Direct experiences are those you experience yourself. The places you have visited, the people you know, and the hobbies and sports you participate in are all good sources of ideas for writing. What unusual or interesting places could you describe? What people do you know well; what is different or special about each of them? What amusing, touching, or memorable events can you share with your readers?

EXAMPLES   *Places:* sitting under the oak tree at the end of the cornfield, the waiting room at my dentist's office
People: how my cousin copes with her handicap
Hobbies: restoring a Model T Ford, raising rabbits as a 4-H project
Sports: tobogganing at the forest preserve, trying out for the swimming team
Work: stocking shelves at my aunt's hardware store

Indirect experiences are those you gain from reading books or newspapers, watching films or television programs, or listening to another person. These experiences can also be good subjects for writing. If you have read several articles about experiments during flights of the space shuttle, you probably know enough to write about this subject. If your great-uncle has told you about the hardships his family faced during the Depression, you might write about his experiences.

EXAMPLES *Reading about the Loch Ness monster:* how scientists have searched for the monster
Tour of the local hospital: how a heart monitor works, why the community needs a trauma center
Nature program you heard on the radio: how animals communicate

Using Brainstorming

19e. Use brainstorming to discover ideas for writing.

Brainstorming is a technique that stimulates thinking and helps writers recall experiences they may have forgotten. When you brainstorm, you concentrate on one subject or category and record all the ideas that come into your mind, even those that seem far-fetched. You can brainstorm alone or in a group. If you are working alone, find a quiet spot, write your subject at the top of a sheet of paper, and let your mind relax.

Record all the ideas that come into your head, since a weak or ridiculous idea often leads to a good one. When you run out of ideas, go over your list. Circle any items that might be good subjects for writing. If you think of additional ideas as you read through the list, add these.

Here are some of the notes one student made while brainstorming about his own experiences:

Places
    The tree house my sister and I built when I was six
    The hayloft of the farm

People
  Canoeing with my grandfather
  My sister's struggle to make the gymnastics team
Part-time Work
  Giving my aunt's terriers a bath
  The pros and cons of a paper route
Hobbies/Crafts
  How to do simple calligraphy
  Collecting unusual bumper stickers
Sports
  Junior high football—is it dangerous?
  Skateboarding—picking the right skateboard
Clubs and Activities
  Raising a seeing-eye dog as a 4–H project

EXERCISE 7. Brainstorming Subjects for Writing.
Choose three areas of experience from the following list. For each of these, spend at least five minutes brainstorming possible subjects for writing. When you have exhausted all your ideas, exchange papers with at least two of your classmates. Ask them to tell you what experiences on your list they would like to know more about.

1. When I was seven . . .
2. Interesting places
3. People I know well
4. Sports and recreation
5. Chores and part-time jobs
6. Clubs and activities
7. Moments I'll never forget

Using a Writer's Notebook

19f. Gather ideas for writing in a writer's notebook.

Many writers keep a written record of their experiences in a special notebook, or journal. Here they describe people they meet, tell about interesting events, and make notes on books and articles they read. They may also include newspaper clippings, quotations, cartoons, advertisements, or photographs that interest them. There is no formula for how to keep a writer's notebook. Some writers simply talk to themselves on paper or list questions for which they would like to find answers. Your writer's notebook may include anything that interests, puzzles, or impresses you—anything you want to remember or explore as a possible subject for writing. The following excerpt shows how one student used her journal.

> Jill is so funny. She's only three, but she tries so hard to be grown up. Yesterday in church she decided she should sing the hymns with everyone else. Of course, she can't read, so she just hums or goes "la-la-la-da." I couldn't help laughing. When she saw me, she got very serious, scowled, and said, "Jenny, I not funny." It's odd. Even when Jill messes up my room, I'm amused. When my nine-year-old sister does something silly or bothers me, I'm annoyed. I know I'm too hard on her. Maybe it's easier to understand brothers and sisters if they're much younger than you are. I wonder if other kids my age have the same feelings.

EXERCISE 8. Keeping a Writer's Notebook. For the next week, collect at least one item daily to put in a writer's notebook. You may want to use a folder for this purpose. The daily entry might be a few sentences you write about an experience. It might also be a newspaper or magazine article, cartoon, comic strip, advertisement, picture, or letter to an editor or advice columnist. Use your imagination in deciding what to include in your notebook.

Using Your Powers of Observation

19g. Use your powers of observation to find subjects for writing.

Rather than waiting for inspiration, good writers use their powers of observation to discover subjects for their writing in the world around them. They train themselves to look closely, to identify details, and to explore the meaning or significance of people, places, events, and problems.

Here is a paragraph one student wrote about the school cafeteria. This writer has not only used his powers of observation to record a variety of specific details about the litter left by students, but he has also thought about the relationship between the poster's message and the condition of the lunchroom.

Twenty minutes after one. The last lunch hour ended fifteen minutes ago. Right now the only sound in the cafeteria is a muffled conversation coming from the kitchen. I'm sitting at a gray formica table near the door to the main hall. A pool of chocolate milk from an overturned carton has worked its way to the edge of the table, where it's dripping slowly to the floor. Under the table on the right, I can see three crumpled napkins, a plate smeared with half-eaten spaghetti and green beans, several forks, a spoon bent into a U, two grease-stained paper bags, and a half-eaten banana. This isn't unusual. All the tables are dotted with abandoned brown plastic trays, lunchbags, and spills. The Pep Club has taped "school spirit" posters on the walls around the room. Behind me a large orange-and-blue sign proclaims, "Be proud of your school." It's hard to be proud of this mess! Why can't school spirit include the lunchroom?

CRITICAL THINKING:
Observing and Interpreting Specific Details

Writers train themselves to be observant. They begin by paying careful attention to the specific details that make up an experience. Often these are *sensory details*—details that describe the sight, sound, texture, smell, or taste of something. Then they search for words and phrases that will help their readers understand what they have observed. Because the ability to observe specific details and find words to describe them takes skill, many writers make frequent sensory observations in their notebooks. One day they might record the postures of and the expressions on the faces of people waiting in a long line; another day they might write about all the sounds they hear in a quiet library or describe the taste of a spicy Mexican dinner.

EXERCISE 9. Observing and Recording Sensory Details.
Choose four of the following experiences or images and describe
each one in several sentences. If possible, try to experience each
sensory detail or observe each image yourself before you translate it into words.

1. The taste, smell, and feel of eating a spoonful of peanut
   butter
2. The expression on the face of someone who is angry
3. The look and feel of a cat's fur
4. The appearance, smell, and feel of a new bar of soap
5. The smell and taste of a teaspoonful of vinegar
6. The look and sound of ice cubes in a glass of water
7. The inside of your school locker and the sound of its door
   slamming
8. The appearance of your kitchen table at the end of a meal
9. The postures and expressions of two students waiting to catch
   a bus
10. The appearance, smell, and taste of a pickle covered with
    chocolate syrup

Considering Your Attitude

19h. Consider your attitude toward your subject.

Attitude is the feeling a writer has about a subject. Good writers
do not always search for unusual or exciting subjects. Instead,
they may adopt a new or unusual attitude that makes even a
common subject interesting. Hundreds, perhaps even thousands,
of writers have produced books and articles on how to play
baseball. The following writer's comments on this overworked
subject are appealing because of his amusing attitude. Rather
than offering serious advice, he gives his readers some tips on
how to act like a pro.

> 1. When going up to bat, don't step right into the batter's
> box as if it were an elevator. The box is your turf, your stage.
> Take possession of it slowly and deliberately, starting with a

lot of back-bending, knee-stretching, and torso-revolving in the on-deck circle. Then, approaching the box, stop outside it and tap the dirt off your spikes with your bat. You don't have spikes, you have sneakers, of course, but the significance of the tapping is the same. Then, upon entering the box, spit on the ground. It's a way of saying, "This here is mine. This is where I get my hits."

2. Spit frequently. Spit at all crucial moments. Spit correctly. Spit should be *blown*, not ptuied weakly with the lips, which often results in dribble. Spitting should convey forcefulness of purpose, concentration, pride. Spit down, not in the direction of others. Spit in the glove and on the fingers, especially after making a real knucklehead play; it's a way of saying, "I dropped the ball because my glove was dry."

3. At the bat and in the field, pick up dirt. Rub dirt in the fingers (especially after spitting on them). Toss dirt, as if testing the wind for velocity and direction. Smooth the dirt. Be involved with dirt. If no dirt is available (e.g., in the outfield), pluck tufts of grass. Fielders should be grooming their areas constantly between plays, flicking away tiny sticks and bits of gravel.

GARRISON KEILLOR

LIMITING THE SUBJECT

A major airline recently offered one year of free travel to anyone who could fly to all fifty states in thirty days. The airline knew few people could cover that much territory in a short period of time. Several people won the contest; many more tried and gave up in frustration. Even the winners commented that the contest was hard work, no fun, and not something they'd do again.

When you write, you are also limited by space and time. You may have two hours to write a one-page paragraph or one week to write a three-page report. Your writing will be easier, more enjoyable, and more interesting and valuable to readers if you make sensible decisions about how much information you can cover in a particular piece of writing.

19i. Limit your subject to an appropriate topic.

A *subject* is a broad area of knowledge covering a large amount of information. The subject *science,* for example, includes all kinds of science from chemistry to astronomy, all scientists, all scientific discoveries, and all the laws and theories associated with science. It covers science from the beginning of time to the present day and into the future. Even if you planned to write a very long book, you would not be able to discuss every aspect of this subject in a lively, interesting way. The subject is far too large. Before you could begin to write, you would have to decide what smaller part of the subject you could cover, and limit yourself to writing only about this topic.

A *topic* is a smaller part of a subject and provides less information. Working with a limited topic means that you can give readers the kind of specific information and details that make writing interesting. How you limit a subject will depend on the *form* of your writing. The form might be a paragraph, a two-page composition, or a ten-page report. Usually, shorter forms of writing require more limited topics. If you are writing a paragraph, you will have to limit your subject to a topic that can be developed in several sentences. For a ten-page report you can select a topic that covers more information.

EXERCISE 10. Recognizing Subjects and Topics. Copy the following list of subjects and topics. Put a check mark next to all the topics you think are limited enough to be developed in a short composition.

1. Railroads
2. Caring for a gerbil
3. How a pencil is made
4. Famous Americans
5. Snoopy, the all-American dog
6. The development of the first railroad
7. Airplanes
8. How a small plane is checked for safety before takeoff

468 < Writing and Thinking

9. Stranded in a blizzard on Christmas Eve
10. Safety precautions for skateboarding

CRITICAL THINKING:
Analyzing a Subject

To discover smaller parts of a subject, you can use the critical thinking skill called *analysis*. When you analyze something, you break it down into smaller, separate parts and think about how these parts are related. Your analysis of a subject could be based on any of the following divisions: examples, features, time periods, places, events, causes, or uses. The smaller parts you create by analyzing a subject may be suitable topics for writing.

EXAMPLE   *Subject:* Monsters
　　　　　Places: Loch Ness (the monster), Frankenstein's castle, the Himalayas (the Yeti)
　　　　　Time periods: Greek mythology (monsters in), the 1950's (monster movies of), the Middle Ages (dragons of), today's science fiction (monsters in)
　　　　　Examples: sea monsters, vampires, King Kong, trolls, dragons
　　　　　People: Mary Shelley (creator of Frankenstein), Dr. Seuss's monsters, monsters children imagine, scientists' explanations of the Loch Ness monster phenomenon
　　　　　Processes: how special effects are used to create film monsters, how to live in a house with a troll under the stairs

If your first analysis of a subject does not uncover topics that are limited enough, continue the process by analyzing, or breaking down, these topics into smaller and smaller parts. The following example shows how this might be done.

EXAMPLE   *Topic:* Movies about monsters
　　　　　People: Bela Lugosi as Dracula, Boris Karloff as Frankenstein's monster, the monsters of Steven Spielberg

Places: the planet of the apes, Transylvania, *Lost World*

Examples: silent films, slapstick monster films, 3–D films, animated monsters

Time periods: the Edison Company's first Frankenstein film, teen-oriented monster films of the 1950's, monster films of the 1980's

Processes: how special effects were used in *King Kong,* how makeup artists designed a face for Frankenstein's monster

EXERCISE 11. Analyzing Broad Subjects for Limited Topics. For this exercise, select a subject from Exercise 10 by which you did not put a check mark. First, break the subject into smaller parts by thinking of divisions. Then write all the limited topics you can think of for each division. Underline answers that could be topics for a short composition.

GATHERING INFORMATION

Small children are usually delighted with their first large box of crayons. Because they can choose from forty-eight or sixty-four colors instead of six, they know they can create better pictures. The same principle applies to writing. Writers know they can write more effectively when they have dozens of details, rather than five or six, from which to choose. As a result, they explore their topics thoroughly before they write, gathering and recording as much information as possible.

19j. Gather information about your topic.

How you gather information for your own writing will depend on your topic. Sometimes, you will use outside sources such as books and newspapers. (Chapter 27 explains how to find information in these kinds of sources.) When you write about your own experiences, you can use one or more of the following prewriting strategies to collect facts and details about your topic.

Using Brainstorming and Clustering

(1) Use brainstorming and clustering to gather information for your writing.

Earlier in this chapter you used brainstorming to recall experiences that you could write about. You can also use brainstorming to remember details about a topic that lie buried in your memory. When you brainstorm, you relax and allow your mind to wander where it will. Brainstorming works because one thought triggers another and, in a wonderful way unlocks memory and floods the mind with forgotten details.

Here is a list of data one writer gathered when he brainstormed about a school cafeteria for the paragraph on page 464:

Sounds are varied	overturned milk cartons
muffled conversation	crumpled napkins
unusually quiet	list of spelling words
mess	bent spoon
food	grease-stained paper bags
half-eaten banana	tables
pool of chocolate milk	formica tops
spaghetti and green beans	several forks
Trash spills over.	plastic trays

Notice that some of these details are single words or phrases; others are complete sentences. How you record your thoughts when you brainstorm is not important; the important thing is to capture all ideas as they come to mind.

Clustering is another way to tap the details and bits of information stored in your memory. To use clustering, write a topic, a word or phrase, in the center of a sheet of paper. Draw a circle around your topic. Now let your mind wander freely over the topic. As details come to mind, write them down and circle them. Use lines or arrows to show how one detail is related to another. A beginning cluster about the writer's school cafeteria might look like the following one.

When other ideas develop, add them to your diagram. As you continue to add ideas, you will probably discover branches of related ideas growing out from the center of the diagram.

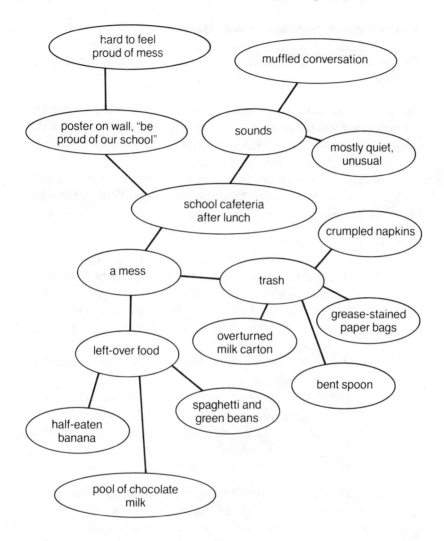

EXERCISE 12. Clustering to Gather Ideas.   For this exercise, select a topic of your choice or one from the list in Exercise
13. Write your topic in the center of a blank sheet of paper. Circle
it, and begin to add ideas around it as they come into your mind.
Continue to add, circle, and connect details until you are sure you
have run out of ideas. Save your work to use later in this chapter.

Asking the 5 W-How? Questions

(2) Use the *5 W-How?* **questions to gather information for your writing.**

Questioning is another prewriting technique for exploring and gathering information about a topic. Reporters use five basic questions (*Who? What? Where? When? Why?* and *How?*) to gather important information for their news stories.

Imagine that you recently spent a weekend observing bald eagles at their nesting area along the Mississippi River. By using the *5 W-How?* questions, you gather information about your experience.

EXAMPLE *Subject:* Bald eagles

Who? About seven hundred people there to observe the eagles; I and my uncle who is a photographer

Where? On land owned by Nature Conservancy near Keokuk, Iowa; where Des Moines River joins the Mississippi

What? To observe bald eagles; almost three hundred eagles in this area

Why? To help carry some of my uncle's equipment; to photograph the eagles

When? Early in the morning, before dawn, when birds are feeding on fish in the river

How? Using telephoto lens

You can gather even more information by following up each of your original questions with additional ones. In the following examples, notice how the writer has used variations of the six basic questions to probe more deeply into the topic.

Where? On land owned by Nature Conservancy near Keokuk, Iowa

Why do the eagles come here? To escape the frozen rivers in Canada and to feed on the gizzard shad

What is the gizzard shad? Small boneless fish

How? Using a telephoto lens

Why? It's difficult for a human to approach a bald eagle.

Why is this difficult? Eagles have keen eyesight and will leave an area if they sense anything out of the ordinary.

EXERCISE 13. Using the 5 *W-How?* Questions to Gather Information. Use the *5 W-How?* questions to gather information on one of the following topics or a topic of your own choice. Write down the questions you ask and your answer for each question. (You may need to do some research to find answers for your questions.)

1. An interesting relative
2. A special event in your community
3. An ideal weekend outing
4. A problem in your school
5. A hobby you enjoy
6. A memory from your childhood
7. Television commercials
8. What your community was like fifty years ago
9. Teen slang or fads
10. Your experiences with violent weather

Asking Point-of-View Questions

(3) Use point-of-view questions to gather information for writing.

Photographers use various articles of equipment to view their subjects from several perspectives. With a zoom lens they can move in to look closely at details and special features. Using time-lapse photography, they can reveal how something changes over a period of time, while a wide-angle lens allows them to show how a subject fits into its natural background. When you write, you can ask questions to examine your topic from all three of these perspectives.

1. *What is it?*

Examining your topic from this perspective, or point of view, is like using a zoom lens. You move in on the topic and ask questions about its definition, appearance, and function. A writer might ask several different questions to gather information from this point of view:

EXAMPLE   *Topic:* Statue of Liberty

How large is the statue? About 151 feet tall and weighs 225 tons

What is it made of? Iron framework covered with hundreds of copper plates; thickness of each plate about one-third inch

What does it look like? Tall woman in long gown with graceful folds, holding torch over her head

What is its function? Symbol of freedom, called "Liberty Enlightening the World"

2. *How does it change or vary?*

Like time-lapse photography, this point of view focuses on how your topic has changed or will change over a period of time. Using this perspective, you could ask questions and gather information about how the Statue of Liberty has changed since it was created.

EXAMPLE   *Topic:* Statue of Liberty

When was the statue built? Built in France, then dismantled and shipped to New York in 214 boxes; arrived on June 19, 1885, but pedestal wasn't ready

What changes occurred? Originally a bright copper; gradually acquired a green patina. Flame of the torch copper at first, then gold. In 1916, 600 pieces of yellow glass installed to make light of torch brighter

Why did the statue need restoration? Torch in danger of collapse; much of the copper corroded. Braces inside the statue weakened; some parts of copper skin deteriorated

How will restoration change the statue? New double-decker glass elevator in base of statue. New railing on old circular stairway of 171 steps and a sturdier platform in the crown

3. *What are its relationships?*

Like a wide-angle lens, this perspective reveals how the topic fits into a larger system or background. From this perspective you can also consider the internal relationships that make up your topic—how one part of the topic relates to another. If you examined the Statue of Liberty from this point of view, you might ask questions about how the monument relates to the area around it and the people who visit it or questions about the relationships between parts of the statue.

EXAMPLE   *Topic:* Statue of Liberty

How does the statue relate to New York City? Placed on Bedloe's Island, now Liberty Island, at entrance to New York Harbor. Tallest structure in the city in 1885.

What meaning does the statue have for Americans today? Close to Ellis Island, where twelve million immigrants landed; first thing many of them saw from decks of the ships that brought them to America.

EXERCISE 14. Gathering Information by Asking Point-of-View Questions.

Using the three different points of view, ask questions to gather information about two of the following topics. Write the questions you ask as well as your answer to each question.

1. A job such as yardwork or baby-sitting
2. A close friend or relative
3. A room in your house or apartment
4. A holiday such as Thanksgiving or the Fourth of July
5. An annual community event or festival
6. A kind of music
7. A nearby tourist attraction or park
8. A hobby
9. A place in your school, such as the locker room or cafeteria
10. An abstract concept such as teamwork, school spirit, or friendship

ORGANIZING INFORMATION

Imagine that you have decided to mount a box of old photographs in an album. Before you begin, you will have to think about a plan or order for the photos. You might start with the oldest and move to the most recent photographs, or you might group them under headings: Family Reunions, Weddings, Holidays, Trips, Comic Situations. Whatever kind of organization you use, you will want to be consistent and logical. A formal shot of your sister's wedding will look out of place among snapshots of your first camping trip.

Once they have gathered information about a topic, writers must also arrange their notes in an order that will be easy for readers to understand and follow.

19k. Eliminate any notes that are not related to your purpose.

A first step in arranging the information you have gathered is to cross out any items that clearly do not relate to your purpose. One writer gathered the following notes for a short paragraph. His purpose is to inform readers about the man for whom Halley's Comet is named. Which item would you eliminate?

> The comet was named after the astronomer Edmund Halley.
> My great-grandfather, who is ninety, saw the comet in 1910.
> Halley developed the theory that paths of comets are controlled by gravity.
> He became interested in comets when he saw a brilliant one over England in 1682.
> Halley also discovered the 75-year orbit of the comet that is named for him.

The second item should be crossed out because it does not give information about the astronomer Edmund Halley.

19l. Classify your notes in related groups.

The next step is to put related items into groups. Your purpose may suggest how your notes can be grouped. For example, if you wanted to tell about the amusing events at your sister's wedding, you would probably group details by the time at which they happened: before the wedding, during the ceremony, and at the reception. If you wanted to describe the three antique cars the wedding party rode in, you would probably put details about each car in a separate group.

CRITICAL THINKING:
Classifying Information

When you classify, you identify items that have something in common. Then you group these items under a heading that explains how they are related.

Here is how one writer classified his notes about the Statue of Liberty:

Design of the Statue
   By French sculptor Bartholdi
   His wife posed as model, but statue has mother's face
   Made four-foot clay model first, then larger models
   Each model—more than 9000 measurements
Construction of Statue
   Wooden molds built from pieces of full-size plaster model
   Copper sheets hammered into shape over mold
   Internal framework designed by Gustave Eiffel
   Frame of four iron piers, ninety-seven feet tall with hundreds of struts and cross-bracing
Transportation to New York
   Finished statue presented to U.S. ambassador on July 4, 1884
   Statue carefully taken apart and packed in boxes
   214 boxes loaded aboard the *Isère*
   Reached New York on June 19, 1885

EXERCISE 15. Classifying Information. Classify the items in the following list under these three main headings:

Facts about comets
The history of Halley's comet

The latest appearance of Halley's comet

Comets only visible when they approach the sun
In November 1985, tail 50 million miles long
Two kinds: those with straight, gaseous tails and those with curving, dusty tails
On latest orbit first visible to naked eye in November, 1985
1577—Queen Elizabeth I forbade anyone to look at comet
Have a small nucleus, a coma, or head, and a tail
Composed of icy particles
Halley's comet—first observation recorded by Chinese in 240 B.C.
Middle Ages—thought Halley's comet would bring famine and plagues
1910—earth passing through tail of Halley's comet; anti-comet pills taken for protection
Usually look pink
Comet at brightest from February to March 1986

19m. Arrange your notes in a logical order.

After you have sorted your notes into groups, the next step is to decide in what order you will present these details in your writing. Frequently, your purpose for writing will suggest an order. For example, the author's purpose for writing about the following items is to tell what happened over a period of time. Such details are usually arranged chronologically—in the order in which they happened.

EXAMPLE *Topic:* How makeup artist turned Karloff into Frankenstein's monster
Details:
    a. Wax applied to eyelids
    b. Invisible wire clamps to pull down corners of his mouth
    c. Corners of forehead and brow built up with layers of cotton strips and adhesive
    d. Gray-green makeup applied
    e. Scar and fake metal clamps added to forehead
    f. Took over three hours for whole process

The author's purpose for writing about the next group of details is to persuade readers by giving reasons. Persuasive details are often arranged, from least important to most important.

EXAMPLE   *Topic:* Student council should volunteer to clean writing off lockers
            Details:
            a. If everyone helps, won't take long
            b. Bring radios and have a party when finished
            c. Graffiti unattractive; suggest lack of concern about our school
            d. If students know lockers cleaned, may stay clean longer
            e. Money saved in fund for another computer

Details that explain how to do or make something are usually arranged in the order in which they should be carried out, but there are other ways to arrange details. Details that describe are arranged to guide the reader's eye—from right to left, top to bottom, or near to far. If your purpose does not suggest an order, choose an arrangement that will be clear and easy for readers to follow. For example, in looking over your notes, you may decide that the notes under one heading should be presented first because your readers will need this information to understand the material under another heading.

EXERCISE 16. Arranging Details in a Logical Order.
Copy the following details, putting them in an order you think is logical. Be prepared to explain why you arranged the details in this order.

1. At 5:13 A.M. on April 18, 1906, a severe earthquake struck the city of San Francisco.
2. In three days nearly five square miles of the city had been destroyed.
3. Rain fell on April 21 and extinguished the fires still smoldering in thousands of buildings.
4. The first severe shock was followed by two lesser earthquakes.

5. On April 19, the fire department had to dynamite buildings in the fire's path.
6. After the three earthquakes, fires broke out across the city.
7. On April 20, shifting winds pushed the fire into new areas, threatening the mansions on Nob Hill.
8. The city's six hundred firefighters sprang into action.
9. Broken water pipes throughout the city hampered the fire-fighters' efforts.
10. Within the week, the city started to rebuild.

REVIEW EXERCISE. Following the Steps for Prewriting. Prepare to write a paragraph on a topic of your choice. Decide on your purpose and audience, and then choose a subject and limit it to a topic that can be covered adequately in a single paragraph. Using at least one of the techniques for gathering information, make a list of specific details to include, classify the details, and arrange them in order.

WRITING

After you have completed the prewriting steps, you are ready to move to the second stage of the writing process—writing a first *draft*, or version, of your paper. Students sometimes think that good writers know exactly what they want to say when they start writing. Actually, few writers work this way. Most produce many drafts before they are completely satisfied. They write, rewrite, and rewrite once more.

WRITING A FIRST DRAFT

19n. Write a first draft.

Creating something new and unique is always a little intimidating. Even if you have planned carefully, you may not be sure of exactly what you want to say. As you begin to write, remember that your goal is not to produce a polished piece of writing. Your first draft is only a beginning—your first attempt at putting your ideas into words and sentences.

Writing is a process of discovery, filled with surprises. As your first draft takes shape, you may discover that you need more information, or you may decide that some of your details don't fit your topic. Perhaps the way you planned to present information is not as clear as you thought it would be. When these situations occur, remember that the writing process is flexible. You can always stop and move back to gather more information or reorganize your ideas. You can even start over.

CRITICAL THINKING:
Synthesis

Whenever you decide how to put together separate elements to create something new, you use the critical thinking skill called *synthesis.* Pioneer families used synthesis when they combined logs, clay, and straw to build frontier cabins. They used synthesis again when they collected scraps of fabric, cut them into interesting shapes, and fit them together to create patchwork quilts. Writers use synthesis when they collect and combine ideas and information to create paragraphs, compositions, letters, and stories.

As you write, what you know about your purpose and audience will guide you in making decisions about how to express ideas. Before you begin a first draft, take a few moments to review the planning you did during the prewriting stage. Think again about each of the following questions:

What do I know about my readers?
What is my purpose for writing?
What order will I follow in presenting my ideas? How will this order help readers understand my topic?

EXERCISE 17. Analyzing a First Draft.   Read the following first draft and answer the questions that follow it.

If it weren't for the whims of an Egyptian ruler, the figure we know as the Statue of Liberty might be standing on the banks of the Suez Canal. It's kind of a neat story; here's what happened. In 1867 Ismail Pasha, the Khedive of Egypt, asked Frédéric Bartholdi, a French sculptor, to design a lighthouse to be built at the entrance to the Suez Canal. The canal was started in 1859 and finished in 1869. Impressed with the colossal Sphinx and obelisks he had seen on an earlier trip to Egypt, Bartholdi prepared drawings and architectural specifications for a lighthouse in the shape of a titanic human figure holding aloft a large torch. For unknown reasons, the khedive did not respond to Bartholdi's design. In 1869, Bartholdi abandoned the project, but he revived it in 1872 when he was asked to submit plans for a monument commemorating the ties between France and America.

1. Is the purpose of this paragraph (a) to persuade, (b) to describe, or (c) to tell what happened?
2. If this paragraph were intended for an audience of third-graders, what words would you change?
3. Is this topic limited enough for a paragraph?
4. Do all the sentences in this paragraph relate to the topic? Which sentence is unrelated and should be removed?
5. Do you think the sentence "It's kind of a neat story: here's what happened" adds anything to the paragraph? Would you advise the writer to put this sentence in the next draft or leave it out?

EXERCISE 18. Writing a First Draft.   Using the prewriting notes you developed for Review Exercise (page 480), write a first draft of a paragraph. You may want to refer to the Guidelines for Writing Paragraphs (pages 535–36) for some extra help before you begin writing.

REVISING

Once you have something down on paper, you can begin to experiment and improve your work, moving around words and phrases, rearranging thoughts, crossing out one word and trying another. When you judge and make changes in your writing, you are *revising*. This is the next stage in the writing process.

REVISING YOUR FIRST DRAFT

19o. Revise your first draft.

Before you revise your writing, set it aside for a short time and do something else. After this short "time out," you will be able to view your writing more realistically and make better decisions about what works and what does not work.

As you reread your paper, put yourself in your readers' shoes. Try to react to your writing as if you were seeing it for the first time.

First, think about the content of your paper. Your job as a writer is to interest and inform your readers. If parts of your paper seem vague or unclear, you may need to add additional or more specific details. If your entire paper seems too general or dull, you may need to limit your topic further. Working with a topic that is too broad often forces writers to make general, rather than specific, statements.

Next, think about your organization. If you are writing a composition of several paragraphs, reread each paragraph to be sure it relates to your topic. Then think about the order in which you present your ideas. Each idea should logically follow the previous one and connect smoothly with the next idea. If you find places where what comes before does not seem to connect with what follows, you may need to reorganize that part of your paper. Ask yourself how each sentence relates to your topic and purpose.

Finally, look at your sentence structure and choice of words. A paper that combines short and long sentences or simple and complex sentences is usually more interesting and readable. A paper with too many short, choppy sentences often becomes monotonous, while a paper made up entirely of long, complicated sentences may be difficult to follow. Try to vary the length of your sentences and the way in which they begin. Finally, look at your choice of words. Is your language suited to your topic and purpose? Perhaps a slang expression has slipped into a persuasive paper about a serious topic. Perhaps too many vague, indefinite words are weakening your descriptive paragraph. Perhaps you can add interest to your narrative by inserting more strong action verbs or concrete nouns. Before you make any changes in your first draft, study the Guidelines for Revising on page 486. You can use these questions whenever you revise your own writing. If you answer "no" to a question, think about how you might improve that part of your paper.

Occasionally, your teacher may ask you to exchange papers with one or more of your classmates and to make comments about their writing. Reading another student's writing provides an opportunity to learn how someone else handles a similar writing situation. Whenever you read and make suggestions about another person's writing, try to be specific and helpful. Before you write or say something, think about how you would feel if someone made the same comment about your writing. Would you understand what they meant? Would the comment help you to improve your work or leave you feeling confused or discouraged?

EXERCISE 19. Analyzing a First Draft. Read the following first draft with the writer's revisions, and answer the questions that follow it.

For thirty dollars, car owners in our state can order ~~really neat~~ "prestige" license plates. Instead of a ~~bunch~~ *meaningless jumble* of letters and numbers~~with no meaning~~, these plates carry a message of six or seven letters. ~~I kept a list of the messages I've seen on these special plates. The messages fall into several categories.~~ *For convenience* ^ Some individuals, like my grandfather, simply have their initials and year of birth (HGD 1918) printed on their plates. ~~I guess that's convenient.~~ My aunt~~who works as~~ a veterinarian has a plate that advertises her profession (DVM 146).

I've also seen plates that read BARBER, THE DOC, TEACH, and PHOTOG, but I'm still wondering about a plate that read KGB SPY. A small group of friendly folks have plates with ~~messages~~ *greetings* like LOVE YA, SMILE, or HELLO. For sports fans, of course, a license plate is another way to show their team loyalty: GO SOX, ILLINI, and METS FAN are examples of this. I haven't figured out ~~one thing~~ *is why* Some drivers have plates that read A KLUTZ, DIZZY, or FAT BOY. Maybe, they like to laugh at themselves. Maybe someone gave them the plate as a gag? My favorite plates are the ones that state the obvious. THE CAR, BACK END, BUMPER, VEHICLE, or MY AUTO fall into this category. Finally, one word of advice: watch out for the car with A GRUMP on the plate. That's my sister and she's not kidding.

1. What do you think is the writer's purpose?
2. Do you think this paragraph was written for an audience of young children, an audience of experts, or students your age?
3. In revising this paragraph, the writer crossed out two sentences. Why do you think these were taken out?
4. Where did the writer make a change to vary the beginning of a sentence?
5. Where did the writer change a general word to a more specific word?

EXERCISE 20. Revising a First Draft.   Revise the first draft that you wrote for Exercise 18, or revise another piece of your writing. Use the Guidelines for Revising on the following page as you consider each word and each sentence. Reread your draft several times as you revise it.

GUIDELINES FOR REVISING

Content and Organization

1. Is the subject interesting and informative for the audience?
2. Is the content suited to the age and interests of the audience?
3. Are ideas expressed in a way that is suitable for the audience? For example, are simpler vocabulary words and less complicated sentences used for younger audiences?
4. Is the topic suitably limited for the form of writing?
5. Is the topic well developed with details suitable for the purpose?
6. Are details organized according to some logical order?
7. Does the arrangement of details reflect the purpose for writing?

Style

1. Does the writing have fresh and exact adjectives and adverbs?
2. Are there vivid verbs to help convey action?
3. Is the sentence structure varied?
4. Do sentences vary in length?

PROOFREADING

When you proofread, you examine each word and sentence in your writing to find and correct mistakes in spelling, grammar, usage, and mechanics. The term *proofreading* comes from publishing. After the printer has made the plates that will be used to print a book or article, a set of trial pages, called proofs, is run off. These proofs are then checked carefully to ensure that all mistakes are corrected before thousands of copies are printed on the press.

PROOFREADING YOUR WRITING

19p. Proofread your writing.

If you made a number of changes, or revisions, in your writing, your paper may be hard to read. In this case, you will probably want to rewrite your paper before you proofread it. Then, if possible, put your paper aside for several hours or for a day or two. Proofreading requires concentration, and you will do a better job when you return to your paper later.

Some writers begin by covering all but the last line of their work with a blank sheet of paper. After they have proofread this line, they move the sheet of paper up to uncover another line. This method of proofreading focuses the writer's attention on words and sentences rather than on the meaning of the paper.

The chart on page 488 shows some of the most common proofreading symbols. You can save time by learning to use these proofreading marks. Before you proofread, look over the Guidelines for Proofreading on this page. The questions on this chart will help you identify the errors students often make when they write.

GUIDELINES FOR PROOFREADING

1. Does every verb agree in number with its subject? (pages 199–214)
2. Are verb forms and tenses used correctly? (pages 227–43)
3. Are troublesome verbs such as *sit/set, lie/lay,* and *rise/raise* used correctly? (pages 235–39)
4. Are subject and object forms of pronouns used correctly? (pages 252–60)
5. Are the comparative forms of adjectives and adverbs used correctly? (pages 269–74)
6. Are double negatives avoided? (page 275)
7. Does every sentence begin with a capital letter? Are all proper nouns and proper adjectives capitalized? (pages 314–24)
8. Are all words spelled correctly? Have spellings been checked in a dictionary? (pages 726–28)
9. Are sentences punctuated correctly? Does every sentence end with a punctuation mark? (pages 336–86)
10. Is every sentence a complete sentence, not a fragment or run-on? (pages 399–415)

EXERCISE 21. Proofreading a Revised Draft. Proofread the draft you revised for Exercise 20 or another paper you have revised. Be sure to check each of the points in the Guidelines for Proofreading on page 487.

REVISING AND PROOFREADING SYMBOLS

Symbol	Example	Meaning of Symbol
≡	at Waukeshaw lake	Capitalize a lower-case letter.
/	a gift for my Uncle	Lower-case a capital letter.
∧	cost ∧cents (fifty)	Insert a missing word, letter, or punctuation mark.
∧	ate two much (o)	Change a letter.
℘	What day is is it?	Leave out a word, letter, or punctuation mark.
ℐ	rakeing leaves	Leave out and close up.
⌒	any body	Close up space.
∾	recieved	Change the order of letters.
tr.	The girl with the dog (in the red dress)	Move the circled words to the place marked by the arrow. (Write *tr* in nearby margin.)
¶	¶ The last step is	Begin a new paragraph.
⊙	Please be patient⊙	Add a period.
∧	Yes∧that's right.	Add a comma.
#	figure#skating	Add a space.
(:)	all of the following items(:)	Add a colon.
(;)	It's not hard(;)I'll help you.	Add a semicolon.
=	his great=grandfather	Add a hyphen.
∨	Linda ∨s work	Add an apostrophe.
stet	a ~~bitterly~~ cold day	Keep the crossed out material. (Write *stet* in nearby margin.)

MAKING THE FINAL COPY

PREPARING A FINAL COPY

19q. **Prepare a final copy of your writing, following directions about the correct form.**

Sometimes you can hand in a paper on which you have neatly made your corrections. Most of the time, you will want to prepare a clear, correct final copy. Be sure you understand directions about the form and appearance of your paper. If your teacher does not give you specific instructions, use the following ones:

1. Use white paper 8½ × 11 inches in size for typewritten papers and ruled composition paper for handwritten ones.

2. Write on only one side of the sheet.

3. Write in blue or black ink, or type. If you type, double-space the lines.

4. Leave a margin of about two inches at the top of the page and margins of about one inch at the sides and bottom. The left-hand margin must be straight; the right-hand margin should be as straight as you can make it.

5. Indent the first line of each paragraph about one-half inch from the left.

6. Write your name, the class, and the date on the first page. Follow your teacher's instructions in the placement of these items.

7. If your paper has a title, write it in the center of the first line. Do not enclose the title in quotation marks. Skip a line between the title and the first line of your composition.

8. If the paper is more than one page in length, number the pages after the first, placing the number in the center, about one-half inch down from the top.

9. Write legibly and neatly. Form your letters carefully, so that *n*'s do not look like *u*'s, *a*'s like *o*'s, and so on. Dot the *i*'s and cross the *t*'s. If you have to erase, do it neatly.

EXERCISE 22. **Preparing the Final Copy.** As your teacher directs, prepare the final copy of the paper you revised for Exercise 20, page 485. Use the manuscript form described on page 489 or another one that your teacher prefers.

CHAPTER 19 WRITING REVIEW

Applying Your Knowledge of the Writing Process. As your teacher directs, prepare a piece of writing about one page in length. Use your knowledge of the writing process to complete the following steps.

1. Decide on a purpose and audience.
2. Develop a limited topic.
3. Gather information about the topic.
4. Group details and arrange them in order.
5. Write a first draft. If possible, put it away for a few days.
6. Revise the first draft one or more times. (Use the Guidelines for Revising, page 486, to help you.)
7. Recopy the revised draft, using correct manuscript form.
8. Proofread the final draft. Use the Guidelines for Proofreading on page 487.

CHAPTER 20

Writing Paragraphs

STRUCTURE AND DEVELOPMENT OF PARAGRAPHS

In writing, the smallest unit in which a complete thought may be expressed is the sentence. Sometimes, however, several sentences are necessary to express an idea. A *paragraph* is a group of sentences that presents and develops one main idea. The skills that you will use in writing effective paragraphs are the same skills that you will need in writing longer papers.

In this chapter you will study the structure and development of paragraphs. You will write and revise many different paragraphs as you follow the steps in the process of writing.

THE STRUCTURE OF A PARAGRAPH

All well-written paragraphs have certain qualities in common. You can improve your paragraph-writing skills by learning to recognize these qualities.

THE MAIN IDEA

20a. A paragraph is a series of sentences that presents and develops one main idea about a topic.

A well-written paragraph presents information about a single topic. Each of the sentences contributes something new to the paragraph; yet, at the same time, each sentence is directly related to the paragraph's main idea.

THE TOPIC SENTENCE

20b. The topic sentence states the main idea of a paragraph.

Although the topic sentence is not always the first sentence in the paragraph, this is its usual position. As the first sentence, the topic sentence tells the reader what the paragraph is going to be about. Knowing this, the reader is able to follow the writer's ideas more easily.

In the following example, the writer is explaining deceptive sales practices. The topic sentence appears in boldfaced type.

Wise consumers have learned to recognize deceptive sales practices. Some store owners, for example, may offer merchandise at "thirty percent off" but may have raised the original prices beforehand. Another deception is that of "bait and switch." A store will advertise an item at a truly low price (the bait). A customer asking for this item will be told that it is inferior in quality to another brand that costs more (the switch).

All of the rest of the paragraph following the topic sentence explains the deceptive sales practices customers have learned to recognize.

Occasionally, the topic sentence may appear somewhere in the middle or at the end of a paragraph, as in the following example:

In the old days, coal miners worked with pick and shovel and hand drill. Today, hand tools have been replaced by power cutters, drilling machines, mechanical loaders, timbering machines, and roof bolters. Electric locomotives, replacing mules, pull larger cars that carry heavier loads. Conveyor belts, too, move coal in a continuous flow through mine tunnels to the cleaning, washing, and loading machines. **In every way, mechanization has vastly increased the efficiency of coal mining.**

In your reading, you will find that some paragraphs do not have topic sentences. In paragraphs that tell about a series of actions, writers often do not state a main idea. Paragraphs that explain, inform, describe, or persuade usually do have topic sentences, however. In this chapter, you will practice writing paragraphs with topic sentences because such paragraphs will help you to develop important writing skills. (You will learn about writing effective topic sentences on page 523.)

EXERCISE 1. Identifying Topic Sentences. In each of the following paragraphs, identify the topic sentence. Be prepared to discuss how the other sentences in the paragraph develop the main idea as stated in the topic sentence.

1

Many people think that the rocket is a recent invention, but it was used as a primitive weapon many centuries ago. The Chinese had rockets in the thirteenth century and called them "arrows of fire." In the fifteenth century, the Italians used rockets that traveled over the ground on rollers. These rockets were made in the shapes of animals. Probably neither the Chinese nor the Italian rockets were very destructive. They were designed to frighten enemies, not to kill them.

2

All lasers contain some material—a gas, crystal, or dye—that emits light waves when an electrical voltage or a light source is applied to them. These waves, unlike those in ordinary light, are perfectly aligned, resulting in a beam with such concentrated energy that it can cut through a 4-inch steel plate. Lasers are classified by the materials that emit the light—for example, carbon dioxide gas or yttrium-aluminum (YAG) crystal.

GORDON GRAFF

3

If one person bicycles a distance in five minutes while another person runs the same distance in ten minutes, who will get wetter when it rains? According to Dr. Gerald Feinberg, professor of physics at Columbia University, the person who is traveling more slowly will get hit by more raindrops. A person traveling at the speed of light would be hit by practically no raindrops, so the slower you go, the more likely you are to get soaked.

4

Many states have names that come from Native American words. The state of Michigan, for example, was once called *Michigama,* an Algonquian name meaning "great water." *Missouri* comes from another Algonquian name for "people of the big canoes"; and *Wyoming* comes from *Mecheweaming,* which means "large plains." Both North and South Dakota are named for a tribe, the Dakota, whose name means "to think of as a friend."

SUPPORTING SENTENCES

It is not enough to have a topic sentence that states a paragraph's main idea. That main idea must then be developed by other sentences in the paragraph.

20c. Other sentences in a paragraph give specific information that supports the main idea in the topic sentence.

A paragraph should have enough information to develop the topic sentence. If it does not, the paragraph is weak; it seems empty, flat, and uninteresting. Usually three or more supporting details are necessary for an effective paragraph.

WEAK   **Members of a group called the Animal Liberation Front "rescued" 260 animals in a middle-of-the-night raid on a university research center.** They claimed the animals were being mistreated. A university spokesman said they were not.

IMPROVED   **Members of a group called the Animal Liberation Front "rescued" 260 animals in a middle-of-the-night raid on a university research center.** The group claimed that they had rescued 80 rats, 70 gerbils, 35 rabbits, 38 pigeons, 21 cats, 9 oppossums, and a baby primate from cruel and inhumane experiments. Vicky Miller, the group's spokesperson, said that the animals were in "safe" shelters and homes. A university official denied that the animals had been mistreated and said that they were now in worse hands.

EXERCISE 2. Improving a Weak Paragraph.   The following paragraph is weak in supporting details. Study the paragraph and the questions that follow it. Using your answers to the questions, develop a working plan for improving the paragraph. Write a topic sentence, and list below it sufficient details for adequate development. Then rewrite the paragraph so that it has enough information to support the main idea as stated in the topic sentence. Write your revised paragraph on a separate sheet of paper.

The gym was very crowded, and the fans were excited. The score had been close all through the game, but in the last minute the home team pulled ahead by four points.

1. What kind of game is being played in the gym?
2. Why is this game important? Who is the home team playing? Which side are you on?
3. What sounds can you hear?
4. Exactly what happened during the last minute of play? Who scored the winning points?
5. What happened when the game ended? What did the players do? What did the fans do?

EXERCISE 3. Improving Weak Paragraphs.   The paragraphs that follow are weak because they lack sufficient details. Revise each paragraph by adding sufficient specific details to support the topic sentence.

1

I remember how I felt the first day I attended this school. The building seemed huge, and there were so many teachers and students I didn't know.
(*Hint:* How did you feel? What did you worry about? What did it feel like to be in a new homeroom? In the halls between classes? In the cafeteria? How was this school different from your previous school?)

2

Deciding to stay in school until you graduate from high school is a decision that will have far-reaching effects. A high-school diploma is necessary for college and for many kinds of vocational training.
(*Hint:* How does having a diploma affect the possibility of getting a job? What are the statistics for unemployment of dropouts? Of high-school graduates? How does a high-school diploma affect a person's ability to earn money? Do you know anyone who has dropped out of high school and has returned? Why did that person return to school?)

3

If I could plan for myself an "ideal" birthday celebration, I'd have no trouble thinking of wishes I'd like to see come true. First of all, I'd like a reunion of all my "best friends" and friends I've really cared about over the years.
(*Hint:* Where would you like to be for that reunion? What would you choose to eat, do, listen to? How would you begin your "ideal day"? If you could invite a famous person to your reunion, whom would you invite?)

4

Playfulness is a characteristic of most young animals. Kittens wrestle with one another. Puppies play a lot, too.
(*Hint:* Add several more details about how kittens and puppies play. What other kinds of young animals have you seen playing—bear cubs, tiger cubs? For every kind of animal that you mention, give specific details about how the animals play. You might visit a pet store and take notes as you observe young animals.)

PREWRITING For each paragraph, ask yourself questions similar to those in Exercise 2. These questions should help you to gather additional information that you can use to develop the paragraph's main idea. (If necessary, consult a reference book to find answers to your questions.) Consider the details you have gathered, and decide which ones support the main idea most effectively. Revise each topic sentence as necessary. Use the list of details and the revised topic sentence as a working plan to write an improved paragraph.

WRITING THE FIRST DRAFT Begin with the topic sentence, and use each detail in a sentence. Include specific details to make your sentences interesting.

REVISING AND PROOFREADING Reread the first draft carefully. Do the supporting sentences give enough information about the main idea? See if you can make the paragraph read more smoothly by combining sentences or by adding transitional expressions (see page 509). Finally, proofread the paragraph to correct inaccuracies in grammar, usage, mechanics (capitalization and punctuation), and spelling.

THE CLINCHER SENTENCE

20d. A *clincher*, or *concluding*, sentence may be used to summarize or restate the paragraph's main idea.

Sometimes a paragraph may be long and complicated or may include details that the writer wants to emphasize. Such a paragraph may end with a concluding sentence that clinches the point made in the paragraph.

A clincher sentence may restate the idea of the topic sentence, or it may summarize the most important details in the paragraph. Sometimes, a clincher sentence makes a comment on the ideas in the paragraph or draws a logical conclusion.

In the following paragraph, both the topic sentence and concluding sentence appear in boldfaced type. Notice how the concluding sentence restates the idea of the topic sentence.

There is still some good outdoor cooking going on in this country, but none of it needs machinery. The first meal that comes to mind is a clambake last summer in Maine. Here is the authentic recipe for a clambake: dig a big hole in a beach. If you have a Maine beach to dig your hole in, so much the better, but any beach will do. Line the hole with rocks. Build a big fire on the rocks and take a swim. When the fire is all gone, cover the hot rocks with seaweed. Add some potatoes just as they came from the ground; some corn just as it came from the stalk; then lobsters, then clams, then another layer of seaweed. Cover the whole thing with a tarp and go for another swim. Dinner will be ready in an hour. It will make you very happy. **No machine can make a clambake.**

CHARLES KURALT

Remember that not every paragraph should have a clincher sentence. A clincher sentence is helpful at the end of a long paragraph, but usually seems out of place in a short paragraph. When you write a paragraph, try writing two or three different versions of a clincher sentence. Then decide whether the paragraph seems stronger with one of these clincher sentences or without any of them.

EXERCISE 4. Writing a Clincher Sentence. Each of the following numbered items includes a topic sentence and several specific details. Using the topic sentence and the suggested information, write a paragraph. You may word the supporting sentences any way you choose. Write at least two different versions of a clincher sentence for each paragraph, and tell which one you think is better.

1. *Topic sentence:* Human beings can distinguish more than five thousand different smells, scientists say, and the "fragrance industry" is growing.
   Details:
      a. Perfumes worn by women—colognes and after-shaves worn by men
      b. Odor control devices—replace bad smells with more acceptable smells

    c. Latest in odor control—room sprays that mask bad odors but have no smell of their own

    d. Dolls that smell like strawberries; greeting cards that smell like roses or chocolate

2. *Topic sentence:* Recently members of the Stepfamily Association of America discussed some of the most common problems teen-agers have with stepparents.

Details:

    a. Children made to feel uncomfortable if they talk about natural parents

    b. Children uncomfortable when forced to call a stepparent Mom or Dad

    c. Children made to feel guilty about enjoying being with a stepparent

    d. Complaints about not having enough time alone with natural parent

    e. Agreement that remarriage of a parent not necessarily a traumatic experience

3. *Topic sentence:* Human beings are capable of great strength and courage when another person's life is in danger.

Details:

    a. Four-year-old boy in Williamstown, Kentucky

    b. Father working under a two-ton truck in family garage

    c. Truck slipped off jack, pinning father underneath

    d. Father shouted to four-year-old to get jack handle; father slipped jack under truck's rear springs and started to jack up truck but couldn't continue

    e. Four-year-old jacked up truck and freed father; went to neighbor who called for ambulance

4. *Topic sentence:* Teen-agers all over the world are probably saying, "Things are different from when you were a kid, Mom (or Dad)"—and they're right.

Details:

    a. Parents who remember when there was no television

    b. Parents who remember when there were no digital clocks; when everyone had to learn to "tell time"

   c. Parents who remember when gasoline cost 38 cents a gallon, and chicken 29 cents a pound.

   d. Parents who remember when mothers didn't work outside the home and when families lived all their lives in the neighborhood where they grew up

UNITY IN A PARAGRAPH

20e. **Every sentence in a paragraph should be directly related to the main idea.**

All sentences in a paragraph should develop, explain, or prove the paragraph's main idea. A sentence that is not about the main idea confuses and distracts the reader. Such a sentence destroys the paragraph's *unity*. Unity is one of the essential qualities of a well-written paragraph.

The following paragraph contains a crossed-out sentence that is not directly related to the main idea, which is in boldfaced type.

> **According to psychologists, certain adult personality traits are a result of a child's place in the family.** Adults who were only children are likely to be high achievers, verbal, and self-confident. They like to work alone and tend to be perfectionists. Firstborn children have most of these same characteristics. ~~My sister Sheila, who is a firstborn, is finishing her second year in medical school.~~ Middle children must compete for their parents' attention, and as adults they are skilled in dealing with people. Adults who were youngest children tend not to be high achievers but work hard to be liked.

The best way to achieve unity in a paragraph is to write an effective topic sentence. (See pages 523–25 on writing effective topic sentences.) As you write, keep checking to see that your supporting sentences are directly related to the topic sentence. Sometimes one sentence will make you think of an idea that is *somewhat* related but which strays from the paragraph's main idea. Such semirelated ideas should be omitted.

EXERCISE 5. Identifying Sentences That Destroy Unity.
Read each of the following paragraphs carefully. On your paper, write the number of the paragraph. If all of the sentences in the paragraph are directly related to the main idea, write *U* (for unity) next to the number. If the paragraph contains one or more sentences that destroy the paragraph's unity, write the sentences you think should be omitted. (Some paragraphs contain several sentences that should be omitted.)

1

Among the Chinese, there are surprisingly few last names. Almost all Chinese last names have only one syllable, and in Shanghai, China's largest city, only 408 one-syllable last names appear in the city's records. The most common are Zhang, Wang, Liu, and Li. Because there are so few last names, many people in China have exactly the same names. For example, almost 5,000 people in Shenyang, Manchuria, are named Li Shuzhen ("fair and precious"). In that same city, 4,300 people have the name Wang Yulan, and more than 3,000 are named Wang Wei. In the United States, the most common last names are Smith, Jones, and White. How many Robert Smiths can you find in your city's phone book?

2

Many people consider the computer the most revolution-ary invention of modern times. It can make calculations with dizzying speed, performing in a matter of seconds feats that would normally take weeks of human labor. If it is programed correctly and information is fed into it, a computer can sort through mountains of data and can provide instant, accurate answers to questions. The abacus, an ancient counting board, is in some ways like a tiny computer.

3

Migrating birds travel at heights far above the 50 to 100 feet at which small birds usually fly. Flocks of thrushes and warblers have been sighted at heights of up to 20,000 feet. Bar-headed geese fly at almost 30,000 feet as they wing their way over Mount Everest, earth's highest mountain. Mount Everest is in the Himalayas on the border of Nepal and Tibet.

Highest-flying of all is the Ruppell's griffon, a type of vulture, which ran into a plane at 37,000 feet over Africa. At this height, humans would die because of lack of oxygen, but birds have air sacs in addition to lungs. These air sacs enable them to get oxygen even at heights where there is very little oxygen.

4

A newly formed company is offering to broadcast messages into space. For a $30.00 fee, the company will send your message to any of the planets in our solar system. Wow, just suppose that you could actually broadcast your own message into space. What would you say? For an additional fee, the company will assist you in writing a message that is appropriate for the planet you have chosen. A brochure describing the service is available from Intraplanet, Inc., 4202 Woodlynne Avenue, Indianapolis, Indiana, 43201.

REVIEW EXERCISE A. Checking Paragraph Unity. Look back at all of the paragraphs you have written so far for the exercises in this chapter. Check each one carefully to make sure that no sentence detracts from the paragraph's unity. Every sentence should be directly related to the paragraph's main idea as it is expressed in the topic sentence. Revise each paragraph as necessary, omitting unnecessary or distracting sentences and ideas.

COHERENCE IN A PARAGRAPH

A paragraph in which the sentences are not in a logical order is difficult to understand. Compare, for example, the following two versions of the same paragraph. Each paragraph contains exactly the same sentences; only their order is different.

UNCLEAR   **A device has recently been developed to en-
            able a blind person to detect objects by sound.** If
            there is no obstacle in front, the blind person hears
            only a steady hum. Many blind people use canes to
            probe for obstacles; this device uses a beam of sound.
            If the obstacle is near, the hum becomes a screech,

warning the blind person to stop or turn around. The blind person wears a transmitter, which sends out the beam, and a receiver, which gives a signal. If, however, the beam of the sound hits an obstacle, the hum grows louder.

CLEAR   **A device has recently been developed to enable a blind person to detect objects by sound.** Many blind people use canes to probe for obstacles; this device uses a beam of sound instead. The blind person wears a transmitter, which sends out the beam, and a receiver, which gives a signal. If there is no obstacle in front, the blind person hears only a steady hum. If, however, the beam of sound hits an obstacle, the hum grows louder. If the obstacle is very near, the hum becomes a screech, warning the blind person to stop or turn aside.

20f. Arrange the ideas in a paragraph according to a definite plan.

Chronological Order

(1) Details in a paragraph may be arranged in chronological order.

When you tell a story, you usually tell it in *chronological order*—the order in which events happened in time. You begin at the beginning, tell what happened next, and complete the story by telling each event in the sequence in which it happened. Chronological order is often used in paragraphs that tell about personal experiences and in paragraphs about historical events.

In the following paragraph about acid rain, notice that the underscored words and phrases help the reader keep track of when the events happened.

The first ominous warning that these polluted rains were destroying aquatic life came from Norway <u>in the late 1950s,</u> when a Norwegian fisheries inspector established the <u>first</u> link between lake acidity and declines in

fish populations. A decade later, Swedish scientist Svante Oden analyzed precipitation data gathered since the 1950s, and found that European rainfall acidity had been increasing steadily. Within the next few years, the Scandinavians were to realize that 5,000 lakes and dozens of streams had been biologically decimated.

JON R. LUOMA

Chronological order is also used in paragraphs that explain a process, such as how to build a kite or how to develop a roll of film. (You will learn more about paragraphs that explain a process in pages 559–60.)

In the following paragraph, the writer tells how to ride a wave on a surfboard.

A new swell approaches, and you decide to ride it in. This is a much trickier feat. You turn your body toward shore and glance coolly over your shoulder to note how big the wave is, how fast it is coming and, most crucially of all, when it will break. Your judgment, let's say, is just right. You are already planing toward the beach when the wave reaches you. It bears you surgingly up and forward, and just then the threatening tracery along its crest breaks, not over you but under you. You can feel its chaotic turbulence beating all along your body. It goes on and on, like some rolling hydraulic engine beneath you, shooting you wildly toward shore. At last it beaches you, with a certain grudging gentleness. Victory.

JOHN KNOWLES

EXERCISE 6. Writing a Paragraph Using Chronological Order.
Use the following information to write a paragraph in which the details are arranged in chronological order.

Topic sentence: In 1872 Susan B. Anthony led a group of women who challenged the laws that kept them from voting.

Details:

a. 1870—Fourteenth and Fifteenth Amendments added to the Constitution; gave blacks the right to vote, but not women

b. After trial Anthony continued traveling, speaking, working for amendment to Constitution giving women right to vote

c. 1920—Nineteenth Amendment ratified, giving American women right to vote

d. At trial Judge Ward Hunt told jury to find Susan B. Anthony guilty; then dismissed jury before they could vote; trial helped the movement for women's vote

e. October 1872—Susan B. Anthony led group of fifteen women; registered to vote in Rochester, New York; insisted that wording in Fifteenth Amendment giving right to vote to "citizens of the United States" applied to women too

f. November 28, 1872—Susan B. Anthony and other women arrested for having voted

g. U.S. government prosecuted only Susan B. Anthony; trial began June 17, 1873

h. November 5, 1872—Anthony and other women cast their ballots in Rochester

PREWRITING Look at the list of details, and arrange them in chronological order. You may eliminate some details or add other information to strengthen the paragraph.

WRITING THE FIRST DRAFT Write the topic sentence as the first sentence in the paragraph. Then write a sentence for each detail. (You may want to combine ideas with several details in one sentence.) Try writing a clincher sentence, and see whether the paragraph sounds better with or without a clincher sentence.

REVISING AND PROOFREADING Reread the first draft to see if all of the supporting sentences are directly related to the paragraph's main idea. Check to see that the ideas are presented in a logical order, and see what you can do to make the paragraph read more smoothly. Focus on each word, replacing vague words with more specific ones. When the paragraph is the best that you can make it, proofread it carefully to eliminate inaccuracies in usage, punctuation, capitalization, and spelling.

Spatial Order

(2) Details in a paragraph may be arranged in spatial order.

When you use *spatial order,* you arrange details according to position. For example, if you were describing a room, you might imagine yourself standing in the doorway of the room. First, you might mention the objects immediately to your left. Then you would mention each object in order as you moved your eyes around the room from left to right. Other spatial orders include near to far, right to left, top to bottom, and inside to outside.

The following description of the earth's composition proceeds from the outer layers of the earth to the inner layers.

Earth scientists have discovered that the earth is composed of a number of layers. The outside layer, called the crust, is hard rock, which varies in thickness. In many places it is twenty or thirty miles thick, but beneath some parts of the sea it has a thickness of only three miles. Inside the crust, there is a layer about eighteen hundred miles deep called the mantle, which is composed of flowing rock. Beneath the mantle is the outer core, a layer about thirteen hundred miles thick and thought to be liquid iron. Finally, there is the inner core, which is a ball of hot, solid metal.

–topic sentence

four layers described in spatial order (outside to inside)

EXERCISE 7. Writing a Paragraph Using Spatial Order. Use the following topic sentence and details to write a paragraph using spatial order. Arrange the details in the order of near to far. You may make up additional details to make the paragraph more interesting.

Topic sentence: Sam sat alone on the beach, watching the people and the ocean.

Details:
   a. Directly in front of him—family with three young children, umbrella, portable crib, blankets
   b. Far out to sea—two ships
   c. Two young couples stretched out on beach towels
   d. Elderly couple on chairs, reading magazines
   e. At water's edge—children building sandcastle
   f. Close to shore—people floating, swimming, bobbing in waves; parents watching children in shallow water
   g. Colorful sails of sailboats beyond the swimmers

Order of Importance

(3) Ideas in a paragraph may be arranged in order of importance.

In persuasive paragraphs and in paragraphs that discuss causes and effects, the ideas and reasons are often arranged in *order of importance.* You may begin with the least important idea and save the most important for last. This arrangement emphasizes the most important idea by leaving it in the reader's mind at the end of the paragraph. On the other hand, you may begin with the most important idea or reason followed by those that are less important.

In the following paragraph the writer gives reasons why a class newspaper is needed.

> **Our class needs a student newspaper.** A newspaper can entertain the class by printing interesting news about students. It can announce important events like a basketball game or Halloween party. The money raised from sales can be donated to a worthy cause or used to buy a gift for the school. Most important, a student newspaper can provide valuable training for students by letting them write for readers their own age.

In this paragraph the writer gives four reasons and arranges them from least to most important. What are the four reasons?

EXERCISE 8. Writing a Paragraph Using Order of Importance. Use the following topic sentence for a paragraph. List all of the supporting reasons you can think of. Choose three of those reasons, and arrange them in order of importance.

Topic sentence: As part of eighth-grade physical education, we should have some all-day hiking trips.

Comparison or Contrast

(4) Ideas in a paragraph may be developed by comparison or contrast.

A paragraph may discuss how two or more objects, people, or places are different or alike. Such paragraphs use *comparison* when they tell the ways in which the subjects are alike. When they tell how the subjects differ, they use *contrast*. Some paragraphs use both comparison and contrast.

In the following paragraph, the writer compares and contrasts the new all-terrain bikes, or ATBs, with those of earlier years.

> Once, when Harry Truman was President and Joe Louis ruled the ring, bicycles were bicycles the way men were men—plain and strong. In those days, you could ride bikes over curbs. They had fat tires and wide, upright handlebars. So what if they only had one speed? Pushing 46 pounds of rubber and steel up a hill would have been very good exercise—if exercise had been invented yet. But then the '50s brought lighter, three-speed English bikes, and the '60s and '70s brought 21-pound ten-speeds, with downturned handlebars and skinny tires, bikes that could *go,* even up hills, but not over curbs. Then, as the '70s waned, there was another development. Out of California came all-terrain bikes. The ATBs have eighteen speeds, weigh 25 to 32 pounds, and are something of a throwback: they are plain and strong, with fat tires and upright handlebars, and you can ride them over curbs. But you can also ride them up hills, and they are light enough to carry up stairs.
>
> DAN LEVIN

EXERCISE 9. Analyzing a Paragraph of Comparison and Contrast. Read the preceding paragraph to answer these questions.

1. Name two ways in which ATBs are different from bicycles of the '40s (when Truman was President). Name two ways in which ATBs are like bikes of the '40s.
2. Name three ways in which ATBs differ from bikes of the '60s and '70s. Name one way in which they are alike.

REVIEW EXERCISE B. Choosing an Order for Developing a Topic. For each of the following topics, tell what kind of order you would use. Number your paper 1–10, and write *CHR* (chronological), *S* (spatial), *I* (order of importance), *C-C* (comparison or contrast).

1. A typical Saturday morning in your home
2. How being in the eighth grade is different from being in the seventh grade
3. What the school cafeteria looks like after lunch
4. Your favorite pair of shoes
5. Why it's important for people to have hobbies
6. How mopeds are different from motorcycles
7. How to kill a mosquito (or housefly or cockroach)
8. A time when you laughed a lot
9. Why there should (or should not) be a law requiring everyone in a car or bus to wear a seat belt
10. Why you should be the first student to go on a space flight

Transitional Expressions

In a well-written paragraph, sentences seem to follow one another naturally. A skilled writer can provide clues that help the reader follow the train of thought more easily. Words and phrases that show the relation of one idea to another within the paragraph are called *transitional expressions*.

20g. Use transitional expressions to show how ideas are related and to make a paragraph read smoothly.

In the following paragraph, the transitional expressions are underlined. Take a careful look at how each one relates the idea in the sentence to the idea of the preceding sentence.

> **The first plastic was invented as the result of a contest.** After the Civil War, the game of billiards became very popular, and a demand arose for billiard balls, which had always been made of ivory. Now there was not enough ivory to meet the demand. Consequently, one firm offered a prize of ten thousand dollars for a good substitute. Hoping to win this prize, John Wesley Hyatt mixed cellulose, nitric acid, and camphor, and produced a substance that was called "celluloid." This new substance was not suitable for billiard balls, and Hyatt did not win the prize. However, the invention turned out to be worth a great deal more than ten thousand dollars. Soon many articles were being made from this plastic. As a result, Hyatt became extremely wealthy.

Transitional expressions are used to show different kinds of relationships.

Expressions that show chronological order:

after	finally	next
afterward	first, second, etc.	now
before	later	presently
eventually	meanwhile	soon

Expressions that show spatial order:

above	below	in the distance
across	beyond	near
ahead	here	next to
around	in front of	outside
behind	inside	to the right (left)

Expressions that link similar ideas:

again	for example	likewise
also	for instance	moreover
and	furthermore	of course
another	in addition	similarly
besides	in a like manner	too

Expressions that link dissimilar or contradictory ideas:

although	in spite of	otherwise
as if	instead	provided that
but	nevertheless	still
even if	on the contrary	yet
however	on the other hand	

Expressions that indicate cause, purpose, or result:

as	for	so
as a result	for this reason	then
because	hence	therefore
consequently	since	thus

Not every sentence in a paragraph requires a transitional expression. In fact, transitional expressions should be used rather sparingly. A paragraph that contains too many transitional expressions may sound stiff and formal. Direct references (pronouns, and key words and phrases) are a more natural way to achieve paragraph coherence.

Direct Reference

A *direct reference* is a reference to a noun or idea mentioned earlier. When you speak and when you write, you use three kinds of direct references: pronouns, key words and phrases, and rewording.

Pronouns

20h. Use pronouns that refer to nouns in a preceding sentence or to the idea in a preceding sentence.

When you speak, you automatically use pronouns to avoid repetition and to make your meaning clear. You would never, for example, say anything like the following sentences:

UNNATURAL   Jenny gets up at 6.00 A.M. every morning to shampoo and blow-dry Jenny's hair. Jenny gets up at 6:00 A.M. every morning to shampoo and blow-dry

Jenny's hair so that Jenny's hair looks shiny, soft, and clean.

Using pronouns allows you to say the same thing in fewer words and much more naturally.

NATURAL   Jenny gets up at 6:00 A.M. every morning to shampoo and blow-dry *her* hair. *She* does *this* so that *her* hair will look shiny, soft, and clean.

Key Words and Phrases

20i. Connect statements by repeating a key word or phrase from a preceding sentence.

In a paragraph, a key word or phrase may be repeated not only for coherence, but also for emphasis. For example, in the paragraph about Jenny, the key word *hair* is repeated; while in the paragraph on page 510, the word *prize* appears three times.

Rewording

20j. Connect statements by using a word or phrase that means the same thing as a word or phrase in a preceding sentence.

By referring back to a preceding idea in slightly different words, you can weave together the sentences in a paragraph. In the following paragraph, the boldfaced words or phrases are reworded in later sentences; the rewordings are underlined.

Another project involving ergonomics (a word derived from the Greek "work" plus "law" or "customs") was conducted by the **design staff** of the General Motors Corporation. The designers studied **how a driver adjusts the seat** in response to various distances and angles between the steering wheel and foot pedals. With space at a premium in new, smaller cars, the designers hoped to be able to reduce the leeway of front-seat adjustment, thus providing more room for rear-seat passengers.

JOHN HOLUSHA

REVIEW EXERCISE C. Arranging Ideas in Logical Order.
Number your paper 1–8 and arrange the following sentences in
logical order for a paragraph explaining a process.

a. Here are some ways to keep houseplants healthy.
b. Don't overwater.
c. Too much water causes root rot and kills houseplants.
d. Fertilize once a month from early spring through early fall.
e. You can test to see whether the soil is dry by pushing your
   finger into the top layer of soil.
f. Use the correct soil mixture so that plants have air and
   water around the roots.
g. Water thoroughly, but let the surface soil dry out thoroughly between waterings.
h. You can add one-third sand or perlite to a soil mixture.

**REVIEW EXERCISE D. Using Transitions to Make a Para-
graph Coherent.** Using the sentences you arranged in logical
order for Review Exercise C, write a coherent paragraph. Use
transitional expressions, pronouns, key words, key phrases, and
rewording to link the ideas in the paragraph.

THE DEVELOPMENT OF A PARAGRAPH

In Chapter 19 you studied the processes of writing and thinking
that take place whenever you write. Now you will work through
the steps involved in writing a one-paragraph composition.

PREWRITING

CHOOSING AND LIMITING A TOPIC

20k. Develop a limited topic that is suitable for a paragraph.

Which of the following are *subjects* (broad, general areas of
knowledge) that you are interested in?

diet	drawing	computers	raising livestock
cars	skating	football	space travel
music	tennis	gymnastics	science fiction
birds	debate	basketball	photography
movies	camping	bicycling	psychology
health	sailing	politics	gardening

If you stop to think about your interests, hobbies, and experiences, you can list many other subjects that you might write about. Take the time right now to jot down four or five subjects that you might write about. Once you have jotted down some ideas about possible subjects, you need to choose one that interests you and that you know something about. Once you have chosen the subject, you need to narrow it to a limited *topic* that can be covered adequately in a paragraph. Suppose, for example, that you chose the general subject "movies." You would need to break down this general subject into its smaller parts.

Brainstorming

Two techniques for limiting a general subject are brainstorming (see page 461) and clustering (see page 470). When you brainstorm for paragraph topics, you will use a paper and pencil or pen. Begin by writing the broad, general subject at the top of the paper, and then jot down whatever ideas come to your mind. While you concentrate on the subject, you are at the same time letting your ideas flow freely.

The following list is the result of one writer's brainstorming for two minutes on the subject "movies." Notice that the list is made up of narrower aspects of the general subject.

Subject: Movies
Ideas: history of movies
silent films—silent film stars
how movies are made
favorite movies—favorite movie stars
Oscars—history of Academy Awards
kinds of movies—Which are most popular?
movie classics—all-time great movies

rating systems for movies
what to eat while watching a movie
watching movies at home with a VCR—pros and cons
money spent in making movies
technicolor and special effects
movies of the future—What will they be like?
jobs involved in making movies
touring a movie studio
foreign films

This list could go on—and on and on. (Give yourself two minutes, and see what other narrower topics you can think of under the general subject "movies.") While all of these topics are more limited than "movies," none are yet limited enough for a paragraph; they are still too broad.

Clustering

The technique of clustering is similar to brainstorming but uses a diagram format instead of a list. See page 522 for a clustering diagram on the topic "Effects of mechanization on coal mining." Brainstorming and clustering are techniques that can be used either to limit a topic or to gather information for writing.

Asking the 5 *W-How?* Questions

The *5 W-How?* questions can help you divide and subdivide a general subject into parts. Some parts may be suitably limited topics for a paragraph, but others may be too broad and have to be limited further. (See pages 466–69 for more information on limiting topics for writing.) For example, if you were using the *5 W-How?* questions to limit the subject "Kites," you might discover the following parts:

General subject: Kites
5 W-How? questions: What is a kite? *What* is the history of kite flying?
Who invented kites? *Who* flies kites?
When were kites invented?

Where were kites invented? *Where* do people fly kites?

Why are kites so popular?

How do kites work? *How* do you build a kite? *How* do you fly a kite?

After writing out the questions, you may want to change the questions to phrases so that you can decide whether the parts are appropriately limited for a paragraph. For example, you could change "Who invented kites?" to "The first kite flyer," a topic that could be handled in a single paragraph. Similarly, you could change "How do you build a kite?" to "How to build a kite," another topic that would be appropriate for a single paragraph.

Some of the questions have created parts that are still too broad, however. "What is the history of kite flying?" can be changed to "The history of kite flying." This subject is obviously still too broad for one paragraph because the history covers hundreds of years and many countries.

When you discover that a part is too broad, you can always use the *5 W-How?* questions to divide it into even smaller parts. In further dividing, you might find the following parts:

General subject: The history of kite flying
5 W-How? questions: What is kite flying?
        Who invented kites?
        When were kites invented?

Sometimes, as in this example, you will find yourself repeating some of the questions ("Who invented kites?" and "When were kites invented?") from your first list. These repeated questions will probably be good topics for a paragraph.

EXERCISE 10. Choosing and Limiting Topics. Choose a subject that interests you. You may use one of the subjects from the list on page 514 or choose a subject of your own. Use the *5 W-How?* questions, brainstorming, or clustering to divide and subdivide the subject until you have three topics that are limited enough for a paragraph topic. Keep a record of the questions, lists, or diagrams that you use to limit the subjects. Be ready to explain what you might include in a paragraph based on each limited topic.

CONSIDERING PURPOSE

20l. Determine your purpose for writing the paragraph.

The most common purposes for writing are to describe (descriptive writing), to tell a story (narrative writing), to explain or inform (expository writing), and to persuade (persuasive writing). Besides these four purposes, there are other purposes as well. For example, you may write to keep in touch with a friend or to record ideas and feelings in a journal. You may also write to entertain someone; usually this involves telling a story.

Your purpose for writing will influence which details you choose to include in your paragraph and will also affect the *tone* of your writing—the way in which you express your ideas. (See pages 452–54 for more information about a writer's purpose.)

In the two paragraph plans that follow, the writer has chosen different details to accomplish a different purpose for each paragraph.

Purpose: To persuade
Limited Topic: Why a mandatory seat belt law should be passed in this state
Details: a. Wording of proposed bill
  b. What citizens can do to support the bill's passage
  c. Reasons for passing the bill

Purpose: To inform
Limited Topic: Results of mandatory seat belt law in one state
Details: a. Statistics (on deaths and serious injuries from automobile accidents) in one state during year *before* mandatory seat belt law went into effect
  b. Statistics from same state during year *after* mandatory seat belt law went into effect
  c. Conclusions drawn from comparing two groups of statistics
  d. Mention of results in other states

EXERCISE 11. Selecting Details to Accomplish a Given Purpose. Each of the following numbered items lists a limited topic and a purpose. For each numbered item, suggest three or four details that might be given in a paragraph with that topic and purpose.

1. *Limited topic: The launching of a space shuttle*
   Purpose: To describe
2. *Limited topic:* Why every student should take a computer course
   Purpose: To persuade
3. *Limited topic:* Interesting information about your community
   Purpose: To inform
4. *Limited topic:* What you like most about your best friend
   Purpose: To explain
5. *Limited topic:* Your favorite place outdoors
   Purpose: To describe

EXERCISE 12. Analyzing a Paragraph's Purpose. Bring to class three different paragraphs from newspapers, magazines, or books. Be prepared to tell the class what you think the writer's purpose was in writing the paragraph.

CONSIDERING AUDIENCE

20m. Consider how your audience will affect your writing.

Before you begin to write, you need to identify your audience. Think about the ways in which you will try to make your writing meet the needs of your specific audience.

1. *Your audience will affect the way in which you limit your topic.* Try to choose a limited topic that your audience will be interested in. [Which of these two limited topics do you think an audience of eighth-graders would be more interested in: (1) a description of the tomb of the ancient Egyptian King Tutankhamen or (2) the story of the curse written on the wall of the tomb

against anyone who disturbed the tomb and of the deaths of the three men who unsealed the tomb?]

2. *Your audience will affect what you say about your limited topic.* Consider, for example, the two paragraphs that follow.

Purpose: To inform
Limited Topic: The song of the mockingbird
Audience: A class of fourth-graders

The mockingbird is famous for its beautiful and unusual singing. Unlike other birds, the mockingbird can imitate the songs of many different birds. Mockingbirds sing at daybreak, all day, and even in the middle of the night. All male mockingbirds sing, but females rarely do. The male mockingbird sings to find a female. Experts say that there are more male mockingbirds than females. They think the male mockingbirds who sing the most are those that are still single—that have not yet found a mate.

Purpose: To inform
Limited Topic: The song of the mockingbird
Audience: College students who are taking a class in ornithology, the study of birds

A recent study has investigated the singing of *Mimus polyglottos* ("many-tongued mimic"), a species of thrush commonly known as the mockingbird. Unlike other species, the mockingbird sings a medley of the songs of neighboring species as well as warbles and trills of its own. The male mockingbird sings (females rarely sing) to attract a mate, and since the male-female ratio is approximately 13:10, the males must compete for available females. A study of banded mockingbirds on a college campus suggests that the best singers—those with the biggest repertoire of imitated birdsongs—are most successful in attracting mates. Dr. Peter Merritt, an ornithologist who conducted a six-year study of mockingbirds, speculates that females choose males who show their intelligence and their ability to protect their families by their stunning display of songs of many species.

The first paragraph makes a series of general statements, while the second is much more detailed and technical. The paragraph for the audience of college students gives specific and technical information: the scientific name of the bird, the male-female ratio, the name of the scientist who did the study, and the length of the study on which the generalizations are based.

3. *Your audience affects the language that you use.* In the mockingbird paragraph for fourth-graders, sentences are short and the vocabulary is simple. Difficult concepts are either not introduced or are explained in simple terms. On the other hand, the paragraph written for college students assumes that the audience knows the meaning of such terms as *species, thrush, banded,* and *ornithologist.* Difficult vocabulary words such as *repertoire* and *speculates* are also included.

EXERCISE 13. Rewriting Paragraphs for a Different Audience. Rewrite the following paragraphs for the audience specified. Pay attention to vocabulary, sentence length, and the way in which ideas are presented.

1. The following paragraph is written for an audience of adults. Rewrite the paragraph for an audience of fifth-grade science students.

   Glacial erosion has a powerful effect upon land which has been buried by ice and has done much to shape the mountain ranges of our present world. Both valley and continental glaciers acquire many thousands of boulders and rock fragments, which, frozen into the sole of the glacier, gouge and rasp the rocks over which the glaciers pass. The rocks are slowly abraded down to a smooth, fluted, grooved surface. Glacial meltwater, from periods of daylight or summer thaw, seeps into rock fissures and joints. When it freezes again, it helps to shatter the rocks, some of which may become frozen into the body of the glacier and be carried away as the glacier moves downslope. Avalanches and undercutting of valley sides add to the rock debris.

   FRANK H. T. RHODES

2. The following paragraphs are from a fourth-grade science textbook, *Concepts in Science*. Rewrite the paragraphs for an adult audience. (If you wish, you may do some research to find additional information on the process of diffusion.)

> Everyone knows what happens to a lump of sugar at the bottom of a glass of water. The sugar dissolves in the water. But not everyone realizes how this happens. As the sugar **dissolves,** it *spreads* through water. No stirring is needed! If it is given enough time, the sugar will spread through every bit of the water.
>
> When a substance spreads in this way, we say that the substance **diffuses.** Sugar diffuses through water. Oxygen diffuses through water. Carbon dioxide diffuses through water. In fact, if a substance dissolves in a liquid, it can diffuse through the liquid.
>
> PAUL F. BRANDWEIN et al.

GATHERING INFORMATION

20n. Gather information about the limited topic of your paragraph.

You can use a number of different methods to gather information for a paragraph. Your goal is to make a list of possible details to support the paragraph's main idea.

If you are writing about something you are familiar with, you can gather information simply by concentrating on your topic with a paper and pencil in hand. You can use the brainstorming technique (see pages 514–15). Write the paragraph's main idea at the top of your paper, and then list whatever related ideas occur to you. When you run out of ideas, look critically at your list. Cross out some of the details and keep those you think are most useful. You can also use the clustering technique (see pages 470–71) to think of specific details to support your main idea. The following clustering diagram shows details that were used to develop the paragraph on page 492–93. Notice that not all of the details were actually used in the paragraph.

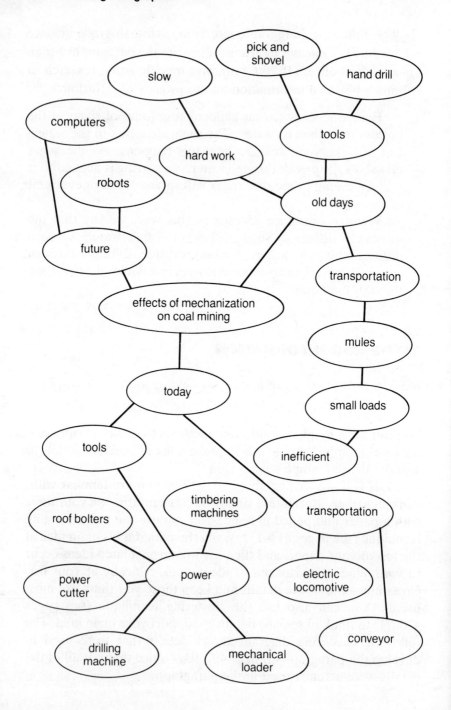

The *5 W-How?* questions can also help you to list specific details and information. Depending on the topic, you may find some of the questions more helpful than others.

If you are writing about an unfamiliar topic, you will need to do some research. You can gather information by interviewing a person who knows a great deal about the topic, or you can use sources in a library. As you interview or read for information, take notes on a sheet of paper or on note cards. You will use these notes when you choose specific information to include in your paragraph.

EXERCISE 14. Limiting Topics and Gathering Information. For each of the following subjects, narrow the subject to a limited topic suitable for a paragraph. (You may have to divide and subdivide several times until you get a topic that is appropriate for the limited space of a paragraph.) Then choose *one* of the limited topics. Use one or more of the techniques discussed in the preceding section to gather information about the limited topic you have chosen. Write a list of details that you might use in a paragraph about the limited topic you have chosen.

1. Fears   3. Popularity   5. The future
2. Records   4. Football

DEVELOPING A WORKING PLAN

20o. Develop a working plan for your paragraph by writing a topic sentence and listing specific details to develop it.

A working plan for a paragraph is a very brief outline. The working plan is made up of the topic sentence followed by a list of supporting details. On page 517 are two working plans for paragraphs on a seat belt law.

Writing an Effective Topic Sentence

The topic sentence performs two important functions. First, it controls what ideas can go into the paragraph by stating a main idea that all other sentences in the paragraph must support. The topic sentence should also arouse the reader's interest. Before you write a first draft, study your list of details to focus your thoughts on what the paragraph's main idea will be. Try writing a topic sentence that states this main idea precisely.

A writer has gathered the following list of details about a computer game. Which of the suggested topic sentences would be most effective for a paragraph based on these details?

Details:

 a. Computer software game—called "Synthetic Adventure—The Flask of Doom"

 b. Created by chemistry professor, Fred D. Williams—teacher at Michigan Tech

 c. Teaches organic chemistry

 d. Player visits planet Organo—people who live there are organic compounds

 e. Goal of game, player's "mission"—finding a DNA molecule

 f. DNA—basic material in all living matter; transmits hereditary characteristics (DNA is what makes seeds grow up to be specific kind of plant, babies grow up to be humans, puppies grow up to be dogs)

 g. Players visit more than 50 locations—accompanied by chemicals (Organo residents); combinations of chemicals produce compounds to solve game's problems

Possible topic sentences:

 a. Students can learn organic chemistry more easily.

 b. A new computer game called "Synthetic Adventure—The Flask of Doom" makes learning the chemical compounds of organic chemistry easier and much less painful.

 c. "Synthetic Adventure—The Flask of Doom" is one of several new computer games.

Of these possible topic sentences, sentence (b) is the most effective. It "covers" the list of details and arouses the reader's interest. Sentence (a) is both dull and too general; it does not even mention the specific game that will be the focus of the whole paragraph. Sentence (c) suggests that the paragraph will be about more than one game ("one of several"), but the details mention only the one game.

Choosing Supporting Details

Before you begin to write your first draft, look again at your list of details. You may find some that no longer "fit" the main idea and should be dropped. You may find that you do not have sufficient details to develop the main idea. In this case, you will have to add more information to your list. Perhaps you will need to choose a different aspect of your topic or select a new topic altogether.

EXERCISE 15. Writing a Paragraph. Use topic sentence (b) and the list of details on page 524 to write an explanatory paragraph for an audience of organic chemistry students. You may omit some of the information given in the list or add information.

EXERCISE 16. Writing Topic Sentences. Each of the following numbered items is a list of details that might be included in a paragraph. For each of the numbered items, write an effective topic sentence. (It does not have to cover all of the details.) Try writing several different versions, and choose the one that you think is most effective.

1. a. More than one third of the approximately sixty million potential voters in the United States not registered
   b. About 80 percent of registered voters vote in Presidential elections
   c. Reasons people don't register: don't care; don't think a single vote can make a difference; don't want to be called to jury duty (voter registration rolls used for jury pool)
   d. Voting in elections a citizen's responsibility; can't vote if you're not registered
   e. Countries that have no free elections; many Americans take right to vote and other freedoms for granted
   f. Importance of registering to vote

2. a. Mobile homes (trailers); way of life for many Americans
   b. Wyoming—18.3 percent of homes are mobile homes; Montana and Arizona—13 percent; Nevada—12.8 percent; New Mexico—12.5 percent
   c. National average—5.3 percent of all homes mobile homes
   d. More in Rocky Mountain states because of "boom and bust" jobs; temporary, immediate homes
   e. More trailers also in Sunbelt states; inexpensive and easily maintained homes
   f. Lowest percentage in Washington, D.C.—1 percent; low percentage of mobile homes in urban Northeast

EXERCISE 17. Writing a Paragraph. Write a paragraph for both of the numbered items in Exercise 16. As the first sentence in each paragraph, use the topic sentence you wrote for the list of details.

PREWRITING Begin by writing the topic sentence. Decide in what order the details would be most effective. You may decide to omit some of the details or to add to the list of information. Make sure that any details you add are directly related to the paragraph's main idea.

WRITING, REVISING, AND PROOFREADING Write the first draft of your paragraph, following the order you have decided on for the supporting information. Try to write a sentence for each item on the list. When you revise, check to see that all of the information is directly related to the topic sentence. During the revising stage, you may decide to combine sentences, vary sentence beginnings, and replace vague words. Before you write a final draft, proofread your paragraph carefully.

CRITICAL THINKING:
Making a Generalization

A *generalization* is a universal statement about a whole group of people, events, objects, places, or ideas.

EXAMPLES   Eighth-grade students are required to take English and mathematics.

All green plants need light in order to live.

Left-handed people are more creative than right-handed people.

You can see that the generalizations are about *all* eighth-graders, green plants, and left-handed people.

You can, of course, make up a statement that is a false generalization, a fallacy. It is only partly true or completely false. (Many people, for example, would not agree with the generalization about left-handed people being more creative.) Here are some examples of false generalizations.

EXAMPLES   All good typists make good secretaries. [Many people who type well would not be good secretaries.]

Elephants can fly. [Only Dumbo flew.]

Scientists are thinner than farmers. [There is no information to back up this generalization.]

Generalizations are meaningful only when they are *valid*–that is, when they are reasonable. In order to be valid, a generalization must be based on factual information or on many specific observations.

20p. The topic sentence of a paragraph usually states a generalization.

EXAMPLE   Mobile homes, often called trailers, are a much more common way of life in the Rocky Mountain states than they are in the urban Northeast.

In making a generalization, you must consider all of the available facts and make a reasonable statement based on those facts. The following generalizations about Americans came from a handbook published by the United States government for foreign students and scholars planning to study in the United States. Notice that the generalizations are stated as topic sentences.

Americans are very informal. They like to dress informally, entertain informally, and they treat each other in a very informal way, even when there is a great difference in age or social standing. Foreign students may consider this informality disrespectful, even rude, but it is a part of U.S. culture.

Americans are achievers. They are obsessed with records of achievement in sports, and they keep business achievement charts on their office walls and sports awards displayed in their homes.

Americans value punctuality. They keep appointment calendars and live according to schedules. To foreign students, Americans seem "always in a hurry," and this often makes them appear brusque. Americans are generally efficient and get a great many things done, simply by rushing around.

UNITED STATES INFORMATION AGENCY,
BUREAU OF EDUCATIONAL AND CULTURAL AFFAIRS

EXERCISE 18. Analyzing Paragraphs Based on Generalizations. Be prepared to discuss each of the following questions, based on the preceding paragraphs about Americans.

1. These paragraphs contain three generalizations. What are they?
2. Do you think these generalizations are reasonable? Discuss each one, explaining your answers.
3. What other valid generalizations can you make about Americans? List your generalizations and a sentence or two to support each one.
4. What valid generalizations can you make about eighth-grade students in your school? List your generalizations and a sentence or two to support each one.

EXERCISE 19. Writing a Paragraph Based on a Generalization. Choose one of the generalizations you have written in answer to questions 3 and 4 of Exercise 18. Write a paragraph based on that generalization, making it the paragraph's topic sentence. Include sufficient supporting details to convince the reader that the generalization is true.

CRITICAL THINKING:
Deciding Which Details Support a Main Idea

How can you judge which supporting details best support the main idea of your paragraph? The critical thinking skill that you use in making such decisions is the skill of *analysis*. When you analyze a paragraph, you decide how the ideas and information relate to each other.

20q. Keep the topic sentence clearly in mind as you decide which details to include in a paragraph.

The following guidelines will help you decide which details to include and which ones to omit. Ask yourself these questions for each detail that you are thinking about including in a paragraph.

1. Is this detail *directly* related to the paragraph's main idea as it is stated in the topic sentence? (Details that are not directly related destroy the paragraph's unity.)

2. How will this detail function within the paragraph? Is it an example of the generalization in the topic sentence? A fact? A reason? (You will learn more about these different types of supporting details on pages 554–557. If you have a clear idea of how each supporting detail functions within the paragraph, you will be more likely to have a logically organized paragraph.

3. Will this detail help the reader to understand the main idea, or will it confuse or distract the reader? Will the paragraph be more forceful and easier to understand with the detail or without it?

Consider the following topic sentence and possible details for a paragraph about voter registration. Which of the details would you choose to include in such a paragraph?

Topic sentence: From the age of 18 on, all American citizens are eligible to vote in elections, but too few take advantage of this privilege and responsibility.

Possible details:
   a. More than one third (approximately sixty million) of those eligible to vote not registered
   b. Only about 80 percent of registered voters vote in Presidential elections.
   c. Voting in elections—a citizen's responsibility; can't vote if you're not registered
   d. Many countries have no free elections; some Americans take right to vote and other freedoms for granted
   e. Where do you register to vote?
   f. Everyone in my family registered to vote
   g. Some reasons people don't register: don't think a single vote can make a difference; don't want to be called to jury duty (voter registration rolls used for jury pool)
   h. Voter registration card—useful as identification

Details a, b, c, d, and g are useful in developing the main idea. The other details in this list should be omitted from a paragraph with the suggested topic sentence.

EXERCISE 20. Choosing Details and Writing a Paragraph. Decide which of the following details should be included in a paragraph developed from the topic sentence. (You will probably omit several.) Be prepared to explain your choices. When you have decided which details to include in the paragraph, write a paragraph based on the information given. If you wish, you may add other details that you think will improve the paragraph.

Topic sentence: Running for office in a class election is a lot of work, but it can also be a lot of fun.
Possible details:
   a. Qualifying for nomination—past grades and conduct examined
   b. Writing campaign speeches—broadcast over radio
   c. Candidates running for same office sometimes best friends: Pat and I both candidates for Vice-President of Student Council
   d. Fun to prepare campaign posters and buttons

e. In city, state, and national elections, electioneering not permitted near polls
f. Tension and suspense while votes counted
g. Day of elections—candidates exhausted, voters still trying to decide
h. Candidates talk to students, try to make themselves known
i. Responsibilities of each student government officer—list each office

WRITING THE FIRST DRAFT

Methods of Paragraph Development

20r. Choose an appropriate method of development for your paragraph.

The main idea in a paragraph may be developed by facts and statistics, concrete and sensory details, reasons, incidents, or examples. You will practice each of these methods of paragraph development in the next chapter when you study four types of paragraphs: narrative, expository, descriptive, and persuasive. Paragraphs may also be developed by a combination of methods.

Using the Working Plan

When you write your first draft, start with your working plan that includes your topic sentence and list of supporting details. Begin your first draft by writing the topic sentence as the first sentence. Then make each of the details listed in your paragraph plan into a sentence. You may decide to combine several details into a single sentence. Some writers try to vary sentence beginnings, structure, and length as they write the first draft. Others leave these matters to the revising stage. Your goal in writing the first draft should be to express what you mean as clearly as possible.

Read the following list of prewriting notes for a paragraph about animal heroes in Japanese folk tales:

Topic sentence: Japanese folk tales include many stories of animals that help or reward people.
Details:

    a. Kindness to animals; Japanese idea of divine spirit, *kami,* in all nature

    b. Animals sometimes become human beings

    c. Story of sparrow whose tongue was cut by washerwoman —punishment for eating woman's rice

    d. Old couple, neighbors of the washerwoman, found and cared for sparrow

    e. Sparrow transformed to human—offered elderly couple two boxes; they chose the small box

    f. Other examples—grateful dog gave mistress supply of silk, which made her rich; pair of mandarin ducks saved lives of servants who kept them from being separated; cat belonging to elderly couple turned herself into a woman to earn money to support the couple

In the first draft that follows, you can see that the writer chose to omit some of these details. (Notice that the paragraph contains some problems in spelling, mechanics, and usage, which will be corrected in the revising and proofreading stages.)

Japanese folk tales include many stories of animals that help or reward people. These stories increase the Japanese belief of kindness to animals, it is based on the believe that *kami* is found in all of nature. *Kami* is a divine presence. One story is about a sparrow, a washerwoman, and an old couple. The washerwoman cuts the sparrow's tongue because the sparrow ate some of her rice. The old couple found and cared for the sparrow. They had been kind to the sparrow even before this happened. The sparrow became a human being. The sparrow offered the couple a choice of two boxes. They chose the smallest box, they found in it unending money. In these folktales the animals become human beings.

EXERCISE 21. Analyzing a First Draft.   Answer the following questions about the first draft of the paragraph on Japanese folktales.

1. Look at the list of prewriting notes on page 532. Which details did the writer not include in the first draft of the paragraph? Do you think the paragraph would be better with these details or without them? Explain your answer.
2. Are the ideas in the paragraph arranged in an effective order? How would you improve the arrangement of ideas?
3. In what order is the story of the sparrow told?
4. How effective do you think the topic sentence is? Try writing other versions of a topic sentence.
5. Does the first draft have a clincher sentence? Try writing several clincher sentences, and see if any one of them improves the paragraph.

REVISING

The *revising* stage is essential in good writing; no writer can possibly expect to get everything right the first time. If possible, let some time elapse between writing your first draft and revising it. This time lapse will help you to look at your writing with a fresh eye to see how you can improve it.

REVISING YOUR FIRST DRAFT

20s. Revise your first draft carefully for content, organization, and style.

Some writers revise even as they write a first draft—changing words, crossing out sentences, or varying sentence starts. Others write three or four or more drafts before they are satisfied that they have a finished piece of writing. Revision involves at least three separate tasks, each of which requires a separate reading.

Revising for Content

Take a long, hard look at the information in your paragraph. The topic sentence should state the main idea clearly and precisely. It should also, if at all possible, make the reader want to read the rest of the paragraph.

The paragraph should contain enough supporting details to develop the main idea. If there are not sufficient details, add more information to strengthen the paragraph. All of the supporting sentences should relate directly to the paragraph's main idea. Cross out any ideas or sentences that destroy the paragraph's unity.

Revising for Organization

Reread the first draft again, this time focusing on coherence. How easy is it to understand what you are trying to say? Are the sentences and ideas in the best order, or do some need to be moved? Consider adding transitional expressions to help improve the paragraph's coherence. Your goal in revising for organization is to make your ideas easy to follow and understand.

Revising for Style

Some writers call this step "polishing." You will polish not only sentences but also individual words. One of the best tests of style is to read the first draft aloud to yourself. Your ear may be able to "hear" where you need to make changes. Read the first draft aloud to see if it has any awkward-sounding spots. To make the sentences read more smoothly, you may want to combine sentences or vary sentence beginnings, length, or structure.

Another important part of style is *diction*—word choice. Take the time to focus briefly on each important word. You may need to replace a vague word or phrase with a more precise one and sometimes substitute a simpler word for a more complicated one. Remember that your goal is to convey your meaning clearly and simply.

Finally, look for unnecessary repetition. Good writing contains no "padding." Check each sentence one more time to see if words or phrases can be omitted without changing a sentence's meaning or detracting from the paragraph in any other way.

Study the following revision of the paragraph about Japanese folktales. See if you can tell why the writer made each change. Do you agree that the change is an improvement? Why or why not? (Notice that the revision also shows changes in spelling and usage made during the proofreading stage, which is discussed in the following section.)

Japanese folk tales include many stories of *grateful* animals that help or reward people, *who are kind to them.* These stories, ~~increase~~ *reinforce* the Japanese *value* ~~belief~~ of kindness to animals, ~~it~~ *which partly,* is, based on the ~~believe~~ *belief* that *a divine presence* kami is found in all of nature. ~~Kami is a divine presence.~~ One *such* story is about a sparrow, a washerwoman, and an old couple. The washerwoman, *cruelly* cuts the sparrow's tongue because ~~the~~ *it had eaten* ~~sparrow ate~~ some of her rice. *A neighboring* ~~The~~ old couple, found and cared for the *wounded* sparrow. ~~They~~ *who* had been kind to the sparrow even before this happened, *and, as a* The sparrow became a human being, *reward for their kindness,* ~~The sparrow~~ offered the couple a choice of two boxes. They chose the *smaller one and* ~~smallest box, they~~ found in it *endless riches.* ~~unending money.~~ In these folk tales the *grateful* animals *sometimes transform themselves into* ~~become~~ human beings.

Keep the following guidelines in mind as you revise your first draft.

GUIDELINES FOR WRITING AND REVISING PARAGRAPHS

1. Do all of the sentences in the paragraph develop one main idea?
2. Does the topic sentence state the main idea of the paragraph? Is the topic sentence clear and precise? Does it arouse the reader's interest?

3. Do the supportive sentences give specific details that support the main idea stated in the topic sentence? Are there sufficient details?

4. Does the paragraph have unity? Is every sentence directly related to the main idea?

5. Does the paragraph have coherence? Are ideas arranged in a logical order? Should any sentences or ideas be moved?

6. Does the paragraph read smoothly? If appropriate, are transitional expressions used to show how ideas are related? Are direct references (pronouns, repetition of key words, substitution of words and phrases) used to make the paragraph read smoothly?

7. Would a clincher, or concluding, sentence improve the paragraph?

8. Does the paragraph contain unnecessary words or phrases that should be omitted?

9. Is every word in the paragraph effective, or can more precise words be substituted for vague or imprecise words?

PROOFREADING

PROOFREADING YOUR PARAGRAPH

20t. Proofread your paragraph and make a final copy.

Proofreading is the last step before copying a final version of your paragraph. When you proofread, you look for mistakes in spelling, capitalization, and punctuation. You also correct usage mistakes—errors in subject-verb agreement or in pronoun usage.

Some people can proofread and revise at the same time, but most writers find it easier to concentrate on one thing at a time. One method is to check spelling first, then punctuation, then usage, and then capitalization. Whatever you do, be sure to spend some time making sure your paper is free from such mistakes. Proofread your final version also, to make sure you have not made any new errors in copying the final draft.

EXERCISE 22. Revising and Proofreading Weak Paragraphs. Use the Guidelines for Writing and Revising Paragraphs to revise each of the following first drafts. You may make up any specific details that you need.

1

Jason has been my best freind since he moved next door last summer. He has a lot of talent. He plays the clarinet really good, he's in a youth symphony and he's also in the school band. Jason also is good in sports, he writes well, and makes friends easily. Jason has a great sense of humor and Jason likes to tell jokes.

2

The horse is a beautiful animal. Wild horses have been used by humans for a long time. They are used on farms and for rideing and for races. Before there were automobiles, the horse was the main means of transportation. The word *horsepower* is the power exerted by a horse when it pulls. *Horsepower* is a unit for measuring the power of a motor, one horsepower equals the force needed to raise 33,000 pounds of anything at the rate of one pound every minute. A horses scientific name is *Equus caballus.*

3

On Sunday afternoons the park is full of people. Parents and children are picnicking. There is always at least two baseball games at one end of the field, touch football at the other. Bicyclists are bicycling, joggers jogging. People are on the lake in rowboats or paddleboats. Lots of people play volleyball, too.

EXERCISE 23. Proofreading a Paragraph. Using the Guidelines for Proofreading on page 487, proofread the following paragraph. Write the corrected version on a separate sheet of paper. You may need to reword the paragraph to correct run-on sentences and sentence fragments.

In the creation myth of the Iroquois tribe, the earth began when the mother of earth fell threw a hole in the sky. She fell into an endless lake but fortunatly with her fell a cosmic tree, it had some magical earth around it's roots. The young woman who fell from the sky was saved from drowning by two swans. Then three animals—Otter, Beaver, Muskrat, and Toad—each dived to the bottom of the lake. To try to get some of the magical earth on the trees roots. Otter, Beaver, and Muskrat drownded; Toad was able to get a single mouthful of the earth, it grew first into an island for the mother of earth to stand on, and then it grew and grew and kept right on growing. Until it became the hole world.

CHAPTER 20 WRITING REVIEW

Writing an Effective Paragraph. For this assignment you will put into practice all that you have learned about planning and developing paragraphs. Your teacher may specify a topic. If not, you may choose a subject of your own or one of the following subjects. Then narrow your subject to a specific topic.

A great sports figure	Exercise
Nightmares	Shopping malls
Anger	Mountains
A modern hero or heroine	Health

PREWRITING Be sure to limit your topic so that it can be adequately covered in a paragraph. After you have decided on your purpose and your audience, list details you might include in the paragraph. Write the topic sentence and choose the details that you plan to use; this is your working plan. Decide also in what order you will arrange your details.

WRITING AND REVISING As you write the first draft, follow your working plan. Once you have completed the first draft, ask yourself these questions:

1. Does the topic sentence clearly state the main idea of the paragraph?

2. Do the supporting sentences provide enough information to develop the topic fully?
3. Is the information interesting and specific?
4. Does every sentence in the paragraph relate closely to the topic sentence?
5. Are the sentences clear and easy to understand?
6. Does the paragraph read smoothly?

PROOFREADING When you have finished revising, proofread your paragraph (see the Guidelines for Proofreading on page 487), and write a clean copy of your final version.

CHAPTER 21

Writing Paragraphs

FOUR TYPES OF PARAGRAPHS

In this chapter, you will practice writing four types of paragraphs. Each type has a different purpose.

1. *Narrative paragraphs* tell a story or relate a series of events.

2. *Descriptive paragraphs* describe a particular person, place, or thing.

3. *Expository paragraphs* inform or explain.

4. *Persuasive paragraphs* try to convince the reader that an opinion is true or that the reader should perform a specific action.

THE NARRATIVE PARAGRAPH

Telling about an incident may be a way of developing a paragraph. A narrative paragraph tells a story or relates a series of events. Sometimes the purpose of a narrative paragraph is simply to entertain the reader by telling about an incident or a situation. A narrative paragraph may also illustrate a point made in the topic sentence.

Prewriting for a Narrative Paragraph

In order to write an interesting narrative paragraph, you must fit many pieces together. The prewriting activities for this kind of writing include thinking about and planning what incident you will write about, for whom you will write, and what details you will select. These steps will guide you in your prewriting.

1. Choose an incident that you can tell about in a single paragraph.
2. List the important events in the incident. Then arrange the events in chronological order, the order in which they occurred.
3. Add specific narrative details (strong verbs, precise nouns and adjectives, descriptive information) to make the story more interesting.
4. Decide whether you will use the first-person or third-person point of view.
5. Determine your audience and your purpose. Consider how both audience and purpose will affect what you write.
6. Write a topic sentence that introduces or summarizes the incident. The topic sentence may make the point that the story will illustrate.

Writing a Narrative Paragraph with an Incident

21a. Develop a narrative paragraph with an incident.

Something that happens is an *incident*. The following paragraph uses an incident to develop the main idea in the topic sentence. Notice that the writer uses *chronological order* to tell about the events that make up the incident. The italicized words help the reader keep track of when the events occurred.

> Not all of Adamson's encounters with his liberated lions have been so uneventful. *Several years ago,* he was out on patrol when he met up with two of his ex-charges, a male named Suleiman and his sister, Sheba. They playfully bounded straight at Adamson. Suleiman grabbed him from behind and

the two of them crashed to the ground. *When Adamson squeezed off a warning shot with his pistol,* the animal—no longer playful—growled and bit deeply into his neck. Adamson *then* jammed the weapon into a fleshy area above the lion's shoulder and fired. *With that,* the lion retreated and Adamson hobbled off, bleeding profusely. He made it back to camp where doctors in Nairobi were radioed to fly up and repair the damage. "I worried *all night* about Suleiman," he recalled sheepishly. "I was relieved *the next morning* when he showed up looking little the worse for wear except for a bullet lodged under his skin."

DICK HUSTON

Writing Narrative Details

A well-written narrative paragraph includes many specific *narrative details*. These details help the reader to picture the events being described. Often, narrative paragraphs use vivid details that combine description (what the writer sees, hears, smells, etc.) with narration (what happens). Compare the following versions of the same event. The first version is dull and uninteresting because it does not contain enough narrative details.

WEAK   The boy was riding a bicycle. He didn't see the barrier and hit it. He fell, and the bicycle fell on top of him. He picked himself up and rode away.

IMPROVED   The sandy-haired boy in cutoff shorts and a yellow T-shirt was riding a rusty green Raleigh. As he rode across the narrow wooden footbridge, the boy turned to watch a least tern dive-bomb into the water for a fish. Looking over his shoulder, he crashed into the metal barricade at the end of the bridge. For a moment he struggled to keep his balance. Then he fell beneath the bicycle, landing on his elbow and crashing against his funny bone. He looked around; no one had heard the crash or seen him fall. The boy rocked and moaned, cradling his elbow. As the terrible pain subsided, he picked up his bicycle and rode slowly away.

Choosing a Point of View

The following paragraph is part of an article about a midwinter ski trip through the Grand Canyon. The writer tells the story from the *first-person point of view*, using the pronouns *we* and *I* to refer to himself in the events he actually experienced. In the first-person point of view, the storyteller *(narrator)* participates in the action.

> *We* clipped on our skis, slung on our packs, ducked under a gate and stepped onto the snow. It was ice. The morning was sunny, but there had been no fresh snow for more than a week, and the surface was solidly frozen. *We* set off at a modest pace, with Quiroz up front. *I* charged up a few hills to assure *myself* I could handle this, then dropped in behind Babbitt and Warner. *My* pack was already heavy.
>
> KENNY MOORE

A narrative paragraph may also be written from the *third-person point of view*. In this point of view, the writer does not take part in the story. Instead, the people in the story are referred to by the third-person pronouns *he, she, it,* and *they*. The paragraphs about George Adamson (pages 541–42) and about the boy on the bicycle (page 542) are written from the third-person point of view. Before beginning a narrative paragraph, always decide what point of view you will use. Do not mix first- and third-person point of view in a narrative paragraph.

EXERCISE 1. Writing a Narrative Paragraph. Use the following information to write a narrative paragraph. Follow each of the prewriting steps (page 541) before you begin to write a first draft of the paragraph. You may make up additional narrative details.

Possible details:
   a. Began to smell burning
   b. Had to pay for repairing window
   c. Nobody in family home, nobody could be reached
   d. Worst part—left vegetables cooking on stove
   e. Last summer—finally learned not to get locked out

      f. Neighbor helped; broke bathroom window and climbed through

      g. Went out of house for just a minute—left keys on kitchen table; door locked behind

PREWRITING Arrange the events in chronological order. Decide whose story this is—will you use the first-person or third-person point of view? Add more specific narrative details to make the paragraph more interesting. Which of the items given can serve as the basis for a topic sentence? Try writing several topic sentences, and choose one that will interest the reader and will at the same time indicate what the story is about.

WRITING AND REVISING Use your list of details as the working plan for your first draft. When you have finished a first version, use the guidelines on page 545 to help you improve your paragraph. Consider adding transitional expressions (*first, next, then,* etc.) to help the reader keep track of the order of the events.

EXERCISE 2. Writing a Narrative Paragraph. Search your memory for an experience that you think would make an interesting narrative paragraph. Write an introductory topic sentence, and tell the incident in a paragraph of approximately 100–150 words. You may choose one of the following topics or a topic of your own.

1. Are animals able to think?
2. An experiment that didn't work
3. Overcoming a fear
4. A time when I laughed a lot
5. A well-kept secret

6. A chore that turned out to be fun
7. A dream adventure
8. A promise that was hard to keep
9. An unexpected friend
10. Taking a risk

PREWRITING Follow each of the prewriting steps on page 541. Make sure that you have sufficiently narrowed your topic so that it is suitable for a paragraph.

WRITING, REVISING, AND PROOFREADING As you write the first draft, keep in mind that the paragraph should be interesting to your audience. Try to include enough specific narrative details so that the reader can actually visualize the incident you are writing about.

GUIDELINES FOR REVISING NARRATIVE PARAGRAPHS

1. Does the paragraph have a topic sentence?
2. Does the paragraph contain enough specific details and vivid words? Is the incident interesting to read about?
3. Are the events or actions arranged in chronological order?
4. Is essential information (characters, time, place) included or explained so that the reader can understand the action?
5. Is the incident told from a single point of view (either first-person or third-person)?
6. Is the language appropriate for the audience and the purpose?

EXERCISE 3. Revising a Weak Narrative Paragraph. Add specific narrative details to improve this first draft. Make up any information you need. The questions following the paragraph may help you to think of additional narrative details.

When Amy was very little, she learned something important about driving a car. She got in her father's car. She locked the doors and released the emergency brake. The driveway was on a hill, so the car coasted backward down the hill. Amy cried. The car stopped moving. It was blocking the street. Amy's father came and got her out.

1. How old was Amy?
2. How fast did the car move down the driveway?
3. How did Amy feel when the car began to move?
4. What did the street look like?
5. How long was Amy in the car?
6. How did Amy's father find out what had happened?
7. How did he get Amy out of the car?

8. What did Amy say to her father?
9. What did Amy's father say to her?
10. What was the "something important" that Amy learned from this experience?

REVIEW EXERCISE A. Writing a Narrative Paragraph. Choose one of the following narrative situations, and write a paragraph based on the incident. You may make up any details you want.

1. You have just found out that one of your family members has won a million dollars in a lottery.
2. You are on a wilderness hike in the Rocky Mountains. You become lost.
3. You are walking with your little sister when you meet a dangerous-looking, growling wild dog.
4. You look out your window and see black smoke pouring from a neighbor's house (or apartment).
5. You learn something interesting when you decide to help an elderly neighbor who lives alone.
6. You answer an advertisement for part-time help at a local supermarket.
7. You work very hard on an incredible idea for a science project.
8. You have to make a campaign speech before the entire student body when you run for class president (or Student Council president).
9. You receive a letter in the mail from the President of the United States, asking you to help with a special mission.
10. You work frantically to write a term paper the night before it is due.

THE DESCRIPTIVE PARAGRAPH

When you write a descriptive paragraph, you are creating a word picture. Your purpose is to help the reader clearly imagine the object, place, or person you are writing about.

Prewriting for a Descriptive Paragraph

Painters and photographers plan the pictures they create. When you create a word picture, you plan by following the steps in the prewriting process. You begin by narrowing your subject to a limited topic. Then you decide on the specific details you will use, and you arrange them in order. The following prewriting steps will help you write vivid, effective description.

1. Try to observe the subject you are writing about. Take notes as you observe.

2. List as many concrete and sensory details as you can. Concentrate on other senses besides the sense of sight.

3. Decide what main impression you are trying to create, and choose only details that support that main impression.

4. Arrange the details in an order that seems logical. If appropriate, use spatial order.

5. Occasionally, use a comparison or figurative language to describe something more vividly.

6. Use specific nouns and strong verbs. Avoid overused modifiers such as *very, extremely,* and *really.*

Gathering Concrete and Sensory Details

When you use *concrete details,* you mention specific objects, places, or people. In the following paragraph, notice how many concrete details the writer has included in a description of a busy harbor scene.

As our bus draws up at the wharf in Chongqing, once known as Chungking, we seem to enter a speeded-up movie. Hordes of people scramble down a crazy-quilt pattern of steps that saw-tooth steeply in two opposing directions, criss-crossing in the middle. It is low tide, and there are more than 300 steps swarming with men, women, and children all scampering down toward the river, carrying bamboo poles balancing baskets of cabbages, apples, mandarin oranges, tangerines, persimmons, radishes, grain, spices, chickens, ducks, fish. Children carry stoves, old men fishing poles and nets, Mao-suited businessmen briefcases. Beside a gangplank, people squat in small groups like coveys of birds, counting produce, rearranging cargo and finally funneling into a green, triple-decked ferryboat with a bright red star at the top. When the boat pulls away an hour later, we have observed more of life and human interaction than at any previous time in China.

BARBARA GOLDSMITH

A *sensory detail* is one that appeals directly to the sense of sight, smell, sound, taste, or touch. When most people are asked to describe something, they describe only what they see. In the following description of a place, notice that the writer includes sensory details that appeal to the senses of smell and hearing as well as sight.

I remember my first walk in a Nigerian rain forest. It is moist and the air is soft, a comforting warm smell actually made by the fungi underfoot. The trunks of the great trees rise straight up and tall, set out like pillars along the nave of a great Gothic cathedral. Clouds float between the branches, drifting patches of vapor that come and go. The trees branch out at about a hundred feet. Where there is a break in the canopy, light streams through against the rising mist in rays that you can see. I remember how an ugly dead growth on the branch of one tree suddenly opened in at the middle and said, "Gronk." It was a giant yellow casque hornbill. I remember, too, how the silence that made me place my feet so carefully was broken as frogs began to sing, then more frogs and more until the song swept into the distance and stopped as suddenly as it had begun.

PAUL COLINVAUX

EXERCISE 4. Gathering Sensory Details. Spend at least three minutes carefully observing a specific example of each of the following objects. For each object, write three sensory details that you could use in a paragraph describing the object.

1. A green pepper
2. A penny
3. A car
4. A chair
5. A telephone
6. A book
7. A pencil
8. A door
9. A toothbrush
10. A shoe

Writing a Paragraph That Describes a Place or Object

21b. A descriptive paragraph may create a main impression about a place or object.

Be sure that your topic sentence identifies the place or object you are describing. Try also to create a mood, reveal an attitude, or summarize the details that you will include in your description.

EXAMPLE   Now blackened with tarnish and badly dented, the old hand mirror held secrets of an elegant past.

In the two descriptive paragraphs you have studied so far, both topic sentences reveal a main impression of the place being described. The dominant impression in the topic sentence about Chongqing harbor is of a bustling place, full of rushing people— like *a speeded-up movie.* The description of the woods has a topic sentence that reveals the writer's attitude toward the place.

Using Precise Language

Use specific verbs and precise modifiers. A descriptive paragraph need not be long, but it should be vivid. Action verbs and specific adjectives and adverbs must be carefully chosen to make a clear picture. Never be satisfied with the first descriptive word or phrase that occurs to you; hunt for the best.

WEAK   People walk quickly down the steps.
VIVID   *Hordes of* people *scramble* down a *crazy-quilt pattern* of steps that *saw-tooth steeply* in two opposing directions, *criss-crossing* in the middle.

WEAK   The dog barked into the base of a hollow tree.
VIVID   The *beagle shrieked* into it, his *bay comically muffled* by the cavity in the tree.

EXERCISE 5. Making Descriptions Vivid. Rewrite each of the following sentences. Add specific nouns, verbs, and precise modifiers to make a clear picture for the reader.

1. A woman answered the door.
2. The student sat at the desk.
3. Someone was using a machine that made a lot of noise.
4. The singer sang a sad song.
5. The audience applauded.
6. The basketball player scored two points.
7. The kitchen was filled with a good smell.
8. The baby cried loudly for a long time.
9. Lou felt bad about the news.
10. The driver got in the car and drove away quickly.

Using Comparisons and Figurative Language

Use comparisons and figurative language to help make a description more vivid. In the following paragraph, Lewis Thomas compares the moon with the "living" earth. To say that the earth is alive is a figure of speech called a *metaphor*. Notice the other italicized figurative language.

> Viewed from the distance of the moon, the astonishing thing about the earth, catching the breath, is that it is alive. The photographs show the dry pounded surface of the moon in the foreground, *dead as an old bone*. Aloft, *floating free* beneath the moist, gleaming *membrane of bright blue sky,* is the rising earth, the only *exuberant thing* in this part of the cosmos. If you could look long enough, you would see the swirling of the great drifts of white cloud, covering and uncovering the half-hidden masses of land. If you had been looking for a very long, geologic time, you could have seen the continents themselves in motion, drifting apart on their crustal plates, *held afloat* by the fire beneath. It has the organized self-contained look of *a live creature, full of information, marvelously skilled in handling the sun.*
>
> LEWIS THOMAS

EXERCISE 6. Writing a Descriptive Paragraph About an Object.
Choose one of the items in Exercise 4 or an object of your own. Write a paragraph of 100–150 words describing the object. Be sure your topic sentence states a main impression.

The Descriptive Paragraph > 551

EXERCISE 7. Writing a Descriptive Paragraph About a Place. Choose one of the following places, or a place of your own, and write a descriptive paragraph of 100–150 words. Follow each of the prewriting steps for descriptive paragraphs on page 547.

1. A crowded department store during a sale
2. The cafeteria during lunch hour
3. An empty football stadium
4. An empty movie theater
5. A beach at night (or dawn, or sunset)
6. A park during a snowfall (or heavy rainstorm)
7. The street outside your home at 5:00 A.M.
8. A room in a museum
9. A classroom during a test
10. The kitchen of a restaurant

Writing a Paragraph That Describes a Person

21c. A descriptive paragraph may describe a person.

All the suggestions that you have read so far also apply to paragraphs that describe a person. Descriptive details about people should be as specific as you can make them. You may write about what they wear, how they move, what their facial features look like, what their voices sound like. The following paragraph describes Julian Lennon, John Lennon's son.

> He is dressed in cowboy boots, faded jeans, a gray T-shirt with cutoff sleeves. His features are soft and sensual in repose, though his face is usually in constant motion: his eyebrows dart up and down, he widens his eyes, tilts his head, and these gestures are, as he is, simultaneously expressive and evasive. His face is pale, dominated by a close-mouthed smile that turns the corners of his mouth straight upward, and by his eyes, which sparkle with the mischief of someone who knows a secret he isn't telling.
>
> ELIZABETH KAYE

EXERCISE 8. Writing a Topic Sentence. Write a topic sentence for the paragraph about Julian Lennon. In your topic sentence, indicate the person you are writing about and the main impression that the paragraph will create about the person.

EXERCISE 9. Writing a Descriptive Paragraph About a Person. Find a photograph in a newspaper or magazine that clearly shows a person's face and body. Observe the photograph carefully, and write a descriptive paragraph in which you convey a main impression of the person. Make up any additional information you wish.

GUIDELINES FOR REVISING DESCRIPTIVE PARAGRAPHS

1. Does the paragraph have a topic sentence that conveys a main impression about the subject?

2. Does the paragraph contain enough concrete and sensory details to support that main impression? Are additional details needed?

3. Does the paragraph contain any unnecessary information that distracts the reader and destroys the paragraph's unity?

4. Are the details in the paragraph arranged in spatial order or in some other logical order?

5. Does the paragraph contain vague words that could be replaced by specific words? Do specific nouns, strong verbs, and precise modifiers make the description exact and interesting?

6. Would transitional expressions make the description easier to understand?

7. Would a comparison or figurative language help the reader to visualize the object, person, or place being described?

REVIEW EXERCISE B. Improving a Weak Descriptive Paragraph. Rewrite the following paragraph. Add specific details, and replace vague nouns and verbs with specific ones. You may make up any additional information you need. The questions following the paragraph will help you think of additional details that will strengthen the paragraph.

The girl walked to the door of the house. She had long hair. She wore ordinary clothes. She looked worried and nervous. She carried something in her right hand. She waited next to the door.

1. What does the girl look like? How old is she? How tall? Is she slim or heavy? What color is her hair? How does she wear it?
2. What exactly is the girl wearing? What color are her clothes? Is the girl's appearance neat or sloppy?
3. How can an observer tell that she is worried and nervous? How does she move? What is the expression on her face?
4. What is she carrying in her right hand?
5. What does the house look like? Why is the girl waiting at the door? What does she do while she waits?
6. What sounds can the girl hear? What can she smell?

THE EXPOSITORY PARAGRAPH

Expository paragraphs give information about a topic or explain something. For example, a paragraph defining the word *democracy* is an expository paragraph of definition. A paragraph that gives a step-by-step report on a science experiment is a *process* paragraph, one that tells how to make or do something. Expository paragraphs are usually developed with facts, statistics, examples, reasons, or some combination of these types of details.

Prewriting for an Expository Paragraph

Whenever you give someone information or an explanation, you want to present your ideas and details as clearly as possible. The surest way to do this is to plan what you will say. In writing exposition, you can organize your plan by using the following prewriting steps:

1. Choose a limited topic that you can cover adequately in a single paragraph.
2. Identify the audience for whom you are writing, and decide exactly what your purpose is.

3. Gather specific information related to your topic. You may need to use reference books and other library sources to look for facts, statistics, and examples. You may also find other kinds of information. Take notes as you read.

4. Write a topic sentence that states your paragraph's main idea.

5. Choose only the information that directly supports the main idea, and arrange the information in a logical order.

Writing an Expository Paragraph with Facts and Statistics

21d. An expository paragraph may be developed with facts and statistics.

A *fact* is a statement that can be proved to be true, and a *statistic* is a numerical fact that has been carefully collected, checked, and recorded. The paragraph that follows is about the career of a professional basketball player. How many facts are included in this paragraph?

> Marques Haynes was on the road again, just as he has been every season since he left Langston nearly 40 years ago. He won't admit to his exact age—"I'm 37½ and holding," the man says—but he figures to be 60 or thereabouts, assuming he was 21 when he graduated from Langston in '46. That was about 12,000 basketball games ago, Haynes estimates, played during an odyssey of more than four million miles with the Globetrotters (1947–'53); the original Harlem Magicians ('53–72); the Globetrotters again ('72–79); Meadowlark Lemon's Bucketeers ('79–81); the Harlem Wizards ('81–83); and finally his own Harlem Magicians again. It is an odyssey that has taken him to 97 countries and to so many American cities, towns, and hamlets that he is hard put, glancing at a map, to find a place he hasn't been.
>
> WILLIAM NACK

The following paragraph uses both facts and statistics to give information about the earth's oceans.

The ocean covers 71 percent of the Earth's surface.
But what we see is, of course, only the top of it. On the
average, the ocean is 2.3 miles (3.7 kilometers) deep. The
total volume of the ocean is about 300 million cubic miles
(1,200 million cubic kilometers). That means if you built a
square tank 36 miles (58 kilometers) on each side and poured
all the ocean water into it, you would have to build the walls
as high as the Moon in order to hold it all.

ISAAC ASIMOV

**EXERCISE 10. Writing an Expository Paragraph Based
on Facts and Statistics.** Write an expository paragraph
based on the information given. You need not use all of the
information.

Details:
  a. Roberto Clemente, one of baseball's all-time great out-
     fielders and hitters
  b. Tried to help others, especially young people in Puerto
     Rico, where he was born and grew up
  c. Humanitarian—person who tried to help others
  d. In 1972 after earthquake in Managua, Nicaragua,
     Clemente appealed to Puerto Ricans on radio and TV:
     contribute food and supplies for Managuans
  e. Raised more than $150,000; 26 tons of supplies
  f. New Year's Eve, 1972—Clemente on flight from San Juan,
     Puerto Rico, to Managua to deliver supplies
  g. Plane took off at 9:00 P.M.; crashed at sea—no survivors
  h. Clemente mourned as *"un gran hombre—un hombre de
     buen corazón"* (a great man—a man of good heart)

Writing an Expository Paragraph with Examples

**21e. An expository paragraph may be developed with exam-
ples.**

Expository paragraphs often contain specific examples (instances) of a generalization made in a topic sentence. In the

following paragraph, the writer uses examples to develop the main idea. What is that idea?

> The story of David with his slingshot slaying the clumsy giant has delighted children for at least three thousand years. David was an early example of a common type of folk hero—the one who fights with skill and daring against superior force and wins. Sometime before David's triumph in the valley of Elah, Odysseus was in Sicily winning his battle of wits against the Cyclops. Similar stories are found in the folklore of nations all over the world.
>
> FREEMAN DYSON

EXERCISE 11. Writing an Expository Paragraph Developed with Examples. Write a paragraph of 100–150 words based on one of the following topic sentences and the suggested examples. You may add facts and examples if you wish, or you may choose a topic of your own.

1. Home accidents are often caused by carelessness that can be avoided.
   a. Dropping pins or needles on the floor—stepped on by bare feet
   b. Overloading electrical outlets
   c. Leaving skates or other toys in halls and on stairs
   d. Leaving medicines and poisonous substances within the reach of small children
2. Through the centuries, people have discovered many ways to preserve foods for long periods.
   a. Pickling and preserving vegetables and fruits
   b. Curing and smoking meats
   c. Canning a wide variety of foods
   d. Freezing fresh fruits, vegetables, meats, dinners
   e. Irradiating fresh fruits and vegetables
3. Team members need to develop many skills to create a championship football team.
   a. Accurate passing
   b. Speed and evasiveness

    c. Determined blocking

    d. Quick thinking

    e. Strength for long passes

4. The American public is deeply interested in sports events.

    a. Sports sections in daily newspapers

    b. Popular magazines that deal solely with sports

    c. TV and radio broadcasts of regular and special sports events

    d. Crowded baseball parks and football stadiums

EXERCISE 12. Writing a Paragraph Developed with Examples. Write a paragraph of about one hundred words in which you use one or more examples to support the idea stated in the topic sentence. Use the following suggestions, or choose a topic of your own.

1. A weekend day can be enjoyable even if it's pouring or snowing outside.

2. Athletes can testify that constant and consistent practice will eventually pay off.

3. When you're prepared for an argument, you never get one; arguments seem always to take you by surprise.

4. People can take many positive steps to keep themselves healthy.

5. If you live in a city, you can do many leisure-time activities for little or no money.

6. We take for granted today many conveniences that were entirely unknown fifty years ago.

7. We should add to our list of national holidays several new ones that honor important people and events.

8. Driving a car seems to bring out the worst in some people, while others remain as courteous behind the wheel as they are on foot.

9. Schools need to try different techniques to prevent students from quitting high school.

10. Everyone dances, but dancing varies greatly in different cultures and in different times.

Writing a Paragraph of Definition

21f. An expository paragraph may be developed with a definition.

A special type of expository paragraph is a *paragraph of definition*. The first step in defining a word is to place it in its general class.

EXAMPLES A *skunk* is a type of *mammal*.
An *oboe* is a *musical instrument*.

A definition goes on to mention the specific characteristics that distinguish the subject from all other members of its general class. For example, the following notes list characteristics that distinguish the skunk from all other mammals.

EXAMPLE *Skunk*—related to weasel; bushy tail; small, about size of cat; black fur, generally with two white stripes down its back; gives off terrible-smelling liquid when it is attacked; nocturnal (active during night, sleeps during day)

In a paragraph of definition, the topic sentence mentions the general class to which the subject belongs and at least one characteristic. Succeeding sentences list other characteristics, examples, and additional information. The following paragraph defines the term *Impressionism* as it applies to painting.

Impressionism is a type of painting that began in France during the 1870's. The Impressionists tried to capture the impression of an object in nature with short brush strokes of pure color. They were especially concerned with the effects of sunlight and often painted outdoors. Impressionist painters include Claude Monet, Camille Pissaro, Alfred Sisley, Edgar Degas, and Pierre Auguste Renoir. Impressionism had a profound effect on paint-

topic sentence
characteristics

examples

importance of

ing. Before Impressionism, artists tried to
paint their subjects almost photographically.
After Impressionism, artists felt free to express themselves in any way they wished.

Impressionism

EXERCISE 13. Writing a Paragraph of Definition. Write a
paragraph defining and explaining one of the following terms.
Use a dictionary or an encyclopedia to gather information.

1. Bat (the animal)
2. Success
3. Diamond
4. Love
5. Microwave oven
6. Responsibility
7. Irrigation
8. Chrysanthemum
9. Iroquois
10. Democracy

PREWRITING Choose one of the terms (or a term of your
own), and write a one-sentence definition. Include in this definition the class to which the term belongs and one of its characteristics. Under this sentence, list as many other characteristics as you
can think of. (Use a dictionary or reference book for help.) Then
list several examples. Arrange the most important details from
your list in a logical order. Begin with the class, then mention
characteristics, examples, and other information.

WRITING, REVISING, AND PROOFREADING Write a first draft
based on your prewriting notes. When you revise, check especially for clarity. Have you defined your term adequately? Have you
left out any important characteristics? If appropriate, have you
given enough examples? Refer to the Guidelines for Revising
Expository Paragraphs on page 561 and the Guidelines for
Proofreading on page 487.

Writing a Paragraph That Explains a Process

21g. An expository paragraph may explain a process.

A *process paragraph* explains how to make or do something.
When you write a process paragraph, assume that your audience

is completely unfamiliar with the process. Your first step is to choose a process that can be explained adequately in a paragraph. For example, you would not write about how to maintain a ten-speed bike; the subject is too general. You would have to choose a limited topic, such as how to check the brakes.

Your most important prewriting task is to list the separate steps that are necessary to complete the process. Next, arrange the steps in chronological order, the order in which they must be done. As part of your prewriting notes, you also need to define unfamiliar terms and list any necessary materials, or tools.

In the following paragraph, the writers explain how to do the basic forward stroke in paddling a canoe.

> In the flat waters of Florida, most of your effort will go into strokes designed to move the canoe forward in as straight a line as possible. **Even people who have never been in a canoe before seem to know instinctively how to execute the forward cruising stroke.** Bring the paddle forward, plant the entire blade in the water, and draw it back slightly past your shoulders. Simple. And by observing a few more points, it can become the kind of stroke you can repeat a thousand times a day without tiring. Be sure to reach forward slightly at the start of each stroke. The power comes when the blade is perpendicular to the surface, not at the end of the stroke as it flattens out in the water. And be sure to draw the paddle back parallel to the center line of the canoe, not the side. Otherwise, your partner will wind up fighting your efforts.
>
> MIKE TONER and PAT TONER

EXERCISE 14. Writing a Paragraph Explaining a Process.
Write a paragraph explaining how to do something. Use one of the following topics or choose one of your own.

1. How to button a button
2. How to take a photograph
3. How to eat spaghetti
4. How to study for a final exam
5. How to do a somersault

6. How to whistle
7. How to telephone long-distance
8. How to blow-dry your hair
9. How to tie a pair of shoelaces
10. How to tell time on a clock with hands

PREWRITING Make sure the topic you have chosen is limited enough for a paragraph. If not, limit it further. Then divide the process into separate steps, and arrange the steps in chronological order. List any materials, tools, or supplies necessary to complete the process, and define any unfamiliar terms. Try to imagine what someone unfamiliar with the process would need to know.

WRITING AND REVISING Using your prewriting notes, tell the reader each step in the order in which it should be done. Consider using transitional expressions (*first, then, next, finally,* etc.) to help clarify the order. When you have finished writing the first draft, reread the paragraph to see if the process is clearly explained. You might have someone else read it to see if he or she can understand what you have written. Use the following guidelines for revising.

GUIDELINES FOR REVISING EXPOSITORY PARAGRAPHS

1. Does the paragraph have a topic sentence that clearly states the paragraph's main idea?
2. Do all of the ideas and details directly support the main idea? Does the paragraph contain enough information?
3. Is the information presented in a logical order?
4. Are sentences smoothly linked to one another by devices that ensure coherence (pronouns, key words and phrases, rephrasing, transitional expressions)?
5. Are sentences varied in structure and length?
6. Are the language and content appropriate for the intended audience and purpose?
7. Can the choice of words be improved?

REVIEW EXERCISE C. Writing Expository Paragraphs.
Write an expository paragraph that gives information about a subject or defines a term or tells how to make or do something. Use one of the following limited topics or a limited topic of your own choice.

1. Equipment and supplies for an overnight hike
2. Work of an airport traffic controller
3. Three most interesting places to visit in this community
4. How to swim underwater
5. How to save money when shopping for food
6. How to wash a car
7. Definition of *termite*
8. Definition of *courage*
9. How to register to vote in this community
10. Qualifications for applying to the police academy

THE PERSUASIVE PARAGRAPH

Persuasive writing tries to convince the reader that an opinion is true. Persuasive writing may also attempt to persuade the reader to do something specific. To accomplish these purposes, a persuasive paragraph presents an *argument*. The argument is made up of an opinion that is supported by reasons and evidence.

Prewriting for a Persuasive Paragraph

To present a convincing argument, you must have your ideas and supporting information well organized so that your readers can follow your train of thought. Sometimes your reasons are so clear and convincing to you that you have difficulty in organizing your argument. You can avoid such difficulty by using the following prewriting steps to create your argument.

1. Choose a topic that is a serious issue, not merely a matter of personal preference.

2. Write a topic sentence that clearly and precisely expresses your opinion on the issue. Check to make sure the topic sentence states an opinion, not a fact.

3. List as many reasons as you can think of to support your opinion. Back up your opinion with accurate facts, examples, incidents, and other information.

4. Identify your audience. Consider what they already know about the topic and what background information you will have to give them.

5. Choose the two or three strongest reasons. Make sure they are different and do not merely repeat the same idea in different words.

6. Arrange the ideas in a logical order. Try the order of importance, with the most important reason first or last.

Distinguishing Fact from Opinion

A persuasive paragraph is based on an opinion about a debatable issue. A fact is not debatable and is therefore not a suitable topic for a persuasive paragraph.

FACT According to a Nielsen survey, children aged 2–5 watch more than twenty-seven hours of TV a week.

OPINION Parents should allow children aged 2–5 to watch no more than fourteen hours of TV a week.

FACT Four out of ten high-school students in this country drop out of school before they graduate.

OPINION The school system should start a system of peer counseling (students counseling each other) to help keep students from dropping out of school.

Choosing a Topic

Keep two things in mind as you choose a topic for a persuasive paragraph:

1. *The topic should be one about which people have differing opinions.*

NOT SUITABLE   Students should learn to write well. [Most people would agree.]

SUITABLE   Every eighth-grade student should be required to write two compositions a week.

NOT SUITABLE   Students should take classes that will prepare them for living in the modern world. [Most people would agree.]

SUITABLE   Every eighth-grade student should be required to take a course in using computers.

2. *The topic should not simply state a preference about a matter of personal taste.* A persuasive paragraph should deal with a serious issue or concern, not with the writer's likes and dislikes.

NOT SUITABLE   Pizza tastes best with mushrooms and onions. [personal preference]

SUITABLE   The school cafeteria should not sell any junk food, including soda, cakes, sweets, and non-nutritious snacks.

NOT SUITABLE   History is more interesting than math. [personal preference]

SUITABLE   Every high-school student should be required to take a one-year course in world history.

Planning a Position Statement for Persuasion

21h. Write a topic sentence that states an opinion about a debatable issue.

The topic sentence for a persuasive paragraph is sometimes called a *position statement.* It should state the writer's opinion clearly and precisely. If possible, the topic sentence should make a specific suggestion.

WEAK   Something needs to be done about the long lines in the school cafeteria.

WEAK   People have to wait too long to buy their lunches in the school cafeteria.

IMPROVED   To relieve the crowding in the school cafeteria, students should be allowed to eat lunch outside of school.

The first two topic sentences merely state the problem (overcrowding in the cafeteria). The third topic sentence states the problem and also suggests a specific solution.

EXERCISE 15. Identifying Effective Topic Sentences.
Some of the following topic sentences are suitable for a persuasive paragraph; others are not. Decide which topic sentences are suitable. If the topic sentence is suitable, write *S*. If it is not suitable, write *NS*, and be prepared to tell what is wrong with the topic sentence.

1. Every eighth-grade student should be required to participate in at least one after-school activity.
2. Something should be done to reduce crime in this community.
3. Handicapped people should be treated fairly.
4. It's much better to live in the quiet country than in a big, noisy city.
5. Drivers and passengers in automobiles should be required to wear seat belts in order to reduce injuries and deaths in automobile accidents.
6. Advertisements for beer and other alcoholic drinks should be banned from TV and radio.
7. Destruction of school property by vandals must be stopped somehow.
8. Bicycling is better than jogging.
9. All students enrolled in physical education classes should do aerobic exercises three times a week.
10. All dog owners should be required to use leashes when walking their dogs.

Writing a Persuasive Paragraph with Reasons

21i. Develop a persuasive paragraph with reasons that build a logical argument.

The topic sentence states an opinion, and the supporting sentences give reasons to support that opinion. Reasons may be statements of facts, statistics, examples, or incidents.

In the following paragraph, the writer states an opinion about a debatable issue. (Notice that in this paragraph the first two sentences express the main idea.) How many reasons does the writer give to support the opinion?

> A state law should be passed requiring all students who participate in extracurricular activities to have grades of 70 or above in all of their academic subjects. If students fail to meet this requirement, they should be suspended from all extracurricular activities. First of all, many students devote so much time to extracurricular activities that they neglect their academic studies. Students need to remember that they are in school to learn, not to play. Second, students need to pass academic subjects because these subjects prepare them for jobs and for their lives as adults. That is the whole point of education. Most important, this proposed law will motivate students to work harder at academic subjects. Given the motivation and extra tutoring, every student can pass all academic subjects and can feel successful in school.

EXERCISE 16. Analyzing a Persuasive Paragraph.
Reread the preceding model paragraph, and answer the questions that follow.

1. How many reasons does the writer give to support the opinion in the topic sentence?
2. In what order does the writer give these reasons? Which is the most important one? Do you agree or disagree that this is the most important reason? Explain why.
3. Can you think of any other reasons to support the opinion? If so, list them briefly.

4. What is your opinion about the proposed law? If you support it, list your reasons briefly, in order of importance. If you oppose it, list your reasons briefly, in order of importance.

5. Ask other people—friends, family, teachers, coaches—what they think of the proposed law. Take notes on what they say.

EXERCISE 17. Writing a Persuasive Paragraph. Reread your answers to questions 3, 4, and 5 in Exercise 16. Write a paragraph stating your opinion about the proposed new law. Give at least three reasons to support your opinion, and arrange your reasons in order of importance. You might use some of the following information if you wish, or you might gather information about the specific situation in your own school.

Details:
   a. At Irving High, 119 of 700 students participating in extracurricular activities failed academic subjects
   b. If new law goes into effect, weaker students may drop out or take easy courses
   c. Only reason some students stay in school is to participate in extracurricular activities
   d. Athletic coaches offering students special tutoring programs
   e. Superintendent of schools: "People don't get breaks on the job or in college; they must learn that lesson in school"
   f. Athletics keeps many students interested in school; teaches important life skills
   g. Educators, many parents, business groups support proposed law—stresses academic excellence
   h. Committee sponsoring new law: "Young people must learn that work takes priority over play"
   i. 52 percent of freshmen on athletic teams failing one or more courses
   j. 40 percent of students at one high school stay after school for extracurricular activities

EXERCISE 18. Writing a Persuasive Paragraph. Choose one of the following topics, or a topic of your own, and write a persuasive paragraph. Be sure to express your opinion clearly and precisely in a topic sentence. Then back up your opinion with at least two reasons. Give information (facts, statistics, examples, etc.) to support your reasons.

1. An eleven-month school year for all students
2. An optional extra period at the beginning or at the end of the school day
3. The elimination of a dress code in schools, allowing students to wear whatever they want to wear
4. A peer-counseling program in which students talk to and advise fellow students who have problems
5. The same minimum wage for teen-agers and adults
6. The drafting of women into the armed services
7. The national rationing of water
8. A law prohibiting cigarette smoking in movie theaters, stores, restaurants, and other public places
9. A law prohibiting the manufacture and sale of leaded gasoline to eliminate lead from the air
10. A law prohibiting the use of animals in medical research

GUIDELINES FOR REVISING PERSUASIVE PARAGRAPHS

1. Is the paragraph about a debatable, serious topic? Is the topic sufficiently limited?
2. Does the topic sentence state the writer's opinion clearly and precisely?
3. Is the topic sentence developed with sufficient reasons that directly support the writer's opinion?
4. Are the writer's ideas clear and easy to understand?
5. Are the writer's ideas arranged in an effective order?

Writing a Letter to the Editor

A *letter to the editor* is a special type of persuasive writing. Letters to the editor appear on the editorial pages of newspapers and magazines. The writer may comment on an issue or problem or on a story or article that appeared in the publication. The writer may also praise or criticize the work of a group or an individual.

A letter to the editor should be brief, concise, and clear. As in a persuasive paragraph, the writer of a letter to the editor should express an opinion and support it with reasons or with other information.

To the Editor:

I believe that this community should have middle schools for grades 6 through 8. Presently, students attend elementary schools from kindergarten through grade 6 and junior high schools from grades 7 through 9. I believe that seventh and eighth-grade students require the close supervision of the middle-school structure. These students are definitely too big for elementary school but too young for the independence of junior high. Therefore, the best solution is to separate this group of young students into a middle school. There they are less likely to be adversely influenced by older teen-agers who have got into one kind of trouble or another. In a middle school, students are also more likely to receive the individual attention of teachers and administrators, who are less burdened by large numbers of problem students. Finally, middle-school teachers, who know their students personally, are more likely to communicate with parents when students need some kind of help.

A CONCERNED PARENT

EXERCISE 19. Writing a Letter to the Editor. Write a letter to the editor in which you agree or disagree with the opinion stated in the preceding letter. Give reasons and information to back up your opinion.

EXERCISE 20. Writing a Letter to the Editor. Choose one of the topics listed in Exercise 18, or choose a topic of your own. Write a letter to the editor of your local or school newspaper. Be sure to express your opinion clearly and precisely in a topic sentence. Then back up your opinion with at least two reasons and specific information.

REVIEW EXERCISE D. Writing a Letter to the Editor. Write a letter to the editor of your school or local newspaper. You may write a letter either praising the work of a specific individual in the school or community or pointing out a problem and suggesting a specific solution. Give reasons and information to support your opinion.

CHAPTER 21 WRITING REVIEW

Writing Different Types of Paragraphs. Write each of the following types of paragraphs:

1. A narrative paragraph about something funny that happened to you or to someone you know
2. A descriptive paragraph about a place (house, apartment, community) where you would like to live someday
3. An expository paragraph giving information about a topic you are interested in
4. A persuasive paragraph or letter to the editor giving specific suggestions about how to improve something in your school or community

PREWRITING For each type of paragraph, refer to the appropriate list of prewriting hints in this chapter.

WRITING AND REVISING Before you begin to write a first draft, make sure that you have a working plan that lists a topic sentence and the details you plan to include in your writing. Refer to the appropriate guidelines in this chapter for revising each type of paragraph. See also pages 533–36 for more informaton about revising paragraphs.

CHAPTER 22

Writing Stories

USING NARRATION AND DESCRIPTION

Have you ever heard anyone described as a "natural storyteller"? Do you know someone who can hold everyone's attention when relating a personal experience? Such persons use gestures, facial expressions, and tone of voice to make their stories vivid and interesting, but they are also careful to organize their stories. They make sure that their stories lead somewhere and end at a definite point, and that what they say is clear to their listeners. They are skilled in the art of *narration*.

Not all storytellers, however, can write a story as well as they can tell it. They may not be as skilled in using words as they are in using gestures and facial expressions. Someone writing a story does not have personal contact with the audience and must rely on words to make contact. Yet, as you know from your reading, written stories can be as interesting, as funny, or as thrilling as a story that is told.

Over the years, fine writers have made us aware of how much can be done with words alone. They have shown that even the simplest story must have a plan behind it, and they have used many effective devices in writing their stories. In this chapter, you will learn the basic principles of planning a story and some of the devices that make a story vivid and interesting.

PREWRITING

CHOOSING A SUBJECT FOR A STORY

22a. Choose a subject that is appropriate for your purpose.

You know that the purpose of any narrative is to tell *what happened*. The story may be a true account or a fictional account, but it usually begins with a problem or a conflict and then tells what happened as a result of that problem. The problem or conflict does not have to be serious nor does it have to be physical. It may be a humorous situation, such as being frightened by a ghost who turns out to be your younger brother looking for his pet turtle. It may be an internal problem, such as a teen-ager's fear of facing other students after doing poorly on a test or after making a mistake in a soccer game.

When you look for a subject for your own story, remember that your readers will be interested in the problems and experiences of other people—your own experiences, those of people you know, or the fictional experiences of people you create out of your imagination.

To search for a subject, start with what you already know. Read through your writer's notebook, looking for notes about experiences that were especially exciting or moving. Perhaps you will find a note about how nervous you were on the day of tryouts for the swimming team. Talk to friends or family members about experiences they have shared with you. One of your relatives might remind you of your visit to the city museum the day the fire alarm went off. Another way to search for subjects is to brainstorm (see pages 461–62), searching your mind for events or moments that stand out because of a problem or struggle and someone's attempt to solve it.

When you have identified several possible subjects for your story, choose the one you find most interesting. If it is a personal experience, be sure it is one that you are willing to share with others.

EXERCISE 1. Identifying Purpose.   The following list contains some subjects that are appropriate for a narrative purpose and some that are not. Number your paper 1–10. For those subjects that are appropriate, write *A*. For those that are inappropriate, write *I*.

1. How my illness spoiled our trip to Washington, D.C.
2. Finding your way around the Smithsonian Institution
3. The importance of participating in athletics
4. How I learned a lesson from a younger person
5. Why students should spend at least one hour studying each night
6. How to cook eggs sunny side up
7. My quarrel with Julian about the class party
8. The difference between reading a science fiction story and watching a science fiction movie
9. The time our car stalled in a blizzard
10. How I took the wrong plane and ended up in the Fiji Islands

EXERCISE 2. Searching for Story Subjects.   Review your writer's notebook, talk to friends and relatives, or brainstorm to remember experiences that could be appropriate for a narrative. Make a list of at least ten problems or conflicts that you could use as the basis for a story. Use one or more of the following questions to guide you in your search.

1. What was the most exciting day of my life?
2. What was the most serious problem I ever had to face?
3. What was the most difficult decision I ever had to make?
4. What experiences of my friends or relatives were especially exciting or challenging?
5. What happened the first time I, or someone I know or have read about, tried to snow-ski, water-ski, skate, give a speech, change a bicycle tire, etc.?
6. What problems have I or other people faced that turned out to be less difficult than expected?

7. If there were one day I could live over again and live differently, what day would that be and how would I live it?
8. What is the worst or best thing that ever happened to me or to someone I know?

EXERCISE 3. **Choosing a Subject for a Story.** From the list of problems or conflicts you developed for Exercise 2, choose one you feel is especially interesting. If it is a personal experience, be sure that you feel comfortable sharing it with others.

LIMITING SUBJECTS TO MANAGEABLE TOPICS

22b. Limit your subject to a specific problem or experience.

Subjects for brief stories, like subjects for brief compositions of any kind, must be limited to a topic that can be handled in a few paragraphs or pages. An appropriate topic for a short narrative is a specific problem or a specific conflict.

A subject such as your great-grandparents' struggles on the western frontier would contain enough action details for a book. A story about all the problems and conflicts you have faced with your best friend would be vague and unfocused. You would be forced to tell about several experiences—the time you were not invited to your friend's party, the time the two of you got into trouble for going to a movie after school, the time your friend loaned you a new tape player, and so forth. As a result, you would not be able to include any of the specific details that make a story interesting to read. If you limited your subject to one of these experiences—the time your friend loaned you the new tape player, for example—you would be able to add precise details and develop your story in an interesting way.

EXERCISE 4. **Limiting a Subject for a Brief Story.** Some of the following subjects are too broad for a brief story and would be more appropriate for a very long story or a book. Others are suitably limited for a story of two or three pages. Number your paper 1–10 and write *B* if the subject is too broad and *L* if the subject is appropriately limited.

1. The history of the English monarchy
2. The time I convinced my friend to enter a skating (or some other) competition
3. The time I forgot to study for a history test
4. An encounter with a runaway horse
5. Flying a balloon across the United States
6. The adventures of a sailor
7. My first hockey game
8. How I lost a race and won a friend
9. My father's childhood in Maryland
10. How I nearly lost my paper route

EXERCISE 5. Limiting Your Subject for a Brief Story.
Decide whether the subject you selected for Exercise 3, or any other subject of your choice, is limited to a specific problem or experience. If it is not appropriately limited, rewrite it so that it is suitable for a brief story. Save your limited subject for later work.

THINKING ABOUT PURPOSE AND AUDIENCE

22c. Think about the purpose and audience of your story.

Throughout the writing process—whether you are planning, writing, or revising—you need to be aware of your purpose in writing as well as the readers for whom you are writing. As you know, the purpose of a story is to tell what happened, to interest the audience in an experience or a problem and its outcome. Keeping that purpose in mind will help you to shape your story and make it more interesting.

Your audience may vary. It may be your teacher and your classmates, another audience your teacher assigns, or a group of people of your own choice. All audiences, no matter who they are, have special needs and interests that you must identify and keep in mind in order to write effectively.

CRITICAL THINKING:
Analyzing the Needs and Interests of an Audience

Analysis is the critical thinking skill you use when you divide something into its parts and study the relationships between the parts. When you are writing, you are concerned with how the needs and interests of your audience will affect what you can write. To analyze the needs and interests of your readers, ask questions such as the following ones:

1. What background information does my audience already have about my story?
2. What background information will my audience need in order to understand my story?
3. What kinds of problems and experiences will my audience find interesting?
4. What can I do to make the problem or experience I want to tell about interesting to my audience?
5. How will my audience's knowledge and background affect the words I use?

Suppose, for example, you are writing a story about the time an alligator climbed your back fence in pursuit of your dog. Your readers will be your classmates in your new school in Minnesota. Your analysis of your audience's needs and interests might be as follows:

1. They know that alligators live in warm climates. They know that alligators sometimes attack small animals and people.
2. They need to know that I was living in Florida rather than in Minnesota. They need to know that an alligator can move fast on land and that it can climb a wire fence.
3. They are interested in daring adventures. They are interested in adventures of people their own age and in adventures with happy endings.
4. I need to get them interested in the danger to the dog and in the idea that an alligator can actually climb a fence. I should wait until the end of the story to let them know that the game officials came in time to save the dog.

5. They will understand almost any word that is a part of my vocabulary. If I use difficult words such as "interceded" and "assault," they may be confused or think that I am showing off.

EXERCISE 6. Analyzing the Needs and Interests of an Audience. Choose one limited subject and one audience from the following lists. Write the subject and audience you have chosen at the top of a sheet of paper. Use the questions on page 576 to analyze how the audience's needs and interests would affect the subject you have chosen. Write out your answers to the questions. Your teacher may ask you to discuss your answers in class.

Limited Subjects	*Audiences*
1. The night we saw a spaceship over our house	a. adults who read a local newspaper
2. Why I came in second in the spelling contest	b. seven-year-old children in Japan
3. How I saved my cousin from the ocean's undertow	c. eighth-grade students in your school

EXERCISE 7. Analyzing the Needs and Interests of Your Audience. Use your limited subject from Exercise 5 or any other limited subject of your choice. Think about the people who will be reading your story. If your teacher has not assigned a special audience, your readers will be your teacher and your classmates. Answer the five questions on page 576. Save your analysis for later use.

GATHERING INFORMATION FOR YOUR STORY

22d. Identify action details, and gather information for your story.

To gather information for a narrative, you must focus on the question *What happened?* If you are writing about a problem or conflict from your own life, you can review your writer's notebook, talk to friends and relatives about what they remember about the experience, or brainstorm to recall any of your own memories about what happened. If you are writing about an experience or a problem faced by someone else, you can ask that person questions about what happened. You can also start with the question *What happened?* when you are writing about an imaginary event. Ask yourself the question, allowing your thoughts to flow freely over everything that *might* happen.

Whenever you are gathering information for a narrative, the *5 W-How?* questions used by reporters will help you collect the details you need. Notice in the following example how a writer might use the *5 W-How?* questions to gather information.

Who was involved in this experience? My mother and I

What happened? Mother left me at home alone while she went to help a sick neighbor. I got scared. I hid under the bed, and I fell asleep. My mother couldn't find me and was afraid I had drowned in the well. She was angry when she found me.

Where did the experience take place? In our home

When did the actions occur? They started when my mother went to visit a sick friend. They ended when I woke up and crawled out from under the bed.

Why is this experience or this problem and its outcome interesting or important? I discovered how easily concern and relief can turn into anger.

How did I feel? I was afraid of being caught by a ghost or a kidnapper. I wondered why my mother was angry.

EXERCISE 8. Gathering Action Details and Information for a Narrative. Using your limited subject and the information about audience you developed for Exercise 7, or using any other limited subject of your choice, gather action details and information for your narrative. You may refer to your writer's notebook, talk to friends and relatives about what they recall, or brainstorm to recall your own memories or to think through imaginary details. Use the *5 W-How?* questions listed above to guide your thinking. Write your answers to the questions on a sheet of paper and save it for later use.

ARRANGING DETAILS AND DEVELOPING A STORY PLAN

22e. Arrange the action details and information for your story.

The actions in a narrative are usually arranged in the order in which they happened, that is, in chronological order. Notice that the following example of a list of action details is arranged in the order in which the actions happened.

mother was called to take care of a sick person
left me at home alone
no problems before dark
sat outside
as darkness came, decided to go in house
felt sleepy
afraid to sleep on top of bed
crawled under the bed
fell asleep
awakened to sound of voices
heard them searching for me
crawled out from under bed and told them I was there
was surprised because my mother was angry with me rather
    than happy to see me

EXERCISE 9. Arranging Action Details for a Story.   On a sheet of paper, list the following actions in the order you think they would have happened.

felt surprised
car suddenly started rolling
Aunt Renée left me in her car while she ran back into the
    house for something.
went through a fence
pretended I was driving
sideswiped a tree
released the brake
smashed into neighbor's house
turned on the car radio

EXERCISE 10. Arranging Action Details for Your Story.
Arrange the list of action details you gathered for Exercise 8 in
the order in which they happened. Save the list so that you will be
able to use it for a later exercise.

22f. Plan your story before you write it.

Before writing any narrative, whether it is a story about your own
personal experience, a story about someone else's experience, or
a fictional story, work out a rough plan to guide your thinking.
Your plan will help you to include all the necessary details.

Such a plan should list the necessary information. If you
divide your plan into five categories—*When, Where, Who, What
happened,* and *How I felt*—you will be likely to include all the
important information. Notice how easily the information gathered with five of the *5 W-How?* questions (page 578) was
converted to create the following plan.

1. *When:* My mother left me alone and went to visit a sick
friend; I was a small child.
2. *Where:* I was at home.
3. *Who:* My mother and I
4. *What happened:* It became dark and I was afraid. I went
into the house and crawled under the bed to hide. I fell asleep.
Mother came home. She couldn't find me. She was afraid I was in
the well. I woke up. I told her where I was. She was angry rather
than happy.
5. *How I felt:* Puzzled that she was angry with me rather than
happy to see me

A story need not end with a statement of how you felt about
the events described. A personal experience narrative often will
suggest the writer's feelings rather than state them. A narrative
about someone else's experiences or about a fictional experience
will often contain only a vague suggestion of the writer's feelings,
or attitude, about the experience.

Read the following personal experience narrative taken from
Barrio Boy. Does it tell *when, where, who, what happened,* and
how the writer felt?

Model Personal Experience Narrative

A neighbor who lived at the other end of the block, across from the orchard, came to our cottage in distress. There was a sick person at their house and help was needed. It was a situation in which I would clearly be in the way. My mother did something unusual; she decided to leave me alone in the cottage. . . .

While the twilight lasted I had no problems. I sat by the back door facing the orchard, thinking of many things, alert for the footsteps of Doña Henriqueta. But as night fell and the darkness deepened, I decided that since I was taking care of the house I might as well be inside of it. . . .

My mother had said that if I felt sleepy I was to get into bed. That would have been very well if she had been there and it was still light outside. Now it was certainly the wrong thing to do. The back door would be open and I might be caught asleep on top of the bed by a ghost or a kidnapper.

I crawled under the bed wrapped in my sarape and wedged myself on the floor as close to the door as possible. I intended to stay awake and crawl out as soon as my mother was home.

I was awakened by voices in the room. By the candlelight I could see feet shuffling by me. People were calling my name. I heard my mother say, "The well. Please look in the well again."

I wormed my way from under the bed, stuck out my head, and said, "Here I am."

I could not understand why a mother should not be overjoyed to find that her son had not fallen into the well and drowned but had only been asleep under the bed. She wanted to know since when I had forgotten that I was to answer instantly when I was called.

ERNESTO GALARZA

EXERCISE 11. Creating a Story Plan. Prepare a story plan and save it for later use. Use the list of details you organized in Exercise 10, or any other limited subject and list of details of your choice.

WRITING

CHOOSING DETAILS

22g. Choose details to make the action vivid.

Reread the model narrative (page 581). Notice the use of details to tell exactly what happened. Suppose the following paragraph were substituted for all but the first two paragraphs in the model. Would the story be as effective?

> When it was dark, I went into the house. Then I felt sleepy, but I was afraid to sleep out in the open. I crawled under the bed to hide. Later I was awakened by voices. My mother was afraid I had fallen into the well. I crawled out and told her I was there.

The use of effective details makes a story vivid. If such details are missing, the reader will lose interest in the story.

(1) Choose specific details.

Compare the following two paragraphs. Which is the more interesting?

1

When the canoe touched the river bank, I told John to push us away with his paddle. Instead he panicked. He got up and tried to climb to the shore. In his efforts, he overturned the canoe. I fell into the water.

2

The canoe glided toward the river bank. I felt a bump as it touched land. "Use your paddle. Push us away," I told John. He put his hand on the side of the canoe and pushed himself to his feet. I yelled at him to sit down, but he wasn't listening. His hands trembled. Awkwardly he teetered on one foot as he reached out to grab a branch that was hanging over the bank. The canoe began to rock. "Sit down!" I yelled. The canoe rocked violently. Suddenly I was thrown from my seat and hit the water with a splash.

Most readers will agree that the second paragraph is the more effective. The first paragraph gives only general information about what happened. The second paragraph tells how John used his hand to push himself up and how he looked (teetering awkwardly) as he tried to leave the canoe. Instead of the general statement *I fell into the water,* the second paragraph gives two specific details: being thrown from the seat and the splash of hitting the water. Also, the second paragraph does more than tell what happened; it *shows* what happened. There is no direct statement about John's panic. A detail, the trembling of John's hands, shows that he was too nervous to follow instructions correctly.

To sum up, the second paragraph is superior in two ways: (1) it gives specific details to make the action vivid, and (2) it avoids general statements and lets the readers draw their own conclusions from the details.

EXERCISE 12. Using Specific Details.   Rewrite one of the following paragraphs. Use specific details to make your readers feel that they are participating in or witnessing the action.

1

There was one minute to go in the last quarter. I caught the pass and ran sixty yards for a touchdown. The crowd cheered.

2

There was a very long line in front of the ticket office when I arrived. I was impatient at first. Then I began to think about something else. When the man behind the window asked me how many tickets I wanted, I was very much surprised.

3

When the leader called on me, I was very nervous. I grew calmer as I explained why our club should donate to the Community Fund. At the end of my speech, the members applauded.

4

The two boys clenched their fists and threatened each other. Each of them wanted to appear brave but did not really want to fight. After the crowd watching them had gone, each muttered a final insult and left.

EXERCISE 13. Writing a Paragraph Using Specific Details. Write a paragraph of fifty to seventy-five words about one of the following situations. Assume that your paragraph is to be part of a longer narrative.

1. Sliding on the ice and bumping into a woman carrying packages
2. Hitting a long, high ball that you think is a home run until the center fielder catches it
3. Being caught in a hailstorm
4. Winning (or losing) a three-legged race at a picnic
5. After riding for twenty minutes, discovering you are on the wrong bus
6. Trying to keep a little boy from crossing the street against the traffic light
7. Helping move furniture during spring-cleaning
8. Saving someone from drowning
9. Making a report to the class
10. Working with your block association

PREWRITING Choose a situation that you find interesting and know something about. If you have not had a similar experience, you may have to draw upon your imagination and write a fictional narrative. Ask yourself the *5 W-How?* questions to gather information about the situation. You may want to use the technique of brainstorming (page 470) or clustering (page 470–471) to gather more specific details. After you have identified several actions and specific details, arrange the actions in chronological order. Write a plan.

WRITING AND REVISING Review your plan and write a first draft. Remember that you need to include specific details to show how the actions occurred. Write freely without stopping to make corrections. If you think of something that you should have mentioned earlier in the paragraph, jot down a note at the side of your paper and come back to it later.

After you have completed your first draft, use the revision guidelines on page 603 and revise your paragraph. Use the proofreading guidelines on page 487 as you proofread your paragraph and make a final copy.

(2) Use specific verbs.

Some verbs describe actions more specifically than others do. The verb *walk,* for example, gives a general idea of an action; the verbs *amble, stroll, swagger,* and *shuffle* give more specific impressions. When used appropriately, such verbs can help the reader form a clear picture of the action. Of course, you should not try to use a vivid verb in every possible situation. If you are simply telling how you get to school in the morning, it would be better to use *walk* than *stroll* or *amble.* If the point is *how* you walk, a more specific verb may be better.

EXERCISE 14. Identifying Specific Verbs. Some of the verbs in the following paragraph are specific, and some are not. List the specific verbs, and be prepared to explain how these verbs make the action vivid.

The circus was a blend of movement, color, and noise. In the center ring, a bareback rider performed. As her horse pranced around the ring, the rider tensed, whirled in the air, and landed neatly on the horse. In another ring, a seal held a large ball in its flippers. A clown dressed in orange, green, and purple tiptoed up and reached out for the ball. The seal yelped. The clown staggered back, threw up his hands, and flopped to the sawdust floor. Above the crowd, aerialists performed their dangerous work. A man swung out on a trapeze, holding a woman by the wrists. Suddenly he released her. As she plunged into space, a third aerialist swooped down just in time and caught her by the wrists.

USING DIALOGUE

22h. **Use dialogue to make your story lively and convincing.**

If you present the direct speech of people, your writing will be livelier and more realistic than if you merely describe their thoughts and feelings indirectly. Direct speech can vividly reveal the personalities of the speakers. Conversation makes a story seem more lifelike and exciting.

In the following passage, the characters are engaged in conversation, but what they say is described—it is not reported directly. The result is a dull, uninteresting paragraph.

> My friends Sue and Edie went abalone fishing at Hondo Beach. When I met them, I asked where they had been. They told me. I asked what an abalone was. Sue said it was a shellfish. I asked how they caught abalone. Sue said they waded out into the water and pried them off the rocks. Edie said the water was very cold, and that the abalone were hard to pry off the rocks. I wanted to know if the abalone were good to eat. Sue said yes, if properly cooked; but Edie said they were awfully tough.

In the following paragraphs, the conversation is written as dialogue. Notice how much more interesting this second version is. Notice also that it is much more convincing. The dialogue not only adds liveliness; it also indicates the personalities of the speakers. Sue and Edie sound like real people, each with a distinct personality, and the dialogue shows their personalities.

> I ran into Sue and Edie on the street.
> "Where'd you go yesterday?" I asked them.
> "Abalone fishing at Hondo Beach," Sue said.
> "What's abalone?" I wanted to know.
> "A shellfish."
> "Like oysters?"
> "No more like oysters," Edie snorted, "than a wheelbarrow is like a motorcycle."
> Sue explained, "An abalone has just one top shell, like a snail. It's open at the bottom."

"You fish for 'em with hook and line?"

"Gosh, are you ignorant!" Edie said.

"They stick to the rocks, underwater," Sue said, "and you wade out—"

"In water that's so cold you turn blue," Edie interrupted.

"—and you pry them off the rocks. It's easy."

"Sure," Edie said, "as easy as prying names off plaques."

"What do you do with them?" I asked.

"Eat them," Sue said.

"If you're crazy enough," Edie said. "By rights, you should use them for shoe soles."

"They're not tough if you remember to tenderize them by pounding before you fry them."

"Personally," Edie insisted, "I prefer slabs of old automobile tire fried in axle grease."

One of the problems in writing conversation is to keep the reader aware of who is talking. There are many ways to do this. How many different ways of revealing who is speaking are shown in the passage above? Notice where the speaker is identified—at the beginning, at the end, or in the middle of the speech. With several speeches, there is no identification, yet the reader knows easily who the speaker is because the author has made it clear.

Remember that, as well as adding life to the story, good dialogue helps tell the story. Dialogue should always do at least one of the following things:

1. Tell something about the characters.
2. Tell some of the actions.

Notice how the dialogue in the above model tells a lot about the characters. Compare that dialogue to the very short bits of dialogue in the model on page 581. Do the words of the mother and child tell something about their personalities or tell some of the actions?

Before you write a story with conversation in it, review the rules for punctuation of dialogue on pages 371–76. Remember these three rules:

1. Place quotation marks before and after words that anyone speaks.
2. Use commas to separate a person's speech from the rest of the sentence.
3. Start a new paragraph to indicate a change of speaker.

EXERCISE 15. Using Direct Quotations. The following story is told without direct quotations. Rewrite it, putting the appropriate lines into direct quotations.

A mean, bullying man borrowed a plow from his meek neighbor and failed to return it. Finally the owner of the plow asked for it. The big man said sorrowfully that he could not return it; rats had eaten it up. When the little man left without his plow, the big man laughed and laughed.

Some days later, the big man found that the buzz saw he used to cut up logs had been ruined by somebody. Furious, he went to his little neighbor and shouted that someone had knocked big chunks out of his fine new saw. The little man suggested that the damage must have been done by cats. Wildly, the big man protested that it couldn't have been cats, that it would take mighty tough cats to bite pieces out of a buzz saw. This was so, the little man agreed; in a country where the rats feed on iron, the cats have to be tough.

EXERCISE 16. Writing Dialogue. Select two of the following situations, and write a short conversation to fit each of them. Let the dialogue show the personalities of the speakers.

1. Two motorists have had a collision; each is saying that the accident is the other's fault.
2. Two small boys are bragging about their dogs.
3. Two friends argue about a baseball hero.
4. A girl insists to her parents that she is old enough and capable enough to have a part-time job.
5. A girl tries to persuade her mother to let her skip piano practice that day.
6. Two girls try to persuade a third girl to invite two particular boys to a party she is giving.

7. A girl tries to make her parents see why it is impossible for her to go to a boy cousin's party.

8. A boy tries to convince his parents that his allowance must be increased.

9. A girl is helping a boy with his algebra, but he would rather talk about sports.

10. An uncle treats his nephew like a baby; the boy tries to convince his uncle that he has grown up.

WRITING DESCRIPTION

22i. Use description to make your story vivid and convincing.

A good description makes the reader see, hear, or otherwise experience something. You have already learned how precise details and specific verbs can make the description of action vivid. Description can also improve a story in other ways. A description of a scene can make a reader feel present at the scene. A description of a person may almost make a reader familiar with that person. Properly used, description can convince the reader that what is happening in a story is real because the details seem real.

The longer your story, the more description you will probably use. There is no place for a long description of a person or scene in a very short story, but even here a sentence or two of vivid detail can make the story more effective. In this part of the chapter, you will learn how to use description to improve your stories.

(1) Use details that appeal to the senses.

Before you can write a good description, you must learn to be a sensitive observer. Notice the sights, sounds, and smells around you; and make a mental list of them. For example, what might you observe in the halls when classes are passing at your school? First, you would *see* the students on their way to their classes. Next, you would *hear* them talking with each other or shouting to students across the hall. Finally, you would *feel* some of them jostling you as you passed them.

Just as you learn about life around you through your senses, so you can make a story lifelike by using details that appeal to the senses. The senses you will use most often are *sight* and *hearing,* but many times you will also use *touch, taste,* and *smell.* The more senses you appeal to, the more convincing your description will be.

Read the following model description. How many of the five senses do the details appeal to?

Model Description

I pushed up the high steps and into the aisle of the bus. The shrill screaming, shouting, and laughing were like a wall of noise in front of me. Because we had been waiting in the rain, the air in the bus was steamy and smelled of wet wool. As I tried to squeeze past the boy ahead of me in the aisle, my books began to slide out of my arms. When I grabbed for them, my right hand struck a hockey stick and was twisted backward painfully. The books slipped away. I saw that every seat was taken, but nobody seemed to be sitting down. The aisle was jammed. Everywhere arms were waving and pushing.

EXERCISE 17. Observing Details. Test your powers of observation on your way home from school. How many details can you observe? To which senses do they appeal? List at least ten details and indicate the senses to which they appeal.

EXERCISE 18. Writing a Description. Organize the list of details you observed for Exercise 17. You will probably want to use chronological order, as in the model description above, or spatial order (page 506). Use your arranged list of details to write a one- or two-paragraph description of your trip home.

EXERCISE 19. Adding Descriptive Details. The following paragraphs might belong to stories in which long descriptions would be out of place. The addition of vivid sentences would improve the stories. Rewrite two of the three paragraphs, following the directions in parentheses.

1

At the end of the debate a gentleman stood up. "I've attended many town meetings," he said, "and I've never heard such nonsense as I've heard tonight." Angrily he tore the meeting's agenda into pieces. (Insert two or three sentences to follow the first. Describe how the gentleman looked and spoke.)

2

My sister had worked on the model boat for months. It had occupied most of her spare time. Lovingly she had carved, sanded, and painted it. Now she held it proudly in her hand, displaying it before us. (Write two or three sentences about the boat.)

3

It was a very unpleasant trip. I was relieved when the plane finally arrived at the airport in San Francisco. (Insert several sentences after the first. Show how the trip was unpleasant. Appeal to at least three of the senses.)

(2) Select adjectives and adverbs carefully, and use them sparingly.

As you remember, an adjective describes a noun or pronoun and tells *what kind, which one, how many* or *how much*. An adverb describes a verb, an adjective, or another adverb and tells *when, where, how,* or *to what extent.*

If you do not try to find the adjective or adverb that gives an exact description, you may rely on dull, tired words that have already been used too often. Notice the use of dull, tired words in the following example:

We had a swell time, because the speaker was very interesting. He made some tremendously good remarks. After he finished, the applause was absolutely fabulous. We all agreed that he was a terrific speaker.

The writer of this passage indicated that the speaker was *interesting* and *terrific*, but these tired words tell little about the speaker or his speech. Was he *stimulating? Thought-provoking? Witty? Persuasive?* Similarly, the applause is described as *absolutely fabulous*, a phrase that has almost no meaning. Was the applause *energetic? Deafening?*

Get into the habit of avoiding such words as *swell, terrible,* and *terrific*. When you encounter these words in your own writing, cross them out and find adjectives and adverbs that are more interesting and more exact in meaning.

Some vague, dull, and overused adjectives and adverbs are

absolutely	funny	nice	tremendous
awful	grand	really	very
cool	great	swell	wonderful
cute	horrible	terrible	
fabulous	neat	terrific	

EXERCISE 20. Using Fresh and Exact Adjectives and Adverbs. Write the following sentences. For the first five, fill in each blank with as fresh and exact an adjective as you can. Supply fresh and exact adverbs for the second five sentences. Use the dictionary if you need to.

1. She refused to give him a(n) —— answer.
2. In spite of his —— suit, he looked shabby.
3. They ate an enormously —— dinner.
4. The actress wore a strikingly —— evening gown.
5. The general handled his troops with —— skill.
6. A frightened child —— asked a question.
7. My new sweater is —— scarlet.
8. After cleaning house, I flopped —— on my bed.
9. The wind was whistling outside, but the Hernandez family sat —— around the fire.
10. Breathing ——, I began to unwrap the presents.

(3) Use description to make characters seem real and interesting.

The persons in a story are called the *characters,* and the place where a story happens is called the *setting.* A story is more convincing if the reader knows something about the characters and setting. If a character is to play an important role in a story, a description will focus attention on that character. For example, at the beginning of *Treasure Island,* the author focuses attention on one important character in the story.

> I remember him as if it were yesterday, as he came plodding to the inn door, his sea chest following behind him in a handbarrow; a tall, strong, heavy, nut-brown man; his tarry pigtail falling over the shoulders of his soiled blue coat; his hands ragged and scarred, with black, broken nails; and the saber cut across one cheek, a dirty, livid white.
>
> ROBERT LOUIS STEVENSON

EXERCISE 21. Writing a Description of a Character. Review the story plan you developed for Exercise 11. Think about a character whom you plan to include in your story. Decide what characteristics or traits make this character interesting. Ask yourself whether anything about this character will affect the action in the story. For example, if the action in the story hinges on the character's quick temper, you will probably need to include that in a description.

You may want to use the technique of brainstorming (page 470) or clustering (pages 470–71) to gather details. If the character is a real person, you might be able to spend some time observing him or her. For example, if the character is your mother, you might listen to the sound of her voice as she encourages your sister with her homework, and you might notice her rapid stride as she hails a taxi in the city.

Make a list of the details you gather, and then arrange them in an order that will make sense to your readers. Then, keeping your details in mind, write a short description of the character.

(4) Use description to make the setting vivid.

Setting may also play an important role in a story. If you were writing about a night spent in a supposedly haunted house, the house itself would be an important factor, and a description of it would make your story more effective. Notice the following description from the beginning of *Losing Battles,* a novel that tells of one day in the life of a large rural family. This beautiful description of dawn shows the importance of the novel's country setting.

When the rooster crowed, the moon had still not left the world but was going down on flushed cheek, one day short of the full. A long thin cloud crossed it slowly, drawing itself out like a name being called. The air changed, as if a mile or so away a wooden door had swung open, and a smell, more of warmth than wet, from a river at low stage, moved upward into the clay hills that stood in darkness.

Then a house appeared on its ridge, like an old man's silver watch pulled once more out of its pocket. A dog leaped up from where he'd lain like a stone and began barking for today as if he meant never to stop.

EUDORA WELTY

EXERCISE 22. Writing a Description of a Setting. Review the story plan you developed for Exercise 11. Think about the setting of the narrative you are planning. Then take a few minutes to brainstorm for details related to that setting. If it is a real setting that is convenient to visit, go there and observe carefully. If not, try to recall every detail. Be aware of your senses and try to recall or observe the sights, sounds, smells, tastes, and feelings that might be related to the setting. If your setting suggests a feeling or mood of mystery, dreariness, brilliance, gaiety, or fear, try to select your details to reflect that mood.

Make a list of these details, and then arrange them in a logical order. Remember that spatial order, the arrangement of details according to location (page 506), is usually appropriate for a description of a place. Then, keeping your details in mind, write one or two paragraphs describing the setting of your narrative.

WRITING A FIRST DRAFT

22j. Write a first draft of your story.

Most good narratives include five basic story elements. It will help to remember these elements as you write:

1. Interesting start
2. Beginning explanation
3. Action
4. Climax
5. Ending

Interesting Start and Beginning Explanation

Your opportunity to reach your readers may begin—and end—with the start of your narrative. If you do not interest your readers in the first one or two sentences, they will likely stop reading and never discover the rest of your story. Read the following paragraph from the beginning of the narrative on pages 604–605.

> Some years ago my friend Chip and I tried to go to the moon, but some apples and pears got in our way. Both Chip and I had seen a television program about reaching the moon. When we talked about the program, we agreed that the important thing was to get up enough speed to overcome the earth's gravity. The rest would be easy. We decided to try an experiment. There was a long block in our neighborhood that ran downhill and then uphill. If we took Chip's wagon and got up enough speed going downhill, we might be able to leave the earth going uphill.

The first sentence of this narrative contains the *interesting start*. It tells the reader what the story is about in such a way that the reader's curiosity is aroused. This sentence also introduces the time, "some years ago," and the characters, "my friend Chip and I."

The rest of the paragraph is the *beginning explanation*. Notice that the paragraph does not supply unnecessary information.

It does not tell how Chip and the writer became friends, nor does it give all the details of their talk about the program. It does, however, include an important description of the setting, "There was a long block in our neighborhood that ran downhill and then uphill."

This paragraph avoids a common problem in story writing: beginning in the wrong place. The writer should not begin the story with getting up that morning or going to school or even with meeting Chip. The real beginning of the story is the decision by Chip and the writer to make the trip.

EXERCISE 23. Writing the Beginning of Your Story. Using your limited subject and the plan you developed for Exercise 11, write a story beginning. Try to include an interesting start. If appropriate, identify the time, the place, and the people. Include any background information that the reader will need in order to understand the action of the story.

Action and Climax

The middle of a narrative is made up of the action and the climax. The action is the series of step-by-step events that happen after the beginning explanation, and the climax is the high point of the story. In the story about the trip to the moon, the second paragraph gives the step-by-step account of the action. Notice how it tells specifically what happened the morning of the attempted trip to the moon.

> The next morning we got up very early. We wanted to reach the block before people started coming out of their apartment houses to go to work. I sat in the front of the wagon. Chip gave a push and jumped on behind me. The wagon went faster and faster. Chip and I cheered. We were sure that we would leave the earth's gravity and would be on our way to the moon. I began to daydream about newspaper headlines and being interviewed on television.

In this story the climax, in the third paragraph, is the wagon crashing into Mrs. Clark's fruit stand. Notice the way in which this climax is made vivid by the use of specific details and effective verbs.

> Suddenly Chip yelled, "Watch out!" Going uphill had made our wagon change direction. We were headed straight for Mrs. Clark's fruit stand. I grabbed the handle of the wagon to steer, but it was too late. We crashed into the fruit stand and almost hit Mrs. Clark. Mrs. Clark shouted. The fruit spilled in all directions.

EXERCISE 24. Writing the Middle of Your Story. Write the middle section of the story you started to write in Exercise 23. Remember that the middle includes a series of step-by-step events that build to, and climax with, the high point of the story. If you plan to use dialogue, you may want to include it in this section. Try to allow enough time to write the entire middle section in one sitting.

Ending

The ending of a story ties up the loose ends. The ending may state how the writer felt about the events of the story, or it may merely suggest the writer's feelings. In this story, the ending tells what happened after the wagon hit the fruit stand. Although we are not told directly, the details about the dented wagon, being grounded, and paying for the damaged fruit give a good idea of how Chip and the writer must have felt. We are not surprised that they did not plan another trip to the moon for a while.

> The story has a sad ending. Out of our savings we paid $9.40 for the fresh fruit that Mrs. Clark lost. Chip's wagon had a big dent in it. I was grounded for sneaking out of the house early in the morning. Chip and I postponed our plans for the next moonshot indefinitely.

Sometimes a story does not contain all five elements. An interest-arousing opening and a strong climax are, of course, assets to a story, but they are not necessities. Many good stories lack them. Nevertheless, keeping the basic elements in mind as you write will help you to organize your story.

EXERCISE 25. Writing the Ending for Your Story. Write an ending for the story you began for Exercises 23 and 24. Remember that the ending should tie up all the loose ends and satisfy the reader that the story is over. Plan your time so that you will be able to write the first draft of the ending in one sitting.

REVIEW EXERCISE. Writing a First Draft of a Personal Experience. Write a draft of a narrative about a personal experience that you would enjoy sharing with others.

PREWRITING Select one of the subjects you identified in Exercise 2 or search for a new subject. Be sure that your subject is limited to a specific experience or problem that is appropriate for a short narrative. Review any notes in your writer's notebook and brainstorm to recall details related to the experience. Use the *5 W-How?* questions to gather all the important details and develop a story plan.

Before you actually begin writing, review the five basic elements of a story. Think about how you will develop each element. Decide whether to include any descriptions of setting and characters and whether you should use dialogue.

WRITING As you write, allow your thoughts to flow freely. If you run out of ideas for the moment, review your story plan. Do not worry too much about accuracy and organization at this stage; just try to keep your ideas flowing and get them down on paper. You will have an opportunity to revise your paper later.

REVISING

REVISING A NARRATIVE

22k. Revise the first draft of your story.

Many writers feel that the revision stage is the most important part of the writing process. It is here, once the first draft is on paper, that the writer can shape and polish the story.

Content

When you evaluate the content of your narrative, you will want to begin by deciding whether you need any additional actions or descriptive details. A missing action or descriptive detail will confuse your readers. For example, if you are writing a story about a friend who was bidding on a vase at an auction, you may need to mention that antique dealers were bidding on the same vase. Otherwise, your readers may lose sight of the central struggle in the story.

The next step is to see if you have included any details that do not belong. Ask yourself: Is this detail necessary in order to understand the story? Does it detract attention from what is happening in the story?

The following story contains one unnecessary sentence. It is underlined.

> Last August I went to an auction with my friend Leslie. She hoped to get a large Rookwood vase for a low bid. However, there were several antique dealers sitting behind us. Just before the bidding started, we heard the dealers whispering excitedly. They would stop at nothing if they wanted the vase.
>
> The auctioneer began calling for bids. Leslie opened with twenty dollars. The dealers raised the bid to thirty. Quickly the bidding reached seventy-five. <u>I noticed Sarah Horne, my art teacher, come in at that point.</u>
>
> One of the dealers said, "Eighty-five."
>
> Leslie called out, "One hundred dollars."
>
> My heart was beating rapidly as the auctioneer cried, "Going, going, gone!" Leslie had bought the vase.

The detail about the teacher is unnecessary. At this point the reader is eager to find out what happened, not to learn who was present. The only persons really necessary to the story are Leslie, the antique dealers, and the writer.

EXERCISE 26. Identifying Unnecessary Details.

In the following story there are five sentences containing unnecessary details. Copy these five sentences on your paper.

The day of the Halloween party, Hope Buchanan told me she was sure that she would win the prize for the best costume. She was coming as Marie Antoinette, and her mother had bought her an authentic eighteenth-century costume, including a wig. Hope's father is a dentist. "What are you coming as?" she asked.

I said, "Oh, you'll see." I didn't have much chance of winning the prize, but I didn't want Hope to know that. All I had was a ghost costume that my mother and I had made out of a sheet. Janet Goodrich was coming as a pirate.

That evening we had lamb chops for dinner. At the dinner table, my mother asked me why I looked so gloomy. I told her about Hope's costume. "We'll have to do something about that," said Mother.

First she got some of Father's medals and pinned them on the sheet. Then she pasted on some gold stars. After I put on the costume, she got my brother Billy's western outfit, took off the holster, and put the cartridge belt around my waist. Billy can be nice, but he is usually a pest. Finally, Mother took a black crayon and drew a beard on the sheet.

Margarita, Dwayne, Jennifer, and Greg were at the Halloween party. To Hope's surprise and my own, I won the prize for the best costume—as the ghost of a dead general!

Organization

Organization refers to the arrangement of information and details in your narrative. You will need to check to see whether all of the actions are arranged in a step-by-step manner in chronological order (the order in which they happened). In the story about the auction, for example, the auctioneer calls for bids before the bidding starts. A reversal of that order would only confuse the reader.

If you have included a paragraph or more of description, you will need to be sure that descriptive details are arranged in a way that will be clear to the reader. Remember that details about setting are usually arranged according to location, and details about people are usually arranged to emphasize the most important features.

Style

The style of your narrative includes all of the details of form—including your choice of words and sentence structure. Are the sentences you have written and the words you have used appropriate for your audience?

Look at the individual words you have used. If you have used weak, vague verbs, the actions will not seem interesting to your readers. For example, the sentence "The reddish-brown dog sat at it owner's feet" tells little about how the dog is sitting. Changing the verb creates a more vivid picture. "The reddish-brown dog *sagged* at its owner's feet."

Study the adverbs and adjectives you have used. Adjectives and adverbs should be precise and vivid, but they are like spices in food. They are necessary for seasoning, but too many of them will spoil the dish. Notice how the removal of unnecessary modifiers makes the second of the following models more effective.

1

The cute, reddish-brown, friendly dog sagged mournfully and wearily at its generous owner's feet. The huge man with the long, massive legs had hunted tirelessly and eagerly all that clear, sunny day. Now he had fallen blissfully asleep in the soft, comfortable easy chair.

2

The reddish-brown dog sagged at its owner's feet. The huge man had hunted eagerly all day. Now he had fallen asleep in the soft easy chair.

You may be tempted to include a great many adjectives and adverbs in your own stories in the hope that they will make your writing more vivid. Using too many modifiers, however, will weaken your description. As you revise your story, the following hints will help you avoid problems with modifiers.

1. *Cut out repetitious modifiers that do not contribute much to a description.* In the passage about the hunter, the elimination of unnecessary adjectives and adverbs resulted in a stronger description.

2. *Use comparisons.* If you want a more vivid and exact way to describe a person or an object at an important moment in your story, make a comparison. Instead of saying "The job was difficult," write that it "was like completing a jigsaw puzzle while blindfolded."

3. *Rewrite some sentences so that nouns and verbs do the work of describing.* For example, the sentence "Suddenly he ran forward and quickly pulled the letter from her hand" can be changed to "He darted forward and jerked the letter from her hand." The verb "darted" replaces "suddenly ran," and the verb "jerked" replaces "quickly pulled."

In revising for style, you should also look at sentence structure. Check to see whether any dialogue you have used is lively and natural-sounding. The sentences in dialogue should be fairly short, as in normal conversation. Try to vary the lengths of your other sentences so that they will not be boring to your readers.

EXERCISE 27. Replacing Overused Adjectives and Adverbs. Number your paper 1–10. After the proper number, replace the overused adjectives and adverbs in italics with words that you think are fresher and more exact. Use your dictionary if you need to.

EXAMPLES   1. I wanted to paint the room purple, but Geraldo thought it would look *funny.*
1. *peculiar*
2. Since Marsha was elected president of the club, she has become *terribly* efficient.
2. *extremely*

1. Sabrena, your birthday party was *nice.*
2. I had an *absolutely terrible* time at the dentist's.
3. It is a *cute* little puppy that often does *cute* tricks.
4. John Brady has recorded a *terrific* new song.
5. Just as we ran out of ideas, Wanetta made a *neat* suggestion.
6. Kim gave a *swell* performance in the class play.
7. Margie's hair looks *horrible* this morning.

8. The homework Mr. Rubin assigned is *really* difficult.
9. David plays the clarinet *awfully* well.
10. We had an *awfully wonderful* weekend at your home.

EXERCISE 28. Omitting Unnecessary Adjectives and Adverbs. The passage below has too many adjectives and adverbs. Rewrite it according to the following directions:

1. Eliminate unnecessary modifiers from the first two sentences.
2. Use a comparison in the third sentence (perhaps to a little dog cautiously approaching a big dog).
3. Rewrite the last sentence so that an exact verb will replace a verb and an adverb.

The shabby, pathetic-looking little man shuffled timidly and fearfully along the dingy, cracked, uneven sidewalk. His old, battered hat jiggled precariously on his head. When he saw Mr. Abercrombie, the banker, coming up the street, he cautiously sidled up to him. Mr. Abercrombie walked haughtily past.

GUIDELINES FOR REVISING NARRATIVES

1. Is the start interesting?
2. Are the characters and the setting introduced in the beginning explanation?
3. Are specific details used to make the action vivid?
4. Have any important actions been omitted?
5. Are any actions included that should be omitted because they are not directly related to the story?
6. Is the dialogue lively and natural-sounding?
7. Are the actions arranged in chronological order?
8. Are specific nouns, verbs, adjectives, and adverbs used to make the story more interesting?
9. Have unnecessary adjectives and adverbs been eliminated from the description?
10. Are the words and sentences appropriate for the readers?

EXERCISE 29. Analyzing a Writer's Revisions. Read the following three paragraphs. This is a revised first draft of three paragraphs of the personal experience narrative you studied on pages 595–97. Think about the changes the writer made for the final version. Then answer the questions that follow the paragraphs.

Some years ago my friend Chip and I tried to go to the moon, but ∧we had trouble. *some apples and pears got in our way.* Both Chip and I had seen a television program about reaching the moon. When we talked about the program we agreed that the important thing was to get up enough speed to overcome the earth's gravity. The rest would be easy. We decided to try an experiment. There was a long block in our neighborhood that ran downhill and then uphill. ~~Children usually roller-skated there.~~ If we took Chip's wagon and got up enough speed going downhill, we might be able to leave the earth going uphill.

The next morning we got up very early. We wanted to reach the block before people started coming out of their apartment houses to go to work. I sat in the front of the wagon. Chip gave a push and jumped on behind me. The wagon went faster and faster. Chip and I cheered. We were sure that we would leave the earth's gravity and would be on our way to the moon. ∧ *I began to daydream about newspaper headlines and being interviewed on television.*

We were headed straight for Mrs. Clark's fruit stand. Suddenly Chip yelled, "Watch out!" Going uphill had made our wagon change direction. ∨I grabbed the handle of the wagon to steer, but it was too late. We *crashed* ~~ran~~ into the fruit stand and almost hit Mrs. Clark. Mrs. Clark *shouted.* ~~was angry.~~ The fruit spilled in all directions.

1. Why did the writer change the ending of the first sentence?
2. Why did the writer remove the sentence "Children usually roller-skated there"?
3. Why did the writer add a sentence at the end of the second paragraph?
4. Why did the writer change the order of some of the sentences in the third paragraph?
5. Why did the writer change "ran" to "crashed" and "was angry" to "shouted"?

EXERCISE 30. Revising Your Own Story.   Revise the draft of the narrative you wrote earlier in this chapter. Use the revision guidelines on page 486 and the Guidelines for Revising Narratives on page 603. Remember that it is often helpful to exchange papers with another student and evaluate each other's papers.

PROOFREADING

PROOFREADING YOUR STORY AND MAKING A FINAL COPY

22l. Proofread your story and make a clean, accurate final copy.

Proofreading is easier if you put your paper away for a few days and come back to it with a fresh eye. You can also improve your proofreading abilities by covering all but the line you are studying at the time and by reading your paper backwards. If you have used dialogue in your narrative, pay particular attention to the punctuation and paragraphing of each speaker's words. Use the Guidelines for Proofreading on page 487 as a reminder of the things to be looking for.

Remember that the final aim of any writing is to have people read and appreciate what you have written. Readers may be unable or unwilling to read a messy paper that does not follow the standards for manuscript form. Review those standards on page 445 before making your final copy.

EXERCISE 31. Proofreading Your Narrative. Using the Guidelines for Proofreading on page 487, proofread the narrative you revised for Exercise 30.

EXERCISE 32. Making a Final Copy of Your Story. Review the standards for manuscript form on page 445 and follow these standards in making your final copy. After you have completed the copy, proofread it one more time to check for any mistakes you may have made as you copied the story.

CHAPTER 22 WRITING REVIEW

Writing a Story About an Imaginary Experience. Write a story about an imaginary experience. It might be about someone's first day on a new job or first attempt at some athletic or artistic task. You may imagine that the experience was your own or someone else's. Remember that writers draw upon their own experiences as well as experiences that they have witnessed or read about when they write fiction. They use their imaginations to change what happened in real life into what might happen in the world they have invented.

Use the process you practiced in this chapter to choose a subject, consider your purpose and audience, gather and arrange information, write, revise, proofread, and make a final copy of your narrative.

CHAPTER 23

Writing Exposition

THE WHOLE COMPOSITION

You have already practiced the writing process in Chapter 19. In this chapter you will use the writing process to write *expository compositions*. The expository composition, like the expository paragraph (see pages 553–62), presents a certain amount of information about a topic. All writing presents some information: a narrative about a neighborhood incident may contain some facts about your neighborhood or house, your neighborhood friends, and so on.

In expository writing, however, the information is the focus. The purpose of exposition is to explain or to inform, that is, to tell the audience something that they may not know and to tell them in a way that they will understand. You can see that exposition is a very important kind of writing. We learn most things we know from other people, and we learn a great many of these things through reading. Through your life experiences you have already gathered a great deal of information that will be interesting or helpful to others. To present it clearly and well, you need the writing skills you will practice in this chapter.

Although the compositions you write in school may be of different lengths—some no longer than a paragraph—the word *composition* usually means a piece of writing of three to five paragraphs, often 250 to 300 words long. Of course, the right length for a composition depends on the topic and the amount of information presented about it. The minimum of 250 to 300 words is mentioned only to give you a general idea.

PREWRITING

CHOOSING A SUBJECT

23a. Choose a subject for your expository composition.

Some of the compositions you write this year will be on subjects assigned by your teachers. Your social studies teacher may ask you to explain your local government. Your English teacher may ask you to explain why you enjoy reading science fiction or biographies of famous artists. For these assignments, you will simply have to be sure that you understand the assignment and know how to find the information that you will need.

At other times, however, you will probably be able to choose a subject of your own. For example, your teacher might give you one of the following composition assignments:

Write a composition explaining how to make *something* or how to do *something*.
Write a composition giving directions to *some place*.
Write a composition giving information about *someone, something, or some place*.

In these cases, choosing a subject may be the most important decision you make in planning and writing your composition. It is a decision that requires careful thought. To choose a subject for your composition, you will really do two things. First, you will search for possible subjects to write about. Then you will select one subject from your list of possibilities.

Searching for Possible Subjects

The best subject to write about is one that you know well. The subjects that you know best come from your personal interests (hobbies, sports), knowledge, and experiences. To search for subjects you know well, you can use any of the following methods.

(1) Examine your personal resources.

Perhaps you know a great deal about stamp or coin collecting: how to start a collection, where to obtain specimens, what pleasures and advantages this hobby offers. Such a subject, which you can write about from your own experience, is an excellent possibility for a composition. If you stop to think about it, there are a number of things you know about. Your whole life—your interests, knowledge, and experiences—is raw material for compositions.

EXERCISE 1. Cataloging Your Personal Resources. In order to use your personal resources for your writing, you need to know what those resources are. Answer the following questions about your interests, knowledge, and experiences. Save your answers for use later in this chapter.

1. What do you think you know a lot about?
2. What activities do you do well?
3. What unusual experiences have you had?
4. What is your favorite school subject?
5. What do you most like to read about?
6. What programs do you most like to watch on television?
7. What are your hobbies?
8. What extracurricular activities do you enjoy?
9. What do you really enjoy doing in your free time?
10. If you could do anything or be anything, what would it be?

(2) Observe the world around you.

Much of what you know has come to you secondhand from books, magazines, radio and television programs, movies, and conversations with other people. Perhaps you have read a great deal about the Egyptian pyramids, the San Francisco earthquake, the early days of aviation, or the special effects in science fiction movies. The knowledge you have about these subjects is a part of your experience, too.

You can begin the search for subjects by observing the world around you. Ask yourself questions such as the following ones:

What is happening around me?
What do I see that I could explain to someone else?
What interests me in what I observe?
What interests me so much that I want to write about it?

For example, suppose that you are asked to write a composition explaining how to do something. To find a subject to write about, you can begin by observing the world around you. You may notice a neighbor planting vegetables in his garden, a friend stringing her guitar, and a relative using a computer.

Now think about your own interests. You may realize that using a computer interests you the most. Starting with your own observations and interests, you have discovered a subject to write about. Of course, this subject is very broad, or general. Nevertheless, you have completed an important first step in the writing process by discovering a broad subject.

EXERCISE 2. Using Observation to Search for Subjects.
Using your observations of the world around you, list at least three broad subjects for each of the following expository writing assignments. For example, for a composition giving information about something, three broad subjects are *sea creatures, painting with watercolors,* and *trees in my neighborhood.*

1. Giving directions to some place
2. Explaining how to do something
3. Giving information about a person
4. Explaining how to make something
5. Giving information about a place

(3) Use a writer's journal as a source of possible subjects.

One source of subjects to write about is a writer's journal, or notebook. Many writers keep journals in which they record their feelings, thoughts, and experiences. Later, when they want to find something to write about, these writers can look through their journals for subjects from their own lives. You may also want to keep a writer's journal. Then, when you need to find something to write about, you can read your own notebook to search for possible subjects. If you decide to keep a writer's journal, remember to record the experiences, thoughts, and feelings that you would feel comfortable sharing with others in public writing such as a composition.

For example, here is a sample journal entry from one young person's notebook:

> We had a speaker at school today—a stockbroker from New York. She explained how stocks are traded at the New York Stock Exchange on Wall Street. In some ways it's much simpler than I expected. If I wanted to buy some stock in a company, I would call my personal stockbroker. This person would place my order with a telephone clerk at the stock exchange in New York. The clerk would talk to a broker there. This broker, who is on the floor of the stock exchange, would actually bargain with other brokers to get the amount of stock I want to buy at the best possible price. After the deal is made, the broker would tell the telephone clerk, who would call my personal broker. I would have to pay for the stock five days later.

If you read this entry in your writer's journal, you might realize that you could write about buying stock, which could be a broad subject for an expository composition. Thinking about this entry might also lead you to other possible subjects, however. Other ideas might occur to you that could also be broad subjects for an expository composition: for example, "becoming a stock-broker" or "the New York Stock Exchange." Keeping a writer's journal lets you record things you can refer to later, but it can also stimulate other ideas.

EXERCISE 3. Keeping a Writer's Journal. Keep a writer's journal for three to five days. This journal can be a notebook or a file folder. In your journal, record the thoughts, feelings, and experiences you want to share with other people. Then, using your writer's journal as a source, list at least five broad subjects for an expository composition. Remember that the purpose of exposition is to inform or to explain. If you already keep a journal regularly, you may refer to any entries you wish.

(4) Use brainstorming to search for subjects.

You can also use brainstorming to search for subjects to write about. When you brainstorm, you write down as many ideas as you can think of all at once. Your aim is to list as many subjects as possible, without judging them. Deciding which subjects you can actually write about comes later in the writing process.

Suppose, for example, that your English teacher had asked you to write a composition giving information about someone or something. To search for subjects, you might brainstorm for ideas using the question "What do I know about?" By brainstorming about *your own knowledge*, you might come up with a list like this:

playing the piano	waltzing on ice skates
planting a vegetable garden	understanding my brother
the local recreation program	snorkeling
being a day-camp counselor	types of cameras
my uncle's trip to Alaska	

After you brainstorm, you can select a subject from those on your list. These subjects are still too broad or general to be suitable for an expository composition, but you have discovered several possible subjects to write about.

EXERCISE 4. Using Brainstorming to Search for Subjects. Use brainstorming to search for at least ten subjects for an expository composition. Focus on your own knowledge. Think up as many answers as possible to the question "What do I know about?" Keep your list of possible subjects. You may want to refer to this list later in the chapter.

(5) Use clustering to search for subjects.

You can also use clustering to search for subjects to write about. Suppose your English teacher had asked you to write a composition explaining how to make or do something. You could use clustering to search for subjects, starting with the question "What do I know how to make or do?" Your cluster diagram might look like this:

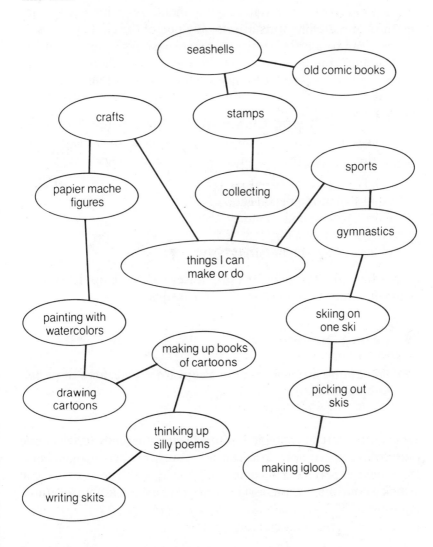

Clustering is like brainstorming. You write a word or a phrase. Then you write all the other words or phrases the first idea makes you think of. You also circle each idea as you write it down, and you connect these circled words and phrases with lines. Each line should connect an idea with the idea it came from.

In this way, you can almost "see" your train of thought. That is, you can see how one idea leads to another and then another and so on. When you cluster, your goal is to think up as many ideas as possible, without judging them. As with each other method of searching for subjects, any one of the circled words or phrases can be a broad subject for an expository composition. As with brainstorming, you will be able to decide whether you can use any of these possible subjects later in the writing process.

EXERCISE 5. Using Clustering to Search for Subjects.
Use clustering to search for possible subjects for an expository composition. Use any one of the following headings to start your cluster diagram:

> Things I am interested in
> Things I can make or do
> Things I know about
> Things I have experienced

Circle and connect the words or phrases you think up. Keep your work in your notebook for use later in this chapter.

Selecting One Subject

(6) Select one subject to write about from your lists of possible subjects.

After you search for possible subjects, you are ready to select one for your composition. You can use your own knowledge, interests, and experiences to help you decide which to use. As you think about the writing assignment you have, ask yourself three questions.

1. What subject interests me the most?
2. What subject do I know the most about?
3. What subject do I have the most experience with?

Suppose that you decided to use clustering to search for subjects. If you made a cluster diagram like the one on page 613, you could ask yourself the three questions just mentioned to choose one subject to write about. You might decide that you enjoy gymnastics, but that you have not had enough experience to explain this subject to someone else. You might also be very interested in painting with watercolors. Still, you might not feel you can explain this subject well. So, you might decide that a subject you really know something about is stamp collecting. This could be the broad subject for your expository composition. You still would need to limit the subject to a manageable size, but you would have chosen a subject that you can explain well.

EXERCISE 6. Selecting a Subject for Your Composition.
Look over the lists of subjects you made in Exercises 1–5. Select a subject for your expository composition from these lists. To do so, ask yourself these questions: What subject interests me the most? What subject do I know the most about? What subject do I have the most experience with?

CONSIDERING AUDIENCE

23b. Think about the audience for your expository composition.

To choose a subject for your composition, you thought about your own interests, knowledge, and experiences. Your attention was focused on yourself. It is also important for you to think about the audience for your composition. Remember that the *audience* is the person or people for whom you write. In expository writing, the audience is especially important because of the purpose of exposition, that is, to inform *someone* about something or to explain something to *someone*.

You can write on any given subject for a variety of audiences. For a school writing assignment, you can write on the same subject for your classmates, your teachers, your parents, or students in other grades. Each of these audiences is very different from the others. This is because each audience has a different background, different interests, and different experiences.

Suppose that you choose "science fiction movies" as a subject for your composition. How you explain this broad subject will depend on who your audience is. For instance, if you are writing for second-graders, you might want to focus on why a movie is labeled science fiction. For your classmates, you might focus on the differences between the special effects in two science fiction movies. For an audience of parents, you might explain why science fiction movies are good entertainment for young people your age. Your audience influences what part of the subject you will explain.

Your audience will also affect how you actually write your composition. For an audience of second-graders, you will have to use simple vocabulary words and easy-to-understand sentences. For an audience of parents, on the other hand, you can use more technical terms and more difficult sentences.

How you think about your subject for the rest of prewriting will be decided by who your audience is. You will have to adjust according to your audience's background and needs. To think about your audience, ask yourself the following questions. They will focus your attention on your audience's background and needs.

1. How can I describe my audience?
2. Is this subject suitable for this audience?
3. What does my audience already know about this subject?
4. What does my audience want to know or need to know about this subject?

As you ask these four questions, you will also be gathering information you can use later in the writing process. You will have to think about your audience when you are gathering information, writing your composition, and revising your draft.

EXERCISE 7. Thinking About Audience.   On page 616, you learned that there are four questions you can ask when you are thinking about the audience for a piece of writing. Below are five audiences paired with five subjects. Answer the audience question included in each item. You may have to write more than one sentence to answer each question.

1. *Subject:* Microcomputers in math class
   Audience: Members of an eighth-grade class
   How can you describe this audience?
2. *Subject:* Safety with strangers
   Audience: First-graders
   What does this audience want to know or need to know about this subject?
3. *Subject:* William Shakespeare
   Audience: Eighth-grade English teachers
   What does this audience already know about the subject?
4. *Subject:* Summer arts festivals
   Audience: Readers of the local newspaper
   How can you describe this audience?
5. *Subject:* Local elementary schools
   Audience: Tenth-graders
   Is this subject suitable for this audience? Why?

EXERCISE 8. Thinking About Your Audience.   On page 616, you read about four questions you can use to think about the audience for your composition. Write a brief answer for each question, thinking about the audience for your expository composition.

LIMITING THE SUBJECT

23c. Limit your subject to a manageable topic.

If you have to write a composition, you may think that a broad, general subject will be better than a smaller one. It is true that there is more to say about "the history of aviation" than about "the Wright Brothers' first flight." The problem is, however, that there is too much that *has* to be said about a large subject.

Whole books have been written about the history of aviation. All that a short composition on this subject can do is make some general statements. A short composition does not have room for the supporting ideas and details that would explain these general statements. Exposition, more than other forms of writing, especially calls for precise, detailed information. The larger the subject, the more details you have to include.

To be effective, your composition should explain a subject that is well chosen and that has been developed well in terms of your audience. When you think about your subject, you should decide whether it is manageable within the limits of the size of your composition. Remember that you only have a limited space in which to explain your subject.

For example, stamp collecting may be an idea for a composition, but this subject is too large. On the other hand, a composition telling how to start to collect and display stamps is a limited topic just right for a short composition. You need to limit, or narrow, your broad, general subject to a manageable topic.

CRITICAL THINKING:
Analyzing a Broad Subject

To limit your broad subject to a manageable topic, you should analyze your subject, that is, divide your subject into its smaller parts. You can divide your broad subject by asking yourself questions about your subject. The following questions will help you limit your subject.

1. What are *examples* of the subject?
2. What are *uses* of the subject?
3. What are *types* of the subject?
4. What are *activities* involving the subject?
5. What *time periods* does the subject include?
6. What *places, people, or events* does the subject include?

As you answer these questions about your subject, you will be dividing it into more limited, or smaller, topics for your composition. Notice, however, that you will probably not be able to use each question with every subject.

You can limit the broad subject "stamp collecting" into smaller, more manageable topics in this way:

Subject: Stamp collecting
Activities: trading with other collectors, joining stamp clubs or societies, attending exhibitions, starting to collect and display stamps
Types: Rare stamps, first day covers, commemorative stamps, specialized stamps (railroads, birds, ships, paintings, etc.)

Any one of the items listed above could be a limited topic for an expository composition.

EXERCISE 9. Selecting Limited Topics.   Five of the subjects listed below are too broad to be good composition topics. Five are limited enough to be suitable. Number your paper 1–10. Write *S* after the number of each suitably limited topic. Write *NS* after the number of each subject that is not suitably limited.

1. The youth of an American President
2. Preparing for an overnight hike
3. Mystery stories
4. Agriculture in South America
5. Profile of a local disc jockey
6. Pioneer life
7. Environmental pollution
8. Starting a vegetable garden
9. Hunting for snakes
10. The women's rights movement

EXERCISE 10. Developing Limited Topics.   For the five broad subjects in Exercise 9, develop at least two limited topics. Remember to use questions to divide each broad subject into its smaller parts.

EXERCISE 11. Developing Your Own Limited Topic.
Using the broad subject you have chosen for your composition, develop a topic that is limited enough for a composition. Use questions to divide your subject into its smaller parts. Be sure to limit, or narrow, your subject enough so that it can be easily explained in a short composition.

STATING THE PURPOSE

23d. State the purpose of your composition.

At this point in prewriting, it is a good idea to think about your topic in a very specific way. That is, you should now write a statement or phrase that plainly indicates what your composition will be about. You should state the purpose of your composition.

You know by now that an expository composition should explain or inform. That is the *general* purpose of exposition. For your statement of purpose, you should focus specifically on what your composition will explain to your audience, or what you will inform your audience about. To do so, you should use phrases such as *to explain, to inform, to show, to indicate,* or *to discuss* in your statement.

For example, for the topic "beginning a stamp collection," you might write a statement of purpose such as this: *to explain how someone can begin to collect and display stamps.* Notice that this statement of purpose focuses on the topic. It is clear that the composition will show how someone can begin to collect and display stamps.

Focusing on your topic in this way will help you later in the writing process. By stating the purpose of your composition, you will know what kind of information you should gather for your composition. This statement of purpose can also be included in the introductory paragraph you write for your composition.

EXERCISE 12. Stating a Purpose. For each limited topic listed below, write a statement of purpose for an expository composition. Remember that you should include phrases such as *to explain, to inform, to indicate, to show,* or *to discuss* in your statement.

1. Muhammad Ali's prizefighting record
2. How Manhattan got its name
3. Making toothpick sculptures
4. Creating fantastic fireworks
5. A space achievement of the 1980's

EXERCISE 13. Stating a Purpose for Your Own Composition. Write a statement of purpose for the topic you have limited for your expository composition. Remember to use one of the key phrases mentioned on page 620. Save this statement of purpose in your notebook. You may decide to include it in the introductory paragraph of your expository composition.

GATHERING INFORMATION

23e. Gather information for your expository composition.

You have now completed the steps in prewriting that help you decide what you will write about in your composition. Now you are ready to focus on your topic even more, by gathering information about your topic. The information you gather—ideas and details—will be what you use to explain your topic to your audience.

As you are learning in school, some topics require you to do library research. You will study how to do that in Chapter 24. For the kind of expository composition you are now writing, your own background of knowledge and experience contains more than enough information. The important thing is to know how to get at this knowledge for your writing.

Three strategies will enable you to gather information for your expository composition. Each one enables you to search your own background or personal resources.

Listing Ideas and Details

(1) List ideas and details for your expository composition.

With this information-gathering method, you simply jot down ideas and details about your topic as quickly as they occur to you. In this way, listing ideas and details is very much like brainstorming and clustering. Your aim here, as with brainstorming and clustering, is to list as many ideas and details as possible. Later on you will have time to decide which ones you should actually include in your composition and how they should be organized.

For example, following is a list of ideas and details for the topic "beginning a stamp collection." Notice that the information is listed as it occurred to the writer, rather than in an organized plan. Notice also that there may be some ideas and details the writer might eventually decide not to use in an expository composition on this topic.

Topic: Beginning a stamp collection
Purpose: To explain how to collect and display stamps
Ideas and details:

educational value
family mail
hobby stores
removing stamps from
  envelopes
fun of watching collection
  grow
learning locations of
  countries
appreciating beauty of
  stamps
stamp dealers

history of postage stamps
learning about people and
  customs of foreign lands
mounting stamps in album
supplies: tongs, hinges,
  album
post office
stamp packets
approval sheets
valuable stamps

EXERCISE 14. Listing Ideas and Details. For each limited topic below, list at least five ideas and details. If your teacher so directs, you may instead select only one topic and list as many ideas as you can about it.

1. Why I hate amusement parks
2. Differences between concerts and record albums
3. How to ride a bicycle safely
4. Why I watch television
5. The care and feeding of small animals

Using a Writer's Journal

(2) Use your writer's journal as a source of information about your topic.

Earlier in this chapter you learned that you could use a writer's journal, or notebook, to search for subjects to write about. This writer's journal can also be used as a source of ideas and details about your topic. The entries you have written contain information about what you have done, seen, thought, and felt. You can use this information in your writing.

The journal entry on page 611 contains ideas and details about how stocks are traded. If you were writing a composition on this topic, you could use this particular journal entry as a source of information on how a stockbroker goes about buying stocks. Your writer's journal could be used for gathering information. When you use a writer's journal in this way, remember that you are free to use more than one entry. Sometimes a series of entries about your experiences may provide the information you need for your composition.

EXERCISE 15. Gathering Information from a Writer's Journal. Keep a writer's journal for three to five days. Remember that you should record the ideas and experiences you feel comfortable sharing with other people. Then list at least two topics you could write about based on your journal entries. After that, list at least five ideas and details from your journal entries that you could use to explain each topic.

As an alternate activity, you can review your writer's journal for any ideas and details that will explain the composition topic you limited in Exercise 11. Write these ideas and details down in your notebook.

Asking the 5 W-How? Questions

(3) Ask the *5 W-How?* questions to gather information on your topic.

Asking questions is often a useful way to find information about a topic. Newspaper writers use one strategy that enables them to gather the basic facts about a news happening. They ask the *5 W-How?* questions: *Who? What? When? Where? Why? How?* The answer to each question gives you a piece of information—an idea a detail—about your topic.

For example, you can use the *5 W-How?* questions to gather information on the topic "being a day-camp counselor."

Who?   Who can be a day-camp counselor?
Young people with day-camp experience, good personal reputations, and some outdoor camping and crafts skills

What?   What do day-camp counselors do?
Supervise children in day camps, give classes in craft projects and outdoor skills, assist the camp directors

When?   When are there jobs for day-camp counselors?
Every summer, usually in one-week sessions in June, July, and August

Where?   Where are there jobs for day-camp counselors?
Local communities, religious groups, community organizations, and groups like the Boy Scouts, Girl Scouts, and Camp Fire Girls sponsor day camps

Why?   Why would someone want to be a counselor at a day camp?
To work with young people, to make some money, and to spend the summer in an interesting environment

How?   How can someone get a job as a day-camp counselor?
Call local religious groups, ask the local parks and recreation department, contact groups such as the Boy Scouts and Girl Scouts. See what jobs they have and what kind of people they like to fill them with.

Notice that these questions enable you to gather many ideas and details about this topic. You could use the answers to each question to write an entire expository composition about being a day-camp counselor.

EXERCISE 16. Asking the 5 *W-How?* Questions.   Select a topic from the following list. Then ask the *5 W-How?* questions (*Who? What? When? Where? Why? How?*) to gather information on the topic. For each question, write at least one answer.

1. My favorite team's greatest accomplishment
2. What I really want to do this summer
3. Recreational opportunities in our community
4. Organizing a teen-age volunteer group
5. The easiest way to learn to play a musical instrument

EXERCISE 17. Using Information-gathering Strategies. You have studied three ways to gather information for an expository composition: listing ideas and details, using a writer's journal, and asking the *5 W-How?* questions. Use any one of these methods to gather information for a topic of your own. Keep the information you gather in your notebook. You will use it later in this chapter.

GROUPING IDEAS AND DETAILS

23f. Group related ideas and details under headings.

Now that you have gathered information about your topic, you are ready to begin grouping closely related ideas and details. This is called *classifying*.

To group your information under headings, you must begin by considering whether two or more ideas have something in common. You must decide whether there is a larger idea that includes them. For example, here are six of the ideas from the topic "beginning a stamp collection" (page 622):

1.   fun of watching collection grow
2.   removing stamps from envelopes

3. learning about people and customs of foreign lands
4. appreciating beauty of stamps
5. learnirg locations of countries
6. educational value

A quick glance probably tells you that some of these ideas and details are related and some are not. There is an obvious connection between numbers 1 and 4, both of which involve pleasure or enjoyment. A similar connection exists between 3, 5, and 6, all of which have something to do with the educational aspect of collecting stamps. Only 2 does not combine with a related idea.

Once you have grouped your ideas by finding the larger idea that they have in common, it is an easy step to give each group a heading. You simply express the central idea of the group in a word or phrase. For example, you can group the following items together, since they both deal with pleasure or enjoyment:

1. fun of watching collection grow
4. appreciating beauty of stamps

You need only choose between *pleasure* and *enjoyment*, and you have a heading for the group. Suppose you choose *pleasure:*

Pleasure
   fun of watching collection grow
   appreciating beauty of stamps

It will be easier to find a heading for the group that includes 3, 5, and 6:

3. learning about people and customs of foreign lands
5. learning locations of countries
6. educational value

You probably realize that 3 and 5 describe specific educational values of collecting stamps. Therefore, the heading for the group is supplied by one of the ideas from the list itself:

Educational value
   learning about people and customs of foreign lands
   learning locations of countries

By following the same general process of grouping ideas and details and adding headings, you could develop a complete list of ideas like the one on the following page.

Pleasure	heading
fun of watching collection grow	} related ideas
appreciating beauty of stamps	
Educational value	heading
learning about people	
and customs of foreign lands	} related ideas
learning locations of countries	
Sources of stamps	heading
family mail	
hobby stores	
post office	} related ideas
dealers: packets, approval sheets	
Displaying stamps	heading
removing stamps from envelopes	
supplies: tongs, hinges, album	} related ideas
mounting stamps in album	

Perhaps the process of grouping is not quite finished yet. The first two headings are, in fact, the reasons for collecting stamps. Therefore, you can combine the first two groups into one:

Reasons for collecting stamps	heading
Pleasure	subheading
fun of watching collection grow	} related ideas
appreciating beauty of stamps	
Educational value	subheading
learning about people and customs	
of foreign lands	} related ideas
learning locations of countries	

Notice that identation is used to show that related ideas and details are grouped under headings.

When you attempt to group the ideas and details you have gathered, you may find that some items do not fit anywhere. Not all the information you have gathered may really suit your topic. Look over the list about stamp collecting on page 622. Two ideas can be eliminated.

history of postage stamps [eliminated because it does not
contribute to purpose of composition]
valuable stamps [eliminated because a beginning collector
would not ordinarily try to collect valuable stamps]

Remember that in exposition, as in most other kinds of
writing, what you leave out can be as important as what you put
in. By omitting an unrelated idea or detail from your list, you can
often improve your paper greatly.

EXERCISE 18. Eliminating Ideas and Details. The following list contains several ideas or details that do not fit the topic
"repairing a bicycle." Decide which items do not fit and copy
them on your paper. Be prepared to explain your choices.

Topic: Repairing a bicycle
Purpose: To show how to make simple repairs on a bicycle
Ideas and details:

adjusting the handlebars	safety helmets
long-distance bicycling	selecting a bicycle
streets vs. dirt roads	locking the bicycle
removing the chain	measuring the height of
locating a tire puncture	the seat

EXERCISE 19. Grouping Ideas and Details. The ideas for
each of the following topics can be organized under two separate
headings. First write down the topic. Then supply appropriate
headings and list related ideas and details under each heading.

EXAMPLE   1. Baking bread
Mixing ingredients; flour; shortening; kneading
dough; setting oven; yeast; salt; forming loaves;
water; letting dough rise
1. *How to bake bread*

Ingredients	*Procedure*
flour	*mixing ingredients*
shortening	*kneading dough*
yeast	*forming loaves*
salt	*letting dough rise*
water	*setting oven*

1. School activities
   Glee club; football; baseball; science club; drama club; gymnastics
2. Model planes
   Balsa wood; sharp knife; cutting out parts; gluing parts together; blueprints; paint; painting; glue
3. Encyclopedias
   Using the index to find information on a topic; gaining additional information from maps and charts; finding topic alphabetically by title; skimming to find needed facts; taking notes on the article

EXERCISE 20. Grouping Your Own Information. Sort into groups the ideas and details you gathered for a topic of your own in Exercise 17. First look for major headings; then list related ideas and details under the headings. Use indentation to distinguish related ideas from headings.

ARRANGING IDEAS AND DETAILS

23g. Arrange your ideas and details into a topic outline or an informal plan.

By now you have limited your topic, gathered supporting ideas and details, and grouped related ideas under headings, omitting those that are not related to the purpose of your composition. Now you are ready to organize or arrange your groups into logical order. You should put your groups into an order that fits your topic. Remember that you want to present information about your topic so that it makes sense to your audience.

As you arrange your ideas, you will be developing a plan that will guide your writing. The purpose of this plan is to show all of the ideas and headings that will go into the composition in the order in which you will explain them. Your plan should also show the relationship they have to each other.

Often the ideas and details themselves suggest the proper method of arrangement. For example, headings for a composition about producing a play might follow the order of time: choosing the play, casting the play, and rehearsing the play. A composition on "our responsibilities," on the other hand, might call for headings arranged from the most general to the most specific: responsibilities to our country, responsibilities to our community, responsibilities to our family, and responsibilities to ourselves.

The major headings for "beginning a stamp collection" may be arranged in order of time. Certainly the idea of "acquiring stamps" belongs before that of "displaying stamps," and "reasons for collecting stamps" comes before either.

Feel free to experiment with the order of your headings until you find the arrangement that presents your ideas in the clearest possible way. Find the order that will make the most sense to your audience. In addition to arranging headings in an order that makes sense, you may have to do the same with supporting ideas and details that fall under these headings. See if these ideas and details should be arranged in a particular order too.

The plan you develop for your composition can be an *informal plan* or a *topic outline*. In an informal plan, you simply arrange your major headings in a logical order. Supporting ideas and details are then indented under the major headings, in the form found on page 627. You can also develop a more formal plan, called a *topic outline*.

EXERCISE 21. Deciding on the Proper Arrangement.

For each of the following topics, indicate the order you would use to arrange the headings for a composition: order of time, general to specific, or specific to general. Be prepared to explain your answer.

1. How to assemble a telescope
2. The importance of being familiar with microcomputers
3. How to prepare for a math test
4. Directions to the Bijou Theater from Edgewater Junior High School
5. My generation's ambitions

EXERCISE 22. Arranging Your Own Ideas and Details.
In Exercise 20 you grouped ideas and details for a topic of your
own. Now arrange your groups, or major headings, into the order
most logical for your composition. Remember that you may also
have to arrange supporting ideas and details into a particular
order for each main heading.

Using Outline Form

Outlines follow a specific form. The outline consists of *headings*,
which state your main ideas, and *subheadings*, which state the
ideas and details that support the main ideas. These are arranged
in a specific way. In the topic outline, words or phrases are used
rather than complete sentences.

The main ideas in the composition are indicated by Roman
numerals (I, II, etc.). These will usually be the heads under which
you grouped related ideas earlier (see pages 625–28). In the
outline for a composition on "beginning a stamp collection," for
example, the first Roman numeral head might be

I. Reasons for collecting stamps

Notice that the heading itself begins with a capital and that it
is not a complete sentence. This will be true of all of the heads in
the topic outline you are developing.

The idea expressed in the first head indicates that several
reasons will be given. If each of the reasons is taken up separately, each will become a subheading under the main heading. These
divisions of the main idea are indicated on an outline with capital
letters:

I. Reasons for collecting stamps
  A. Pleasure
  B. Educational value

Notice that the subheadings are indented to show that they are
divisions of the idea marked by the Roman numeral. Since the
subheadings are divisions, there must be at least two of them. An
outline should never have just one subhead under a main head.
The reason for this is that subheads are used to divide the main

heads into smaller parts, and whenever you divide *anything*, you must end up with at least two parts.

IMPROPER   I. Reasons for collecting stamps
                       A. Pleasure
              II. Sources for the collector

If the only reason for starting a collection is pleasure, then the Roman numeral heading should be revised and the single subheading omitted:

BETTER   I. The pleasure of collecting stamps
             II. Sources for the collector
               (etc.)

If either or both of the subheadings can be further divided, a further indentation is made and the new and smaller ideas are marked with Arabic numerals (1, 2, etc.):

  I. Reasons for collecting stamps
     A. Pleasure
        1. Fun of watching collection grow
        2. Appreciating beauty of stamps
     B. Educational value
        1. Learning about people and customs of foreign lands
        2. Learning locations of countries
 II. (etc.)

For most short papers, these levels of headings and subheadings will be sufficient. If you wish to make still smaller divisions, the following skeleton outline shows how it is done:

  I.
    A.
       1.
       2.
          a.
          b.
    B.
 II. (etc.)

The complete topic outline for "beginning a stamp collection" would look something like the following one.

Title: Beginning a Stamp Collection [title not part of outline]
Purpose: To give reasons for collecting stamps and to show how
  to get started

   I. Reasons for collecting stamps   main heading
     A. Pleasure   subheading
       1. Fun of watching collection grow   }
       2. Appreciating beauty of stamps   } subheadings
     B. Educational value   subheading
       1. Learning about people and customs }
          of foreign lands   } subheadings
       2. Learning locations of countries }
  II. Sources for the collector
     A. Family mail
     B. Post office
     C. Hobby stores
     D. Stamp dealers
       1. Packets
       2. Approval sheets
 III. Stamp display
     A. Supplies
       1. Album
       2. Hinges
       3. Tongs
     B. Procedure
       1. Removing from envelopes
       2. Mounting in album
 IV. Specialization

Notice that a fourth main idea has been added to provide a
conclusion for the composition. Notice also, though, that the
word *conclusion* is not used in the outline. The writer has told
how to start a collection; he wants to end by giving the audience
some idea of a more advanced kind of collecting. How to write a
conclusion is discussed later in this chapter.

EXERCISE 23. Completing an Outline. Copy the incomplete outline at the left. Then fill in the blanks with the items
given at the right.

Title: Our Science Club
Purpose: To explain how our science club began and to show its
activities

I. Formation of club
   A. ——
   B. ——
   C. ——
      1. Campaigning
        for office
      2. ——
   D. Writing the club
      constitution
II. ——
   A. ——
      1. Government
        laboratories
      2. ——
   B. Projects
      1. ——
      2. ——
   C. Talks by eminent speakers
   D. ——

Holding elections
Tours of laboratories
Recruiting members
Discussions of current scientific
   developments
Raising an ant colony
Choosing a name
Industrial laboratories
Electing officers
Club activities
Studying a bacterial mold

EXERCISE 24. Developing an Outline. Arrange the following ideas and details into an outline. Include a statement of
purpose. Your outline, like the one on page 633, should have
three levels.

Title: Taking a Camping Trip
Major ideas:
   Camp health and safety
   Planning
   Setting up camp
Supporting ideas and details:
   Selecting equipment   Dry ground
   Making a fire   Safety when hiking
   Safety tips   Arranging the wood
   Setting up tents   Tents
   Presence of fuel   Purifying water

Knives, hatchets, and axes	Safety in the water
	Choosing a campground
Chopping wood	Bedding
Selecting clothing	Food, pans, plates, spoons,
Personal health	etc.

EXERCISE 25. Developing Your Own Outline.   Prepare an outline on a topic of your own. You may want to develop an outline for the information you grouped and arranged in Exercises 19 and 20. Remember that this outline will guide the writing of your composition, so be sure it includes all the items you want to explain in your composition.

WRITING

WRITING A FIRST DRAFT

23h. Write a draft of your expository composition: the introduction, the body, and the conclusion.

In Chapter 22 you learned that a narrative should have a beginning, a middle, and an end, also known as the introduction, body, and conclusion. The same is true of the expository composition; it should also have an introduction, a body, and a conclusion. Each of these sections plays a different part in presenting your topic to your audience.

As you write the draft of your expository composition, allow your writing to flow freely. Concentrate on putting down your ideas about your topic. After you write this draft, you will be able to revise and proofread. Right now you should simply focus on expressing your thoughts about your topic.

As you write this draft, you may notice that new ideas about your topic occur to you. Include these ideas in your draft, even though they do not appear in your outline or informal plan. Thinking up new ideas as you write is both natural and predictable in a creative process such as writing.

You may find it helpful to keep three questions in mind as you begin to write your draft. These questions will focus your attention on your purpose for writing, your audience, and your topic:

1. What is my purpose for writing?
2. Who is my audience?
3. How can I best explain this topic to my audience?

Writing the Introduction

The *introduction* to an expository composition should indicate the general purpose and topic of your composition. In this way the introductory paragraph prepares your audience for the rest of your composition. Notice that the sample composition on pages 639–41 begins, "Stamp collecting is a very popular hobby for several reasons." This introductory paragraph not only briefly gives the basic idea of the paragraph, but also leads to the basic purpose of the composition—to tell how to begin a stamp collection. You may want to include your statement of purpose in your introductory paragraph.

EXERCISE 26. Writing an Introductory Paragraph. Write an introduction for your expository composition. Be sure you include a sentence that states your composition's general purpose and topic; in this way, your audience will know what to expect when they read your composition.

Writing the Body

The *body* is the longest part of a composition and contains most of the information. It carries out the purpose indicated by the introduction to the composition. As you write the body of your composition, be sure to refer to your informal plan or outline. Either one of these can guide your writing, since each shows how you have planned your composition. In the sample composition on pages 639–41, the body consists of the second, third, fourth, fifth, and sixth paragraphs. These paragraphs develop ideas given in parts II and III of the sample outline on page 633.

You may find that you can discuss each main heading in your plan or outline in a separate paragraph. Sometimes, however, you may discuss an especially long or complicated main idea in more than one paragraph. At other times, you may discuss more than one main idea in a single paragraph. How you form paragraphs depends on your main ideas or headings: how much information do they contain, and how difficult are they to explain?

Using Transitional Words and Phrases

To help your audience follow your ideas throughout a piece of writing, you should connect ideas and details. You can do this by using transitional words and phrases. These are expressions that join ideas or details. In Chapter 20 you studied one use of transitional words and phrases—to connect *sentences* within a paragraph. Transitional words and phrases are also used to make smooth connections between *paragraphs* in a composition. By showing how one idea relates to another, transitional words and phrases enable your audience to follow your train of thought throughout your composition.

As the following list indicates, most transitional words and phrases can join paragraphs as well as individual sentences.

besides	even more	next
finally	in addition	on the other hand
first	in fact	then
for example	moreover	therefore
furthermore	nevertheless	thus

It is especially important to use transitional words and phrases in expository writing. When you are writing to inform or explain, you need to be sure your audience is following each point you make. This is particularly true of compositions that explain how to make or do something and of compositions that give directions. For each of these expository compositions, success depends on understanding how each step relates to the next. For example, if you were explaining how to make toast, you would probably use words or phrases that show time order: "*First* place the slice of bread in the toaster, *then* push the handle down, and *finally* remove the toast when it pops up."

EXERCISE 27. Finding Transitional Words and Phrases. Locate an expository paragraph in an encyclopedia, newspaper article, magazine article, how-to manual, cookbook, or textbook. If you are permitted to cut the paragraph out, paste it to a sheet of paper; then circle all the transitional words and phrases in the paragraph. If you cannot cut the paragraph out, simply write down all the transitional words and phrases it contains. Do they help you to follow the writer's train of thought? Be prepared to explain why these transitions are or are not effective in this particular paragraph.

EXERCISE 28. Writing the Body. Write the body for a composition on your own topic. Use your informal plan or outline as a guide. Remember that you can write one paragraph for each major idea or heading in your plan or outline. Also remember to include transitional words and phrases to connect sentences and paragraphs in your composition.

Writing the Conclusion

The *conclusion* brings the composition to a definite close. It should not be long or complicated. To write a conclusion, ask yourself one question: What do I want my audience to think about my topic after they read my composition? One way of concluding a composition is to sum up some of the points you made earlier in the composition. For example, notice that the last sentence of the sample composition on page 641 restates the main idea of the first paragraph. In a short composition, the conclusion —like the introduction—does not have to be longer than one or two sentences.

EXERCISE 29. Writing the Conclusion. Write the conclusion for your expository composition. Ask yourself what you would like your audience to think about your topic; then try to make this point in one or two sentences.

Studying a Sample Composition

The sample composition that follows was developed from the topic outline on page 633. The outline's main headings appear in the margin to show how the outline and the composition are related.

As you study the sample composition, notice how the first paragraph begins with a sentence that suggests the purpose of the composition. Each paragraph in the body then explains the main headings in the outline. Notice how some main ideas are given more space than others, depending on how much explanation they require. Finally, notice how the last paragraph brings the composition to a definite end.

BEGINNING A STAMP COLLECTION

Stamp collecting is a very popular hobby for several reasons. Collectors gain pleasure from the varied colors and designs of the stamps, while they enjoy the fun of watching their collections grow. In addition, stamp collecting has educational value. Stamps often tell the collector much about a country's important customs, events, and famous citizens. Furthermore, collectors soon learn to find out the exact location of a country. Often they are interested enough to find out other important facts about that country.

introduction (reasons for collecting stamps—I, A–B in outline)

transition

transition

Beginning collectors can start with family mail. A variety of stamps can be collected from the letters and packages the average family receives. If a relative or family friend happens to be living overseas, another valuable source is available.

body (acquiring stamps—II, A in outline)

In addition, the collector can get domestic stamps at the post office. Some large post offices have special windows for new stamps, but all post offices have the new stamps. Foreign stamps can often be bought in hobby stores or ordered from stamp dealers.

(II, B–C in outline); transition

In fact, stamp dealers who advertise in magazines (often in magazines popular with young people) are an important source of stamps for all collectors. Most dealers offer beginners a packet of assorted stamps at a low price. After collectors have acquired many common stamps, they may be interested in dealers' approval sheets. Stamps on an approval sheet are usually less common than those in the packets; each is mounted and priced separately. Collectors keep any stamp they want and send their money and the remaining stamps back to the dealer.

(II, D in outline; transition)

Most collectors display their stamps in albums. Albums for beginners usually have pictures of some of the stamps and sections for the different countries. Besides an album, a collector needs stamp tongs—a sort of tweezers—and hinges, small bits of gummed paper that connect the stamp to the album page.

(displaying stamps—III, A in outline)

Stamps taken from the family mail, as well as many included in the packets that come from dealers, have to be removed from the part of the envelope to which they are still sticking. To remove a stamp, the collector first places it face down on a blotter and moistens the envelope paper with warm water. After

(outline III, B)

transition

transition

the paper is thoroughly soaked, the stamp can usually be removed easily. By working slowly and carefully with the tongs, the collector can avoid tearing or otherwise damaging the stamp. To mount the stamp in an album, the collector allows it to dry, <u>then</u> folds a hinge with the gummed side out, moistens it, and attaches the stamp to the page.

transition

After beginners have had a taste of the pleasure of collecting, they are likely to want to specialize. For example, they may wish to concentrate on stamps of a particular country, or on those that have ships or certain animals on them. Whether they specialize or not, however, they are certain to gain much enjoyment and knowledge from their hobby.

conclusion
(specializing—IV in outline)

restates first sentence

EXERCISE 30. Studying an Expository Composition.
Answer each of the following questions about the sample composition on pages 639–41. Be prepared to explain your answers.

1. Who is the audience for this composition? Why do you think so?
2. If you were writing this composition, what information would you add? What information would you omit? Why?
3. How could the writer of this composition form paragraphs differently and still explain the topic clearly?
4. Select any one paragraph in the composition. Write down its topic sentence, and then list all the ideas and details that support this topic sentence. Also compare these ideas and details to those listed in the outline. How are the composition and outline similar or different on this point?
5. Do you think the writer successfully explained how to begin a stamp collection? Why or why not?

GUIDELINES FOR WRITING EXPOSITORY COMPOSITIONS

Prewriting

1. Select a topic you understand well enough to explain to someone else. You will probably have difficulty explaining a topic you do not understand well.

2. Be sure to limit, or narrow, your topic well so that you can discuss it clearly and thoroughly in a few paragraphs.

3. Ask yourself what someone unfamiliar with your topic might want or need to know about your topic. Then gather information for your composition with your audience in mind.

4. Determine if any technical or unusual words need to be defined. Your audience may need help with the meanings of some words.

5. Group and arrange ideas and details so that your topic will make sense to your audience. This organized information makes up an informal plan or outline that can guide the drafting of your composition.

Writing

6. Write an introduction that includes a statement indicating your composition's general purpose and topic.

7. Use your outline or informal plan as a guide to follow when you draft the body of your composition. Be sure to connect your ideas smoothly by using transitional words and phrases.

8. Write a conclusion that leaves your audience thinking about your topic, either the main points or other related ideas.

Revising

9. After you write a draft of your composition, check to see that you have included enough information to explain this topic to your audience. Ask yourself if you have presented ideas and details in an order that will be clear to your audience. Check that the words and kinds of sentences you have used fit your audience.

Proofreading

10. Proofread your composition for mistakes in spelling, grammar, usage, punctuation, and capitalization *before* and *after* you prepare a final copy for your intended audience.

REVIEW EXERCISE. Writing an Expository Composition.
Following the Guidelines for Writing Expository Compositions,
write a composition on a topic of your own. Follow the steps in
the writing process as you plan and draft this composition.

REVISING

REVISING A DRAFT

23i. Revise the draft of your composition for content, organization, and style.

After preparing your draft, you are ready to revise for content,
organization, and style. You should look over your draft to see
where you can make changes to explain your topic better or to
inform your audience in more detail about your topic.

Three strategies may help you to revise your draft more
easily. First, try to put your draft aside for a while before you
begin revising. Sometimes thinking about your draft for a few
days allows you to see its strengths and weaknesses more clearly.
Second, read your draft aloud to yourself. If something sounds
confusing or does not make sense to you when you read your
draft aloud, it is possible that the same thing will happen to your
audience. Third, ask a classmate to read your composition and to
suggest places where you might improve your draft. Someone
else's comments can often be very helpful.

CRITICAL THINKING:
Evaluating a First Draft

To revise your composition, you use the critical thinking skill of
evaluation. *To evaluate* means to judge, or to determine if
something measures up to your standards. You use the critical
thinking skill of evaluation when you explain why your school
soccer team just played its best game ever: you judge the team's
performance by comparing it to your idea of what makes a great

soccer game—perhaps fast action, quick saves by the goalkeeper, and fancy dribbling and passing. You judge your team's game in terms of some standards.

When you revise your composition, you are evaluating your draft in terms of some standards. The standards you use to judge your draft relate to its content, organization, and style.

Content is what you say about your topic. This includes the ideas and details you use to develop your major ideas about the topic. *Organization* is the arrangement of those ideas and details so that your explanation of the topic will make sense to your audience. *Style* concerns the words you use and the kinds of sentences you write; for example, short and simple or long and complicated. Both your choice of words and your choice of sentences should fit your topic and your audience.

You can use the following questions to begin to evaluate the first draft of your composition.

1. Are there any ideas or details I should add to explain my topic better?

2. Are there any ideas or details I should omit because they do not help to explain my topic better?

3. Are there any ideas and details I should replace with other, more exact ones?

4. Are there any sentences or paragraphs I should rearrange, or put into a more logical order for this particular topic?

5. Are the words and kinds of sentences I have used suitable for my topic and audience?

A revised first draft of the third paragraph of the sample composition (page 640) follows. As you study the paragraph, notice how the writer made several changes to improve the draft.

¶ *In addition*

1. The collector can ~~also~~ get ~~local~~ *domestic* stamps at the post office.

2. *Foreign* ~~Unusual~~ stamps can often be bought *(in hobby stores)* or ordered *(from stamp dealers)* ~~Some~~

3. ~~really~~ large post offices have *special windows for* ~~places to buy~~ new stamps, but

4. all post offices have the *new* ٨ stamps. ~~Some of those foreign~~

5. ~~stamps are really incredible!~~

After you study the revised paragraph, you may realize that the writer made the following kinds of changes:

1. In lines 1, 2, and 3, the writer substituted words or phrases that are more suitable for the paragraph.

2. In lines 4 and 5 the writer deleted, or omitted, a sentence that did not help to explain the topic. In lines 1 and 2 a word was also omitted.

3. In lines 2, 3, and 4, the writer rearranged two sentences so that ideas would be in a more logical order.

4. In line 1 the writer added a transitional phrase to connect this paragraph to the one that comes before it.

5. In lines 2 and 4 the writer added words to explain the topic more specifically.

Use the five questions on page 644 and the following guidelines to revise any expository composition you write.

GUIDELINES FOR REVISING EXPOSITORY COMPOSITIONS

1. Is the topic interesting and informative for the audience?
2. Is the content suited to the age and interests of the audience?
3. Does each paragraph in the body help to explain at least one part of the topic?
4. Does every idea or detail support the topic without repeating it?
5. Are details organized according to the order that makes sense for this particular topic?
6. Are transitional words or phrases such as *first, furthermore,* and *on the other hand* used to show the order of ideas or the connections between ideas?
7. Are ideas expressed in a way that is suitable for the audience? That is, are simpler vocabulary words and less complicated sentences used for younger audiences?
8. Are technical terms or unusual vocabulary words explained?
9. Does the writing have fresh, exact, and vivid adjectives, adverbs, and verbs?
10. Is there a variety of sentences, smoothly and clearly written?

EXERCISE 31. Studying a Writer's Revisions. For each of the following sentences, the writer revised by (1) adding, (2) deleting, (3) substituting, (4) rearranging words or phrases, or (5) adding transitional words or phrases. Four of the five kinds of revision were used. Indicate what kind of revision was used and the purpose of the revision.

EXAMPLE   1. The Everglades‸is 100 miles long and 50 to 75 miles
             ‸ a marshy grassland in southern Florida ‸
             wide.

           1. *Kind of revision?* Adding a phrase
              Why? To identify the topic (the Everglades) more
              clearly

1. To locate the Big Dipper, seven stars in the Great Bear
   constellation,‸look for the North Star,‸look for the two
            first   *then*
   stars that point toward the North Star in the front of the
   cup, and‸look for the stars that form the dipper's handle.
         finally

2. The Great Lakes is a ~~humongous~~ chain of freshwater lakes
                        an extensive
   in North America.

3. Our international backpacking expedition takes us to
   Great Britain in October, ⟨the Great Salt Lake in September,⟩ and Australia's Great Sandy Desert in November.

4. The Great Wall of China‸is an earth and stone defensive
                          ‸ over 1500 miles long ‸
   wall that stretches across northern China.

EXERCISE 32. Revising for Content, Organization, and Style. Part of the following paragraph has been revised for content, organization, and style. Study the writer's revision. Finish revising the paragraph, using the guidelines on page 645.

¶ Preparing onionskin ⟨*for examination under a microscope*⟩ is a simple process. Materials you   need

are a microscope slide and cover slip, water, tissues, a   knife, tweezers, a medicine dropper, an onion, and a little dilute iodine. Put ~~some~~ a small drop of water on the slide. First Clean a slide and cover slip with a paper tissue. Loosen an inner layer of onion and ~~chop~~ cut off a piece (about ¼" square). With ~~teeny weeny~~ tweezers, ~~get~~ peel the onionskin off ~~of~~ one side of the small piece ~~of onion~~ onion. Get the onionskin in the drop of water on the slide and get the cover slip on it. Supposedly, if you hold an onion under running water when you peel it, your eyes will not tear. My sister always cries when she peels onions. She must not know about the water trick. To see them better, place some of the iodine stuff on the cover slip. It will ooze under the cover slip lots and lots faster if you get one corner of a blotter to the water at the opposite side of the cover slip. Peep at the slide under the microscope.

EXERCISE 33. Revising Your Own Composition.   Revise the expository composition you wrote in the Review Exercise on page 643 or in Exercises 26, 28 and 29. Be sure to refer to the Guidelines for Revising Expository Compositions on page 645.

PROOFREADING

PROOFREADING YOUR EXPOSITORY COMPOSITION

23j. Proofread your expository composition.

After you revise your draft, you should check your writing for any mistakes in spelling, grammar, usage, and mechanics. By correcting these mistakes, you will make it easier for your audience to understand the ideas you are trying to communicate about your topic.

In order to proofread, you should read over your composition several times. Each time you should concentrate on a different aspect; one time you should check for correct spelling and proper capitalization, another time for correct punctuation, another time for correct verb forms and tenses, and so on. By focusing on one item at a time, you should notice any errors more easily.

While you are proofreading, you may want to use the list of revising and proofreading symbols on page 488. You can also use the following list of proofreading guidelines to proofread any expository composition you write.

GUIDELINES FOR PROOFREADING EXPOSITORY COMPOSITIONS

1. Are all words spelled correctly? Have word meanings been checked against a dictionary?

2. Does each sentence begin with a capital letter? Are proper nouns and proper adjectives capitalized?

3. Is every sentence a complete sentence, not a fragment or a run-on?

4. Are sentences punctuated correctly? Does every sentence end with a punctuation mark?

5. Do plural verbs have plural subjects? Do singular verbs have singular subjects?

6. Are verb forms and tenses used correctly? Are troublesome pairs of verbs such as *sit/set* and *lie/lay* used correctly?

7. Are subject and object forms of pronouns used correctly?

8. Are the comparative forms of adjectives and adverbs used correctly?

9. Have double negatives been avoided?

10. Are words correctly divided at the ends of lines?

11. Are there proper margins? Are new paragraphs indented?

12. Is the paper neat and legible, with no messy crossed-out passages?

EXERCISE 34. Proofreading a Paragraph. The following paragraph contains ten errors in spelling, grammar, capitalization, punctuation, and usage. Proofread the paragraph, locating each error and correcting it on your own paper. The lines of the paragraph are numbered for you.

1   The late Dr. Frank E Lutz of the American Musuem of
2   Natural History in New York City once told the director of
3   the museum that he could collect 500 insect species in in his
4   own yard. Dr. Lutz lived in a suburb of New York city, and
5   their yard was only 200 feet long and 75 feet wide. Yet he was
6   a specialist in the study of insects, and he felt sure that he
7   could find, at least 500 species in his yard the director of the
8   museum could not beleive Dr. Lutz's claim, but the director
9   was mistaken. Dr. Lutz collected 1,042 species of insects in
10   his yard and has fun doing it.

EXERCISE 35. Proofreading Your Expository Composition. Proofread the composition you revised in Exercise 33. Determine where you made errors in spelling, grammar, usage, and mechanics and correct each mistake. Refer to the Guidelines for Proofreading Expository Compositions on page 648 and to the list of revising and proofreading symbols on page 488. If you and a classmate exchange compositions, you can double-check each other's proofreading.

PREPARING THE FINAL VERSION

MAKING THE FINAL COPY

23k. Prepare the final copy of your expository composition.

The final draft is the final copy of your composition. This is the version you will pass along to your audience. When you prepare this copy, be sure to use correct manuscript form. (See Chapter 18.) Follow any special instructions your teacher may give you.

After you make this final copy of your composition, be sure to proofread it again. It is easy to omit words or to make accidental errors as you recopy your draft. Proofreading one more time will allow you to catch these accidental mistakes before your audience reads your composition.

EXERCISE 36. Preparing a Final Copy. Prepare a final copy, or final draft, of any composition you have written in this chapter. You may decide to prepare a final draft of the composition you revised and proofread in Exercises 33 and 35. As you prepare this draft, concentrate on avoiding the kinds of errors students tend to make at this stage of the writing process. Be sure to proofread again before you pass your composition on to your audience.

CHAPTER 23 WRITING REVIEW 1

Writing an Expository Composition. Following the steps of the writing process, write an expository composition on a topic of your choice. As you plan and draft your composition, be sure to refer to the Guidelines for Writing Expository Compositions on page 642. You should also refer to the revising guidelines on page 645 and to the proofreading guidelines on page 648 after you have written your draft. If your teacher allows, you may also want to share your composition with your classmates after you have revised and proofread.

CHAPTER 23 WRITING REVIEW 2

Studying Your Expository Writing. What you have learned about writing exposition in this chapter applies to the expository writing you do in all your school subjects. Select an expository paragraph or composition you have written for one of your other classes, such as a paper for a science or social studies class. Read your paper, then answer the following questions:

1. Who is your audience for this paper?
2. What did you do to adjust to your audience's needs when you wrote this paper?
3. Did you follow the steps in the writing process when you wrote this paper? Why or why not?
4. What part of the writing process would you use differently to improve your paper? Why?
5. How do you think knowing about the writing process can help you to improve your writing in your other classes?

CHAPTER 24

Writing Exposition

SUMMARIES AND REPORTS

All through school, you will be called upon to find information and to report on it in your own words. No skill that you study this year will be more useful—not just in your English class, but in all of your other courses as well.

WRITING SUMMARIES

The simplest kind of report is the *summary,* an account in your own words of a longer piece of writing. As with other forms of writing, preparing a summary involves prewriting, writing, and revising steps.

PREWRITING

Considering Purpose and Audience

24a. Consider the purpose and the audience for a summary.

The *purpose* of a summary is to provide a short account of a longer piece of writing. To accomplish this purpose, include only the main ideas of the original article. Leave out unimportant details, examples, anecdotes, statistics, and so on.

The way in which you write the summary depends on the age and background of the audience. Sometimes a summary is written for the same audience as was the original article. If so, use the same kinds of sentences and vocabulary in your summary as in the original article. At other times, however, your summary is for an audience younger or older than the original audience. Generally speaking, use shorter sentences and less difficult vocabulary for the younger audience. For some audiences, you may also need to define terms and to give some background information.

EXAMPLE

Original:

Insects are one of the most common forms of life on earth. Just think of the different kinds you have seen right around your home. Certainly you've seen ants and wasps, and, if you have a lawn or garden, you've probably seen grasshoppers and maybe even beetles with bright red spots on their backs.

With insects so common, most people haven't thought much about the fact that some insects are very dangerous. Throughout history, and up until this very minute, certain insects have been killing people and spreading disease. One of the many types of mosquitoes, for example, is currently blamed for one million deaths each year in various parts of the world, and for ten times that many cases of various illnesses.

DONALD CAUSEY

Summary for eighth-grade students:

Insects, one of the most common life forms, are all around us. Because they are so common, however, many people do not realize how dangerous some of them are. A certain kind of mosquito, for example, causes many deaths and illnesses all over the world.

Summary for second-grade students:

An *insect* is a small animal that has three pairs of legs. Insects are all around us. Because people see them so often, they may not realize that they can be dangerous. Some insects, however, are very dangerous. One kind of mosquito, for example, causes many deaths and illnesses.

EXERCISE 1. Deciding on Main Ideas. The following three paragraphs are from an article on one kind of dangerous insect—army ants. Read the article carefully, deciding which are the main ideas that should be included in a summary. Then answer the question that follows the paragraphs.

To get the full picture of what a swarm of army ants looks like, imagine a tide of them up to 33 yards (30 m) wide moving through the jungle at speeds up to 38 yards (35 m) an hour. A swarm this big makes a crackling and hissing sound in the jungle somewhat like rain coming through the trees.

The eerieness of a swarm of army ants is increased by the fact that, en masse, they have—just as their name suggests—a distinctly military appearance. In fact, many species of army ants travel in a classic pincher formation that is shaped something like a *V*. This pincher formation allows an army— of people or ants—to encircle an enemy and fall upon it suddenly from all sides.

A feature of army ants that makes them so dangerous is their constant hunger for fresh, live food. Unlike ordinary ants, which usually scurry about looking for bits of dead food, grains of sugar, fresh leaves, and so forth, army ants kill what they eat. Their diet includes anything that comes in their path—grasshoppers, baby birds in a low-hanging nest, lizards, snakes, and rats. There have even been reports of army ants attacking penned livestock and, within minutes, tearing whole cows to pieces.

DONALD CAUSEY

Each of the following items is from the article on army ants. Which of them should be included in a summary?

Details:
  a. Army ants can move in wide swarms up to speeds of 35 meters an hour.
  b. The swarm sounds like rain as it comes through the jungle.
  c. Many army ants travel, like a military formation, in a V.
  d. One reason army ants are so dangerous is that they are always searching for fresh, live food.
  e. Examples of the kinds of food regular ants eat are grains of sugar and fresh leaves.

Gathering Information

24b. Gather information for the summary by taking notes.

To write a summary, first read through the article carefully, looking for main ideas. During this first reading, do not take notes. Instead, concentrate on understanding what you read. Then, read over the article again, this time jotting down the main ideas. In taking notes, be certain that you use your own words.

EXAMPLE

Original:

> **Halley's comet**, *HAL eez*, is a brilliant comet named for the English astronomer Edmond Halley. Before Halley made his investigations, most people believed that comets appeared by chance and traveled through space in no set path. But Halley believed that comets belonged to the solar system and took definite paths around the sun at regular intervals. He found that the paths taken by certain comets in 1531 and 1607 were identical with the path of a comet observed in 1682. He decided that the same comet made all these paths. He predicted that it would reappear in 1758 and at fairly regular intervals thereafter. The comet was seen in 1758 and made its closest approach to the sun in 1759. It appears an average of every 77 years and was seen as long ago as 240 B.C.

Halley's comet can be seen only as it nears the sun. In August 1909, scientists at Helwan Observatory in Egypt photographed the comet when it was about 300 million miles (480 million kilometers) from the sun. On April 24, 1910, it came as close as 55 million miles (89 million kilometers) to the sun. In early May 1910, the comet's head was as brilliant as the brightest stars. Its tail stretched about two-thirds the distance from the horizon to directly overhead. On May 21, 1910, the earth is believed to have passed through the comet's tail. The comet was last observed in this orbit with a camera on July 1, 1911.

On Oct. 16, 1982, astronomers at the Palomar Observatory in California made the next sighting of Halley's comet. They photographed the comet when it was about 1 billion miles (1.6 billion kilometers) from the sun. The comet was expected to make its closest approach to the sun on Feb. 9, 1986.

JOSEPH ASHBROOK

Notes:

1. Comet named for English astronomer Edmond Halley
2. Seen on an average of once every 77 years
3. Visible only when it nears the sun
4. In 1910, as bright as a star—tail stretched high above horizon
5. Later that year, earth may have passed through comet's tail
6. Was expected to pass closest to sun in 1986

Notice how the writer of these notes concentrates on the years the comet approaches the earth or the sun, and on what the comet looks like. The notes do not include details about exact distances and exact days.

EXERCISE 2. Taking Notes. The following paragraphs are from an article about the use of computers to help paralyzed people move their arms and legs. The young woman, Nan Davis, whose legs are paralyzed, has worked with Dr. Jerrold Petrofsky in his computer program. First, read the paragraphs carefully, looking for the main ideas. Then, as you read the paragraphs a second time, make notes on the main ideas.

Dr. Petrofsky knew that Nan's *muscles* had not been damaged. The problem was that the damage to her spinal cord prevented Nan's brain from sending nerve signals to her muscles.

Dr. Petrofsky believed that electrical impulses, controlled by computer, could substitute for blocked nerve signals. In a limited way, he thought, the computer could do the brain's job.

"The computer puts electrical impulses into the muscles to make the muscles move," he explains. "There are sensors on the leg that tell the computer how much the muscles are moving. The computer can change the impulses it sends to produce nice, smooth movement."

Dr. Petrofsky knew that muscles lose their strength when they are not used for a long time. He began teaching Nan how to exercise in a new way. He used the computer to stimulate her leg muscles. This enabled Nan to lift weights and pedal a stationary bicycle.

Nan began taking part in an experimental fitness program in the doctor's lab. She was one of a number of volunteers in the program. Technicians would tape three rectangular electrode pads to her legs. The electrodes were wired to the Apple II. A special program, written by Petrofsky and his research partner, medical doctor Chandler Phillips, was started. Slowly but surely, Nan's legs began moving.

Her progress was dramatic. Thanks to this fitness program, Nan's leg muscles began growing again. "You can't get discouraged with [Dr. Petrofsky], because he never gives up," says Nan.

Dr. Petrofsky's experiments showed that computers could help people exercise paralyzed muscles. The freedom this brought meant a lot to Nan: "I could go in, get on the bicycle and work out, and get the same feeling that you would," she says. "I feel like I have more energy."

While Nan and the other test subjects worked on strengthening their muscles, Dr. Petrofsky and his research team were developing a walking system. The hardware for this system filled shelves and sprouted wires and cables. The heart of it, however, was a Z–80 microchip—the kind of chip used in TRS–80 computers.

After her months of work in the fitness program, Dr. Petrofsky decided that Nan was the best candidate to try the experimental device. On a November night in 1982, he gathered Nan and his team in the lab. The university had announced a press conference for the next day to demonstrate the walking system—and Nan had yet to take her first step.

She parked her wheelchair between a pair of handrails. She slipped into a special parachute harness that would pull some weight off her feet, easing the stress on her still-fragile bones. At the other end of the platform, Dr. Petrofsky stood before the equipment that was supposed to make her walk.

"Power up," he called. Nan leaned forward and rose from the wheelchair. With the computer controlling electronic sensors on her legs, Nan moved forward—step by halting step. The next day, in front of reporters from around the world, Nan walked again.

TIMOTHY R. GAFFNEY

WRITING

Writing the First Draft

24c. Write the first draft of a summary that is one third or less the length of the original article.

Using your notes, write the first draft of your summary. Use your own words, but follow the organization of ideas in the original summary.

EXAMPLE

Original:　AMERICAN ECONOMIC SUCCESS

The United States is one of the richest nations in the world. Most Americans enjoy a high standard of living. A nation's **standard of living** is the well-being of its population based on the amount of goods and services they can afford. On the average, we have more money to spend, and more goods to buy, than the people of most other nations. Our economic system produces more goods and services than any other in the world.

What makes all this possible? There are a number of reasons for our economic success. First of all, the United States is a land of great natural resources. We have timber, minerals, energy resources, a good climate, and fertile soil in abundance. In addition, we always have had energetic and inventive people. They have taken our resources and turned them into needed and desirable products.

Furthermore, our system of government has ensured the right of private enterprise—that is, the owning and operating of businesses by individuals rather than by the government. It has protected the right of individuals to own property and make a profit. Finally, the United States has developed an economic system in which most of its people can find work and earn financial success.

WILLIAM H. HARTLEY *and* WILLIAM S. VINCENT

Summary:

The United States is one of the wealthiest nations on earth. Americans, who provide more goods and services than any other people, have a high standard of living. They can afford to buy many goods and services. America is economically successful because it is rich both in natural resources and in industrious people. Our system of government, which ensures the right of people to own businesses and to make a profit, also contributes to our economic success.

EXERCISE 3. Writing a First Draft of a Summary. Using the notes provided, write a first draft of a summary of the article on Halley's comet, pages 655–56, or of the article on pages 657–58.

EXERCISE 4. Writing a First Draft of a Summary. The following paragraphs are from an article about people who worked to improve lives for many other people. First, read the article carefully, looking for main ideas. Then read the article again, this time making notes on the main ideas. Finally, use your notes to write a first draft of a summary that is one third or less the length of the original article. Your teacher may ask you to turn in your notes with the first draft of your summary.

HELPING THE DISADVANTAGED

Many people were unwilling to live in isolated communities and abandon all the customs and patterns of ordinary life. They were nonetheless sincerely interested in improving society. Some devoted their energies to helping people in need. Samuel Gridley Howe, a Boston doctor, specialized in the education of the blind. In the 1830s he founded a school, the **Perkins Institution**. He developed a method for printing books with raised type so that blind people could learn to "read" with their fingertips. Howe's greatest achievement was teaching Laura Bridgman, a child who was both blind and deaf, to read in this way and to communicate with others through signs called a manual alphabet. Another of his pupils, Anne Sullivan, learned the manual alphabet to communicate with Laura. She later became the teacher of Helen Keller, a remarkable woman who lost her sight and hearing as an infant.

Another Massachusetts reformer, Dorothea Dix, practically revolutionized the treatment of the mentally ill. Dix was a schoolteacher. One day in 1841 she was asked to teach a Sunday school class in a jail in Cambridge, Massachusetts. When she went to the jail, she discovered to her horror that insane and feeble-minded people were being kept there and treated like ordinary criminals.

Thereafter, Dix devoted her life to improving the care of the insane. She visited prisons all over the country and wrote reports describing conditions and exposing their faults. Dix insisted that insanity should be treated as a disease and that it could be cured. Through her efforts many states set up asylums for the care of the mentally ill.

JOHN A. GARRATY

REVISING

Revising the Summary

24d. Revise the first draft of your summary.

Like other forms of writing, summaries can be improved by revision. If possible, put your first draft aside for a few days before you begin to revise it. Keep the original article until you have completed your revision, as you may need to check details.

The following guidelines can help you in revising your summary.

GUIDELINES FOR REVISING A SUMMARY

1. Are only the main ideas of the original included in the summary.
2. Is the summary suitable for the audience?
3. Is the summary written in the writer's own words?
4. Does the organization of ideas in the summary follow that of the original?
5. Is the summary one third or less the length of the original?

EXERCISE 5. Revising a Summary. For this exercise, use the first draft of a summary you wrote for Exercise 3 or for Exercise 4. Check your first draft against the Guidelines for Revising a Summary given above, making changes to improve it. When you have finished the revision, recopy the summary. Before handing in your final draft, proofread it for errors. (See the Guidelines for Proofreading on page 487.)

REVIEW EXERCISE. Writing and Revising a Summary. Using what you have learned in this chapter, prepare a summary of one of the kinds of materials listed after these instructions. Follow these steps: (a) read the article looking for main ideas; (b) read the article a second time, taking notes on the main ideas; (c) use your notes to write a first draft; (d) check your first draft against the Guidelines for Revising a Summary on page 661, making necessary changes; (e) recopy the summary; (f) proofread the final draft for errors; and (g) make a final copy.

1. An interesting magazine or newspaper article
2. An encyclopedia article
3. Part of a chapter in your science or social studies book
4. A magazine profile of a historical figure or a celebrity
5. An editorial from your school or local newspaper

WRITING LONGER REPORTS

A more challenging kind of report, which you will often be asked to write, requires you to gather and organize information from a number of sources. In writing this kind of report, there are four basic steps:

1. Developing a limited topic
2. Gathering information
3. Organizing the information
4. Writing and revising the report

PREWRITING

Developing a Limited Topic

24e. Develop a limited topic.

Sometimes your teacher will assign a report topic; at other times you may be asked to develop your own. If you begin with a broad subject, such as animals, astronomy, or computers, you must limit it in the same way you would a composition topic (see pages 617–19). Your factual report will probably be a short one, only several paragraphs long. The topic should be one about which you can give detailed information in that space.

EXERCISE 6. Choosing Limited Topics. Some of the following topics are suitably limited for a factual report; others are too broad. On a piece of paper, write down the topics that are limited enough for a short factual report.

1. The flea: a dangerous insect
2. The role of women in the settlement of the West
3. How astrology works
4. How falcons are trained to hunt
5. The history of UFO's
6. The harmful effects of sugar
7. The U.S. Camel Corps—how it began and what happened to it
8. Unicorns and other mythical animals
9. How television changed the sport of football
10. Three famous tricks of Houdini—how they were done

24f. Consider the purpose and audience for your report.

The purpose of a factual report is to present factual information. Select a topic about which you can find information in reference sources such as encyclopedias and dictionaries, not a topic that you can know about only from your personal experience. For example, you may have had an exciting experience participating in a bike-a-thon to support diabetes research. Your experience riding in the bike-a-thon is a personal one; you will not find information about it in reference sources. However, you could write a factual report about diabetes—its causes, effects, and possible cures.

The topic you develop should be interesting to your audience. Most audiences are interested in new or unusual topics or in fresh information on well-known topics. For example, by the eighth grade almost everyone has heard reports on topics like Christopher Columbus's voyages to the New World; on when, where, and how dinosaurs lived; and on Halley's comet. Few people probably know, however, what Christopher Columbus was really like as a man. They may not know why skeletons of dinosaurs, which lived in swampy marshlands, are found today in dry, desert climates. Nor may they have thought about the effects of Halley's comet on business. For example, companies could make much money selling T-shirts, binoculars, telescopes, and the like. Cruise ship companies could book cruises to the Southern Hemisphere, where the comet can best be seen. Each of these items gives fresh information about a well-known topic.

24g. In developing a limited topic, consider your library resources.

For a factual report, you will need these library sources—books, magazine articles, newspaper articles, and other reference materials. If your topic is too technical or too new, you may not find the information that you need. Before you make a final decision on your topic, check your library resources.

EXERCISE 7. Choosing Report Topics. Some of the following topics are suitable for a factual report; others are not. On a piece of paper, make a list of the suitable topics. (Unsuitable topics may be based on personal experience or they may be uninteresting to the audience. They may also be too new or too technical for available sources.) Be prepared to explain why the topics you did not list are unsuitable.

1. How computers are used to help paralyzed people walk
2. The first walk on the moon
3. How and why hypnotism works
4. Why the class-sponsored carwash was a failure
5. The invention of the telephone
6. How the latest biological developments prolong life expectancy
7. The feeding habits of the male strap-toothed whale
8. What I learned about crazy diets
9. Buffalo Bill—the man behind the name
10. Magnetic resonance readings for medical diagnosis

EXERCISE 8. Developing a Limited Topic. For this exercise, you will develop a limited topic for your factual report. You may use a topic already mentioned in this chapter, you may select a topic from the following list, or, with your teacher's permission, you may develop a topic of your own. (Some of the topics in the following list need further limiting.)

1. Computer voices in stores and cars
2. Life in the coldest place on earth
3. Life in the hottest place on earth
4. The invention of fireworks
5. An endangered species: the humpback whale
6. What a Supreme Court justice does
7. A Chinese teen-ager at school in China
8. Egyptian mummies
9. Stonehenge: an ancient observatory?
10. How silk is made
11. Superstitious beliefs about owls
12. Legends about werewolves
13. The first railroad car for passengers
14. Jackie Robinson—how he broke the color barrier in Major League baseball
15. The Japanese samurai warrior
16. The sword swallowers and fire-eaters of India
17. The tradition of foot binding in ancient China
18. The Cajuns of Louisiana—their history and their culture
19. The history of the hamburger
20. The different movie versions of the Frankenstein story

Gathering Information

24h. Find sources of information about your topic.

Usually, the reference section of your library is the best place to begin gathering information. An encyclopedia or other general reference work will usually provide you with a good introduction to your subject. Depending on your subject, you may find additional information in more specialized reference books (pages 743–45).

Reference books usually provide a general introduction to a subject. For more detail, you must find books and magazine articles about it. To find books on your subject, you will use the card catalog (pages 738–40). Unless your subject is a broad one, it may be treated in *parts* of several books but not be the subject of a whole book itself. In this case, you will need to use the indexes of the books the card catalog directs you to in order to find the information you need.

To find articles about your subject in magazines, consult the *Readers' Guide to Periodical Literature* (pages 745–46).

24i. Record the sources from which you gather information.

For each source in which you find information, make a *source card.* (Use a 3 × 5-inch note card or slip of paper.) Different kinds of sources will require different types of source cards. On each type of source card, write the following information.

An encyclopedia source card:
1. The name of the author of the article, if there is one
2. The name of the article (in quotation marks)
3. The name of the encyclopedia (underlined)
4. The year of the edition

EXAMPLE

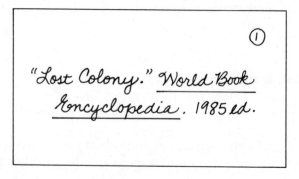

(*Hint:* Notice the punctuation on the card. A period comes at the end of the article's name [before the quotation marks]. A period also follows the name of the encyclopedia. Note that *edition* is abbreviated as *ed.*)

A book source card:

1. The name of the author (last name first)
2. The title of the book (underlined)
3. The place of publication
4. The name of the publishing company and the year of publication

EXAMPLE

> ②
>
> Kupperman, Karen Ordahl.
> Roanoke: The Abandoned
> Colony. Totowa : Rowman
> & Allanleld, 1984.

(*Hint:* Place a comma between the author's first and last names. A period comes after both the author's name and the book's title. Notice the colon after the place of publication and the comma between the name of the publishing company and the year of publication.)

A magazine or newspaper source card:

1. The name of the author, if there is one
2. The name of the article (in quotation marks)
3. The name of the magazine or newspaper (underlined)
4. The date of the magazine or newspaper
5. The page numbers of the article

EXAMPLE

> ③
>
> "'Lost Colony':— a Mystery
> now Solved?" U.S. News &
> World Report, July 9, 1984,
> p. 61.

(*Hint:* If the article begins on one page and then continues later in the magazine, put a comma between page numbers. A hyphen between page numbers means that the article is on all pages between the numbers. Study the punctuation on the card.)

Note that each source card has a circled number in its upper right-hand corner. As you fill out each source card, number it in this way. Later, when you begin taking notes, you can mark each note card with this number, instead of having to write out the name of the source.

EXERCISE 9. Gathering Information.   For this exercise, use the limited topic you have developed for Exercise 8. Using your school library, look up four sources of information about the topic. Find at least one encyclopedia article, one book, and one magazine or newspaper article about your topic.

EXERCISE 10. Preparing Source Cards.   Using 3 × 5-inch note cards or slips of paper, prepare a source card for each source you have found for Exercise 9. Use the correct format for each source card. Give each source card a number, beginning with 1.

Developing a Working Outline

24j. As you read about your topic, develop a working outline.

Suppose you are preparing a report on the "lost colony." (The "lost colony" was a settlement on Roanoke Island off the coast of

North Carolina. Established by English settlers in the sixteenth century, the colony simply disappeared.)

In the library, you have found an encyclopedia article, two books, and a magazine article about your topic. After reading the encyclopedia article, you decide that you will deal with the following three main topics in your report:

  I. Departure of colonists from England
 II. Arrival of colonists on Roanoke Island
III. Disappearance of colonists

These topics are the beginning of a working outline that can guide your research. You now know, for example, that you need to find information on each of these three topics.

EXERCISE 11. Developing a Working Outline. First, read one of the sources that you found for Exercise 9 that gives general information about your topic. After reading the material, write down three topics that you think you will cover in your report. Save your working outline to help you in your research.

Taking Notes

24k. Take notes on your reading.

Your reading will include encyclopedia articles, parts of books, and magazine articles. You cannot hope to remember all of the details of information that you collect. Consequently, you will need to take notes.

The most efficient way to take notes is to write them on cards or slips of paper, using a different card for each note. Early in your reading, you will find that the subject matter of your report falls into a number of general divisions or topics. Once you have three or four of these, you can use them as headings for your note cards. When you find information that would come under one of these headings, write the heading at the top of the card and underline it. Then write your notes under the heading. Underneath the note, write the page number(s) on which you found the information.

EXAMPLE

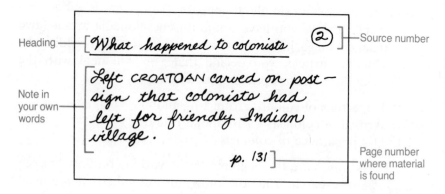

The number in the upper right-hand corner means that this note was taken from the source on card number 2 *(Roanoke: The Abandoned Colony).* Use separate note cards for each heading and for each source. For example, the note in the above example is about what happened to the Roanoke colonists. You might also find information on that topic in an encyclopedia and a magazine article. You would then have three note cards with the same heading but different source numbers.

Before you begin taking notes, read over your source material, looking for main ideas. Then, as you read back over your material, jot down notes. There are three ways that you can take notes.

1. You can *paraphrase*, or put the material into your own words.

2. You can *summarize* the material by giving only the main ideas.

3. You can quote from the material by using quotation marks around the writer's exact words.

EXAMPLE

Original:

If they did indeed go to Croatoan, the mist of history closes over them there. They may have stayed and intermarried with the Indians. Over a century later the explorer John

Lawson, writing in 1709, said he saw the ruins of the fort on Roanoke and found some guns and coins there. And he said the surviving Indians of the Hatteras area claimed to have white ancestors.

DAN LACY

Paraphrase of information:

If colonists went to Croatoan, they were lost to history— may have intermarried with Indians there. One hundred years later, explorer named John Lawson saw ruins of fort on Roanoke, also guns and coins. Lawson said Hatteras Indians believed they had white ancestors.

Summary of information:

If colonists went to Croatoan, they were lost to history. Explorer later found evidence of colonists of Roanoke. Hatteras Indians believed they had white ancestors.

Paraphrase of information, with quotation:

If colonists went to Croatoan, "the mist of history closes over them there"—may have intermarried with Indians. One hundred years later, explorer named John Lawson saw ruins of fort of Roanoke, also guns and coins. Lawson said Hatteras Indians believed they had white ancestors.

EXERCISE 12. Taking Notes. For this exercise, use the sources you found for Exercise 9. Prepare at least ten note cards. At the bottom of each note card, tell whether your note is a paraphrase, a summary, a quotation, or a combination of these.

Organizing the Report

24I. Organize your notes according to their headings.

Now you must prepare to use the notes that you have made for your report. Eliminate notes that contain information that is duplicated or facts that do not fit your limited topic. Next, sort the cards in piles according to their headings. Each pile will contain all the information on one topic. By eliminating and sorting you have organized your information and are ready to shape your final outline.

24m. Make a final outline based on your notes.

Study this final outline for the report on the Roanoke Island colony.

I. Departure of colonists from England
   A. Purpose of colonists
   B. Purpose of earlier explorers
II. Arrival of colonists on Roanoke Island
   A. Disappearance of earlier explorers
   B. Beginning of colony
      1. Need for food and supplies
      2. Return of leader to England
III. Disappearance of settlers
   A. John White's return to Roanoke
   B. Absence of settlers
      1. Missing houses and household goods
      2. Carved sign
   C. Ideas about disappearance
      1. Spanish ships
      2. Hostile Indians
      3. New life with friendly Indians

EXERCISE 13. Preparing an Outline. Using the note cards you made for Exercise 12, prepare an outline for your factual report. Before you begin, study the sample outline above.

WRITING

Writing the First Draft

24n. Using your final outline and your notes, write the first draft of your report.

As you write the first draft of your report, observe the following suggestions.

1. Remember that a factual report is a kind of expository composition. As such, it has the same basic parts: *introduction, body, conclusion.* It has an interesting, limited topic sufficiently developed with specific details. (Before you begin writing, review the material on expository composition, Chapter 23.)

2. Be certain that you understand all the terms you use. If necessary, look up the words in the dictionary.

3. Use your own words in writing the report. It is tempting to copy a passage from a book, but copying is not writing. Introduce quotations only when they are particularly apt or striking.

4. Put every necessary detail into your report, but omit unnecessary items. Stick to your topic.

5. Give details in their proper order, using your outline as a guide.

6. At the end of the report, list the sources from which you got your material.

CRITICAL THINKING:
Analyzing a Model

Looking at the parts of a model report and the way they work together can help you to write your own report. As you read the sample report that follows, notice these specific parts. (Note that the paragraphs in the sample report are numbered. This numbering is for convenience in discussing the report.)

1. *The topic*—Is it suitably limited for a short factual report? Is it suitable for the audience?

2. *The introduction*—Does it interest the reader?

3. *The body*—What specific information about the topic is given in these paragraphs?

4. *The conclusion*—Does it signal, in an interesting way, that the report is coming to an end? Does it avoid repeating the same ideas as the body of the report?

5. *The individual paragraphs*—Does each paragraph in the report have a main idea? Is that idea adequately developed with specific details?

6. *Unity*—Does each paragraph develop the topic?

7. *Coherence*—Are ideas in the report arranged in a logical order? Have transitional words and phrases been used to show the relationships between ideas?

ROANOKE: THE LOST COLONY

1   In May 1587 a group of 117 men, women, and children sailed from England, headed for the part of the New World they called Virginia. As the travelers said goodbye to their native land, they never expected to return home. Their purpose was to begin a new life across the ocean—to build houses and to plant crops. They were to be the first English settlers in that vast new land.

2   Although these settlers were the first English people who intended to make their homes in Virginia, they were not the first to reach the land. In both 1584 and 1585 groups of Englishmen had landed in the New World. These groups, however, had come for a much different reason. Their purpose was to find a base for English ships in the New World. From the base, English ships could easily attack the ships of England's great enemy, Spain, sailing in the nearby Caribbean. Both groups of explorers landed on Roanoke Island, off the coast of present-day North Carolina. To their disappointment, the early explorers found that the waters there were too shallow to be used as ports for their ships. All but fifteen of the men in these two groups returned to England.

3   On July 22 the ships carrying the third group of English people—the settlers—anchored off Roanoke Island. On the island, they found that the fifteen men left behind from the earlier group had disappeared. All that remained was the skeleton of one sailor lying across the path. The few huts that the men had built stood in ruins, overgrown with twisted vines. These new settlers would have to begin again.

4   The Roanoke colonists set to work to build new houses. By August 18, less than a month after they landed, they must have already felt a tie to their new home. On that day Virginia Dare became the first English child born in the New World. The colonists intended to plant crops and to learn to hunt and fish, but it would be a long time before they could take care of themselves. At the end of the year, they would need more supplies. John White, a leader of the expedition and the grandfather of Virginia Dare, agreed to return to England with a group of sailors. There he hoped to gather more supplies and to return to Roanoke Island before the year was out.

5   John White never saw his new granddaughter or the other settlers again. On his return to England, he found that England's enemy, Spain, was gathering a vast fleet of ships. With these ships, called the Armada, Spain intended to gain control of the seas and, in this way, to dominate England. To defend England, Queen Elizabeth ordered all ships to remain at home. It was not until three years later that John White was able to return to Roanoke with the promised supplies.

6   As White finally approached the shore of Roanoke, one day before his granddaughter's third birthday, he called out to the colonists through the dark night. There was no answer. The sailors landed and crossed the island looking for the colonists. In the sand were footprints that the sailors knew must have been made by Indians. The English colonists would have worn shoes. The colonists' houses had been torn down, the planks taken away. All of the colonists' clothes and household goods were gone also. Near the huts, carved in the bark of a tree, were the letters CRO. Nearby, on a post, the word CROATOAN had been carved.

7   Now, John White thought he knew where the colonists might have gone. Before he had left three years earlier, he and the colonists agreed on some signs. If the colonists had to leave Roanoke for some reason, they were to carve the name of the place where they were going. Croatoan was a village of friendly Indians on an island fifty miles away.

White thought that the colonists, probably near starvation after three years with no supplies, had gone there for help. White was comforted that there was no cross carved in the tree above CROATOAN. A cross was the colonists' signal that they were in danger.

8   The next day, White planned to sail from Roanoke to Croatoan to search for the colonists. Because of violent storms, however, the ships had no choice but to sail for England. John White never again returned to Roanoke.

9   What happened to the settlers on Roanoke Island remains a mystery. Some historians believe that Spanish ships may have landed and carried them away. Others believe that the settlers were captured and killed by hostile Indians. There is, however, another possible solution. In southeastern North Carolina, not far from the original Roanoke, live the descendants of a group of Indians called the Lumbees. Unlike most brown-eyed descendants of Native Americans, many of the present-day Lumbees have blue eyes. Many of them also have the English names of some of the English settlers, names like Bailey, Dale, and Cooper. Perhaps the colonists, in the three years of their isolation, began a new life with their Indian neighbors.

10   The next group of settlers to the New World came to Jamestown, Virginia. With them they brought records kept by John White about the experiences of the Roanoke colonists. Those records helped the new colony to succeed. That is why, even though Jamestown is recognized as the first English settlement in the New World, the Roanoke settlers will always be remembered for their important role in America's history.

Sources

Kupperman, Karen Ordahl. *Roanoke: The Abandoned Colony.* Totowa, N.J.: Rowman & Allanheld, 1984.

Lacy, Dan. *The Lost Colony.* New York: Franklin Watts, 1972.
" 'Lost Colony': A Mystery Now Solved?" *U. S. News & World Report,* July 9, 1984: 61

Smelser, Marshall. "Lost Colony." *World Book Encyclopedia.* 1985 ed.

(*Hint:* Notice that sources are alphabetized by the last name of the author. If there is no author, use the title of the article.)

EXERCISE 14. Analyzing a Model Report. On a piece of paper, answer the following questions about the model report on pages 674–76.

1. What is the limited topic for this report? Is it a suitable topic for a short factual report?
2. Do you think that the topic for this report is an interesting one for most eighth-grade students? Why?
3. The first paragraph of this report is the introduction. Do you think that the introduction should capture the attention of most readers? Why?
4. The conclusion simply does not repeat the ideas in the report. What does it do instead?
5. Write a paragraph in which you summarize what you learn about the topic from this report.
6. What is the topic sentence of paragraph 2? What details develop the main idea that is expressed in the topic sentence?
7. What is the topic sentence of paragraph 7? What details develop the main idea that is expressed in the topic sentence?
8. This report has unity because each paragraph develops the limited topic. What does paragraph 4 tell you about the topic?
9. What information does paragraph 9 give you about the topic?
10. This report has coherence because its ideas are arranged in a logical order. In paragraph 1, the English settlers leave England for the New World. What happens to the settlers in paragraph 3? What has happened to them in paragraph 6?

EXERCISE 15. Writing a First Draft. Using your outline and notes (from exercises 12 and 13), write a first draft of your report. Be certain that the report is in your own words.

REVISING

Revising Your Report

24o. Revise your report.

If possible, put your first draft aside for a few days. This time away from your writing will help you to look at it more objectively.

Whether you work alone or in revision groups, the following guidelines will help you to improve your report. As you read over your first draft, check it point by point against the suggestions in the guidelines.

GUIDELINES FOR REVISING A FACTUAL REPORT

1. Does the report have a suitable limited topic.?
2. Is the topic suitable for the audience?
3. Is there sufficient factual information to develop the topic?
4. Is the report written in the writer's own words? Is the material paraphrased or summarized as appropriate?
5. Does quoted material have quotation marks around the writer's exact words?
6. Are all details in the report related to the topic?
7. Are details given in a logical order?
8. Does the report have an interesting introduction and conclusion?
9. Do paragraphs in the report have a main idea that is expressed in a topic sentence? Is the main idea developed with details?
10. Are sources listed at the end of the report?

EXERCISE 16. Revising Your Report. Using the revision guidelines in this section to help you, make changes in your first draft to improve your report. See also the general Guidelines for Revising on pages 486. Ask your teacher directs, recopy your report. Before you hand in the final draft, proofread your paper carefully. (See the Guidelines for Proofreading on page 487.) Your teacher might ask you to hand in your source and note cards, your outline, and your first draft, as well as your final draft.

WRITING A BOOK REPORT

A book report gives two kinds of information: what the book is about and what you think of it.

PREWRITING

24p. Think about the purpose and audience for your book report. Think also about gathering specific information from your book.

Prewriting Hints for Writing a Book Report

1. *The purpose for writing a book report is to inform your audience about the book's content and about your opinion of the book.* In the first part of a book report, you usually tell what the book is about. If you are reporting on a novel, indicate the background of the story—time, place, main characters. For a nonfiction book, summarize the important information given. If you are reporting on a biography, indicate why the person written about is important, and mention chief incidents in that person's life.

In the second part of a book report, you usually tell your reaction to the book. This part of the report is important because it tells how carefully and thoughtfully you have read the book.

2. *Use specific details from the book.* Whether you are telling about the book's content or your reaction to the book, support what you say with specific details from the book. You may even want to quote words or sentences from the book. For example,

notice the first paragraph of the sample book report, on page 681. The writer of the report says that the book is about eight people who have made important contributions to the lives of many other people. Then the writer mentions the specific contributions of two of these people. In the second paragraph of the report, on page 681, the writer gives one reason for liking the book. In the rest of the paragraph, the writer gives details to support the reason.

In preparing a book report, use your note-taking skills (see pages 669–71). After you have read the book, jot down notes about its content and about your reaction to the book. Look up details about the plot and the characters that you may have forgotten.

3. *Summarize information about the book.* Avoid getting bogged down in details. You cannot possibly give every detail of the plot in a novel or every piece of information in a nonfiction book. Instead, concentrate on important details about the plot and the main characters. Discuss the main ideas in a nonfiction book.

EXERCISE 17. Preparing a Book Report.   With your teacher's guidance, select a book for your report. After reading the book, make notes about its content and about your reaction to it. On a piece of paper, make a list of specific details from the book. For a novel, jot down details about the plot, the setting, and the main characters. For a nonfiction book, make notes about important information. For both types of books, make notes about specific details to support your reaction.

WRITING

24q. Write a first draft of your book report.

In preparation for writing your own report, read the following sample report. As you read, ask yourself these questions:

1. What is the book about?
2. What specific details does the writer give about the book's content?
3. What is the writer's reaction to the book?
4. What specific details are given to support the writer's reaction?

A Report on *Shortchanged by History: America's Neglected Innovators*, by Vernon Pizer

1   *Shortchanged by History: America's Neglected Innovators*, by Vernon Pizer, is the story of eight Americans who have "fallen through the cracks of history." Each of these people has made an important contribution to the lives, health, and safety of millions of people, but each has been forgotten. Among these people is the man who designed and built the first flour mill. This same man also built, in the early 1800's, a steam-powered vehicle that actually moved across roads under its own power and then left behind its land wheels to become a boat. Another one of these people discovered the process for separating red and white blood cells to make plasma. The plasma, which could be dried and safely stored, has saved the lives of countless burn and wound victims.

2   I like this book because each of the eight accounts reads like an exciting adventure story. James Eads, for example, worked on a Mississippi riverboat during the mid-1800's. Underneath the treacherous waters of the Mississippi, all up and down the river, were wrecks of riverboats. James Eads thought there should be a way to recover the cargo and the engines of the wrecks lying at the river's bottom. While in his early twenties, Eads invented a diving bell that, carrying two men, could be lowered through the heavy currents. Through the open bottom of the diving bell, the men could attach lines to the submerged cargo. Air pumped from the salvage boat above kept water out of the bell. Before his first bell was ready, Eads was asked to recover a cargo of gold ingots. Unable to refuse the challenge, Eads fitted a huge wooden

barrel with weights and descended through the raging current. Much to everyone's astonishment, the twenty-two-year-old Eads rescued the entire cargo.

3   Another reason I like *Shortchanged by History* is that each of the people described in the book had great moral courage. Sara Josephine Baker, for example, became a physician in 1898, a time when most people did not approve of women doctors. Because she wanted so much to help people, Dr. Baker became a health inspector for New York City. In her job, she was sent to the place with the worst living conditions in the city—a place called "Hell's Kitchen." Going by herself from tenement to tenement, Dr. Baker worked especially to improve the health of infants. When she began her work, as many as fifteen hundred babies were dying in New York each week. Battling the constant prejudice against women doctors, she trained a team of nurses to go into the slums to teach health education. She established free clinics for mothers and their babies throughout the city. Before her work ended, she was responsible for reducing the death rate of infants in New York City by 50 percent.

4   In the world today, names such as Alexander Graham Bell, Thomas Edison, and Wilbur Wright are remembered. The author of *Shortchanged by History* helps us to recognize the important contributions of eight other Americans.

EXERCISE 18. Writing the First Draft of a Book Report.
Using the notes you have made for Exercise 17, write the first draft of your book report.

REVISING

24r. Write a revised draft of your book report.

Use the following guidelines for help in preparing a revised draft of your report.

GUIDELINES FOR REVISING A BOOK REPORT

1. Are the book's title and author mentioned early in the report?
2. Is the title of the book underlined when it is mentioned?
3. Does the report give information about both the book's content and the writer's reaction to the book?
4. Are specific details from the book used to support the writer's statements about the book? Are specific reasons given to support the writer's reaction to the book?
5. For a novel, are the time, place, and main characters of the story indicated in the report? Is enough of the plot revealed to give readers a general idea of the story?
6. For a nonfiction book, does the report give a summary of important information?

EXERCISE 19. Revising the Book Report. Check the first draft of the book report that you wrote for Exercise 18 against the Guidelines for Revising Book Reports above. As you do, make changes to improve the first draft. As your teacher directs, recopy your paper for submission. Use the Guidelines for Proofreading on page 487 to check your report for errors in usage and mechanics.

CHAPTER 24 WRITING REVIEW

Applying Your Knowledge of Summaries, Reports, and Book Reports. Following your teacher's instruction, complete one or more of the following items.

1. The following paragraphs are from the book *Shortchanged by History: America's Neglected Innovators.* Following the prewriting, writing, and revising steps that you have learned in this chapter, write a summary of the paragraphs. The summary should be one fourth to one third the length of the original. Use your dictionary to look up any words in the paragraphs that you do not understand.

History has, for the most part, dealt kindly with America's creative giants, recording their innovations and accomplishments, rendering them the recognition and praise they richly merit. But history is a chronicle recorded by people, and people are merely fallible humans, so the chronicle is flawed. There are gaps in it, unaccountable omissions from the list of those who wielded an important influence over the shaping of the nation, unwarranted slightings of many of the country's significant innovators.

Largely overlooked, for instance, is Philip Mazzei, an Italian who settled in Virginia in 1773 to establish an experimental farm. However, it was not in farming practices but in a far different field that he bestowed on America a gift of supreme importance. Deeply committed to improving conditions for the common man by eliminating bigotry and repressive government, he wrote stirring articles and delivered ringing speeches urging the cause of independence. President John F. Kennedy observed two centuries later that the moving words of the Declaration of Independence—"All men are created equal"—can be traced to Mazzei.

Or consider Mary Engle Pennington, who in the late 1800's when it was still considered "unladylike" for a woman to enter the sciences, earned her doctorate as a chemist and then went on to contribute more than any other single individual to raising the nutritional level of the food that America eats. During a notable career that ended in 1952 when she was eighty, Dr. Pennington devised many of the techniques and health standards of the milk, egg, and poultry industries; she established methods for the safe storage and transportation of perishable foods, improved the design of home refrigerators, and helped develop the processes that resulted in creation of the modern frozen-foods industry.

2. Develop for a factual report a limited topic other than the topic you have already used to write a report. Using this new topic, complete, as your teacher directs, any or all of the following exercises: Exercise 9, Exercise 10, Exercise 11, Exercise 12, Exercise 13, Exercise 15, and Exercise 16.

3. For this exercise, choose a different type of book from the one you have already reported on in this chapter. For example, if you have already reported on a nonfiction book, choose a novel. Then follow the prewriting, writing, and revising steps that you have learned in this chapter to write a book report.

CHAPTER 25

Writing Letters

SOCIAL LETTERS, BUSINESS LETTERS

Letters from friends usually bring enjoyment. It is interesting to learn what they have seen and done recently, what they think, and what has happened to other friends. However, you will not receive many letters unless you write letters.

When you begin to write a letter, you may think: But I don't have anything to say! A moment's thought will show that this is untrue. What do you want to learn from friends' letters? What questions do you want answered? Probably they have the same kinds of questions to ask you.

SOCIAL LETTERS

PREWRITING

Deciding What To Say

25a. In a friendly letter, write about the things that interest you and the person to whom you are writing.

Before you write a friendly letter, jot down your ideas. Include news that will interest your friend. Think of your friend's letter to you. Were there any questions or comments that need a reply? As you write, keep in mind the person who will receive your letter. You would not send the same kind of letter to a friend you met at summer camp as to your favorite uncle.

1849 West Sixth Street
Los Angeles, California 90014
April 14, 1986

Dear Tom,

You asked what Carl and I have been up to lately. Well, Carl is taking care of a horse for friends of his parents, but he's afraid to ride it. I said I'd ride it. You know me — no brains.

That horse jumped suddenly high into the air and tried to throw me off. I stayed on, though, until it reared straight up and fell over backwards. Carl's dad ran over to me. He was mad, but all he said was that maybe we'd better put the horse back in the stable.

You asked what I'm doing for the Science Fair at school. Carl and I have taken photographs of cloud formations. We are mounting these photographs for an exhibit on weather forecasting.

How about letting me know what you're doing?

Sincerely,
Bill

A Friendly Letter

Study the example of a friendly letter (page 687). Would you say that Bill is thinking of his friend Tom as he writes? Why? How would this letter be different if it were written to Bill's grandmother?

WRITING

Writing a Friendly Letter

25b. Choose stationery and ink that are appropriate for a friendly letter.

Use letter stationery. White is always appropriate, though other colors may be used.

Write in ink, never in pencil. (If you can type *well,* type your letters.) Avoid ink blots and erasures. Keep your writing neatly spaced and properly aligned; crowded lines that climb or stagger or droop give a bad impression. Make your margins wide; try to keep them equal on top and bottom as well as on the sides.

Try to estimate in advance how long your letter will be. A brief letter may require only one page. If you use folded stationery and the letter runs to two pages, do not write on the back of page one but skip over to page three. If the letter is longer than two pages, use the page order of a book; write the second page on the back of the first, and so on.

25c. Follow generally accepted rules for the form of a friendly letter.

The form of a friendly letter is not hard to master. Study the following instructions and sample letter.

1. Heading

The *heading* tells when and where the letter was written. It consists of three lines, placed at the upper right corner of the page. The address of the writer is placed on the first two lines, and the date on which the letter was written is placed on the third. Note that a comma is used between city and state and between the date of the month and the year. The ZIP code number appears several spaces after the state and on the same line. There is no punctuation at the ends of the lines.

18 Prince Street
Houston, Texas 77008
April 14, 1986

Dear Bob,

_____

_____

_____

_____

_____

_____

Sincerely yours,
Jim

Form of a Friendly Letter

Two kinds of headings are appropriate in a friendly letter. The example shown on this page is in *block style*. That is, the second and third lines of the heading begin directly below the beginning of the first line. Another style that is often used for handwritten friendly letters is *indented style,* in which the heading looks like this:

2534 Polk Place
Portland, Oregon 97235
May 6, 1982

2. Salutation

The *salutation* begins at the left-hand margin and is placed a short distance below the heading. In a friendly letter, it is followed by a comma.

3. Body

The *body* of a friendly letter is the message, what you have to say. It may begin directly below the end of the salutation, or may be indented about an inch from the left margin. The first line of each paragraph that follows must be indented the same distance.

4. Closing

The *closing* for a friendly letter may be *Your friend, Sincerely, Sincerely yours,* or any similar phrase you like, except *Yours truly* and *Very truly yours,* which are used only on business letters. The closing is placed just below the final line of the letter, beginning a little to the right of the middle of the page, and is followed by a comma. Only the first word of the closing begins with a capital.

5. Signature

The signature in a friendly letter need be only your first name. Center it under the closing. Always write the signature by hand, even if you have typed the rest of the letter.

EXERCISE 1. Writing a Friendly Letter. Make a list of experiences you have had in the last few days. Using this list as a basis, write a letter to a friend of your own age. Follow the instructions on the preceding pages concerning both content and form.

EXERCISE 2. Writing a Friendly Letter. Using the list you prepared for Exercise 1, write a letter to a relative or to an adult friend. As you write, keep in mind the receiver of your letter. In class, discuss how your two letters differ.

Addressing the Envelope

The envelope of a letter should be addressed with care. The letter may not be delivered if the address is carelessly written. The ZIP code number should always be included. There should always be a return address so that the post office may return the letter if your correspondent has moved.

Susan Froelich
597 Spruce Street
Kansas City, Kansas 66143

       Miss Astrid Addison
       89 Kirkland Street
       Cambridge
       Massachusetts 02127

A Model Envelope

Study the example above and the following instructions.

1. Place the return address in the upper left corner of the envelope.

2. Place the address of the person to whom the letter is going just below the middle and to the left of the center of the envelope.

3. If the letter is going to an adult, write a title before the name: *Mr., Mrs., Ms., Dr.,* and so on. Do not put a title before your name in the return address.

4. Write the state on a separate line, as in the example, or on the same line as the city. Put a comma after the city if the state is written on the same line. Place the ZIP code number several spaces after the state.

5. If you use *Post Office Box, Rural Free Delivery,* or *Rural Route* in the address, you may use abbreviations: *P.O. Box 351, R.F.D. 1,* or *R.R. 1.*

EXERCISE 3. Addressing Envelopes. Using your ruler, draw the outlines of four envelopes. Address each envelope. Use your own return address.

1. miss edna a burns   16 casita way
   omaha nebraska   68138
2. mrs h b byerley   111 orchid way
   st louis missouri   63179
3. ms ellen craig   p o box 753
   butte montana   59601
4. dr n t bain   r r 8
   winamac indiana   46996

EXERCISE 4. Writing a Friendly Letter. Choose one of the following situations, and write the letter it suggests. If you prefer to invent your own situation, you may do so. Address an envelope for your letter.

1. You are visiting relatives in another city, and they have taken you to see a World Series game. Write to your parents, telling them about the visit and the game.
2. A friend who lived nearby has moved some distance away. Give her recent news about your neighborhood and ask questions about her new home and neighborhood.
3. You are a CB radio operator, and you have been exchanging messages with a CB radio hobbyist in another town. Invite him to visit you. Describe the members of your family and tell

him about the fun he will have on his visit. If you like, tell him about other CB operators you have contacted.

Folding the Letter

If your letter stationery consists of a folded page, fold it in half and insert it, fold first, into the envelope. If the stationery is a single sheet of the same width as the envelope, fold the bottom third up, then the top third down, and insert it into the envelope, with the last fold first. See the illustrations on page 702.

Writing Social Notes

25d. **Write prompt, courteous social notes.**

Social notes are written for a limited purpose, such as to extend or accept an invitation, or to thank someone for a gift or favor. Such notes generally follow the form of a friendly letter and are written on personal stationery. If they are brief, they may be written on correspondence cards.

Since you will have many occasions to write social notes, you should learn to write them properly.

The Bread-and-Butter Note

Occasionally you are invited to visit friends or relatives who live out of town, and you spend several days with them. After you return home, you must write a note to your host—your friend's parents, or the adult or adults really responsible for your comfort —to thank them for their kindness to you. This note, commonly called a "bread-and-butter" note, should be written promptly. Tell your hosts how much you enjoyed your stay and appreciated their efforts to make your visit pleasant. Mention some of the things they did for you. Your hosts will be interested, too, in what kind of trip you had returning home, so it is appropriate to mention that briefly.

Study the sample bread-and-butter note. Notice that, like the thank-you note, it follows the form of a friendly letter.

34 Casa Grande Drive
Berkeley, California 94713
August 6, 1986

Dear Mr. and Mrs. De Stefano,

Ever since I got home, I've been thinking about the wonderful week I spent with your family in Yosemite Park. The park had always been a sort of picture album place to me, and now I've got my own snapshots of it! But the outdoor scenery was only part of the pleasure of camping with your family. Waking up in the morning to the smell of frying bacon and eggs, hiking up the steep trails and coming back to cool off with a swim in the river, sitting around the campfire singing and telling stories — I'll remember these things for a long time. Thanks ever so much for having me as a guest.

Please tell Helen I'll send her some of my snapshots as soon as they are ready.

Sincerely yours,
Nora Davis

A Bread-and-Butter Note

The Thank-You Note

After receiving a gift or favor from someone whom you cannot immediately thank in person, you should write a thank-you note. Always write promptly. A delay gives the impression that you do not really appreciate the gift. A thank-you note will seem less like a duty letter if you write about something else as well, and if you give specific reasons for your gratitude.

Study the following thank-you note. Has Tony thanked his uncle properly?

641 Ardmore Avenue
Philadelphia, Pennsylvania 19153
June 3, 1986

Dear Uncle Harry,
  Thanks ever so much for the model plane engine. I'm having a lot of fun with it. The other boys tell me that a Junior Wasp model like this is very dependable. It starts easily and runs with no trouble. I've been running it on a breaking-in block. It's surprising how much roar such a tiny engine has! I'm eager to finish building my model. I know this engine will really make it zoom.
  The folks gave me some fine birthday presents too, but I suspect that I'll remember this birthday most of all because of your wonderful gift.
                    Your nephew,
                    Tony

A Thank-You Note

EXERCISE 5. Writing a Bread-and-Butter Note. Write a bread-and-butter note expressing thanks for the hospitality you received on a recent visit, or imagine that you were in one of the following situations, and write a bread-and-butter note.

1. A friend's family has taken you with them on a camping trip; you went canoeing along a mountain stream.

2. While your mother was ill in a hospital, you stayed with your grandmother. She lives on a big farm.
3. An uncle has taken you to an amusement park and paid for all your rides.
4. An aunt has taken you on a trip to New York City, where you visited the Empire State Building, the United Nations Building, the Statue of Liberty, and went to a show at Radio City Music Hall.
5. You spent your summer vacation with your older married sister and her husband. They live in a nearby town and have two small children.

EXERCISE 6. Writing a Thank-You Note. Write a thank-you note and address an envelope for one of the following situations, or choose a situation of your own.

1. A friend, who lives in another city, has sent you a new sweater for your birthday.
2. An aunt, who owns her own company, has sent you a share of her company's stock for graduation.
3. Your grandmother, who lives in another town, has sent you ten dollars for your birthday.
4. An older cousin is with the army in Europe. He knows you have been collecting dolls since you were seven. He has sent you a set of dolls in the native costumes of various countries.
5. A family friend, on a trip to Mexico, has sent you a fine, brilliantly colored blanket.

REVISING AND PROOFREADING

Revising and Proofreading Social Letters

Use the following guidelines to help you revise and proofread your friendly letters and social notes. Be sure to ask yourself these questions as you revise your letters.

GUIDELINES FOR REVISING AND PROOFREADING SOCIAL LETTERS

1. In a friendly letter, has the writer included news the other person would like to know or would find interesting? Has the writer answered any questions that may have been asked in the friend's last letter?

2. Has the writer organized his or her letter so that the person who is reading it can follow it easily?

3. In a note of thanks, has the writer been specific about what he or she is grateful for?

4. Is the letter neat? Has the writer used pen or typed the letter?

5. Is the form correct, with each of the parts correctly placed?

6. Are the address and date in the heading?

7. Is the salutation suitable? Does a comma follow the salutation?

8. Is the first line of the body indented? Is the first line of each paragraph that follows indented the same distance?

9. Are the sentences grammatically correct and properly punctuated?

10. Is the closing appropriate? Is the first word in the closing capitalized? Does a comma come at the end of the closing?

11. Is the address on the envelope complete? Is it correctly placed?

BUSINESS LETTERS

Business letters are important in our daily lives. You may have already written some to order goods from a firm or to request information from an institution or government department. Later you may write business letters to apply for a job or entrance to a school or to make reservations for a vacation trip.

PREWRITING

Planning a Business Letter

When you plan your business letters, the following steps will be helpful to you.

1. *Consider your purpose.* Think about why you are writing the letter. Are you ordering goods? Asking for information?

2. *Consider your audience.* Keep in mind to whom you are writing. What does the audience already know? What does the audience need to know?

3. *Consider your tone.* In a business letter you want to be courteous. Your letter will make a better impression if the tone is polite and reasonable. If you must make a complaint in a letter, do so courteously.

4. *Gather your ideas.* Jot down exactly what you want to say or whatever information you intend to convey. Include as much information as you feel necessary to explain the situation.

5. *Be brief.* Check to see that you have not included any unnecessary information. However, do not leave out any important details; if you do, the reader of the letter will not be able to fulfill your request promptly.

WRITING

Writing a Business Letter

25e. Follow generally accepted rules for the form of a business letter.

Business firms use printed business stationery in two sizes: $8\frac{1}{2} \times 11$ inches and (for brief letters) $5\frac{1}{2} \times 8\frac{1}{2}$ inches. You should use unruled white paper of standard typewriter size; $8\frac{1}{2} \times 11$ inches. If you type well, it is always advisable to type your business letters. If you do not type well, however, write carefully with pen and ink.

Make your letter neat and attractive. Center it on the page, leaving equal margins on the right and left sides and on the top and bottom. Avoid ink blots, erasures, and crossed-out words. Write only on one side of the page.

The form of a business letter is somewhat different from that of a personal letter. One important difference is that a business letter always includes an *inside address.* Study the following example and instructions.

```
                        567 Hardwood Street
                        San Diego, California 92128
                        December 10, 1986


Mr. John Anders
Acme Sporting Goods Company
33 Norton Avenue
Cleveland, Ohio 44105

Dear Mr. Anders:

        _____

    _____

    _____

    _____

        _____

                    Very truly yours,

                    Donald Hayes
                    Donald Hayes
```

Form for a Business Letter

1. Heading

A business address always requires a complete heading: street address on the first line; city, state, and ZIP code number on the second line, with a comma between the city and state; date on the third line, with a comma between the day and the year. It is better not to abbreviate the month and the state.

Block style, not indented style, should be used in the heading of a business letter.

2. Inside Address

A business letter, for filing purposes, requires an inside address, which gives the name and the address of the person or the firm (sometimes both) to whom you are writing. A comma is used between the city and state, and the ZIP code number appears several spaces, or about one-quarter inch, after the state. Place the inside address four typewriter lines below the heading and on the other side of the page, flush with the left-hand margin.

3. Salutation

The salutation is placed two typewriter lines below the inside address, flush with the left-hand margin. It is followed by a colon, not a comma as in a friendly letter.

The kind of salutation you use will vary. If you are writing to a person whose name you have used in the inside address, you say *Dear Mr.——:* (or *Dear Miss——:* or *Dear Mrs.——:* or *Dear Ms.——:*).

EXAMPLE   Ms. S. E. Sorenson, Circulation Manager
Astronomy Magazine
67 East Eighth Street
New York, New York 10003

Dear Ms. Sorenson:

If you are writing to a person whose name you do not know, but whose official position you do know, you say *Dear Sir:* or *Dear Madam:*

EXAMPLE   Public Relations Director
State Oil Company
317 Bush Street
Dallas, Texas 75243

Dear Sir:

     or

Dear Madam:

If, however, you are writing to a group or a company, you may use an impersonal salutation *(Customer Service:, Editors:)*. You may also use either of these salutations: *Gentlemen:* or *Ladies and Gentlemen:*. When you use the salutation *Gentlemen:*, it is generally understood that the group you are writing to may be composed of both men and women.

EXAMPLE   Bradley Electronics Corp.
56 La Mesa Drive
Lafayette, California 94549

Mail Order Department:

4. Body

The first sentence of the body of a business letter begins two typewriter lines below the salutation. This first line may be indented about an inch or the length of the salutation. The first lines of all paragraphs in the body should be indented the same distance. (If you are using a typewriter, indent five spaces.) Keep the left-hand margin straight; keep the right-hand margin as straight as you can.

5. Closing

The form for the closing of a business letter is *Yours truly* or *Very truly yours* or *Sincerely yours*. The closing should begin a little to the right of the middle of the page. Only the first word is capitalized. A comma follows the closing.

6. Signature

Directly below the closing, in line with it, sign your full name in ink. If you are typing the letter, type your name below your written signature. Never put a title (Mr., Mrs., Miss, etc.) before your handwritten signature.

Yours truly,
Margaret Nolan

Very truly yours,

John Anderson
John Anderson

7. Envelope

The return address and the address on the envelope of a business letter are written and placed exactly as they are on the envelope of a friendly letter. The "outside" address should be the same as the inside address.

8. Folding the Letter

If the letter is written on $8\frac{1}{2} \times 11$-inch paper and is to be put into a long envelope, fold the sheet up a third of the way from the bottom, then fold the top third down over it.

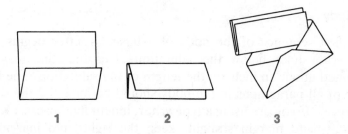

If the sheet is to go into a small envelope, fold the page up from the bottom to within a quarter of an inch of the top; then fold the right side over a third of the way, and fold the left side over it. Insert the letter into the envelope with the last fold at the bottom of the envelope.

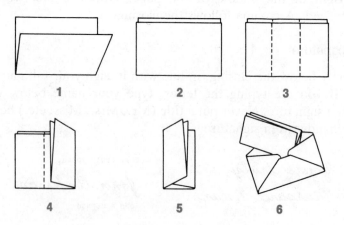

EXERCISE 7. Writing a Business Letter; Addressing an Envelope. The following paragraph contains all the information needed for a business letter. Write the letter in correct form and arrangement on a sheet of business stationery. Address an envelope for it.

32 Berenda drive, Flagstaff, Arizona 86001 december 2 1986 Acme outfitting company inc p.o. box 289 milwaukee wisconsin 53248 customer service department kindly send me your mail order catalog on sporting goods and hunting and fishing equipment thank you yours truly judy muller

Writing the Order Letter and the Request Letter

25f. Become familiar with the two common kinds of business letters: the *order* **letter and the** *request* **letter.**

The Order Letter

When writing an order letter, be sure to identify the merchandise you want by its catalog number, or by the place you saw it advertised, and by its price. State whether you are charging the merchandise or paying for it by cash, check, money order, or C.O.D.

> ☞ **NOTE** You will order many items of merchandise not by letter, but by order blank. When you use an order blank, be sure to follow the directions carefully and fill in all the blanks. No cover letter is necessary.

EXERCISE 8. Evaluating an Order Letter. Scan the advertisements in a catalog, newspaper, or magazine. Select an item you would like to have, and write a letter ordering it. Exchange letters with a classmate. Evaluate that letter. Check to see whether (1) it follows the business letter form; (2) it identifies exactly the item wanted; (3) it states how the item is being paid for.

```
                                    89 East First Street
                                    Kankakee, Illinois 60901
                                    March 10, 1986


        Standard Equipment Company
        448 Westwood Boulevard
        St. Louis, Missouri 63107

        Mail Order Department:

             Please send me the field glasses, No. 791,
        which you advertised for $11.98, postpaid, in
        the February 17 issue of the Farm Gazette.
        I am enclosing a money order for $11.98.


                             Very truly yours,

                             Rachel Beam

                             Rachel Beam
```

Model Order Letter

EXERCISE 9. **Writing a Business Letter.** Choose one of the following situations and write the letter it suggests. Address an envelope for the letter.

1. You ordered a pair of rabbits, New Zealand Giants, from Beyer's Mail Order Mart, 88 H Street, Augusta, Georgia 30915. Instead you received a set of "rabbit ears" antennae for a television set.
2. You ordered a cashmere sweater from the Chic Shop, 49 Sierra Road, Philadelphia, Pennsylvania 19154. When it arrived, it was the wrong size and color.
3. You ordered a first baseman's glove from Harold's Sporting Goods, Inc., 724 Freneau Parkway South, Bangor, Maine 04401. Instead, you received a catcher's mask.

4. You ordered (enclosing full payment) a pair of work gloves from Mercantile Mail Order Company, 97 West Ivy Street, Akron, Ohio   44153. You received twelve pairs of mittens.
5. For your mother's birthday, you ordered a sweater from Gifts Galore, 819 West Drive, Dubuque, Iowa   52018. In your letter you enclosed a money order. Your mother's birthday is a week away, and the sweater has not yet arrived.

The Request Letter

Occasionally you have to write to get information or to ask for a pamphlet or a catalog or samples. In such a letter you are, of course, asking a favor; be brief, clear, and courteous.

34 Addison Place
Boise, Idaho 83742
December 2, 1986

Air-Industry, Inc.
10 West Norton Avenue
Los Angeles, California 90037

Publicity Department:

    Our eighth-grade class at Brice Junior
High School is studying the use of helicopters
in farming operations. If you have a free
brochure describing your helicopters and how
they are used on farms, we would appreciate
receiving ten copies.

                Yours truly,

                Martha Ames

                Martha Ames

Model Request Letter

EXERCISE 10. Writing a Request Letter. Write to a department of your city or state government, asking for free pamphlets or leaflets about the duties and services of the department. Address an envelope for your letter, but do not mail the letter unless you are seriously interested in the information.

EXERCISE 11. Writing a Business Letter. Write a letter for one of the following situations. Address an envelope, but do not mail the letter unless you are serious about your request.

1. Your class has been studying wildlife conservation. You would like some maps showing the great "flyways" on the continent of North America used by migrating birds. Write for such maps to the Fish and Wildlife Service, United States Department of the Interior, Washington, D.C.
2. Your group wishes to visit a famous museum in your area (or the Guggenheim Museum in New York City, New York, or the Hearst Castle in San Simeon, California). Write for information about visiting hours and fees. Ask whether a reduced rate is possible for your group. Inform the management of the museum of your group's purpose in making the visit.
3. Write to the United States Government Printing Office, Washington, D.C. Ask if they have publications on a particular subject such as national monuments. Write why you are interested in this subject.

☞ **NOTE** The United States Postal Service recommends the use of two-letter codes for states, the District of Columbia, and Puerto Rico. The service also recommends the use of nine-digit ZIP codes. When you use these codes, the address should look like this:

EXAMPLE   Ms. Linda Ramos
6 Northside Dr.
St. Joseph, MO   64506–1212

The two-letter code is in capital letters and is never followed by a period. The following is a list of two-letter codes for states, the District of Columbia, and Puerto Rico.

Alabama AL	Montana MT
Alaska AK	Nebraska NE
Arizona AZ	Nevada NV
Arkansas AR	New Hampshire NH
California CA	New Jersey NJ
Colorado CO	New Mexico NM
Connecticut CT	New York NY
Delaware DE	North Carolina NC
District of Columbia DC	North Dakota ND
Florida FL	Ohio OH
Georgia GA	Oklahoma OK
Hawaii HI	Oregon OR
Idaho ID	Pennsylvania PA
Illinois IL	Puerto Rico PR
Indiana IN	Rhode Island RI
Iowa IA	South Carolina SC
Kansas KS	South Dakota SD
Kentucky KY	Tennessee TN
Louisiana LA	Texas TX
Maine ME	Utah UT
Maryland MD	Vermont VT
Massachusetts MA	Virginia VA
Michigan MI	Washington WA
Minnesota MN	West Virginia WV
Mississippi MS	Wisconsin WI
Missouri MO	Wyoming WY

REVISING

Revising a Business Letter

Use the following guidelines to help you revise and proofread your business letters for clarity and appearance. Be sure to ask yourself the questions as you revise your letters.

GUIDELINES FOR REVISING AND PROOFREADING BUSINESS LETTERS

1. Has the writer stated what he or she wanted to? Has the writer included all the information that is necessary?
2. In an order letter, is the letter brief and to the point?
3. In a request letter, has the writer made his or her request courteously?
4. Is the letter attractive? Is the form correct, with each of the parts correctly placed?
5. Does the heading give the complete address and the full date? Are commas used to separate the city from the state and the day of the month from the year?
6. Is the inside address accurate, complete, and properly spaced?
7. Is the salutation appropriate? Is it followed by a colon?
8. Is the first line of the body indented? Are the first lines of the following paragraphs indented the same distance?
9. Is the closing appropriate? Does the first word begin with a capital letter? Do the other words begin with a small letter? Does a comma follow the closing?
10. Is block style used correctly in the letter? Is the address on the envelope identical with the inside address on the letter?
11. Is the address on the envelope accurate, complete, and correctly placed?
12. Has the letter been folded to fit the envelope?
13. Is the return address on the envelope?

CHAPTER 25 WRITING REVIEW 1

Writing a Friendly Letter. Choose one of the following situations, and write the letter it suggests. If you prefer to invent your own situation, you may do so. Use the Guidelines for Revising and Proofreading Social Letters both *before* and *after* you write your letter.

1. You are a 4–H Club member. At a recent 4–H convention you made friends with a member from another part of the state.

Write a letter to your new friend, telling about recent club activities and the exhibit you are busily preparing for the 4–H Club county fair.

2. You have recently attended a wedding. Write to a friend or relative, describing the events of the wedding: the ceremony, the reception, the behavior of the bride and bridegroom and their parents, and your own reactions.

3. You have been elected secretary of your club. Write to a friend or relative, describing the club, its purpose, and its members.

4. Write to an older brother or sister at college. Tell about your own progress at school, and ask questions about college life.

CHAPTER 25 WRITING REVIEW 2

Writing Business Letters. Write a letter for each of the following situations. Use the Guidelines for Revising and Proofreading Business Letters both *before* and *after* you write your letters. Address an envelope for each letter.

1. Write an order letter to Travis Novelty Company, 18 Meadow Street, St. Louis, Missouri 63128, for the following merchandise: 2 giant balloons, at $.85 each; 18 pencils, with the name "Pat" printed in silver, at $.35 each; and 1 box of birthday candles, at $1.35. You are enclosing a money order to cover the total cost.

2. Write a request letter asking for the summer schedule of plays at the Beacon Summer Theater, Portsmouth, Rhode Island 02871; inform the theater that you represent a group and need information on group ticket rates.

PART SIX

AIDS TO GOOD ENGLISH

CHAPTER 26

Using the Dictionary

ARRANGEMENT OF A DICTIONARY, INFORMATION IN A DICTIONARY

ᛋ	Early Phoenician (late 2nd millenium B.C.)	ᛉ	Early Etruscan (8th century B.C.)
ᛃ	Phoenician (8th century B.C.)	ᛉ	Monumental Latin (4th century B.C.)
ᛯ	Early Greek (9th–7th centuries B.C.)	M	Classical Latin
Λ	Western Greek (6th century B.C.)	ന	Uncial
M	Classical Greek (403 B.C. onward)	ന	Half Uncial
		ന	Caroline miniscule

When using most words, you rely on your own experience as to their meaning, pronunciation, and general appropriateness. You have been accumulating this kind of experience about words since you first learned to talk; but no matter how extensive your experience with words, there will be times when it fails to provide the specific information you need. In such situations, you should turn to your dictionary.

A good dictionary tells you what meanings a word has, how it is usually spelled and pronounced, what its history is, and, often, the kind of situations in which it is appropriate or inappropriate. If you are not yet making sufficient use of the dictionary, this chapter will show you how to do so.

Since dictionaries differ from one another in their methods of presenting information, a textbook can treat only the general features that dictionaries have in common. The best guide to the use of your dictionary is the introductory section that explains the arrangement of entries, the system of showing pronunciations, and special features of that particular book. You should take the time to read the introductory section to find out how your dictionary goes about the job of presenting information. Finding an entry will not be much help to you if you do not know how to interpret the information.

ARRANGEMENT

26a. Learn how to find a word in the dictionary.

The words in a dictionary are listed in alphabetical order. This does not mean simply that all words beginning with a particular letter are lumped together in one section. It means that words having *a* as a second letter come before those that have *b* as a second letter, and so on through all the other letters in the word. To find whether *force* or *form* comes first, you have to look at the fourth letter; to decide between *reconcile* and *reconciliation,* you have to look at the ninth. Running through the alphabet nine times is a lot of trouble. If you are still hazy whether *q* comes before *s,* or *m* before *n,* you will save yourself time and effort by getting it straight right now.

Two special problems should be kept in mind: abbreviations and entries of more than one word.

Some dictionaries explain abbreviations in a special section, but most dictionaries define them in the main part of the book right along with the other entries. In such dictionaries, abbreviations are entered according to the letters in them, *not* according to the complete words that they stand for. The abbreviation *pt.* (meaning *pint* or *part*) comes after *psychology,* even though both words that the abbreviation can stand for would come before *psychology.* In a dictionary, the abbreviation *St.* (for *saint*) comes after *squirt* and before *stab.* A name like *St. Denis,* however, would appear under the full spelling—*saint.*

Two or more words used together as a single word (*open season, prime minister*) are treated as though they were a single word. Thus *open shop* appears after *openly* because *s* comes after *l*.

EXERCISE 1. Arranging Words, Phrases, and Abbreviations in Alphabetical Order. Arrange the following words, phrases, and abbreviations in alphabetical order.

watermelon	dept.	Mrs.	munificence
department	st.	departmental	munificent
curtain	curvature	curtail	water moccasin
stateside	static	mudguard	water wheel
municipal	muddy	mt.	department store

Where you open a dictionary to find a word makes a difference. You can find *municipal* if you open at the *s*'s and leaf back to the *m*'s, but it would be better to open at the *m*'s in the first place. This is how to open near the place you want.

1. *Divide the dictionary into thirds.* Think of your dictionary in three parts, consisting of the following groups of letters:

abcde   fghijklmnop   qrstuvwxyz

The parts do not look equal because more words start with some letters than with others. However, if you try these divisions, you will get three fairly equal sections. Your first objective is to open to the third of the dictionary in which the word you want is to be found.

EXERCISE 2. Using the Divisions of the Dictionary. After the appropriate number, indicate in which third of the dictionary (first, middle, last) you would find each of the following words.

1. falcon
2. recruit
3. equation
4. opportunity
5. robin
6. cryptic
7. stability
8. pensive
9. decimal
10. fable

2. *When you have found the right third, find the letter you want.* As you get used to thinking of the dictionary in thirds, you will gradually come to know in what part of each third to look for particular letters. It helps to know, for example, that more words begin with *s* than with the letters *u, v, w, x, y,* and *z* combined.

EXERCISE 3. Using the Divisions of the Dictionary. Place your dictionary on your desk in front of you and leave it closed. Your teacher or another student in the class will call out a letter at random. Suppose you hear *g* called. You will then open your dictionary near the beginning of the middle third and call out the number of the first page you find that has words beginning with *g*. The winner can then call out the next letter for the class to find. If you are not clear about which letters belong in which third, it will help to have them written out in front of you.

3. *When you have found the right letter, begin looking at the guide words.* Guide words are printed in boldfaced type at the top of each dictionary page. The one on the left is the same as the first word defined on that page; the one on the right is the same as the last word on that page. Words that fall between guide words in the alphabet will appear on that page. A word that comes alphabetically before the first guide word will be found on a page toward the front, and one that comes after the second guide word will be found toward the back.

In using guide words, you will find it useful to have a general idea of the number of words beginning with a particular letter. If you are looking up *stanchion,* for example, and open to a page that has the guide words *size* and *skinner,* you can safely turn several pages at a time because you know that the *s*'s take up many pages. On the other hand, if you are looking up *yucca* and open to a page with the guide words *yawn* and *yet,* you had better turn one page at a time because it does not take long to get through the *y*'s. In general, look closely at the guide words on each page when you are close to the page you want, and turn several at a time when you are further from it.

EXERCISE 4. Using Guide Words. Number your paper 1–15. Suppose that the guide words *needy* and *neither* appear on a particular dictionary page. After the proper number, make a plus sign if the corresponding word would appear on that page. Write *before* if it would appear on an earlier page and *after* if it would appear on a later page.

EXAMPLES　1. nefarious
　　　　　　 1. +
　　　　　　 2. navy
　　　　　　 2. *before*

1. negative	6. ne'er-do-well	11. negligent
2. necessary	7. newcomer	12. Neanderthal
3. needle	8. noble	13. nemesis
4. nearsighted	9. neediest	14. New Zealander
5. neophyte	10. necktie	15. negotiate

FINDING THE RIGHT MEANING

26b. Learn to find the meaning you want.

Most English words have a number of different meanings. Some common words, like *run,* for example, have thirty or more. When you go to the dictionary, you are usually interested in a particular meaning of a word—one that will fit into the particular sentence or situation in which you heard or read the word. Nevertheless, it is a good idea to scan all of the meanings given. By doing so you will form a general impression of the range of meanings that word may have. When you have read them all quickly, you can focus on the part of the entry that seems most closely related to the meaning you need.

　　Each separate meaning of a word is explained in a numbered definition. Some dictionaries use letters within numbered definitions to distinguish between closely related meanings. To see how this works, examine the following dictionary entry for the word *offensive.*

¹of•fen•sive \ə-'fen-siv\ *adj* **1 a** : of, relating to, or designed for attack ⟨*offensive* weapons⟩ **b** : being on the offense ⟨the *offensive* team⟩ **2** : giving unpleasant sensations ⟨*offensive* smells⟩ **3** : causing displeasure or resentment : INSULTING ⟨an *offensive* remark⟩ — **of•fen•sive•ly** *adv* — **of•fen•sive•ness** *n*

²**offensive** *n* **1** : the act of an attacking party ⟨on the *offensive*⟩ **2** : ATTACK ⟨launch an *offensive*⟩

From *Webster's School Dictionary.* © 1980 by Merriam-Webster Inc., publishers of the Merriam-Webster ® Dictionaries.

Suppose you want to find the meaning of *offensive* in the sentence "The child was scolded for making such an offensive remark." By recognizing that the word is used as an adjective in this sentence, you can concentrate your search on the entry that gives definitions for the adjective (*adj.*) *offensive.* Definitions 1 and 2 do not fit the context, but definition 3 does. What is more, the illustrative example for 3 provides a context very similar to the one you have in mind.

Now look back at the sample entry and notice that *offensive* is listed again, this time as a noun (*n.*). This particular dictionary gives separate entries for each part of speech. The small numeral 2 before the entry word shows that it is the second entry for the same word. Other dictionaries may not list parts of speech in this way. They may have all the definitions of a word in one entry, with each part of speech in its own subgroup. The following definition, taken from a different dictionary, illustrates the latter method. Notice that the definitions for the noun subgroup, marked by *–n.* for *noun,* begin with the numeral l.

of•fen•sive |ə fĕn'sĭv| *adj.* **1.** Offending the senses; unpleasant: *an offensive smell.* **2.** Causing anger, displeasure, resentment, etc.: *offensive language.* **3.** |ô'fĕn'sĭv| *or* |ŏf'ĕn'-|. Of an attack; aggressive; attacking: *an offensive play in football.* *—n.* **1.** An aggressive action; an attack: *their third major offensive of the war.* **2.** An attitude of attack: *take the offensive.* **—of•fen'sive•ly** *adv.* **—of•fen'sive•ness** *n.*

Whichever dictionary you use, you will find meanings more rapidly if you know your parts of speech.

EXERCISE 5. Finding the Correct Meaning in the Dictionary. Below are three groups of sentences, each group followed by a dictionary definition. Number your paper 1–10. After the appropriate number, write the number (3) or the number and letter (2b) of the definition that gives the correct meaning of the word as it is used in the sentence.

1. This morning we had a *rough* exam in science.
2. Mrs. Logan made a *rough* sketch of the model.
3. Joan's coat is made of *rough* material.

> **¹rough** \\'rəf\ *adj* **1 a** : having an uneven surface : not smooth **b** : covered with or made up of coarse and often shaggy hair or bristles ⟨a *rough*-coated terrier⟩ **c** : difficult to travel over or penetrate : WILD ⟨*rough* country⟩ **2 a** : characterized by harshness, violence, or force **b** : DIFFICULT, TRYING ⟨a *rough* day at the office⟩ **3** : coarse or rugged in character or appearance: as **a** : harsh to the ear **b** : crude in style or expression **c** : marked by a lack of refinement or grace : UNCOUTH **4** : marked by incompleteness or inexactness ⟨a *rough* draft⟩ ⟨*rough* estimates⟩ [Old English *rūh*] — **rough•ly** *adv* — **rough•ness** *n*

From *Webster's School Dictionary.* ⓒ 1980 by Merriam-Webster Inc., publishers of the Merriam-Webster ® Dictionaries.

4. The pet owner claimed that he *trains* bullfrogs to dance.
5. Astronomers will *train* their telescopes on Halley's comet.
6. I *train* the ivy to grow around the window frame.
7. Ms. McConnell *trains* every morning for the marathon race.

> **²train** *vb* **1** : to direct the growth of (a plant) usually by bending, pruning, and tying **2 a** : to teach something (as a skill, profession, or trade) to ⟨was *trained* in the law⟩ **b** : to teach (an animal) to obey **3** : to make ready (as by exercise) for a test of skill **4** : to aim (as a gun) at a target **5** : to undergo instruction, discipline, or drill [Middle French *trainer* "to draw, drag"] **syn** see TEACH — **train•able** \\'trā-nə-bəl\ *adj* — **train•ee** \trā-'nē\ *n*

From *Webster's School Dictionary.* ⓒ 1980 by Merriam-Webster Inc., publishers of the Merriam-Webster ® Dictionaries.

8. Paying your bills promptly will help you establish a good *credit* rating.
9. Oscar winners often share the *credit* with their co-workers.
10. How many *credits* do you need in social studies before you can graduate?

cred•it |krĕd′ĭt| *n.* **1.** Belief or confidence; trust: *I placed full credit in the truthfulness of the state records.* **2.** Reputation or standing: *It is to his credit that he worked without complaining.* **3.** A source of honor or distinction: *a credit to his team.* **4.** Approval, honor, or acclaim for some act or quality; praise: *They shared the credit for the book's success.* **5.** Certification that a student has fulfilled a requirement by completing a course of study. **6.** An acknowledgment of work done, as in the production of a book, motion picture, or play. **7.** A reputation for repaying debts and being financially honest: *He has good credit at all stores.* **8. a.** A system of buying goods or services by charging the amount, with payment due at a later time: *buy on credit.* **b.** Confidence in a buyer's ability and intention to pay at some future time: *The store extended credit to him.* **c.** The period of time allowed before a debt must be paid. **9.** The amount of money in the account of a person or group, as at a bank. **10.** In accounting: **a.** The amount paid on a debt. **b.** The right-hand side of an account, on which such payments are entered. —*modifier: a credit risk; a credit rating.* —*v.* **1.** To believe; trust: *He credited her explanation for the delay.* **2.** To give honor to (a person) for something: *They credit him with founding modern biology.* **3.** To attribute (something) to a person: *Some credit the song to Haydn.* **4.** To give academic credits to (a student). **5.** In accounting: **a.** To give credit for (a payment). **b.** To give credit to (a payer).

CONTENT

26c. Learn what different kinds of information a dictionary gives you about words.

So much information is packed into the typical dictionary definition that some of it is likely to be overlooked if you are not careful. Most of the following explanations correspond to the labels on the sample dictionary column on page 721. Consult the sample column as you study these notes so that you do not overlook any of the information that your dictionary has to offer.

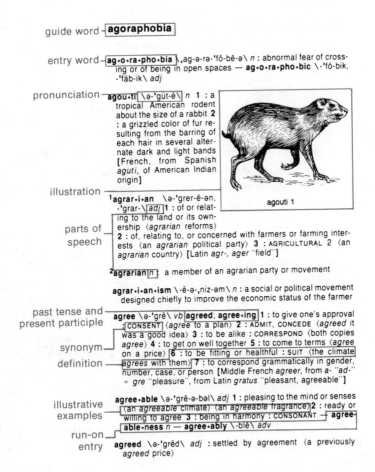

guide word — **agoraphobia**

entry word — **ag·o·ra·pho·bia** \,ag-ə-rə-'fō-bē-ə\ *n* : abnormal fear of crossing of or being in open spaces — **ag·o·ra·pho·bic** \-'fō-bik,
-'fäb-ik\ *adj*

pronunciation — **agou·ti** \ə-'güt-ē\ *n* **1** : a
tropical American rodent
about the size of a rabbit **2**
: a grizzled color of fur resulting from the barring of
each hair in several alternate dark and light bands
[French, from Spanish
aguti, of American Indian
origin]

agouti 1

illustration

1agrar·i·an \ə-'grer-ē-ən,
-'grar-\ *adj* **1** : of or relating to the land or its ownership (*agrarian* reforms)

parts of
speech — **2** : of, relating to, or concerned with farmers or farming interests (an *agrarian* political party) **3** : AGRICULTURAL 2 (an
agrarian country) [Latin *agr-*, *ager* "field"]

2agrarian *n* : a member of an agrarian party or movement

agrar·i·an·ism \-ē-ə-,niz-əm\ *n* : a social or political movement
designed chiefly to improve the economic status of the farmer

past tense and
present participle — **agree** \ə-'grē\ *vb* **agreed**; **agree·ing** **1** : to give one's approval
: CONSENT (*agree* to a plan) **2** : ADMIT, CONCEDE (*agreed* it
was a good idea) **3** : to be alike : CORRESPOND (both copies

synonym — *agree*) **4** : to get on well together **5** : to come to terms (*agree*
on a price) **6** : to be fitting or healthful : SUIT (the climate

definition — *agrees* with them) **7** : to correspond grammatically in gender,
number, case, or person [Middle French *agreer*, from a- "ad-"
+ gre "pleasure", from Latin *gratus* "pleasant, agreeable"]

illustrative
examples — **agree·able** \ə-'grē-ə-bəl\ *adj* **1** : pleasing to the mind or senses
(an *agreeable* climate) (an *agreeable* fragrance) **2** : ready or
willing to agree **3** : being in harmony : CONSONANT — **agree·
able·ness** *n* — **agree·ably** \-blē\ *adv*

run-on
entry — **agreed** \ə-'grēd\ *adj* : settled by agreement (a previously
agreed price)

From *Webster's School Dictionary.* © 1980 by Merriam-Webster Inc., publishers of the
Merriam-Webster® Dictionaries.

1. *Entry word.* The word to be defined is called the *entry
word.* It appears in boldfaced type. You use the entry word to
locate a definition, to get the correct spelling of a word, and to
find out how it is divided into syllables, if it has more than one
syllable. Most dictionaries also indicate words that are capitalized
by beginning the entry word with a capital letter. However,
capitalization may be indicated in other ways, especially in
dictionaries not specially designed for high-school students. If

there is more than one acceptable spelling of a word, the alternative is usually listed immediately after the entry word.

EXAMPLE   **moustache** or **mustache**

In most cases the first spelling listed is the one that most people prefer to use. You will never go wrong by using the first spelling given in any dictionary.

2. *Illustration.* Sometimes the best way to indicate the meaning of a word is through an illustration. *Agouti* on page 721 is such a word. The definition tells you the meaning of this word; the illustration *shows* you the animal itself.

3. *Pronunciation.* The pronunciation of a word is usually indicated immediately after the entry word by means of a special respelling, which is explained in detail on pages 731–33. The dictionary from which the sample column on page 721 was taken uses slant lines (\\) to enclose the pronunciation respelling, but many other dictionaries use parentheses to enclose the respelling. The sounds represented by the symbols in the pronunciation respelling are explained in a key that usually appears inside the front cover of the dictionary. A shorter key may appear at the bottom of each page or of every other page. (For more about pronunciation, see pages 730–33.)

4. *Definition.* The definition gives the meaning or meanings of a word. When a word has more than one meaning, each meaning is defined separately in a numbered definition. (Some dictionaries use letters to distinguish between meanings so closely related that they are defined in a single numbered definition.)

5. *Illustrative example.* For many words, and for different meanings of the same word, sample contexts are provided to show how the word is used. Do not overlook sample contexts. They often provide essential clues to the meaning of a new word. For example, a *hoax* is a kind of trick, but you cannot say that you have "taught the dog a hoax." Illustrative examples often provide the clues that will prevent you from making mistakes in usage.

6. *Synonyms.* Synonyms are words that have similar meanings. In the sample column on page 721, for example, *consent* is

given as the synonym for *agree*. (The word *consent* is printed in block letters to indicate that it is a synonym.) Words that are synonyms can be used alike in some contexts but not in others. For example, the words *deep* and *profound* are synonyms when the subject is mystery. The words *stern* and *rear* are synonyms when one is sailing on a boat.

7. *Run-on entry.* Many English words have companion forms that are closely related to them in meaning. Dictionaries include these words at the end of an entry as *run-on entries.* At the end of the adjective *bad,* for instance, you may find the notation "**—bad′ly** *adv.* **—bad′ness** *n.*" Although often no definitions are given in a run-on entry, a part-of-speech label is provided for each companion form. Some dictionaries also give the pronunciation for the companion form. (For more about companion forms, see pages 761–62.)

8. *Part of speech.* The part of speech is indicated by an italicized abbreviation:

n.	noun	*adv.*	adverb
pron.	pronoun	*prep.*	preposition
v. or *vb.*	verb[1]	*conj.*	conjunction
adj.	adjective	*interj.*	interjection

Many English words can be used as more than one part of speech. For such words, a dictionary will indicate how the definitions are related to the part-of-speech labels. In some dictionaries, all the definitions for one part of speech are grouped together after the label, as on page 721. Other dictionaries provide consecutively numbered definitions, with the part-of-speech label after each numeral. The most frequent usages are given first. The second method is used in the following entry.

---

[1] Unabridged dictionaries and those designed for older students distinguish between verbs like *wonder* in the sentence "I wonder" and verbs that require another word to show who or what is receiving the action; for example, *hit* in "The batter hit a home run." Such dictionaries label verbs like *wonder,* in the first example, *v.i.,* and verbs like *hit,* in the second, *v.t.* The abbreviation *v.i.* stands for *intransitive verb; v.t.* stands for *transitive verb.* Transitive verbs always have to have an object—a word showing who or what was affected by the action expressed by the verb.

smart [smärt] **1** *adj.* Quick in mind; intelligent; bright; clever. **2** *adj.* Keen or shrewd. **3** *adj.* Witty and quick but not deep: *smart* remarks. **4** *adj.* Sharp and stinging: a *smart* cuff on the ear. **5** *n.* A sharp, stinging sensation. **6** *v.* To experience or cause a stinging sensation: eyes *smarting* from smog; The cut *smarts.* **7** *v.* To feel hurt, sorry, irritated, or upset: He still *smarted* over their rude remarks. **8** *adj.* Clean, neat, and trim in appearance. **9** *adj.* Fashionable; stylish: a *smart* outfit. **10** *adj.* Vigorous; brisk; lively: to move at a *smart* pace. — **smart'ly** *adv.* — **smart'ness** *n.*

A dictionary also provides the following information:

Usage label. Not all words entered in a dictionary are equally acceptable in all situations. A usage label is a mild warning that people use a word (or use a particular meaning of a word) only in certain situations. For example, the label *slang* indicates a word that may be used in certain informal situations but is likely to call attention to itself when used in other situations. Another label, *archaic,* indicates that a word was once common but is now rarely used. A third label, *dialect,* indicates that a word is used in only one part of the country. The introduction to your dictionary explains the meaning of all the usage labels employed by your dictionary.

Origin. For some words, school dictionaries provide information about the history of a word, usually by indicating the language from which it was borrowed. Such information may appear near the beginning of the definition or at the end, as in the following example:

dex·ter·ous [dek'strəs *or* dek'stər·əs] *adj.* **1** Skillful in using the hands or body; adroit: a *dexterous* billiard player. **2** Mentally quick; keen. — **dex'ter·ous·ly** *adv.* ◆ *Dexterous* comes from a Latin word meaning *skillful,* which in turn comes from a Latin root meaning *on the right* or *right-handed.*

Encyclopedia information. A small number of dictionary entries deal with people and places. There are better places, including encyclopedias, to find out about important people and places than in a dictionary—these are described in Chapter 27. However, if all you need is a general identification or location, the dictionary will usually provide it, as in the following entry:

Pierce (pirs), **Franklin** 1804–69; 14th president of the U.S. (1853–57)

EXERCISE 6. Writing Synonyms of Words. Number your paper 1–10. Write a synonym for each of the following words. If necessary, use the dictionary.

1. coax
2. development
3. distinct
4. diversity
5. final
6. find
7. happy
8. melancholy
9. perhaps
10. plain

EXERCISE 7. Understanding Usage Labels. Copy from your dictionary the usage labels for five of these words. Be prepared to explain what the labels tell you and how they would affect your use of the words.

1. afeared
2. corny
3. davenport
4. gabby
5. loco
6. lorry
7. ope
8. petrol
9. pone
10. raspberry

EXERCISE 8. Finding Run-on Entries for Specific Words. Copy from your dictionary a run-on entry for each of the following words.

1. celebrate
2. cold
3. negative
4. rapid
5. reform
6. fair
7. foolish
8. smooth
9. suppress
10. thin
11. liquidate
12. mobilize
13. turgid
14. water
15. weigh

EXERCISE 9. Writing Definitions According to Parts of Speech.

Copy from your dictionary two definitions for each of the following words, each definition for a different part of speech. Following the definitions, indicate the parts of speech by using part-of-speech labels.

EXAMPLE   1. flower
  1. a. *The part of a plant that normally bears the seed,*
     n.
    b. *To blossom; to bloom, v.*

1. back	5. maneuver	9. register
2. chance	6. match	10. tag
3. holiday	7. net	
4. Chinese	8. range	

EXERCISE 10. Finding Information About Persons and Places in the Dictionary.

Look up the following persons and places in your dictionary. Be able to tell what information the dictionary provides about them.

1. Ruth	6. Orinoco
2. Helen of Troy	7. New Delhi
3. Emily Brontë	8. Maria Montessori
4. Port Said	9. Sequoya
5. Majorca	10. Tierra del Fuego

SPELLING

26d. Learn to use your dictionary for spelling and capitalization.

If you are not sure about the spelling of a word, you should look it up in the dictionary. Occasionally, it may be difficult to find. If you do not know the initial letters of *gnaw, knife,* and *pneumonia,* you might look for these words under *n.* Fortunately, most words in the dictionary are easier to find. In English, the spelling of the initial sound of a word is much more regular than the spelling of sounds in the middle or at the ends of words. To find how most words are spelled, simply follow the principles of alphabetical order and let the guide words help you.

Variant Spellings

A dictionary occasionally gives two spellings for a word: *abridgment* and *abridgement, coconut* and *cocoanut, partisan* and *partizan.* Both spellings are correct, but usually a dictionary indicates which spelling is more usual by listing it first. Thus *abridgment,* listed before *abridgement,* is considered the more common spelling in several dictionaries.

EXERCISE 11. Finding Variant Spellings of Specific Words. Copy from your dictionary a variant spelling for five of the following words. Be able to tell whether one spelling is preferred.

1. cantaloupe
2. demon
3. fantasy
4. frowsy
5. honor
6. judgment
7. likeable
8. mold
9. rickshaw
10. salable
11. savior
12. sulfur

Unusual Plurals

If the plural of a noun is formed in an unusual way, a dictionary will give the plural form with the abbreviation *pl.* preceding it. For example, the plural of *datum* is given as *data.* Some dictionaries list plurals that are formed in the regular way if there is a chance that the plural will be misspelled. The plural of *valley* might be given *(valleys)* so that no one will make the mistake of ending the plural in *–ies.* Always read the entire entry of a word to be sure of knowing its correct plural form.

Unusual Verb Forms

If a verb forms its past tense, its past participle, or its present participle in an unusual way, a dictionary will list these irregular forms. On page 721, the past tense and present participle forms of *agree* are given. The past participle form is not provided since this is the same as the past tense form. In the entry for *freeze,* a dictionary lists all three forms: *froze, frozen, freezing.*

Comparatives and Superlatives

If the comparative and superlative forms of an adjective are spelled in an unusual way, a dictionary provides these forms either near the beginning or the end of an entry. Sometimes the abbreviations *compar.* and *superl.* are used.

> **love·ly** [luv′lē] *adj.* **love·li·er, love·li·est**
> **1** Having qualities that make people love one:
> a *lovely* child. **2** Beautiful: a *lovely* rose. **3**
> *informal* Enjoyable; pleasant: to have a *lovely*
> time at a party. **—love′li·ness** *n.*

EXERCISE 12. Finding Unusual Spelling Forms for Specific Words.

Copy from your dictionary the unusual spelling forms (if any) for the following words. After the forms, write *(1)* if they are unusual plurals, *(2)* if they are unusual verb forms, or *(3)* if they are unusual comparatives and superlatives.

EXAMPLE 1. swim
1. *swam, swum, swimming (2)*

1. city	5. index	9. rise
2. choose	6. individuality	10. rob
3. defy	7. mad	
4. good	8. needy	

CAPITALIZATION

In English, proper nouns are capitalized, while common nouns are not. You should be familiar with the rules for capitalization given in Chapter 13. If you are not sure about capitalizing a certain word, the dictionary might help you by showing or stating whether or not the word is usually capitalized.

Sometimes a word should be capitalized in one sense but not capitalized in another. In such a case, the dictionary indicates which meaning requires a capital. For example, some dictionaries print *Mass*, meaning "a religious ceremony," with a capital; but *mass*, meaning "a large amount or number," appears uncapitalized. *Pole*, meaning "a native of Poland," is printed with a capital; *pole*, meaning "a slender piece of wood," is not capitalized.

EXERCISE 13. Using the Dictionary for Capitalization. Look up the following words in a dictionary to see when they are capitalized. Be able to explain why they are or are not capitalized in each usage. Your dictionary may not give capitalized uses for all the words.

1. cupid
2. democrat
3. devil
4. episcopal
5. japan
6. calliope
7. nativity
8. pope
9. senate
10. west

SYLLABLE DIVISION

A dictionary divides all words into syllables. *Agreeable* on page 721 is divided into three syllables. Knowing the syllables of a word may help you to spell the word. In addition, if you have to divide a word at the end of a line when you are writing, you must know the syllables to divide it correctly. (See page 447.)

If your dictionary uses small dots or dashes between the syllables of a word, as on page 721, be careful not to confuse these marks with a hyphen. Look up a hyphenated word like *mezzo-soprano* or *open-minded* to be sure you can tell the difference.

EXERCISE 14. Dividing Words into Syllables. Copy the following words, dividing them into syllables. Use the same method to indicate syllable division that your dictionary uses.

1. absolution
2. comma
3. endurance
4. extra
5. flexible
6. junior
7. penetrating
8. severity
9. socialize
10. underdog

PRONUNCIATION

26e. Learn to use your dictionary for pronunciation.

One of the most important pieces of information given in a dictionary is the pronunciation of a word. This information usually comes immediately after the entry word and is enclosed within slant bars (as shown on page 721) or within parentheses. Be careful not to confuse the pronunciation indication with the spelling of a word.

The Accent Mark

In words of two or more syllables, one syllable is always pronounced with greater force than the others. A dictionary indicates which syllable needs emphasis by using an *accent mark*. Most dictionaries use one of two kinds of accent marks: either the mark ' appearing before the syllable or the mark ' placed after the syllable. Both marks appear well above the center of a letter. Look at the pronunciation indication for *agree* on page 721. Which of the two accent marks is used?

In a word of three or more syllables, a dictionary usually indicates two accent marks, one primary, the other secondary. The word *elevator* has a primary accent on the syllable *el* and a weaker accent on *vat*. Dictionaries generally show the secondary accent in one of three ways. When the mark (´) is used to indicate primary accent, the secondary accent is indicated by a weaker mark (ʹ) or by two marks (ʺ). When the primary accent (ˈ) is used, the secondary accent is a similar mark placed at the bottom of a syllable (ˌ). In the word *agoraphobia* on page 721, where does the secondary accent mark occur?

EXERCISE 15. Dividing Words into Syllables and Indicating Accented Syllables.   Copy the following words, dividing them into syllables, and indicate the accented syllables. Use the kinds of accent marks that are used in your dictionary.

1. aristocrat	5. hornpipe	9. sarcasm
2. detrimental	6. masquerade	10. similarity
3. distribution	7. Olympian	
4. frugal	8. revolt	

Pronunciation Symbols

A dictionary uses pronunciation symbols to indicate the pronunciation of a word. Most symbols are regular letters of the alphabet, but they are used more strictly than in ordinary writing. For example, the letter *c* can have several different pronunciations, as in the words *city, control,* and *cello.* A dictionary would indicate the beginning sounds of these words as *s, k,* and *ch.* To show the pronunciation of vowels, which is harder to indicate than the pronunciation of consonants, a dictionary uses *diacritical marks*—special symbols placed above the letters.

Indicating pronunciation is among the dictionary maker's most difficult tasks; thus it is not surprising that dictionaries vary in their use of symbols. To use the pronunciations given in your dictionary, you must become familiar with the symbols it uses. A key to these symbols usually appears inside the front cover and sometimes on each page as well. In addition, your dictionary probably includes a thorough explanation of its pronunciation symbols in the introduction. Study this explanation carefully.

In this chapter you will study several diacritical marks that are used by most dictionaries.

Long Vowels

To indicate a long vowel, a dictionary generally uses a diacritical mark called a *macron*—a long straight mark over the vowel. When a macron is used, the long vowel is said to have the sound of its own name.

EXAMPLES   main   /mān/
               mean   /mēn/
               mine   /mīn/
               moan   /mōn/
               immune   /imūn/

Notice the use of the macron in the pronunciations of *agoraphobia* and *agree* on page 721.

Short Vowels

The vowels in the words *mat, head, bid, dot, could,* and *cut* are called short vowels. Dictionaries differ in their methods of showing the sound of short vowels.

One method uses a symbol called a *breve* (pronounced *brēv*) over the vowel. Another method is to leave short vowels unmarked.

EXAMPLES   mat   (măt)   or   /mat/
              head   (hĕd)   or   /hed/
              bid   (bĭd)   or   /bid/

Sometimes, when all that we pronounce in an unaccented syllable is the sound of the consonant, the pronunciation indication in certain dictionaries may omit the short vowel altogether.

The Schwa

Most recent dictionaries use an upside-down *e*, called a *schwa*, to represent the neutral vowel sound "uh." This sound occurs in the phrase *the pen* (thə pen) and in the following words.

minute (min′ət)
Karen (kar′ən)
permit (pər mit′)
police (pə lēs′)
busily (biz′ə lē)

Most dictionaries use the schwa for the "uh" sound only when it occurs in unaccented syllables, but several dictionaries use this symbol when the sound occurs in accented syllables and in one-syllable words. Consult your dictionary to see how it uses the schwa sound.

EXERCISE 16. Finding the Pronunciations of Specific Words. Copy from your dictionary the pronunciation of each of the following words. Follow the practice of your dictionary in using parentheses or slant lines to enclose the pronunciation. Be able to explain all the diacritical marks used.

1. diet
2. erase
3. bumblebee
4. matriarchy
5. nation
6. poverty
7. puny
8. revolve
9. seldom
10. sidesaddle

EXERCISE 17. Finding the Pronunciations of Specific Words. Follow the directions in Exercise 16.

1. appetite
2. collection
3. debatable
4. fraternal
5. gelatinous
6. heritage
7. major
8. Manila
9. radiator
10. slippery

REVIEW EXERCISE. Understanding the Arrangement and Content of Dictionaries. Use complete sentences in writing the answers to the following questions. If necessary, look the information up in the chapter.

1. Define
   a. synonym
   b. macron
   c. guide word
   d. schwa

2. Name three kinds of information about spelling that a dictionary provides.

3. After which of the following words would *mother-in-law* occur in a dictionary?

    a. motherly   c. motherhood
    b. mother   d. motherland

4. What kind of information is given by the following terms: *slang, informal, archaic*?

CHAPTER 27

Using the Library

ARRANGEMENT OF A LIBRARY, REFERENCE MATERIALS

You can carry about in your head only a limited amount of information, but you can find out almost anything you want to know if you know where to look for it. Your best place to look for information is a library, whether it is your school library or a public library. To use a library efficiently, you must understand its system of arranging the books, magazines, pamphlets, and other materials it contains so that you can find what you want easily and quickly.

THE ARRANGEMENT OF A LIBRARY

Fiction

27a. Learn to locate books of fiction.

In most libraries all books of fiction are located together in one section. The books are arranged on the shelves in alphabetical order according to authors' last names. For example, if you were looking for *The Good Earth* by Pearl S. Buck, you would go to the fiction section and find the books by authors whose last names begin with *B*. Among these, you could easily locate books by Buck. You might find a number of these and have to look along the shelf to find *The Good Earth*. To help you do this, the library arranges books by the same author also in alphabetical order according to the first word in the title, unless that word is *a*, *an*, or *the*. If the first word is *a, an,* or *the,* the second word of the title is used for alphabetizing. *The Good Earth* would come then in the *G* position.

☞ **NOTE**   Books by authors whose names begin with *Mc* (such as McDonald) are arranged as though the name were spelled *Mac*; *St.* is arranged as though it were spelled out, *Saint*.

EXERCISE 1. Arranging Books of Fiction.   Number your paper 1–10. After these numbers, write the authors and titles of the following books of fiction in the order in which the books would be arranged in the library.

1. *The Light in the Forest* by Conrad Richter
2. *Curtain* by Agatha Christie
3. *Jane Eyre* by Charlotte Brontë
4. *Dirt Track Summer* by William Campbell Gault
5. *Crooked House* by Agatha Christie
6. *The Incredible Journey* by Sheila Burnford
7. *The Friendly Persuasion* by Jessamyn West
8. *Wuthering Heights* by Emily Brontë
9. *The Tamarack Tree* by Betty Underwood
10. *The Martian Chronicles* by Ray Bradbury

Nonfiction

27b. Learn the Dewey decimal system of arranging nonfiction.

The Dewey decimal system is named after Melvil Dewey, the American librarian who developed it. Under this system, books are classified under ten headings, and each heading has a number. The numbers and headings are as follows:

000–099   General Works (encyclopedias and other reference materials)
100–199   Philosophy
200–299   Religion
300–399   Social Sciences (economics, government, etc.)
400–499   Language
500–599   Science
600–699   Technology (engineering, aviation, inventions, etc.)
700–799   The Arts (architecture, music, sports, etc.)
800–899   Literature
900–999   History (including geography, travel, and biography)

The number given to a book is known as the book's call number. To see how the Dewey system works, take as an example Arthur Zaidenberg's *How to Draw Cartoons.* Since the book is about art, its number will be in the 700's. Within this broad category, the numbers 740–749 are used for books on drawing and decorative arts. Books on freehand drawing are given the number 741. By means of a decimal, the classification is narrowed further. The number 741.5 is given to books about drawing cartoons, and 741.5–Z is the call number for the book *How to Draw Cartoons.*

Biographies are arranged in alphabetical order according to the names of the persons written about, not according to the names of the persons who wrote the biographies. For example, *The Helen Keller Story* by Catherine Owens Peare will appear among the K's. The call number may consist of **B** (for biography) with **K** (for Keller) under it: $\frac{B}{K}$. Or it may consist of 92 with **K** under it: $\frac{92}{K}$. Some librarians use the B; others use the 92, which is a short form of the Dewey number (920) for biography. Still others use 921.

EXERCISE 2. Classifying Nonfiction According to the Dewey Decimal System.   Within which number range in the Dewey decimal system would you find each of the following?

EXAMPLE   1. A book on modeling in clay
              1. *700–799*

1. A book about Greek philosophy
2. A book about travels in Africa
3. A book about the development of the French language
4. A book about the Presidency
5. A collection of biographies of pioneer men and women
6. A book about baseball
7. A book about the Bible
8. A history of Portugal
9. A book about English poetry of the eighteenth century
10. A book about organic chemistry

THE CARD CATALOG

You can find out the call number of any book in the library by looking the book up in the card catalog.

27c. Learn to use the card catalog.

The card catalog is a cabinet with small drawers that contain file cards arranged in alphabetical order. These cards represent all the books—fiction and nonfiction—in the library. For each book of fiction there are at least two cards, an *author card* and a *title card*. For each book of nonfiction, there are usually three cards, an *author card*, a *title card*, and a *subject card*. If the book is by two or more authors, there is an author card for each name.

Each card provides a different means of finding a book. If you are looking for a book by a particular author, you would look for the *author card*. If you know the title of the book but not the name of the author, you would look for the *title card*. If you need information about a particular subject (rockets and rocketry, for instance) but do not have a specific book or author in mind, you would look for a *subject card;* that is, you would look for cards with the word *ROCKETS* at the top.

Study the following sample cards and explanations:

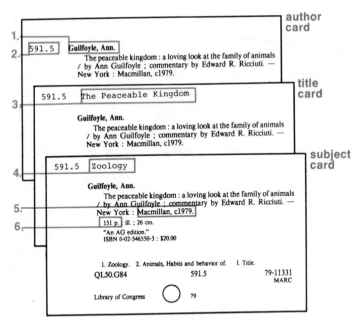

Principal Items of Information on a Card

1. *Name of author.* This information appears first on author cards, which are filed alphabetically under the author's last name. All books by one author are then arranged in the alphabetical order of titles. An author's birth date is often given after the name.

2. *Call number.* This Dewey decimal number tells you where to find the book in the nonfiction section of the library.

3. *Title of book.* On title cards this information appears first. Title cards are filed alphabetically in the card catalog according to the first word of the title, not counting the words *a, an,* or *the.*

4. *Subject.* The subject of a book appears first on subject cards. Like author cards and title cards, they are arranged alphabetically in the card catalog.

5. *Publisher and date of publication.* The date of publication is an important guide if you want recent information on a subject. If you were looking for facts about last year's baseball

season, you would not choose a book published early last year because the information could not have been compiled then. You will save time on research by checking each source's date of publication to make sure that you are using the most current edition of that source. The place of publication is often given before the publisher's name.

6. *Number of pages.* Occasionally this fact will be useful. Obviously, a book about the history of the Supreme Court that is only seventy pages long cannot give much detailed information on the subject.

7. *"See" and "see also" references.* Sometimes a subject card has a "see" reference or a "see also" reference sending you to another card in the catalog. For example, if you looked up *Revolutionary War,* you might find a card saying, "See United States—History—Revolutionary War." If you looked up *Diving,* you might find, "See also Skin Diving."

EXERCISE 3. Using the Card Catalog. Using the card catalog, list the call number, title, author, and date of publication of one book on each of five of the following topics.

1. French Impressionist painters
2. Lasers
3. Birds of Europe
4. Baseball
5. Florence Nightingale
6. South America
7. American poets and poetry
8. Computer games
9. Japanese Americans
10. Scientists

REFERENCE BOOKS

27d. Learn to use the reference books available in the library.

The section devoted to reference books is one of the most important parts of a library. These books contain information on a great many subjects or tell where such information can be found. Once you become familiar with the reference books in your library, they will prove a valuable aid to your studies.

Encyclopedias

An encyclopedia contains articles on a wide range of subjects. These articles are written by experts and present information not only through words but through pictures, charts, and maps. Many articles, especially articles about cities, states, and countries, contain lists of facts and tables of figures. When you are writing a report, an encyclopedia article will give you a good overall view of the subject and may also suggest more detailed sources of information.

You will likely find the following three encyclopedias handy for most reports:

Compton's Encyclopedia
World Book Encyclopedia
Collier's Encyclopedia

All these encyclopedias consist of many volumes and arrange their articles alphabetically by subject. The guide letter or letters on the spine of each volume will help you to find information about a particular subject. Guide words at the top of each page will help you to find a specific article. Use them as you would use guide words in a dictionary. (See page 716.) If you cannot find an article under a particular subject, look for similar subjects or for a larger subject that includes yours. For example, information on *supersonic flight* can probably be found in an article on *aviation*.

You can also find information in an encyclopedia by using the index. Most encyclopedias have indexes, but the indexes are not always located in the same place. For example, the index of *Collier's Encyclopedia* is the last volume, while the index in *Compton's Encyclopedia* is at the end of each volume. You can use the index to locate maps, charts, tables, and illustrations, as well as articles about a particular subject. Usually there is a guide to using the index at the beginning of the index itself.

The index in the last volume of the *World Book Encyclopedia* is in somewhat different form. It is a "Reading and Study Guide," which is arranged by subjects. Each subject is divided into a series of smaller subjects for which a list of articles available in the encyclopedia is given.

EXERCISE 4. Using an Encyclopedia. Look up two of the topics below in an encyclopedia and take half a page of notes on each of them. Below each group of notes, write the title of the article, the name of the encyclopedia, the volume number, and the number of the page on which you found the information.

EXAMPLE   1. The tourist industry in Hawaii
               1. *Each year, several million tourists enjoy vacations in Hawaii. They spend about $3 billion dollars. The busiest months are July, August, and December. In 1903, business people on the islands established an agency that later became the Hawaii Visitors Bureau. The bureau, with state assistance, conducts advertising campaigns to attract tourists.*
                  "Hawaii," World Book Encyclopedia, *volume 9, page 102*

1. Soft-coal mining in the United States
2. The paintings of Mary Cassatt
3. Famous volcanoes
4. Dinosaurs
5. The Battle of Hastings
6. The origin of bowling
7. Penguins
8. The native tribes of Australia
9. The rules and strategy of backgammon
10. The invention of the Diesel engine
11. The statues on Easter Island
12. How to care for a pet
13. Ambergris, its origins and uses
14. The electron microscope
15. The population and industries of Maine
16. The building of the Appian Way
17. The ruins at Angkor Wat
18. Mesmerism
19. Stonehenge
20. Electronic music

Atlases

Atlases are reference books made up mainly of maps. Often they contain much other information, such as the population figures for cities, states, and countries; principal crops; natural resources; and major industries.

Atlases are of several kinds. Some contain maps for all the countries of the world. Others contain maps for a particular country only. Historical atlases show how countries have changed through the years, while economic atlases show such things as trade routes and natural resources. Some of the common atlases are

The Encyclopaedia Britannica Atlas
Hammond Contemporary World Atlas
National Geographic World Atlas
Rand McNally Popular World Atlas

Atlases will prove valuable in your history and geography courses. You should learn about the different kinds of information that atlases provide and become thoroughly familiar with at least one atlas.

EXERCISE 5. Using a World Atlas. Consult a world atlas and write answers to two of the following questions.

1. Name three national parks in California.
2. List three important geographical features (rivers, plains, deserts, lakes, etc.) of each of the following countries:
   a. Brazil   b. Algeria   c. England
3. List the countries that border on each of the following:
   a. Switzerland   b. Venezuela   c. Turkey
4. List four major products of each of the following countries:
   a. Bolivia   b. Ethiopia   c. Pakistan   d. Iraq
5. In which country is each of the following cities situated?
   a. Volgograd   b. Riyadh   c. Jena   d. Sapporo
6. List the following states in order of population, beginning with the most populous:
   a. Illinois   c. Virginia   e. Maine
   b. Alaska   d. Ohio   f. California

Almanacs

An almanac consists in large part of lists of miscellaneous information, including sports statistics, names of government officials, population figures, and birth and death rates. In addition, an almanac is a good place to find much recent information, since almanacs are published annually and give many facts about the preceding year. For instance, if you want a review of the important events of last year, you should consult this year's almanac.

Three useful almanacs are *The World Almanac and Book of Facts, Information Please Almanac,* and *The CBS News Almanac.* The various kinds of information in an almanac are not always organized alphabetically or according to any other kind of logical, systematic arrangement. The best way to find information in an almanac is to use the index. In *The World Almanac* the index is at the front of the book, while in the other almanacs it is at the back.

EXERCISE 6. Using an Almanac. Consult one of the almanacs mentioned above and write answers to two of the following questions:

1. Give the birth dates and birthplaces of the following persons (look up "Personalities, noted" or "Celebrated persons").
   a. Eudora Welty   d. Robert Redford
   b. Steven Spielberg   e. Jesse Jackson
   c. Chris Evert Lloyd
2. Give the names of the Secretaries of State during the administration of the following Presidents:
   a. John Quincy Adams   d. William Taft
   b. William Harrison   e. Warren Harding
   c. Abraham Lincoln
3. Who won the Nobel Prize for physics in 1923? 1938? 1946? 1970? 1976?
4. Give the name of the author and title of the novel that won the Pulitzer Prize for fiction in each of the following years: 1926, 1928, 1947, 1955, 1959, 1980.

Biographical Reference Books

A biographical reference book contains short biographies of famous persons. The following are among the most useful of these books. Find out whether they are in your library.

Who's Who and *Who's Who in America*—useful for principal biographical facts about living persons only.

Webster's Biographical Dictionary—very short biographies of famous persons, modern and historical.

Contemporary Authors and *Contemporary Authors: First Revision*—interesting profiles of modern writers.

Current Biography—lives of persons currently prominent in the news. Published monthly.

The *Readers' Guide*

27e. **To find a magazine article, use the** *Readers' Guide.*

To find a magazine article on any subject, you use a very valuable reference book called the *Readers' Guide to Periodical Literature.* Published eighteen times a year, the *Readers' Guide* indexes articles in more than one hundred magazines. Every year the issues are collected and published in a large volume. You can look up an article by its subject (like *Tutenkhamun*) or by its author. To save space, the listings use abbreviations. If you are in doubt about the meaning of the abbreviations, you should consult the keys in the front of the *Readers' Guide.*

Study the excerpts (on the following page) from an issue of the *Readers' Guide.* The marginal notes will make clear the information given.

Suppose you are writing an article about ancient Egypt and wish to include some information about King Tut's tomb. The *Readers' Guide* (see the following page) would lead you first to the subject *Tutenkhamun,* then to the subdivision *Tomb,* and finally to an article by W. H. Honan in the *New York Times Magazine* of December 17, 1978. The entry for this article gives the following information:

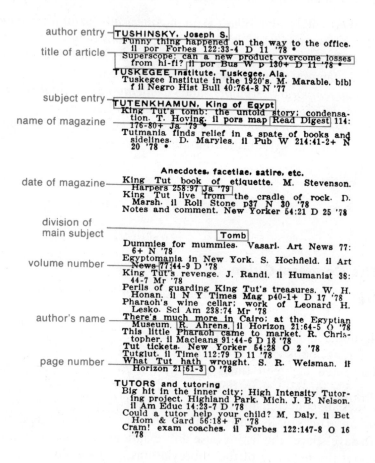

author entry

title of article

subject entry

name of magazine

date of magazine

division of main subject

volume number

author's name

page number

An article about King Tut's tomb titled "Perils of Guarding King Tut's Treasures" by W. H. Honan can be found in the *New York Times Magazine.* The article, which is illustrated (il), begins on page 40 and is continued on later pages (p40–1+) of the December 17, 1978, issue (D 17 '78).

EXERCISE 7. Using the *Readers' Guide*. In the *Readers' Guide*, find an article listed under any five of the following subjects. Copy the entry for the article. Be ready to explain the information for the entry.

1. Scandinavia
2. Phonograph records
3. Lakes
4. Colleges and universities
5. Personnel management
6. Space probes
7. Elephants
8. Coal
9. Submarines, atomic-powered
10. Washington, D.C.

THE VERTICAL FILE

27f. To find a pamphlet, use the vertical file.

Besides books and magazines, pamphlets can be helpful to you when you are studying a topic. The U.S. Government publishes hundreds of pamphlets each year. In addition, state and local governments, businesses, colleges and universities, and health and other organizations publish pamphlets regularly. Your librarian files these pamphlets in a special filing cabinet called a vertical file. Sometimes newspaper clippings of special interest will also be included. Each pamphlet or clipping is placed in a folder and filed in alphabetical order by subject. For current information, you will find the vertical file very helpful. Ask your librarian whether a file folder is available on the topic you are studying.

MICROFILM AND MICROFICHE

27g. Use microfilm and microfiche to find information.

To save space, many libraries store some magazines, newspapers, and documents on microfilm or microfiche. *Microfilm* is a roll or reel of film containing photographically reduced pages.

Microfiche is a small sheet of film containing photographically reduced pages. Both microfiche and microfilm can contain hundreds of pages. To use the microfilm and microfiche, you use microfilm and microfiche projectors, respectively. Each machine enlarges the microscopic images to a readable size. Your librarian can tell you which publications are stored on microfilm and microfiche, where the microfilm and microfiche are located in the library, and how to use the microfilm and microfiche projectors.

COMPUTERS

27h. Use computers to find information.

Some libraries have computerized their book lists, periodical lists, and catalogs. If this is the case, then you will have to use the computer to find the lists of books and periodicals in the library. Instead of looking through the card catalog or the *Readers' Guide,* you would type the information you need into the computer—for example, "subject: plant collecting." The computer would search for the titles and locations of books and periodicals on your subject. Then it would print the information onto its screen. The computer might even be able to give you a printout, or a printed list. Your librarian can tell you what kinds of computer programs the library has, where the computers are located, and how to use the computers.

REVIEW EXERCISE. Using Library Reference Tools. Number your paper 1–20. Write the reference tool from the list on page 749 to which you would turn first to get information on the corresponding subject in the list below.

1. Latest developments in cancer research
2. History of the Nobel Prize
3. Source of the Mississippi River
4. Antarctica—climate, terrain, etc.
5. Motion Picture Academy Award winners in 1980
6. Title and author of a library book on outer space

7. Diplomatic career of James Russell Lowell, the American poet
8. Origins of jazz music
9. Titles of novels by Joy Adamson (1910–1980)
10. Population of Naples, Italy
11. Natural resources of the Rhineland in Germany
12. A list of magazine articles on a recent international crisis
13. The work of Grant Wood, American artist
14. Winners of the World Series since 1977
15. The title of a book in the library on the Revolutionary War
16. Height of Mount Everest
17. Facts about the present Secretary of State
18. History of Italian opera
19. Facts about Ralph Ellison, the American author
20. The biography of a person who has only recently become prominent in the news

SUMMARY LIST OF LIBRARY REFERENCE TOOLS

The card catalog
Computers
Microfilm or microfiche
Reference books
    Encyclopedias
    Atlases
    Almanacs
    Biographical reference books
        Who's Who
        Who's Who in America
        Webster's Biographical Dictionary
        Contemporary Authors
        Contemporary Authors: First Revision
        Current Biography
    Readers' Guide to Periodical Literature
The Vertical File

CHAPTER 28

Vocabulary

LEARNING AND USING
NEW WORDS

The books you have read, the games you play, school subjects, hobbies—all your interests are reflected in your vocabulary. It is no surprise, then, that teachers and parents rely on vocabulary growth as one way of measuring success in school. Knowing many words, of course, does not make anyone a good student automatically, but hardly anyone does well in school without developing a good vocabulary.

Although there is no simple way to acquire a large vocabulary, there are ways in which you can learn and remember more of the words you encounter every day. This chapter will give you practice in using these methods. It will also introduce you to a number of words that are widely used in the books you will be reading this year and in the future.

To keep a record of your progress and to refresh your memory, set aside a section of your notebook in which to enter the new words you learn. Along with this list of words, write a definition and a sentence or phrase illustrating how each word is used. You can begin your vocabulary notebook with any unfamiliar words that you encounter in the following diagnostic test.

DIAGNOSTIC TEST

Number your paper 1–25. After the proper number, write the letter of the word or phrase that is closest in meaning to the numbered word.

EXAMPLE 1. hamper   a. build   c. hinder
                               b. revise   d. search

      1. *c*

1. abashed   a. beaten   c. lowered
                     b. ashamed   d. fallen

2. adept   a. skillful   c. proud
                b. bold   d. lazy

3. amity   a. boredom   c. anger
                b. hatred   d. friendship

4. belligerent   a. dull   c. swift
                       b. warlike   d. gentle

5. crony   a. old woman   c. candy
                b. tower   d. friend

6. deluge   a. opinion   c. excitement
                b. illusion   d. flood

7. dexterity   a. sugar   c. handiness
                  b. duplicate   d. kindness

8. fatigue   a. war   c. fatalist
                b. weariness   d. explosion

9. guffaw   a. laugh   c. loosen
                b. retire   d. drive

10. haughty   a. moderate   c. proud
                b. smiling   d. slow

11. humdrum   a. melodious   c. aggressive
                  b. loud   d. dull

12. levity   a. simple lever   c. earnestness
                b. excessive speed   d. lack of seriousness

13. menace   a. army   c. song
                b. threat   d. rival

14. pallid   a. pale   c. sleepy
                b. excited   d. calm

15. pedagogue a. teacher c. politician
       b. learning d. politics
16. primitive a. undeveloped c. violent
       b. prominent d. religious
17. raze   a. lift   c. destroy
       b. attack   d. repel
18. remorse a. repetition c. justice
       b. guilt   d. reason
19. revile   a. abuse   c. rebuild
       b. correct   d. bury
20. seraphic a. telegraphic c. angelic
       b. intelligent d. serious
21. sinew   a. novelty c. disappointment
       b. excitement d. strength
22. tepid   a. unlucky c. alone
       b. lukewarm d. rushing
23. unique   a. singular c. uneven
       b. together d. heavy
24. vehement a. energetic c. timid
       b. serious   d. laughing
25. visage   a. cage   c. face
       b. news   d. tang

LEARNING NEW WORDS

Occasionally we see or hear a word used alone, but most of the time we encounter words used in combination with other words. If the word is unfamiliar, these surrounding words often supply valuable clues to meaning.

28a. Learn new words from context.

The *context* of a word means the words that surround it in a sentence and the whole situation in which the word is used. The context of the word supplies the main clue to the meaning of *inedible* in this sentence:

The cook was told not to use toadstools in the stew because they are inedible.

Since the cook was warned against using the toadstools in a stew, it stands to reason that something *inedible* is something "not fit to eat." If you know that much about toadstools already, you can be even surer about your guess.

Many common English words have several meanings. The context often provides clues to their meanings. For example, *pound* means one thing in a grocery store, another in a story about a dogcatcher, and still another in a British movie. Context clues will aid you in understanding these words when you encounter them in your reading.

EXERCISE 1. Using Context Clues to Define Words.

Number your paper 1–10. For each italicized word in the sentences that follow, write the letter of the definition that is closest in meaning. You will not need all the definitions in the list. Check your answers in the dictionary.

a. calm	e. pronounced	i. fearful
b. peak	f. honesty	j. confused
c. guidance	g. government	k. round of applause
d. magic	h. swung to hit	l. without success

1. Mrs. Tompkins has been the treasurer for twenty-seven years, and no one doubts her *integrity.*
2. The angry mob gathered at the palace to express their disapproval of the *regime.*
3. At thirty, Lisa Chin is at the *summit* of her tennis career.
4. The fortuneteller claimed that she had *occult* powers.
5. He is so *timorous* that he can not sleep in the dark.
6. Unhappy, the baby *flailed* angrily at the bars of her playpen.
7. At the end of the play, the enthusiastic audience gave the actors a rousing *ovation.*
8. She could not solve the puzzle because it *bewildered* her.
9. The doctor spoke comforting words to *allay* the patient's fears.
10. The speaker *articulated* her words with care.

EXERCISE 2. Using Context Clues to Define Words.
Follow the directions in Exercise 1.

a. aloneness   e. good luck   i. disaster
b. reduce   f. ambition   j. insult
c. bravery   g. respect   k. joy
d. avoid   h. get well   l. imaginary

1. The soldiers bowed to the emperor as a sign of *deference*.
2. The earthquake, a *catastrophe* that caused hundreds of deaths and thousands of injuries, came unexpectedly.
3. Harold has a *fictitious* playmate, whom no one has ever seen.
4. Luke finds it extremely difficult to make friends because he has lived the greater part of his life in *isolation*.
5. After a successful operation, a patient usually remains in the hospital to *recuperate*.
6. With a roar, the crowd expressed its *jubilation* at the football victory.
7. People should not attempt to *evade* their duties as citizens.
8. If the railroad keeps on losing money, it will have to *curtail* its services.
9. Jose's *aspiration* is to win the lead in the school play.
10. Private Lewis showed such *valor* in battle that he was promoted to corporal.

Related Word Forms

28b. Learn the related forms of new words.

Some words can be used as different parts of speech without changing their spelling. The word *iron* can be a noun, an adjective, or a verb: a piece of *iron*, an *iron* bar, to *iron* a dress. More often, however, something is added or taken away from the word to change it from one part of speech to another. The ending –*ly* can be added to most adjectives to make them adverbs (*soft, softly*), and the ending –*ness* is often added to make them nouns (*softness*). You will study more about such changes later in this chapter. The main thing now is to be aware that a new word may have related forms that are just as useful as the one you have encountered. When you can learn two or three new words with no more effort than it takes to learn one word, why not do it?

EXERCISE 3. Writing Related Forms of Specific Words.
The first part of each numbered pair contains an italicized word used as a particular part of speech. The second part of each pair contains a blank in which a related form of the same word will fit. Number your paper 1–10. After the proper number, supply the appropriate form. Use your dictionary if you need to.

EXAMPLE   1. an act of *valor*
           a ——— action
        1. *valorous*

1. a *coherent* explanation
   to explain with ———
2. to *aspire* to something
   noble
   a noble ———
3. an *isolated* farmhouse
   to live in ———
4. to *evade* responsibilities
   an ——— of one's duty
5. to *coerce* a person
   to get something by ———

6. a *futile* attempt
   to try ——— to do
   something
7. the *tumult* of a battle
   a ——— scene
8. the *validity* of an argument
   a ——— reason
9. *appropriate* behavior
   to behave ———
10. a skillful *diplomat*
    skill in ———

Using the Dictionary

28c. Learn to find the meaning you want in your dictionary.

If you cannot guess the meaning of a word from context, you should go to your dictionary. Context is still important, however. Most words have a number of different meanings, and the best way of finding the one you want is to look for the definition that fits the context in which you originally encountered the word. Consider the following sentence.

Your jokes are in poor taste, Harold, and we can dispense with any more of them.

Dispense has the following meanings: (1) to give; (2) to distribute; (3) to get rid of; (4) to get along without. By trying each of these meanings in place of the word *dispense* in the example, you can easily eliminate all of the choices except the last one—the meaning you want.

Which of these numbered meanings for *dispense* fits the following sentence?

The Red Cross dispensed clothing to the flood victims.

Dictionaries often supply sample contexts to help you distinguish between the various meanings of a word (see pages 717–18). Such phrases can be very helpful in showing you how to use the new word in your own speech and writing.

EXERCISE 4. Finding the Correct Meaning of a Word.
The italicized words in the following sentences have a number of different meanings. Using your dictionary, select the meaning that best fits each sentence, and write it after the proper number.

EXAMPLE   1. A candidate for the presidency is likely to be an *eminent* political figure.
   1. *prominent*

1. The doctor said that there was nothing to be feared from the *benign* swelling.
2. The old man gave us a *benign* smile.
3. The professor's lecture *illuminated* the subject for us.
4. With the flick of a switch, he can *illuminate* the garden.
5. As we drove into the valley, a beautiful *pastoral* scene unrolled before us.
6. The minister attended to his *pastoral* duties.
7. Your argument seems *valid* and has convinced us all.
8. Since this is a *valid* contract, you will have to live up to it.
9. The manager's *bland* words calmed the angry customer.
10. I don't like this cereal because it is too *bland*.

EXERCISE 5. Defining Words. The following two columns consist of a list of words and a list of definitions for these words. Number your paper 1–10. After the proper number, copy the letter of the definition that is closest in meaning. Refer to a dictionary when necessary. You will not use all the definitions in the second column.

1. chronic	a. calm and serious
2. appalling	b. to climb rapidly
3. sedate	c. numerous
4. forgo	d. shocking
5. prodigy	e. person having special abilities
6. myriad	f. arrival of an important event
7. debonair	g. give up
8. advent	h. slowly falling
9. decrepit	i. lively and gay
10. pewter	j. heavy silver-gray metal
	k. law or principle
	l. continuing for a long time
	m. foolishly happy
	n. feeble

REVIEW EXERCISE A. Defining Words. The words in this exercise have been chosen from those you have studied so far. Number your paper 1–20. After the proper number, write the letter of the word or phrase nearest in meaning.

1. evade   a. run   c. trick
         b. avoid   d. lose

2. coerce   a. cooperate   c. refuse
         b. lag behind   d. compel

3. pastoral   a. finely made   c. of the past
         b. about rural life   d. richly perfumed

4. fictitious   a. handsome   c. musical
         b. invented   d. genuine

5. regime   a. airplane   c. government
         b. boating   d. regulation

6. catastrophe   a. crowd   c. royalty
                b. disaster   d. fortune

7. summit   a. dessert   c. peak
                b. rebellion   d. leap

8. illuminate   a. go as   c. argue with
                b. light up   d. seem like

9. valor   a. courage   c. wisdom
                b. laziness   d. vanity

10. tumult   a. disturbance   c. motive
                b. accident   d. hatred

11. bewilder   a. prepare   c. confuse
                b. bewitch   d. lose

12. eminent   a. small   c. prominent
                b. permanent   d. clever

13. curtail   a. correct   c. finish
                b. build   d. reduce

14. timorous   a. unreliable   c. trusting
                b. afraid   d. royal

15. flail   a. restore   c. beat
                b. chase   d. impress

16. integrity   a. honesty   c. misery
                b. loyalty   d. treachery

17. recuperate   a. lessen   c. duplicate
                b. refill   d. recover

18. coherent   a. clear   c. mistaken
                b. scrambled   d. recent

19. aspiration   a. relief   c. ambition
                b. slogan   d. notion

20. benign   a. evil   c. dangerous
                b. kind   d. pale

PREFIXES, ROOTS, AND SUFFIXES

Some words can be divided into parts, and some cannot. Those that can be divided, like *workbook* and *unhappy,* often consist of parts that mean something separately. By learning how to divide words into their parts, you can sometimes discover additional clues to meaning.

The basic part of a word is called a *root*. A part added before the root is called a *prefix*; a part added after the root is called a *suffix*. Becoming familiar with the common prefixes and suffixes discussed here will provide you with helpful leads to finding the meaning of a large number of new words.

Prefixes

28d. Learn how common prefixes change the meaning of words.

The following common prefixes occur in thousands of English words.

PREFIX	MEANING	EXAMPLE
auto–	self	automobile
bi–	two	bimonthly
circum–	around	circumference
con–	together	concord
de–	down or from	degrade
dis–	away or apart	disagree
ex–	out	expel
im–	not	impractical
mis–	wrong	misjudge
multi–	many	multiply
pre–	before	preview
semi–	half or partly	semiprecious

EXERCISE 6. Using Prefixes to Define Words. Number your paper 1–10. After the proper number, give the meaning of the italicized word in each of the sentences. Be prepared to tell how the prefix of the word helps determine its meaning. Use the dictionary if necessary.

1. The assistant principal *convened* the student council to draft a new student code of conduct.
2. An artillery shell completely *demolished* the hut.

3. He gave some *preposterous* excuse for not passing the test.
4. Our newspaper is published *biweekly*.
5. Laura Chou was born in Hong Kong and was not brought to the United States until she was six years old; therefore, she is *bilingual*.
6. Some of the czars of Russia were cruel *autocrats* who were feared by the people.
7. To call Alvin a worker is a *misnomer* because he is always asleep with a broom in his hands.
8. Mrs. Boscombe cut small *semicircles* of paper with the sharp scissors.
9. The *dissatisfied* members of the council held a protest meeting.
10. Mrs. Boone is a thorough housekeeper, and her apartment is always *immaculate*.

EXERCISE 7. Using Prefixes to Define Words. Follow the directions for Exercise 6.

1. Ferdinand Magellan, the Portuguese sailor and explorer, *circumnavigated* the globe.
2. The girl held a large, *multicolored* ball in her hands.
3. The mechanic had to *dismantle* the motor to find the faulty part.
4. Holding a lantern, she slowly *descended* the cellar stairs.
5. Because Mr. and Mrs. Harrison are a *congenial* couple, they rarely quarrel.
6. The theft of the jewels showed careful planning and must have been a *premeditated* crime.
7. We finally *dissuaded* Tom from writing a letter to the author.
8. Archimedes is supposed to have *exclaimed* "Eureka!" when he made an important discovery.
9. The Pueblo Indians have observed this custom since time *immemorial*.
10. The Whitmore Construction Company is building a group of *semidetached* houses on this block.

EXERCISE 8. Using Prefixes to Define Words.   Follow the directions for Exercise 6.

1. Frank has become so efficient at packaging toys that he moves like an *automaton*.
2. The people, angry over years of misrule, *deposed* the unjust king.
3. Remember Shakespeare's *immortal* words: "This above all, to thine own self be true."
4. The Smiths own *extensive* lands in this valley.
5. Mrs. Slocum showed how to *bisect* an angle.
6. Is the prisoner truly sorry for his *misdeeds*, or is he only sorry he was caught?
7. Ms. Feinstein stayed in a *semiprivate* hospital room.
8. The prisoner was allowed to move freely within a *circumscribed* area.
9. Next year our city will hold its *bicentennial* celebration.
10. Melba MacHenry Gardner, who donated the money for our new Civic Center, is a *multimillionaire*.

Suffixes

28e. Learn to recognize common suffixes when they occur in *companion forms.*

Sometimes adding a suffix will result in a word that is a different part of speech than the original word. For example, the suffix *–ly* added to the adjective *free* results in *freely*, an adverb. The suffix *–ly* occurs at the end of an adjective or an adverb but never at the end of a noun. Therefore, words ending in this suffix are never nouns. (When the letters *–ly* occur at the end of a noun such as *lily*, they are not a suffix but part of the basic word.)

There are many English words to which suffixes can be added. The new words formed by adding suffixes are *companion forms* of the basic word. Adding suffixes to the root *free* results in the companion forms *freedom* and *freely*. If you are on the alert for companion forms and learn some common suffixes, you will often be able to guess the correct meanings of new words. One fact to keep in mind is that the spelling of the root may change when a suffix is added. For example, when *–ly* is added to *gay*, the resulting word is not *gayly* but *gaily*. When *–ition* is added to *repeat*, the resulting word is spelled *repetition*.

Learn the following suffixes that occur in nouns.

SUFFIX	MEANING	EXAMPLE
–hood	condition	childhood
–ness	quality	goodness
–ance, –ence	state, act, fact	independence
–ation, –ition, –tion	action or state	celebration
–ity, –ty	quality	ability
–ment	result or action	employment

EXERCISE 9. Using Noun-forming Suffixes. Number your paper 1–10. Form nouns from the following words by using the suffixes just listed; then give the meanings of the new words. In some cases it will be necessary to change the spelling of the root. Check your answers in the dictionary.

EXAMPLES 1. kind
1. *kindness—the quality of being kind*
2. create
2. *creation—the act of creating*

1. replace   4. accept   7. fragile   9. improvise
2. likely   5. intense   8. aspire   10. friendly
3. articulate 6. man

The following suffixes occur in adjectives.

SUFFIX	MEANING	EXAMPLE
–ish	like or suggesting	foolish
–able, –ible	able	tolerable
–ous	having the quality of	religious
–esque	like	statuesque
–some	like or tending to	tiresome

EXERCISE 10. Using Adjective-forming Suffixes. Number your paper 1–10. Form adjectives from the following words by using the suffixes just listed; then give the meanings of the new words. Check your answers in the dictionary.

1. lone
2. picture
3. harmony
4. devil
5. grace
6. baby
7. luxury
8. depend
9. meddle
10. riot

The following suffixes occur in verbs.

SUFFIX	MEANING	EXAMPLE
–ate	cause to become	animate
–en	make or become	deepen
–fy	make or cause	fortify
–ize	cause to be	motorize

EXERCISE 11. Using Verb-forming Suffixes. Number your paper 1–10. Form verbs from the following words by using the suffixes just listed; then give the meanings of the new words. Check your answers in the dictionary.

1. captive
2. system
3. strength
4. nausea
5. glory
6. active
7. civil
8. sweet
9. illumine
10. beauty

EXERCISE 12. Identifying and Defining Words with Suffixes. Each of the following sentences has a word with a suffix that you have learned in this chapter. Number your paper 1–10. Find the word in each sentence. After the proper number, copy the word and underline the suffix. Then write the meaning of the word. In some cases, you may be able to guess the correct meaning. In others, the root of the word may not be familiar to you. Check *all* your answers in the dictionary.

EXAMPLE   1. Gerry's arrogance has caused him to be disliked by many people.

1. *arrogance—state of being arrogant*

1. The beautiful scenery provided the artist with inspiration enough for fifty pictures.

2. The sentries in the prison camp were not allowed to fraternize with the enemy.
3. Job prayed to be relieved of his afflictions.
4. At Thanksgiving time the store had a window display showing the courageous Pilgrims.
5. The two countries formed an alliance to help each other in the event of war.
6. The refinement of her manners is proof of her strict upbringing.
7. This company believes that it has an obligation to please all of its clients.
8. The coat of shellac guaranteed that the table surface would be durable.
9. Factories should not be allowed to fill our waters with waste products that might contaminate them.
10. *Carmen* is regarded as one of the most melodious of all operas.

USING EXACT WORDS

28f. Use the exact word in your speaking and writing.

In English, many thousands of words are available to help you express exactly what you mean. If you use the same few words to describe many different people or things or actions or situations, you are not taking advantage of the variety of your language. Avoid overworked words that are used in so many different contexts that they lose precise meanings. *Good* is one such word. If you were to refer to someone as "a good person," would you mean that he is capable, kind, or dependable? If you were to say, "I had a good day," would you mean an enjoyable, a productive, or a tranquil day? *Good* might be the first word that occurs to you to describe a person or a day, but a moment's thought will usually supply a better word to express your meaning. Of course, the greater the stock of words at your command, the easier it will be for you to substitute a fresh, precise word for a trite one.

Using Adjectives to Describe

The English language is rich in adjectives. You should learn to use adjectives to express your meaning exactly. In talking about a book you enjoyed, for example, you might say it was *interesting*, but how much more expressive you would be if you called it *exciting* or *engrossing* or *stimulating*! Build your vocabulary by taking time to find the exact adjective to express your thought.

EXERCISE 13. Selecting Precise Adjectives.   Each of the following sentences contains a vague or overworked adjective, in italics, which should be replaced by a more precise word. Number your paper 1–10. After the proper number, write the more precise adjective from the list preceding the sentences. You will not need all the words in the list. Use the dictionary, if necessary, to check your answers and make corrections.

eccentric	decrepit	devout	tangible
casual	customary	insipid	eligible
titanic	burly	appalling	boisterous
fragrant	sallow	fluent	

1. That rice pudding had a rather *flat* taste.
2. The *old* car drove slowly down the road.
3. The damage done by the hurricane was *shocking*.
4. The *muscular* sailor pushed against the door.
5. Paul is regarded as *odd* because he puts mustard on ice cream.
6. When we began to sing and shout, our counselor warned us that we were being too *lively*.
7. With a *great* effort, Samson tore down the pillars of the Philistine temple.
8. The foreman of the jury said that no *real* evidence of guilt had been produced.
9. No student who is failing one or more subjects is *qualified* for a student council position.
10. The roses were *sweet-smelling*.

EXERCISE 14. Selecting Precise Adjectives. Number your paper 1–5. After the proper number, write an adjective from the following list that conveys an idea appropriate to the sentence. You will not use all the words in the list. Use the dictionary, if necessary.

diverse	feasible	abundant
latent	oratorical	excessive
resolute	homogeneous	pertinent

1. Ms. Henderson's plan seems to work well.
2. Once Fran sets a goal in life, nothing will stop her from reaching it.
3. Your statement is very much to the point.
4. Anna has talent, but it needs to be developed.
5. All the women in this group are the same age and height, and all have the same interests.

Using Verbs to Express Action

Your ability to express yourself is directly dependent on your verb vocabulary. Verbs give action and color to your sentences. The following exercise includes a number of verbs that are important for you to know.

EXERCISE 15. Selecting Verbs to Complete Sentences. Number your paper 1–10. After the proper number, copy the verb whose meaning best completes the sentence. Change the tense if necessary to fit the sentence, and use your dictionary. You will not need all the verbs in the list.

soar	restrain	capitulate	browbeat
saturate	liberate	stray	wheedle
diverge	carouse	restore	elapse
confiscate	pollute	obliterate	

1. Because they could not pay their taxes, the government —— their property.

2. The fighter was badly beaten but refused to —— to his opponent.
3. Realizing that the bird would die in captivity, the girl took it to the woods and —— it.
4. As the plane —— above the clouds, the earth disappeared from view.
5. Several hours —— before the weary hikers returned home.
6. She is extremely timid and allows people to —— her.
7. Skillful detective work —— the stolen painting to its rightful owners.
8. The two hunters parted company when their paths —— .
9. Two centuries of wind and weather have almost —— the words carved on the stone.
10. Although we may be tempted to overeat, we should —— ourselves.

Using Adverbs to Modify Verbs

Because adverbs answer such questions as *How? When?* and *Where?* in connection with verbs, they are a very important part of your vocabulary. The exactness and vividness of your writing and speaking depend a great deal on your using adverbs well. In the exercise that follows, there are a number of adverbs for you to learn. Many of these adverbs are formed from words in the list beginning on page 774.

EXERCISE 16. Using Adverbs to Modify Verbs. Number your paper 1–10. After the proper number, write an adverb from the list that answers the question. You will not need all the adverbs in the list. Use the dictionary, if necessary.

immensely	resonantly	superficially
covertly	scrupulously	rigidly
abruptly	urgently	cautiously
excessively	anonymously	ostentatiously

1. How did the conscientious bookkeeper keep the company's records?

2. How did the woman who found there were burglars in her house call for the police?
3. How did the opera star sing the low notes in his aria?
4. How did the audience like the actor's superb performance?
5. How did the newly engaged girl display her engagement ring?
6. How did the tired student check her homework?
7. How did the little boy try to get a cookie from the cookie jar when his mother was in the next room?
8. How would a person stand if imitating a statue?
9. How does a doctor leave a dinner party upon receiving an emergency call?
10. How does a person cross a busy city street during rush hour?

Synonyms and Antonyms

A *synonym* is a word that means nearly the same thing as another word. Sometimes a dictionary will define a word in terms of its synonym: One definition of *benign* is "kind." Although words that are synonyms are close in meaning, they rarely have *exactly* the same meaning. At times you will be able to use one of several words in a sentence, but at other times only the exact word will do.

Pleasure, delight, and *joy* all have roughly the same meaning, yet each expresses a different shade of meaning. *Pleasure* is the most general of the three words; it covers a variety of situations, none of them very specifically. *Delight* indicates a sharp feeling of pleasure that lasts only a short time. *Joy* may indicate a deep and long-lasting happiness. In the following sentence, which of the three words fits most exactly?

I receive great —— from my study of mathematics.

Pleasure fits, of course, but is not very specific. *Delight* does not fit very well because the feeling indicated in this sentence would seem to last for some time. The synonym that most exactly expresses the desired meaning is *joy.*

When you look up a word in a dictionary, you will often find several synonyms listed. Be sure you understand the exact meaning of each synonym. To help you to distinguish between synonyms, some dictionaries give *synonym articles*—brief explanations of a word's synonyms and how they differ in meaning. Your own reading will also help you. The more often you encounter a word in different contexts, the better you will be able to determine its meaning.

EXERCISE 17. Selecting Synonyms to Complete Sentences. Number your paper 1–10. After the proper number, write the synonym you have selected that best fits the sentence. Use the dictionary to learn the exact meaning of each synonym.

1. My jacket is made of a new (fabricated, imitation, synthetic) material.
2. Our (invincible, victorious, triumphant) army never has been and never should be defeated in battle.
3. The monks in several medieval monasteries kept (histories, annals, records) summarizing the important events of each year.
4. Medieval artists had a special (fashion, technique, system) for making stained-glass windows.
5. The young couple fondly (fed, nourished, sustained) their baby daughter.
6. You can imagine how (ridiculous, shaming, humiliating) it was to be spanked in front of all my relatives.
7. Her (guess, conjecture, estimate) that there would be a test the next day was based on the fact that Mrs. Brown had assigned no homework that night.
8. Although the lawyer stayed within the law, he relied on (guile, deceit, fraud) to win his case.
9. Under the new government, many citizens were (dispossessed, deprived, divested) of their rights.
10. After studying the problem I formed a working (theory, hypothesis, supposition), which I tested by experiment.

The antonym of a word is a word with the opposite meaning. *Bad* is the antonym of *good*, and *happy* is the antonym of *sad*. Sometimes an antonym of a word is formed by adding a prefix meaning *not*: an antonym of *wise* is *unwise*. Knowing the antonym of a word will often help you to understand the word's exact meaning (or at least one exact meaning). For example, knowing that *dexterity* is the antonym of *clumsiness* will lead you to a correct meaning for this word. A dictionary sometimes lists antonyms at the end of an entry for a word.

EXERCISE 18. Selecting Antonyms for Specific Words. Antonyms for words in the first column may be found in the second column. Number your paper 1–10. After the proper number, write the letter of the correct antonym. You will not need all the words in the second column. Use the dictionary, if necessary.

1. frustrate	a. tiny	
2. contemptible	b. dawn	
3. colossal	c. ornamental	
4. impertinent	d. spiteful	
5. upbraid	e. satisfy	
6. twilight	f. wordiness	
7. brevity	g. biased	
8. neutral	h. probity	
9. functional	i. courteous	
10. random	j. eventual	
	k. admirable	
	l. orderly	
	m. praise	

SPECIAL VOCABULARIES

Each of your school subjects has special words that you must learn if you are to understand the concepts. Some of the words are new, while others, which are used in everyday speech, have special meanings in a particular subject.

A textbook often calls attention to these new words by printing them in italics or in boldfaced type. Printing a word in a special way shows that it is important. Often a definition immediately follows the word. If not, turn to the back of the book to see if there is a glossary—a short dictionary of special words. There, you will usually find a definition for the word. Always use a glossary when a textbook provides one. It is one of the most valuable features of a book.

EXERCISE 19. Defining Mathematics Words. The words in this exercise are used in mathematics books designed for students in your grade. Write each word on your paper, and follow it by a short definition. Then write a short sentence using each word correctly. Use a dictionary or the glossary in your mathematics book.

acute	exponent	numeral	radical
bisect	intersection	obtuse	radius
diameter	irrational	quotient	rational

EXERCISE 20. Defining Social Studies Words. The following words are likely to appear in your social studies assignments. Follow the directions for Exercise 19.

History: blockade, capitalism, carpetbagger, depression, filibuster, gerrymander, initiative, recall, referendum, sharecropper, totalitarian, vassal

Geography: fiord, meridian, monsoon, plateau, precipitation, topography, tributary

EXERCISE 21. Defining Science Words. The following words are likely to appear in your science assignments. Follow the directions for Exercise 19.

antibody	electron	fulcrum	radiation
atom	embryo	nebula	satellite
condensation	friction	neutron	spectrum

28g. Use the words from specialized vocabularies in your everyday speaking and writing.

Many words in a special field are often used outside the field. *Condensation* and *inertia* are often found in nonscientific books, while *exponent* and *radical* can be used by a political speaker as well as a mathematician. Learn the meanings of these words as used outside their fields. Use them in your own speaking and writing when they help to express your ideas exactly.

EXERCISE 22. Using Special Words in Everyday Writing.
The following words used in mathematics, science, and social studies have meanings outside these fields. Use these words appropriately in the blanks in the sentences. You will not use all the words.

blockade	embryo	initiative	radical
condensation	fulcrum	intersection	satellite
diameter	inertia	obtuse	vassal

1. Harriet displayed great —— in forming a drama club and recruiting members for it.
2. When you have trouble getting started on your work, you are suffering from —— .
3. The newspapers have called Mayor Tompkins "a —— of special-interest groups."
4. George is so —— that he didn't get the joke even after she explained it.
5. The department store has been completely reorganized; you will discover some pretty —— changes when you go there.
6. To save space, the magazine published a —— of Madeleine L'Engle's new book.
7. The fugitive ran up the stairs to the attic and ——d the entry by pushing a heavy table against the wooden door.
8. Ann met us at the —— of Vernon Street and Third Avenue.

REVIEW EXERCISE B. Defining Words. The words in this exercise have been chosen from all those you have studied in this chapter. Number your paper 1–30. After the proper number, write the letter of the word or phrase that is closest in meaning to the numbered word.

1. abundant
   - a. house
   - b. plentiful
   - c. sloppy
   - d. crowded

2. affliction
   - a. aviation
   - b. guardian
   - c. report
   - d. misery

3. appalling
   - a. revealing
   - b. annoying
   - c. shocking
   - d. rewarding

4. boisterous
   - a. lively
   - b. supporting
   - c. treacherous
   - d. weak

5. concord
   - a. sympathy
   - b. conformity
   - c. agreement
   - d. boredom

6. covertly
   - a. swiftly
   - b. gaily
   - c. badly
   - d. secretly

7. decrepit
   - a. decoyed
   - b. feeble
   - c. wise
   - d. proud

8. deference
   - a. pressure
   - b. deceit
   - c. respect
   - d. loyalty

9. divest
   - a. clothe
   - b. deprive
   - c. retreat
   - d. amble

10. extensive
    - a. large
    - b. thin
    - c. visual
    - d. highly respected

11. feasible
    - a. expensive
    - b. fearful
    - c. missing
    - d. workable

12. flail
    - a. shrink
    - b. beat
    - c. reveal
    - d. forget

13. homogeneous
    - a. alike
    - b. different
    - c. thoughtful
    - d. respected

14. immaculate
    - a. forgetful
    - b. spotless
    - c. cowardly
    - d. intelligent

15. jubilation
    - a. anniversary
    - b. ceremony
    - c. terror
    - d. rejoicing

16. nourish
    - a. hate
    - b. regret
    - c. love
    - d. feed

17. ovation
    - a. honor
    - b. action
    - c. recipe
    - d. applause

18. premeditated
    - a. deliberate
    - b. fiendish
    - c. foolish
    - d. great

19. random   a. close   c. aimless
               b. emotional   d. knowing

20. resolute   a. reserved   c. enduring
               b. determined   d. miserable

21. restrain   a. hold back   c. dress up
               b. teach   d. remember

22. rigidly   a. stiffly   c. cleverly
               b. stubbornly   d. rudely

23. saturate   a. wring out   c. treat badly
               b. imitate   d. fill completely

24. sedate   a. noisy   c. calm
               b. healthy   d. honest

25. stray   a. wander   c. lonely
               b. direct   d. puzzled

26. synthetic   a. tiring   c. careless
               b. expensive   d. artificial

27. technique   a. detail   c. instruction
               b. method   d. reason

28. titanic   a. metallic   c. backward
               b. huge   d. alive

29. upbraid   a. climb   c. reverse
               b. misread   d. scold

30. wheedle   a. grow   c. coax
               b. correct   d. crawl

Word List

The following list of 300 words should form the basis of your vocabulary study for the year. You have already encountered many of them (or related forms) in this chapter. When you encounter a new word, add it to your vocabulary notebook. Write a definition of the word, and use the word in a sentence.

abuse	activate	advantageous
acceptance	adapt	advent
access	adept	aeronautics
accessory	adequate	affliction
accommodations	adjacent	aggressive

alliance
anonymous
antibiotics
anxiety
appalling

aristocrat
aroma
articulate
aspiration
assumption
attain
automaton
badger
baffle
bankrupt

barbarism
basis
baste
bewilder
blockade
boisterous
boycott
burly
calamity
calculation

capital
casual
catastrophe
category
censorship
charitable
chronic
circulate
circumnavigate
clarify

climax
colossal
commute
complement
condemn
confederation
confide
confiscate
conjecture
consecutive

considerate
contagious
contemporary
controversy
convert
creative
customary
decade
deceased
deceive

dedicate
deduction
defy
delegate
demolish
denial
depose
derive
descend
despise

detach
dictate
dilapidated
dilute
diminish

dingy
diplomat
disagreeable
discord
disintegrate

dismantle
dispatch
dispense
dissect
distraction
durable
eccentric
ecology
elegant
eligible

embarrass
emigrate
eminent
emphasize
endorse
enhance
epidemic
erosion
essay
evacuate

exaggeration
exertion
extensive
falter
famine
famished
feasible
felony
ferocious
fictitious

folklore
foresight
foreword
fortnight
fragile
fragment
fraudulent
frequency
gallery
generate

glorify
gnarled
gracious
grieve
hamper
harmonious
haughty
haven
hilarious
homicide

hospitable
humidity
humiliate
hydraulic
hypothesis
illuminate
immense
immigrate
immune
imperative

imply
impose
improvise
impulsive
inanimate

inclination
incomparable
inconsiderate
indelible
inevitable

inflexible
ingenious
inherit
inquisitive
insoluble
integrity
intelligible
intensity
intentional
intercept

intervene
intrigue
invariable
isolation
jeopardize
jubilation
knoll
latent
liable
liberate

literal
malfunction
malnutrition
manageable
maroon
massage
meddlesome
memento
menace
menagerie

miscellaneous
misdeed
modify
monopoly
morale
multicolored
multitude
mutual
myriad
nationality

negligent
neutral
notify
nourish
novelty
obituary
obscure
occupant
occurrence
omission

optimism
pacify
pamphlet
parasitic
persistent
pessimistic
petty
pewter
phenomenon
photogenic

picturesque
pious
planetarium
pleasantry
pollute

populate
posterity
potential
prearrange
predicament

premier
premiere
presume
primitive
privilege
probable
probation
propaganda
proposal
provision

pulverize
pun
punctual
quaint
quench
rebate
recuperate
refuge
regime
remorse

remote
resolute
respiration
restore
restrain
revelation
rigid
riotous
romantic
ruthless

sable
salutation
sanctuary
sarcasm
satire
saturate
secluded
sedate
sincerity
sinew

spacious
sphere
sterile
strategy
successor

summit
superficial
sustain
synthetic
tangible

tariff
tarnish
technology
temperament
testify
therapy
thrifty
thrive
titanic
transit

tumult
unique
upbraid
urban
urgent
valid
valor
verify
vitality
warranty

CHAPTER 29

Spelling

IMPROVING YOUR SPELLING

English is a language that is not consistent in its representation of sounds. For this reason, learning to spell in English is a challenging task. You have already learned to spell many thousands of words, but there are probably others that give you trouble. You can increase your ability to spell provided you approach the task slowly and easily—and provided you have the will and patience to learn.

GOOD SPELLING HABITS

These are a few of the things you can do to improve your spelling:

1. Keep a list of your own errors.
2. Use the dictionary as a spelling aid.
3. Spell by syllables.
4. Avoid mispronunciations that lead to spelling errors.
5. Proofread your papers to avoid careless spelling errors.

1. *Keep a list of your own errors.* As your ability to spell improves, you will notice that some words seem to be especially difficult for you. But don't be discouraged; make your own

spelling book. The best way to master words that you find troublesome is to list them and review them frequently.

2. *Use the dictionary as a spelling aid.* A dictionary is a writer's best friend. Get the habit of consulting a dictionary whenever you have a spelling problem.

3. *Spell by syllables.* If you have trouble spelling long words, break them up into syllables. A syllable is a part of a word that can be pronounced by itself. The word *remember* has three syllables: *re·mem·ber.* Most syllables have no more than three or four letters, and certainly you can learn that many. A long word then becomes a group of short parts, and you can learn it syllable by syllable.

4. *Avoid mispronunciations that lead to spelling errors.* If you listen and speak carefully, you will be less likely to misspell words because you are not pronouncing them correctly. Be sure that you say *chimney,* not *chimbly; library,* not *liberry; modern,* not *modren.*

5. *Proofread your papers to avoid careless spelling errors.* Half the trouble in spelling comes from careless haste. Whenever you do any writing, proofread your paper for errors in the spelling not only of difficult words but also of the ordinary, easy words that you may have misspelled through carelessness.

SPELLING RULES

The following rules are helpful, even though there are exceptions to them. If you learn them thoroughly, you will find it easier to spell correctly.

ie and *ei*

29a. Except after *c*, write *ie* when the sound is long *e*.

EXAMPLES	believe, relief, field, deceive, ceiling
EXCEPTIONS	neither, leisure, seize, weird

Write *ei* when the sound is not long *e*, especially when the sound is long *a*.

EXAMPLES   reign, weight, eight, freight, height, sleight
EXCEPTIONS   friend, mischief

–cede, –ceed, –sede

29b. Only one word in English ends in *–sede—supersede;* only three words end in *–ceed—exceed, proceed,* and *succeed;* all other words of similar sound end in *–cede.*

EXAMPLES   concede, recede, precede

EXERCISE 1. Writing Words with *ie* and *ei*. Write the following words, supplying the missing letters (*e* and *i*) in the correct order. Be able to explain how the rules apply to each word.

1. fr . . . nd
2. p . . . ce
3. rec . . . ve
4. c . . . ling
5. w . . . ght
6. bel . . . ve
7. br . . . f
8. h . . . ght
9. n . . . ghbor
10. fr . . . ght

EXERCISE 2. Writing Words with *–ceed, –cede,* and *–sede*. Write the following words, supplying *–ceed, –cede,* or *–sede*.

1. pre . . .
2. pro . . .
3. con . . .
4. inter . . .
5. super . . .
6. ex . . .
7. suc . . .
8. re . . .

Adding Prefixes

A prefix is one or more letters added to the beginning of a word to change its meaning.

EXAMPLES   un + able = **un**able
           pre + arrange = **pre**arrange

29c. When a prefix is added to a word, the spelling of the word itself remains the same.

EXAMPLES il + logical = **il**logical
in + elegant = **in**elegant
im + perfect = **im**perfect
un + selfish = **un**selfish
dis + trust = **dis**trust
mis + apply = **mis**apply
over + see = **over**see

EXERCISE 3. Writing Sentences for Words with Prefixes.

Number your paper 1–25. Write correctly the words formed. Then choose ten of the words and use each of them in a sentence.

1. il + legal
2. in + exact
3. im + migrant
4. in + equality
5. dis + order
6. mis + inform
7. re + enter
8. over + rule
9. il + liberal
10. un + natural
11. in + active
12. mis + use
13. over + rated
14. re + establish
15. dis + similar
16. mis + interpret
17. im + probable
18. over + run
19. il + legible
20. mis + trust
21. semi + annual
22. in + numerable
23. dis + array
24. un + necessary
25. im + material

Adding Suffixes

A suffix is one or more letters added to the end of a word to change its meaning.

EXAMPLES care + less = care**less**
walk + ed = walk**ed**
comfort + able = comfort**able**

29d. When the suffixes *–ness* and *–ly* are added to a word, the spelling of the word itself is not changed.

EXAMPLES   mean + ness = mean**ness**
casual + ly = casual**ly**

EXCEPTIONS   Words ending in *y* usually change the *y* to *i* before
–ness and *–ly:* misty—mist**iness**; happy—happ**ily**.
One-syllable adjectives ending in *y* generally follow rule 29d: shy—shy**ly**.

29e. Drop the final *e* before a suffix beginning with a vowel.

EXAMPLES   line + ing = lin**ing**
approve + al = approv**al**
desire + able = desir**able**

EXCEPTIONS   In some words, the final *e* must be kept to retain
the soft sound of a *c* or *g:* notice + able =
notic**eable**; courage + ous = courag**eous.**

**29f. Keep the final *e* before a suffix beginning with a conso-
nant.**

EXAMPLES   hope + less = hope**less**
care + ful = care**ful**

EXCEPTIONS   true + ly = tru**ly**
argue + ment = argu**ment**
judge + ment = judg**ment**

EXERCISE 4. Writing Words with Suffixes.   Number your
paper 1–20. Write correctly the words formed.

1. mean + ness
2. final + ly
3. love + able
4. shine + ing
5. true + ly
6. one + ness
7. notice + able
8. outrage + ous
9. pretty + ly
10. advantage + ous
11. change + able
12. please + ing
13. hope + ful
14. place + ing
15. remove + al
16. study + ing
17. happy + ness
18. come + ing
19. sudden + ness
20. cordial + ly

29g. With words ending in *y* preceded by a consonant, change the *y* to *i* before any suffix not beginning with *i*.

EXAMPLES   cry + ed = cri**ed**
           lovely + ness = loveli**ness**
           bury + al = buri**al**
   but   cry + ing = cry**ing**

Note that words ending in *y* preceded by a vowel generally do not change their spelling when a suffix is added.

EXAMPLES   pray + ing = pray**ing**
           pay + ment = pay**ment**
           boy + hood = boy**hood**

29h. With words of one syllable ending in a single consonant preceded by a single vowel, double the consonant before adding *–ing, –ed,* or *–er*.

EXAMPLES   sit + ing = sit**ting**
           swim + ing = swim**ming**
           drop + ed = drop**ped**

29i. With words of more than one syllable ending in a single consonant preceded by a single vowel, double the consonant before adding *–ing, –ed,* or *–er* if the word is accented on the last syllable.

EXAMPLES   occur' + ed = occur**red**
           begin' + er = begin**ner**
           permit' + ing = permit**ting**

If the word is *not* accented on the last syllable, the final consonant is not doubled before a suffix.

EXAMPLES   trav'el + er = traveler
           can'cel + ed = canceled
           sten'cil + ing = stenciling

EXERCISE 5. Writing Words with Suffixes.   Number your paper 1–20. Write correctly the words formed.

1. study + ed
2. hurry + ed
3. study + ing
4. hurry + ing
5. bid + ing
6. quiz + ing
7. drop + ed
8. fit + ed
9. race + ing
10. stop + ed
11. cry + ed
12. joke + ing
13. deploy + ing
14. prefer + ed
15. permit + ed
16. beg + ed
17. plan + ed
18. admit + ing
19. run + er
20. bat + er

THE PLURAL OF NOUNS

Plurals are formed in several ways, most of them covered by rules. To learn irregular plurals, you should enter them in your private spelling list and memorize them.

29j. Observe the rules for spelling the plural of nouns.

(1) The regular way to form the plural of a noun is to add an —s.

EXAMPLES desk, desks
idea, ideas

(2) The plural of some nouns ending in s, x, z, ch, or sh is formed by adding —es.

EXAMPLES pass, passes
fox, foxes
buzz, buzzes
clutch, clutches
dish, dishes

EXERCISE 6. **Writing the Plurals of Nouns.** Number your paper 1–10. Write the plurals of the following words:

1. wish
2. pilot
3. machine
4. match
5. automobile
6. porch
7. dance
8. mechanic
9. reflex
10. box

(3) The plural of nouns ending in _y_ preceded by a consonant is formed by changing the _y_ to _i_ and adding _–es_.

EXAMPLES   army, armies
country, countries
city, cities
pony, ponies

(4) The plural of nouns ending in _y_ preceded by a vowel is formed by adding _–s_.

EXAMPLES   journey, journeys
key, keys

(5) The plural of most nouns ending in _f_ is formed by adding _–s_. Some nouns ending in _f_ or _fe_, however, form plurals by changing the _f_ to _v_ and adding _–s_ or _–es_.

EXAMPLES   grief, griefs
belief, beliefs
shelf, shelves
knife, knives
thief, thieves

(6) The plural of nouns ending in _o_ preceded by a vowel is formed by adding _–s_; the plural of nouns ending in _o_ preceded by a consonant is formed by adding _–es_.

EXAMPLES   _o_ following a vowel:

radio, radios
curio, curios
patio, patios

_o_ following a consonant:

tomato, tomatoes
echo, echoes

EXCEPTIONS   Eskimos, silos, pianos, sopranos, altos

Note that many nouns ending in *o* that pertain to music are exceptions to this rule.

(7) The plural of a few nouns is formed in irregular ways.

EXAMPLES   child, child**ren**   goose, **geese**
             ox, ox**en**   mouse, **mice**
             woman, wom**en**   foot, **feet**
             tooth, **teeth**

EXERCISE 7. Writing the Plurals of Nouns. Number your paper 1–25. Write the plurals of the following nouns:

1. city	10. galley	19. soprano
2. chimney	11. calf	20. echo
3. company	12. knife	21. child
4. foot	13. leaf	22. tooth
5. donkey	14. belief	23. mouse
6. valley	15. roof	24. hero
7. lily	16. rodeo	25. woman
8. goose	17. volcano	
9. library	18. mosquito	

(8) The plural of compound nouns consisting of a noun plus a modifier is formed by making the noun plural.

EXAMPLES   passer-by, passers-by
             maid of honor, maids of honor
             brother-in-law, brothers-in-law

(9) The plural of a few compound nouns is formed in irregular ways.

EXAMPLES   drive-in, drive-ins
             fourteen-year-old, fourteen-year-olds

(10) Some nouns are the same in the singular and plural.

EXAMPLES   trout, salmon, sheep, Sioux, deer, moose

(11) The plural of numbers, letters, signs, and words considered as words is formed by adding an apostrophe and *s*.

EXAMPLES   1900   1900's   +   +'s

ABC   ABC's   *and*   *and*'s

EXERCISE 8. Writing the Plurals of Nouns.   Number your paper 1–10. Write the plurals of the following nouns:

1. sheep
2. weekend
3. trout
4. daughter-in-law
5. *a*
6. teen-ager
7. guard of honor
8. deer
9. cupful
10. 1800

EXERCISE 9. Writing the Plurals of Nouns.   Number your paper 1–25. Write the plurals of the following items. After each plural, write the number of the subrule under rule 29j (1–11) that applies.

EXAMPLE   1. proof
1. *proofs (5)*

1. child
2. ox
3. 100
4. *t*
5. shelf
6. belief
7. cry
8. monkey
9. sister-in-law
10. sheep
11. piano
12. spoonful
13. Eskimo
14. knife
15. clutch
16. radio
17. potato
18. lass
19. alto
20. *and*
21. baby
22. chef
23. arpeggio
24. pulley
25. wax

WORDS OFTEN CONFUSED

The words grouped together in the following lists are frequently confused with each other because their pronunciation or spelling is the same or similar. Study them carefully, and learn to distinguish both their meanings and their spellings.

accept	*to receive with consent; to give approval to* Many of his contemporaries did not *accept* Copernicus' theory that the earth moves around the sun.
except	*[verb] to leave out from a number; [prep.] with the exclusion of; but* We were *excepted* from the assignment. Everyone will be there *except* Mark.
advice	*a recommendation about a course of action* Good *advice* may be easy to give but hard to follow.
advise	*to recommend a course of action; to give advice* I *advise* you to continue your music lessons if you possibly can.
affect	*to influence; to produce an effect upon* The explosion of Krakatoa *affected* the sunsets all over the world.
effect	*the result of an action; consequence* It has long been observed that the phases of the moon have an *effect* on the tides of the earth's oceans.
all right	*everything is right* or *satisfactory* [This must be written as two words. The spelling *alright* is never correct.] Maria did *all right* in the track meet. Was my answer *all right*?
all ready	*all prepared* or *in readiness* The players are *all ready* for the big game.

already   *previously*
Our class has *already* taken two field trips this year.

EXERCISE 10. Selecting Spelling Words to Complete Sentences.
Number your paper 1–10. After the proper number, write the word given in the parentheses that makes the sentence correct.

1. Everyone likes to give (advice, advise).
2. The (affect, effect) of the victory was startling.
3. Why did you (accept, except) Carla from the class rule?
4. The scientists were (all ready, already) to watch the launching of the rocket.
5. The coach (advices, advises) us to stick to the training rules.
6. Her weeks of practice finally (affected, effected) her game.
7. Most of the rebels were offered a pardon and (accepted, excepted) it, but the leaders were (accepted, excepted) from the offer.
8. Juan has (all ready, already) learned how to water-ski.
9. Do you think my work is (all right, alright)?
10. Whose (advice, advise) are you going to take?

---

altar   *a table for a religious ceremony*
The *altar* was banked with lilies.

alter   *to change*
The outcome of the election *altered* the mayor's plan.

---

all together   *everyone in the same place*
The director called us *all together* for one final rehearsal.

altogether   *entirely*
Your story is *altogether* too late for this issue.

brake	*a device to stop a machine* Can you fix the *brake* on my bicycle?
break	*to fracture; to shatter* The winner will be the one who *breaks* the tape.
capital	*a city; the seat of a government* Olympia is the *capital* of Washington.
capitol	*building; statehouse* Where is the *capitol* in Albany?
choose	[present tense, rhymes with *lose*] *to select* Will you *choose* speech or civics as your elective next year?
chose	[past tense, rhymes with *grows*] *selected* Janet *chose* to play in the band rather than in the orchestra.

EXERCISE 11. Selecting Spelling Words to Complete Sentences.   Number your paper 1–10. After the proper number, write the word given in parentheses that makes the sentence correct.

1. The building with the dome is the (capital, capitol).
2. By working (all together, altogether) we can do the job easily.
3. Because she loved dramatics, Alice (choose, chose) a difficult part in the school play.
4. Be careful not to (brake, break) those dishes.
5. That book is (all together, altogether) too complicated for you to enjoy.
6. The candles on the (altar, alter) glowed beautifully.
7. We don't know whether to (choose, chose) band or orchestra.
8. A car without a good emergency (brake, break) is a menace.
9. Will Joan's accident (altar, alter) her plans?
10. Tallahassee is the (capital, capitol) of Florida.

clothes   *wearing apparel*
One can learn a lot about a historical period by studying its fashions in *clothes*.

cloths   *pieces of fabric*
You'll find some cleaning *cloths* in the drawer.

---

coarse   *rough; crude*
The beach is covered with *coarse* brown sand.

course   *path of action; planned program or route* [also used in the expression *of course*]
The wind blew the ship slightly off its *course*.

---

consul   *a representative of a government in a foreign country*
Who is the American *consul* in Nigeria?

council   *a group of people who meet together*

councilor   *a member of a council*
The king called a meeting of the *council* and informed the *councilors* that the royal treasury was nearly empty.

counsel   *advice; to give words of advice*

counselor   *one who advises*
When choosing a career, seek *counsel* from your teacher.
Who is your guidance *counselor*?

---

desert
[des′ ert]   *a dry, sandy region*
The Sahara is the largest *desert* in Africa.

desert
[de sert′]   *to abandon; to leave*
Most dogs will not *desert* a friend in trouble.

dessert
[des sert′]   *the final course of a meal*
Fruit salad is my favorite *dessert*.

EXERCISE 12. Selecting Spelling Words to Complete
Sentences. Number your paper 1–10. After the proper number, write the word or words given in the parentheses that will make the sentence correct.

1. Each class has four representatives on the student (council, counsel).
2. The guide threatened to (desert, dessert) us as we crossed the (desert, dessert).
3. Most young people are very much interested in (clothes, cloths).
4. Your guidance (councilor, counselor) can be of great help to you.
5. The (coarse, course) for the cross-country race is a rugged one.
6. The cleaning (clothes, cloths) must be washed after each use.
7. Do we have a Canadian (consul, council) in this city?
8. (Coarse, Course) gravel lined the driveway of Margarita's house.
9. The meal didn't seem complete without (desert, dessert).
10. The members of the losing team looked to their coach for (council, counsel).

---

formally   *with dignity; following strict rules or procedures*
The Governor delivered the speech *formally.*

formerly   *previously; in the past*
Formerly I knew the Zubalsky family very well.

---

hear   *to perceive sounds by ear*
Dogs can *hear* some sounds that are inaudible to people.

here   *in this place*
The campsite is right *here.*

---

its | [possessive of the pronoun *it*]
Mount Fuji is noted for *its* beauty.

it's | [a contraction of *it is* or *it has*]
It's an extinct volcano.
It's been a long time.

lead | [present tense] *to go first; to be a leader*
[lēd] | A small town in New Hampshire often *leads* the nation in filing its election returns.

lead | *a heavy metal*
[lĕd] | A *lead* pencil actually has no *lead* in it.

led | [past tense] *went first*
The Governor *led* the slate with an impressive majority.

loose | [rhymes with *noose*] *not securely attached; not fitting tightly.*
If a tourniquet is too *loose*, it will not serve its purpose.

lose | [pronounced lo͞oz] *to suffer loss*
Vegetables *lose* some of their vitamins when they are cooked.

EXERCISE 13. Selecting Spelling Words to Complete Sentences. Number your paper 1–10. After the proper number, write the word or words given in parentheses that will make the sentence correct.

1. (Its, It's) a long way from (hear, here) to the park.
2. The plumber is removing the (lead, led) pipes and putting in brass ones.
3. We don't want to (loose, lose) you in the crowd.
4. Before the club takes up new business, the secretary (formally, formerly) reads the minutes of the previous meeting.

5. (Its, It's) too bad that the tree has lost (its, it's) leaves so early.
6. Do you (hear, here) me, Ann? Come (hear, here) now!
7. The Yankees were ten runs behind, and it seemed certain that they were going to (loose, lose).
8. The marshal (lead, led) the class into the chapel.
9. Had Pepita ever done any running (formally, formerly)?
10. That (loose, lose) bolt can cause trouble.

passed	[past tense of *pass*] *went by* Our airplane *passed* over the Grand Canyon.
past	*that which has gone by; beyond* Some people live in the *past.* They moved *past* the dozing sentry.
peace	*security and quiet order* We are striving for a world of *peace* and prosperity.
piece	*a part of something* Some people can catch fish with a pole, a *piece* of string, and a bent pin.
plain	*simple, common, unadorned; a flat area of land* A *plain* jackknife is often as useful as one with several blades. What is the difference between a prairie and a *plain?*
plane	*a tool; an airplane; a flat surface* The *plane* is useful in the carpenter's trade. Four single-engine *planes* are in the hangar. Rhoda says she likes *plane* geometry.
principal	*the head of a school; main or most important* The *principal* is the chief officer of a school. What are the *principal* exports of Brazil?

principle   *a rule of conduct; a main fact or law*
She listed some of the *principles* of economics.

quiet   *still and peaceful; without noise*
A *quiet* room is needed for concentrated study.

quite   *wholly or entirely; to a great extent*
Winters in New England can be *quite* severe.

EXERCISE 14. Selecting Spelling Words to Complete Sentences. Number your paper 1–10. After the proper number, write the word or words given in parentheses that make the sentence correct.

1. A bright smile often makes a (plain, plane) face attractive.
2. The summer was (quiet, quite) over before the beginning of school brought a (quiet, quite) household once more.
3. This is an important (principal, principle) in mathematics.
4. On July 20, 1963, the moon (passed, past) between the earth and the sun, causing a total eclipse.
5. A (plain, plane) is a useful tool.
6. Save me a (peace, piece) of that blueberry pie.
7. Our (principal, principle) is leaving the school this year.
8. We should try to learn from (passed, past) experience.
9. The nation was working hard to attain (peace, piece).
10. Cattle were grazing over the (plain, plane).

shone   [past tense of *shine*]
They polished the silver until it *shone.*

shown   [past participle of *show*] *revealed*
A model of the new school will be *shown* to the public next week.

stationary   *in a fixed position*
Most of the furnishings of a space capsule must be *stationary.*

stationery   *writing paper*
I need a new box of *stationery.*

---

than   [a conjunction used for comparisons]
The Amazon River is longer *than* the Mississippi River.

then   *at that time*
If the baby is awake by four o'clock, we will leave *then.*

---

there   *a place* [also used to begin a sentence]
Go *there* in the fall when the leaves are turning.
There were no objections.

their   [a possessive pronoun]
Their team seems very skillful.

they're   *they are*
They're taller than most of our players.

---

threw   [past tense of *throw*] *hurled*
Our pitcher *threw* four balls in succession.

through   [a preposition]
Have you ever seen a ship go *through* the locks of a canal?

EXERCISE 15. Selecting Spelling Words to Complete Sentences.   Number your paper 1–10. After the proper number, write the word or words given in parentheses that make the sentence correct.

1. We go (there, their, they're) often, for the children can get (there, their, they're) instruction in swimming, and we can see how (their, there, they're) progressing.
2. She has more (stationary, stationery) than she'll ever use.
3. The stars (shown, shone) brilliantly.
4. The city was so much larger (then, than) I expected.
5. The desks in our art room are not (stationary, stationery).

6. We often hear the planes break (threw, through) the sound barrier.
7. Sue will have the first ride; (than, then) it will be your turn.
8. The goal posts on the football field have been made (stationary, stationery).
9. We were (shone, shown) all the points of interest in the downtown area.
10. The pitcher (threw, through) a wild ball that almost hit the batter.

to	[a preposition, also used with the infinitive of a verb] A visit *to* Chinatown is an exciting treat. Many small nations are eager *to* become independent.
too	*also; more than enough* We have lived in North Dakota and in Alaska, *too.* It is *too* cold for rain today.
two	*one plus one* Americans can visit *two* foreign countries without leaving the continent.
weak	*not strong; feeble* My mother likes to drink *weak* tea.
week	*seven days* Your pictures will be ready in about a *week.*
weather	*condition of the air or atmosphere* *Weather* prediction is an important branch of meteorology.
whether	[a conjunction] *if* Jane Gordon is wondering *whether* the bond issue for the new school will be approved.

whose	[a possessive] *Whose* report are we hearing today?
who's	*who is* or *who has* *Who's* read today's newspaper? *Who's* representing the yearbook staff?
your	[a possessive] *Your* work in math is improving.
you're	*you are* *You're* right on time!

EXERCISE 16. Selecting Spelling Words to Complete Sentences.

Number your paper 1–10. After the proper number, write the word or words given in parentheses that make the sentence correct.

1. Lack of exercise made the runner's legs (weak, week).
2. (Weather, Whether) we'll go or not depends on the (weather, whether).
3. (Whose, Who's) books are you carrying?
4. Find out (whose, who's) going if you can.
5. Allen thought algebra was (to, too, two) difficult for him (to, too, two) master.
6. (Your, You're) a long distance off your course, captain.
7. We took (to, too, two) (weaks, weeks) for our trip.
8. The (weather, whether) was cloudy in Orlando, Florida.
9. Would you enjoy a trip (to, too, two) Mars, Flo?
10. Aren't you using (your, you're) compass?

50 Spelling Demons

ache	built	cough	don't
again	busy	could	early
always	buy	country	easy
answer	can't	doctor	every
blue	color	does	friend

guess	minute	straight	trouble
half	often	sugar	wear
hour	once	sure	where
instead	ready	tear	which
knew	said	though	whole
know	says	through	women
laid	shoes	tired	
meant	since	tonight	

250 Spelling Words

In studying the following list, pay particular attention to the underlined letters. These letters are generally the ones that present most students with the greatest difficulty in correctly spelling each word.

abandon	appearance	carrier
absolutely	application	ceiling
acceptance	appreciation	challenge
accidentally	approach	choice
accommodate	arguing	choir
accompany	argument	chorus
accomplish	article	circuit
achieve	assistance	colonel
acquaintance	authority	column
acquire	basis	coming
actually	beginning	commercial
advertisement	believe	committees
against	benefit	competition
aisle	boundary	completely
amount	bouquet	conceive
analysis	bulletin	condemn
anticipate	business	congratulations
anxiety	canceled	conscience
apology	capacity	conscious
apparent	careless	control

convenience
courteous
criticism
cylinder
dealt
deceit
decision
definite
definition
describe

description
desirable
despair
develop
difficulties
disappointment
discipline
discussion
diseased
distinction

distribution
doctrine
duplicate
economic
eligible
embarrass
engineering
enthusiasm
equipped
eventually

exactly
exaggerate
excellent
existence
experience

experiment
explanation
fascinating
favorite
February

finally
flu
forty
fourth
friendliness
generally
governor
grammar
gratitude
guarantee

guardian
gymnasium
hatred
height
heroine
hesitate
humorous
hypocrite
ignorance
imagination

immediately
incidentally
individual
inferior
initial
inspiration
intelligence
interfere
interrupt
involve

judgment
knowledge
laboratory
leisure
lengthen
lieutenant
loneliness
luncheon
majority
manufacture

marriage
mechanical
medieval
military
mourn
multiplication
muscular
mystery
naturally
necessary

nickel
nonsense
nuisance
numerous
obvious
occasionally
occurrence
opinion
opportunity
orchestra

originally
paid
parallel
parliament
patience

performance
personal
personality
persuade
philosopher

picnicking
planned
pleasant
possess
precede
preferred
prejudice
privilege
probably
procedure

professor
pursuit
qualified
realize
receipt
recognize
recommend
referring
regularly
relieve

repetition
research
response

rhythm
satisfied
saucer
schedule
scissors
sense
sentiment

separate
sergeant
shepherd
similar
simply
solemn
source
sponsor
straighten
subscription

succeed
success
sufficient
suggest
suppress
surprise
surround
suspense
suspicion
tailor

temperament

tendency
theory
therefore
thorough
tobacco
tonsils
tradition
tragedy
transferred

tries
truly
unanimous
unnecessary
unsatisfactory
until
useful
using
utilized
vacuum

variety
various
vein
view
villain
violence
warrant
weird
wholly
writing

CHAPTER 30

Studying and Test Taking

SKILLS AND STRATEGIES

For many of your classes, you will be expected to complete assignments on your own. You may have to read a chapter in your textbook and answer questions at the end of the chapter; you may have to read to prepare for a writing assignment or you may have to study for a test. You will also be required to take tests to show that you remember and understand what you have studied. This chapter will help to make your studying more effective and your test taking more successful.

STUDY SKILLS

You study to gain information about a topic and to understand and evaluate knowledge that you have acquired. The following strategies and skills can help you improve your study skills.

Following the SQ3R Study Method

30a. Use the SQ3R Study Method.

The *SQ3R Method* is a study method developed by Francis Robinson, an educational psychologist. This method is easy to follow and can be very useful in many study situations. The SQ3R Method consists of the five following steps.

1. *Survey.* Survey your selection by glancing quickly at the title, the subheadings, important terms in **boldface** and *italics,* and all charts, diagrams, illustrations, summaries, and questions. In addition, read the introduction and the summary paragraph quickly to find the main ideas.

2. *Question.* Make a list of questions that you want to be able to answer after you have read the selection. One way to do this is to change the subheadings into questions. For example, if the subheading in a social studies selection is *The Industrial Revolution,* you might write *What was the Industrial Revolution?* In some cases these kinds of questions are given before or after a selection. At other times your teacher may give you a list of questions.

3. *Read.* Read your selection *carefully* to find answers to your questions. Look for main ideas and supporting details. Look up any unfamiliar words. Take notes as you read.

4. *Recite.* Read the questions that you have written down. Think carefully about the answers, and recite them in your own words. (Refer to your notes to make sure your answers are correct.) Write down the answers to the questions.

5. *Review.* Review the selection by asking yourself the questions again. This time, try to answer them without looking at your notes. Then check your answers by consulting the selection and your notes. Immediately after you have finished checking your answers, review the selection once more to reinforce your knowledge.

EXERCISE 1. Applying the SQ3R Method to a Homework Assignment. Select a homework assignment in your science or social studies textbook. Follow the steps of the SQ3R Method to complete the assignment. Write the answer to each question as you work through the steps.

1. *Survey.* a. What is the title? b. What are the subheadings?

> c. What are the new terms in boldface or italics? d. What charts, illustrations, diagrams, or summaries are there? e. What do the introductory and summary paragraphs tell you?

2. *Question.* Make a list of questions that you want to be able to answer after you have read the selection. Turn the subheadings into questions. (If your teacher has assigned specific questions, use those instead.)
3. *Read.* Take notes of the main ideas and important details.
4. *Recite.* Recite the answers in your own words. Write down the answers to your questions.
5. *Review.* Review your answers to the questions.

Adjusting Your Reading Rate to Your Purpose

30b. Adjust your reading rate according to your purpose.

Depending on what you are reading, you may need to read quickly or at a moderate rate or slowly and carefully. You should learn to adjust your reading rate to your purpose.

(1) Scan to find information quickly.

Scanning means to read quickly to find *specific* information, such as facts, dates, or names. For example, you scan a dictionary to find a particular word by moving your eyes quickly down the page until you find the word you seek. Materials that you scan frequently include the telephone directory, indexes, and tables of contents.

(2) Skim to get a general idea of what the selection covers.

Skimming means to read at a fast rate to get the *general* idea of what a selection covers. In the Survey step of the SQ3R Method, you skim when you quickly read the title, subheadings, charts, diagrams, key terms, introductory and summary paragraphs, and any questions.

(3) Read closely to understand the main ideas and details.

Reading closely means to read slowly and thoughtfully. You read closely to identify not only the main ideas but also the supporting details. You read closely to find answers to study questions. In the Read step of the SQ3R Method, you read closely.

(4) Read recreational materials lightly.

Reading lightly means to read at a fast rate. You are not concerned with learning main ideas and details. Light novels and some magazines are examples of materials that you read lightly.

EXERCISE 2. Determining Reading Approaches for Particular Situations.   Determine the appropriate reading approach (scanning, skimming, reading closely, or reading lightly) for each of the following situations. Be prepared to explain your answers.

EXAMPLE   1. You need to find the term *parentheses* in the index in this book.
   1. *scanning*

1. You need to find rule 30c in this chapter.
2. You want to get a general idea of what the next chapter in this textbook will cover.
3. You completed the Survey and Question parts of the SQ3R Method for your social studies assignment. Now you need to read the selection.
4. You want to read a novel for entertainment.

Recognizing Main Ideas

30c. Find the main ideas of the material being studied.

The main idea of a piece of writing is the most important point that the author wants to make. Sometimes the main idea is stated.

Sometimes it is implied, or suggested. For effective studying, it is important that you recognize main ideas.

(1) Main ideas may be stated.

The main idea of a piece of writing is usually stated as a complete sentence. For example, the main idea of a paragraph about cats may be *Cats are easier to care for than dogs are.* The main idea of a paragraph about a particular cat may be *My cat is a lovable pet.*

The following paragraph is from "Bears," by Ben East. The topic is "a bear track." The main idea is *A bear track is calculated to send shivers up the human spine.*

> A bear track is calculated to send shivers up the human spine. You stare at the footprints, printed big and deep in the sand of a woods road or the mud along a stream bank, and you say to yourself, "A bear walked here, in the black of night, cloaked in darkness, furtive and silent. On what bloody errand was he bent? What prey did he finally find? Did he surprise and brain a young deer? Sniff out a wild turkey on her nest? Raid a pigpen on some settler's brush-bordered farm? Or did he only tear a log apart for ants? What would have happened if I had met him face to face?"
>
> BEN EAST

Note that the main idea in this paragraph is stated in the first sentence. The main idea may also be stated in the middle or at the end of a paragraph.

(2) Main ideas may be implied.

Sometimes the main idea is implied, or suggested. When a main idea is implied, you will need to read closely, examine details, and state the main idea in your own words.

For example, in the paragraph below from "Nature's Medicines: Spearmint," the main idea is implied.

> Ancient Greeks used to perfume their arms with spearmint so they could smell its refreshing scent wherever they went. Romans placed fresh sprigs of spearmint on their dining

tables and in their sleeping chambers. Today many gardeners simply go out to their spearmint patches and breathe deeply. The smell is said to help them if they are nervous or have a headache.

LOIS WICKSTROM

The subject of this paragraph is "spearmint." What does this paragraph tell us about spearmint? The first sentence tells us that ancient Greeks used spearmint as a perfume. The second sentence tells us that Romans used spearmint to scent their homes. The third and fourth sentences tell us that today many gardeners grow spearmint and breathe in its scent for relief of nervousness or a headache. These details add up to the main idea of the paragraph: *People have appreciated the scent of spearmint for thousands of years.*

EXERCISE 3. Finding the Main Idea. Write the stated or implied main idea for each of the following paragraphs.

1

The January wind has a hundred voices. It can scream, it can bellow, it can whisper, and it can sing a lullaby. It can roar through the leafless oaks and shout down the hillside, and it can murmur in the white pines rooted among the granite ledges where lichen makes strange hieroglyphics. It can whistle down a chimney and set the hearth-flames to dancing. On a sunny day it can pause in a sheltered spot and breathe a promise of spring and violets. In the cold of a lonely night it can rattle the sash and stay there muttering of ice and snowbanks and deep-frozen ponds.

HAL BORLAND

2

Though ski areas around the world have installed "alpine engineering" units to combat uncertain snow conditions, the demand for good snow cover is especially intense in the Eastern U.S. The major population centers of New York and Boston produce many avid skiers who take to the hills and mountains of Vermont, New Hampshire, and upstate New

York in search of downhill thrills. The owners of ski resorts in these areas know that if skiers are disappointed by the condition of the slopes, they may go elsewhere—out West, or to Europe. Or the resort owners may lose these skiers to another winter sport. These owners have learned that good snow is a must, whether it falls from the sky or is made by machine.

BRIAN MCCALLEN

3

The tropical sun beat down upon the baked earth as the temperature rose to a blistering 105 degrees. Even in the extreme heat the scientists continued their work. Finally, the months of labor were about to pay off. The scientists moved in closer to the excavation for a better look. They had spent several months at this site. The soil had been carefully removed inch by inch. Slowly, the object of their work appeared. As they peered into the pit they saw the remains of a brontosaurus.

PHILLIP EICHMAN

4

Imagine waiting all your life for a dream to come true! Some people achieve greatness during their lifetime. Others are recognized only after their deaths. John James Audubon was labeled a failure for most of his life. He knew a small measure of success before he died. Years later, organizations were named for him, and his monumental work was finally recognized for the magnificent achievement that it is.

ELEANOR P. ANDERSON

Finding Details That Support Main Ideas

30d. Find details that support main ideas.

In addition to identifying main ideas, you will need to identify the details that support main ideas. Details may include reasons, examples, or descriptions. Often you will need to recall these kinds of details for tests.

In the following paragraph, the main idea is expressed in the topic sentence (the first sentence.) The other sentences contain details that support the main idea.

> Are you prepared to give your pet lifetime care? Even a fully grown pet is totally dependent on you for all of its needs. Every day, you must provide it with food and water, change its litter box or walk it and make sure that it gets sufficient exercise. You're also responsible for keeping it clean, watching over its health and taking it to the vet if necessary. What's more, you'll have to train and discipline your pet so that it doesn't become a nuisance, and give it attention and affection so that it remains loving and companionable. When your pet becomes a senior citizen, he will probably need even more affection and care.
>
> ALICE HERRINGTON

The main idea of the paragraph above is *You must be prepared to care for a pet throughout its life.* The rest of the paragraph contains details that support this main idea. (1) You must feed the pet, care for its needs, and make sure that it gets exercise. (2) You must keep it clean and healthy. (3) You need to train your pet and give it attention and affection. (4) When your pet ages, you will have to give it additional love and care.

EXERCISE 4. Using Supporting Details to Answer Questions. Read the following paragraphs, noting the main ideas and the supporting details. Then complete the assignment that follows each paragraph.

1

That first winter in St. Catharines was a terrible one. Canada was a strange, frozen land, snow everywhere, ice everywhere, and a bone-biting cold the like of which none of them had ever experienced before. Harriet rented a small frame house in the town and set to work to make a home. The fugitives boarded with her. They worked in the forests, felling trees, and so did she. Sometimes she took other jobs, cooking or cleaning house for people in the town. She cheered on these newly arrived fugitives, working herself, finding work for them, finding food for them, praying for them, sometimes begging for them.

ANN PETRY

1. The details in the paragraph above are reasons that explain why the first winter in St. Catharines was hard for Harriet Tubman. List at least four of these reasons.

2

In ancient times an elephant was as powerful and feared a weapon as a missile with a nuclear warhead is today. Generals depended on these animals, and it isn't hard to understand why. A group of elephants could trample an army or batter down the walls of a city. When sent into battle carrying a tower full of armed men, an elephant was the equivalent of a modern armed tank. Warrior elephants could inflict tremendous physical damage on the enemy, but that wasn't the most important reason for using them. When soldiers saw elephants for the first time, they were often so frightened that they forgot to fight; they simply dropped their weapons and ran. Horses panicked and refused to charge, and the elephants won easy victories. In the ancient world, elephants were such valuable weapons that every king wanted to have some, and a few rulers, like Queen Semiramis of Assyria, went to incredible lengths just to get hold of a few of these remarkable animals.

SUZANNE JURMAIN

2. Write four sentences explaining why the elephant, in ancient times, was powerful and feared. Use your own words.

Distinguishing Between Fact and Opinion

30e. Distinguish between fact and opinion.

Most of what you read and hear contains both facts and opinions. It is important to be able to distinguish between these two types of information.

(1) A statement of fact contains information that can be proved true or false.

A statement of fact contains information about things that have happened in the past or are happening in the present. For example, here are three statements of fact.

> Amelia Earhart was born in 1898.
> Oranges are a source of vitamin C.
> Edgar Allan Poe wrote "The Raven."

(2) A statement of opinion expresses a personal belief or attitude. It contains information that cannot be proved true or false.

An example of a statement of opinion is a prediction about the future, since a prediction contains information that cannot be proved true or false at the present.

The following examples are three statements of opinion.

> It will be sunny on Father's Day.
> Birthday parties are fun.
> Soccer is a more exciting game than baseball.

Sometimes a statement of opinion contains expressions such as "Everyone knows that . . ." or "The truth is that . . ." or "It's a fact that . . . ." Do not let these expressions mislead you into thinking that a statement of opinion is a statement of fact.

Remember also that not everything presented as a statement of fact is true or accurate. Be prepared to use some reliable source to establish that a given statement is true. Among the common sources you might refer to are direct experience, an expert, an encyclopedia, a dictionary, an almanac, or some other authoritative reference.

EXERCISE 5. Distinguishing Between Facts and Opinions. Number your paper 1–10. After the proper number, write whether each of the following items is a fact or an opinion. If it is a fact, write some kind of evidence or a source (such as direct experience, an encyclopedia, a science textbook, or an almanac) that you could use to determine that it is truly a fact.

EXAMPLES   1. The Bill of Rights was ratified in 1791.
          1. *fact—social studies textbook*
          2. Oranges are more delicious than apples.
          2. *opinion*

1. Twenty-six times two equals fifty-two.
2. The United Nation's Children's Fund (UNICEF) aids children and teen-agers in developing countries.
3. UNICEF is the most helpful of all children's organizations.
4. Denver is the capital of Colorado.
5. Everyone knows that Denver is the best place for skiing.
6. The Pilgrims landed at Plymouth on December 26, 1620.
7. The school day should be longer.
8. Stamp collecting is dull.
9. Blue jeans are the most comfortable of all clothing.
10. Yosemite National Park is the most interesting of all the national parks.

Taking Effective Study Notes

30f. Take effective study notes.

Notes that you take while reading your textbooks will help you remember what you have read.[1] Your notes should be brief, but you need to be able to understand them. The following strategies will help you to take effective study notes.

    1. Make sure that you have read your selection once closely.

    2. Take your notes on sheets of paper rather than on note cards.

    3. Use the section title and subheadings in your textbook as the subject and topics in your notes. Leave room for main ideas and details under the topics.

---

[1] See pages 854–55 for strategies in taking notes from class lessons.

4. As you read, look for statements that introduce main ideas; such as, *The invention of the cotton gin affected the South in these two important ways.* Be aware of transitional words or phrases, such as *first, next, therefore, however, more importantly,* and *on the other hand,* which often introduce main ideas.

5. Write the main ideas and details under the topics.
6. Use your own words.
7. Use words, phrases, or short sentences.
8. Use abbreviations when possible. Omit articles *(a, an, the).*
9. Review your notes soon after you have taken them.

Now read the following passage about how to make an artificial ant colony. Then read the sample study notes for the passage.

The simplest way to have an artificial ant colony to study in your home is to take a large jar and fill it with soft black earth. Then find a colony of small black or brown ants. You must dig this colony out with a *trowel,*[1] keeping a sharp eye out for the queen, who is much larger and fatter than the small workers. When you find her, put her into the jar along with a couple of hundred workers. They will quickly get busy making passageways down into the earth, and if you feed them a little sugar, honey, meat, and bread crumbs each day, they will make their ant town right in your jar. To see their passageways under the earth, cover the jar to the level of the dirt with black cloth or paper, and take this off only at rare intervals. When you do take it off, you will see passageways running next to the glass and will be able to watch the ants going about their work underground.

VINSON BROWN

Study Notes: How to Make an Artificial Ant Colony
—Fill large jar with soft black dirt.
—Find colony of small black or brown ants.
—Look for queen—fatter, larger.
—Put her and about two hundred others into jar with dirt.
—Feed each day—sugar, honey, meat, bread crumbs.
—Cover jar up to level of earth with black paper.
—Seldom take paper off.

[1] *trowel:* a tool with a scoop, used for digging up plants in gardens.

—Will be passageways running down sides of jar.
—Can watch ants working.

EXERCISE 6. Taking Study Notes. Select a homework assignment in your science, social studies, or English textbook. Take study notes, using the strategies on pages 812–13. Be prepared to share your notes.

Writing a Summary of Study Material

30g. Write a summary to help you understand your study material.

A *summary* is a brief composition that covers the main ideas and important supporting details of a piece of writing. It should be approximately one third the length of the original writing and should be written in your own words. Study the following steps for writing a summary.

1. Skim the selection.
2. Read the selection closely, looking for the main ideas.
3. Read the selection again, this time identifying not only the main ideas but also the supporting details. Look up any unfamiliar words. Take notes as you read.
4. Identify the author's main ideas and important supporting details. (You might put a check mark [√] next to those ideas in your notes.)
5. Using complete sentences, write the summary. Include only the author's main ideas and *important* supporting details. Be sure to use your own words.
6. Revise your summary to make sure that you have covered the main ideas and important supporting details.
7. Revise your summary until it is approximately one third the length of the original piece of writing.

Now read the passage on page 813 again. Then read the following example summary for that passage. Note how the 179 words in the passage have been summarized in 59 words, approximately one third the length of the original.

Summary

To make an artificial ant colony, fill a jar with earth. Then find an ant colony and put the queen (the largest ant) and about two hundred other ants into the jar. Feed them every day. Cover the jar to the top of the earth with black paper. Remove the paper when you want to see the ants working.

EXERCISE 7. Writing a Summary. Select a homework assignment in your science, or social studies textbook. Write a summary of one passage, using the strategies on page 814.

PREPARING FOR AND TAKING TESTS

Not all tests are the same. Some tests are designed to measure how well you remember specific information; others determine how well you understand ideas. Some questions ask you to write brief answers; others ask you to write a paragraph or more. You can learn skills and strategies that will help you to prepare for and take different kinds of tests.

Preparing for Objective Tests

Objective tests measure how well you remember specific information, such as dates, names, terms, and definitions. Objective tests include multiple-choice questions, true-or-false questions, fill-in-the-blank questions, short-answer identifications, and matching questions.

30h. Prepare for objective tests by studying the specific information that will be included on the test.

Follow these steps to prepare for objective tests.

1. Know what will be included on the test, for example, Chapter 3, "Establishing the English Colonies," pages 54–89.

2. Gather the materials that you will need, such as your textbook, study notes, and homework assignments.

3. Review your notes and assignments. Pay attention to names, dates, terms, and definitions. If your notes are not clear, reread the appropriate section in your textbook.

4. Make up questions that might be on the test. Then answer these questions. (Use your notes to check your answers.)

Taking Objective Tests

Follow these steps to take objective tests.

1. Read the directions closely. Note *exactly* what the directions ask you to do; for example, "Answer *three* of the following five questions."

2. Skim the rest of the test. Note how many questions there are, which ones are difficult, and which ones are easy. Complete the easy ones first; then work through the more difficult ones.

3. Note how much time you have for the test, and figure out how much time you can spend on each question. (Plan on spending less time on the easy questions and more time on the difficult ones.)

4. If you do not understand some point on the test, ask your teacher.

In addition, keep in mind these points about the specific kinds of objective tests.

Multiple-choice Questions

Multiple-choice questions ask you to choose the correct choice from three or more options. Follow these steps when answering multiple-choice questions.

1. Read the question carefully.

2. Read *all* of the choices *before* you answer the question.

3. Eliminate choices that you know are incorrect. (Usually there will be one or two.)

4. Think carefully about the remaining choices. Based on what you know, determine which choice makes the most sense.

Now look at the following multiple-choice question and the solution.

EXAMPLE   A single entry word in the dictionary appears divided into two parts to show (a) that it is sometimes written as two words (b) the origin of the word (c) that the word consists of two syllables. [Having studied the dictionary, you would be able to eliminate choice *b*—information about origin follows the entry word. Of the two remaining choices, choice *c* makes more sense—the single word is divided into two syllables, not spelled as two words. The correct choice is *c*.]

True-or-false Questions

True-or-false questions ask you to determine whether a given statement is true or false. Follow these steps when answering true-or-false questions.

1. Read the entire statement carefully.
2. Look to see if *any* part of the statement is false. If this is the case, mark the statement false.
3. If all the parts of the statement are true, mark the statement true.

Now look at the following true-or-false questions and the solutions.

EXAMPLES   1. In 1875 Edison invented the phonograph. [This statement is false. Though Edison invented the phonograph, he invented it in 1877, not in 1875.]
2. The sun is the center of the solar system. [All parts of this statement are true; therefore, the statement is true.]

Fill-in-the-blank Questions

Fill-in-the-blank questions ask you to fill in the missing word or words that correctly complete the sentence. Follow these steps when answering fill-in-the-blank questions.

1. Read the question carefully.

2. Write a specific answer, using the terminology found in your notes or textbook.

3. Try to fill in all the blanks.

Now look at the following fill-in-the-blank questions and the solutions.

EXAMPLES 1. A —— gives inventors exclusive rights to make and sell their inventions. [patent]

2. Jimmy Carter was elected President in ——. [1976]

3. Sandra Day O'Connor was the first woman ever appointed to ——. [the United States Supreme Court]

Note that the first statement asks you to fill in a term, the second statement asks you to fill in a figure, and the third statement asks you to fill in a name. Note also that all answers are appropriate to the subject matter being tested.

Short-answer Identifications

Short-answer identifications usually ask you to answer a question with a word or a phrase or with one or two sentences. Follow these steps when answering short-answer identifications.

1. Read the question carefully.

2. Write a specific answer, using the terminology found in your notes or textbook.

3. Try to answer all questions.

Now look at the following short-answer identifications and the solutions.

EXAMPLES 1. In American politics, what does ERA stand for? [the Equal Rights Amendment]

2. Who was Nelson A. Rockefeller? [Nelson A. Rockefeller was a former New York State governor who was chosen by President Ford as Vice-President.]

Notice that each of the answers is specific and that the terminology is appropriate to the subject matter.

Matching Questions

Matching questions ask you to match the items in one list with the items in another list. Follow these steps when answering matching questions.

1. Read the directions carefully. Sometimes the directions will explain that there are more items in one list than in the other list but that you do not have to use all items. At other times the directions will explain that you may use items in one list twice.

2. Read both lists and see how they are related. For example, one list might contain the names of the famous people, and the other list might contain descriptions of their accomplishments.

3. Skim through the items. Identify the easy ones and the difficult ones. Do the easy ones first.

4. Complete the rest of the test by making informed guesses, that is, by using clues to help you.

Now look at the following matching questions and the solutions for a test on a chapter titled "The Constitution of the United States."

EXAMPLES

1. To accuse an official in the executive branch or a judge in a federal court of wrongdoing
2. Proposal for a law
3. Set number of members required to conduct the business of Congress
4. A change or an addition to a constitution
5. Provision that allows Congress to stretch its powers to meet new situations

a. impeach
b. bill
c. amendment
d. quorum
e. elastic clause

Note that the list on the left contains definitions, and that the list on the right contains the corresponding terms. First, you might identify items 1, 2, and 4 as easy items and match item 1 with *a*, item 2 with *b*, and item 4 with *c*. Then, of the two remaining choices, you could examine the words in item 5 and determine that the word *stretch* is a clue: something that can be stretched is said to be elastic. Thus you would match item 5 with choice *e*. Last, you would correctly match item 3 with choice *d*.

EXERCISE 8. Applying Test-taking Skills. Write the answers to the following questions:

1. Identify ten key terms that might appear in an objective test on this chapter.
2. Using the terms you chose, prepare for a test on this chapter by writing sample questions. Include two of each of the following types of test questions:
   a. multiple-choice
   b. true-or-false
   c. fill-in-the-blank
   d. short-answer identifications

Preparing for Essay Tests

Essay tests are intended to measure how well you understand what you have learned. Essay tests ask you to express your understanding in one paragraph or more.

To prepare for essay tests, you should reread the appropriate sections of your textbook and your notes to identify main ideas and important supporting details. Study these main ideas and details until you understand them. Try answering any questions in your textbook that ask you to write a paragraph or paragraphs. In addition, try making up your own essay questions.

Though there is no single *right* answer on an essay test, as there usually is on an objective test, your teacher will want to see specific details in your essay answer. Therefore, while studying, gather main ideas and important supporting details so that you can use them to write complete, well-supported answers.

Taking Essay Tests

30i. **Plan your time and your answer for an essay question.**

Follow these steps when taking an essay test.

1. Read the directions closely. Note whether you have a choice of questions to answer.

2. Skim the rest of the test. Note how many questions there are, which ones are easy, and which ones are difficult.

3. If you have a choice of essay questions, decide which one(s) you will answer.

4. Figure out how much time you can spend on each question. (Remember to leave enough time to plan, write, and revise your essay answer.)

5. Begin by reading the directions carefully. Note *what* task you are being asked to do, for example, to *compare* (point out likenesses *or* differences between) two characters or to *explain* (give reasons for) the causes of a war. In addition, note *how many* tasks you are being asked to do; for example, the following directions ask you to do two tasks: *Paul Bunyan and Pecos Bill have some traits and interests in common and some differences. Briefly describe the character and adult activities of each; then discuss any differences between the two legendary characters.*

6. Work through the stages of the writing process.

   a. *Prewriting.* Gather ideas for your answer. Write a sentence that expresses your main point. Be sure your sentence uses the key words of the question.

   b. *Writing.* Use your prewriting notes to help you write your answer. Depending on the amount of information you gathered, you will write your sentence either as the topic sentence of a paragraph or as the thesis statement of a composition. Be sure everything else you write develops the main idea expressed in this sentence.

   c. *Revising.* In most cases you will not have much time for revising. Reread the question and your answer to make sure that you have answered the question.

   d. *Proofreading.* Proofread your paragraph for inaccuracies in grammar, usage, spelling, and mechanics.

Answering the Different Kinds of Essay Questions

30j. Know the different kinds of essay questions and what is expected in the answer for each type.

Essay questions generally ask you to complete one of several tasks. Each of these tasks is expressed in a verb. The following list shows key verbs and the tasks each verb signals.

Essay Test Questions

KEY VERB(S)	TASK
analyze	Take something apart to show how each part works.
compare	Point out likenesses *or* differences.
contrast	Point out differences.
compare and contrast	Point out similarities *and* differences.
describe	Give a picture in words or an account of.
list, outline, trace	List events, show development.
discuss	Examine in detail.
explain	Give reasons for something's being the way it is.
demonstrate, illustrate, show	Provide examples to support a point.
interpret	Give the meaning or significance of something.

Now read the following example essay question:

EXAMPLE   Contrast the Pilgrims' reasons for coming to North America with those of the Jamestown settlers.

This essay question asks you to point out the differences between the Pilgrims' reasons for coming to North America and those of the Jamestown settlers. The sentence that expresses your main idea might be *The Pilgrims' reasons for coming to North America were different from those of the Jamestown settlers.* Your details would include the Pilgrims' main reason for coming to North America (religious persecution in England) and the Jamestown settlers' reasons (lack of jobs in England, conflict with the government). You would provide details to support these reasons. You might arrange your essay test answer by first expressing your main idea, next discussing the Pilgrims' reasons, and then discussing the Jamestown settlers' reasons.

EXERCISE 9. Analyzing Essay Questions. For each of the following sample essay questions, identify the key word or words that state the specific task in the question. State briefly what task you must do to answer the question.

EXAMPLE   1. Explain why the United States replaced the spoils system with the merit system for hiring federal employees during the late 1800's.

1. *Explain—give reasons for the replacement of the spoils system with the merit system.*

1. Compare the Treaty of Versailles with President Wilson's Fourteen Points.
2. Interpret Robert Frost's poem "The Road Not Taken." Be sure to give reasons to support your point of view.
3. The conflict of the myth of Antigone involves two strong wills. In a single paragraph, explain the struggle between Antigone and Creon.
4. Describe the geography and climate of Costa Rica.
5. Several selections presented in this unit focus on beliefs that are part of America's heritage, particularly belief in independence, tolerance, and personal freedom. Choose two selections you have read, and in a brief essay show how they demonstrate characteristic American beliefs. Identify the selections by title and author.

PART SEVEN

SPEAKING AND LISTENING

CHAPTER 31

Speaking

FORMAL AND INFORMAL SPEAKING SITUATIONS

Learning how to speak well and comfortably before groups or in unfamiliar situations is an important part of every young person's education. This chapter will help you to improve your speaking skills.

MAKING ANNOUNCEMENTS

To announce a bit of information or an event to other students, you will not need to make extensive preparation or elaborate notes. Nevertheless, you should write down the information you are to give and check it over to be sure it includes all the essential facts. You have already used the *5 W-How?* questions to gather information for your writing. These same questions, also known as the journalist's questions, can help you organize information for your announcement. Does your announcement tell *who, what, when, where, why,* and *how?*

31a. In making an announcement, be sure to include all the necessary facts.

Most announcements should include the following information: (1) the kind of event, (2) the time, (3) the place, (4) the admission fee, if any, and (5) special features. The following example includes four of these items, omitting only the admission fee.

EXAMPLE   The Microcomputer Club meeting that was scheduled for this afternoon has been postponed because of the storm. Instead, the Microcomputer Club will meet next Tuesday, January 15, at 3:05 P.M. in Room 27. All members and any other interested students are invited for a program called "Using Computers to Create Sound Effects."

Go over the facts of an announcement several times in your mind before you speak. If you are not sure that you will remember them all while you are speaking, carry a note card with the information written on it. You can glance at this card as you speak.

Use a normal rate of speaking, and make sure that you give your audience time to take in what you are saying. Speak loudly enough so that everyone will hear.

EXERCISE 1. Correcting Announcements. Each of the following announcements omits essential items of information. What are these items? Rewrite each announcement so that it includes all the necessary information.

1. Students in Ms. Robertson's and Mr. Cleveland's classes who are going to the art museum tomorrow should be ready to leave at 11:15. The only expense will be for lunch in the museum cafeteria.

2. The Junior Philharmonic needs more members. Even if you are not sure of your musical talent, why not come to a rehearsal and join the preparation for the next concert program?

3. There will be a Thanksgiving party on Saturday, November 18, in the school auditorium. All students are invited. Profits from the party will go to the Resource Center Fund.

EXERCISE 2. Preparing and Delivering Announcements. Prepare and deliver an announcement for one of the following events or for an actual event taking place at your school. Give all the necessary information, using the *5 W-How?* questions as a guide.

1. An excursion sponsored by the Drama Club
2. Copies of your school yearbook on sale
3. A 4–H Club meeting
4. Tryouts for the play *You're a Good Man, Charlie Brown*
5. A book fair
6. A soccer game between two classes
7. An open house at school for new students
8. A five-mile bicycle race to benefit handicapped children
9. The annual Spring Talent Show
10. The eighth-grade class trip to Washington, D.C.
11. The annual Varsity Awards Dinner
12. Teacher Recognition Day
13. A science fair
14. The all-county gymnastic meet
15. The Winter Carnival

PREPARING AN ORAL REPORT

31b. Learn how to prepare an oral report.

As you study this part of the chapter, you might notice several similarities between planning an oral report and planning a piece of writing. In fact, you use the same skills to organize each form of communication: choosing a suitable subject, limiting the subject to a topic, and gathering and arranging information. You might recognize that these skills are the prewriting steps in the writing process. For a review of these prewriting steps, you might find it helpful to refer to pages 452–79 in Chapter 19.

Oral reports and written reports, which are discussed in Chapter 24, are planned in much the same way. Also, both oral and written reports have the same purpose: to present information or to explain something about a subject. Still, there is one important difference: Oral reports are not written out word for word. Instead, you make some notes to help you remember your material as you speak. Be sure to use the following steps to prepare oral reports for any of your school subjects.

(1) Choose a suitable subject for your oral report.

If you are given a subject to report on, you have no problem of selection. If you are asked to choose your own subject, however, you can find subjects to talk about just as you find subjects to write about. You can use the methods discussed in Chapters 19 and 23 to find subjects for your talk: observation, brainstorming, clustering, and a writer's journal.

It is important for you to choose a suitable subject, that is, one that is right for your report. Two ideas can guide your choice. First, focus on your interests and experiences. By discussing a subject you know about or are interested in, you will be able to speak confidently and enthusiastically. Your confidence and enthusiasm should also make your report more interesting to your audience.

Second, select a subject that will interest your audience. A report on how to identify types of clouds might bore some people; a report on how to repair leaky faucets might bore others; and a report on how to hang up your clothes properly would bore everybody. But a report on ways to earn money after school or on a new probe of a distant planet or on the discovery of an ancient city buried under a lava flow would be likely to interest many of your listeners.

EXERCISE 3. Choosing Suitable Subjects. Suppose that you must give an oral report that explains a subject to your classmates. Using your interests and experiences and your audience's interests as guides, list at least five subjects that would be suitable for your report.

(2) Limit your subject to a narrow topic.

It is important to select a subject that is suitable for your report. Once you have chosen a subject, you should limit it. That is, you should narrow your subject to a topic that can be covered reasonably well in the time you have for your report. Remember that the purpose of an oral report is to give information about or to explain a particular subject to an audience. If the subject is too large, you will not be able to achieve this purpose.

To limit a subject to a narrow topic, you should divide it into smaller parts. Suppose you chose the subject "dinosaurs" for an oral report in science class. This subject is very broad—there is a great deal of information about many aspects of dinosaurs that you could discuss.

To limit this broad subject, divide it into smaller parts: "how scientists identify dinosaur bones," "the climate when dinosaurs roamed the earth," "two explanations for the dinosaurs' disappearance," and "places to see dinosaur exhibits in the United States." Notice how each topic focuses on a small part of the broad subject "dinosaurs." You could easily develop an oral report on any one of these limited topics. Depending on the time you have to present your report, sometimes you may need to continue narrowing your subject to even more limited topics. For more help on limiting subjects, see pages 466–468 in Chapter 19.

EXERCISE 4. Limiting Subjects. Each of the following subjects is too broad for an oral report. Limit each to at least two narrow topics by dividing it into smaller parts. If your teacher prefers, you may instead limit the broad subjects you selected in Exercise 3. Keep the report's explanatory or informative purpose in mind.

1. Laser light shows
2. Modern transportation
3. Great cities
4. The American West
5. Clothing
6. Schools
7. Community recreation
8. Fireworks
9. Insects
10. Women writers and artists

(3) Gather information for your report.

Once you have a limited topic, your next step is to gather information for your report. There are at least three sources for such materials: (1) your own ideas and experiences, (2) other people who know something about your topic, and (3) books and periodicals. Consult all of these sources, and get as much information as you can.

Remember that the methods you use to gather information for your writing can also be used to gather information for your oral report. These methods include using a writer's journal, brainstorming, clustering, changing your point of view, and asking the 5 W-How? questions. You may want to refer to the information gathering sections of Chapters 19 and 23 for more help. Be sure to write notes or brief summaries of the information you are gathering. You will use these notes to prepare your oral report.

EXERCISE 5. Gathering Information. Gather information for an oral report. Use any one of the narrow topics you developed in Exercise 4, or use another narrow topic of your own. Be sure to write notes or brief summaries of the information you gather.

(4) Prepare an outline of your oral report.

From your notes, prepare an outline for your talk. (Refresh your memory on how to prepare an outline by looking at pages 631–33 in Chapter 23.)

Suppose that you have decided to give a report in your science class on shooting stars. You have often observed shooting stars and have wondered what they are and why they occur. Having discovered that shooting stars are meteors, go to the library (see Chapter 27, pages 735–49) and read articles on meteors in various reference works. On cards or slips of paper, copy items of information you want to use. Study these notes until the material is familiar to you. From the notes, prepare an outline. The outline might have four main headings:

    I. Time: when meteors are seen
   II. Nature: what the characteristics of meteors are
 III. Place: where and why meteors are seen
 IV. Fate: how speed, size, and course determine the final end of meteors

Under each of these headings, arrange your material in logical order. For some topics, you will give the major ideas first, with the details following them. For other topics—such as how to conduct an experiment—you will arrange ideas in chronological, or time, order. The logical order you use depends on your topic. Once you have settled on the content and structure of your report, you are ready to think about how to deliver it.

EXERCISE 6. Preparing an Outline.   Using the information you have gathered on your topic, prepare an outline of your oral report.

(5) Write note cards to use as reminders when delivering your report.

It is not necessary to write out a speech word for word and memorize it. Instead, read and reread your material and your outline until they are so familiar that you need only an occasional reminder to help you talk freely about your topic.

Write these reminders on 3- × 5-inch note cards. Arrange the cards to correspond to the order of your outline. These cards make up the body of your oral report.

Include the subheadings under the main idea on the card.

Reminder cards do not have to contain complete sentences; key words or phrases will do. Remember: These cards are not to be read aloud. They are meant to aid your memory.

A reminder card for a talk on shooting stars might look like this:

I. Time
   A. More after midnight than before
   B. More in the fall than in any other season
   C. Five per hour - 500 per minute

When giving your speech, you would start with this card. The items on the card are reminders. The main point tells what this part of the speech is about; the subheadings identify details to discuss. You might start your speech by saying:

> We are all familiar with shooting stars, or meteors. Often, on summer evenings, we have seen them streak across the dark sky. Most of us, however, are unaware that we can see more shooting stars after midnight than before and that we can see more in the fall of the year than in other seasons. Usually, about five shooting stars per hour can be sighted. However, when meteor showers occur, sometimes as many as five hundred meteors fall each minute. . . .

In some cases it is wise to write full and exact details on a note card. If, for example, you want to give the ingredients of a recipe or the measurements of material needed to make a greenhouse or statistics on World Series baseball games, it is wise to write out the full details on a note card so that you can read them off when you need them.

You may want to use direct quotations from people whom you have interviewed. (Direct quotations will not only make your talk livelier but will give it the weight of authority.) Write out quotations exactly as given, to avoid misquoting the person you interviewed.

If you are explaining a process to your audience, it may be helpful to have charts and pictures. You may also want to use the chalkboard to write figures and dates or draw illustrations. A reminder card can tell you when to use these visual aids.

You may need only a few reminder cards if the material of your speech is very familiar to you—perhaps just one for each main heading, plus one or two additional cards with details to support some point requiring exact information. No rule can be set for how many cards you will need; prepare as many as you think necessary.

As you speak, hold the cards in your hand. Glance at the top card, and talk on the subject it lists. Then move this top card to the bottom, uncovering the next topic of your speech. Continue this process until you have spoken on every topic listed on your cards.

As you practice your speech, practice using your note cards also. You should be able to use them smoothly so that they do not distract your audience.

(6) Plan an interest-arousing introduction and a strong conclusion.

It is helpful to write out an exciting first sentence, one that will arouse your audience's interest. Memorize this sentence so that you can look at your audience and speak the sentence naturally.

Similarly, it is helpful to work out a strong ending statement for your talk—a sentence or paragraph that ties your main ideas together. You may write this statement out on a card. However, try not to spoil the effect of a good speech by reading the last part of it. (For more help in writing introductions and conclusions, see pages 636 and 638 in Chapter 23.)

EXERCISE 7. Completing an Oral Report. Prepare note cards and plan an introduction and a conclusion for a topic of your own. You may want to use the topic and information you have developed in previous exercises. When you have completed this activity, you will be ready to deliver your oral report.

REVIEW EXERCISE A. Planning an Oral Report. Plan a short oral report on one of the following topics or on a topic of your own. Be sure to follow each of the steps explained in this chapter.

1. UFO's: reality or illusion?
2. Progress made to save the whales
3. Tree grafting: how to raise pears on an apple tree
4. What makes an airplane fly?
5. The monster called Sasquatch
6. An interesting part of the city that many people don't know about
7. Today's pony express
8. Why _____ is the best career

9. Comparing American football and English rugby
10. Family birthday customs in China
11. Can cars run on solar energy?
12. My choice for a personal hero
13. The career of my favorite artist or musician
14. Programs I'd like to see on television
15. A hobby that earns money

DELIVERING AN ORAL REPORT

By planning your oral report, you have focused on the content of your speech: *what* you will explain to your audience about your topic. Since your planning is for a speech, it is also important for you to consider *how* you will communicate this content to your audience. Delivering your speech effectively will complete the circle you began by planning your speech thoroughly. As you deliver your report, you need to think about nonverbal communication, pronunciation and enunciation, and expression.

Nonverbal Communication

People often communicate with unspoken, or nonverbal, signals. For example, someone who cannot talk may use sign language to converse. An umpire at a baseball game raises one thumb in the air to say, "You're out!" A car driver signals a left-hand turn by extending the left arm.

Nonverbal communication—also called body language—is also an important part of giving a speech. An audience will read, or interpret, a speaker's gestures and body movements in the same way that they will listen to words. Such nonverbal signals, therefore, should communicate exactly what a speaker wants to say.

31c. Learn how to use nonverbal signals as you speak.

You can improve your speech by using firm posture and natural gestures.

Stand straight. Keep your weight on both feet. If you are sitting, place both feet squarely on the floor, and keep your back straight in the chair. Good posture communicates confidence.

Look at your audience as you speak. Glance around the room, and try to focus on the faces of your listeners. Eye contact is an effective way to hold the audience's attention. If you are using note cards, glance—but do not stare—at them as you speak. You should be looking at your audience during most of the speech, not at your cards. While speaking, try to smile occasionally. Smiling usually helps to relax the audience.

Keep gestures under control. Although it is natural to feel nervous about giving a talk, avoid nervous, random gestures, such as fidgeting with your hair or your note cards.

Think about what gestures may mean. Choose gestures that help rather than hinder your spoken words. Keeping your hands in your pockets, for example, is a gesture that suggests you are not well prepared to give the speech. Scratching your head suggests that you are not sure of what to say next. Avoid any gestures that detract from your message.

Pause for transition. A short pause between parts of your speech can be a nonverbal signal to your audience that you are about to introduce another topic. A pause can also give you a chance to take a deep breath and relax.

EXERCISE 8. Thinking About Nonverbal Communication. Try to write down at least five different forms of nonverbal communication that you notice at school, at home, on television, or anywhere else. Next to each form, write what you think it means. Prepare to compare and discuss your list with your classmates.

Pronunciation and Enunciation

31d. Pronounce words correctly, and enunciate carefully.

Your audience must hear your speech plainly. An audience that must strain to hear becomes restless, and a talk that is not heard is wasted.

Take care to speak correctly and distinctly. In many cases the meaning of a word varies with the way it is pronounced. Remember that if your words are mispronounced or if you mumble or run words together, your audience will have difficulty in following you.

Vowel Sounds

Each vowel in our language may be pronounced in different ways. In some words vowels or combinations of vowels have sounds that you might not expect from the spelling. Make sure you use standard pronunciation for the following words:

despite	fertile	opaque	thorough
despot	genuine	suite	through
drought	mischievous	superfluous	victuals

Consonant Sounds

As important as pronunciation is *enunciation*, the careful sounding of every syllable. Be especially careful with words that end in *–ing* and words that contain similar consonants—*p* and *b, m* and *n, t* and *th*.

For practice, say the following groups of words aloud, taking care to make the consonant sounds clearly distinguishable so that no one in the room mistakes the word you used.

d—t		*t—th*	
do	to	tank	thank
dent	tent	taught	thought
din	tin	bat	bath
done	ton	tinker	thinker
dare	tear	mutter	mother
and	ant	ton	thumb
send	sent	ten	then
bed	bet	rat	wrath
wed	wet	tat	that
madder	matter	wetter	weather

b—p		*v—f*	
blank	plank	vendor	fender
bin	pin	veil	fail
bowl	pool	viewer	fewer
robe	rope	vault	fault
bunk	punk	veal	feel
Benny	penny	vision	fission

EXERCISE 9. Practicing Vowel and Consonant Sounds.

Practice reading aloud the following tongue twisters. Prepare yourself to read them to the class.

1. She said severely, "Son, shun the hot sun, or your poor back will burn pitifully."
2. She sells seashells at the seashore.
3. The tinker muttered thanks in a thin, throttled tone.
4. Jane's chuckles and antics jarred her ailing aunt and uncle.
5. The tank of thin tin was dank and dented.
6. In the still, chill silence of the church, Benny's penny clattered tinnily in the cup.
7. Chunks of junk smashed the vendor's fender.
8. The mole delved twelve feet under the thin turf.
9. His mother muttered that wetter weather would wash his wrath away.
10. Penny's robe, belted with rope, was tugged snug at the throat.

Omitting Sounds

Take care not to omit sounds that belong in words. Here is a list of words frequently subject to nonstandard pronunciation.

arctic (not "artic")
asked (not "ask" or "ast")
exactly (not "zactly" or "exackly")
finally (not "finelly")
library (not "liberary")
mystery (not "mystry")
probably (not "probly" or "proely")

EXERCISE 10. Including Frequently Omitted Sounds.

Use five of the words in the preceding list in sentences to be spoken aloud in class. Be sure to include all the sounds in each word.

Adding Sounds

Take care not to add sounds to a word—either inside a word or at the end. Do you use nonstandard pronunciation with any of these words?

arithmetic (not "arith*uh*metic")
athlete (not "ath*uh*lete")
barbarous (not "barbar*i*ous")
chimney (not "chim*b*ley" or "chim*uh*ney")
column (not "col*y*um")
corps (the *p* and *s* are silent)
elm (not "el*u*m")
height (ends in *t*, not *th*)
scent (the *c* is silent)
subtle (the *b* is silent)
umbrella (not "umbrell*er*" or "umb*e*rella")
vehicle (the *h* is silent)

EXERCISE 11. Practicing Frequently Mispronounced Words.

Practice each of the preceding frequently mispronounced words. Form a pair with a classmate, and take turns pronouncing each word twice. Be sure not to add sounds that do not belong in each word.

Changing Position of Sounds

Be careful not to change the position of a sound within a word. Sometimes such nonstandard pronunciation is based on the similarity of a word to another word that is almost like it in spelling. *Perspire* and *prescribe*, for example, have first syllables that are almost alike. *Perspire* is often mispronounced *prespire,* and *prescribe* is often mispronounced *perscribe.*

Here are some words whose sounds are often transposed.

apron (not "apern")

cavalry (not "calvary")

children (not "childern")

contradict (not "conterdict")

modern (not "modren")

EXERCISE 12. Pronouncing Words Correctly. Review all of the preceding lists. At your teacher's request, be prepared to write words on the board and to pronounce them.

REVIEW EXERCISE B. Practicing Mispronounced Words. Here is a list of frequently mispronounced words. Be prepared to read them aloud to the class. Use the dictionary if you are not sure of the correct pronunciation.

admirable	hearth	partner
architect	hurtle	remembrance
bade	incomparable	scythe
champion	indict	superfluous
favorite	infamous	theater
film	jostle	toward
finale	jubilant	tremendous
gape	mischievous	yacht
gesture	museum	
handkerchief	ogre	

Running Words Together

Another form of mispronouncing words is running them together when speaking. Telescoping words makes a wreckage of sense. Too often, for example, we run together the words of such a sentence as *I'm glad to meet you* into *Gladdameecha*.

EXERCISE 13. Pronouncing Words Distinctly. Translate the following mangled words into understandable language.

didja	gonna	woncha
gotcha	whereya	harrya
thankslot	lemmetry	didjaseer
gimeyahan	whadideedo	wassamadawichoo
wachasay	begyaparn	wyncha

Expression

31e. Learn to speak with expression and meaning.

We give meaning to language not only by our choice of words but also by the *feelings* we put into them—the tone of voice, the grouping of words, the emphasis, and the variety of tone. The tone and emphasis we use can greatly influence the meaning our words convey. Differing emphases on certain words or syllables can convey different meanings and emotions.

You can increase the effectiveness of your speech by giving attention to your tone of voice and to the amount and kind of expression you use.

EXERCISE 14. Speaking with Expression. Study these sentences before reading them aloud. The class will discuss how well each person expresses the different feelings.

1. You are taking care of a six-year-old. Tell her, "Susan, put that puppy down!"
   a. Say it as if the mother dog, growling furiously, is getting out of her box to leap at Susan.
   b. Say it as if you know Susan is going to plead with you to buy the puppy and you don't have the money.
2. Someone has just walked through your room with muddy feet, leaving tracks on the rug. You ask, "Kyle, did you just walk through my room?"
   a. Say it as if you have told him before to stay out of your room.
   b. Say it as if you have just cleaned your room.
3. A new dress has just been delivered to your house. Today is your birthday. You ask, "Mom, Dad, did you buy this dress for me?"
   a. Say it as if the dress is exactly what you have been hoping for, but you can't believe that your parents would be so extravagant.
   b. Say it as if you are bitterly disappointed.

4. You have started on a long walk when you discover that your small brother is walking behind you. You tell him, "Andy, go home and go to bed."
   a. Say it as if he is feverish with a bad cold, and you are very worried about him.
   b. Say it as if you've told him before that he could not come along.

EXERCISE 15. Changing Tone and Emphasis. See how many meanings you can put into the following remarks by varying your tone and the words you emphasize.

1. I'll go now, if you don't mind.
2. I'd like some steak, too.
3. Bring all your money tomorrow.
4. I told you not to play with him.
5. You earned all that money yourself?
6. Did you say yes?
7. He will do the dishes, and you, Preston, will sweep.
8. Did you promise to help him, Laura?

EVALUATING A SPEECH

31f. Learn to evaluate another person's report politely and constructively.

Often, after a student has given a report, the class is asked to evaluate the talk. The purpose of such an evaluation is to help the speaker improve by getting reactions. Another purpose is for the group to give recognition to the fine qualities as well as the weak points of the talk.

Be clear and definite. Whether praising a talk for its fine qualities or pointing out its weaknesses, always give reasons for your evaluation. Be generous with praise. If you find serious faults in a talk, it is wise to begin by discussing strong points, then going on to show how the talk might have been even stronger if certain faults had been corrected.

WEAK   "I thought it was very interesting."

BETTER   "His description of Mount Rainier was very interesting because his details were so sharp that I could almost see the mountain trail."

"I like her story of exploring the cave because she built up so much suspense."

WEAK   "I just couldn't follow the talk."

"He did not convince me."

BETTER   "Her explanation was clear and easy to follow except in a couple of places, and I wonder if she left out some steps."

"He convinced me that fishing in the river should be limited for a while, but I'd like more proof that dumping factory waste into the river is the real reason why fish are scarce."

Do your part in helping the class to establish an atmosphere of kind and constructive evaluation. When you evaluate a classmate's oral report, try to use the following guidelines.

1. Give praise when it is merited.
2. Avoid discussing trifles, or small points of little importance.
3. Point out strengths as well as weaknesses.
4. Be definite and constructive.

Your class may decide to use an evaluation sheet like the one on page 845 for evaluating speakers. After a talk each listener rates the speech, and the sheets are collected and given to the speaker.

EXERCISE 16. Delivering an Oral Report. Deliver the talk that you prepared in Exercise 7 or in Review Exercise A. Remember the importance of nonverbal communication, pronunciation and enunciation, and expression.

EXERCISE 17. Evaluating an Oral Report. Write a paragraph evaluating a talk someone has given in class. Use the following evaluation sheet as a basis for your evaluation, but also give your opinion of the talk as a whole.

EVALUATION SHEET

Speaker ———————————————

Topic ———————————————

Critic ———————————————

	Very good	Good	Fair	Weak
Introduction				
Organization				
Conclusion				
Use of notes				
Posture				
Gestures				
Voice				
Pronunciation				
Other comments				

PARTICIPATING IN GROUP DISCUSSIONS

Another situation in which you can use your speaking skills is the group discussion. Throughout your schooling and later in adult life, you might often join with other people to discuss important issues or to explore solutions to problems. To help your group meet its goal—that is, to discuss an issue or problem intelligently and fairly—you need to learn how to participate in a group discussion.

You already have some experience with participating in group discussions, although you may not have studied how a group discussion can proceed as smoothly as possible. You often converse with friends, teachers, and family members. These conversations are an informal, or unplanned, form of group discussion. They do not necessarily involve exploring an issue or solving a problem; you simply join others to talk.

You may have already participated in group discussions that are more focused or planned than informal conversations, however. In school your teachers may have asked you to meet with classmates to discuss school-related topics, for example, ways to involve parents in tutoring, how to raise money to buy band equipment, or reasons for allowing students to help plan lunch menus. As a community member, you may have served on a committee that discussed how young people can help teach adults to read or how to prepare for citywide competitions at the local swimming pool.

Think about the group discussions you have participated in. Some may have had a discussion leader and an audience, whereas others may not. Some discussions may have gone very smoothly: the group discussed an issue or problem and came up with creative or useful ideas. In other cases, the group may have argued constantly and therefore accomplished very little, so that the time spent together may have been wasted. To make a group discussion worthwhile and satisfying, you should learn how to participate in a group discussion. Knowing how to discuss intelligently and fairly involves several simple rules based on courtesy and common sense. By following these rules, you and your fellow group members should be able to express your ideas in an atmosphere of consideration and respect.

31g. Learn to participate in a group discussion.

(1) Be sure the discussion topic is manageable.

You have already learned the importance of having a manageable topic when you plan a piece of writing or an oral report. Your discussion topic should also be narrow, or limited, enough for the time you have available. Suppose your group wants to discuss ways to expand your school's extracurricular activities. If you only have thirty minutes for your discussion, you should divide this broad subject into smaller parts and discuss each one separately at a different time. For example, your group could instead discuss ways to expand after-school musical activities. This topic is more manageable for the time you have.

(2) Learn the duties of each participant in a group discussion.

A group discussion can have three different participants: a discussion leader, speakers or discussion members, and an audience. While not every discussion has all three, you should learn the role each participant should play. The *discussion leader* organizes and guides the discussion. He or she introduces the topic and the speakers, asks questions, keeps the speakers on the topic, and summarizes the discussion's main points. The *speakers* actively participate in the discussion. They should listen carefully and courteously to the other speakers, speak clearly, and stay on the topic. The *audience* should also listen quietly and carefully, and audience members can ask questions when the discussion leader invites them to do so.

(3) Prepare thoroughly for a discussion.

Whenever possible, prepare for the discussion beforehand. Gather information about the discussion topic by reading magazines, books, and encyclopedias and by discussing the topic with people who know about it. If each group member has spent some time studying and thinking about the topic, the discussion should proceed smoothly and intelligently.

(4) Be sure all group members have a chance to participate in the discussion.

Because some people feel more comfortable expressing their ideas in a group, it is always possible that one or two group members will dominate, or take over, the discussion. A group discussion should have *all* group members participating equally, however. Be sure that all members have a chance to express their ideas on the topic. Listening respectfully to each other should make group members feel comfortable in sharing their ideas.

(5) Listen with an open mind.

Members of a group discussion, who have different interests and experiences, often express ideas and opinions that may be very different from your own ideas and opinions. As you hear these different ideas, listen with an open mind. Remember that a group discussion should be a learning experience that allows an exchange of ideas. If someone else's ideas make sense, be prepared to change your own mind freely.

(6) Focus on the discussion topic only.

With several people meeting together, it is easy to get off the subject and to start discussing ideas that are not related to the group's discussion topic. Remember that your group is talking together for a specific purpose; you must therefore stay on your topic. Help your group to accomplish its purpose. Stay on the topic yourself, and politely remind your fellow group members to stay on the topic if the discussion begins to wander.

(7) Listen attentively to every speaker in the group.

Every speaker in your discussion group should have your full attention. Listen carefully to others as they express their ideas about the discussion topic, and avoid chatting with members of the group while a speaker is discussing the topic. Rules of courtesy that apply to informal conversations are especially important in group discussions as well. Allow one speaker to talk at a time, and avoid shouting when group members happen to disagree on a point. Instead, calmly discuss your different ideas, and allow each person to contribute his or her views on the point of disagreement.

(8) Continue to improve your participation in group discussions.

It is likely that you will participate in group discussions throughout your schooling and your adult life. Learning to be a better participant in a group discussion is therefore an important skill to work on. One way to improve is to focus on the seven preceding rules of courtesy and common sense for a group discussion. Another way to improve is to ask yourself several questions after a group discussion. These questions will focus your attention on how well the discussion went and whether it accomplished its purposes:

a. Did group members prepare beforehand? Did everyone demonstrate that they had studied and thought about the topic before the group met?

b. Did all group members contribute in some way to the discussion?

c. Did all group members understand and fulfill their role in the discussion?

d. Did the group stay on the discussion topic?

e. Did group members show respect and courtesy toward one another?

You and the members of your group should ask yourselves these questions after your discussion. Try to answer *yes* to each question, and work to improve how you participate in a group discussion.

EXERCISE 18. Participating in a Group Discussion. Join a discussion group your teacher assigns you to, or form a discussion group with three or four classmates. Select one of the following topics or a topic of your own, and discuss it in the time period your teacher assigns. Remember that your group has a specific purpose to accomplish during this time. Your teacher may also direct you to select a discussion leader who will guide your group's work.

1. Three reasons for allowing students to help establish school rules

2. Our class's most memorable contributions to school life

3. How to raise money for school projects without having bake sales or carwashes

4. A famous man and a famous woman that young people can respect

5. Three things you can do to contribute to a happy family life

EXERCISE 19. Evaluating a Group Discussion. After your group completes its discussion in Exercise 18, evaluate your group's work. Use the five questions on page 849 to evaluate your discussion, and be prepared to discuss your evaluation in class.

EXERCISE 20. Evaluating a Group Discussion You Observe. Observe a group discussion—one your classmates are having or one on a television news program. Use the five questions on page 849 to evaluate what you observe. Be prepared to explain whether the group accomplished its purpose and to discuss how the group could have improved its work together.

CHAPTER 32

Listening

IMPROVING YOUR LISTENING

Listening well is an important part of learning. In school, at home, and among friends, you can learn more by listening well to others.

LISTENING TO MEDIA

You may spend many hours each week watching television and listening to the radio. You may also go to the movies often. It is good to have the fun and relaxation that such entertainment provides, but you owe it to yourself to develop a critical appreciation of what you see and hear.

32a. Choose radio programs, television programs, and movies intelligently.

You can learn a great deal from radio, television, and movies if you plan ahead and decide what you want to see and hear. Newspaper reviews, suggestions from friends, and your own interests should guide your choice of these media.

EXERCISE 1. Identifying Preferences for Particular Movies and Radio and Television Programs. Look at the television, radio, and movie schedules for the next week. Make a list of the shows you want to see or hear. Next to each show, give the reason for your interest. In class, compare your list with your classmates'. Did you list the same shows? Do you have the same reasons?

LISTENING TO INSTRUCTIONS

A large part of what we listen to is not only enjoyable—it is informative. Our daily life depends on people telling other people things that are useful for them to know. As students, much of your listening is done for the purpose of gaining information.

32b. Listen alertly to directions and class assignments.

You can save time and avoid errors by listening carefully to directions. If the directions are lengthy, jot down each step on a piece of paper. Do not interrupt with questions while the directions are being given. Wait, and ask your questions when the speaker has finished. Be sure that you have noted *all* the instructions and have understood them. Repeat them aloud if necessary.

EXERCISE 2. Following Oral Directions. Someone in the class will read the following directions aloud. See if you can follow the directions after hearing them. You may want to jot each step down on a piece of paper.

Take out a piece of paper and write your name in the upper left-hand corner. Beneath your name write the day you were born.

Draw a line down the middle of the page. Mark the left column with the letter *A* and the right column with the letter *B*. In column A, write the months of the year that begin with the letter *J*. In column B, write the days of the week that begin with the letter *T*. Compare the lists. If column B has more words, fold your paper in half.

LISTENING TO OTHERS

32c. Listen to talks and oral reports with an open mind.

The basis of good listening is *interest* and *purpose*. You listen very attentively to something that interests you. You also listen attentively to, and remember vividly, information that will serve a purpose that you consider important.

When listening to a talk, ask yourself: *How can this information be of real help to me?* If you can determine ways in which the content is important to you, listening and remembering will be easier.

Suppose, however, you are listening to a talk on how a particular club serves the community. You may not be very interested. The club has staged a benefit dance to buy a record player and records for a local hospital. To you, this is of no immediate concern. You could fog your mind in a daydream now if you wished; but if you pay attention, you may discover that the club also sponsors trips for students, or that it compiles job opportunities for students seeking summer employment.

Sometimes you know what you are listening for—as when you listen to directions or assignments. At other times you should keep an alert, open mind—you may learn something unexpectedly useful.

EXERCISE 3. Determining Purposes for Listening.
Suppose the following people spoke in assembly programs at your school. What would be your purpose in listening to each?

1. The manager of a local department store talks on "How to Tell a Bargain from a Rip-off."
2. A graduate of your school gives a talk on two years spent with the Peace Corps in South America.
3. A professional guitarist speaks on "What to Listen for in Music," illustrating points on the guitar.
4. The head of a research laboratory gives a talk on new ways of using solar energy.

32d. Listen actively.

If you intend to use the information you are hearing, you must be alert to grasp the ideas presented. You must select the ideas that you can use. You must retain them so clearly that you will remember them later when you need them.

(1) Listen for the speaker's purpose.

Sometimes, while listening to a talk, you want to know the speaker's intention. Is the speaker trying to persuade you to do something? Are you expected to agree or disagree with the speaker? In such situations, concentrate on grasping the speaker's point of view. Ask yourself why the speaker wants you to do something or why the speaker holds certain opinions.

(2) Listen for a few main ideas.

Listen to grasp the *main points* of the speech: the reasons the speaker gives for taking action or the ideas with which the speaker supports one side of an issue. If a speaker gives information or relates an experience, try to understand and remember each main idea presented.

When you are listening for the main ideas of a speech, it is often helpful to pay special attention to the start and finish of the talk. A speaker's introduction often presents the main points that will be developed, and the conclusion often sums them up. An able speaker makes an effort to emphasize important ideas so that you can easily recognize them.

EXERCISE 4. **Listening for Main Ideas.** Select six short news stories in a newspaper. Read each story aloud. Listeners will write down, in their own words, the main idea of each story. Compare the answers.

(3) Listen for specific details.

On some occasions your purpose in listening to a talk will be to get specific details. Suppose, for example, that you are listening to a talk on how to start a model airplane engine or how to decipher a secret code or how to tell edible mushrooms from poisonous ones. A general idea of the method will not be sufficient; you will want exact details.

EXERCISE 5. Listening for Specific Details. This activity requires listening carefully to detailed information. Your teacher will read aloud a set of instructions or directions. When the teacher has finished, write the details of the instructions or directions from memory. When you are finished, the teacher will reread the instructions and ask you to check the accuracy of what you remembered.

(4) Evaluate nonverbal signals such as gestures.

A speaker may use gestures for emphasis. Some of these gestures may be appropriate; for example, a comedian will often rely on gestures to draw laughs. Other gestures may be inappropriate; for example, nervous speakers will often wave one or both hands in the air as they speak. The best gestures add to a speech and communicate nonverbally what the speaker is trying to say.

EXERCISE 6. Evaluating Nonverbal Signals. Watch a popular comedian or another personality speaking. Notice how gestures are used. Describe these gestures to your classmates and indicate what they mean to you.

32e. Listen critically. Distinguish fact from opinion. Judge whether statements are backed up by evidence from dependable sources.

When you listen to a speaker, you do not wish to be fooled by trickery or unreliable sources of information. Ask yourself questions as you listen: Is this statement a fact or an opinion? If the speaker is presenting it as a fact, is it backed up with proof from a dependable source or a trustworthy expert? Is the speaker talking from experience?

Know the difference between fact and opinion. A fact is a statement that can be proved true or false, such as, "Winter temperatures averaged 12° Celsius this year." An opinion is a statement that cannot be proved true or false, such as, "It feels colder this winter than last."

Study the following examples. Can you see why two are opinions and two are facts?

OPINION The library facilities in this school are inadequate.

FACT In the library, there are 10 books available for this assignment, but there are 150 students who must do the assignment at once.

OPINION The referee is being unfair to our players!

FACT The referee has given our players three penalties in the last five minutes.

EXERCISE 7. Distinguishing Between Fact and Opinion.

If you heard the following statements, would you accept them as fact or interpret them as opinion? After each number on your paper, write *fact* if you think the statement would be a fact or *opinion* if you think it would be an opinion. Be prepared to explain each choice.

1. We ought to irrigate our desert lands with fresh water made from sea water.
2. A tornado in Kansas today wrecked fifty homes.
3. Sunbathing is harmful.
4. Stanford beat Oregon at football today, 28 to 14.
5. There's no place like home.
6. TV comedies are all alike.
7. Mrs. Currier gives too much homework.
8. American cars give the best value among low-priced compacts.
9. The orchestra has improved greatly this year.
10. Mrs. Townsend has never been introduced to my family.

INDEX
AND
TAB KEY INDEX

Index

D

Dangling participle, 280–81
Dates, commas with, 353
Declarative sentence, defined, 21
Definition, paragraph of, 553, 558–59
Demonstrative pronoun, 45
Dependent clause = Subordinate
  clause
Description
  adjectives and adverbs in, 549,
    591–92, 601, 765, 767
  comparisons in, 602
  details for, 589–90, 592–93
  diction in, 547, 549, 550, 601
  gathering information for, 589–90
  in narration, 541–42, 589–94, 599,
    600, 601–02
  model, 590
  observation for, 547, 589–90
  of character, 592–93
  of person, 551, 589–90
  of place or object, 549–50, 589–90
  of setting, 589–90, 593–94, 600
  order of importance for, 600
  purpose of, 453
  sensory language for, 548, 591–94
  spatial order for, 478–79, 506, 547,
    600
  verbs in, 549–50, 585, 601–02, 766
  See also Descriptive paragraph
Descriptive paragraph, 540, 546–51,
  552
  comparisons in, 547–48, 550
  concrete and sensory details in,
    547–48, 551
  defined, 540
  figurative language in, 547–48, 550
  main impression in, 547, 549
  observation for, 547
  organizing, 547
  precise language in, 549
  prewriting steps for, 547–48
  purpose of, 540, 546
  revising, 552
  spatial order for, 547
  topic for, 547
  topic sentence of, 549
  writing a first draft, 549–51
Desert, dessert, 791

Details, specific
  arranging, 478–79, 483
  choice of, determined by purpose,
    456, 476
  classifying, 476–77
  concrete and sensory, 547–48
  gathering, 469–75, 547–48, 622
  identifying, in studying, 808–09
  observing and interpreting, 464
  revising, 482–84
  sensory, 464, 548, 589–90
  See also specific types of writing
Development, methods of
  for descriptive paragraph, 549–50,
    551
  for expository paragraph, 554–60
  for narrative paragraph, 541–44
  for persuasive paragraph, 562–65,
    566
Dewey decimal system, 736–37, 739
Diacritical marks
  accent, 730–31
  breve, 732
  macron, 732
  vowel sounds, 732–33
Diagraming
  adjectives, 51–52
  adjective phrases, 119–20
  adverbs, 73
  adverb phrases, 119–20
  complements, 97–98, 99
  complex sentences, 181–82
  compound sentences, 178
  compound subjects, 25–26
  compound verbs, 26
  coordinating conjunctions, 25–26,
    98, 99, 105–06, 178
  direct objects, 97–98, 99
  gerund phrases, 136–37
  indirect objects, 99
  infinitive phrases, 137
  nouns and adjectives, 51–52
  participial phrases, 136
  possessive pronouns, 52
  predicate adjectives, 105–06
  predicate nominatives, 105–06
  prepositional phrases, 119–20
  purpose of, 24
  simple subjects, 24–26

Tab Key Index

Key to
English Workshop Drill

To supplement the lessons in *English Grammar and Composition, Second Course*, there is additional practice in grammar and usage, punctuation, capitalization, composition, vocabulary, and spelling in *English Workshop, Second Course*. The following chart correlates the rule in the textbook with the appropriate lesson in *English Workshop*.

Text Rule	Workshop Lesson	Text Rule	Workshop Lesson	Text Rule	Workshop Lesson
1f–g	19	9a–b	93	20a	110
		9c	94–97	20b	111–112
2a	1			20e	110
2b	2			20f	114
2c	3	10a–b	74–75	20g–j	114–115
		10c–d	76–77		
3a	4–5	11a	18	21a	116
3b	6			21b–c	117
3c	7	13d	66–67	21d–g	118
3d–f	9	13e	68	21h–i	119
		13g	69		
4a	8,15			22a–h	124
4b	8,16	14a–d	43	22i	123–124
4c	8	14f–g	44	22j–l	124
4d	8,17	14h	20		
		14i–j	44	23a–d	120,125
5a	57–58	14k–l	45	23e–g	121,125
5b	57	14m	46	23h	125
5e–j	58			23i	122,125
5k–l	57	15b–c	49	23j–k	125
		15d	50, 57		
6a–c	25	15e–g	49	24p–r	126
6d	26–30	15h–i	50		
6e	35–38	15l–m	47	25a–d	127
		15n	48	25e–f	128
7a–b	20				
		16a	55	26b	11, 33, 72
8a	83	16b	56	26e	12, 24
8b	84	16c	57		
8c	85	16e	60–61	28a	11
8d–f	87			28b	23
8g–i	88	17a	102–103	28c	11
8l	86	17d–f	104	28f	64
8m	84	17g	105–108		
				29d–i	42, 53, 65, 73

8
E 9
F 0
G 1
H 2
I 3
J 4